MW01627500

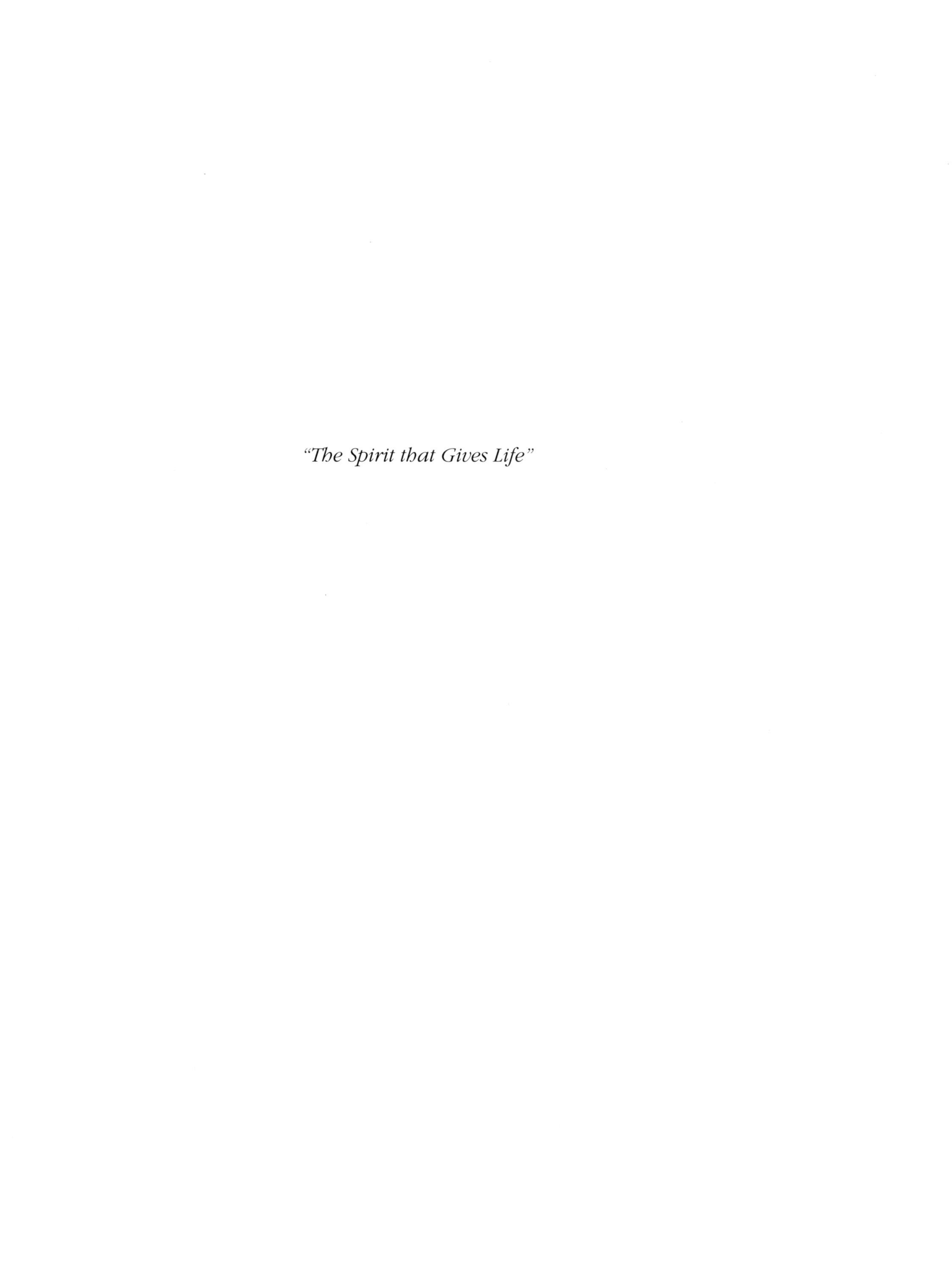

"The Spirit that Gives Life"

"The Spirit

The History of
Duquesne University,
1878–1996

that Gives Life"

by Joseph F. Rishel

with additional research by
Paul Demilio,
Duquesne University Archivist

Duquesne
University Press

This book is published by Duquesne University Press
600 Forbes Avenue
Pittsburgh, PA 15282–0101

Library of Congress Cataloging-in-Publication Data

Rishel, Joseph Francis, 1945–
The spirit that gives life: a history of Duquesne University, 1878–1996 / by Joseph F. Rishel, with additional research by Paul Demilio.
p. cm.
Includes bibliographical references and index.
ISBN 0–8207–0268–4 (acid-free paper)
1. Duquesne University—History. I. Demilio, Paul. II. Title.
LD1733.D82R57 1997
378.748'86—dc21 97–4680
CIP

Contents

Illustrations

Foreword

An entire century and almost two decades have passed since the priests and brothers of the Congregation of the Holy Ghost created the Pittsburgh Catholic College. From this humble beginning on the second floor of a commercial building to its prominence as one of the leading Catholic universities in America, the fascinating narrative of Duquesne University of the Holy Ghost is unfolded in the first comprehensive and official history of the University. It is a magnificent work authored by Professor Joseph Rishel, a professor of history at Duquesne.

The history of Duquesne University is a microcosm of the history of Southwestern Pennsylvania and America over the last 119 years. The history of higher education over this period also unfolds through the prism of a private Catholic college which was to become a University. It is a history of challenge, tribulation and triumph. Most important, it is a history of faith and hope and love.

Through wars and depressions, victories and defeats, Duquesne has provided education for tens of thousands who have become leaders in the four corners of the globe, many of whom would not have had the advantage of higher education without Duquesne. As this history appears, Duquesne stands as a leader in higher education with more students than ever before, a beautiful campus and state-of-the-art technology in nine schools.

Over this entire period, massive changes have occurred at Duquesne to react to the felt needs of students and society. The Mission of the University, however, has never changed. From its inception to the present and into the future, Duquesne University is a Catholic university in the Spiritan tradition, sustained through a partnership of laity and religious. It serves God by serving students—through commitment to excellence in liberal and professional education. It combines genuine academic excellence with a profound concern for moral and spiritual values through the maintenance of an ecumenical atmosphere open to diversity and through service to the Church, the community, the nation and the world.

This purpose, this philosophy, this Mission has never wavered. There are many heroes in the Duquesne story. We are pleased to share the story of their creativity, indefatigable efforts and sacrifices with you. We are very proud of this noble enterprise called Duquesne University where education is not only for the mind, but for the heart and the soul.

John E. Murray, Jr.
President

Preface

The history of Duquesne University has been one of heroic sacrifice on the part of many people. It has been one fraught with perils and hardships, but it has also one of opportunities seized and realized. From its humble beginnings in rented quarters, Duquesne has grown, not merely to physical greatness, but to become a positive influence in the region, the nation, and the world.

When confronted with the daunting task of composing the first definitive history of Duquesne University of the Holy Ghost, it was not the intent of the author to write a thematic history of the University's development. Rather, I wished to show the effort and attainment of every administrative body, school, department, and student organization. I wished to place the Duquesne student in the classroom, in the dorms, on the teams, in the chapel, and as part of any number of organizations. I wished to present as much of university life in its intricacies as I could possibly include. My purpose was twofold: first, to show the dedication of the people who built Duquesne from its initial vision as directed by the Holy Spirit, "who gives life" to this University; and second, to give each individual associated with Duquesne a sense of familiarity with the campus, schools, and activities and to place those experiences into the wider continuum of the university's existence. If the history proves to be a vast compilation of facts and details, the author hopes that they will all prove to be significant to some portion of the readership, who will relive experiences recalled by these references. Hopefully, enough stories have been included to interest all. I hope that the readers will find it enjoyable.

Duquesne's early history bears a striking resemblance to that of the early Christian Church. Reluctant to face the challenges and decisions of an uncertain future, the apostles huddled together awaiting that first Pentecost that would give life to the Church. Similarly, Father Strub reluctantly struggled with the task of establishing the college. Feeling that such a work was not compatible with the essential missionary work of his Spiritan order, the Holy Ghost Fathers, he would have rather settled for something less, a trade school or, possibly, an orphanage. He only accepted to undertake the Pittsburgh bishop's request and establish the college under the hope that it would one day include a seminary for the preparation of priests for the order's North American missions. Strangely, the seminary was the only aspect of the university not to materialize in the midst of schools, departments, and programs that Strub could scarcely have imagined. But then, it was the Holy Spirit, not just the plans and hands of men, that was to determine the direction of Duquesne's growth.

The initial steps in the history of the early Church and in the history of Duquesne were marked by countless difficult decisions that would frame the vision and the workings of the body that was to follow. Strub thought much about the launching of his college and the necessary considerations to ensure its success. He communicated these thoughts in a barrage of epistles to his superior in France. He requested specific personnel, he worried over possible sites, he gave advice on how the priests should dress and act so as to be accepted in this American society. Many of his plans resulted in personal disappointments as things did not work out as he had hoped. Disasters smaller than his had aborted other attempts to establish a Catholic college in Pittsburgh. Yet, Duquesne, like the early church, survived in the face of seemingly unsurmountable obstacles and opposition.

Just as the early church embraced all but consisted largely of the poor and the dispossessed, Duquesne found itself servicing a Catholic population near the bottom of the economic structure, despite their high hopes and ambitions. Resources were always scarce, but the college strove to do the best with what it had and to generously share of its meager stores to give deserving students a chance they could not afford on their own. Despite Duquesne's recent financial posture, the University, though no longer facing the scarcities that characterized most of its existence, has visions that still outstrip its resources and yet strives to do all it can to surpass the expectations of other universities in similar circumstances. Duquesne has always embarked upon each new venture on a proverbial shoestring and put its faith in the Holy Spirit to provide the backing. Ever hoping to embrace more, the University, like the Church, will begin to die if it should ever begin to feel comfortable and complacent.

This book has been arranged into chapters based on a chronological arrangement of the administrations of the University presidents. It is convenient to describe events as occurring in the Hehir Administration or while Father Kirk was president. Although one individual hardly constitutes the sentiments of an entire faculty, the receptiveness, flexibility, and enthusiasm of the president influences the ability of the university to grow and the direction which that growth will take.

In the history of the Church, saints who were deeply in tune with the Holy Spirit, periodically led the people of God to gigantic leaps of faith. Through its history, that faith has waxed and wained. In a similar pattern, the history of Duquesne University had periods of retrenchment and peaks of high productivity and accomplishment. It was one of these golden eras that has prompted this work, a time in which the Holy Spirit's inspiration is an almost tangible presence. Because of this, this book is dedicated to the memory of Father Henry J. McAnulty, C.S.Sp.

I wish to thank my wife Helen who not only helped mightly with indexing the *Duquesne Duke,* but also for her help in reading the manuscript and suggesting changes. I would also like to thank my children, Jonathan, Emily, Marjorie, and Elizabeth, who endured the writing of this manuscript for more than three years and who suffered abbreviated vacations because of it. Someday I hope my children will claim Duquesne as their Alma Mater and see this history with new eyes. I would also like to thank the following for their assistance and encouragement: Michael P. Weber, Henry J. McAnulty, C.S.Sp., Vernon Gallagher, John E. Murray Jr., Henry Koren, C.S.Sp., Charles J. Fenner, C.S.Sp., Sean Hogan, C.S.Sp., Paul Demilio, Charles Ruch, Sean Farragher, C.C.Sp., Patricia E. Jakub, Margaret Daniels, Betty Beaman, Stephen Strasser, James Sawa, Frank Dutkovich, James Caputo, Perry Blatz, Bernard Weiss, Christine Lober, John Dowds, Susan Wadsworth-Booth, Constance Ramirez, Sally Lutz, and Elizabeth Ward. I hope the work is worthy of the effort they have expended on my behalf.

I would also like to thank in a special way those who wrote dissertations that aided in the writing of this book: William Clees, Francis Hanley, Michael Kupersanin, Eileen Gimper, and James Fitzpatrick.

1. A College is Born

Duquesne University owes its beginnings to the strenuous efforts of the Holy Ghost Fathers and, in a strange and perverse way, to Otto von Bismarck's *Kulturkampf* of the 1870s. The Holy Ghost Fathers, also known as the Spiritans, were a Roman Catholic order of priests and brothers founded in France in 1703. Their seminary early gained a reputation for academic excellence, one destined to mark their extensive missionary activities around the world. Indeed, it is difficult to separate their educational and missionary work.[1] After near extinction during the French Revolution, the order rebounded in the nineteenth century and founded, in Ireland, Blackrock College and Rockwell College and Seminary,[2] both of which strongly influenced Duquesne University. But it is not from Ireland alone that Duquesne traces its origins.

From Germany to Pittsburgh

The Holy Ghost Congregation was extremely active in Germany. There, they and their dynamic provincial superior of the German province, Father Joseph Strub, C.S.Sp.,[3] ran headlong into the nationalistic ambitions of the German chancellor, Otto von Bismarck. Perceiving the Roman Catholic Church as a social and political threat to the newly united Germany, Bismarck, in an attack known as the *Kulterkampf*, went so far as to close the schools of religious orders. The Iron Chancellor exiled Father Strub and the Holy Ghost fathers from Germany in 1872.[4] This was the first in a series of difficulties that led paradoxically to the successful establishment of the university we know today.

Father Strub and five other priests emigrated to America and briefly settled in Ohio. A few years later they relocated again when they learned of a demand for German priests in Pittsburgh, where industry had attracted many European immigrants, many of whom were Catholic.[5] Indeed, the Catholic population of the Diocese of Pittsburgh, which at the time embraced nearly all of western Pennsylvania, was about 60,000.[6]

Ecclesiastical Difficulties

In April of 1874 Bishop Domenec invited Father Strub to serve as rector of St. Mary's Church in Sharpsburg, just north of Pittsburgh. It was hoped that St. Mary's could be used as a base of operation in opening a school for young Catholic men. Attempts to establish a college in Pittsburgh had already met with three successive failures,[7] probably because the bishops could not staff the schools themselves. This fourth attempt was different in that it was to rely on a faculty having only minimal parish duties to distract it from its major goal. Although Father Strub was reluctant to establish a college, he accepted the challenge in the expectation that it could serve also as a scholasticate for the preparation of priests for his congregation (despite the superior general's wishes that all Spiritans be educated in France). However, a stumbling block was thrown in his way when in 1876 the Diocese of Allegheny City, containing Sharpsburg and St. Mary's, was carved from the Diocese of Pittsburgh, initiating a chain of events that delayed the founding of the college for two years. Bishop Domenec left Pittsburgh to become the ordinary of the newly created diocese, and quickly became embroiled in a dispute with Bishop John Tuigg of Pittsburgh over the responsibility of the old diocesan debt, and went to Rome to plead his case. He resigned—and died!—before he could return.[8] Realizing that a mistake had been made in creating the

Diocese of Allegheny, the Holy See did not appoint a successor to Bishop Domenec. Instead, Bishop Tuigg became administrator of both dioceses, and the Allegheny Diocese was formally reincorporated into the Pittsburgh Diocese in 1889.

In 1878, Bishop Tuigg finally gave Father Strub permission to open a college in the city.[9] That, and his best wishes, were all he gave. No money, land, or building were available. He promised, though, "I'll send a letter to be read in all the churches and I'll recommend your college warmly." It was then announced to the faithful that Father Strub and his confreres were to give instruction in the classical, scientific, and commercial subjects, along with religious training.[10] The institution was to be named the Pittsburgh Catholic College of the Holy Ghost.

Laying the Groundwork

Even before the ecclesiastical difficulties had been resolved, Father Strub was engaged in securing the necessary personnel to operate the college and in preparing them for work in the United States. "You can't wear the religious habit[11] outside the community," he warned the superior general in Paris, "so make sure they all come with Laics and use them in the journey in order to get accustomed to them. . . . You wouldn't believe how much laughter and hilarity we aroused on our arrival in New York. . . . It is a waste of money carrying a habit and hat that can't be used." Also, he enjoined, "Be careful to send no one without English. . . . You have no idea how useful the English language is here. I might even say necessary!" Still another concern was that the Irish and German elements of the staff be balanced. Strub believed the Pittsburgh community would perceive German teachers as more industrious, productive, and disciplined than the Irish.

For president, Strub asked for the best man he knew, Rev. J.E. Raffe, C.S.Sp., of Blackrock College. But Raffe refused the position:

> The system of education demanded by public opinion in America is not one of serious classical studies. I could. . . . be of service there if it was a question of showing people how to appreciate Aeschylus, Sophocles, [or] Homer. . . . but that is not what is wanted in America. Physics, Chemistry, Mechanics—their minds are tuned to inventions, sewing machines, threshing machines, artificial manures—but I have never made a special study of applied science.[12]

Apparently immune to Celtic charm, Strub specifically asked that the rector *not* be Father William Patrick Power, C.S.Sp, an Irishman, but Power was selected nonetheless. Strub accepted the choice on the condition that Power arrive in plenty of time to prepare for the opening of the college.

Power, however, was delayed until January 1879 so the German-born Father John Bernard Graff was sent from Ireland to serve during the interim. Father Strub was not too happy with him, either. He felt Father Graff was unsuited to the work of establishing a new school since he functioned best "in a well-established community where he can simply follow the tradition of the house. Here he would have to start from zero and he would spoil everything." Graff, however, performed better than expected. Along with three Holy Ghost brothers, he awaited the arrival of the rest of the staff. Fathers Michael Dunne and John Quinn arrived just four days before the scheduled opening. Father Francis Salles arrived four days after classes began, and his knowledge of English was so limited that he was unable to teach. Father Hiezmann joined the faculty but was in failing health. A lay teacher later was added to round out the staff of six. Interestingly, the ethnicity of the priests was similar to that of the student body, as three were Irish and two were German.

After various attempts to secure a centrally located building, on August 3, 1878, Strub signed a lease for the use of the second floor (later to include the third floor also) of the Smith Building at the corner of Wylie Avenue and Federal Street. This location is now where Crosstown

Boulevard passes over Center Avenue immediately north of Chatham Center. The rental was $2,000 per year.[13] As celebrated in the folklore of Duquesne University, this was a truly ecumenical location. The street floor of the Smith Building housed both a Scottish Presbyterian tailor, and a German Lutheran baker. The Presbyterian caused the Catholic school no problems, but the aroma of baking bread from the Lutheran's shop permeated the entire building and made it difficult for the students to concentrate on their studies!

An advertisement for the Pittsburgh Catholic College was placed in the August 24, 1878, edition of *The Catholic*, the diocesan newspaper. It listed the courses of study and tuition costs, which, oddly enough, were expressed in terms of costs per month rather than by semester.[14] There were a Classical Course, a Commercial Course, a Preparatory course (the nineteenth century equivalent of high school), and a course for younger boys.[15] The latter two were intended to prepare students for the college. This arrangement—the preparatory school would survive until 1941—was not unusual. It imitated a system used by Catholic colleges in Europe and introduced to the United States by the Jesuits that combined three years in an academic preparatory school with three years in a humanities-oriented college.

A Humble Beginning

The Pittsburgh Catholic College officially began on October 1, 1878, fully one month behind schedule. Instead of Bishop Tuigg's wildly optimistic prediction that 500 students would enroll, only 40 students presented themselves.[16] The bishop himself was partly responsible for the poor turnout. As an Irishman, Tuigg was disappointed to learn that the expected Irish rector would be temporarily replaced by German-born Graff. His enthusiasm cooled considerably, and the warm endorsements he had promised did not materialize.

Father Strub had left two weeks after the opening to establish the Holy Ghost fathers in another state, Arkansas, since he hoped to avoid provoking Tuigg's ill will toward the college on his account. Strub had supported Bishop Domenec in the dispute between Domenec and Tuigg. Strub's absence, however, was not enough to elicit the bishop's favor, and Tuigg continued to be unfriendly for quite a while. Even after Father Power's arrival, Tuigg refused to grant the Holy Ghost fathers serving at the school the right to exercise any priestly functions there. They could not celebrate Mass at the school (only in the parishes) or hear the confessions of any of their students.

In an effort to demonstrate the quality of education at the fledgling institution, an oral public examination "that must have terrorized the students" was held at the close of the first school year. Invitations were sent to parents and selected clergymen of the diocese. "The answering was most satisfactory and confidence was inspired."[17] Enrollment for the fall term of 1879 grew to 124 and increased again the following year. Gradually, the bishop began to change his attitude toward the Pittsburgh Catholic College, and the clergy of the diocese followed suit.

Finding a Permanent Foundation

The school needed both a charter and a permanent location convenient to students from all parts of the city. On July 7, 1882, only one month following the petition, the state charter was granted:

> To support and maintain a college for the instruction of youth in all branches of a thorough moral and secular education, including languages, the liberal arts and sciences, and also the preparation and education of youths destined for the Catholic Priesthood and to confer the usual scholastic degrees, and also to engage in and support missionary and congregational undertakings in the Catholic Church.

After the legal position of the college was established,[18] a suitable permanent location was found on a bluff of ground overlooking the Monongahela River known as Boyd's Hill.[19] Here a Dr. A.G. Walter had built a private two-story hospital in the 1850s. The doctor's heirs were willing to sell both the building and the adjacent lots, but not to the Pittsburgh Catholic College, so Father Power had to use a third party whose religious affiliation was unknown to the heirs in order to secure the property. Since dormitory space was needed, the hospital was not demolished. Instead, a one-story foundation was prepared on the east side of Colbert Street and the building was moved to the new location—after spending the winter in the middle of Colbert street when the moving operation proved too difficult to complete until the spring. Housing both faculty and students who could walk to the Wylie Avenue location, the building was named St. John's Hall and later was changed to St. Mary's Hall. On its original site the college erected the imposing five-story structure that came to be known as "Old Main."

Building "Old Main"

The building now serving as Duquesne's Administration Building has been "Old Main" to generations of Duquesne students. In 1885 it was an awesome structure, with five stories, each 14 to 15 feet high, and an open cupola that was for years the highest point on the Pittsburgh skyline. Since the development of the modern skyscraper with its steel frame was in its infancy at the time, the building was made with load-bearing walls ranging from 36 inches thick on the lower floors to 25 inches on the top floor. The architect was a local man, William Kaufman. Called Victorian Medievalistic, the building's distinctive style features horizontal bands of stone, giving "a curious striped appearance that, architecturally speaking, was quite fashionable after the mid-century, although it had practically disappeared after 1900."[20] The cupola was removed in 1949 to make way for the University radio station antenna. Extensive renovation in the early 1960s unfortunately truncated the once graceful chimneys and removed the interior woodwork and open stairways.

For its time, the building was considered quite spacious, so spacious that it housed both students and faculty. The fifth floor contained a combination chapel / auditorium with a sanctuary at one end and a stage at the other. The setup was quite ingenious. Folding doors separated the sanctuary when the stage was in use, and the seats had reversible backs to allow the worshippers / audience to face in either direction. The basement held a bakery, cafeteria, laundry, gymnasium, physical exercise rooms, and a locker room. The rest of the building was devoted to classrooms, labs, and dormitories. The odd mixture of classrooms and dormitory rooms on the same floor probably reveals the age differentials among the students, who were segregated by floor. This same separation was undoubtedly reflected in the existence of five eating facilities and two libraries.

Although the building was undeniably grand for its time, the site was less satisfactory. The surrounding land was so uneven that students would enter the school by stepping from a hill to the porch that ran along the second story in the rear of the building. Furthermore, the area behind the school was already much subdivided into lots, and outside sports had to be played on the surrounding streets. Also, nearby there was a brickyard,[21] complete with the humming engines and grinding of rock with the resultant dust and dirt.

Erecting a large five-story building must have been a daunting prospect to even the most optimistic of the Holy Ghost fathers. Since the college had practically no funds, the entire $150,000 cost of the building was borrowed from the Knights of Columbus and the American Province of the Holy Ghost Fathers. By 1886, the college was paying $6,000 annually in interest when its total income was only about $10,000 a year. Such a burden proved impossible to sustain for any length of time, and the American Province eventually forgave some $60,000 that the college still owed on its debt.

The site for the building required considerable preparation as about thirty feet of ground needed to be scraped off. Even the excavation for the building itself was accomplished with great difficulty; the stone and clay had to be blasted out.[22] A brickyard was established to utilize the clay for bricks. In what was to become the single most widely known fact of Duquesne's history, the bricks were handmade at the college-owned brickworks by the Holy Ghost brothers, though a contractor was hired to actually build the building.

The cornerstone was laid at the archway entrance facing Bluff Street in April 1884. Bishop Phelan and a crowd estimated by some at 25,000 attended the celebration.[23] Dedication day followed on Sunday, May 3, 1885, with parade, complete with flags and banners representing area parishes.The sermons, in English and German, reflected the foreign-born character of the Catholic population.

The new building should have ushered in a period of growth for the school, but this was not to be the case. The shortage of English-speaking priests reached critical proportions in the 1880s. In addition, disease, mostly tuberculosis, weakened a faculty that had earlier survived the ravages of smallpox.[24] The situation was so disheartening that on more than one occasion the closing of the school was considered. Nevertheless, it slowly, steadily grew. The Pittsburgh Catholic College had accomplished what three-fourths of all Catholic colleges founded before 1900 had failed to do: it had survived. And it did far more than that. From its very beginning, it established a reputation of offering an excellent education and of graduating young men of sound moral principles who were a credit to the college and the community.

A large part of its success can be attributed to a very remarkable Irishman, Father John Murphy.

An Irishman Learns about Pittsburgh

Like Fathers Strub and Graff before him, Father Power's tenure was brief. Only two months after the dedication of the new building, he was assigned to St. Mary College in Trinidad. He was succeeded by Father John Willms, C.S.Sp., who led the college for a single year.[25] Finally, on August 19, 1886, with the installation of the Very Reverend John Toohill Murphy, C.S.Sp., the Pittsburgh Catholic College of the Holy Ghost at last received a 13-year period of continuous leadership.[26] It was also to begin a much longer 44 years of governance by Irish-born, Irish-trained clerics, who strengthened ties with Rockwell and Blackrock Colleges in Ireland.[27]

The philosophy in which Father Murphy was trained stressed classical education for the purpose of producing cultured gentlemen who would enter law, medicine, and the priesthood. Father Murphy was soon to learn, however, that the children of immigrants were not yet being admitted to the professions in numbers large enough to warrant this kind of curriculum. Still struggling for middle-class status, the Catholic population viewed their children's education as a vehicle for upward occupational mobility from manual labor to white-collar office jobs. Their immediate need was for a job-related education, not a college degree with study in Latin and Greek. Of Pittsburgh's major steel companies, only the firm controlled by Andrew Carnegie would employ Roman Catholics in high-level administrative positions where a college degree might be useful. And, anyway, in the nineteenth and early twentieth centuries, for much of the population, Protestant and Catholic, the normal age for beginning a working career was 12 to 14 years. Thus, for a family to do without the additional income that a child could bring to the household—and pay tuition besides—constituted a considerable sacrifice.

From the day of its founding, the high school "commercial" course had always been the most popular at the college and would remain so well into the twentieth century. As late as 1911, nearly 72 percent of the graduates (60 students) received high school certificates. This reflected larger national trends with about seven out of every ten students at American Catholic colleges in 1907 enrolled in the modern-day equivalent of a high school department.

To ascertain the needs of the College's approximately 250 students, Father Murphy conducted a survey of the educational needs of the community soon after his arrival. He concluded that this heavily industrialized city needed students trained in physics and chemistry. Courses in these subjects were added to the curriculum, and, thanks to the generosity of both clerics and laymen, a well-equipped laboratory was established. In 1889, only three years after Father Murphy's arrival, the college conferred its first bachelor's degrees. Six were awarded in both the arts and the sciences.

Despite the findings of the educational requirements survey, Father Murphy expanded the scope of the liberal arts curriculum, enlarging the Classical Department, and added three special interests of his own: dramatics, debating, and elocution. Long a devotee of forensics, Father Murphy was a noted speaker. He also enlarged the Commercial Department. With so many new courses, Pittsburgh Catholic College was well on its way to becoming a university.

Having a special love for dramatics, Father Murphy personally directed, in 1891, a student presentation of *Alcestis* performed in the original Greek. The play had never before been performed in Pittsburgh, its intellectual nature not being well suited to the town. As Father Murphy put it, "[t]he hazardous nature of such an attempt, especially in our city of industry and commerce, caused many of our friends to fear that we would not be able to interest or even to draw a numerous audience, especially since the tickets were $1.50 and .75. A smashing success nevertheless crowned the efforts of our young Hellenists." The play netted $1,000. The audience doubtless did not understand a word of it, but Father Murphy wisely provided verbal introductions to each act and programs having a synopsis of each act.

The proceeds from *Alcestis* were used to purchase shelving and furniture for the library—a room that had been funded with the proceeds of an earlier student production, *The Athenian Captive*, performed at the Opera House in 1883. That thespian effort had netted about $1,200.[28] Successful as the plays were, they were hardly sufficient to settle the college's funding problems. The Pittsburgh Catholic College served a student body in generally precarious financial circumstances. Since its founding, the college had reduced or waived entirely the tuition of some needy students. Nonetheless, a number of deserving boys were compelled to discontinue their studies due to a lack of funds. A so-called Burse's Foundation was established in 1887 to attract $1,000-per-donor contributions from clergy and laity to assist such boys, but even when the thousand-dollar stipulation was dropped, contributions were not forthcoming. The vast majority of the Catholic population in Pittsburgh simply did not have the financial resources to help. The college could not begin to grant scholarships until 1900.

In 1887 the College lowered tuition by 20 percent to $50.00 a year for day students. This was made possible only through the sacrificial efforts of the Holy Ghost Fathers, who worked without pay. These dedicated men also journeyed "to the parishes of the Diocese, aiding the pastors in conducting services and substituting for the regular pastors when they had to be absent from their churches . . . the priests . . . used this meager income from these labors for the school's operating capital."[29]

1. Rev. Joseph Strub, C.S.Sp., founder of the Pittsburgh Catholic College. Strub, of the Holy Ghost Congregation in Germany, settled in Pittsburgh a few years after he and other Holy Ghost fathers were exiled from Germany.

In 1874, Bishop Domenec of the Pittsburgh Diocese urged Strub to establish a college. Despite his original reluctance, he opened The Pittsburgh Catholic College of the Holy Ghost on October 1, 1878, with 6 faculty and 40 students. Father Strub left Pittsburgh to establish the Holy Ghost fathers in Arkansas two weeks after his college opened.

2. Pittsburgh Catholic College began in rented quarters on the second floor of this building on Wylie Avenue.

This location is now where Crosstown Boulevard passes over Center Avenue, just north of Chatham Center. First floor occupants included a tailor and a baker. The aroma of baking bread filled the whole building, often making it difficult for the students to concentrate on their work. Classes were held in this building for eight years.

Pittsburgh *Post-Gazette*

3. In 1882, the college acquired its first building. Saint Mary's Hall was originally built as a hospital by Dr. A. G. Walters. His heirs wanted to sell the property — but not to the college. Through a third party, rector William Power arranged to acquire the building on Boyd's Hill, a bluff overlooking the Monongahela. The building was moved across the street to a site now occupied by the Bayer Learning Center. Saint Mary's, shown here as it appeared in 1936, served at different times as a student dormitory, a convent, and offices. It was razed in 1971.

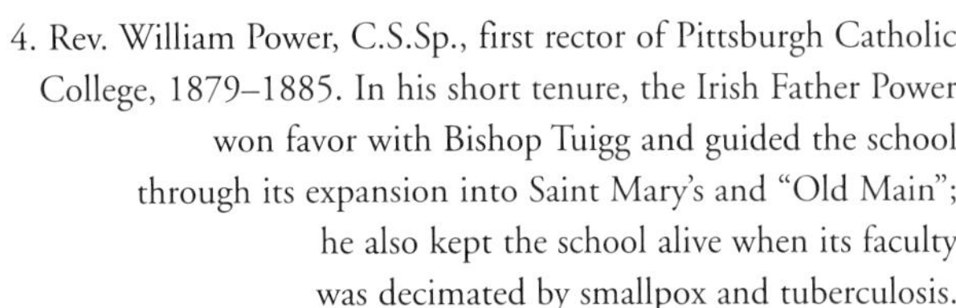

4. Rev. William Power, C.S.Sp., first rector of Pittsburgh Catholic College, 1879–1885. In his short tenure, the Irish Father Power won favor with Bishop Tuigg and guided the school through its expansion into Saint Mary's and "Old Main"; he also kept the school alive when its faculty was decimated by smallpox and tuberculosis.

Two months after the dedication of Old Main, he was assigned to St. Mary College in Trinidad.

5. This pen and ink drawing is one of the only surviving illustrations of the Administration Building, newly completed in 1885. Constructed on Boyd's Hill, the original site of Walters's Hospital, this five-story building housed a chapel/auditorium, a bakery, cafeteria, laundry, gym, two libraries, classrooms, labs, and dormitories for faculty and students. For decades it was known simply as the "main building"; only later did it become "Old Main."

6. Rev. John Willms, C.S.Sp., Rector, 1885–1886. Father Willms led Pittsburgh Catholic College for only one year. He followed the Rev. William Power, C.S.Sp., and was succeeded by the Very Reverend John Toohill Murphy, C.S.Sp.

7. This 1888 photograph depicts a virtual pantheon of Pittsburgh Catholic College luminaries. *Seated l. to r.*, Fr. McDermott (coached the college's first football team, lobbied for Duquesne University to receive state funding in 1913), Fr. Griffin (secured an organ with 1,290 pipes for the chapel in 1896), Fr. Murphy (president, 1886–1889), Fr. Strub (college founder), Fr. Roth, Fr. Willms (rector, 1885–1886), Fr. Quinn (one of the six faculty teaching when the college opened in 1878). *Standing*, Fr. Phelan (later Provincial of the Holy Ghost Order), Fr. Hehir (president, 1899–1930), Fr. Gross.

Throughout its early history, the college's fate often swung on the relationships between these men. The importance of ethnicity and of conflict between ethnic groups was a national issue in the 1890s. Posed together here, they reveal none of the ethnically-based antagonisms so prevalent between them.

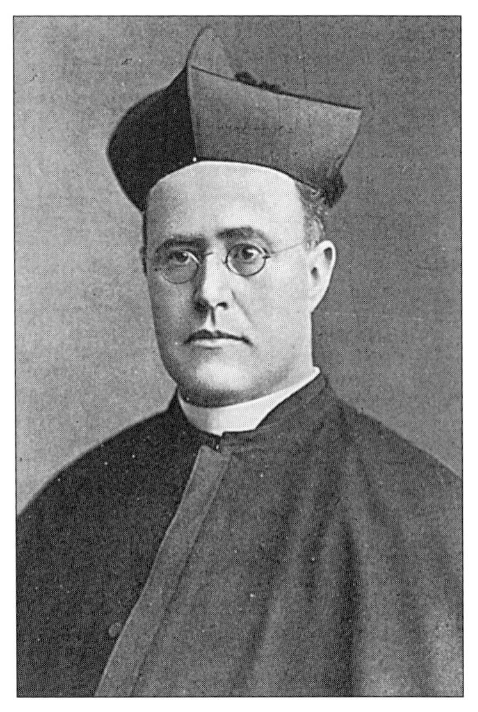

8. As president of Pittsburgh Catholic College, from 1886–1899, Father John T. Murphy, C.S.Sp. at last brought the stability and direction so desperately needed by the fledgling school. He soon saw that his own classical training alone would not meet the needs of Pittsburgh's students; he added classes in physics and chemistry to the curriculum, and he established a well-equipped laboratory. He also expanded the liberal arts curriculum, adding specialties in his own favorites, dramatics, debating, and elocution. He insisted that instruction take place only in English, a stance that alienated many Pittsburghers of German descent.

In 1887 Murphy established the Association of Past Students, predecessor to the Duquesne University Alumni Association.

9. Father Murphy's pump. In 1889, the dam of the South Fork Hunting and Fishing Club on the Conemaugh River burst, causing the Johnstown Flood and contaminating Pittsburgh's city water system. Father Murphy had a 150-foot well dug behind Old Main. The pump atop it was a gathering spot for students until it was capped in 1938. Shown here in this 1931 photo are student athletes Aldo "Buff" Donelli, Joe Pesci, Al Benedict, and Andy Smeaton.

10. In the 1880s and '90s, Pittsburgh Catholic College wrested its playing fields from the tenements surrounding it. Old buildings were razed, the area was fenced, and trees were planted along its borders. In 1900 a grandstand was built; it stood across the playing field from Old Main. Here part of the grandstand doubles as an outdoor church in a benediction service. Note the row of young trees and the Frick Building in the background.

11. From the beginning, athletics were included in the Pittsburgh Catholic College curriculum, in order to compensate for the strains of scholarly study. The Holy Ghost fathers saw athletics as something to do rather than something to watch. Student field days, with calisthenics, gymnastics, and dumbbell exercises were perhaps equal to varsity sports in importance. This 1910 photo shows an outdoor gymnastic drill. The students appear to be from the Preparatory School, a division similar to a modern high school.

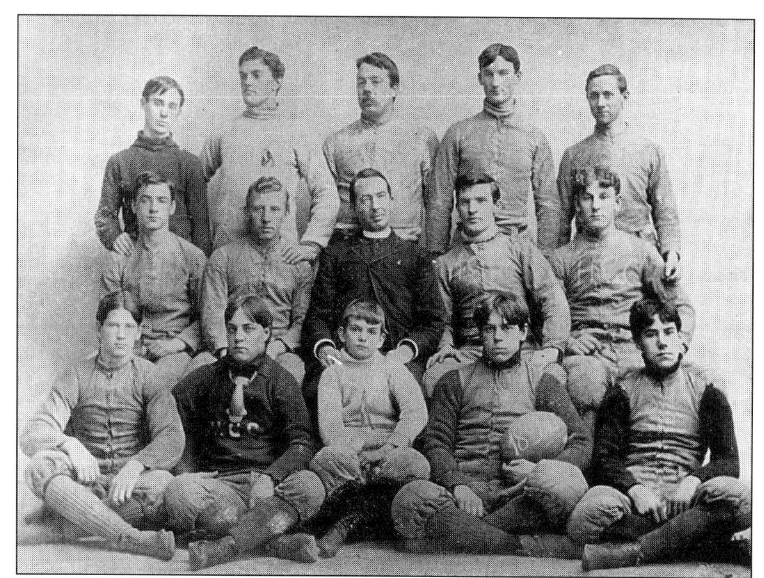

12. The 1894 football team. In 1891, football, or "American Rugby," was one of the first team sports organized at the college, and on one of the earliest teams was a student named Henry McDermott. Several years later, Father McDermott returned to teach at his alma mater, and he coached teams for several years. The young boy serving as the mascot was probably a student in the Grammar School. In the 1880s, an eight-year-old boy could begin his education at Pittsburgh Catholic College and stay until he achieved a Bachelor's degree.

Student Life in the Nineteenth Century

After the move to the Bluff, the college began to accept boarders as well as day students. Whether a student traveled to school each morning or rose in the dormitory at the required time of 6:15 a.m., he had to be in class at 9:00 a.m. or be refused admittance. In other words, there was no such thing as "tardy." One was either on time or marked absent. A student who was absent was required to supply an excuse from his parents and could not be readmitted to classes until the note was countersigned by the president or his representative. Classes ended at 2:30 p.m. Boarding fell into two groups, full boarders and half boarders (those who went home for the weekend). On Sundays the full boarding students were permitted to sleep until 6:40 a.m.!

In accordance with nineteenth century customs, students' days were strictly regulated. Attendance at Mass, study times, classes, and recreation were all carefully delineated. The day ended with night prayers in the chapel, and it was "lights out" at 9:00 p.m. On Sunday evening students went to a Benediction service at 7:15, followed by a concert and night prayers. The regimen was purposefully designed to prevent any impropriety. Even students' correspondence, except to parents or guardians, was subject to the supervision of college authorities, and publications of any sort were not delivered to the students until they had been examined and approved. Permission to leave the campus was granted only upon the written request of a parent.

The strict discipline produced a camaraderie among the boarders that was very valuable and enjoyable. Indeed, it was to prevent the loss of this sense of attachment that Father Murphy established the Association of Past Students in 1887, a predecessor to the Duquesne University Alumni Association.

The College Magazine

Beginning in the fall of 1894, the first issue of the *Pittsburgh College Bulletin* was published, presenting a collection of articles, essays, and poetry reflective of the liberal arts orientation of the school. In its first four years, the magazine was a quarterly publication, but general interest was sufficiently great that it became a monthly in October 1898. Its name was changed to the *Duquesne Monthly* in 1911. It held the distinction of being the oldest continuously published college periodical in the city.

The Versatile, Imaginative Father Murphy

Father Murphy seemed especially gifted in dealing with unexpected crises. In 1889 the dam of the South Fork Hunting and Fishing Club on the Conemaugh River burst, causing the Johnstown Flood and making Pittsburgh's drinking water even more undrinkable than usual. Only the foolhardy drank Pittsburgh's water without boiling it anyway (the city did not build a water filtration plant until 1908), but after the flood, the floating wreckage and animal carcasses made the contamination overwhelming. Since the college buildings were served by the city lines, the faculty and students were at risk to whatever diseases might be present in the water. Father Murphy to the rescue! He had a 150-foot well dug behind Old Main. The pump atop it quickly became a gathering spot for students and remained so until it was capped in 1938 at the urgings of health officials who objected to the use of a common dipper.[30]

"To Keep the Body in a Sound State": Pittsburgh Catholic College Athletics

The Holy Ghost fathers' ideal, according to the *Pittsburgh College Bulletin*, was "to keep the body in a sound state to compensate for the strains of study." The emphasis was on an intramural program with "every student an athlete trained in one or more branches . . . football, baseball, basketball, soccer and handball." Yet the property owned by the college was too small to permit outdoor sports—until,

> [a]t much expense and not a little diplomacy, the tenement houses [behind the college] were bought up and leveled to the ground. Mounds of clay were carried off and turned into bricks, and finally the brickyard itself disappeared. In March 1894, the Miller property was purchased [with other properties soon to follow], and steps were at once taken to have Eagle Street closed and incorporated with the college grounds.[31]

Gradually all of the property bounded by Bluff, Colbert, Locust, and the now nonexistent end of Shingiss Street[32] was purchased. By 1910 all of this property, with the exception of its northwest corner, had been secured. The northwest corner was a giant hole in the ground mined out by the brickyard. The old gymnasium (now the Rangos School of Health Sciences) was later built on this site. The story of how some tenement houses were displaced is a curious one:

> The late Brother Adolph . . . for a while was chief engineer, directing the blasting of the rocks and the leveling of the grounds. Little by little he approached the houses on the hill and the old foundations became insecure. The tenants had to abandon the houses. Thus one after the other they disappeared. At one time the brother had undermined the hill to quite an extent and had dug a tunnel cave. When a blast had been prepared in the cave, his voice rang out with the familiar "fire" and everyone scampered for cover. For they knew that the brother meant business, as one or other occasions the rocks and dirt were driven out of the tunnel as from the mouth of a cannon, scattering the rocks and dirt over the grounds, leaving marks on the building and endangering those within reach.[33]

The quadrupling of the college property made genuine outdoor athletic activities possible. Handball courts were built along Bluff Street. A wall and fences were constructed, ground was sodded, and an avenue, fourteen feet wide and lined with alternate poplar and maple trees, was made to run along the borders of the site. A grandstand was erected opposite the college buildings that seated 600 spectators, many of whom donned the school colors, dating from the Holy Ghost Order, of red and blue.

Athletics was seen as an aid to the student in developing self-control as well as good health. The 1904 catalog advertised that "every possible opportunity is given to the students of the College to secure the relaxation of mind and body necessary to the proper development of their health, as well as to the successful maintenance of discipline." The YMCA was a source of wholesome recreation for Protestant boys, but local Catholic parishes lacked the resources to provide similar programs. The December 1914 issue of the *Duquesne Monthly* addressed the concern thus: "The desire for recreation is natural and legitimate. The young men of today are bound to have it and if they cannot find it in their parish lyceum, they will seek it either in pool rooms, theaters, or on street corners, all of which are very often the occasion of sin. . . . Therefore, let us hope that our Catholic lyceums will soon realize the important position they hold in influencing our young men and that they will succeed in keeping them interested."

From the viewpoint of the College's treasurer, athletics had yet another practical value; it was a means of encouraging students to board on campus. "The boarders have an extra hour's apparatus work every Saturday morning—another reason why some of our day scholars ought to join the ranks of the resident students."[34]

Besides the expectation that every student participate in sports, the school also organized official teams. There were neither paid coaches—the Holy Ghost Fathers coached varsity teams—nor an established intercollegiate schedule. In 1891 football, which at the time was called "American rugby," was among the first team sports organized.[35] In the first few years of competition, the school played athletic clubs, YMCA teams, as well as other local colleges, including Western University. In the fall of 1897 their schedule included Bethany, Washington and Jefferson, Geneva, and West Virginia. The regulations that were later to characterize intercollegiate athletics had not yet been formed when the college hired a football coach in 1898. So Mr. Van Cleve, already a college graduate, was a player as well as a coach.[36] Moreover, so-called "tramp athletes" who were not students but played for several colleges during a single season, were in the Pittsburgh Catholic College lineup.

Baseball was played on the same newly acquired grounds that the football team used. "Excellent nines were sponsored and tales too numerous to mention are related to Bluffite diamond and gridiron warriors of the Gay Nineties."[37] In June of 1899, however, the *Bulletin* lamented "that during the past season our [baseball] teams have not been sufficiently supported to keep them on the field." That same issue went on to credit playing baseball as a means to football success since the same athletes played in both sports. To the *Bulletin* it was only logical that "if we succeed in equalling the excellent records made in past years we can safely begin the next Football season with assurance of success."[38] The baseball schedule (which in 1901 began on April 20 and ended on June 19) was as bizarre to moderns as the football schedule. The 15 games included such opponents as the Carnegie Steel Company, Polish Athletic Club, and Past Students Association (Alumni), as well as West Virginia University, and Washington and Jefferson College. In 1901 the team even played the Pittsburgh Pirates major league team, to whom they lost by a score of 17 to 3.[39]

Important though the varsity sports may have been to school spirit, it should be noted that the philosophy of the Holy Ghost Fathers saw athletics essentially as a participatory activity rather than as a spectator function. Therefore, student field days—with calisthenics, pyramid building, dumbbell exercises, track, and so on—practiced outdoors, and involving the entire faculty, were perhaps equal to varsity athletics in importance. In sum, physical education was seen as an integral part of the process of creating the whole man, fit in mind and body.

The Building of the Chapel

The spiritual formation of the individual was, of course, considered more important than the physical development, and Father Murphy earnestly desired a *real* college chapel for the religious services that were being held in the fifth floor chapel / theater of Old Main. It was decided to build a chapel connected directly to the back of the main college building where the land had already been leveled. In addition to using less land, the chapel would be symbolically as well as physically connected to the main college building. This was made possible when the city vacated Bonus Alley behind Old Main in 1893. However, the business depression that had begun the year before hindered the fundraising efforts of the college, and Father Murphy had to be satisfied with half a chapel for a while. A wooden sanctuary was constructed at the uncompleted end.[40] The chapel was not finished until 1904.

The chapel is of red brick matching the main college building but without the intervening stone layers.[41] At the corners, stone towers were constructed with castle-like merlons and crenels, a curious touch for an ecclesiastical building. The inside is vaguely Gothic in style. The magnificent stained glass windows, made in Munich, Germany, were donated—along with many of the other interior appointments, such as the side altars and confessionals—by generous friends of the college. Their names, or those of whomever they wished to memorialize, are inscribed at the bottom of each window directly on the glass. Through the efforts of Father Griffin, an organ with 1,290 pipes was installed in 1896.[42]

In 1897 Father Murphy secured from Rome the relics of St. Romulus, the boy martyr. These were placed beneath the high altar along with a full-size wax image of the saint. The image was contained in a glass case in view of the congregation until the 1950s when a remodeling of the altar covered it completely. There it lay undisturbed and "more or less forgotten" until 1968, when, in another renovation of the chapel, it was discovered by some astonished workmen.

The basement beneath the chapel was equipped as a theater, for Father Murphy made no secret of his love of the dramatic arts. It was he who inaugurated the custom of a yearly play. The stage was also used as a debating platform, and, most commonly, as a place from which to address the students. In later years, generations of Duquesne students would remember the theater as the scene of some of their largest undergraduate classes.

Father Murphy could take pride in the work of the Holy Ghost Fathers, but like the chapel that was not yet complete, neither was his work. This, however, would be left to others, for in June of 1899, Father Murphy was transferred to Ireland to become head of Blackrock College.[43] His successor was as competent and energetic as he. His name was Rev. Martin A. Hehir, and his presidency was to last 31 years.

2. A University is Born

An Irishman, born and bred, Father Martin A. Hehir, came to the Pittsburgh Catholic College as a newly ordained Holy Ghost Father in 1884,[1] became vice president in 1892, and succeeded Father Murphy as president seven years later. It was under his guiding hand that the college would become a university and grow to become the seventh largest Catholic school in the United States. Never, before or since, would one man be such an overshadowing figure to the school.

When Father Hehir became president, the college prospectus listed the divisions as (1) the Collegiate, which was the regular college course leading to a B.A. Degree; (2) the Academic, the high school department; (3) the Commercial, to prepare one to enter business; (4) the Scientific, a preparatory course leading to the study of medicine, engineering, or one of the exact sciences; and (5) the Grammar, the equivalent of the grade school. It was possible for a boy to begin his schooling on the Bluff at age eight and stay until he received a college degree.

The Student Body

A study conducted by the U.S. Immigration Commission revealed that some 51 percent of the immigrants' children making up the student body at Pittsburgh Catholic College were Irish, 31 percent were German, 9 percent Polish, 4 percent Hungarian, and 4 percent "Bohemian."[2] This was in 1908, but even as late as 1928, Irish names predominated, making up about 40 percent of the school's graduation list. The importance of ethnicity and of the inevitable conflict between ethnic groups, especially the Irish and the Germans, can scarcely be overemphasized. Indeed, it was a nationwide conflict in the 1890s. Consequently, Father Murphy's opposition to instruction in any language other than English had been interpreted by Germans as hostile and lost him the support of the area's German clergy, as well as several of his own confreres. Actually, Father Murphy feared that perpetuating any foreign language would only serve to isolate that ethnic group and deprive it of its rightful influence in American society. Nevertheless, the school could not afford an enrollment decline, so Father Murphy stepped down. Happily for the future of the school, Father Hehir quickly repaired relations with the German clergy and enrollment began to climb once more.

But it climbed slowly, very slowly. Despite the growth of the city—by 1910 Pittsburgh had a population of 533,905—the growth of Pittsburgh's only Catholic college was typified by its 4 percent increase from 1910 to 1911—going from an enrollment of 375 to a total of 390 in all divisions. And most of those were in the noncollege divisions. Still, the area's Catholic population tended to view Pittsburgh Catholic College as *the* primary institution of higher learning.

Father Hehir had accurately assessed the competitive nature of his adopted country. In his 1902 commencement address, he had declared, "Never before in the history of this country has the struggle for supremacy been keener than at the present moment. Victory lies with the most intelligent, with the best educated." At that time the percentage of the nation's total labor force that was classified as blue collar was 48 percent as compared with 62 percent for the Catholic labor force. Accordingly, the president had begun a reorganization of the school in which the College Division was made into a four-year school clearly separate from the Preparatory School.

He also had established, in 1900, complete scholarships of $1,000 each for boys selected by the pastors of each of the parish schools in Pittsburgh and Allegheny City, reactivating the long dormant Burses Fund. The absence of a Catholic upper class able to fund such scholarships is underscored by a 1916 list of donors to the Burses Fund. The list is composed entirely of the bishop and the priests of the diocese. This fund might have constituted the first real step taken by the school in building what could be described as an endowment, but it did not occur. Father Hehir "had his own free and easy bookkeeping system which could allow for a promising young man who could not afford the education it was apparent he would appreciate."[3] Both the Burses Fund and the pay-if-you-can system were administered in a completely nondiscriminatory fashion, which doubtless did much to raise the good will of the Germans toward the Irish-born president.

Fighting City Hall

Despite Father Hehir's apparent insouciance regarding money, he apparently was a good administrator. When he took office in 1899, the college debt, incurred largely as a consequence of the construction of Old Main, had been reduced only $20,000 in 13 years. It was still $130,000. By 1909, however, the school was debt-free. But taxes were a concern. For reasons not entirely clear, the tax status of the college was uncertain, and the city of Pittsburgh maintained that the college was not exempt from its real estate taxes. (The assessment for 1901 amounted to $2,000.36.) On the advice of its lawyers, the college had not paid any taxes since its move to the Bluff. Father Hehir feared that at any time the city might decide to foreclose. Not wanting the matter to be drawn out any further, Father Hehir asked the law firm that regularly represented the college to initiate court action. In March 1902 the court decided in favor of the college. "This sword of Damocles, so long suspended over the head of the staff, was thus removed and occasioned no little rejoicing and congratulations."[4] Still another potential disaster had been averted. With that financial uncertainty out of the way, Father Hehir felt justified in finishing the chapel. Work was completed in 1904, just in time to celebrate the college's 25th anniversary.

The University Charter

For two years, Hehir and the college faculty had considered applying to the state for elevation to university status. The socioeconomic condition of Catholics had improved steadily during the last quarter of a century. Professional occupations, heretofore largely closed to them, were beginning to open up. A story from 1911 has an old millhand at a Pittsburgh factory saying of the Irish, Germans, and Welsh that "some of them are still in the better paying jobs in the mills; but mostly you'll have to look for them among the doctors and lawyers, office holders, clerks, accountants, salesmen."[5] And therefore, "if preparation for the professions was not to be exclusively under non-Catholic auspices in the Pittsburgh area, it was incumbent upon Duquesne to move towards university status. Other established urban Catholic schools such as St. John's, Marquette, DePaul, and Loyola of Chicago all took this step between 1906 and 1909."[6]

Through most of the nineteenth century, any institution of higher learning with the power to confer degrees could obtain a charter from the county court in whose jurisdiction it was located. These lax circumstances changed abruptly in 1895, when the Pennsylvania General Assembly set forth a new and precise manner of incorporating all "institutions of learning with power to confer degrees in art, pure and applied science, philosophy, literature, medicine and law and theology . . ." Among other things, the act required the applying institution to have at least $500,000 in assets and at least six full-time professors. The college could easily meet this second requirement as it had 16 Holy Ghost fathers on staff, including Father Hehir, and eight full-time lay professors. Six other laymen taught part-time, and nine Holy Ghost brothers were classified as "auxiliaries." The first requirement, $500,000 in assets, was more problematic.

A special College and University Council made up of educators from across the Commonwealth would rule on the application. In the 15 years of the council's existence, no application from a Catholic college had yet come before it! Pittsburgh Catholic College became the first, on June 18, 1910, when it applied to become the "University of the Holy Ghost" with powers to confer advanced degrees in law, medicine, dentistry, and pharmacy. The council had convened so infrequently its members did not know exactly how to proceed, nor were they certain of the extent of their powers. Still, the attorneys handling the application, the firm of Watson and Freeman, were given ample warning that the examination process was not to be taken lightly and that the Carnegie Foundation was likely to oppose the college's petition. But it appeared that heaven had provided an ally for the school, right there on the council. Dr. Nathan Schaeffer, secretary of the council, acted as an informal conduit of information to the bishop of Harrisburg and thus aided the cause immeasurably. A forewarned Father Hehir began to muster his forces with all the preparation of a general about to do battle. Letters of endorsement were obtained from every bishop in Pennsylvania and two from outside the state, the mayor of Pittsburgh, the area's representative in Congress, and a host of Catholic organizations including the Knights of Columbus, the Knights of St. George, the Catholic Mutual Benefit Association, and the Ancient Order of Hibernians. In his letter to the council, representative of many others, Bishop Canevin of Pittsburgh argued that one fourth of the population of Pennsylvania was Catholic and lamented "we have not so far even one center of complete University education for our people and our families."[7] The hearings dragged on for nine months. But, despite Father Hehir's sinking hopes, they were dragging on to a positive conclusion. Certainly, no observer would have predicted it, and who is to say when the tide turned?

Harry F. Stambaugh, the attorney representing the college, perceived the main hurdle as a matter of satisfying the $500,000-asset requirement. In this belief, he posed endless and minute questions to the parade of witnesses who appeared on behalf of the college. No asset was overlooked; even the handball courts, the steam boiler in the basement, and the stained glass windows in the chapel did not escape scrutiny.

The testimony revealed that the college owned an eight-acre farm used as a summer retreat by the college faculty and students. The college also had a "scientific fund," money donated to purchase laboratory equipment, of $2,000, plus $11,340 in a scholarship endowment (the Burses Fund) invested in first mortgages on Pittsburgh real estate. Not including the free teaching services of the Holy Ghost fathers, reckoned at $20,000 a year, these constituted virtually the entire endowment the college had at the time. The inventory of equipment owned by the college gives an interesting view of its facilities in 1910:[8]

Libraries		10,200
Commercial Hall & Office	5,660	
Physics & Chemistry Apparatus	4,300	
Draughting Room	400	
Stationery Office		2,250
Father's Offices and Rooms	2,500	
Parlors	1,100	
Musical Instruments	3,425	
Furniture of Class Rooms & Study Halls	2,600	

Chapel and Hall Equipment (18 stained-glass windows, 8 altars, confessionals, stations, etc. Gymnastic apparatus, Pool and Billiard tables, chairs, etc.)	23,230		
Clocks, Pictures, Statues, etc.		700	
120 Beds & Bedding		2,000	
Dining Room Furniture			300
Kitchen, Scullery, Refrigerator		1,300	
Laundry, Electric Plant, Boiler, Heater		1,750	
Bakery, Store Rooms, Cellar		1,800	
Hand Ball Courts, Dressing Rooms, Well and Pump	3,600		
Shoemaker's Shop		250	
Tailor's Shop		100	
Carpenters Tools and Supplies			250

In October 1910 the situation took a decided turn for the worse when the council visited the campus and that of its sister institutions in the city. Henry S. Drinker, a member of the executive committee, concluded that there was "no necessity for another medical or law school in the Pittsburgh region for the needs of that particular locality or of the Commonwealth at large."[9] This opinion was almost certainly influenced by the Carnegie Foundation, which had filed a report opposing the establishment of any additional medical schools in Pennsylvania. And more bad news was forthcoming. Since the college had presented so many letters of endorsement and attached such importance to the letters from the bishops, the council asked what funding the school might count on from them. This inquiry elicited the fact that "the Archbishop [of Philadelphia] was not prepared at the time to say to what extent the Catholic Church in Pennsylvania would guarantee financial support to the University."[10] A desperate Father Hehir then contacted the Knights of Columbus. He was told that "the organization is presently involved in a similar campaign for the Catholic University of America and will be unable to help until that campaign is over."[11] Letters of endorsement were easier to obtain than money or even pledges of money.

From this shaky situation, though, somehow the college emerged once again victorious. The members of the council, most of whom were connected with other colleges and universities in the state, appeared to be decidedly *not* in favor of granting university status, yet in the end they voted unanimously to do so. The final meeting took place in Governor Edwin S. Stuart's office on December 30, 1910. Still acting as the attorney for the college, Mr. Watson made a final plea on its behalf. Reiterating Bishop Canevin's figures on the number of Catholics in the state, Mr. Watson added that the university would "be open to all the other people of the State whatever their religious belief." Whether it was his eloquence or some other tool of Providence, the council members were all swayed to let the "University of the Holy Ghost" have its chance.

Only the matter of the school's assets remained to be settled, and this meant that the petition now went back to where it started, in the Allegheny County Court of Common Pleas. The judge ordered fact-finding and appointed the Pittsburgh city engineer, two real estate businessmen and a builder to place a valuation on the property and buildings. They were the same men who had testified on behalf of the College before the Council in October! There was now little doubt as to the court's decision. The Pittsburgh Catholic College was found to have $730,485 in assets, well in excess of the required amount. At long last, on the 30th day of March, 1911, Judge Robert Frazer announced that the petition for a change in the school's charter was granted. The corporation was now the University of the Holy Ghost and its charter was changed to permit it "to confer degrees, in the sciences of law, medicine, dentistry and pharmacy." It thus became the first Catholic university in Pennsylvania and, at the time, the only Catholic university between Washington, D.C., and South Bend, Indiana. There was rejoicing in the halls of Old Main, the *Pittsburgh Catholic* ran banner headlines, and Father Hehir, now called Chancellor Hehir, breathed a sigh of relief.

The following June, when Father Hehir spoke at the university commencement exercises, he made clear the enormity of what had been accomplished:

> Let us not fail to bear in mind that there is not a single Catholic in that Council. . . . the charter was secured because we fought for it . . . it was a study to notice the expression of surprise on the countenances of the members of Council at Harrisburg when a clergyman from Pittsburgh in the name of the College, in the name of the Catholics of Pennsylvania, advanced reasons, such as they never heard before, why we should have a Catholic University in the State. They were more than astonished, they were dumbfounded that we demanded such a thing, and I doubt if some of them have fully recovered up to the present.

A New Name: Duquesne University

The University of the Holy Ghost was to exist under that name for less than two months. Hardly had the court granted the new title when a controversy erupted among the faculty. Some wanted "to retain the distinctive title of the religious order under whose auspices and general direction the new institution of higher learning was to be conducted," but others felt embarrassment at having "the vulgarity and apparent profanity of associating, especially in newspaper language, the sacred name of the 'Holy Ghost' with the expressions of these profane occasions." Perhaps some faculty members were horrified by the prospect of sports headlines with titles such as "Holy Ghost Whips _______" or worse, "_______ Whips Holy Ghost."

A petition to delete "The" in the University's title and substitute the word "Duquesne" explained:

> Said corporation desires to insert in its corporate title some additional and more distinctive name which will also indicate the locality in which the visitation is situated; and has selected the word "Duquesne" from Fort Duquesne which was the name of the first settlement made on the site of the present City of Pittsburgh and was derived from the name of the Catholic governor of the Province of Canada at the time when such settlement was made.[12]

On May 27, 1911, the name was formally changed to "Duquesne University of the Holy Ghost," which in 1935 was shortened to "Duquesne University." In 1960 the full name was restored. The name "Duquesne" was by no means unique.[13] An elite downtown business club had used the name since its founding in 1873. The nearby municipality of that name had existed since 1891. The Allegheny Light Company had changed its name to Duquesne Light Company in 1903, and scores of businesses were to use it as the century progressed. Indeed, the name became so popular that a song in a 1947 Pittsburgh Playhouse musical alluded to it: "No one knows the reason, no one can explain; but everything you look at is named Duquesne."

The Preparatory School

After the college became a university, the administration decided that a grammar school was no longer appropriate. Also, if new academic programs were to be created, the space would doubtless be needed. Beginning in 1911, the registrar's dockets show no new students admitted to the grammar school, and gradually it was phased out.

The Preparatory School was an entirely different story, however. Duquesne could not really depend on a supply of students from the diocesan high schools. In 1909 only 887 students were enrolled in all of the diocesan high schools combined, and of those who did go on to college, it was by no means certain that they would choose Duquesne. Of the 60 students graduating from the Preparatory School in 1911, a sizable majority, 43, received high school certificates. Eliminating it, therefore, was unthinkable if Duquesne were to remain financially sound. Its divisions were consolidated into a single school officially called the Duquesne Preparatory School, and it became more recognizable as a modern high school, the largest Catholic high school in the diocese.

Founding a School of Law

It was neither the grammar school nor the prep school that most occupied Father Hehir, however. No sooner had the new charter been granted than he set about founding a school of law. This followed an established pattern among Catholic universities. A law school was much less expensive and complicated to start and maintain than a medical school. In addition, it was far more compatible with the rest of the curriculum at an essentially liberal arts school. "Also," according to Duquesne history professor, Bernard J. Weiss, "it was viewed as producing the type of public men who could best assume leadership roles in both the Catholic and larger secular society to the credit of Catholicism."[14]

The law school opened to its first class of 12 students in September 1911 in three rented rooms on Fourth Avenue in the heart of Pittsburgh's financial district. Its first dean was the Honorable Joseph Swearingen, President of Common Pleas Court #4. Judge Swearingen had a statewide reputation and was assisted by another well-respected man of law, John Laughlin, Esq., "widely known and highly esteemed as one of the most prominent and brilliant of the younger members of the Bar."[15] Harry Stambaugh, Esq., who had represented the Pittsburgh Catholic College in its petition for a university charter, was also named to the school's first faculty.

Judge Swearingen was concerned that the school teach the spirit as well as the letter of the law. He wished to create "a thoroughly efficient Law School of the highest character and the broadest range in the determination of its specific and collateral courses," in which the students "would be taught the fundamental principles of legal ethics, and of justice, rights and duties, at every point of view." His goal was the training not only of successful attorneys, "but broad-gauged, cultural gentlemen."[16]

A student could be admitted to the law school who had graduated from an accredited four-year college or university. However, according to the *Duquesne University Bulletin* of 1911, a student 18 years of age could also be admitted by passing a general education examination. The school awarded both a bachelor of laws and master of laws degree.

Duquesne University was unique in offering night classes that afforded an opportunity for middle-class young working men to enter the legal profession. These men already had full-time white-collar jobs during the day, largely lower-paid positions in offices and banks.

Of the original class of 12, all passed the Bar examination in 1914, and were celebrated in a dinner presided over by Father Hehir. The surnames of this first graduating class revealed the primarily German, Irish, and English composition of the student body.[17] The law school's enrollment continually outgrew its accommodations, forcing it into a succession of relocations.[18]

A State Subsidy?

The rented locations, convenient though they might have been, underscored the neverending problem of funding. Despite the phasing out of the grammar school, there was not enough space because the university simply did not have enough money to build additional buildings. Endowment income was miniscule and tuition income insufficient to fund the needed expansion. While it was true that Duquesne's tuition in 1914 was about half the amount charged by the University of Pittsburgh, it could not be substantially increased without causing a serious strain on the financial resources of the students.

The university decided to seek funding from the state legislature. For nearly 40 years, the legislature had been making appropriations to Protestant church-related colleges, but no funds had ever been voted for a Catholic college or university. Aware of this, Father Hehir wisely decided to change some of the wording in the university's charter: the phrases, "and also the preparation and education of youths destined for the Catholic Priesthood," as well as, "And also to engage in a support of missionary and Congregational undertakings in the Catholic Church," were deleted. An amount of $210,000 was requested—$150,000 for a new building and $60,000 for maintenance.

Father Hehir and Father McDermott made several trips to Harrisburg to discuss the bill with members of the General Assembly. To their relief, the Appropriations Committee approved the full amount and sent it to the Senate, where there was no opposition. It passed the first and second readings in the House without much serious discussion, but opposition surfaced on the third reading. A prolonged debate centered almost exclusively on the fact that no previous appropriation had ever been made to a Catholic institution.

Finally, at ten minutes past midnight on June 10, 1913, the House of Representatives voted—somewhat surprisingly in view of the acrimony of the debate—162 to 3 in favor of the Duquesne University Appropriation Bill. It was then sent to Governor John K. Tener for his approval. At this time, the Knights of Pythias and various Masonic societies fell on the bill tooth and nail. Nevertheless, Father Hehir felt confident that the governor would sign the bill. A Pittsburgher, Tener had grown up near the campus, played baseball on the college playing field, and knew several of the Holy Ghost Fathers. He had even received support for his gubenatorial candidacy from the Knights of Columbus. To the amazement of nearly everyone at the university, though, the governor vetoed the bill. Disappointment blanketed the campus, and Father Hehir plotted his next move.

Since Governor Tener's term was due to expire in less than two years, the best course of action was to wait for a new governor, who, it was hoped, would prove more sympathetic to the needs of the university.[19] Father Hehir waited until 1915 for a second attempt. This time the university sought the reduced amount of $100,000 for maintenance only. No money for a new building was sought because it was learned that state funding entitled Pennsylvania to hold a lien against the university in the amount of the building's cost in the event it were used for noneducational purposes. The second try went much like the first; the bill was approved by the Appropriations Committee and sailed through both houses of the legislature, this time without a single dissenting vote. But, like his predecessor, Governor Martin G. Brumbaugh vetoed the bill.

Still a third attempt was made in 1917. The bill's sponsors again proposed $100,000 for maintenance, but this time the Appropriations Committee reduced the amount to $25,000. Once again the bill passed through the legislature without difficulty and went to the governor. This time Father Hehir succeeded in getting Governor Brumbaugh to sign the bill, but not before he further reduced the amount to $15,000.[20] The amount was especially disappointing in view of the sums then being approved for other colleges and universities in the state. Still, it increased revenue by about 10 percent, it placed Duquesne University on the regular appropriations list, and gave hope of increased amounts in future years. Certainly, appropriations were urgently needed every year. In 1920, a year for which figures are available, total receipts amounted to $133,156.53 and total expenditures amounted to $123,247.56. The university was in a fight for its existence, and the prayers of its supporters must have swung another battle its way, for in 1919 the legislature voted $50,000 for maintenance. No dissenting votes were cast in either chamber, and Governor William C. Sproul signed the bill. The General Assembly had voted funds for some 69 Protestant church-related colleges, institutions, and hospitals; to have vetoed only Duquesne's funding would have been so glaringly prejudicial as to have caused a public outcry.

Enter Mr. Collins

A recent battle may have been won, but in this life the war is never over, and Duquesne University took a serious hit in 1920 from one Willis Collins, who brought suit alleging that the Appropriation Bill of 1919 violated the Pennsylvania State Constitution. Article 3, Section 18 of the 1874 Constitution then in effect stated, "No appropriations . . . shall be made for charitable, educational or benevolent purposes, to any person or community nor to any denominational or sectarian institution, corporation, or association." Four Protestant hospitals in various locations around the state elected to go to court as a group. Duquesne University elected to fight its legal battle alone.

Thus began the case of *Willis Collins v. Harmon M. Kephart, State Treasurer of Pennsylvania, and Duquesne University of the Holy Ghost, of Pittsburgh*. The bill of complaint against all 69 colleges charged that they were operated by a particular religious denomination, that devotional exercises were carried on, that the students received religious instruction, and that other religions were not tolerated. The lawyers for the plaintiff also entered a complaint against Duquesne University stating:

> That the By-laws and Rules of Government of Duquesne University of Pittsburgh provide substantially that all the officers and governing body shall be composed of members of the Roman Catholic Priesthood and Church, and that said institution shall be under the control and domination of the same, and that all property of said institution shall be owned and controlled by officials of the said church.

At the trial that began in September 1920, the lawyers for the plaintiff argued that an appropriation was made to a nonexistent institution, "Duquesne University of Pittsburgh." Basing their case on a narrow interpretation of the charter, they averred that the university was under the control and direction of the Holy Ghost Fathers of the Roman Catholic Church and that a majority of the officers of the school must profess that faith. They also claimed that most of the textbooks had to be approved by the Catholic hierarchy and that non-Catholic students were obliged to attend religious services against their will. Both of these latter claims were completely unfounded.

Although the court dismissed the case, Mr. Collins immediately filed an appeal with the Supreme Court of the State of Pennsylvania, and this court held that the purpose of Article 3 was indeed to prohibit the state from giving recognition, directly or indirectly, to any particular religious denomination—even though that institution might bestow its benefits on others not of its faith. Noting that church-related colleges had been receiving state aid for 40 years, the court nevertheless ruled that being generally assented to by public authority did not give the practice legality. Finally, addressing itself to Duquesne University, the court ruled that a college is within the prohibitions of the state constitution when its name indicates a relationship with a specific religious denomination that supplies most of the faculty members, and where it appears that religious services of this denomination are held in its chapel, and a course in its doctrines is given in its curriculum, even if attendance at either chapel or class are not compulsory. Hence, "We can but conclude that the institution in question is sectarian and denominational, within the inhibition of the constitution, and may not receive state aid." A seven-year legislative and court battle had come to an unsatisfactory end. Father Hehir and the Catholics of Pennsylvania could not help but wonder why no such court ruling on public funding had occurred until Duquesne University was the recipient.

But the administration was not preoccupied with the issue of state funding. It was preoccupied with the growth and development of the university. And it was looking to a higher source than the state government for that.

Founding A Business School

Despite the closed door to state funding, the university survived—and expanded. Back in 1913 it had founded a business school, the School of Accounts, Finance, and Commerce. Housed downtown in a single room in the George Building, the same building where the Law School was located, the business school grew steadily through the years, offering night courses for young men already in business as well as day classes for full-time students.[21]

Dr. William M. Walker, the first dean, was recruited from the Wharton School of Business of the University of Pennsylvania. The program he organized provided practical instruction in the principles of accounting, banking, and general business. As he put it,

> The student is able to acquire in the classes of this school a thorough practical and concise knowledge of business procedure such as cannot be had outside the University, except by long years of tedious study and grinding experience. The man who learns merely by observation and home reading, or who depends upon his daily experience for improvement, is dissipating his energies and wasting his opportunities for a much better and more thorough knowledge can be gained in the University with the expenditure of but a fraction of the energy and time thus consumed.[22]

The school began with 14 students and three professors. By 1918 the faculty had grown to 12—five CPAs, one Ph.D., and six others holding law degrees. All of the faculty were successful businessmen in their own right.

Until 1931, the school offered a two-year certificate program in "Commercial Science" (which required four years of study in the night school). The bachelor of science in economics required eight years in the night school or four years in the day school. The day school also offered a six-year combination course in economics and law leading to a combined bachelor of science in economics and a bachelor of law degree.

Using the same procedure as the University of Chicago, the Duquesne Business School was one of the first to base graduation requirements on comprehensive examinations. And Duquesne was the first to introduce the industrial engineering approach to its courses and to require philosophy courses and specified readings outside of the business field in preparing future businessmen to deal with both business and social life.

Since the business school began its first year rather late and with very little public notice, the administration decided to open the second year with an elaborate exercise. In his speech, Father Hehir made a scathing observation on the abbreviated courses offered by some business colleges:

> We always discountenanced the deceptive system of so-called business colleges, which sell diplomas and scholarships, and turn out bookkeepers by the score, after five or six months. This we consider a deception to parents, an injustice of young men and an insult to business methods. All true educators believe in the necessity of a broad general education at the beginning; then comes specialization, according to the states of life young men embrace.

> This holds true for all the professions, and it holds true, especially in our age and country for business men.

The school was also rightfully proud of its commercial library, serviced by a full-time librarian. This library, built around the core of books brought from the Wylie Avenue location when the college moved to the Bluff, was the most complete collection of its kind in the city next to the main branch Carnegie Public Library.

The founding of the business school reflected both change and continuity at Duquesne. In the days before the university charter, the single largest group of students was enrolled in the high school Commercial Department. For most of them, the educational process ended with a high school diploma. These graduates gained entrance, on at least a modest scale, to the white-collar business world. As the century approached its second quarter, the marketplace became more sophisticated, and the university fulfilled its new higher requirement. By 1928 some 1160 students were enrolled in the business school, accounting for 49 percent of the total student body. Actually, among all Catholic colleges and universities in the late 1920s, students enrolled in schools of business administration in much higher percentages than students in non-Catholic schools. At the University of Pittsburgh, for instance, enrollment in the business school accounted for only 6 percent of the student body. The trust that students placed in business education at the college level, as opposed to climbing the corporate ladder thorough experience and seniority, proved to be well founded. Graduates of the School of Business Administration of Duquesne University assumed executive positions in the city, throughout the United States, and even abroad. In 1915, seven of the eight graduates of the CPA class received certificates in a city that up until that time had only 18 certified accountants.

Oratory, Debate, and Drama

Not all of the expansion in the wake of the university charter was of such a practical nature. A weekly "playlet" and an annual play had been an established tradition at Duquesne. Oratory and debate were also frequent additions to the calendar of events. One of Father Murphy's dreams was realized in the fall of 1913 when the School of Speech Arts and Drama was founded.[23] He chose an experienced actor and producer of the outdoor pageant-drama *Hiawatha*, Dr. Clinton Lloyd, to head the new school. The school was "planned to meet the requirements of the orator, debater, instructor, platform reader, actor and all those whose success in life depends in whole or in part on their ability to express their thoughts and feeling with conviction, gracefulness, and magnetic clearness." A complete and comprehensive course in stage direction was also available, and in later years the program added a course in "Shakespearean Interpretation."[24] Enrollment was so low that it was difficult to justify the drama school's existence, and in 1940 it was discontinued. But the Red Masquers drama club, which the school had birthed in 1914, survived and continued to perform in the theatre under the college chapel.

New Departments: From Social Services to Latin American Commerce

In 1916, Duquesne founded its School of Social Services as an outgrowth of the Department of Economics and Sociology begun in 1911. The school was an early experiment in adult education, designed for businessmen, charity workers, priests, and candidates to the priesthood to receive training and practical field experience. Covering family welfare, child welfare, community work, medical social service, industrial service, and a parish school service, the two-year program led to a diploma.

Also dedicated to the betterment of the community was the Sanitary Science and Public

13. Rev. Martin A. Hehir, C.S.Sp., president (1899-1930), came to the Pittsburgh Catholic College as a newly ordained Holy Ghost father in 1884. He became vice president in 1892 and succeeded Father Murphy as president seven years later. It was under his guiding hand that the college would become a university and grow to become the seventh largest Catholic school in the United States. Never, before or since, would one man be such an overshadowing figure to the school.

14. The new chapel, begun under the resourceful Father Murphy's direction in 1893, quickly became the spiritual center of Duquesne. Renovated many times after its completion in 1904, its interior, shown here in 1938, was an ornate form of Victorian Gothic. Its stained glass windows were made in Munich, Germany, and donated by friends of the college. Thanks to the efforts of Father Griffin (photo 7), chapelgoers enjoyed the music of an organ with 1,290 pipes. The chapel connected directly to the back of the main building, and its red brickwork matched that of the older structure, although it did not have the intermittent stone layers included in the earlier building. The corners were castle-like stone towers ornate with merlons and crenels, a curious touch for an ecclesiastical building. The wax image of St. Romulus, the boy martyr, was a visible part of the altar until the 1950s. The relics themselves rested beneath the altar.

15. The Marquis Du Quesne, first governor of New France (in what is now Canada). The first settlement made on the site of Pittsburgh was named Fort Duquesne in his honor, and, by the 1900s many city sites and businesses had adopted the name. On May 27, 1911, the two-month-old University of the Holy Ghost became "Duquesne University of the Holy Ghost," and eventually, simply "Duquesne University." In 1960 the full name was restored.

Pittsburgh City Photographer

16. This photo, taken in 1916, demonstrates the degree to which the Administration Building (on the left), sitting atop Boyd's Hill and crowned with its elaborate cupola, dominated the Pittsburgh skyline.

17. The Honorable Joseph M. Swearingen, President of Common Pleas Court #4 and first dean of the Duquesne University of the Holy Ghost Law School, 1911–1929. He wanted a school in which students "would be taught the fundamental principles of legal ethics, and of justice, rights, and duty at every point of view. The law school opened with a class of 12 students in September 1911, in three rented rooms on Fourth Avenue, in the heart of Pittsburgh. Of these original 12, all passed the bar examination in 1914.

18. The George Building on 4th Avenue in 1911. This downtown site was chosen as the home of the Law School so that office workers by day could conveniently attend night classes. In Pittsburgh, Duquesne University was unique in offering night classes, creating an opportunity for middle-class young working men to enter the legal profession. No day classes were offered.

19. One of Father Murphy's dreams was realized in the fall of 1913, when the School of Speech Arts and Drama was founded. A weekly "playlet" and an annual play soon became traditional at Duquesne. Although at this time a few women were admitted to the university on a case-by-case basis, there were none in this 1913 student production of *Why Smith Left Home.*

20. Collegiate football was played by very loose rules in the early 1900s. In 1903, so many "Hillmen" were injured in one game that President Father Hehir banished varsity football the next season. But students continued to field intramural teams. Shown here is a 1919 football team. Art Rooney, later to rise to fame with the Pittsburgh Steelers, is in the second row, sixth man from the left. His brother Dan Rooney is in the same row, second from the left.

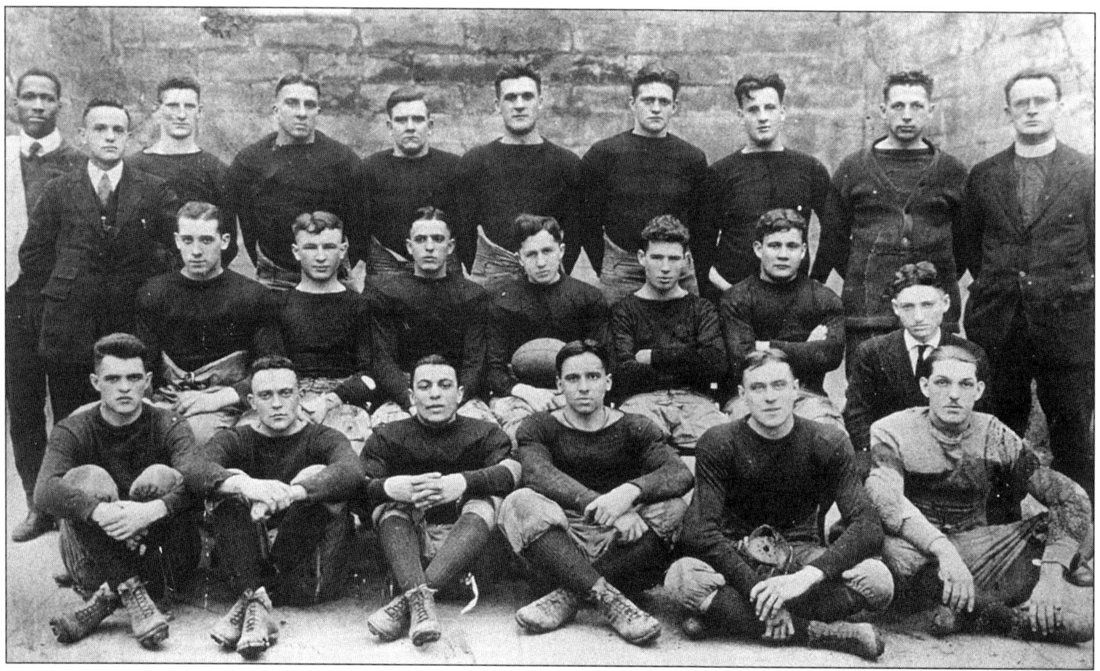

21. Baseball initially fared far better than football at Duquesne. The university fielded winning teams for almost 20 years. Known as the "Dukes," the "Bluffites" or the "Hillmen," they played both local teams and teams from as far away as Milton, Massachusetts. The 1916 team appears here. Standing third from left is Cumberland Willis Posey (Posey Cumbert). An African American from nearby Homestead, Posey joined the National Negro League's Homestead Grays in 1911. Two years later he was captain of the team. Next he joined the Hillmen at Duquesne, where he contributed to both baseball and basketball, playing until he was 27, although there is no record of him ever enrolling as a student. Later, he became a nationally known baseball organizer, manager, and owner, leading the Grays to the National Negro League pennant for eight consecutive seasons.

22. The entire 1907 graduating class of the Classical Department. Study of the classics was one of the earliest courses of study at the university, and one dear to Father Hehir, trained in the classics at Blackrock College, Ireland. His position in the center of the group is both literal and symbolic; students of this discipline were "his" boys.

23. Duquesne University of the Holy Ghost, with its strong ethnic and historical ties to Germany, found it especially important to enthusiastically and openly support the United States' participation in World War I. In the summer of 1917, Duquesne initiated a military training program and formed two infantry companies that practiced drills on the playing fields behind Old Main. Duquesne bought 100 guns at $4 each to arm its reserves. By 1918, over 220 students had enlisted in the nation's armed forces; at least 15 died there. That same year, the school gave up its new School of Social Services to establish and maintain a unit of the Students Army Training Corps (SAT), complete with barracks and infirmary. Shown here is part of the SAT squadron, Dec. 3, 1918.

24. A chemistry lab in 1916. This program included the Sanitary Science and Public Health Department, which worked with the Allegheny County Board of Health to prepare chemists for government work, primarily in analyzing food and milk. Some of these students might have been enrolled in Duquesne's Pre-Medical Program, designed in 1913 to help students meet the State Board of Examiners' qualifications for medical school candidates. Note that there are no lab whites; coats and ties were standard dress.

Health Department, which operated in conjunction with the Allegheny County Board of Health in preparing chemists for government work, primarily in the analysis of food and milk.

Before World War I, Duquesne had departments of Vocal and Instrumental Music, Fine Arts, Pre-Medical, and even Spanish Language and Latin American Commerce. One of these departments, Pre-Medical, begun in 1913, was designed to meet the qualifications of the State Board of Examiners for specialized preparation of medical school candidates in lieu of the scientific course. The program's success was demonstrated in its Class A rating and affiliation with medical schools throughout the country.[25]

Founding a Graduate School

The School of Graduate Studies was established in 1911. The following year, Duquesne began offering summer courses attended primarily but not exclusively by underclassmen. A few students who wished to pursue work beyond the bachelor's degree made special arrangements with the faculty for graduate courses. Within three years of the founding of the graduate school, the number of graduate students had increased sufficiently to warrant the formation of the Committee on Graduate Studies to organize and supervise the work. In 1924 Rev. James F. Carroll, C.S.Sp., S.T.D., was appointed to head both the graduate school and the College of Arts—obviously a man of far-ranging talents. The College of Arts, which traces its origins to the very founding of the Pittsburgh Catholic College, remained the nucleus of the university and home of many departments, among them music, languages, education, history, philosophy, and classics. Only in the 1920s did Education and Music become separate schools.

Athletics and "College Spirit"

When Father Hehir assumed the presidency in 1899, collegiate athletics were not seen as spectator sports but as an integral part of the curriculum for all students. But that began to change. Looking back on the pre-war era, the January 1924 issue of the *Duquesne Monthly* observed Notre Dame's early realization of the value of public recognition through varsity sports:

> Ten years ago Notre Dame was reckoned a pretty fair school, a school with an unimpeachable reputation, but not known to any vast extent than any one of six or eight Catholic institutions spread throughout the land. But Notre Dame was more than just "pretty fair," she had more than a mere reputation. Notre Dame had vision . . . Cannot Duquesne learn something from Notre Dame? Cannot the Red and Blue take the chance of the Blue and Gold?

Father O'Hara, president of Notre Dame, claimed that the school made $4 million from football in ten years, money they were able to put into their educational programs and facilities.[26]

Not only had the Red and Blue failed to "take the chance of the Blue and Gold" in using football publicity to advance its national reputation, it had frequently suffered criticism for its lack of "college spirit." The December 1919 issue of the *Duquesne Monthly* commented,

> College spirit may be defined as that which makes college life what it is. Taking the college spirit of our present students as a criterion, the college life at D.U. is a pretty poor one. Let us examine our consciences. Must we not admit it—we are a passive and indifferent lot. Some of you do not even know how many teams we have. This is an unhappy and dangerous state—unhappy for the players and students, and dangerous for the institution.

Duquesne's "college spirit" had waxed and waned over the years, depending on the particular sport—football, baseball, or basketball—and on the tenor of the times.

Collegiate football was played by very loose rules back in 1903, when "a certain disastrous conflict with Wash-Jeff [Washington and Jefferson College] left so many Hillmen on the injured list that Father Hehir . . . put exceedingly conclusive quietus on further tussling." Varsity football was discontinued after the season despite this view from the *Pittsburgh College Bulletin*:

> For various reasons (which we need not discuss here, as they seemed good to our betters) no Varsity football team was organized. But football and football enthusiasm has by no means died out among the students. In fact, there is more life and activity on the campus these sunny days of Indian Summer than at any other season of the year. Five [intramural] teams have been organized and good schedules arranged by all. (Nov. 1904)

The Pittsburgh Catholic College was not the only school concerned about unnecessary roughness in football, and rule changes were effected two years later, but they "were found wanting."[27] In fact, "association football"—that is, soccer—became more popular than regular football for a while, considered safer and of more physical benefit. The administration refused to reactivate varsity football until 1913, and then it lasted only two seasons—two losing seasons (2–4 and 0–5). It reappeared in 1920 with similarly disappointing results. Even the athletic determination of Art Rooney, later of Pittsburgh Steeler fame, and his brother Dan, was not sufficient to field a winning team. Happily, their own careers on the Bluff ended in a blaze of athletic glory.

Baseball fared better at Duquesne. Shortly after the turn of the century, the college sponsored the formation of the Athletic Association to raise funds for the baseball team. "A small fee is levied on the members each month, which with a little more aid, will enable the 'Varsity Team' to appear on the Campus with new uniforms," explained the *Pittsburgh College Bulletin* in March 1901. Membership was a matter of school spirit. The Athletic Association even asked its members to sell season tickets to baseball games. The season began in late April and ended in June. Although the college played schools as far away as Curry College in Milton, Massachusetts, most games were played with local opponents, both collegiate and noncollegiate. Some games were extraordinary. In 1914 Duquesne played the Chinese University of Honolulu at Forbes Field. "The Orientals played the game like veterans, though the runs made by the Dukes were scored when the pitcher lost his head for a few moments in the antepenultimate sessions," exulted the *Duquesne Monthly* in July 1914. The term "Dukes" may have been an official name, but it was used interchangeably with "Bluffites," and "Hillmen." These were halcyon days for Duquesne baseball, when winning was a tradition. In 1907 the team compiled a 19–1 record.

The winning baseball team of the first two decades on the Bluff hit hard times with America's entry into the First World War. "In the spring of 1918 it was discovered that not enough men of college rating were left on the enrollment rosters to warrant as feasible an attempt to continue baseball." When play was resumed the following year, the impetus had been lost. Duquesne's baseball record from 1919 to 1924 resembled its football team's losing record.

The baseball team produced a number of colorful characters, perhaps the best known of which was Gregory I. Zsatkovich of the class of 1907. In 1919 the *Duquesne Monthly* acclaimed him as "the first and only American president of a European state." The state, Zsatkovich said, was to be called Rusinia. The article reported that, "He will shortly depart for Prague, the capital of Szecho-Slovaki . . . and one of his first unofficial acts will be to encourage the formation of a baseball league, and to introduce baseball as the new national game." The article went on to "wish the new president unlimited success in his undertaking," and expressed the hope that his new state would prosper. The congratulations were premature as Rusinia never gained independence and probably did not adopt baseball. Zsatkovich did become the governor of Carpatho-Ruthenia, operating as an autonomous state in federation with Czechoslovakia for two years following World War I. That Mr. Zsatkovich was a persuasive individual cannot be doubted;

in his graduating class he won the gold medal for oratory.

His son, Gregory I. Zatkovich [sic], Jr., as an editor of the *Duquesne Monthly*, produced the article from which the foregoing quotes are taken, and further reported that Gregory Sr. had been born in a gypsy camp where his mother had taken refuge on a visit to her homeland. An old gypsy woman had prophesized that Gregory would someday rule the country of his birth. The family had immigrated to the United States when he was five. Following the war, he was sent as an envoy of the International Peace Conference and served as governor until the reorganization of the government, then returned to his Pittsburgh law practice.

Another glittering figure in both baseball and basketball at Duquesne from 1916 to 1918 was an African American known as Posey Cumbert. His real name was Cumberland Willis Posey and his nickname "Cum." From nearby Homestead, he had attended Penn State before joining the national Negro League's newly formed Homestead Grays in 1911. In two years, he became captain of the Grays "and worked at organizing them into a semi-professional team."[28] Posey then made his way to Duquesne University. He did not graduate and probably had little academic attachment to the university. As a professional athlete, though, he contributed much to both the baseball and basketball teams with his stellar performances until, at age 27, his financial obligations made it impossible to remain. He later achieved fame as a baseball organizer, manager, and owner before his death in 1946, having brought the Grays to the National Negro League pennant for eight consecutive seasons. Cumbert's acceptance at Duquesne gives ample indication of the social "openness" of the school at a time when such an attitude was rare indeed.

Despite the interest that the likes of Zsatkovich and Cumbert might have generated in the game of baseball, it was basketball that led Duquesne into athletic fame in the post-World War I era. Yet at first the administration hesitated to establish varsity basketball. In a 1904 article titled "The Basket-ball Question," *The Pittsburgh College Bulletin* claimed that the game was overly strenuous "and not at all conducive to healthy physical development." Its objections centered around the "wildness" of the game, and the fact that it was played indoors:

> Basket-ball is a close second to Foot-ball for "wildness," without its open-air recommendation, being played in a hall, usually a small one. The style of play is so fast and furious that very little time is given for regular breathing—a thing not exactly beneficial to heart and lungs. Besides, the dust raised by the contestants and the stamping of spectators, does not materially increase the ozone of the little air that manages to circulate within the narrow walls. (Feb. 1904)

It was ironic that outdoor sports were the ones considered healthy in a city where the smoke was so heavy that it frequently darkened the sun at midday. In any case, the administration overcame its misgivings and established basketball as a varsity sport in 1914. *The Bulletin*, renamed the *Duquesne Monthly*, forgot the objections of student writers and called basketball a "big success," rejoicing that "Duquesne, aiming as ever to rank with the leading colleges in the country, has decided to introduce basketball, and, with this view, has devoted every effort to secure a winning team." And win they did. The first game was played, and won, against Bethany College in the "new" gym under the college chapel on January 9, 1914.

The *Duquesne Monthly* gave an interesting account of the athletic facilities that had been moved out of Old Main after the erection of the college chapel:

> The first difficulty to be encountered was the apparent lack of proper floor space, not that our gymnastic hall was not large enough, but rather precisely that it was too large and long. To obviate this difficulty a cage was ordered, and after passing through the deft fingers of the Brother engineer of the house, who worked increasingly at it during the

Xmas holidays, it has turned out to be "a thing of beauty." By a most ingenious system of hollow steel tubes at the four corners revolving on swivels, and with the aid of ropes and pulleys the gymnasium can be transformed in a moment from a theatre into a basketball floor; the nets may be raised at will, and even the baskets may be lowered or removed out of sight in a twinkling of an eye. (Jan. 1914)

World War I Exacts its Toll

In a politically wise move, given the German origins of the university, Father Hehir presided over a flag-raising ceremony shortly after the U.S. entry into the Great War. He exhorted the students:

> There are or should be, gentlemen, two great loves in the soul of man—the love of God and the love of country. I feel inclined to say, after the example of our Divine Master, when He said that the love of God and of our neighbor are one, that the love of God and our country are one. I do not believe that a man can love his country with true patriotic love, unless he has the love of God in his soul. I believe that the more a man loves God, the more genuine, the more disinterested, the more self-sacrificing, is his love of country and the flag of his country.[29]

The sacrifice so ringingly declared by Fr. Hehir was soon to follow. In the summer of 1917, Duquesne initiated a program of military training and instruction about the Constitution and the structure and workings of the federal government. By the fall semester, the program was expanded with the formation of two infantry companies that performed military exercises and drills on the playing field in back of the Administration Building. Duquesne purchased 100 guns at $4 each for the program since it was under university auspices and not a part of the regular army. By the beginning of 1918 some 220 Duquesne men had enlisted in the nation's armed forces. A service flag was blessed and raised in their honor on February 26, 1918. Duquesne followed the course of the war by recording the names of those students and alumni killed in action in the *Duquesne Monthly*. The first Duquesne man killed in the war was Albert A. Mountain, who died at Ourcq River, France, on July 30, 1918. In all, seven Duquesne men were killed in the war and another eight died while serving in the military. Most noncombat deaths were due to influenza, pneumonia, and meningitis.

No citizen could honestly question Duquesne's unswerving loyalty to the Allied cause. Apparently none did, as Duquesne seems to have escaped the suspicions that were directed toward German parishes and fraternal organizations in the city. The university joined enthusiastically in the great crusade to make the world safe for democracy. Holy Ghost fathers who celebrated Mass at neighboring German-speaking parishes ceased speaking in German—at least officially. (At many such parishes, the pastor continued to deliver the sermon in German at the earliest Mass.) The university even discarded its school song, originally written in 1912 by Father Malloy. The words were not offensive, but according to the *Duquesne Monthly*, they had been set to the melody of "a certain national hymn which at the epoch fell into disrepute." The national hymn referred to was, of course, the German national anthem, *Deutchland Uber Alles*. In 1915 and again in 1917 students composed new melodies to fit the original lyrics, but, observed the *Duquesne Monthly*, both these attempts, while meritorious, lacked something or other that would give a song enduring popularity among the old grads and underclass men." Not until 1920 would the university have an official alma mater.

By the fall of 1918, yet another sacrifice was made by the university on behalf of the war effort: the Army established a unit of the Students Army Training Corps (SATC). Because the university had so little space, this program forced the discontinuance of the School of Social Services, founded only two years earlier. The university did manage to house the 175 men, including some third- and fourth-year high school boys, in the campus theater beneath the chapel. They were drilled on campus and instructed in the Vandergrift Building. St. Mary's Hall was designated for use as their infirmary. When campus barracks space proved inadequate, the university secured the use of the lyceum at nearby Epiphany Parish. The two infantry companies were divided into approximately 100 men each to drill Monday and Thursday evenings under the supervision of three Army captains and a colonel. They were considered members of the United States Army subject to call to active duty at any time. According to special regulations, college courses were modified to be of direct military value.

When the war ended in November of 1918, the SATC was rapidly demobilized. It was immediately replaced by the Reserve Officer Training Corps (ROTC), which was approved by the university administration on December 12, 1918. By September 1919, registration stood at 81 students. ROTC students were to wear uniforms on drill days, receive credit for military science courses, and replace physical education requirements with drill. By 1920, though, the university found ROTC economically and physically hard to support with its hard-pressed resources.

End of An Era

Although crowded into a small number of buildings, and overextended in its offerings, after the war, Duquesne University stood posed for a period of great growth. Still primarily a school through which the children and grandchildren of immigrants ascended into the ranks of business and the professions, Duquesne University had appreciably widened its view of the world. In doing so, it had, in turn, gained greater acceptance by the larger society. When, for example, the university began the SATC on October 1, 1918, it did so on the same day as some 400 other colleges and universities, public and private. In ways both real and symbolic, this represented a greater degree of participation in national life than ever before possible. Its students and alumni had fought in the Great War with the same dedication that had moved the nation. Some had given their "last full measure of devotion" on the battlefields of France.

Although Duquesne and other Catholic institutions were far from being fully assimilated into the social fabric of American life, as the 1920s would soon reveal, gone were the days when a neighboring football team "refused to play the representatives of a Catholic institution."[30] Its varsity teams publicized the name of the university throughout the region, playing Catholic and non-Catholic colleges alike. Its alumni were a testament to the excellence of its academic programs. Still greater numbers of youths were demanding admission to colleges and universities across the land,[31] and Duquesne University readied itself for the new era with high resolve and great expectations. Its student population had grown sixfold from 1911 to 1921 (390 to 2221 enrollment). Faculty had increased dramatically as well, with, necessarily, a decreasing proportion of Holy Ghost fathers to lay professors. By 1928, only 24 of the 109 faculty members were Holy Ghost fathers. But their influence always was (and would continue to be) greater than their numbers.

3. Fifty Years of Service

In 1920 Duquesne University of the Holy Ghost stood on the brink of a great decision. It could continue with the status quo, with all the restrictions that implied, or it could meet the challenges of the postwar era, with all the risks that implied. Admissions had surged following the war, on a campus so cramped for space that many activities had already been moved to rented quarters in the city's downtown. Enrollment in 1920 totaled 2086 students, and by the following year the school was full to bursting with 2221 students.[1] Yet, with no major endowments, Duquesne was unable to expand and develop the campus on the Bluff. The School of Social Service had been discontinued and other newly established schools were in jeopardy. Plans for new schools, such as the proposed School of Pharmacy, had to be put on hold. The university was like a flourishing plant in a pot too small for it. Father Martin Hehir was determined to nurture that burgeoning life: he launched the "Million Dollar Fund Campaign" to, in effect, buy a bigger "pot." Bishop Canevin, who had held the post of University Chancellor since 1911, happily granted permission for the university's first ever fundraising drive.[2]

Father Hehir Learns about Fundraising

The dates for the campaign were set as October 9 to October 19, 1920: ten days for raising a million dollars worth of pledges. Professional fundraisers were hired.[3] To help inform the public, news releases appeared in the local papers headlined "Duquesne Enrollment Will Crowd Quarters" (*The Pittsburgh Sun*), "Duquesne Badly Needs New Building" (*The Leader*), "Enrollment Large at Duquesne University" (*The Pittsburgh Press*), and so forth. An article in the *Post* written by Dr. Arthur A. Hamerschlag, President of Carnegie Institute of Technology, stated, "Duquesne University should have the support of every person in Pittsburgh in its quest for means to advance the cause of education in this community."[4]

President Hehir sent postcards to all Catholic homes in the Pittsburgh Diocese explaining Duquesne University's appeal for funds and the reasons for the campaign. Bishop Canevin wrote a letter to the clergy and laity of the Diocese urging them to support higher education just as they had supported elementary and secondary education. After recounting the accomplishments of the school in launching so many students into careers, despite the lack of endowment money and due largely to the free labors of the Holy Ghost fathers, he appealed thus:

> Duquesne University now asks for funds, scholarships and endowments, not to enrich the Congregation of the Holy Ghost, but to erect new buildings and establish or complete various departments of a University, so that all the opportunities and advantages of a University training may be given to thousands of ambitious, talented scholars at rates that even the poor can afford to pay.[5]

In another letter to alumni and friends, Father Hehir emphasized that the money was needed for buildings, salaries, and scholarships. He said:

> We feel confident that our loyal alumni and our many friends in and around Pittsburgh will not be deaf to our appeal, and they will contribute according to the means given them by a bountiful Providence, to enable us to continue the work of higher Christian education in the community for the benefit of our state and country, and for God's honor and glory.[6]

The final meeting before the campaign began was held at the William Penn Hotel on October 7, 1920, where final instructions were given to 500 volunteers. The kickoff dinner, held two days later at the Syria Mosque, was an historic event where the alma mater was sung in public for the very first time. Enthusiastic speeches were delivered by The Honorable James Francis Burke, Bishop Canevin, the mayor, Dr. Hamerschlag, and Father Hehir.

Then, what had seemingly been so carefully put together disintegrated to a degree that stunned and confused the organizers. The meeting on October 11 was attended by only a small percentage of workers and when the campaign ended on October 19, pledges amounted to far, far less than a million dollars. The lights burned late in the halls of Old Main as the university administration pondered the reasons for a failure of such magnitude. They concluded that although the campaign was well organized, very possibly the Catholic population of Pittsburgh reacted unfavorably to the use of out-of-town professional fundraisers. Moreover, the vast majority of the work had been done by laymen. Perhaps, they reasoned, the response would have been better if the clergy and church-affiliated organizations had been more active in the campaign.[7]

In a second attempt, the professional fundraisers were dismissed, and two Pittsburgh businessmen, Robert W. Egan and George McSwigan, who had declined to handle the first campaign due to the other obligations, were approached again and this time agreed to take up the torch. Bishop Canevin himself headed the undertaking.

When a new general campaign committee was selected, it consisted of Catholic businessmen, lawyers, and merchants. The second drive was set for November 6 to November 15—again, ten days. *The Pittsburgh Catholic* and *Pittsburgh Observer* carried front-page coverage on October 21. Full-page ads were placed in most of the local papers. The *Pittsburgh Catholic* was used to a far greater extent in the second campaign and included articles on the disappointment and embarrassment of the failed October drive. Mr. Willis McCook, a lawyer and financier, agreed to be general manager and presided over the formal reopening of the campaign at the November 6th rally and dinner at Kaufmann's Department Store auditorium.

Perhaps most important, the Knights of Columbus, who had not been able to help Duquesne financially at the time it was applying for university status, could and did help in this endeavor, supplying 8,000 members to visit every home in the diocese (which in 1920 was estimated at about 500,000 souls). A work force of 8,000 as opposed to the 500 in the October drive—which had quickly dwindled to an even smaller number—increased contributions enormously. Also, parish priests made a greater effort this time to impress their congregations with the importance of Duquesne University to the diocese. Each of the parishes conducted a special collection. Through the Alumni Association alone, $305,902 was pledged.[8] In response to Father Bullion's presentation about how he, as the son of an immigrant family, was given the opportunity to attend Duquesne, some 80 businessmen, a number of whom were not Catholic, contributed $55,000.[9] At a meeting held at the William Penn Hotel, 50 priests associated with Duquesne pledged to raise $250,000.[10] By November 11, Bishop Canevin had instituted the "Canevin Limit Club" in which Catholics could pay a special tribute to the bishop by contributing a minimum of $1,000 over two years. It is perhaps indicative of the socioeconomic standing of Catholics that in a diocese of half a million, it was estimated that only 500 families would be able to make such a contribution.[11] Eventually, about 300 families became members, a true indication of the high regard Pittsburghers had for their bishop.[12]

Ten days after the November kickoff, at the closing dinner, also at Kaufmann's, Mr. McCook reported that the million-dollar goal had not only been achieved, but surpassed. He further announced that a member of the university's advisory board, Frank McGillick, president of McGillick Savings and Trust Company, had given $50,000, a sum which McCook personally was matching with an additional $50,000.[13] After a round of thanks, the assembly sang "Holy God, We Praise Thy Name."[14] The Holy Ghost fathers expressed their appreciation in a full-page advertisement in *The Pittsburgh Catholic*. The ad made no mention of the order's own monumental contribution to the campaign: $169,495.22.

The Expansion Begins

Although the campaign pledges totaled $1,800,000, the money actually raised fell far short of that sum because of a brief but sharp depression in 1921. Only about $300,000 of the pledges was actually received.[15] Compounding the shortfall was the final court decision on state allocations to sectarian institutions. On December 1, 1921, the state was ordered to cease the $50,000 yearly appropriation. The university appealed the decision, but in vain. Despite these disappointments, Fr. Hehir promised that the money would be used for new construction and boldly went ahead with plans for a new academic building, a gymnasium, and a central heating plant.

Two days after the closing of the campaign, the Right Reverend J.F. Regis Canevin resigned his See as Bishop of Pittsburgh. He had truly kept his promise to support Duquesne, made at the time of the petition for the university charter. At commencement ceremonies on June 21, 1921, Fr. Hehir thanked him for his guidance and support.

> My esteem and veneration for him forbid any laudatory remarks, nor do I know any man who dislikes praise more than he. During his term as Bishop, he presided over our commencement Exercises. In securing our charter his recommendations and prudent suggestions were carried out. We are more than grateful for his support. As a mark of our gratification to his Grace, the first of our new buildings to be erected will be called Canevin Hall as a slight recognition for his goodness; I further, as President of the University, confer on him the highest honor the University can bestow, that of Doctor of Laws.[16]

The decision regarding the respective locations of the new buildings was delayed due to incomplete plans for the new Liberty Bridge and Tunnel complex across the Monongahela River and through Mount Washington. The city had not decided on the location of the traffic ramps leading to the bridge or the final status of Shingiss Street between Locust and Bluff Streets.

The Liberty Bridge project turned out to be very important to the university's building plans. Prior to the bridge project, the western end of the Bluff was a jagged hill festooned with unsightly bill boards. To provide the ramp approach to the bridge, the hill was sharply cut away, leaving a sheer drop of 115 feet just beyond the edge of the university playing field. Fearing that the campus would literally slide onto the bridge approach, engineers constructed a sloping concrete retaining wall, the largest of its type ever successfully built.[17] An abandoned coal mine penetrating the Bluff, and posing an unknown danger from possible land subsidence, was carefully backfilled. The city still continued to hold onto the upper part of Shingiss Street, much to the annoyance of Father Hehir, who complained that "loafers" on this part of Shingiss had "become a regular nuisance."[18] The street existed only on paper, and, had it been paved, would have been even steeper than originally planned.[19]

When the plans for the bridge approach were finalized, the university was able to proceed with its own building plans. The combined bids for the new buildings amounted to $494,972.13. The gymnasium and heating plant were planned as contiguous structures but having the appearance of a single building. An ideal site was selected, the diggings of the long defunct brickyard at the corner of Colbert and Locust streets. The academic building was to be located a little farther up the hill at the corner of Colbert and Vickroy Streets.

The "Look" of the University

Father Hehir was concerned about the architectural integrity of the campus—that is, that the buildings would truly look like college buildings. They were built in red tapestry brick with stone trim. Interesting architectural details made them distinctive in their own right yet harmonious with each other. On its first story, Canevin Hall was built with five layers of stone alternating with brick, an architectural variation of the Administration Building. In view of the care given to their appearance, it was unfortunate that both buildings were built up to the sidewalk, allowing no space for lawns or shrubbery in front. Only the planting of a row of ginkgo trees in 1936 next to the curb on Vickroy Street provided some visual relief from the otherwise unbroken line of brick and concrete.

The gymnasium was an ambitious undertaking for the small university. Designed to meet projected growth in enrollments, it was to seat 1200 spectators. The *Pittsburgh Catholic* described its features:

> The dressing rooms, located on the mezzanine level, will be as easily reached from the basketball floor during winter as from the football and baseball fields in their seasons. Another unique feature is that, instead of diminishing the area of the campus, on whose edge it has been built, the gymnasium actually increases it considerably; the roof is really a prolongation of the athletic field and will afford room for several additional tennis and handball courts.

Stone detailing on the building was beautifully done in a scholastic / ecclesiastical style. The front entrance of the gymnasium was built into a university tower incorporating a classical Greek discus-thrower in relief.[20] A dramatic, if invisible, symbol of Duquesne's faith in the future was the heating plant, having three boilers but built with room for three more. An open house to which the general public was invited to view the facility was held in the newly completed gymnasium on December 4, 1923.

The academic building was a four-story structure housing classrooms, lecture halls, libraries, and a fully equipped cafeteria with kitchen and storage facilities. It was designed to be fireproof, since the only wood used in the structure was in the window frames, doors, and chalkboard moldings. And it bore the Duquesne University coat of arms carved in stone, in high relief, above its south entrance.

The Symbols of the University: A Coat of Arms and an Alma Mater

The newly designed coat of arms was the work of Reverend John F. Malloy, A.M., of the English Department, the same man responsible for writing the lyrics of the school alma mater. The talented Father Malloy had long been interested in heraldry and emphasized the tradition in his classes. When he designed the university coat of arms, he followed strictly the rules of heraldry, incorporating elements from the shield of the Marquis Duquesne as well as elements evocative of the university and the Holy Ghost fathers. The coat of arms was then passed on to the Pierre de Chaignon La Rose, one of the greatest experts on heraldry in America at the time, who slightly altered and approved the original design.

The coat of arms (which became the basis for the design of the university seal) shows a black lion with red tongue and claws on a silver field, holding a red book with gilt edges. The upper third of the shield is divided into a blue section and a red section and bears the figure of a silver dove with a golden halo. Father Malloy explained the significance of the symbols:

> The black lion in the silver shield is adopted bodily from the arms of Marquis Duquesne, whose name the university bears; the book is added for a "difference," as kings-at-arms allow, and to indicate the coat is that of a school. The tinctures, azure and

gules—blue and red—are the heraldic equivalent both of the athletic colors of the school and those of the Congregation of the Holy Ghost.

The haloed dove in silver (the heraldic white) is the readily recognized symbol of the Holy Ghost, titular of the University. The many implications of the motto, "It is the Spirit that giveth life," make it a particularly happy choice.[21]

Joseph Carl Breil, an 1888 graduate who had made a career in composing music to be played in accompaniment to movies of the day, including the epic *Birth of a Nation*, composed a song for a school hymn.[22] In his letter to Father Hehir, he explained:

Back in the middle eighties I used to trudge up the Bluff every day to the Pittsburgh college to get my "education." Since then I have developed into a composer of some distinction and am known practically over the world wherever better music is cultivated.

I am sending you a song of mine; perhaps one of your poets could arrange a text for it and it could be adopted as the Duquesne University hymn. I would be pleased to learn that such a thing has been done.[23]

Father Malloy, who later became a Trappist monk, wrote the lyrics to what was to be the *alma mater*. It was officially adopted on October 5, 1920, and sung for the first time in public at the opening dinner of the campaign at the Syria Mosque four days later.

Al - ma Mater, old Duquesne guide and friend of our youth - ful days, we, thy sons, a gal lant train our loy - al voic - es raise. The hours we spend at thy Moth - er's knee, and drank of wis - dom's store, shall e'er in mem'ry treas - ured be, tho' we roam the whole world o'r. Then for - ward ever, dear Al ma Ma - ter, o'er our hearts un - ri - valed reign. On ward ev - er, old Al - ma Ma - ter! All hail to thee, Du - quesne!

The alma mater as originally written had two additional verses, with the last two sentences in the present composition sung as a refrain.

Monongahela's rugged shore
Firm upholds thy classic halls;
Forge's clang and traffic's roar
Sweep round with noisy calls;
Thy voice, tho' graver, gentler still,
Our sluggish will o'er powers,
And wakes ambition's eager thrill
In youthful breasts like ours.

On thy campus' broad expanse
For thine honor we have fought;
For the Red and Blue's advance
Right nobly we have wrought;
And in the glow of life's young morn
Beneath thy smile of pride,
Enduring friendships we have sworn;
We are brothers true and tried!

The Bishop is Honored

As promised at the conclusion of the Million Dollar Fund Campaign, Father Hehir named the new academic building Canevin Hall in honor of the bishop who had so staunchly supported the university. Moreover, the now Archbishop Canevin was asked to officiate at the laying of the cornerstone of the building that was to bear his name. Indeed, the archbishop himself lifted the cornerstone into place in what was to be the first building of its kind in the diocese named for a bishop. The hollow cornerstone contained a copper box with photographs of Archbishop Canevin, Bishop Hugh C. Boyle, Bishop Alexander Le Roy (superior general of the Congregation of the Holy Ghost), and Very Reverend Eugene Phelan, C.S.Sp. (provincial of the Holy Ghost Order in the United States).[24] The box also contained catalogs of the various schools of the university, copies of the *Duquesne Monthly*, a copy of the last annual report of the president of the University, current city newspapers, and specimens of coins in circulation. The main document enclosed was an embossed parchment in Latin and English, placing the event in history by giving the names of those who had important political and ecclesiastical offices.[25] Almost a year after the cornerstone laying, the completed Canevin Hall was dedicated on October 28, 1923.

The Women of the University

Although Canevin Hall is only 166 feet long, it has entrances at both the east and west ends, and a side entrance facing south. Apparently acting on his own and without considering its overtones, Father Hehir issued a directive that women students must enter Canevin Hall "by their own entrance on the south side of the building."[26] In view of the simple fact that there were no other women's entrances on campus, it was a curious regulation indeed. Although various interpretations have been ventured for his actions, it is likely that they simply reflected Father Hehir's Victorian attitude that women were frail, delicate creatures who deserved to be protected from the more raucous male students.[27] But it should be noted that if Father Hehir held Victorian attitudes, this was because he *was* Victorian. When he was born in 1855, her reign had yet 46 more years. In any case, the regulation was short-lived; the flapper of the Roaring Twenties had no desire for a separate entrance, regardless of the motivation, and they ignored the directive.

Women were by no means newcomers to Duquesne University. Duquesne's first woman student was Sister Mary Fides Shepperson of the Sisters of Mercy. She was admitted as a special case—an examination was given—in the fall semester of 1909. She received a bachelor of arts degree in 1911, and a master of arts degree in 1913. Finally, in 1915, because of increasing demand, women were admitted to the schools of Law, Business, and Theatre Arts. Since Chicago's DePaul University had admitted them as a matter of policy just a year earlier, it has traditionally laid claim to being the first Catholic college to admit women.[28] Duquesne's admittance of women five years earlier makes its claim of being the first, albeit not as a matter of policy, better than any other.[29] Father Hehir, however, would not admit women to the College of Arts—the last school not open to them—until the fall of 1927.[30]

Official policy notwithstanding, from 1911 to 1927, some 214 women graduated from Duquesne University, of whom all but 40 were nuns. In this group, 205 bachelor's degrees were earned and three advanced degrees. The first Ph.D. to be awarded to a woman was in 1923. The School of Law conferred its first L.L.B. on a woman in 1918.[31] Five others were to earn that degree in this period.

New schools founded by the university after 1915 accepted both men and women from the beginning. An exception was the first Pharmacy class. There were, however, three women in the second class. And in the 1920s Duquesne granted 60 credits toward a bachelor of science in nursing to any graduate of an approved three-year school of nursing—all women—who wished to continue studies beyond the R.N. level.

Duquesne also had women faculty members at an early date. Margaret Hall, a chemistry major from Bryn Mawr, taught a summer course for women in industry in 1915. In the fall of that same year, Marie G. Corriols became the first full-time woman member of the faculty, joining the Department of Modern Languages.[32]

In September of 1928 Maria Gertrude Blanchard was appointed as the first Dean of Women, a part-time position, since she was also the first university librarian. In 1934 Miss Blanchard resigned the deanship and devoted her energies entirely to the library. Also in 1928, Alice Walton was made coach of the newly established women's basketball program.

Women found representation and camaraderie through various campus organizations. Mary Catherine Donnelly founded the Duchess Club in 1924 "to foster sociability, to promote friendship, to encourage scholarship, and to cooperate with all student activities"[33] for women at the university. In 1928, with the blessing of the university chancellor, Bishop Boyle, the Women's Guild of Duquesne University was founded to work with the Dean of Women in sponsoring activities. Alpha Phi Omicron, the first sorority on campus, was also founded in 1928, with Helen Jacobson from the School of Accounts as its first president.

In 1930 Elizabeth O'Donnell, writing in the *Duquesne Monthly*, summed up the attitude of many women toward Father Hehir and Duquesne University:

> This acceptance by the University of women students into its halls of learning created a debt of gratitude for us toward our Reverend President, Father Hehir, for it was during his administration and with his approval that the portals of the university were thrown wide for our entrance. Through his efforts, it was made possible for the women of Pittsburgh to share in the benefits of a higher education under Catholic auspices.
>
> Because of the great service he has rendered to the women of Pittsburgh, he has won an undying appreciation, which can only end with life, for the learning and culture in which he has given them a share will withstand the acid test of time.

The School of Pharmacy

With the additional space that Canevin Hall provided, the university began to implement plans for the establishment of additional schools. The first of these was the School of Pharmacy. At the time of the petition for the university charter, the Holy Ghost fathers had declared that a definite need for one existed in Western Pennsylvania. Dr. Hugh C. Muldoon, head of the Department of Chemistry and Dean of the School of Pharmacy at Valparaiso University in Indiana, was chosen as the school's first dean and was to head it for 25 years. Muldoon received his formal education at Union University, Massachusetts College of Pharmacy, Harvard, and Valparaiso. His selection was yet another indication of Duquesne's wider, less local scope following World War I.

Amid great fanfare and the obligatory round of speeches, the School of Pharmacy was formally opened on September 23, 1925. It received approval from the Pennsylvania State Board of Pharmacy in its very first year of existence and was duly registered. In addition, the school met all the requirements of the American Association of Colleges of Pharmacy and set what were viewed as high individual standards from the start. Three different programs were offered: degree of graduate of pharmacy (Ph.G.) for a three-year course in preparation for retail pharmacy and hospital dispensary work, the degree of pharmaceutical chemist (Ph.C.) for a four-year course in preparation for general pharmaceutical and chemical manufacturing and control, and the bachelor of science in pharmacy (B.S.Pharm.) for a four-year course in preparation for teaching, business, or special work. Among areas of additional training in the fourth year were pharmaceutical and chemical manufacturing and control, analytical chemistry, bacteriology, and food, drug, and water analysis. Laboratory experience was given a high priority and, in their final year, students served an internship actually dispensing medicines in hospitals under the direction of the staff pharmacists.[34]

Typifying the university's emphasis on producing well-rounded students, the pharmacy school faculty included specialists from Schools of Law, Accounts, and Arts and Sciences, all in an effort to give students management and legal background as well as a broad grounding in the sciences.

The first class was limited to 50 men. Beginning in 1926 the school accepted both men and women. The class list of pharmacy students for 1926 recorded three women out of a total enrollment of 49. Candidates had to be at least 17 years of age, graduates of a four-year high school course or equivalent, of good moral character, and had to apply to the Bureau of Professional Education for a Pennsylvania State Preliminary Certificate. After graduation from the pharmacy school, to become a registered pharmacist, one had to pass the state licensing examination after acquiring three years' experience in dispensing drugs.[35]

Dean Muldoon was not only a prolific scholar and author—he wrote *Lessons in Pharmaceutical Latin, Organic Chemistry for Students of the Medical Sciences*, and *Laboratory Manual of Organic Chemistry*—he also was editor of *Science Counselor* and advisory editor of the *American Pharmacy* textbook series. He was an able administrator and an innovative teacher as well. His Pharmaceutical Association, instituted to keep students current on new developments in the field and to give them experience in addressing large groups, later became a student branch of the American Pharmaceutical Association. He also started the annual Pharmacy Night Program to demonstrate to the public and non-pharmacy students the importance of the field. Many years later, in June 1953, he was awarded the Remington Honor Medal in Pharmacy for outstanding service as an educator, author, and scientist.

The School of Music

The curriculum of the College of Arts had offered vocal and instrumental music courses since the original prospectus of the college in 1878. Prior to World War I, this core of course offerings was expanded in the creation of the Department of Vocal and Instrumental Music within the College of Arts. The next major step was taken in the autumn of 1925 when President Hehir brought the Reverend James B. Parent from Belgium and Professor Joseph A. Rauterkus, who had studied in Belgium and at the Carnegie Institute in New York, to the university to develop plans for a School of Music. Although both of these talented young men had ties with the area, they also had a broader, more international exposure. The School of Music was opened in the fall of 1926 with Professor Rauterkus as dean.

The school offered a four-year course leading to the B.A. in music and instruction in piano, organ, violin, and all the conventional band and orchestral instruments. From the beginning, the School of Music accepted men and women who wished to major in music or pursue an interest. Offerings in the junior and senior years included "melody writing, Gregorian Chant, and other forms of musical composition."[36] Professor Rauterkus also conducted the student "symphonie [sic] orchestra" and the band.[37] The School of Music grew rapidly; just five years after its founding some 113 students were enrolled.

The Library

In 1927 the university acquired a three-story brick apartment house next to Science Hall on Vickroy Street directly across the street from Canevin Hall. Desperately needed, this building was converted into a library on the first and second floors with music studios on the third. The library collection had grown largely from donations, much of which came from priests. Part of the history collection, for example, was a gift from the estate of Monsignor A.A. Lambing, a historian of some note locally. Since the law school library was located on the second floor, the remaining space proved inadequate to house all of the main library holdings. Fiction and periodicals remained in the old library on the second floor of Old Main. The improvement, though small by later standards, was enormous in its time. Whereas in 1910 the total university holdings were only 7027 books, by 1928 the entire collection of the university, including the libraries of the Schools of Law, Pharmacy (housed in Canevin), and Business (also in Canevin), amounted to 19,950 volumes. The university hired its first full-time professional librarian in 1928, but it was not to have a building entirely devoted to library use for another decade. The hiring of a professional librarian was of such significance that it appears in the otherwise sparsely worded minutes of the board of directors.

The School of Education

Duquesne University's School of Education was founded in 1927 by Holy Ghost Father Raymond Kirk, then only 26 years old, who was later to become president of the university. In December 1929 the Pennsylvania State Council of Education approved Duquesne University as a degree-granting institution of the bachelor of science in secondary education. Thus the School of Education officially uses 1929 as its founding date despite a long history of teacher preparation dating from the earliest days of the college.[38]

Since the early 1900s Duquesne had assisted the religious orders of the diocese in preparing nuns to teach in parochial schools. Many candidates at this time came to the sisterhood without a high school diploma. Since it was expected that the state would soon require this, in 1912 Father Hehir opened a summer school to afford the sisters an opportunity to finish their high school studies. The university even went so far as to recognize the motherhouses as university branches so that the professors could hold daily instructions there. This practice continued until 1930 when the Pennsylvania Department of Public Instruction ruled that these motherhouse high school courses would no longer be accredited by the state.

Official classes in education at the college level were begun by the School of Finance in 1910, when it offered extension courses to train teachers of commercial courses. By 1916 the College of Arts was offering educational instruction (pedagogy) courses in the junior and senior years. Requirements for high school teachers through the College of Arts were listed in the *Duquesne University Bulletin* in 1923, and an actual course leading to the degree of bachelor of arts in education appeared in 1925.

When Duquesne opened its School of Education in 1927 it offered two degrees: the bachelor of arts in education, which embraced English, Latin, Greek, history, modern languages, and music; and the bachelor of science in education, which included the fields of biology, physics, chemistry, and mathematics. The student teaching requirement was fulfilled by teaching in the university prep school. Students were also required to select a minor field of study. Thus, the School of Education met the state requirements for state certification of public school teachers from the very beginning, even before it was officially accredited. With accreditation, student teaching was broadened to include the Pittsburgh Public School District. After lengthy negotiations in February of 1929, Father Kirk succeeded in persuading the principal of nearby Fifth Avenue High School to accept Duquesne students. The *Duquesne Duke* referred to it as a "most notable achievement," and indeed it was; negotiations with other public school principals proved futile. Throughout the 1930s, Fifth Avenue High School remained the only Pittsburgh public school to accept Duquesne's student teachers.

Along with the conventional undergraduate day classes, classes at the School of Education were scheduled in late afternoon, evening, and Saturday for those who were employed full time. Summer courses were also offered. The Saturday and summer classes were especially well attended by the sisters who were struggling to obtain their undergraduate and graduate degrees while teaching in the parochial schools. Duquesne contributed greatly to the diocesan parochial schools by offering reduced tuition rates to nuns, brothers, and priests.

A Change in Campus Atmosphere

As the Duquesne student body grew, and as the number of schools within the university proliferated, the sense of intimacy that once characterized the small turn-of-the-century college was in danger of being lost. The atmosphere of belonging that the small size once so easily provided, was replaced gradually by collegiate symbols such as the *alma mater* and the coat of arms, and by student organizations. These organizations—which before World War I simply did not exist—were essential in providing a sense of identity to the university student of the Roaring Twenties.

Student government at Duquesne rested in the Student Senate, established in 1922 under the direction of Dr. John A. Moran, Vice-Dean of the School of Accounts, Finance, and Commerce. The purpose of the senate was to "promote unity within the school and to work with the faculty in furthering progress of the school."[39] The Student Senate was responsible for such additions to student life as the Junior Prom, instituted in 1925; the establishment of a student newspaper, the *Duquesne Duke*, in 1925; the operation of a program of intramural sports; and the first student assembly in April of 1928. The decade following the end of World War I also saw the establishment of numerous clubs, fraternities, and societies to enhance student life on campus. Gamma Phi, founded in 1916 as a business fraternity, was the first fraternity on campus. Kappa Sigma Phi was founded as a catholic fraternity in 1924. Phi Alpha was founded in 1927 as a nonsectarian organization, evidence of Duquesne's increasing heterogeneity.

In November 1924 the Student Senate met to discuss problems in organizing a student newspaper. They decided that the editor would have complete control over the paper and the following month elected Henry X. O'Brien to fill that position. In 1968 Duquesne's former newspaper editor became a justice on the Pennsylvania Supreme Court.

The purpose of the paper was to present the news of the school while it was still fresh "in the breezy, entertaining manner only possible to a newspaper."[40] The *Duquesne Duke* claimed to have sprung from an unauthorized freshman periodical, each copy individually hand-drawn on theme paper and later mimeographed for circulation in the 1924–1925 school year. This collection of cartoons, caricatures, and intimate disclosures, lampooning everything and everyone, was titled the *Duke's Mixture*. It was so popularly received on campus that editor Bill Kelly introduced a motion before the senate to have it made an official newspaper, but he had to give up the humorous and often satirical viewpoint for a more serious orientation, agree to a modification of the name and allow it to be under the control of upperclassmen before it was officially adopted. Originally it was published every other Thursday and was heralded for its role in bringing about union in the school and becoming "a force in shaping student opinion and student policies."[41] It was soon elevated to the status of a weekly.

The *Duke* joined the *Duquesne Monthly* as a forum for student views. Originally published as the *Pittsburgh College Bulletin* in 1894, the *Monthly* was a literary magazine that featured articles, stories, and poems by Duquesne students. In addition, it carried campus news and sports, as well as a section reporting on alumni. The *Monthly* was essentially a magazine with everything rolled into one publication.

The university's efforts to publish yearbooks, *The Grand Duke* in 1926 and *The Monacle* in 1929, were both financial disasters. Publication of a yearbook was suspended with the depression in 1930. It did not appear again until 1947 as *The Grand Duke*. After a single issue, the yearbook disappeared again until 1956, at which time it established itself as an annual publication under the title *L'Esprit Du Duc*.

The Red Masquers Enter the Roaring Twenties

Among the groups on campus that came into greater prominence in the twenties was Duquesne's drama club, the Red Masquers. Established in 1914, the group was organized by students "who desired to produce plays and playlets more frequently than had hitherto been done, to write plays of their own, to read plays intelligently and appreciatively, and to train themselves to be discriminating playgoers."[42] Duquesne had a tradition of dramatic productions from its earliest days in the weekly playlet and the presentation of *Alcestis* in the original Greek. Performances were given each spring in a downtown theater.

In the first decade of Pittsburgh Catholic College's existence, tragedies and dramas were presented; later comedies became popular. The establishment of the Red Masquers further elevated drama in importance at Duquesne. The campus theater stage was outfitted with a proscenium arch, curtain, stage sets, and lighting. At last theatrical productions could be staged on campus instead of rented downtown theaters.

In its first 12 years, the group performed 127 works, including tragedies, comedies, farces, pageants, and tableaux. The highlight of each year's productions was the Christmas play, which was often taken on the road to suburban parishes, orphanages, and other institutions during the holidays. In fact, the group's very first production in 1915 was a Christmas play—or actually a collection of playlets, orchestral numbers, carols, a violin solo, and a piano duet. It was performed for free. Nearly a thousand climbed the hill on that cold night. The Christmas play became a tradition.

The success of the Red Masquers was all the more notable for the fact that the students actually wrote and performed many original plays. Much care was lavished on sets, original scores, and costumes, all of which were made at the university. Since the Department of Drama was open to women by the 1920s, they were able to assume the feminine roles that had been performed by males in the early days of the college, and the productions grew even more popular with the community. Certainly, the drama club fulfilled the creative desires of many students in many ways. There were writers, actors, musicians, and all the people involved in creating sets and costumes. There were opportunities for various types of artistic expression and the development of God-given talents.

The Student Assembly: A Pulpit for "Daddy Hehir"

One tradition that continued throughout the Hehir years was the student assembly. The custom of periodic assemblies endured throughout his administration and imparted not only a sense of intimacy, but elevated President Hehir to that of a father figure. Indeed, most students knew him by no other appellation than "Daddy Hehir." When notices of an assembly were posted, no compulsory attendance was required, but practically every student came. At the assembly Daddy Hehir would speak to the students about anything that happened to be on his mind. A frequent topic was student behavior. He admonished the students to be good "boys and girls"—he never called them anything else—as the Lord wanted them to be. On one occasion an assembly had been called just before a dance in the gymnasium. In his familiar Irish brogue, Father Hehir told the amused multitude, "I want every boy in bed by ten o'clock and the girls with them."[43] It was a momentary embarrassment, but was one of many occurrences that endeared Daddy Hehir to the students.

The Class Ring: A Blue Stone Becomes Red

Attendant to the establishment of the collegiate traditions and organizations, Duquesne University adopted an official class ring. A high school ring was already in existence, but along with the adoption of the *alma mater* and university coat of arms came a strong desire to establish an official ring design. The class of '25 formed a committee that standardized the ring as an octagonal deep blue stone held in place by four corner prongs. The decision for the blue stone was made in the face of considerable student opposition favoring a red stone. Students had the option of purchasing a plain stone or one with an Old English Style "D" embossed in gold. Only in the fall of 1938 did the initial become standard. The sides of the ring showed a modification of the university coat of arms: the dove, representing the Holy Ghost and the teaching order that founded the school, above the rampant lion, from the coat of arms of the Duquesne family, holding a book, the symbol of learning. Finally, in 1927 the blue stone was replaced with the ruby red stone that so many more students favored and that is standard today. Over the years the size of the stone was increased, and in 1936 the prong setting was replaced with a continuous bezel to seal the stone in place.

The ring was so popular that prep school students, intending to enter the university, began buying it instead of the high school ring, much to the annoyance of upperclassmen. To calm them, the university issued a ruling in 1929 that students had to be members of the junior or senior class to be eligible to buy the ring.

Athletics in the Twenties

The renaissance spirit of Duquesne in this period of building and growth was reflected in a renewed interest in athletics. For the first time, Duquesne University had an athletic director to coordinate sports on the Bluff. The post was first filled by Father Eugene McGuigan in 1920, who had coached basketball since 1914. Although affectionately known as "Father Mac," he was commonly called "Coach Gene Martin" in newspaper accounts. The alias surname was taken from Martin Hehir to prevent the name of a Holy Ghost father from being associated with the rowdiness of athletics. Father Mac coached football, baseball, and basketball. Sadly, Father Mac was transferred in 1923, only months before the opening of the new gymnasium.

Prior to 1925, games with other schools in all sports had been scheduled informally in a we'll-work-it-out arrangement. Afterwards, Duquesne was part of an increasingly bureaucratized system, scheduling contests through Francis P. McDermott's office, a kind of sports command center for the university. McDermott was the new coach and athletic director. Despite the team losses under his coaching (all seven games lost in 1925 and five of seven lost the next year), McDermott performed a valuable service for Duquesne athletics:

> But if Frank McDermott found fortune against him in the herculean task of plastering Duquesne on the football, he unquestionably earned all honor for outstanding success in establishing Bluffite sports upon a solid and most cleanly basis. An organizer and an enthusiastic promoter of the Tri-State Conference, he gained for the Red and Blue the utmost respect and confidence of every institution in the district.[44]

Football Agony to Ecstasy

Although McDermott was not blamed for the poor showing of the football team, critics questioned why Duquesne was not able to field as capable a team as many other smaller colleges and universities. They felt that the fault lay in Duquesne's policy of not awarding scholarships to draw the right football talent. The *Duquesne Monthly* of December 1926 even proposed assessing each student $15 for scholarships so that Duquesne could successfully compete on the gridiron.

In 1927 McDermott resigned as football coach. The position was then given to Elmer Layden, one of Notre Dame's famous "Four Horsemen" under Knute Rockne. Layden came to the Bluff in a most roundabout, perhaps providential, way. Father Martin Brennan, an assistant pastor in New Castle, Pennsylvania, had informed his parishioner, Joe Green, of the Duquesne coaching opening. Green had been Layden's college roommate for a year at Notre Dame and recommended him for the post.[45]

Following the announcement of Layden's position, optimism soared on campus. An enthusiastic student body heralded his two-year appointment as coach and athletic director as marking a change in the Dukes' football fortunes. Layden, on the other hand, found his joy over the substantial salary of $6,500 a year dampened when he saw the extent of the task he was about to undertake. As he described it:

> Varsity football had languished to a point where the team had only eleven jerseys with numbers and only enough other spare parts to make up thirty-

Pittsburgh City Photographer Collection

25. The building of the Liberty Bridge, which would span the Monongahela River, and the Tunnel through Mount Washington turned out to be very important to Duquesne's building plans in 1921. Prior to the construction of the Liberty Bridge and its approaches, the west end of the Bluff was a raw unsightly hillside festooned with billboards, as shown in this May 1920 photo. Engineers finally replaced the hillside with a sloping concrete retaining wall, the largest of its type ever successfully built.

26. Father Hehir named the new academic building after the university's Chancellor, Bishop Canevin, one of the school's staunchest supporters during years of fundraising. The Right Reverend J.F. Regis Canevin officiated at the laying of the cornerstone for Canevin Hall on October 29, 1922. In this photo, Bishop Canevin is in the center holding the aspergillum. The hollow cornerstone contained a copper box that held photos of Canevin, Bishop Hugh C. Boyle, Bishop Alexander Le Roy (superior general of the Congregation of the Holy Ghost), and Very Reverend Eugene Phelan, C.S.Sp. (provincial of the Holy Ghost Order in the United States), catalogs of Duquesne's schools, several issues of the university magazine, the *Duquesne Monthly*, current city newspapers, a copy of Hehir's last annual report, and some coins then in circulation. There was also a main document, written in Latin and English, placing the event in a historical context by listing the names of important political and ecclesiastical office holders. The completed Canevin Hall was dedicated on October 28, 1923.

27. Sister Mary Fides Shepperson, of the Sisters of Mercy (the same order that nursed the university's founder and new faculty through a smallpox epidemic in 1881), was Duquesne's first woman student. She gained entrance in the fall of 1909 by special examination. Preparing the way for many women, she received a Bachelor of Arts in 1911 and a Master of Arts in 1913. Other women followed, admitted as "special cases" until 1915, when, due to increasing demand, women were admitted to the Schools of Law, Business and Theater Arts, and most new schools as they were founded. Father Hehir, a true product of the Victorian Era, did not admit women to the College of Arts until 1927. Between 1911 and 1927, some 214 women graduated from Duquesne; all but 40 were nuns. The first woman to earn a Ph.D. from Duquesne did so in 1923.

28. Dean Hugh Muldoon, the first dean of the School of Pharmacy, 1925-1955. He came to Duquesne from a position as Dean of the School of Pharmacy at Valparaiso University. Thanks to the space offered by its new buildings, Duquesne implemented its plans for new programs. The School of Pharmacy had been on the planning list since 1910. It opened in September 1925, and it won the approval of the Pennsylvania State Board of Pharmacy that same year. The first class was limited to 50 men. Dean Muldoon was a prolific scholar, author, and editor. He opened a student branch of the American Pharmaceutical Association, to keep students current on new developments in their field. In 1953, he received the Remington Honor Medal in Pharmacy for outstanding service as an educator, author, and scientist. Suffering from terminal cancer, Muldoon resigned the deanship in 1955 and died less than one year later.

29. Around 1925, football at Duquesne was active again, despite the fact that they lost all seven games in 1925 and five of seven in 1926. In 1927, Elmer Layden, one of Notre Dame's famous "Four Horsemen" under Knute Rockne, became football coach to the Dukes. That year they won half their games. In 1928, Layden won funding for 36 athletic scholarships from the university treasurer. That year, 240 men tried out for the team, and the Dukes finished with 8 wins and 1 loss. In 1929, they were undefeated. In this photo, tight-lipped and nervous, Layden watches a Duquesne–Carnegie Tech football game in 1931. Assistant coach Joe Bach is on the left.

30. President Hoover (center) poses with the unbeatable Duquesne football team on the White House lawn, November 8, 1929. The president shows no signs of concern over the Wall Street "crash" that had occurred just two weeks earlier.

31. Fans of the Dukes rapidly outgrew their unlighted home field on the Bluff. In 1929, the graduate manager of athletics took a big risk for his team; he borrowed money from his father to rent Forbes Field for Duquesne's first night game. Around 27,000 people watched them win 27 to 7, and box office proceeds reached $45,000. After a few more night games, the Dukes became known as the "Night Riders." Layden wanted to photograph the team on horseback (an image that echoed Layden's fame as one of the "Four Horsemen"), and he borrowed mounts from the Pittsburgh Police Department to do it. Players Clark and Benedict pose in this 1930 photo. Note the billy clubs hanging from the saddles.

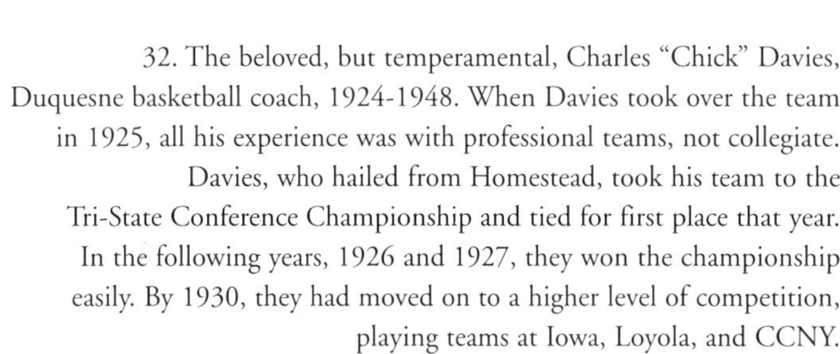

32. The beloved, but temperamental, Charles "Chick" Davies, Duquesne basketball coach, 1924-1948. When Davies took over the team in 1925, all his experience was with professional teams, not collegiate. Davies, who hailed from Homestead, took his team to the Tri-State Conference Championship and tied for first place that year. In the following years, 1926 and 1927, they won the championship easily. By 1930, they had moved on to a higher level of competition, playing teams at Iowa, Loyola, and CCNY.

33. The baseball team in 1922. Baseball, the star in Duquesne's crown before World War I, was scarcely played after 1918. Travel costs and a shrinking number of teams to play led the university to officially drop it from the sports program in 1926. Baseball did not return as an intercollegiate sport until 1948. This team reflects the Holy Ghost fathers' ideal mixture of spirituality and sports; out of these 13 players, 6 entered the priesthood. Middle row, first on the left, is Father Eugene McGuigan, first athletic director for Duquesne (1920-23). Father Mac coached baseball, football, and basketball. First row, on the right, is Samuel Weiss. Weiss attended Duquesne on one of President Hehir's "informal scholarships"; later, as Judge Weiss he generously supported the university.

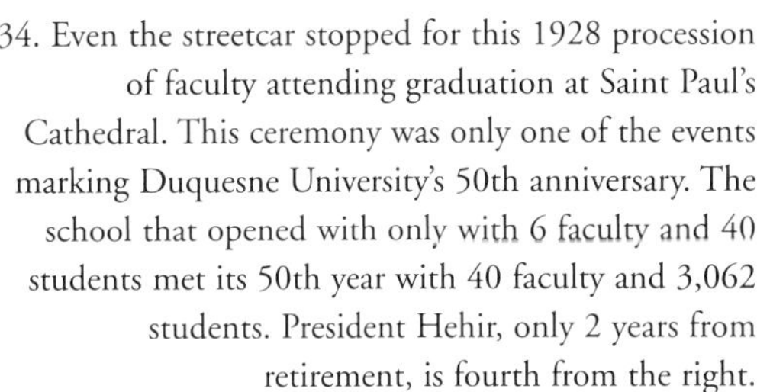

34. Even the streetcar stopped for this 1928 procession of faculty attending graduation at Saint Paul's Cathedral. This ceremony was only one of the events marking Duquesne University's 50th anniversary. The school that opened with only with 6 faculty and 40 students met its 50th year with 40 faculty and 3,062 students. President Hehir, only 2 years from retirement, is fourth from the right.

35. Father Hehir's 31-year presidency (1899–1930) was the longest by far of any Duquesne president. He is shown here at the very end of his remarkable administration, which made a small liberal arts college a university with a range of programs in arts, sciences, and social services. Under his administration, relations between Duquesne and the Diocese of Pittsburgh had been marked by cooperation, respect, and mutual commitment. This was particularly important in a time when Catholics were still not accepted as full participants in American life. President Hehir, in the confines of that era, helped Catholic young people enter professions for which they were gifted and overcome some of the prejudice against them.

36. The city of Pittsburgh continued to grow around the university. This photo shows early stages in the construction of the Boulevard of the Allies, May 25, 1922.

Pittsburgh City Photographer Collection

five makeshift uniforms. The athletic field had been built over an old brick yard and resembled a junk yard more than a gridiron. Part of it was naked of grass. The remainder was covered with a form of tumbleweed. My first day on the scene I was cautioned by my manager about kicking extra points. When the ball cleared the goal posts at one end of the field, it plunged 500 feet or so down the bluff. You had to have a streak of mountain goat in you to be a football manager at that university.[46]

The team used to pay neighborhood boys to retrieve the football each time it went over the wooden fence around the field, in the expectation that they might have to fight off those who otherwise would run away with it.

Layden was comforted by the support offered by Father Hehir and Hugh Muldoon, dean of the pharmacy school, whom he described as "a real lover of football, who wanted to see Duquesne rise in prominence."[47] He had great praise as well for Brother Ammon and "Brue" Jackson, who were "mighty helpful in getting things done."

Just as Posey Cumbert had lifted baseball at Duquesne in an earlier day, Brue Jackson, as Layden's trainer and close associate, brought vitality and enthusiasm to football in 1927. Layden was impressed by the philosophy of the school that had brought a talent like Brue to work for him:

Cleveland Kim "Brue" Jackson is a story by himself. Brue was the first Negro to become the starting quarterback at Braddock High School just outside of Pittsburgh. Brue's dad wanted him to go to college, and so Brue dutifully presented himself at Duquesne in 1925 because it was then what is now called integrated. How it came to be integrated nobody seems to remember. Brue says he thinks it may be because the Holy Ghost Fathers also ran missions in Africa. Whatever the reason, Brue was not the first Negro to apply for admission. Others were already there, and three Negroes were on the football team when I arrived as coach. Three of my better linemen on the 1929 team—Sammy Pratt, Moko Lesser, and Leo Silverstein—would not show up for the West Virginia game because it fell on Yom Kippur. The priests who ran Duquesne were not in the business of letting color or creed get in the way of education.[48]

In his first year as coach, Elmer Layden's Dukes won half their games, a far better performance than that of their predecessors. It was then that Layden requested scholarship money from the university treasurer, Father J.P. Danner, known as "Old Tight Fist" Danner.[49] Layden described Father Danner as one "who practiced the vow of poverty he had taken to enter the Holy Ghost Fathers;" he undoubtedly imposed it on the entire school. However, some of the meager scholarship money was made available and helped draw player talent to Duquesne.

We had about 35 or 40 candidates for football at the start of the 1927 season. We had more than 240 candidates for the start of the 1928 season. Word had spread through the hills of Pennsylvania that a disciple of Knute Rockne had arrived at Duquesne, bent on making a football power. For the first and only time as a coach, I staged tryouts. I had only 36 scholarships to give and I explained first that we did not have an engineering school. This made no impact since most of my candidates had come to me after visiting other tryout camps run by Pitt and Carnegie Tech.

The package I could offer these boys consisted of tuition and room and board in return for playing football and working at a part time job. Their room was really a cot in the gymnasium until basketball season began. After that, they were relegated to a loft above the main building; or, if they were especially lucky, Dean Muldoon might put them up in his apartment. Many of these youngsters came from the coal fields of Pennsylvania. They had no desire to follow their dads into the mines. They left home with the clothes on their backs and little else. They were not expected to return, and Duquesne was their last stop in search of three square meals and an opportunity to keep away from the mines.[50]

This passage not only tells about athletics on the Bluff, it also reveals much about the role Duquesne University played in facilitating upward socioeconomic mobility to those whom it educated.

The boys played hard, giving Duquesne's 1928 squad a record of eight wins to only one loss. They outscored their opponents that season by a 118–32 point margin. Layden was also able to schedule a game against Washington and

Jefferson, a "football entity" ranked only slightly behind Pitt and Carnegie Tech and a previous Rose Bowl participant. This game was the highlight of the 1928 season, with many fans accompanying the team to Washington, Pennsylvania. It was a hard fought 6–6 tie until Duquesne scored a dramatic touchdown in the final minutes to win 12–6. Later that day a victory parade was held through the streets of Pittsburgh. President Hehir, returning from the Eucharistic Congress in Sydney, Australia, hurried back for the game and rode in one of the lead cars. If there had been a shortage of school spirit in support of the teams in the past, it certainly was not evident during the Layden years.

The 1929 season produced the first undefeated team in Duquesne history, although there was a 7–7 tie with West Virginia University. This season also witnessed a bold financial experiment when Duquesne introduced night football to the city of Pittsburgh. Layden writes:

> Once you get a taste of the big-time, you begin to wonder how you can make it pay off. Father Danner, our treasurer, was beginning to wonder when this team that had beaten W and J was going to begin returning some revenue. So was I. Both of us knew it was nearly impossible to expect a big box office return from games we played on our home field [on the Bluff]. At best, 5,000 people could fit in. The time had come to see just what kind of attraction Duquesne football really was in the Pittsburgh area.
>
> John D. Holahan, my student manager of athletics in 1927, had stayed as graduate manager of athletics. I've been told that John borrowed money from his dad to help us rent Forbes Field for our first night game. Forbes Field . . . had some grass, which put it way ahead of our home field. We scheduled the 1929 Geneva game for a Friday night. Riding a wave of optimism, we printed 10,000 tickets, twice as many as we had been selling. We ran out of tickets long before the kick-off. Our attendance for this first experiment in football under the lights was later placed at 27,000.[51]

Not only did Duquesne win 27–7, but the take at the gate was unprecedented. John Holahan rented an armored car to bring the gate receipts to the Bluff. He woke up an astonished Fr. Danner and proceeded to pour out close to $45,000 from the strongbox onto his desk.[52]

With night football at Forbes Field such a success, Layden tried to gain publicity for his team through some imaginative promotion:

> Our nickname changed from the "Dukes" to the "Night Riders." To capitalize on this new name, I had the team's picture taken on horses. . . . Since Father Danner did not have enough funds for the rental of horses, we borrowed them from the mounted unit of the Pittsburgh Police Department. You could see the billy clubs hanging from the saddle cloths.[53]

The city was beginning to take notice of Duquesne's football team. The University of Pittsburgh and Carnegie Institute of Technology competed each year for the city college football championship, and Mayor Charles H. Kine criticized city council for not expanding the competition to include Duquesne:

> I am a trustee of all three schools, and I would like to see the trophy competed for by all three schools, Pitt, Tech, and the Dukes. It is a mistake that only two of our three largest schools compete for this trophy. I am going to ask City Council to correct the error in the future and to specify in the terms of the trophy's award that the Duquesne team also be included as a competitor. . . . So, in the future, you Pitt and Tech boys will have to prove that you are really the city champions by beating the Dukes—if you can.[54]

Father Hehir was a guest of honor at the banquet in which the mayor cited team captain "Buff" Donelli of Duquesne as the best college player in Pittsburgh.

Basketball Gains a Level Playing Field

Football was not the only big sport on the Duquesne campus. By 1923 the university had a modern gymnasium, and basketball was able to take its rightful place in Duquesne's athletic history. Because the university had lacked a proper facility before then, Duquesne basketball had suffered greatly. Duquesne used the slanted floor of the theater below the chapel as a gymnasium in a space so large that a steel cage was constructed and lowered for the games to demarcate the court. The prospect of having to play the game on a slanted floor made it understandably difficult to persuade teams to compete with Duquesne at home. To better describe the beauty of the new facility, the *Duquesne Monthly* outlined the previous situation:

> For years past Duquesne has been forced to one of two alternatives, either to entertain out-of-town cage outfits in the old, slant-floored gym under the chapel, or to rent Motor Square Garden or Montifiore Hall. For obvious reasons both the procedures were unsuitable. Certain schools, seizing on conditions here as an excuse, refused to encounter Duquesne in the Bluffites' home diggings. Red and Blue quintets worked continually at a disadvantage. Forced to meet rival aggregations on unfamiliar ground, often before openly hostile crowds, they saw hard-earned records shattered, felt victory that was logically theirs, torn from their exhausted grasp. But all this had been changed. No institution can now ignore Duquesne's plea for home games without laying itself open to the ancient charge of "dogging it." It is to be hoped that in the future none of Duquesne's little playmates will draw down such an accusation.[55]

Now that Duquesne had a facility worthy of the game, Coach Charles R. "Chick" Davies propelled Duquesne's basketball team into national prominence and more than filled the new 1200-seat gymnasium. Bill Campbell, basketball coach at Duquesne during the 1923–1924 season, recommended Chick Davies for his position although Chick's experience had all been on the professional, not the collegiate level.[56] Chick Davies, like Campbell, was a native son, hailing from Homestead. In his first season as Duquesne's basketball coach, his team tied with Waynesburg for the Tri-State Conference championship. In the two following years, 1926 and 1927, the Dukes had the championship to themselves before withdrawing from the conference and moving to a higher level of competition. Not only did the teams get tougher, but the season, expanded from 20 to 28 games, became more demanding in 1930, when Duquesne played Iowa, Loyola of Chicago, Adrian, Elmhurst, Alfred, John Carroll, American, Catholic, Colgate, St. Bonaventure, Seton Hall, Manhattan, and CCNY. The Davies basketball dynasty continued until 1948.

Baseball Disappears—for a While

Baseball, the star in Duquesne's crown before World War I, was scarcely played at all after the war and was officially dropped in 1926 because of the extensive travel costs in arranging a schedule. Other local colleges were also abandoning baseball at this time, making it increasingly difficult to play nearby teams. Although baseball was played on an informal basis sporadically in the 1930s, it would not return as an intercollegiate sport until 1948.

Tennis is Formalized

Paul Sullivan had helped form an informal tennis squad with fellow undergraduates in 1923. In 1924, Brother Ammon assisted with the completion of the asphalt courts on top of the new gymnasium and an indoor court that was laid out on the basketball floor at the conclusion of the season. The two men persuaded Grant ("Pop") Siverd, captain of the Shady Side Tennis Club team, to coach without pay. The lack of financial backing led to two fundraising ventures, a "Campus Hop" held in the gym, and Pittsburgh's first indoor tennis exhibition. After his graduation from Duquesne's law school in 1928, Paul Sullivan, who had been an outstanding player, began coaching.

Duquesne competed with Pitt, Tech, Geneva, Grove City, Westminster, Bethany, Notre Dame, Cornell, and Michigan (the first Big Ten school played by any Duquesne team) under Sullivan's leadership. Joe Short, who played in the early days after the war, was Duquesne's most outstanding tennis player. Despite the activity of the team, the two tennis courts built on top of the gymnasium were allowed to fall into disrepair, and home matches were moved to public courts.

Track Emerges—and Submerges in the Thirties

Elmer Layden, Duquesne's phenomenal football coach, established track and coached it himself starting in 1928. Brother Ammon helped him lay out a 330-yard track around the football field, the largest the site would allow, although conventional tracks measured 440. His most impressive athletes were Joe Pesci and Tom Schnellbach, whom he referred to as his "two-man team" of 1931. Pesci ran the distances and Schnellbach the sprints to run up an impressive point total for the small school team. But track and field as a collegiate sport at Duquesne did not survive the mid-thirties.

Duquesne's Fiftieth is Celebrated: "Years of Weary Toil"

In 1928 the university celebrated its fiftieth anniversary. And a celebration it was! The observances, scheduled over the first two weeks in June, were opened with a Pontifical High Mass. The Duquesne University Golden Jubilee Pageant, *The Spirit Giveth Life*, by the Reverend John Malloy, C.S.Sp., and Paul Sullivan, was performed at the Syria Mosque. Truly a Duquesne production, it was the work of 11 committees representing every department. A cast of 500 students was directed by Dr. Lloyd, still dean of the drama school, and a musical score was arranged by Dean Rauterkus and Father Parent, both of the School of Music.

In an article titled "Fifty Years of Service," the June issue of the *Duquesne Monthly* reviewed the history of the university in glowing and heroic accounts. A poem by John P. Desmond, A.B., class of '29, titled "The Golden Jubilee," though somewhat morose in tone to modern ears, captured the spirit of the times. The obstacles had been surmounted, and the "burdens leaden like" turned to "gold."

Fifty years of weary toil have passed
To come no more, since first the Red and Blue,
The banner of old Alma Mater, flew
The breeze on these our hills, our stronghold fast.
Our benefactors true, before the mast
For all these years, have seen and weathered
through
The worst of storms and tempests,—Noble crew!
With courage endless; Aye! 'twill ever last.

Those willing hearts their duty never shirked.
Their spirit never purchased was, nor sold
Their bodies weighted down were often irked
By burdens leaden like, till flesh grew cold.
But now the alchemy of time has worked
Through fifty years. The lead that was, is gold.[57]

Though it was a time for celebrating, it was also a time for faith, because the university still had no access to state funding, nor had its fundraising efforts succeeded in developing the endowment so critical to its future growth. Virtually none of Duquesne's students came from wealth, and, as one historian notes, most of its graduates became local businessmen, lawyers and teachers, nearly all of relatively modest means. The university's tuition, its only consistent source of income, had to be kept within the means of those who attended the school, and in 1928 was $150, half that charged by the University of Pittsburgh."[58] Duquesne still depended on what had so often been referred to as the "consecrated endowment," the contributed services of the Holy Ghost fathers. But this contribution was proportionally reduced as the faculty size increased. At the time of the application for the university charter in 1910, the school had 40 faculty members, of whom 25 were Holy Ghost fathers, nearly two-thirds of the total. By the fiftieth anniversary, however, they were less than a fourth of the total, only 24, while the teaching staff had grown to 109.

Considering the inadequate resources, the growth of the university had been truly remarkable. The ten-year period from 1911 to 1921 saw a sixfold increase in student enrollment, and the 1920s shattered even the record, with the student body growing from 2,086 in 1920 to 3,062 full-time students (of which 720 were in the prep school) in 1928. Duquesne University had become the seventh largest Catholic school in the country. Equally impressive, Duquesne's enrollment that year was almost three times that of Villanova College, the state's second largest Catholic school.[59]

Duquesne's growth was the result of both the widespread appeal of its pragmatic approach and the quickening pace of Catholic assimilation into the larger society. The increase in the number and size of its professional schools indicated the broadening career opportunities available to Catholics. Despite the fact that this era witnessed an increase of nativism (evidenced by the growth of the Ku Klux Klan) and the limiting of European immigration, 1928 gave both symbolic and tangible demonstration of the integration of Catholics into the mainstream of American life—for it was in that year that Al Smith, an Irish Catholic, was nominated for the presidency of the United States.

At Duquesne the ethnic composition of the student body stayed surprisingly similar to that of earlier generations. The Irish and Germans still dominated the school, with the Irish constituting the larger group. Distinctly Irish surnames made up 30 of the 73 graduates from the business school, and 20 of the 45 graduates in law. The Jewish community, despite its impoverished beginnings, made an early move into the professions with five graduates from the new School of Pharmacy. Meanwhile, Slavic and Italian surnames were increasing in the prep school. In dramatic contrast to Duquesne, at the University of Pittsburgh foreign-born students and those of foreign descent constituted only six percent of the student body.

Mount Mercy College

In 1929 a second Catholic college was founded in Pittsburgh. The Sisters of Mercy founded Mount Mercy College (now Carlow College), a school for women, at their motherhouse in the Oakland section of the city. Fearing that Mount Mercy would not be granted state accreditation in time for the first graduation, Sister M. Irenaeus, president of the school, came to Father Hehir for help. The result was an agreement unique in the histories of both institutions. On September 30, 1930, Duquesne leased Mount Mercy's property for a nominal sum of $1 per year, in effect, making Mount Mercy a branch campus of Duquesne. Fifty-two students enrolled that year in "Mount Mercy College of Duquesne University." They met the same entrance requirements as Duquesne students, and their records were kept by the Duquesne registrar. Professors hired by Mount Mercy had to be approved by Duquesne, for the contract provided that their names also be listed in the Duquesne University catalog. In the words of the agreement, Duquesne University exercised "a general supervision over the work at Mount Mercy College." Accounts of Mount Mercy social events were even reported in the *Duquesne Duke*.

When state accreditation was received in 1933, the agreement was amicably ended. The friendly relationship between the two institutions, however, continues to this day, and they have long had an agreement whereby students from either school may cross-register for courses at the other school.

Daddy Hehir Departs

Forming an affiliation with Mount Mercy was the last major act of the Hehir administration. The fall of 1930 brought rumors of Father Hehir's resignation after 31 years as president. Nearly a month after the first rumors appeared in the newspapers, the official announcement was made on October 13, 1930. The Superior General of the Congregation of the Holy Ghost was reassigning Father Hehir as Superior of Holy Ghost Apostolate College at Cornwells Heights near Philadelphia.

Daddy Hehir was leaving. Sadness permeated the campus. This was a man whose ear and heart were always open to students, just as his office door was always open—with no secretary to "screen" his visitors. Monsignor Francis Glenn, a student at Duquesne 1929–1934, recalls never seeing Father Hehir sitting down; rather, he stood at a high rolltop desk, occasionally walking in and out of his office talking with whomever chanced to pass.[60] No one was more accessible—and knowledgeable! Maintaining a highly visible profile, Father Hehir was a staunch supporter of and participant in college events. Practically nothing occurred on campus of which he wasn't aware. He knew what the sports teams were doing, what the departments were doing, and what the various student groups were doing. And he knew who was flunking, who was having problems at home, and who needed money.

In one well-known story, Father Hehir asked Samuel Weiss, a Jewish student, about his plans. Weiss replied that he was leaving Duquesne as he had no money. Father told him to go to class instead. Many years later when that student became Judge Weiss, he recounted that he didn't have to pay at the time, but that he had been paying the annual tuition ever since. His long-time support of the university is now memorialized in the Board Room named in his honor. The story of Samuel Weiss is typical of the way Daddy Hehir *noticed* his students. He noticed because he cared. And the students knew they would miss his caring—and his helping.

The faculty and administration would miss him as keenly as the students. His work on behalf of the university was tireless. Because of it, a liberal arts college had been brought to university status, replete with many thriving new schools and departments. His efforts befitted his motto, *Non recucum laborem*, ("I do not refuse to work"). What Hehir had done, he had done well. Moreover, one of his gifts as an administrator was his ability to choose the right men to head the new schools and supply them with both the necessary autonomy and support. His trust in his deans, and his good working relationship with them, was apparent in the fact that all the founders of the various schools still headed those schools at the time of his retirement (except for one who retired for reasons of health).

The Athletic Department was certainly sorry to see him go. Though careful not to allow intercollegiate athletics to interfere with scholastic purposes, Father Hehir had, within the school's limited means, made a provision for a variety of sports programs. "A sound mind in a sound body" was his motto. He did what he could to provide opportunities for developing that sound body, to the delight of spectators as well as sports participants.

The effects of Martin Hehir's departure were felt beyond the university campus. Under his administration, relations between Duquesne University and the Diocese of Pittsburgh had been marked by cooperation, respect, and mutual commitment. This was particularly important in a time when Catholics were still not accepted as full participants in American life. Father Hehir was able to work within the confines of that era to help Catholic young people enter the professions they were gifted for and overcome some of the prejudice against them. The Catholic community was grateful.

At a testimonial dinner, Mayor Charles H. Kline spoke of his long association with Father Hehir and the religious bigotry they had battled in Harrisburg in pursuit of state appropriations while Kline was a state senator. Bishop Boyle remarked on Father Hehir's priestly role in contributing so much strength and talent toward the spiritual welfare of the student body—and everyone else his life had touched. The Sisters of Mercy at Mercy Hospital thanked him for his friendship and his support of their School of Nursing.

The Catholic community had been greatly enriched by this Holy Ghost father, but so had the community at large. The president of the Pittsburgh City Council, John S. Herron, spoke of Father Hehir's role in making Duquesne University an integral part of the city and on his role as citizen: "We who are in public life appreciate men like Father Hehir, constructive and educational men that will give you the benefit of their thoughts and their advice. . . . who will encourage you when you feel that you are slipping."[61] Dr. S.S. Baker of Washington and Jefferson College spoke of Father Hehir's contributions as an educator and as an administrator who made the university known not only in local circles, but throughout the country. James Francis Burke, advisor to President Hoover, applauded Father Hehir for building not only an institution of stone and marble, but one of "ideas and men." John E. Laughlin, vice-dean of the law school, referring to the priest's personal generosity, jokingly called him a "failure"—a man without a dollar in his pocket who had built a university valued at $2 million in physical assets alone. Finally, Mr. Reis proclaimed, "there is no other living man in the city of Pittsburgh who by his work and his labor has rendered so much good and has radiated such a wonderful influence over this community as he has."[62]

In his farewell speech, Father Hehir expressed his dreams for a new science hall, laboratory, auditorium, and administration house for the faculty. He was still planning. As many of his listeners knew, he had frequently commented that if ever he had the money he would immediately start a School of Medicine and Dentistry! No one doubted the sincerity of his concluding statement: "My last prayer and wish is that Duquesne University grow and flourish."[63]

A few short years after that good-bye dinner on November 4, 1930, while acting as superior of the Senior Seminary of the Holy Ghost Order in Ferndale, Connecticut, Martin Hehir became critically ill with cancer. Realizing that he was never to recover, he announced his desire to die in his beloved city of Pittsburgh, and on June 19, 1935, in Mercy Hospital, only three blocks from Duquesne University, he had his own "graduation" from this life at the age of 79.

It was summer, and some students were washing walls in Canevin Hall. Someone came over and asked if anyone had been an altar boy. Another server was needed for the funeral mass. One of the undergrads, although he hadn't served for years and never met Father Hehir—but was apparently less enthusiastic about washing walls than the others—volunteered. His name was Henry J. McAnulty. Together with the other participants, young Henry celebrated Father Martin Hehir's funeral mass in the Duquesne chapel.

Daddy Hehir had come home.

4. Enduring Hard Times

When the hard times of the 1930s hit, Duquesne was under an administration of an entirely different nature than before. Perhaps its somewhat somber tone was fitting for that economic cataclysm known as the Great Depression.

The Scholar-President

A mathematician took the helm of Duquesne University after Father Hehir's departure. The Reverend Jeremiah Joseph Callahan officially succeeded Father Hehir on January 4, 1931, and promptly astonished a throng of newspaper reporters by explaining his contradiction of Einstein's theory of relativity. He had recently published the first book of a two-volume work titled *Euclid or Einstein? A Proof of the Parallel Theory and A Critique of Metageometry*, which evoked considerable interest but was widely disputed by mathematicians.[1] Father Callahan claimed to have "solved the problem [of geometric trisection of the angle] which has baffled mathematicians for 2000 years."[2] He was wrong: it is not possible to trisect an angle with only a straightedge and compass. But, as one Holy Ghost father said of him, "Father Callahan was the one man I knew who never had a doubt."

The first president of Duquesne who was a native-born American, and an alumnus of the school, Jeremiah Callahan was born in Bay City, Michigan, in 1878 and graduated from the Pittsburgh Catholic College before studying for the priesthood at St. Vincent's Seminary in nearby Latrobe, Pennsylvania.[3] He had been president of Holy Ghost Apostolic College in Cornwells Heights, Pennsylvania, when, upon the recommendation of Father Hehir, he was selected to assume the presidency of Duquesne.

A Grand Beginning

Inaugural ceremonies were held at the Schenley Hotel and at Soldiers and Sailors Memorial in the Oakland section of the city on April 30, 1931. Certainly one of grandest presidential inaugurals in Duquesne history, the gala event was attended not only by the Duquesne University administration and faculty, but by representatives of 140 universities, colleges, academies, and learned groups throughout the United States. It was a fitting welcome for a man who was a brilliant scholar. Unfortunately, it is extremely difficult to remain a serious scholar while serving as a university president, as Father Callahan proved with near disastrous results. The attention and energy required by the one vocation steals from that required by the other.

In many ways Father Callahan was the direct opposite of his predecessor, the affable and gregarious Father Hehir. Though he took his meals with the other Holy Ghost fathers, Father Callahan did not really associate with them.[4] He lived in a private apartment, consisting of a bedroom and a bath, which he had specially constructed adjoining the administration building. He was little interested in the details of administrative work. Many of the day-to-day decisions were made at various times by W.S. York Critchley, dean of the School of Education; Father Kirk, also dean of the School of Education (before and after Critchley); Father Manning, dean of men; and Father Brannigan, dean of the College of Arts. Other deans acted with considerable autonomy, almost by default. Father Callahan was so detached that he took two-month vacations—he called them sabbaticals—in the midst of the school year. His brief appearances before the students normally consisted of formal lectures having little to do with the modern-day world or the students' lives but instead devoted to such topics as the science of language, Greco-Roman antiquities, and mathematical theories. With time, his aloofness became more pronounced. Even his occasional presidential messages printed in the *Duquesne Duke* disappeared entirely after his Christmas message of 1932. It is doubtful that these messages were missed by students weary of being told that "Duquesne has no room for the shirker," (September 29, 1932) or that in seeking "first the kingdom of God . . . We have failed miserably" (December 15, 1932).

Father Callahan's entire philosophy of education differed dramatically from Father Hehir's. When Father Hehir assumed the presidency, he surveyed the needs of the community and changed Pittsburgh Catholic College from a basically liberal arts school, emphasizing the classics, into an institution directed toward more practical studies in the commercial and accounting fields. As more occupational opportunities opened to the Catholic community, the university responded with the opening of professional schools. Father Callahan, however, saw the chief purpose of a university in the shaping of a "gentleman" through a liberal education. In his inaugural address he stated his position:

> The tendency of a liberal education is toward intellectual refinement and education of the taste. Liberal education would lead to the possession of the manners and the mental attitude of a gentleman, the complete and perfectly rounded out man of the world.

He criticized practical educational theories as a waste of energy, claiming that "modern education has lost its way and is wandering in the swamps and bush lands of terra incognita."

Economic Shock Waves

Prices in the nation fell as the Great Depression deepened, but Duquesne University continued to maintain its cost of tuition at $225 per year, the same as it had charged in 1929. A hard-pressed college-age population found it difficult to meet even this comparatively modest fee, and enrollment declined for four consecutive years. In 1929 the student body numbered 2751, but by 1933 it had fallen to 2116. The loss of nearly a fourth of the student body dealt a severe blow to the school, dependent as it was on tuition income. The prep school suffered even greater losses. Its enrollment of 720 in 1928 had fallen to 308 by 1932 and still further to 247 the following year.

The Depression slowed, but did not stop, the piecemeal property acquisitions the University had been making in the last years of the Hehir administration. In 1929 alone some 13 houses were acquired, all but one of which were located on Locust and Vickroy Streets on the block occupied by Canevin Hall. This gave the University ownership of about three fourths of that block. While the plans for a new science hall were quietly being shelved, 12 additional properties were acquired and renovated from 1930 to 1938 at a cost of $482,439.71. This was an enormous undertaking in view of the fact that tuition income in 1929 (the last "good" year prior to the onset of the Depression) amounted to only $450,348.07.[5]

The low prices of real estate during the Depression encouraged the administration to purchase other property not on the Bluff. The university had been conducting its downtown operations in rented space in the Vandergrift Building. The board of directors purchased the Fitzsimons Building in 1932, at the very bottom of the Depression, when the cost of $195,000 was less than the assessed valuation of the land on which it stood.[6] Since the seven-story building provided more than ample space, the university was able to rent out the lower floors to private interests.[7] Unfortunately, after the purchase, it was discovered that the elevators needed to be replaced, costing the university an additional $70,000. Two months later the university purchased a building from the Slovak Society on the corner of Hooper and Ivanhoe Streets at a cost of $20,000. This was converted into the music school. In 1934 it purchased a house at 903 Bluff Street, adjoining the new music school, which was named Saint Cecelia's Hall. The ROTC garage was purchased in 1936 at a cost of $12,500.

Altogether 22 houses on the Bluff were purchased in the period of 1929–1938. Those occupied by renters were generating over $20,500 annually by 1941, at which time the campus had grown to 10.75 acres (as compared to two acres in 1885) and included 16 buildings occupied by the university. Many of the houses were converted into departmental offices; and some were used as dormitories, the most notable of which is now called Laval House but was originally called Varsity Hall since it housed student athletes. The increasing size of the university eventually prompted the hiring of a superintendent of buildings[8] and, in March of 1938, the first campus policeman. "Cap," as he was affectionately called, wore no uniform. He faced virtually none of the problems currently confronting campus police across the country; one of his major duties seems to have been keeping neighborhood children off the football field.

As tuition income plummeted—in 1932 alone, it fell about $30,000 from the previous year—and as property acquisitions continued, the university found itself amid oceans of red ink. By June of 1933, the treasurer reported to the board of directors that the university was $400,000 in debt. This indebtedness exceeded the entire annual income of the university—$374,515. Of this amount, $282,973 was tuition income. Duquesne's financial position became so precarious that it was borrowing amounts as small as $5,000 for a 45-day period just to meet its immediate obligations. The state of the university finances, however, was never disclosed to the student body. Throughout the Depression, the *Duquesne Duke* gives no mention of the university's financial condition. But Bishop Boyle knew. He even "offered the assistance of his own financial advisor to reduce the interest on the debts of Duquesne."[9]

Hard times encroached on the university only gradually. A full year after the Crash of '29, the university football team and student supporters arranged for a special charter train for the Loyola game, and 200 Duquesne students journeyed to Chicago. As late as Christmas of 1930, the university was still able to arrange holiday jobs for its students with the Pennsylvania Railroad. Even in November of 1931, an editorial in the *Duke* remained optimistic about employment after graduation being the direct and inevitable result of diligence and scholarly attainment. By May of 1933, though, this optimism had evaporated. In a poll of graduating students, the *Duquesne Duke* found that "no senior is certain of a job." Graduates from previous years were still searching for positions. This critical situation was addressed by a graduating senior in the spring of 1934:

> There is some sort of saying somewhere to the effect that an education is the key to world conquest; that a boy or girl with a high school diploma can step immediately into a position, any one with a college degree can practically set his own hours and salary.
>
> Some years ago this was the gospel truth. But these days a college student has nothing similar to expect. In an era when some of those holding an M.A. or Ph.D. are walking the streets, it is somewhat discouraging to the student who will in June leave college with his degree . . . Statistics reveal that there are great numbers of college graduates who have yet to secure their first job.
>
> About the only thing that can be done now is to wait till the ultimate ends of the present administration are accomplished.
>
> A great many students upon graduation are continuing with post-graduate work. Certainly they can't go wrong in this move, and in time they may probably realize great benefits from their post-graduate studies. This, however, is beyond the means of the majority of graduates.[10]

Duquesne graduates were by no means alone in their search for jobs that did not exist. In February 1934, *Elementary School Journal* estimated that "70 percent of the [college] grating classes of the past three years have not found employment." Job prospects were to remain bleak for many years. As late as 1937, a writer in the *Duquesne Monthly* questioned the value of a liberal arts college education as a vehicle for occupational success: "Here's the dilemma in our educational system. A student spends four years learning how to live, and graduates to find himself unable to make a living."[11] The writer cited a poll of Duquesne alumni revealing that 95 percent "urge that a college education be supplemented with a little technical training."[12] This was a far cry from Father Callahan's vision of a liberal arts curriculum turning out cultured gentlemen.

Duquesne Tries to Help its Graduates—and the Community

Because of the poor job outlook, in May of 1932, the School of Business Administration began a job placement service open to all students and graduates of Duquesne University for full- or part-time employment. Given the times, it may have been wishful thinking, but the university hoped that Duquesne alumni would hire Duquesne graduates in a situation where alumni support alumni. The School of Education opened its own placement service in 1936, after an attempt two years earlier had failed.

The university was sympathetic to the plight of the general public as well as that of its own students and graduates. With so many people having free time as a result of their unemployment, Carnegie Public Library of Pittsburgh experienced a 46 percent increase in library use from 1929 to 1932. This literate element in the population provided Duquesne with an opportunity to make a significant educational contribution. Under the direction of A.B. Wright, dean of the School of Business Administration, Duquesne University opened the School for the Unemployed in 1933. The purpose of the school was purely one of enlightenment—a place for the unemployed adults in the city to attend free courses offered by volunteer instructors in such areas as English, economics, government, history, and psychology. To enter the school, one was required to have completed a minimum of two years of high school, be at least 30 years of age, be certified as unemployed, and be unable to pay tuition. The non-credit classes ran for ten weeks, in the newly purchased Fitzsimons Building downtown. The popularity of the program was attested to by the 275 students who completed the course. The most popular class offered was "Written Composition" and the least popular was, surprisingly enough, "Study of Money."

If the course did nothing to benefit the university financially or to increase the students' academic credentials, it fulfilled Father Callahan's purpose of promoting liberal arts studies for their own sake. More than that, it gave the unemployed with time on their hands a place to go to find intellectual stimulation, purpose, and inspiration in the midst of hopelessness and despair. Father Callahan wrote, "One man admitted that he was seriously considering suicide until his enrollment, and that the inspiring talks of his teacher dispelled this desperate inclination."[13] The School for the Unemployed gave students an opportunity to meet others in circumstances similar to their own and in productive and optimistic surroundings. The sense of camaraderie felt by the adult students led 70 of them to attend a reunion that fall. An unexpected by-product was the considerable good will and favorable publicity that the program generated for Duquesne University.

Financially, though, Duquesne University was hardly in a position to help anybody. The declining enrollment and the shrinking resources of those who did manage to stay in the university made Father Hehir's old system of benevolent bookkeeping impossible. Then came Franklin D. Roosevelt and his New Deal programs to the rescue.

Duquesne and the New Deal

In February of 1934 the Civil Works Administration (CWA) helped finance the cost of education by providing jobs for students at their respective colleges and universities. The hastily drawn directives of the CWA were soon replaced by the more organized Federal Emergency Relief Administration (FERA), which permitted 12 percent of the full-time student body to work a maximum of 50 hours per month at 30 cents an hour. Initially only ten percent of full-time students were permitted to work at any college or university, but the huge waiting lists—there were 200 students on Duquesne's—caused the government to shorten the hours permitted (originally 30 hours a week) and thus allow broader participation. Until the fall of 1938, students did not actually receive a paycheck; the money was sent directly to the university to defray the cost of tuition. A student working under FERA could conceivably earn enough to cover 80 percent of that cost. In the summer of 1935, the program was continued under the National Youth Administration (NYA) which was a part of the Works Progress Administration (WPA). The NYA had the same guidelines as its predecessors except for an additional provision that especially qualified students who devoted all of their time to their studies were not required to work. In 1938 alone, Duquesne received $20,790 in NYA funds, enough to cover the cost of 2,598 credit hours.[14]

Under FERA, students had been employed at the university doing research, clerical work, and "work on the campus and in the cafeteria."[15] But as part of the NYA effort to supply laborers with "socially desirable work which would not be otherwise performed,"[16] many strong, young backs later were employed in campus beautification. This arduous work required the removal of rubbish, brickyard, and construction debris; followed by scraping and leveling; planting shrubs, trees, and lawns; and removing the fences that bordered the campus playing field. These efforts toward beautification were initiated by a gift of trees and shrubbery planted beside Canevin Hall and along Colbert Street in the spring of 1936. Six of these 36 ginko trees still survive between Canevin Hall and Our Lady of Victory Walk. Several more donations of trees, ivy, and shrubs were received and student efforts in planting them were elaborate. A writer in the *Duquesne Duke* quipped, "Probably the most attractive aspect of the project is the shrubbery arrangement which spells 'Duquesne.' Since seeing these letters I've wondered how the little plants knew enough to come up in the right places. I didn't even know they could spell."

The St. Patrick's Day Flood

The peak of NYA employment on the Bluff came in March of 1936 as a result of a natural disaster, the worst flood in Pittsburgh's history. Popularly known as the St. Patrick's Day Flood, it began on March 16 when the waters of the Allegheny and Monongahela Rivers inundated many of the city's downtown streets and other low-lying areas, leaving 74 persons dead and more than 100,000 homeless. With electric power out and most other services curtailed or nonexistent, the normal operation of nearly every school and business in the city was interrupted. On St. Patrick's Day commuter students stayed home as the waters rose still higher. Duquesne science professors managed to bring an antiquated generating system back to life, thus making the Duquesne campus an island of light in an otherwise dismal darkness. The Bluff was also a source of fresh water. Since the pumping station was flooded, the city had ceased supplying water, making Father Murphy's pump beside the administration building more valuable than ever. These factors, along with its elevated proximity to the water-soaked Golden Triangle, made Duquesne an ideal hub for relief operations. The gymnasium, the campus theater, and Varsity Hall all became substitute city police stations. Campus streets were filled with police cars and motorcycles. Fifty makeshift beds were set up in the gym, and those students who yet remained on the Bluff served thousands of sandwiches and cups of coffee to the relief workers. Duquesne football players were recruited to serve as auxiliary police, complete with badges. They assisted in maintaining security and "Some of the squad . . . helped Pittsburgh 'dig out'."[17]

Duquesne continued to be a base of operations long after the waters subsided, delaying the reopening of the university until March 26. Even after that date the campus was crowded with "refugees" from the university's only downtown location, the Fitzsimons Building, which stood in six feet of water. Classes normally held there were moved to the administration building and Canevin Hall. It was quite some time until the mud was cleaned out and the elevators were certified safe for public use. Much of the downtown cleanup was accomplished by Duquesne students working under the NYA. The *Duquesne Duke* missed its March 18th issue, and even the following week's issue could not be published through the regular printer.

The entire disaster tested the university's mettle and it was not found wanting, despite the absence of President Callahan, away on a "sabbatical."

A Grant Produces a Guide

Duquesne's first WPA grant was awarded to its School of Graduate Study to hire unemployed teachers to carry on research in the field of education. Duquesne selected five studies from the choices provided by the WPA: assessing ways of sharing information on student hygiene, determining factors in high school that relate to success in college, creating a digest of Pennsylvania state laws related to education, and assessing practices of teaching English to bilingual children. A year later, the graduate school's work on one of these projects had expanded to include a thorough analysis and simplification of all Pennsylvania school laws. The *Guide to the School Laws of Pennsylvania*, by Profs. Remaley and Carney, became such a valuable resource that a state contract was secured for updating supplements, and the authors soon began work on a second volume of Pennsylvania court decisions pertaining to school cases.

The Coeds of the Thirties

Among the changes of the 1930s were those brought by the vastly increased number of women students. When they first appeared, they were a rare sight on this once all-male campus. As their numbers grew, the men were less inclined to give way every time one smiled at them. The *Duquesne Duke* reported in 1929 that the university had officially ended the coed practice of line-crashing in the cafeteria. Although the ladies themselves ended the use of their own entrance to Canevin Hall, they later made its use a part of the Freshman hazing. They busied themselves with the formation of an array of social, athletic, religious, and scholarly organizations of their own. In February 1938 a coed section to the *Duquesne Duke* was introduced—two full columns dealing with fashions, etiquette, personality hints, occupational opportunities for coed graduates, and a column titled "Co-ed Musings."

Despite Father James F. Carroll's 1930 explanation of the Pope's encyclical advocating complete separation of the sexes in an educational setting, and despite speculation that Duquesne's "merger" with Mount Mercy College might result in a move in that direction, the coeds were on the Bluff to stay. The percentage of women students grew steadily, from 32 percent in 1933 to 41 percent by 1940, amounting to 1,221 women students. St. John's Hall, a men's dormitory, was converted into a girls' dormitory and renamed

St. Mary's Hall for the fall semester of 1934. Only two years before, the women had been housed in just two rooms on the second floor of the library building. St. Mary's Hall gave them two floors of dormitory rooms and a first floor open to the entire university community for a lounge, reception area, and the office of the Director of Social Activities for Women.[18] By November of 1935 the women were already conducting a drive to redecorate!

Campus Life During the Depression

Paradoxically, the Depression was a time of high spirits on campus. The high level of participation in student activities was never again to be equaled. Adding to the fraternities, sororities, and organizations born during the Hehir years were many new ones, covering almost every conceivable field of interest, plus an explosion in the number of sports teams. Economic constraints were such that some social events had to be canceled, and some young men had to forgo inviting coeds out; but there was a widespread attempt to share the cost of dates, and only the most stoic would have agreed with Father Callahan's assertion that the "economic stress through which we are passing has not been an unmixed evil. It has been the means of trimming off many of the frivolities of life."[19] Indeed, most students made a concerted effort to avoid trimming anything that enriched their extracurricular lives. The campus teemed with activity—athletic, musical, dramatic, literary, religious, philosophical, and purely social in nature. And freshman hazing was an undeniably "frivolous" part of that activity.

The incoming class had to subject itself to an official hazing known as "Freshman Rules." Over the years Freshman Rules were either emphasized or downplayed according to the enthusiasm of the current sophomore class for browbeating and humiliating the newcomers. The requirements involved the wearing of red and blue "dinks," performing the Alma Mater and other school songs on demand, parading through the streets of town in strange apparel, and doing chores for sophomores. Initially spread out over the whole first semester, Freshman Rules were eventually formalized into an official week or so of misery. Student Senate plans to rescind them in the fall of 1929 met with great opposition from upperclassmen who claimed that the practice was most necessary in cutting the "arrogant Frosh" down a proverbial peg or two since timid freshmen were a rarity. "This is because they are nearly all graduates of Duke Prep and as such consider themselves part proprietors of the institution."[20]

Although slight variations appeared from year to year, the basic Freshman Rules for women were as recorded in the *Duquesne Duke* 1933: They were to have their official hazing week from October 2 to October 6, at the end of which time they would be officially initiated into the student body at a special ceremony. Coeds met for a tea at the beginning of the year, and were formally welcomed, given insights into college life to help them feel at home, supplied with a sophomore "big sister" to serve as an advisor, and informed about Freshman Rules. During the initiation week they were to

1. Wear armbands until Christmas.
2. Address all girls by name, inquiring as to the name of anyone with whom they were unfamiliar.
3. Wear no jewelry.
4. Use only the Vickroy Street entrance to Canevin Hall.
5. Wear no hats or gloves to class.
6. Refrain from talking to boys.
7. Be courteous to all upperclass women.
8. Offer to carry books for sophomores.
9. Wear no makeup.
10. Attend the October 5th Tea Dance.
11. Learn the Alma Mater.

Freshman men had their formal hazing period from October 6 to November 11. They were expected to:

1. Wear a red tie done in a Windsor knot on campus and to all athletic events.
2. Recite the Alma Mater, college yells, and college songs on demand from any sophomore.
3. Carry a five-cent box of matches for use of upperclassmen who might need a light (although Freshman men and coeds were generally not allowed to smoke on campus themselves during the Freshman Rules).
4. Use only the Vickroy Street entrance and back stairs of Canevin Hall from October 6 to October 27.
5. Wear one light sock and one dark sock from October 6 to October 27 with pants cuffs rolled up to reveal the socks.

Generally the Freshman Rules were well accepted and got the school year off to a joyful beginning, sparking occasional articles in the *Duke* about freshmen making beds in Varsity Hall or parading at noon through the streets of Pittsburgh at the bidding of sophomores. President Callahan officially ended freshman hazing in the fall of 1937, citing episodes from the previous fall when some belligerent freshmen engaged some sophomores in fights. But by the next fall, students had come up with a new "tradition" to replace the old hazing: the Soph-Frosh Mud Battle. Along with the mud-slinging (generously photographed for the *Duke*), the event included a greased-pole-climbing contest to capture the class flag, a bonfire, a rally, and after the cleanup, an informal dance in the gym. By 1941 even the mud battle was replaced by a comparatively tame sophomore-freshman tug-of-war. But the Freshman Rules would not stay dead. They revived themselves in later years, although without their previous verve or rigor.

Fraternities and Sororities

Having survived freshman hazing, students were eligible later to join a Greek fraternity or sorority and undergo yet another hazing. On the Duquesne campus, these generally followed a pattern of moderate humiliation, exemplified by the sack races of pledges on downtown streets. Duquesne was never known for excesses of behavior. In an age when college life included goldfish swallowing and cramming into phone booths on some campuses, Duquesne students were content merely to race turtles: the first Fraternity / Sorority Turtle Derby was held in the cafeteria in the spring of 1939.

Potential members were introduced to the fraternities at the open smokers and to the sororities at tea parties. The fraternities also hosted university-wide affairs. Gamma Phi, the oldest fraternity on campus (founded in 1916) traditionally hosted the University Thanksgiving Dance; Kappa Sigma Phi held the Easter Ball; Phi Alpha, the Annual Spring Frolic; and the Interfraternity Council sponsored the winter dance.

Delta Phi Sigma fraternity was founded in the fall of 1929 for students in the evening school, amidst an outcry from the day-school fraternities who claimed that Delta Phi Sigma was recruiting and pledging members from among full-time students before they were able to meet the more stringent academic requirements for the other fraternities. At length this was resolved and Delta Phi Sigma was able to enrich the social lives of evening students.

By 1937 Duquesne University had seven sororities: Sigma Lambda Phi, Alpha Phi Omicron—the first sorority on campus (founded in 1928), Epsilon Eta Phi, Delta Mu Delta, Sigma Phi Delta, Theta Sigma Delta, and Lambda Kappa Sigma.

The Greek organizations flourished with the founding of both honorary societies and social groups, many with a common ethnicity. Omega Psi Phi (1937) was the "Negro" fraternity; Sigma Epsilon Phi (1934) was for students of Greek nationality. The Jewish fraternity at Duquesne, Phi Delta Rho, organized in 1927, became a chapter of Phi Alpha national fraternity in 1934 and was joined by Jay Sigma Delta Jewish sorority (1936), which went national as Theta Sigma Delta (1937). Alpha Phi Delta fraternity and Sigma Phi Delta sorority, both founded in 1937, were for students of Italian descent.

Although some "Greeks" endured, others were short-lived. In 1941 Gamma Sigma still appeared on the list of officially recognized student organizations, but Omega Psi Phi, Sigma Epsilon Phi, and Beta Pi Sigma were gone. Among sororities, Sigma Phi Delta and Lambda Kappa Sigma had been replaced by Alpha Delta, Delta Sigma Theta, Pi Omega Pi, and Sigma Phi Alpha.

Honoraries included Epsilon Eta Phi (1936), the business administration sorority; Beta Alpha Phi (1937), business administration fraternity; Alpha Tau Delta (1939), the nursing sorority; and Sigma Tau Delta (1939), the English fraternity. Lambda Kappa Sigma was an honorary sorority for pharmacy students. The coeds of Epsilon Eta Phi (Epsies) made a significant contribution, beginning in the year of their founding, by organizing a cooperative book exchange for the first two weeks each semester. In general, the "Greek" impact on campus life was beneficial—and was far greater than the size of membership would suggest. In 1938, for example, only 8 percent, or 245 students, belonged to a fraternity or sorority.[21]

Clubs, Teams, Associations, Publications, and All Kinds of Organizations

Although participation in student organizations was encouraged, the *Bulletin of Duquesne University, 1929–1930* makes no mention of fraternities or sororities on campus. The catalog does list the Alumni Association, the Athletic Association, which "maintains departmental and 'Varsity teams' in football, basketball, tennis, and track," the Red Masquers, the University Orchestra, Band, and Glee Club, four literary societies, religious sodalities, the Catholic Students' Mission Crusade, and three university publications: The *Duquesne Monthly*, the *Duquesne Duke*, and *The Monocle*.

The *Duquesne University Bulletin, 1937–38* lists a full range of organizations for women:

> Social life for the Women students at Duquesne flourishes under the auspices of numerous women's organizations including: Women's Student Government Association, Women's Athletic association with its hockey, basketball, volley ball, tennis, archery, swimming, badminton, and inter college play days, and seven sororities. . . . Students are urged, moreover, to develop their talents along musical and dramatic lines by participating in the entertainments given at frequent intervals by the University Orchestra, the Glee Club, and the Band.

By 1937 the school had three distinct alumni groups: the general Alumni Association, the Women's Alumnae Association, and an organization for the religious, the Sisters Alumnae. In 1940 these organizations were joined by yet another, the Priests Alumni Association of Duquesne University.

Literary groups included a campus debating society, the Duquesne University Debating Society, and another for the evening school, the Duke Owl Debating Society. The Spectator Club of the College of Arts and Letters was a senior honorary study group that ran open-forum discussions and, oddly enough for a study group, hosted dances and social affairs. The women students of the summer sessions, Saturday School, and late afternoon and evening classes conducted their own forums through an organization known as The Duquesne University Forum. The Evening School Association offered its students social affairs and a planned program of intramural athletics. The Student Senate, composed of four elected delegates from each school, governed under the firm control of the university administration. It was replaced in 1937 by an appointed Dean's Council. The Monogram Club, composed of student athletes who had earned a "letter," promoted scholarship and sportsmanship. Wherever an interest or a need existed, an organization seemed to spring up to meet it. Some of the organizations, such as the Newman Club for Catholic Students and the Young Men's Hebrew Association, were city-wide, with members from Carnegie Tech, the University of Pittsburgh, Pennsylvania College for Women (Chatham), and Mount Mercy as well as Duquesne, coordinated through branches on their respective campuses. In a number of cases these branches became independent organizations in their own right.

Nearly every school and department had an attendant organization of interested students. Music students and members of the music ensembles organized the Jarmus club in January 1930, taking their name from Dean Joseph A. Rauterkus's initials and the suffix "mus" from music. The Music School still offered an opportunity to participate in the university orchestra, band, and Glee Club, although at various times different groups came into existence, including a Polyphonic Choir, a girls' orchestra, the Madrigal Singers, and a Schola Cantorum for the study and performance of sacred music. In 1939 the music school was to sponsor another group, a swing band known as the Swingcopaters, who were immensely popular in their introductory concerts and various social affairs.

The Law Club hosted the moot courts each year, and starting in December of 1931, held monthly dinner debates. The moot courts enjoyed great popularity on campus with extensive converage in the *Duke*. The 1932 case in which a coed sued for breach of promise was argued so well that it resulted in a hung jury and created a sensation. The 1936 moot court, a combined effort by the law school and the pharmacy school, dealt with an accidental death due to a pharmacist incorrectly dispensing first aid. It provoked similar enthusiasm.

Pharmacy students could become members of the Pharmaceutical Association, which hosted the Annual Pharmacy Night each spring. The format changed over the years from featuring student speakers to students performing experiments in the labs while guides explained their work, to demonstrations. The Tesla coil was the big hit of 1934; glass-blowing and scientific crime detection evoked interest in 1939. Also featuring exhibits, and a formal program, the event drew approximately 3,500 visitors each year. On several occasions, other departments contributed to the evening. For example, the university orchestra performed at the one annual event, and the Red Masquers presented a short play at another. An extremely active group, the Pharmaceutical Association hosted an annual Ladies' Day as well, during which coeds gave 20-minute presentations. The group also held a carnival and dance each year.

Pre-med and other students in the School of Science joined the Science Club. The Science Club gave occasional shows of experiments, and beginning in 1937, it published a monthly science periodical. And in 1935 it conducted a weekly science seminar in conjunction with the future pharmacists.

Father Kirk, as dean of the School of Education, proposed the formation of a Practice Teacher's Club in 1936 that was supplanted by Future Teachers of America (FTA) in 1939. Duquesne's Raymond V. Kirk Chapter was the first FTA in the state. Students from the School of Business Administration were transferred to the School of Education in 1932. Under the old system, these students, studying to teach commercial courses, took a minor in education; now they were part of the School of Education, enrolled in a program culminating in a new degree, the Bachelor of Science in Commercial Education, and taking their major courses through the School of Finance. These potential teachers of commercial subjects organized as the Commedukes. They held an annual typing contest, put out a publication named for the organization, and did much of the planning for the celebration of the School of Education's 10th anniversary in April of 1939.

The School of Business Administration had

representation on campus not only through its honorary fraternity (Beta Alpha Phi) and honorary sorority (Epsilon Eta Phi), but also through the women in the evening division. The members of Beta Alpha Phi began bi-monthly radio presentations in 1936 over KQV on such topics as "Steel in Relation to Pittsburgh," "Glass and Its Place among Pittsburgh's Industries," and "Why America Should Return to the Gold Standard."

The university's International Relations Club was formed in the spring of 1934 and reorganized by Dr. C. Kelly, political science professor, in the fall of 1936 under the Carnegie Endowment for International Peace. This national organization donated current political library resource materials each year to all the participating schools.

A number of clubs studying various cultures were started on campus, some of which were linked to language departments. The *Duquesne Duke* announced the formation of the Jewish Student Society of Duquesne University in November 1933. The Italian Cultural Club organized the following year, and the Spanish Club was founded by second- and third-year Spanish students in April of 1935. In January 1936 the *Duke* announced the reformation of the Italian Cultural Club, "taking a lead from the French Department." Oddly, the formation of the French Club had not been reported. Students of Polish descent expressed an interest in organizing a club on campus in October 1936 after Madame Krolowna came to the university to teach Polish as a regular credit course in the day and as a graduate course at night. A member of the Polish nobility—hence the title "Madame"—she was also "Doctor Krolowa," having earned a Ph.D. from the University of Warsaw in 1935.

The city-wide Polish Intercollegiate Club had been founded in March 1930, followed by the Intercollegiate Lithuanian Club a year later. Then National Folk Festivals, sponsored by the WPA, became popular. The Spring Folk Pageant first appeared in Pittsburgh in 1936 under the auspices of the NYA and the direction of Frank McGowan, a sociology professor at Duquesne.[22] This increasing community interest in ethnicity was reflected in the growth of ethnically-oriented clubs, fraternities, and sororities on the Bluff, the most distinctive of which became the Tamburitzans.

The Tamburitzans

A group whose name would soon be synonymous with Duquesne and with the city of Pittsburgh was the Duquesne University Tamburitzans. The descendants of East European immigrants, who just 20 years before were scarcely to be found on the Bluff, were now enrolling in large numbers. Practically none of the ancestors of these students came from the upper classes of their respective countries. Rather, they were everyday people steeped in the folk traditions of their homelands. Fearing that these rich and distinctive East European folk cultures might be lost in the great American melting pot, Dr. Lester Pierce in 1937 organized the Slavonic Tamburitza Orchestra under the musical direction of Matt L. Gouze. The group derived its name from the *tamburitza*, an ancient traditional stringed instrument related to the lute. Dr. Pierce, of the School of Education, was not himself of East European descent but took a special interest in that culture.

It all began in Minnesota, where Dr. Pierce was on the faculty of St. Thomas College in St. Paul. He took a trio of musicians—Matt L. Gouze, Frank Gouze, and Anthony Antoncic—in 1932 and after adding two more performers, moved part of the group to St. Edward's University in Austin, Texas. An eastern tour in the 1936–1937 school year brought the American Tamburitza String Orchestra to Pittsburgh and to Duquesne. The group was a sensation, and Dr. Pierce was impressed with the support it received from ethnic groups in the area. Through the efforts of the Croatian Fraternal Union, he was able to negotiate to join the faculty of

Duquesne University and move his Slavonic orchestra to the campus. Only half a dozen Duquesne students (all male) applied the first year. They received their musical training at night and gave primarily instrumental performances. Because they were such a novelty, they performed about 200 times a season, mainly as benefit concerts, to gain increased exposure. In their second season, KDKA radio arranged for a 13-week, nationwide series of broadcasts on a program known as "Slavonic Serenade."

Their resources were not great. The group traveled in a second-hand 1929 Cadillac pulling an eight-bunk trailer. Renamed the Duquesne University Tamburitza Orchestra, the group made its first tour in October of 1937 when it played at the Nebraska State Teachers' Convention. Unfortunately, it could not become financially self-supporting, and Duquesne was hard-pressed to keep itself financially afloat during this period, and so could not afford to continue its sponsorship.

Although the Second World War brought more hard times, it also provided an opportunity. Since its founding, the group had been composed entirely of men. The first woman to join the group was soprano soloist, Mary Verlich, in the 1939–1940 season. As the men went off to war, it was the influx of young women, some not even affiliated with Duquesne University, that kept the group alive. During the war, a reporter from the *Duquesne Duke* first referred to them as the Tamburitzans, a name that has remained ever since. The efforts of the Tamburitza Scholarship Fund Committee and the dedication of the performers, who even as servicemen would join the troupe while on leave, maintained a nucleus for growth into a world-renowned institution after the war.[23]

Theater Arts on Campus

The Red Masquers, Duquesne's drama club, was revived in October 1931. Dr. Clinton Lloyd, dean of the School of Theater Arts and Dramatic Literature, directed an active schedule of production and playwriting despite his occasional incapacitation from a heart ailment. Enthusiasm for the drama club was heightened by the participation of a dynamic student, Samuel Kwok Ying-Fung, who came to America from China seven years before to study modern American drama. He was a frequent speaker on campus on the subject of Sino-Japanese relations. His winning entry in the Red Masquer one-act playwriting contest, *From the Spray of Time*, was broadcast by the group over KDKA radio. This gave the drama students an idea: the following year they performed radio dramas on a regular basis on Monday nights over station WWSW. When Dr. Lloyd died in April of 1936, the directorship of the Red Masquers was assumed by Father R.T. Jones. The troup rallied to complete preparations and stage the Broadway musical *Dulcy* that spring despite the loss of their beloved mentor.[24]

The Red Masquers were not the only ones hosting plays and productions on campus. Indeed, they had some very stiff competition. The Monogram Club hosted an annual musical review at the Nixon Theater every spring, which in 1937 became known as *Topper and Tails*. The production in 1939 had a cast of 40! The Newman Club players, under the direction of Madeline Skelly Foust, who later became head of the Drama School as well as serving as dean of women, also entertained the campus. Madeline Foust was not only an enthusiastic director but also a gifted playwright, and her passion play, *The Other Kingdom*, was regularly revived during the Lenten season. It was under her guidance that the School of Theater Arts and Dramatic Literature became known as the School of Drama. She also was the one who instituted the practice of producing all the required props, scenery, and costumes at the university rather than renting the materials. The School of Drama, under her leadership and that of Mr. Alfred L.

Golden, who briefly left the university to become a scriptwriter in Hollywood, was so dynamic and so ambitious in its offerings that the Red Masquers were unable to draw sufficient participation from the student body for their own productions and were temporarily disbanded in 1936. They became active again in 1941.

Duquesne as a Catholic Institution

Duquesne, of course, maintained a high Catholic presence in its social organizations as well as its academic offerings. The Catholic Student Mission Crusade (CSMC) was particularly active. As the name implies, it was dedicated to spreading the faith and supporting missions by organizing drives and benefits. In May 1936, for example, the CSMC hosted a convention at Duquesne involving a Mass, a rally with a pageant on the Crusades, exhibits of foreign and home missions, and conferences.

The Newman Club for Catholic Students, named for John Henry Cardinal Newman, the English scholar who converted to Catholicism as a result of his study of the Anglican Church, had maintained a presence at many American colleges and universities since its founding in 1914. Duquesne's branch was associated with the other Pittsburgh schools. Although it included study groups, its primary function was social. It sponsored dances and parties, put on plays (as mentioned earlier), and had its events listed in the *Duquesne Duke*. In 1931, through the efforts of Frank Murphy and Paul G. Sullivan of Duquesne, it spawned an alumni branch known as the University Catholic Club, which sponsored an annual "Dry Mass" in which all the prayers and actions of the Mass were acted out and explained but no actual consecration was performed. The University Catholic Club had to compete for members with the Catholic Alumni Club of Pittsburgh.

Philosophical, theological, and moral issues regarding the Catholic faith were explored through the Catholic Action of Duquesne University. This group met with speakers who presented such topics as the pope's labor encyclicals, birth control and "occultism, exorcism, and mysticism."

And to make absolutely sure that there were enough Catholic activities on campus, the Catholic Club was formed in January of 1938 for the "furtherance of Catholic education among the students of the University." It was the Catholic Club that sponsored the 1939 Lenten drive, assessing each student 50 cents for chapel repairs.[25] The *Duquesne Duke* published the names of the university groups with 100 percent contributions from their members. Among the first groups listed were the cafeteria workers, the university library staff, the Catholic Club, and the Tamburitza Orchestra.

In February of 1932 the first issue of the *Student Digest* made its appearance. This magazine for Catholic high school and college students was published regionally with an advisory staff of professors from Duquesne, the University of Pittsburgh, and Seton Hill.

The religious orientation of the school, despite its open policies of acceptance of students regardless of creed, displayed itself in the annual college retreat. The weekend retreat featured simultaneous men's and women's programs on a voluntary basis. Originally a Lenten retreat, it was later moved to the fall and made compulsory for Catholic students (about 85 percent of the student body) with the suspension of classes during the morning presentations each day for a week. Although students of other faiths were welcome, they were not required to attend.

This Catholic presence at Duquesne extended beyond the students to offer parish priests an opportunity for further study following ordination. This program was so well accepted that in the fall of 1935 Bishop Boyle waived the junior priests' examination for those priests who enrolled in the program.

College for Alumni

Beginning in November of 1939, the university sponsored a College for Alumni that was open to the public as well as Duquesne graduates. Professors from different disciplines in the university lectured as part of a series lasting for seven consecutive Sundays. Each Sunday, alumni and their guests could choose from among three non-credit lectures given concurrently in the old and new libraries and the theater. Over 700 persons attended these general-interest talks on topics such as Nazism, biological discoveries, and family ethics. Successful though the alumni College was, it ended after American entry into World War II and was not revived again until 1953.

The Role of Radio

The students, organizations, schools, and departments of the university made frequent use of radio broadcasting facilities around Pittsburgh. By 1932 news from the Bluff and the other city colleges and universities was being broadcast three times a week on WWSW's "Campus Notes." That spring the station aired a Duquesne student presentation, "Why We Go to College," in which Duquesne students discussed their parents' aims of advancing their children's financial futures and gaining prestige and their own aims of entering the college social scene. The program's success prompted a regular Wednesday night news program called "Duke Notes" and a Monday night program, "Duquesne Bandwagon," composed of sketches done by members of the *Duke* staff with background music supplied by students from the Music School. In 1940 a house purchased 11 years earlier by the university was outfitted as a studio for broadcasts over KQV.

College students were frequent listeners to radio, and the famed broadcast of Orson Welles's *War of the Worlds*[26] caused as much panic among the athletes living in Varsity Hall as elsewhere in the country. One of the football team members tuned into the program already in progress and spread the alarm. It caused such a commotion that the incident was even reported in the *Duke*, which quipped, this "leads us to believe that Charlie McCarthy isn't the only dummy in the world."[27]

Money Troubles

The funding of social events was a delicate subject during the Depression. Neither the university nor its students had much disposable income. Many dances ran a deficit, and a fund-raising drive to pay for new band uniforms that cost $1,200 netted only $200. After months of student preparation, Father Callahan canceled the Junior Prom of 1933 "in view of the seriousness of general economic conditions." Only a week later, the administration further announced that all off-campus social affairs were prohibited for the rest of the schoolyear and that hereafter campus affairs were to be limited to Duquesne students only.

Devising ways to save money was a universal concern. The *Duquesne Duke* included articles on the propriety of Dutch-treat dating, how to hitch-hike, and on an unsuccessful effort by students at Duquesne and the University of Pittsburgh to get student reductions on streetcar fares. One enterprising business freshman, Bob Powell, capitalized on the enthusiasm for the football team by selling Duke hatband feathers, gathered at the poultry yard, dyed red, and glued to handcut letters. The university had no plan of comparable effectiveness in funding its social events and extracurricular academic activities, and campus life lost some valuable outlets for creativity and sociability.

Father John Manning Takes Control

In 1935 Father John J. Manning came from Cornwells Heights to assume the post of dean of men, replacing Father John Malloy, who became principal of the prep school. Known popularly as "Gentleman Jim," owing to his good looks and dapper appearance, Father Manning was determined to take control of the chaotic and often unprofitable social scene. He did this with a certain personal charm that produced mixed reactions from the student body. For some the charm outweighed the onerous burdens imposed by Father Manning's control: permission to hold an event to be requested at least a month in advance, financial reports due within two weeks of the affair, cash ticket sales only, return of all unsold tickets, and most onerous of all, 20 percent of the gross to be turned in to the university. Before Father Manning's intervention, three different student organizations had scheduled three major dances in a 12-day period, so his supporters could logically point to the need for scheduling help. However, his controlling hand was strongly resented by the academic clubs. When he announced that intercollegiate debate competition was being dropped in favor of a less costly schedule of city-wide debates and discussion groups, every single officer of the Debate Society, elected the previous spring, resigned en masse.

Even among his supporters, Father Manning did not endear himself to those in fraternities when he had a series of notices printed in the *Duquesne Duke* concerning the unpleasant consequences in store for those who were delinquent in submitting financial reports on profits from social affairs. He even complained about the fraternities cutting into the profits of the university class dances—the Freshman Frolic, the Sophomore Hop, the Junior Prom, and the Senior Ball—by holding competing affairs. Not content to alienate only the Greeks, he further accused class dance chairmen of viewing the position not as serious obligation but as a "social plum." Therefore, he insisted that each applicant for the position of dance chairman have the endorsement of 20 class members. A man of his word, he disqualified two of the four candidates for chairmanship of the Junior Prom, claiming that their papers were not in order. This resulted in the resignation of the elected chairman, a public outcry in the *Duke*, reconsideration of qualifications, and a new election. When in May of 1937, Father Manning forbade fraternities to open their functions to the general student body, the Inter-Fraternity Council lost its reason for existence and the Greek organizations lost an important source of revenue.

By spring the student body was so demoralized that not enough candidates ran for office to fill the seats on the Student Senate. The elections were abolished, and to the amazement of nearly everyone, the Student Senate was disbanded in the fall. Father Manning replaced the Student Senate with a newly formed Dean of Men's Council, branded by the *Duquesne Duke* as being merely an honorary body directly under his control, with no real authority.

Father Manning softened a bit when he lifted the ban on open fraternity dances in November and shortly thereafter replaced the unpopular 20 percent assessment with a five-cent-per-ticket charge. But by then most students—and some faculty—were chafing under his too-firm hand.

Even the Dean's Council eventually proved recalcitrant to Manning's control. In January 1938 the president of the council resigned over a scheduling conflict. The Monogram Club was denied permission to hold its annual Homecoming Dance in conjunction with the Alumni Association because Homecoming fell at Thanksgiving and the Thanksgiving Dance had already been promised to Gamma Phi. Although it was pointed out to Father Manning that both dances were a long-standing tradition and drew from different constituencies, he refused to yield. The Alumni Dance was permitted, but the Monogram Club was not allowed to co-sponsor. With his popularity near the vanishing point, Father Manning wisely accepted a year-long exchange scholarship to Italy, and Father Anthony Lechner was appointed to the position of dean of men.

Father Lechner had a history at Duquesne of "picking up the pieces." He had been principal of the prep school when he was called to serve as university treasurer with the resignation of Father Goebel. When Father Goebel returned, he filled in for Father Carroll as Dean of the College of Arts and Letters during his world tour and assumed the deanship of the School of Music and the position of dean of men during Father Manning's sabbatical. When Father Manning returned the following year, he was ready to do battle once again. But he was not in good health and resigned soon after.

The Typical Duquesne Student of the 1930s

In an editorial, the *Duquesne Duke* answered public allegations of wildness on the part of college students in general by presenting a very different picture of the Duquesne student in particular:

> We have here a student body of whom fifty percent, at a conservative estimate, are assisting themselves through college by some outside occupation. The hours worked vary anywhere from one to eight hours a day. The occupations are wide in their scope, running from bell hops to locomotive fireman.

Working one's way through college, while by no means unique to Duquesne, was certainly characteristic of it. So was high scholastic achievement. Despite the onset of the Depression and the reduced number of applicants, the university tightened its admission requirements. As always, applicants in the upper three-fifths of their high school graduating classes were admitted automatically, but now those in the lower two-fifths could be admitted only if they took an examination given by the Pennsylvania Department of Public Instruction, whereas before a letter of recommendation from the high school principal sufficed.[28]

The *Duquesne Bulletin* of 1933 recorded the most detailed admission requirements in the history of the University. Entrance requirements were stated in high school units, each representing a full year's study in that subject in an approved secondary school. The new requirements resulted in three different categories of undergraduate students attending Duquesne: regular, irregular, and special students. Regular students were those who met all the admission requirements and had graduated from an accredited high school or who had transferred from another college or university where they had previously met the admission requirements. Students who did not meet the admission requirements were given conditional admission status as regular students and allowed to pursue college studies while they made up the deficiencies. Irregular students also had to satisfy the entrance requirements but were required to register for less than 12 credit hours per semester. Special students, who did not have to meet the entrance requirements, were those who wished to receive college credit for their course work but were not enrolled in a degree program.

The College of Arts, and the Schools of Pharmacy, Education, Science, and Accounts (later Business Administration) led the university in the adoption of letter grades instead of numerals in 1930. The university required a C average to graduate. But determining who had a C average was more complicated than merely balancing an A against a D on a student's transcript, as not all courses were three credits. The university adopted a new grading system in the fall of 1938 using quality points: an A was 3 points, B was 2, C was 1, D was 0, and F was -1. Thus a 1.0 was the minimum Q.P.A. (Quality Point Average) a student could have at graduation. Not until 1966 did Duquesne adopt the four-point system that most of the nation's colleges were shifting to in the 1930s.

Faculty Changes in the 1930s

One unexpected benefit of the Depression was the availability of many gifted faculty. Through nationwide searches, Father Callahan was able to secure exceptional people of diverse educational backgrounds and experience. Until this

37. Rev. Jeremiah J. Callahan, C.S.Sp. (1931–1940), succeeded the beloved Father Hehir as president of Duquesne University January 4, 1931, and promptly used his first day as president to explain to attending journalists his contradiction of Einstein's theory of relativity. He was wrong, of course, but, as one Holy Ghost father said of him, "Father Callahan was the one man I knew who never had a doubt." The mathematician-turned-president proved to be an unfortunate choice in the Depression years. Despite the fact that Father Hehir had recommended Callahan, the two men had radically different views of education. Hehir shaped Duquesne to meet the professional needs of the growing city of Pittsburgh and its Catholic community with practical business-oriented studies and a variety of professional schools. Callahan, however, felt the chief purpose of a university lay in shaping "gentlemen" through liberal education.

Callahan's tenure was rife with controversy, imprudent spending and wavering guidance. In 1939, a new provincial forced Callahan's resignation by transferring him to a poor African-American parish at Isle Brevalle, Louisiana.

38. This architect's rendering of a science complex, planned for the lower end of Locust Street, but never built, was one of the many casualties of the Great Depression. Prices in the nation fell as the Depression deepened, but Duquesne University maintained its tuition at 1929 prices, $225 a year. Prospective students found it difficult to meet this fee, and enrollment declined over four consecutive years; Duquesne, tuition-dependent and unendowed, lost a quarter of its student body.

39. Pittsburgh Mayor Scully, Pennsylvania Governor Earle, and Fr. Callahan, president of Duquesne, at a Duquesne-Pitt football game in October 1937. Fr. Callahan looks less than comfortable in the rainy weather.

Courtesy Pittsburgh *Post Gazette*

40. One significant development in 1937 was the opening of Duquesne's School of Nursing under Dean Mary Tobin. Duquesne had offered a program in nursing as part of the College of Liberal Arts since 1926. In 1933, Tobin came from the Yale University School of Nursing to direct the Duquesne program. She was invaluable in building a strong program. She maintained correspondence with Yale, Columbia, and the Army School of Nursing, and implemented the latest ideas in nursing care in her program. She heavily emphasized education and public health nursing, and she added courses in chemistry, zoology, and hospital laboratory techniques. She persuaded nationally known educators to come teach in her program. In 1937, the strong and growing program became an independent school, with Tobin as dean, and two years later they received national accreditation and membership in the Association of College Nursing.

41. Despite the Depression, the university continued to purchase homes both on and off the Bluff. This building, christened Varsity Hall, housed basketball and football players. Now called Laval House, it is one remnant of the old neighborhood. The university purchased more than 23 buildings between 1929 and 1938. As tuition income plummeted and property acquisition continued, Duquesne found itself in debt — $400,000 in 1932. The school's annual income was $374,515.

42. Despite their empty pockets and dubious job futures, during the Depression Duquesne students created a social life that was livelier than ever, and social clubs abounded. Some attributed this to the steadily growing numbers of women students on campus; they provided the impetus, if not the organization, for many events. Here student members of the Monogram Club sell tickets to a dance at the William Penn Hotel.

43. A group whose name would soon be synonymous with Duquesne and Pittsburgh was the Duquesne University Tamburitzans. In 1937, descendants of East European immigrants who just 20 years earlier were scarce at the university, were enrolling in large numbers. These students represented an everyday people steeped in the folk traditions of their homelands. To preserve their distinctive traditions, Dr. Lester Pierce, a member of the St. Thomas College School of Education in Minnesota, organized the Tamburitza Orchestra. The group derived its name from the tamburitza, an ancient stringed instrument related to the lute. By 1938, the group had moved to Duquesne and found a strong base there. Beginning with six male students, the group soon expanded to include women, then Pittsburghers unaffiliated with the university. This photo shows the Tamburitzans performing in St. Louis during their 1938–39 tour. Walter Kolar, later to become director of the troupe, is on the right.

44. The Tamburitzans on tour visited the Empire State Building in February, 1938. Their resources were spare: the entourage traveled in a second hand 1929 Cadillac which pulled an eight-bunk trailer. Fifth from left (standing in the middle row) is Dr. Lester Pierce, founder of the troupe; center right and wearing a scarf is Matt Gouze, their first director.

45. As part of its real estate buying spree, Duquesne purchased a building, located at the corner of Hooper and Ivanhoe streets, from the Slovak Society for $20,000. In 1932 the School of Music was established there. The school underwent several changes, including curriculum reorganization. In the 1930s, its original five programs became two curricula, a conservatory program for performing musicians and the Public School Music Program for teachers. Duquesne University became a center for the training of church organists and choir directors. This photo shows the building as it appeared in 1953.

46. Duquesne's first (1920) ROTC program was disbanded by student referendum almost immediately after World War I ended. But as World War II grew nearer, and the student newspaper carried more articles on international and political affairs, the demand for a new ROTC grew. One survey showed that students were three to one in favor of a unit, if participation was not mandatory, and ROTC returned to the Bluff in 1936, boasting one of the only field-artillery divisions in the area as well as up-to-date motorized equipment. In 1937, a coed unit was formed. Here Battery A, 1st Dukes Field Artillery, stands ready for gun drill in 1938.

47. The only new construction on the Bluff during the Depression was Duquesne's first library building, built exclusively for that purpose. The library had outgrown its small space in Old Main, then the three-story apartment building that housed it after 1928. Students routinely used the downtown branch of the Public library, the Carnegie. When the public library restricted their access to its shelves in 1930, it was the students and university librarian M. Gertrude Blanchard who made the effort to establish adequate facilities. In December of 1938, an anonymous alumnus gift of $50,000 made possible the construction of the new library at the corner of Colbert and Locust; total cost: $67,000. The library was completed in 1939, and soon became very popular. Student use increased to the point where the library had to issue I.D. cards to keep track of borrowers. This was the first form of student I.D. at Duquesne. In this photo, note the utilitarian architecture used, so different from existing structures on campus, and from the plans for the canceled Science building. This library survives today as the westernmost part of the Law School building.

48. Bluff athletics were crucially important in helping Duquesne students relieve the worries of the Depression. As chiefly a commuter school, Duquesne needed a common area of interest to rally the student body, and sports provided it. In this photo, Duquesne students hail a football victory laying to rest their opponent in a make-believe coffin. Such celebrations typified the cross-town rivalries of the 1930s.

49. Alan Donelli returns a punt against Carnegie Tech, in a 1939 game. His coach was his older brother, Aldo "Buff" Donelli, who took over the team that year. The Dukes won the game.

50. Football at Duquesne did very well under coach Elmer Layden, alumnus of Notre Dame football, and under the coaches who succeeded him after he returned to Notre Dame as head coach in 1934. The school hired one of its own alumni, Aldo T. "Buff" Donelli, in 1939. This was the same year that the University of Pittsburgh dropped Duquesne from its schedule, amid charges that Pitt resented the smaller school's growing reputation. Appearing here is the 1941 football team, the only undefeated, untied team in Duquesne history. The team included 16 seniors who had played together for three years, including two All-Americans, John Rokisky and Al Demao. These Dukes were ranked fifth in the nation by the Associated Press.

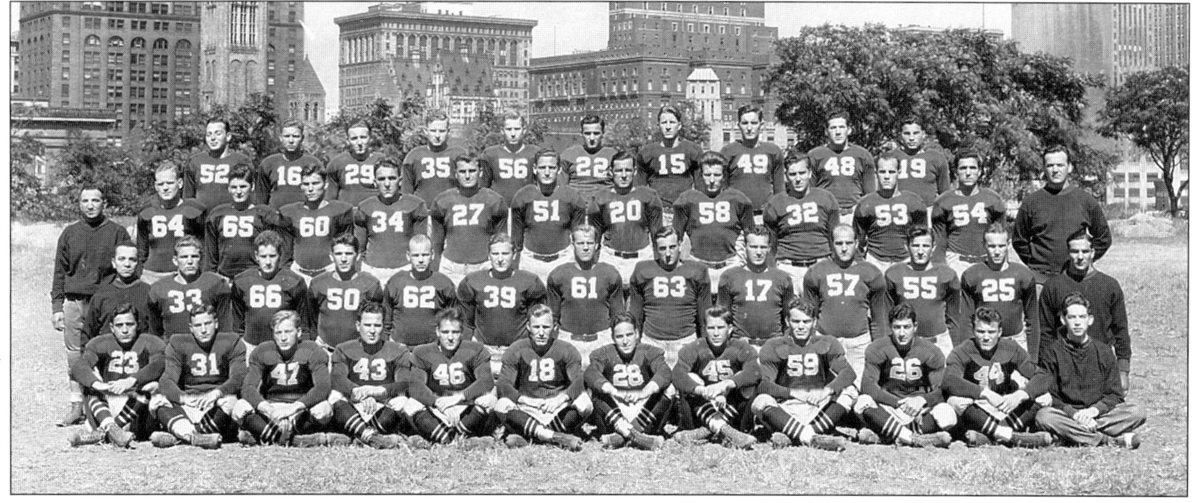

51. The Dukes played and won against Mississippi in the Florida Orange Bowl in 1936. In 1939, they received and declined offers from the Orange Bowl, the Cotton Bowl, and the Los Angeles Olympics Bowl, so many fans were surprised when Duquesne received no bowl bid in December of 1941, despite their undefeated record. The *Pittsburgh Press* ran this cartoon illustrating its disappointment. Some felt the Dukes were excluded because the team did not belong to a conference, and that the organization to which the team belonged counted more than the quality of the play.

52. Basketball also rallied the campus with win after win under the coaching of Chick Davies, and the team challenged ever larger and more powerful schools, and won. Again, the University of Pittsburgh, after losing the city championship to Duquesne in 1939, dropped the smaller school from its schedule. The 1933-34 basketball squad, pictured here, was a powerhouse, winning 47 games and losing two.

53. The basketball team took on teams from larger and better funded schools, and they kept on winning. Here the 1940 Dukes pose with canes and top hats as they prepare to go to New York to play in the National Invitational ournament. On the far right is their talented and temperamental coach, Chick Davies.

54. In this photo, Duquesne players (left to right) Becker, Widowitz and Lacey rebound against the DePaul team in January 1941. Basketball at Duquesne was suspended again in 1943 because so many of its players and fans turned their energies to World War II.

55. Duquesne officially began hockey as a varsity sport in 1937 using the Duquesne Gardens as its home ice. That same year, the editors of the Duquesne Duke, (the school newspaper), audaciously claimed the city championship: "The university played its first, last, and only game of the year when it defeated Carnegie Tech skaters...4-0." The game lasted 10 minutes and took place in the period breaks of a game between two other teams. Father Louis Dietrich (back row, first on the right) coached the team for several years in the thirties. All sports on the Bluff were suspended during World War II. Several of Dietrich's players would, as alumni, be responsible for reestablishing hockey at Duquesne in the 1970s.

56. This Pittsburgh *Sun-Telegraph* photo shows Father Callahan with belongings packed and apparently ready to step down as Duquesne's president. The faculty and many administrators complained of his "lack of leadership" and his "disregard of constitutional safeguards" to the Holy Ghost father overseeing the university, Fr. Christopher Plunkett. When Callahan left for his European "sabbatical" in February, 1936, he had informally agreed to resign when he returned. Indeed, he resigned in May, then reversed himself, refusing to leave office. Duquesne's board of directors reinstated him, and he held on to his position for another four years.

time, most faculty members had had local roots or connections, but now local jobs were not always available, so those universities still hiring had their pick from a national pool. Father Callahan reported that the faculty had obtained undergraduate degrees from 49 colleges and universities and graduate degrees from 31 different educational institutions in the United States and abroad.[29] In 1933 one fourth of the faculty had held doctorates; by the end of the decade one third did. A down side to this new faculty profile was that many of these talented professors did not remain at Duquesne very long. In some cases, they taught for less than a year, and the turnover in faculty was upsetting to the smooth operations of the university.

School of Pharmacy—National Recognition

With membership in the American Association of Colleges of Pharmacy, the School of Pharmacy discontinued its three-year degree program, and beginning in 1932, a full four years of study for the Bachelor of Science in Pharmacy was required. Dean Muldoon did much to advance Duquesne's Pharmacy School's reputation through his radio broadcasts. His first program, "How Medicine Began," was broadcast over Station KDKA in 1935 in celebration of National Pharmacy week. From this initial broadcast followed a weekly presentation entitled "Your Good Health" on WCAE. Muldoon was also very active in science education at the high school as well as the college level. In 1935 he began publication of *The Science Counselor*, a nationwide quarterly publication presenting teaching methods and scientific information for Catholic high school teachers. The publication was so popular that by 1942 other Catholic colleges, including St. Bonaventure, Villanova, and Loyola of Los Angeles, had begun similar publications.

Course offerings increased, with physiological chemistry added in 1935, and the number of laboratory facilities was expanded to handle the growth in laboratory studies. The School of Pharmacy became so well recognized that its entire faculty and a majority of its students accepted an invitation from the Eli Lilly Drug Company in Indiana to be their guests at a special three-day presentation of tours and demonstrations. By 1944 the Pharmacy School had graduated 292 students. Most had gone on to own their own stores, and more than one out of ten had earned advanced degrees.

Law School—Small in Size but High in Quality

The Law School experienced several changes in leadership. Judge Swearington, founder of the school, was replaced upon his retirement in 1929 by John P. Egan who, like so many others, had come all the way through the Duquesne system. Egan had enrolled as a student in the prep school in 1904 and earned his M.A. in the law school. He then taught in the prep school before his appointment to the university faculty. As dean he immediately lengthened the law school program to four years. Although this resulted in a drop in freshman enrollments from 100 to 70 students, it greatly enhanced the professional reputation of the school. As late as 1940, the law school still had only 70 students, but its quality remained high. Of the 17 graduates who sat for the State Board of Examiners that year, all but three passed. In the spring of 1930, the law school awarded a degree to its first black graduate, Joseph W. Givens. He was 31 years old and had worked at various times as a storekeeper, railroad man, janitor, and city employee to put himself through school. His success was applauded by the *Duke*, which also noted that seven of the 14 law school graduates that year were sons of lawyers.

The law school still held classes only as an evening school, ten hours per week, 34 weeks per year. In 1932 it moved from Canevin Hall to the Fitzsimons Building. A 1933 report disclosed that the faculty consisted of a dean and two other full-time professors. The rest of the faculty were part-time instructors, most of whom taught a single course in their area of expertise. Although law students still received a Bachelor of Laws Degree, the report also noted that 95 percent of the students had already earned a bachelor's degree.

Egan resigned from the deanship after becoming a judge of the Court of Common Pleas of Allegheny County, although he continued to serve on the faculty. He was replaced as dean by John E. Laughlin, who in turn was replaced (after his death) by a succession of acting deans until C. Gerald Brophy assumed the position in 1941.

School of Education—Conforming to State Requirements

The School of Education, founded by Father Kirk, went though several changes in administration during the Depression years. Father Callahan had brought W.S. York Critchley in the fall of 1935, ostensibly to head the school but also as de facto administrator for the university. Critchley reorganized the course structure of the School of Education to conform to state requirements, and as a result of his efforts, state approval was obtained for music education, business education, graduate education, educational administration, and elementary education. When Critchley resigned, Father Kirk returned to reassume the deanship, but it passed to C. Gerald Brophy and Dr. Kathryn Redman as acting deans as Father Kirk was elevated to the presidency instead. Later, Dr. A. Lester Pierce, the founder of the Duquesne University Tamburitza Orchestra and author of a syndicated column on education, as well as host of a weekly radio show on the NBC network, became dean of the school. In 1944 he was succeeded by Father George A. Harcar, who directed the new graduate-level programs in guidance, school administration, and library science.

School of Business Administration—the Most Popular School

In 1931 the School of Accounts, Finance, and Commerce changed its name to the School of Business Administration. Under the leadership of Dr. Albert B. Wright, dean from 1932 to 1954, the school continued to be the most popular in the university. Even in 1932, hardly a promising year for American business, some 859 students were enrolled, comprising over a third of the student body. Before the hard financial times of the 1930s, half the students in the university were enrolled in this school. It is perhaps a measure of the effect the Depression had on male students that their number in the School of Business fell from 1,145 in 1929 to 672 by 1932, a 41 percent decrease, while the number of women students in that same period decreased from 271 to 181, a 31 percent decrease. The Depression did not reduce the school's effectiveness, however. In 1941 the university reported that "since 1932 all graduates of this school who have taken the Pennsylvania State Certified Public Account examination have passed successfully."[30]

The business school celebrated its silver jubilee in April of 1938 with exhibits of trends in advertising, journalism, and office equipment. The school had an enrollment of 1,500 and at the same time occupied the fourth to the seventh floors of the Fitzsimons Building as well as the second floor of Canevin. In its 25-year history, more than 20,000 students had enrolled. Always progressive in outlook, it had featured such experiences as field trips to the steel-making operations of the Edgar Thompson Works in Braddock as an integral part of its curriculum.

School of Music—and a Game of Musical Chairs for its Leadership

Just after the elevation of the department to a School of Music in 1927, a dizzying array of leadership changes began. First came the physical moves. The school had begun on the first floor of the Administration Building, then moved in 1928 to the third floor of the library building on Vickroy Street across from Canevin. In 1932 it was established at the corner of Hooper and Ivanhoe, in a building the university purchased from the Slovak Society. An evening division was begun that year in the Fitzsimons Building.

And there were curriculum changes. The school was reorganized in the 1930s from its original five programs into two curricula, the conservatory program for performing musicians and the Public School Music program for teachers. The efforts of Father Carlo F. Rossini, professor of music and chairman of the Diocesan Music Commission, made Duquesne University a center for the training of church organists and choir directors.

But now came many leadership changes. During the Callahan administration, Dean Rauterkus was replaced with another handpicked outsider, Mr. Daniel L. Healey, who had been a leading tenor for the Philadelphia Opera. When Father Bryan was appointed acting president of the university during Father Callahan's sabbatical, Mr. Healey and five other professors in the music school announced that they were leaving immediately following commencement. Administration of the music school was given to Father Kirk of the School of Education, while Teresa Dempsey, a professor in the music school, served as acting dean. Father Callahan complained that the music school was too aloof from the university, operating as an independent body. He gave the deanship of the school to Father John J. Manning, dean of men, in 1937. (Father Anthony F. Lechner served as acting dean in 1939 during Father Manning's year of study in Italy.)

School of Nursing—with an Emphasis on Public Health

One of the most significant developments on campus at this time was the establishment of Duquesne's School of Nursing in 1937. Interest in the preparation of qualified nurses rose with the establishment in the 1900s of settlement houses and reform groups concerned about the public welfare, diseases such as tuberculosis, handicaps such as blindness, and the special needs of children and pregnant women. But the great impetus toward the establishment of university-based nurses' training came following World War I, as the nurses became increasingly aware of deficiencies within the profession.

In 1926 the Catholic Hospitals of the Pittsburgh Diocese had urged Duquesne to begin a nursing program under the College of Liberal Arts and Letters that made it possible for a graduate of one of the diploma schools of nursing (St. Joseph's, Mercy, St. John's, St. Francis in New Castle, and Providence in Beaver Falls) to receive two years of college credit toward a bachelor of science degree.[31] The program required the study of English, history, psychology, language, public speaking, political science, and either philosophy or sociology. A class in religious instruction was required for Catholic students. The curriculum was changed in 1933 to include a class in United States history and one in either medieval or modern history. English literature was added, but psychology, political science, and public speaking were dropped.

Mary Walton, a graduate of Mercy Hospital's School of Nursing and president of the Catholic Nurses' League of the Diocese of Pittsburgh, chaired the committee formed to raise money for a collegiate nursing school at Duquesne. Mary W. Tobin was made head of the new department. She was resident director of the Yale University School of Nursing when brought to Duquesne. Her election proved invaluable to Duquesne in building a strong department. She maintained correspondence with Yale, Columbia, and the Army School of Nursing, which kept her informed of the latest thinking in the field.

Mary Tobin placed a heavy emphasis on education and public health nursing. The curriculum was changed to include academic work in chemistry and zoology with a choice of electives in either nursing education or hospital laboratory techniques. Two separate programs for students in nursing were offered: a two-year course for the full or part-time registered nurse who had already graduated from a hospital diploma program, and a five-year basic course for students who had no previous nurses' training. Duquesne was the first school in Pennsylvania to combine the academic and practical training in a course leading to a bachelor of science in nursing. The students spent their first two academic years at the university and all the summers and their final three years in residence at an affiliated hospital or agency. Nursing arts, dietetics, and specialized nursing in the areas of pediatrics, obstetrics, medicine, surgery, and operating room duty were taught in conjunction with clinical experience at Mercy Hospital.[32]

Although the faculty of the affiliating hospital nursing schools taught the majority of clinical courses, the Duquesne University staff included one full-time faculty member and five part-time instructors in addition to Mary Tobin. Many of these were nationally known educators whom she had persuaded to come to Pittsburgh. The nursing faculty offered day, evening, and Saturday classes in order to accommodate full and part-time students. The department was housed in two rooms of a building called Power Hall on Vickroy Street across from Canevin Hall.

On March 15, 1937, the Department of Nursing Education at Duquesne University was elevated to the status of an independent school. Mary Tobin then became its dean.[33] The State Council of Education approved the program at the end of 1937 following a site visit to the university. The curriculum developed in 1936 remained essentially the same until the 1940s. Of its courses, perhaps the strongest was "Public Health Nursing" under Carla B. Rue, which led to the approval of Duquesne's public health nursing courses by the National Organization of Public Health Nursing in 1938. Public health nursing had been recognized as a pressing need since the passage of the Shaeppart-Towner Act of 1921, which allotted funds for public health nursing in maternal and pediatric health and to help promote the public health curriculum at Duquesne. Duquesne became quite an educational leader in this field. It was chosen as the site for the meeting of the 1938 advisory committee with community members in all phases of public health. The committee petitioned the city council for increased appropriations to implement recommendations from the Allegheny County Health Department for public health nurses, particularly school nurses. Their request was denied.

National recognition and accreditation accompanied Duquesne's School of Nursing's acceptance for membership in the Association of Collegiate Schools of Nursing in the spring of 1939 after three years of reports and site visitations.

As enrollment in the basic five-year nursing course grew from 11 students in 1938 to 24 students in 1939, and then to 36 in 1940, the two-year graduate nurse program declined from 280 in 1938 to 248 in 1940. More students were choosing Duquesne for their entire nursing education. New affiliations included St. John's and St. Joseph's hospitals to accommodate the increased enrollment. In response to requests from employed nurses in the two-year degree program that extension courses be offered in their locales, Duquesne's School of Nursing offered selected courses at hospital sites. Thus it fulfilled the university-wide policy of responding to a need wherever it may arise.

ROTC—its Reemergence

Nursing was not the only new program in the 1930s. An ROTC field artillery unit began operations on campus in the fall of 1936. Originally established at Duquesne in 1920 under the

National Defense Act, the ROTC program was disbanded after a few years following a student referendum. But as the political situation in Europe became more strained, and the *Duquesne Duke* carried an increasing number of articles on international economic and political affairs, the demand for a local ROTC unit grew. A survey taken by the *Duke* showed the students three to one in favor of a unit if participation were not mandatory. Its establishment was announced as including one of the only field-artillery divisions in the area as well as "up-to-date motorized equipment." A building at 815 Locust Street was leased for use as a garage to house cargo and reconnaissance trucks as well as field pieces. The first year, 163 students enrolled. By the next fall it was announced that if 250 men enlisted, they would qualify as a regiment and would be supplied by the government with band instruments. Such "enticements" produced no rush of enlistments; 196 men joined. A regiment was formed in 1938 when 262 men enlisted. It is interesting to note that enlistments bore no relationship to world events. When the war in Europe began in September of 1939, enlistments in the ROTC fell to 182, and by the fall of 1940 had recovered to only 228.

An ROTC pistol squad held its first practice at the Hunt Armory in March of 1936. In the spring Duquesne's ROTC unit received a blue-star rating for excellence, even though an inspection cited a lack of indoor training facilities.

The reestablishment of ROTC brought a new face to social life on campus. The ROTC supplied the honor guard for the Homecoming Queen and the Senior Queen and reinstituted the Military Ball as one of the most prestigious events of the year. In 1937 the coed unit was formed. This honorary body was outfitted in uniform and appeared at official functions, reviews, and parades with the student officers who had sponsored the coeds for membership. The ROTC even had its own honorary society for cadets known as the Scabbard and Blade.

Cadets who completed the full four years of training received commissions but they did not enter into the army. Rather they returned to civilian life to pursue their chosen careers. When the United States entered World War II in December of 1941, these officers in the Reserve Corps were immediately called to active duty to lead the thousands of men drafted into service.

The spring of 1937 brought the first announcements of other military training positions, although not offered at the university. A summer camp in Pittsburgh, open to both male and female students, offered Naval Reserve training. The navy was also offering aviation training. The Army Air Corps offered cadetships to young men with two or more years of college experience at the Air Corps Training Center at San Antonio, Texas. These positions were advertised frequently in the *Duke* in the years preceding the United States entry into the Second World War.

The Library Grows—and Students Gain ID Cards

Among the growing concerns on campus was the extent of the library holdings. While urban colleges and universities normally had on-campus reference libraries for their own students and faculty, they tended to rely on the main branch of the public library for research purposes. Every university in the city, including Duquesne, informally followed this practice. Since the main branch of Carnegie Public Library was inconvenient to the Bluff, Duquesne students routinely went to the downtown branch, which obtained the books they requested from the main branch. When the downtown branch moved from the City-County Building to the Union Trust in November of 1930, it announced that it would no longer request books from the main branch in Oakland. There were other annoying provisions to the new policy as well. Students were no longer permitted to borrow reference books or fiction.

Predictably, the administration did not react, but students were not willing to take this turn of events lying down. The *Duke* mounted a campaign to have the new policy rescinded. At the request of its editors, over 300 students sent protest letters and with considerable effect. The following month, the director of Carnegie Public Library expressed the hope that "some means can be devised to serve Duquesne students more conveniently" and offered to have students' book requests shipped directly to the Duquesne University Library. The apparent victory of the *Duke* proved hollow, since the Duquesne Library did not have enough space to handle the anticipated demand and would not be able to implement such a system until a new library was built. Good feelings were restored when in October 1934 the director of Carnegie Public Library visited the Duquesne University Library and wrote a letter to President Callahan praising the university librarian and the "marked development which has been made during these depression years."[34]

M. Gertrude Blanchard, the University librarian, made great efforts to establish adequate facilities and to enlarge the university's holdings. Donations of books from bequests and gifts were recognized weekly in the *Duquesne Duke*. Various fundraising benefits were held for the library. Graduating students were requested to donate a book as a farewell gesture, and alumni were appealed to for contributions. In December of 1938 an anonymous alumnus gift of $50,000 made possible the construction of a new library at the corner of Colbert and Locust streets, the only new construction on the Bluff during the Depression.[35] Its immediate construction resulted in the delay of spring football practice, since the contractor dumped the excavated dirt on the playing field. The library was completed in June of 1939.

Despite the Depression, the old library collection had been increasing by more than 2,000 titles per year, and when it was moved into the new building, numbered over 50,000. The library also subscribed to some 276 periodicals. Two additional librarians were hired. With a seating capacity for 160 persons and open for 51 hours per week, the library quickly gained in popularity. As patrons increased, the library needed to issue identification cards to borrowers. Thus began the first form of student identification on the Bluff.

The Student Union—Too Popular

The same alumnus who donated money for the library also requested an activities building. Accordingly, the first floor of the old library building on Vickroy Street was converted into an art deco style student lounge with a radio, phonograph, and easy chairs. The second floor provided rooms for student organizations. This was, in effect, Duquesne's first student union. It opened in December of 1939.

The lounge was extremely popular with the students, perhaps too popular. An English professor, Father Francis Thornton, who had been in charge of its decoration, had imagined sedate students sitting quietly, engaged in literate conversation. He was soon to be disillusioned. In fact, Father Thornton was so shocked by students sitting on the arms of easy chairs, leaving newspapers strewn on the floor, and even dancing to the music of the phonograph, that he issued rules prohibiting all three of these actions. He went on to complain that students had the "bad habit of placing chewing gum wrappers and candy bar covers in the ashtrays." These conditions inevitably attracted the attention of Father Manning, dean of men, who ordered the lounge closed at 6:00 p.m. instead of 9:00 p.m. and required groups who wished to use the meeting rooms after closing time to obtain permission one full week in advance. And the entire lounge was closed periodically each time a new infraction occurred. Indeed, it was closed more than it was open, until finally, in February 1941, after some furniture, a vase, and some phonograph records were broken, Father Manning and the dean of women, Kathryn Redman, closed it "indefinitely." Neither Manning nor Redman would talk to student reporters, and both were unmoved by periodic railings against the closing by *Duke* staffers. Even an April Fool's issue announcing its reopening and calling the dean "Dictator Redman" failed to produce the desired result. Yet, on a Middle States Association of Colleges and Secondary Schools questionnaire asking, "What provisions are made for comfortable . . . conditions for . . . students?" the university answered "The student lounge has been refinished, and is open from 8:00 a.m. to 4:00 p.m."

Pearl Harbor provided the excuse to turn "indefinitely" into permanently. In January 1942 the lounge was closed "for the duration of the emergency," its use being restricted to wartime purposes such as first aid and home nursing courses. It was never reopened. The students continued to do what they had been doing for nearly a year: congregating in Canevin Cafeteria.

Athletics Lift Spirits in the Depression Era

Bluff athletics were of crucial importance in helping Duquesne students relieve the worries of the Depression. As a commuter school Duquesne sorely needed a common area of interest to rally the student body. Sports became so prominent in the 1930s that President Callahan was questioned about whether Duquesne wasn't overemphasizing athletics. His response that "the Greeks of Homer's time trained more rigorously than football players of today" reflects the support he gave to the athletic program as it branched out into new areas.

Football under Elmer Layden thrived. Layden had made the Duquesne Dukes such a power that they were asked to withdraw from the Tri-State conference following the undefeated 1929 season. Since they were relatively unknown by the bigger schools, they hoped the intersectional games against Providence, Loyola of Chicago, and North Dakota would win them a reputation. And they did. Duquesne first played Carnegie Tech in a post-seasonal charity game in 1931. Pitt became a regular season rival in 1932. The 1933 squad won nine of its ten games and went on to a history-making defeat of Miami University of Florida in the first Festival of Palms (later known as the Orange Bowl) on New Year's Day, 1934. The victory was the Dukes' farewell gift to Elmer Layden, who, after seven years at Duquesne, announced plans to become head coach at Notre Dame. While at Duquesne, his teams had secured a collective tally of 48 wins, 16 losses, and six ties. A rally was held in his honor on January 23, 1934 which he later recalled in his autobiography:

> The whole Duquesne student body turned out at the gymnasium to send me off to Notre Dame. My departure was even broadcast by a local radio station. The president of the university spoke. His vice-president of the university spoke. Joe Bach, who had been named to succeed me, spoke. The head cheerleader led cheers. Yet what really choked me up was Brue Jackson, who sang a song. Brue had often entertained our team with his songs and piano playing. Already he was picking up a side dollar doing night club work and later made quite a name for himself in show business. This particular day, he was on the end of the program and sang "I Wish I Had My Old Pal Back Again."
>
> Certainly I was leaving a lot of old pals and I never did meet a better bunch.[36]

One of Layden's former Notre Dame teammates, Joe Bach, took over the head coaching position. He had been Layden's line coach and before that, one of the "Seven Mules" who blocked for the "Four Horsemen" at Notre Dame. Christy Flanagan, also a Notre Dame grad, was appointed athletic director and served as Bach's backfield coach. Bach was popular at Duquesne. He wrote a weekly football column for the school newspaper, "How to Watch the Game," and coached the team in an eight-to-two season. But opportunity soon presented itself, and he left to coach Pittsburgh's professional football team, then known as the Pirates.

Christy Flanagan moved up to the head

coaching position for the 1935 season. After his single season in which the team won six of its nine games against such strong opponents as Rice, Kansas State, Washington University, Oklahoma A and M, Detroit, and Catholic University, he resigned to join his father in the Texas oil business. Duquesne's team won the city football championship that year due to its victory over Carnegie Tech, which had defeated Pitt. Winning teams were becoming harder to field because athletic scholarships were disallowed by the Middle States Association in 1931. Duquesne had asked permission to continue the 16 scholarships that had already been awarded, but the last of those ran out in 1934.

The last of the Notre Dame coaches at Duquesne was John P. "Little Clipper" Smith, Flanagan's assistant. Under Smith, the 1936 squad shut out Waynesburg, Rice, and Geneva before taking on Pitt for the first time in three years. Realizing the immensity and power of the opponent and not wishing the outcome of the game to influence their decision, Duquesne University officials magnanimously renewed Smith's contract for the following year before the game commenced. The seven-to-zero victory against the mighty Pitt Panthers even got a round of congratulations from the *New York Times*: "The valiant Dukes, representing a little school of about 1300 students on the city's bluffs, set out to get their first victory in three tests against the Panthers—and did."[37] The season ended with seven wins and two losses (to West Virginia Wesleyan and Detroit University), but Duquesne's victory over Carnegie Tech secured the city championship for the Dukes again. Duquesne went on to the Orange Bowl, where it squeaked by Mississippi State, 13–12, and received a rousing welcome upon its return:

> Thousands of followers and classmates greeted the conquering Duquesne University football squad on its arrival at the Pennsylvania Station last night at 11:25 p.m. The Duke gridders, weary from the long train ride, were pleasantly surprised by the enthusiastic throng which greeted them on their return from Miami in tribute to their brilliant 13–12 triumph.
>
> The welcome celebration climaxed one of the most successful seasons in the athletic history of Duquesne. Loyal followers cheered wildly and sang the school songs as the train bearing the squad pulled into the train shed a few minutes late . . . Radio announcers succeeded in detaining the coaches and some of the gridders for a few hurried words to audiences of WWSW and KDKA . . . Among those interviewed were Rev. Father J.J. Callahan and Graduate Manager John Holahan.[38]

That same New Year's Day, the University of Pittsburgh defeated the University of Washington in the Rose Bowl. Mike Basrak, a senior, became the first player at Duquesne to be named an All-American. He had asked his dad if he could try out for Duquesne's freshman team and was told "no" since he had a good job in the mines. When he asked again he was told that if he left his job to go to Pittsburgh, he couldn't come back. Mike was hungry enough for an education to risk it. He had been a freshman during Elmer Layden's last year as coach and was remembered fondly:

> Mike was a center and came to us, as many boys did, right out of the coal fields . . . Mike likes to remind me how poor we were at Duquesne, how the footballs we used looked like watermelons. "Then one day you came out with a new football" he tells me, "and I asked if I could just feel it, because I knew as freshman I could never get to play with it." That was Duquesne.[39]

If it was not Duquesne in reality, it was the Duquesne of myth and legend. Although a caricature, the memory of those Depression years survives to this day.

The 1937 team under Little Clipper Smith won six but lost four, including both the University of Pittsburgh and Carnegie Tech games. Before the Pitt game, Father Thomas R. Jones, a philosophy professor at Duquesne, made a deprecating comment regarding the Pitt players at the pep rally, that they "play for their weekly paychecks." The University of Pittsburgh reacted with outraged indignation, and Father Jones was pressured to resign. Evidently, however, he harbored no ill will toward Duquesne. Before leaving, he donated a large number of his books to the university library.

Duquesne's football fortunes continued to decline as the 1938 season brought only four wins to six losses, including defeats by both city teams. In fact, the toy fox terrier, Dukie, trained by a member of the ROTC department to stand at attention on his hind legs during the playing of the Alma Mater, bark for the team, and snarl at opponents, received more publicity than the players. Sadly, Dukie was killed by a speeding automobile that winter. The football team had its leanest win record since before Elmer Layden came to the Bluff. In March of 1939 Coach Smith resigned "in the best interests of the university."

After 12 years of Notre Dame coaches, the university started looking for one of its own alumni. Although several names were mentioned, the *Duquesne Duke* speculated that the post should go to Elmer Layden's impressive captain of the 1929 squad, "Buff" Donelli:

> This plan would end the reign of Notre Dame products that began when Elmer Layden came here in 1927 and mark Aldo T. "Buff" Donelli, assistant coach last year and freshman coach since 1930, as the most likely successor to Smith.

Donelli was hired as head coach and as athletic director as well, in charge of intercollegiate and intramural athletics, men's and women's physical education, business affairs of the athletic department, training programs, and publicity. Local radio broadcasting of Duquesne's games on KQV started in 1932, but in 1939 Duquesne's games were broadcast over a nationwide network. Under the leadership of an all-Duquesne alumni coaching squad, the 1939 team scored eight victories to one tie, trouncing both Pitt and Carnegie Tech to regain the city championship. Despite offers from officials of the Cotton Bowl, Orange Bowl, and Los Angeles Olympic Bowl, Duquesne decided not to enter post-season competition. The University of Pittsburgh dropped Duquesne from its schedule at the end of the 1939 season amid charges that Pitt resented Duquesne's growing national reputation at its expense.

Basketball also rallied the campus with incredible successes under Chick Davies, only to have World War II result in a suspension of play. Riding the crest of success from the 28-game schedule of 1930, the Dukes took on Pitt and Carnegie Tech in 1932. Although Duquesne continued to play basketball against Carnegie Tech, Pitt severed its basketball relations with Duquesne in 1939 when the school discontinued competition against Duquesne on the gridiron.

The Duquesne basketball team had become such a powerhouse that they encountered Westminster in 1934 with a 23-game winning streak. But here they encountered opposition of a different sort than they usually encountered on the court. The fact that Duquesne was a Catholic school playing a Presbyterian school brought to the surface a religious intolerance that was characteristic of the 1930s. Professor Kupersanin's insightful interview with Ken Duffey gives a vivid account:

> The Dukes had a twenty-three game winning streak going into that Westminster game at New Wilmington. Westminster was exceptionally strong, too, and had administered the loss that had preceded that streak. The fans were giving the Duquesne team a hard time during the first half—an unusually hard time. There were all sorts of remarks about Catholics, the Pope, and so on. Duquesne fell behind. At half-time, Chick was pacing the floor in the locker room muttering, "They hate us out there, they really hate us." He would punctuate his remarks by slamming a ball off a wall now and then.
>
> Chick himself was a Welshman, and a Protestant. So was his brother Audley, a substitute on the team. The star of the team, Paul Birch, was a Protestant as was Dudey Moore. The three other starters were Marty Reiter, Irv Brynner, and Art Feldman who were all Jewish. Finally, Birch asked, "Coach, why do they hate us?" Chick yelled, "They hate us because we're Catholic!"[40]

Duquesne lost the game by three points, but Paul Birch became Duquesne's first All-American basketball player that season as Coach Davies led his team on to another winning streak of 24 consecutive games.

The 1935 season was almost perfect. The only defeat was by one point to the University of Pittsburgh, and Duquesne was so proud of its team that it sold autographed pictures. Chick Davies also wrote a column for the *Duquesne Duke* for two years. The student newspaper gloried in the team's triumphs.

Amid all these victories, 1938 was the only losing season. Despite the team's failings that year, Chick Davies was awarded a new contract, and the fans honored him with an ovation each time he appeared on the floor. President Callahan assured him that he would remain "professor of basketball" as long as he wished and applauded the team's efforts:

> I consider our season this winter to have been successful because it embodied the elements of true success; our team kept its chin up in adversity and instead of losing courage after defeat was actually playing better at the end than at the start.[41]

Although baseball was discontinued in 1926, the Depression saw a great variety of sports teams on campus. Tennis continued under Paul Sullivan, who took over coaching in 1928. Golf, coached by Emil Loeffler, a professional golfer at the Oakmont Country Club, became a varsity sport in 1932. Elmer Layden's track and field squad, though small, was marked by impressive talent, although it did not continue past 1935. Father Louis Dietrich directed an ice hockey team for several years during the thirties. Although the university did not officially play hockey until the 1937–1938 school year, the student editors of the *Duquesne Duke* were audacious enough to claim the city championship in the sport the year before, as reported in an article on March 18, 1937: "The University hockey team played its first, last, and only game of the year when it defeated Carnegie Tech skaters by a score of 4–0. The game, a very brief contest lasting only ten minutes, was played between periods of the Hornet-Eagle game on Wednesday evening, March 10. Duquesne is now city champ in hockey as well as football."

The end of the decade saw boxing instituted. And plans for a rowing team on the Allegheny River to compete with the other local universities were advanced, but considered in the end prohibitively expensive.

The combination of administrative support, superb coaching, and dedicated athletes willing to give their all for the opportunity to be at Duquesne produced a level of athletic success far above what the size and resources of the university would warrant. Duquesne's athletic prominence so outstripped its means that the 1940 Middle States evaluators questioned how the school could have accomplished so much.[42] Duquesne's athletic endeavors, as well as its scholarly ones, were marked by excellence and intensity.

There has been much discussion concerning the profitability of athletics in this era that later generations would look back on as a golden age. Did Duquesne make money on football and basketball? Financial records for that time are incomplete, but an operating statement from 1937 does survive. It reports income from athletics at $105,873 (football accounted for $98,119 of this amount). Total income from all sources was $586,225 (tuition income accounted for $376,193 of this amount.) So the answer appears to be yes; the university did make money on football and basketball. It is small wonder that after the war other universities would discover this source of revenue.

Father Callahan Departs—But not Without a Struggle

On February 12, 1936, Father Callahan boarded a train for his annual "sabbatical." Billed as a visit to "prominent European educational institutions and old world cultural centers," his leaving was shrouded in mystery. The *Duke* reported rumors of "shakeups in the Administration." His departure was preceded by a farewell dinner marked by a testimonial signed by all of the deans and the vice-president, declaring "our utmost confidence in him as an able administrator" and "expressing the earnest desire for a long and happy term of service as President of Duquesne University." It was a peculiar expression of support; some wondered why it should be necessary.

Father Callahan hadn't been gone a fortnight when the predicted shakeup began. Pleading ill health, the vice-president and treasurer, Father H.J. Goebel, suddenly resigned. So did W.S. York Critchley, whom Father Callahan had hand-picked to head the School of Education the previous fall. Critchley "severed all connections" with the university and offered no explanation for his actions. It was later learned that he had submitted false academic credentials and had not in fact earned a Ph.D. from Cambridge University. The board of directors elected Father Stephen J. "Pop" Bryan, C.S.Sp., vice-president, making him ipso facto acting president. What was not widely known, though Goebel and Critchley surely must have known it since they were so closely identified with Callahan, was that Callahan had privately agreed to resign after returning from his sabbatical. He had made this agreement with Father Christopher J. Plunkett, American Provincial of the Holy Ghost Fathers, who had received mounting complaints from a number of lay faculty and Holy Ghost fathers about a lack of presidential leadership at the university. As a result of "Callahan's disregard of constitutional safeguards," it was reported, morale on campus was low, and "the bishop and his clergy, as well as a number of parents were rapidly losing confidence."[43]

After his return from Europe, Father Callahan publicly announced his resignation at the end of May. When it appeared that he might be leaving under something of a cloud, though, he changed his mind. At this juncture, Father Plunkett fired President Callahan. But Father Callahan simply remained in office, claiming that only the board of directors had the authority to remove him. The board consisted of six Holy Ghost fathers, among whom was, interestingly enough, Father Plunkett. It finally met on June 22. Its tantalizingly brief minutes tell us that J.J. Callahan was elected president (of the board of directors) by a secret ballot. (It should be noted that never before had a secret ballot been taken.) Only a single passage gives a hint of a rift: "As head of the Provincial Council of the American Province of the Fathers of the Holy Ghost, C.J. Plunkett desired to have it recorded that he nominated [Father] F.A. Retka for the office of President." Before the vote, Father Brannigan had resigned from the board. Father Goebel, who had earlier resigned as vice-president, apparently never did resign from the board. So the attempted ouster of Father Callahan did not work. Despite the presence of the provincial at the meeting, the board did not remove Father Callahan either as president of the board or of the university. Since Father Plunkett had no desire for controversy—it was he who moved that Callahan's election be made unanimous—Father Callahan continued in office for another four years.

He might have held on even longer, but Father Plunkett died suddenly of pneumonia in 1939 and was succeeded by Father George J. Collins, who was not afraid of controversy. Father Collins transferred Father Callahan to a poor African-American parish at Isle Brevalle, Louisiana. The president resigned obsequiously in February of 1940, "to bring this internal dissatisfaction to an end."[44] His retirement to take up pastoral duties and pursue the life of a scholar ended the bad press that the university had been receiving and brought calmer times to the Bluff.

5. War and Peace

When Father Callahan resigned his position in 1940, the university board of directors ratified the Holy Ghost Provincial's appointment of the very organized Reverend Raymond V. Kirk, C.S.Sp., to be the next president of Duquesne University.[1] Duquesne was in for another kind of shake-up under this man's administration—an onslaught of efficiency.

The Reorganization Man

Father Kirk, a native of nearby Mt. Pleasant, Pennsylvania, had graduated from both the Duquesne prep school and the university and had also taught in the prep school (after doing parish work for a year in New York City's Harlem). He had a gift for administration. While still in his twenties, he "did the organizational work that made State Certification of the School of Education possible."[2] He then served as dean of the School of Education until his appointment as President. Kirk appointed Dr. Kathryn Redman to fill his place as acting dean of the School of Education, making her the first woman to hold such a position in the university.

During the course of his studies for a doctorate in education at New York University, Raymond Kirk had come under the influence of Dr. Daniel E. Griffiths, a professor of educational administration who had gained recognition in that field.[3] Griffiths taught and Kirk believed that there was much that American higher education could learn from the organization and efficiency of most business corporations. As president of Duquesne, Father Kirk immediately put these beliefs to work. His first act was to reorganize the administration so that class scheduling, curriculum, and changes in faculty status and promotion fell under the jurisdiction of the university vice-president, Reverend John J. Sullivan. The idea was to achieve greater efficiency by centralizing these functions and to more effectively employ the position of vice-president.

Beginning in the fall term of 1940, the curriculum was entirely revamped with the introduction of a core curriculum. The first two years, called a Junior College, where some students might wish to terminate their education, consisted of basic cultural courses—English composition, logic, ethics, philosophy of literature, and social studies. Having completed this, the student could then go on to pursue an area of major academic interest.

In good corporate form, Father Kirk also devised the first organization chart for the university. Other efficiencies were introduced. For example, the drama school, which was graduating only two or three students a year, was made a department in the College of Arts and Sciences. As another example, Duquesne's various alumni groups were organized into one federation. (The original member organizations in the new federation included the newly established Federation Board, the Sisters Alumnae, Women's Club, Women's Guild, Duchess Club, and Nurses Alumnae.) Alumni news from all the organizations was printed in the *Duquesne University Alumni Federation Quarterly*, begun in December 1940. During the war years, the Alumni Federation held an annual fair to promote the Student Loan Fund with various organizations sponsoring booths. The clubs also helped with the government's war bond drive and with fundraising for the financially strapped university. If not for their organization into one group, it is doubtful the alumni could have achieved so much.

Kirk inherited from Callahan a $450,000 university debt. Tuition income of $432,326 during the 1940–1941 school year helped keep Duquesne in the black, but it did not produce enough surplus income to seriously reduce the debt. Then in May of 1941, the Knights of Columbus came to Duquesne's rescue, even as they had in ages past. Assuming the entirety of the debt and accepting the university buildings as collateral, the Knights gave Duquesne a ten-year mortgage at 3 1/2 percent per annum.

The Rosanoff Affair

Making changes in the university's organizational or financial posture was a far different matter than making changes where faculty and personalities were concerned. Control from the president's office had been practically nonexistent throughout the Callahan years, and Father Kirk's more aggressive administration inevitably met with some individual cases of resistance, none more spectacular than the Rosanoff imbroglio.

Dr. Martin A. Rosanoff, one-time research assistant to Thomas Edison and winner of the American Chemical Society's Nichols Gold Medal, had been professor of chemical research at Duquesne since 1933 and dean of the graduate school since 1934. Dr. Rosanoff was a distinguished professor of international reputation, but his administrative abilities as a dean left much to be desired. Amid mounting protest from a number of faculty members, though not all, President Kirk relieved the 65-year-old Rosanoff of his deanship. Along with four other faculty members, Rosanoff resigned from the faculty in a noisy protest. With the involvement of the press, the controversy became a public one. Father Kirk was cast as something of a villain by one local magazine, which erroneously claimed that during his first year as president "almost two dozen professors and instructors out of a faculty of 200 members have resigned or have been discharged."[4] In 1941 Rosanoff entered suit against the university, and after two trials and the passage of ten years, finally settled out of court for $2,800.

Sixteen Points

Tensions between the faculty and the president were further exacerbated when President Kirk promulgated his "sixteen points" at the beginning of the 1940–1941 academic year. Printed in pamphlet form, the points gave reasons why a tenured faculty member could be discharged. The list included the following "discrediting acts":

> To question the existence of a personal God.
> To maintain that religion had its origin in human ignorance.
> To teach any other proposition inconsistent with Catholic doctrine.
> To question the testimony of personal consciousness as a criterion for objective certitude.
> To question the duty of religion for all men.
> To question creation as a volitional act of God.
> To question the immortality, spirituality, individuality of the human soul.
> To suggest that the natural moral law is the result of mere custom or convenience.
> To question the physical freedom of the human will.
> To question the immortality rights bestowed by the Deity commonly called natural rights.
> To support any idea that fosters racial, or religious, or class hatred.
> To deny that Civil Authority is derived from God, or to question the fact that Civil Authority is bound by moral law.
> To foster materialistic Communism or any other form of political theory that would destroy the American form of government.
> To fail to realize that an inculcation of patriotism is a duty incumbent upon all members of Duquesne University faculty.
> To cast aspersions on the adherents of any form of religious belief.[5]

The faculty, 40 percent of whom were not Catholic, objected to the fact that many of the points began with the words "to question." Since it is the nature of a professor to question, such a ruling was at odds with the purpose of higher education. Worse still was the added injunction that these points were applicable outside the classroom. The pamphlet stated that "any overt act, even extra-mural, that might compromise Duquesne University's ideals is sufficient grounds for Duquesne University to terminate immediately any agreement as to tenure previously entered into with them." The issue of academic freedom was raised. However, none of the faculty voiced any serious distress over the points, and apparently no one was ever dismissed for violating any of them.

The Struggle for Accreditation

By 1940 it had been increasingly important for an institution to be accredited by the regional accrediting association where the school was located. In Pennsylvania, this was the Middle States Association of Colleges and Secondary Schools. The university applied for accreditation, and in February of 1935, "the Commission voted, without dissenting voice, to place Duquesne on the approved list."[6] But accreditation had not been obtained easily. Duquesne had labored with near heroic effort to upgrade the qualifications of its faculty, to increase the library holdings, and to strengthen its course offerings.

Upon the return of the Middle States inspection team five years after the initial accreditation, the university had been further improved. But Kirk's 16 points and the publicity they generated overshadowed the many improvements that had been made. When the commission met in November of 1940, it voted in a split decision not to include the university on the approved list. Although Duquesne was restored in 1942, the struggle had taken its toll on Father Kirk, who in the meantime had suffered a severe heart attack.

At least one member of the Middle States inspection team was highly critical of the action the commission took in 1940. A month after the university was restored, Dr. Roy Deferrari wrote to President Kirk saying that Duquesne "should never have been taken from the list"[7] of accredited schools. Previously, Deferrari had written to the secretary of the association saying that the commission had been unfair to Duquesne in the two preceding years. Never again was Duquesne's standing before Middle States similarly questioned. The entire episode was soon to be only an unpleasant memory as concerns of even greater proportions occupied the full attention of the university.

World War II Begins

The long-expected war in Europe finally broke out in September of 1939. Nearly two years before, in a poll of some 300 students on campus, the *Duquesne Duke* asked, "Would you go to fight on foreign shores if drafted?" Sixty-four percent said they would not. The war's coming did little to change student opinion. Two months after the beginning of the war, the magazine *America* asked students, "Do you personally favor the entry of the United States as an armed force in the present European War?" Obviously fearing that they would be the "armed force," a thumping 98 percent said no. And 44 percent foresaw the inevitable and believed "that the United States will eventually be drawn into the European War."

For the entirety of the 1939–1940 school year, the university was more absorbed in the new curriculum, the thrill of live radio broadcasts from the Bluff, and the Duquesne Dukes winning the city football title than the war in Europe. The October 5, 1939, issue of the *Duke*, the first to appear after the war began, did offer advice to male students on "what to do if the war comes" by comparing the relative merits of the army and navy. But a federal program designed to create a "civilian aviation reserve" by teaching students how to fly never got off the ground that year at Duquesne. The students could not fit the 107-hour course into their schedules.

Father Federici's Close Call

Father Salvatore Federici, a professor of history, along with three other Holy Ghost fathers, were in France in 1940 when Germany invaded. They left Bordeaux aboard the liner *Washington*, which was overcrowded with 1,800 passengers. When Father Federici awakened at five o'clock on the morning of June 11, he noticed that the ship had stopped. The lifeboats were suspended and ready for lowering. When the passengers were in the lifeboats, the *Washington* turned and headed at full speed toward the Spanish coast some 180 miles away. By now it was clear to all that this was not a drill; they were being chased by a submarine. Unknown to the passengers at the time, the submarine had given them ten minutes to abandon ship when the captain decided to make a run for it. Either the submarine did not wish to sink an American ship at this time, or the *Washington* outran the sub, but for whatever reason, they were spared.

The whole affair caused quite an international stir. The official German news agency called reports of the incident "brazen lies." Father Federici safely returned to the United States and later it was he, as director of admissions, who would welcome thousands of returning veterans from a war that so nearly claimed his own life.

The Draft Comes to Duquesne

As the students were returning to the Bluff for the start of the fall term, Congress was busy passing the first peacetime conscription bill in the nation's history. It called for drafting 900,000 men between the ages of 21 and 36 for a period of one year. Students in advanced ROTC were deferred. Since it did not include men under age 21, almost all freshmen and sophomores were unaffected. So were seniors, for no student was drafted until he had completed the academic year. The university aided draft registration by canceling all afternoon classes on October 16, 1940, so that students and qualifying faculty could register.

In the fall of 1940 the Civilian Pilot Training Corps began at last, an indication of a changed mood on campus. Thirty-two students applied for the 20 openings allotted to Duquesne. By government order, 10 percent of the corps' positions were reserved for women. The students, all of whom had to be over age 19, received classroom training on campus, but the 35 hours of flying were taken at the Greensburg and Butler airports. The locations of these airports proved too inconvenient for Duquesne students; the next semester only eight students registered. Finally, in the fall of 1942, when nearby Bettis Field was secured, 32 students enrolled in the program. Enrollment automatically made one a member of the Enlisted Reserve Corps of the U.S. Army Air Force.[8]

By the fall of 1940, the Nazis had invaded the Soviet Union, and Great Britain was fighting for its very existence. The deteriorating European situation exercised a decidedly adverse influence over Duquesne's enrollment. Fearful of being drafted, potential freshmen and even some upperclassmen hesitated to register for classes. In an effort to stem the anticipated enrollment decline, President Kirk issued a message in May of 1941 urging the students not to interrupt their studies despite the uncertainty of the times. He reminded them that many courses, such as chemistry, biology, and pharmacy, were essential to national defense and that these programs might be of more importance in the long run than immediate military service. Kirk appointed Dean Muldoon of the pharmacy school to act as chairman of the Deans' Committee in assisting students in securing educational deferments. He also advised students who might be called up by their draft boards to ask for an approximate time of induction so that they would be able to decide whether to enroll for the following semester, informing them that if the call came late in a term, local draft boards were authorized to postpone induction until the end of the semester. His conclusion focused on the needs of the future:

In a truly literal sense, the Universities of the nation are the strongholds of American civilization. During the emergency, and for many years after, America will need its trained citizenry. Upon the college men will rest the responsibility of post-war rehabilitation. In urging you, therefore, to the fulfillment of every patriotic duty, I remind you that America needs an alert and disciplined and superior citizenry to bear the burdens of the days of war, and the equally severe days of peace which will inevitably follow. I commend you to God, and your patriotic conscience.[9]

Kirk's words could not stop the inevitable. From the 3010 total in the fall of 1940, enrollment fell to 2741 at the beginning of the 1941–1942 school year. This may have been partly a result of the passage of the draft extension bill, or because of the general atmosphere of uncertainty, but in any case, it took its toll entirely from among the male students. While the number of women students had been climbing steadily since the bottom of the Depression and would continue to do so until 1942, the number of men had peaked in 1939. Thereafter, their number began to fall, decreasing by more than 300 from 1940 to 1941 alone. Although men still outnumbered women 1487 to 1254, one student probably reflected the feelings of many when she complained in the September 18, 1941 issue of the *Duke*, "If Congress passes many more of these Draft Extension Bills, by the time the draftees are released we'll all be too old to get married."

Closing the Prep School

At the same time, the university experienced yet another contraction with the closing of the prep school. Once such an integral part of Duquesne, it had gradually become administratively separate. As a result of the restructuring in 1929, the *Duquesne Duke* had announced then that "its divorce from the University is almost complete." Its enrollment had experienced a slow decline as parishes began their own high schools and especially after the diocese opened the tuition-free Central Catholic High School in 1927. From more than 700 in 1927, it had fallen to 251 students by 1934. Since a Middle States Association accreditation report suggested that a college should not maintain a preparatory school in conjunction with its other operations, the university sought to satisfy the request and at the same time reverse the decline in the student body by physically separating the prep school from the rest of the campus. (No prep school students took college courses, nor were any college students permitted to take prep school courses. It was not unusual, however, for prep school faculty to "graduate" and begin teaching in the college.) When the Hancock Public School building became available, at the intersection of Webster and Seventh Avenues downtown—which was coincidentally only a block from Duquesne's original Wylie Avenue location—the university purchased and moved the prep school there in 1937. Even so, the high school student body continued to shrink. Though early in 1940 Father Kirk proclaimed that "the Prep School is, and always will be, part of the University,"[10] his statement soon proved to be wishful thinking, following as it did the opening of yet another tuition-free diocesan high school, North Catholic. When the student body fell to 100, the school was forced to close in the spring of 1941, and a part of Duquesne passed into history.

Of course, the times were much changed from the days when the prep school was founded. The university no longer needed to provide its own supply of high school students. As of 1941, there were 5817 students enrolled in private high schools in Allegheny County, the vast majority of whom were in parochial schools. Moreover, there were 69,790 students in public high schools in the county, some of whom would pursue higher education at Duquesne University. Nevertheless, the closing of the prep school was supposed to be temporary, and from time to time its reopening was seriously discussed. Perhaps it was hard to let go of such a characteristically "Duquesne" piece of the university, with all its memories of the Holy Ghost fathers investing their efforts in the younger members of society.

"War Affects Faculty, Students"

On December 7, 1941, the Japanese bombing of Pearl Harbor brought the United States into World War II. Four days later the headlines of the *Duquesne Duke* read, "WAR AFFECTS FACULTY, STUDENTS." It certainly did. Patriotism flared. When the National Youth Administration slashed student pay and hours by a third, no one complained. When history professor, Dr. Erna Risch, offered a knitting class to make socks and sweaters for soldiers, 150 girls showed up for her lessons. A frightened *Duquesne Duke* asked, "could Duquesne be bombed?[11] It received an answer when eleven faculty members and eight students were trained by the Pittsburgh Council of Defense as auxiliary firemen and taught how to mobilize communication facilities "in the event of an emergency."[12] The School of Nursing offered first aid classes. Pharmacy students learned first aid and were taught how to drive ambulances by the Mercy Hospital staff. Starting with Dean Muldoon himself, a pharmacy school phone chain was set up that could be activated on a moment's notice. The entire campus became caught up in a sense of emergency and excitement.

It did not last. The enthusiasm that rose on the Bluff immediately after Pearl Harbor was impossible to sustain, and by February 1942, the dean of women had to call a meeting of all women students to reprimand them for their lack of cooperation in the war effort. Two months after the first knitting classes, not so much as a single glove had been returned. At the nursing school's first aid classes, "sometimes only the instructor was there."[13]

The federal government was urging all colleges to adopt a three-semester year. The university's fears that students would not register for the extended summer classes featuring six additional weeks were confirmed when a survey revealed that a majority of students would not take them. When the Marines came to the campus to explain a deferment program they were offering, attendance at the meeting had to be made mandatory for fear no one would attend. By March of 1942, the major excitement on the Bluff seemed to be the auditions in the campus theater for Fred Allen's Collegiate Talent Search, scheduled to be broadcast over radio station WJAS. The *Duke* told the students how "important" their vote was since they would determine which Duquesne students would "perform before 28 million listeners." By semester's end, however, it was a sobered and saddened student body that bade farewell to Duquesne's seniors. The *Duquesne Duke* of May 1942 editorialized,

> We don't feel much like joking, for when the class of '42 tucks its sheepskins under its collective arms and trundles off into the blue, a lot of fine fellas and girls will be staggering down the hill for the last time.

Father Kirk's advice to remain in school as long as possible went increasingly unheeded. By the fall of 1942, enrollment fell to 1954 students. It was to fall yet again to 1360 in the fall of 1943. The nadir of student enrollment was reached in the second semester of the 1943–1944 school year with 1270 students registered. Of this group, only 305 were men. With the disappearance of most draft-age males from campus, many organizations shut down, and a number of programs were suspended.

Athletics as a Casualty of War

The decade had begun with great optimism. Coach Buff Donelli's 1940 football season was almost as good as the previous year, his first, with seven wins and one loss. The high point of the season was the game against the University of Mississippi, for which Duquesne arranged a special excursion train for the fans at a cost of $20.00 for the fare and game admission. The Mississippi game proved to be Duquesne's only loss that season.

The 1941 season brought Duquesne a perfect, undefeated, untied record in all eight games. The team included 16 seniors who had played together for three years, including two All-Americans, John Rokisky and Al Demao. They had been rated fifth in the nation by the Associated Press and were eagerly looking forward to a bowl game bid. Duquesne was bitterly disappointed, however, when slots went to lesser teams and it was not even considered. Many felt that Duquesne had been excluded because it did not belong to a conference, and that the organization to which the team belonged counted more than the quality of play. Duquesne's failure to get a bowl bid was even more painful in retrospect, because only days later the United States entered the Second World War. With the draft and enlistments, Duquesne would not be able to field such a mighty team again.

Despite the diminished field of players, Duquesne continued to play football in the 1942 season, chalking up six wins in the nine game schedule. Several Duquesne alumni had moved on to the Pittsburgh professional team, the Pirates, now renamed the Steelers. They had asked Buff Donelli to coach for them as well, so he served both on the collegiate and professional levels. Elmer Layden, retired as Notre Dame coach and now the National Football Commissioner, was approached about this supposed conflict of interest and was forced to act:

> One of the toughest jobs I had to perform as commissioner of the NFL was asking Buff to make up his mind about which team he was going to coach. At the time, and this was during World War II, he was coaching the Steelers for pay and Duquesne for free. Buff chose his old College when the chips were down.[14]

It was to be the last season for Duquesne to play football until after the war. Later generations of students would look back on these glory years of Duquesne football with a sense of longing. But surely no student body had ever or would ever need those dazzling successes as much as that Depression-racked one.

Despite the war, Duquesne held onto basketball through the 1942 and 1943 seasons after which it, too, had to be suspended. The gymnasium which was considered so spacious in 1923 was reworked early in 1942 to seat 2000, but even this proved to be inadequate for the crowds who came to see the Dukes play.

Just before the war, the varsity team was outshined by the freshman team, which became known as the "Iron Dukes." Its ethnic composition was described as follows by the *Duquesne Duke* of March 20, 1941:

> The personnel of the Iron Dukes is one that, if drawn to the attention of Herr Hitler, should make him crawl into a hole, for it explódes his theory of racial superiority. The boys that have made the Red and Blue of the University synonymous with basketball superiority are descendants of five different nationalities and their coach Charles "Chick" Davies, of another. Debnar is an Austrian; Kasparik, a Pole; Milkovich is Serbian; Widowitz is Russian and Moe Becker, Jewish. Charles Davies, the molder of this basketball "league of nations" is a Welshman, and can be looked up to as the man that proved that any nationalities can work together amicably towards any goal they set.

The team had impressive 51 wins to 10 losses in their three years of play. Despite an average height of barely six feet, these "giant killers" won through style and accuracy, producing All-American Moe Becker in 1941. Duquesne played in both the National Invitational and the NCAA tournaments at the conclusion of the 1940 season and in the National Invitational Tournament at the end of the 1941 season.

After the attack on Pearl Harbor, all spring sports were canceled for the duration of the war because of the difficulty in obtaining equipment, the lack of traveling facilities, and the expected loss of athletes to the armed services. In September 1943, "Duquesne was the first university to announce the giving up of sports for the duration" of the war.[15] Although basketball made it through the 1943 season as the last holdout, the war superseded all, and Duquesne athletics had to hunker down and await better times.

Educating the Army

Better times seemed far away in 1942, and university officials gave serious thought to closing. Seventy-one colleges across the country had already closed or soon would.[16] Enrollment at Duquesne was less than half of its prewar high. But perhaps this university that had been so covered with the prayers of its founders was not meant to close, even temporarily, for once again, there was a fortuitous turn of events. A 1942 army survey of college and university instructional, housing, and recreational facilities resulted in the selection of Duquesne University as a training site for the first group of 350 officers and cadets in the Army Air Corps. Although Duquesne did not realize a windfall—the government paid only what the university normally charged for tuition, room, board—this influx of Air Force cadets and the financial payments attendant to their coming brought new life to campus and literally kept Duquesne from closing its doors.[16] A serendipitous family connection made it all possible. Father Kirk's brother was the Pittsburgh city treasurer who "knew a lot of people and through his political friends, he got this contract with the Air Force. . . . and they brought trainloads of cadets in here . . . and saved the University."[17]

Classrooms in the administration building were converted into dormitory rooms. Lavatories and showers were installed. Two floors of Canevin Hall were reserved for use by the cadets as classrooms for study halls. Through much schedule juggling, the university was able to conduct ten classes concurrently, with 35 men in each class, and still continue its regular classes.

Known formally as the 328th College Training Detachment, the cadets spent five months at Duquesne, with one fifth leaving each month for flight training as new cadets took their place. Along with physical fitness and military drill, their course of study included College English, United States History, College Mathematics, Physics, World Geography, Airplane Identification, Meteorology, Radio Code, and Military Science. Although the courses were taught by 35 Duquesne faculty members, the cadets did not take classes with the regular students, nor did they receive college credit through the university. After the war, however, many veterans who pursued their education under the G.I. bill would petition to receive credit for the courses taken at Duquesne and other institutions of higher learning.

"In all, 937 men were afforded academic training . . . from April 4, 1943 to May 25, 1944, the last scheduled departure date."[18] In its final report on the program, the university congratulated the faculty for bearing the "extraordinary burdens both of energy and time" that the army's College Training Detachment placed on them. It also noted that a "commendation is due them for their voluntary service in aiding weaker students, by tutoring them beyond scheduled hours."[19]

In January of 1943 Father Edward M. Smith, faculty representative for the army, announced an eight-month meterology course for civilians, Army enlisted men, and members of the Army Enlisted Reserve Corps. Applicants received a rank of Aviation Cadet, pay of $75 per month, a food allowance of $2.25 per day, quarters, tuition, and clothing. Completion of the course earned the student a commission as second lieutenant in the Army Air Corps and placement on active service for the duration plus six months.

The Army was apparently satisfied with the course of instruction and the accommodations given at Duquesne, for no sooner had the

College Training Detachment left when the Army Specialized Training Reserve Program (ASTR) for Pre-Aviation Cadets arrived. These men, members of the 3330th Service Command, were 17-year-olds who had recently graduated from high school and had enlisted in the Army Air Corps Reserves. Not yet on active duty, they were required to enroll in the ROTC. The first group of 213 ASTR cadets arrived in July 1944. Only 166 actually finished the program. Twenty men left when they reached eighteen and one-half years of age, thus rendering them ineligible for the program. The others either voluntarily withdrew or were dismissed because of disciplinary, academic, or health reasons. In October this group was replaced by 177 new cadets.

The conditions of their stay at Duquesne were much the same as the College Training Detachment had been. The university controlled the academic part of the day, but for the rest of the day the cadets were subject to regular military discipline. The university also supplied a chaplain, but the cadets were free to attend the church of their choice.

The syllabus for the American history course is characteristic of the times. It gives the objective of the course as "unreservedly in consonance with the ideas and ideals for which the nation is fighting. Each student should be thoroughly impressed throughout with a sense of the personal responsibility which rests upon him to preserve and strengthen the American Way of Life."[20]

Through these programs even those faculty who could not go to war were able to aid the war effort on the homefront. The programs had another benefit, one that was entirely unexpected. It concerned a contingent from Alabama. As Father Henry McAnulty later recalled,

> When the word got out that Duquesne was a Catholic school . . . half the guys wanted to jump off the train, but . . . they weren't here more than a couple of weeks when they really fell in love with the place. Some of them had never met a real live priest. We had some great guys here in those days, young priests, very active and some of them were very athletic and played ball with the guys. It was a lesson of ecumenism in itself.[21]

The ASTR program ended in April, 1945, only a month before Germany's surrender.

Student Life During the War

With many of its students in the service, the character of student life lost much of its lightheartedness. Air raid wardens were appointed, and drills were held, with professors instructed to dismiss classes as soon as they heard the signal. The campus had become predominantly female. The colleges and universities in Pittsburgh held a cooperative dance during Intercollegiate Week in the spring of 1944 for which the admission price was two books and two three-cent stamps to send the books to "fellow students behind barbed wire, war prisoners for the duration."[22] All the local colleges sent representatives to a war bond rally at Soldiers and Sailors Memorial Hall and pushed war bond sales at their respective institutions. Father Vernon Gallagher directed the Red Cross Blood Bank at Duquesne, selecting student chairmen from the university's schools and departments to encourage competition for the most blood donated. And the students were urged to attend one of the five Masses that were offered daily in the university chapel for the safe return of servicemen.

Many features of the campus now were specific to the war years. For example, the Bishop's Program for Polish Rehabilitation in Pittsburgh included a one-year training course as "social work aides" for the rebuilding of Poland and the cause of Poland's people. Twenty-six graduated from the course in 1945.

The War Affects Nursing Students

When Ruth D. Johnson took over control of the nursing school with the resignation of Mary

Tobin in 1944, the number of nurses available for the advanced courses was small, since many were already serving in the armed forces while the rest were trying to take up the slack on the homefront. Due to efforts to recruit women into the nursing field for the war effort, however, the basic program had 77 enrolled. The program was compressed to accelerate training under what was termed the "Victory Plan." The university also participated in the Cadet Nurse Corps where senior cadet students served army assignments at Deshon Hospital, Butler, Pennsylvania, and Ashford General Hospital, White Sulpher Springs, West Virginia. The Public Health Nursing program was divided into a degree and certificate of public health plan and a certificate alone plan. Both were recognized as sufficient preparation for school nursing in Pennsylvania.

The war brought unforeseen difficulties in clinical training for Duquesne nurses. With the decline in the birth rate during the war, Mercy Hospital could no longer offer the student nurses obstetrical experience. Mercy also raised its laboratory fee, which the university was hard-pressed to meet. These difficulties led Duquesne to formulate plans to make its program independent of Mercy Hospital and award its own diploma, pin, and uniform. Western State Psychiatric Hospital's decision not to accept Duquesne students for clinical studies also left the school searching for another institution.

At the end of the war, the U.S. Cadet Nurse Corps was terminated, and many nurses returned home from the service eager to pursue further full-time study on the GI bill. But in 1945 Duquesne's total enrollment in the nursing programs was 207, far less than the prewar figure, and it took years to build it up again.

The James DeLuco Story

Wars invariably produce bizarre occurrences and Duquesne has a story of its very own. After his graduation from Duquesne's Business School in 1943, James DeLuco of Pittsburgh went into the army. The following October he was shipped overseas, where he served as a private first-class in the infantry. DeLuco's unit was caught in the German advance during the Battle of the Bulge and he was captured in January 1945. It was at the Gerolstein prisoner-of-war camp that DeLuco lost his Duquesne ring. "A German officer, . . . took the ring from me while they were going over us to see if we had anything worth taking. The ring was all I had," DeLuco recalled.[23] He was twice transferred to other camps before he was liberated by the American Third Army in April 1945. After being confined to a field hospital for observation, Jim was shipped home in June.

A U.S. military policeman who was guarding the German prisoners of war noticed the ring. It was being worn by the same officer who had taken the ring from DeLuco at Gerolstein. Seeing the words "Duquesne University," and "Pittsburgh" on the ring, the officer realized that it had been stolen and seized it. The M.P. later sent the ring to his wife in New Jersey with instructions to write to Duquesne University to find a 1943 graduate with the initials J.D.L. When Father Federici received this letter in February of 1946, a search was made of the university's records that turned up DeLuco's name. He had long since given up hope of ever seeing his ring again and had purchased another. When his younger brother, Carmen, later went to Duquesne, Jim gave the second ring to him.

"Our Lady of Victory"

As a lasting memorial to those who served and died in the war, the university planned a campus shrine to Our Lady of Victory. Even before the war was won, Dr. A. Lester "Pop" Pierce had conceived of the idea for this victory shrine, which on Labor Day 1945 finally was dedicated. Situated between Canevin Hall and the library, the six-foot statue of the Blessed Mother holding the child Jesus, both adorned with crowns, was made in Chicago, by Daprato Studios. Terraced gardens surrounded the pedestal. The centerpiece was the outline of the letter "V" for victory, poured in concrete as a planter for flowers in front of the statue. This "V" has since been replaced with one that slopes upward towards the Marian shrine. The top part is now a bar extending entirely across the arms of the "V," thus transforming the letter into a triangle. Since flowers are now planted in the middle of the triangle, all evidence of a "V" has been lost.

The original plan called for a V-shaped lily pond, but the idea was opposed by the head of landscaping, Brother Gerard Keating. Brother Jerry, as he was affectionately known by generations of students, feared that the students would throw each other in and that it would attract neighborhood children. Thus the lily pond never materialized.

For its dedication, the *Alumni Quarterly* announced that all "servicemen and women, on furlough or discharged, are requested to honor the occasion by appearing in their dress uniforms." Two years later the garden was the scene of another service in memory of those who had not returned. Each fall the shrine became the focus for Duquesne's Armistice Day ceremonies. Following the mass and invocation, the names of university dead—underclassmen, graduate students, faculty, and alumni from both world wars—were read before the flag was lowered to half-staff as the ROTC fired a rifle salute.

Over the years the landscaping has been reworked several times. In 1982 the Marian statue was placed on a pedestal of bricks matching those of the new law school. It has since been dedicated with plaques to Duquesne alumni who served in Korea, Vietnam, and most recently, in Grenada, Panama, and the Persian Gulf War.

The Silver and Gold Books

Students, faculty, and alumni who served in the war were recorded in the *Silver Book* placed on display at the vestibule of the Duquesne chapel. The Alumni Office identified 1284 Duquesne men and women who served in all branches of the armed services. Placed with the *Silver Book* was the *Gold Book*, a record of those from Duquesne who had given their lives during the war. The list was appallingly long. Seventy-seven men from the university and 20 graduates of the Preparatory School gave their lives in World War II. Both books were supposed to remain permanently in the chapel's vestibule, but in the 1970s a city fire marshall ordered their removal and they have since disappeared. Fortunately, the Duquesne Archives has lists of names of those who served and those who died in the war.

Changing the Guard

Seeing Duquesne University through these dark days was a great strain on Father Kirk. Still suffering from his heart ailment, he was forced to suspend his activities in 1945 for what was to have been a six-month recovery period, during which presidential duties fell upon the shoulders of Father Francis P. Smith, C.S.Sp. But Father Kirk's health continued to fail, and he was forced to resign the presidency in June of 1946. Having saved Duquesne University from becoming another casualty of the war, he retired to St. Mary's Seminary in Ferndale, Connecticut, where he died the following May at the age of 46, an indirect casualty of the Second World War.

At the end of the war, conditions at Duquesne were changing so rapidly that a special kind of administrator was needed, one who could deal effectively with the problems that postwar expansion would pose. Father Smith, like so many other college presidents, had been an excellent professor but found that his classroom skills were not readily transferable to an administrative capacity. Although he practiced responsible fiscal management, he could not visualize a building plan for Duquesne's future needs nor the fundraising campaign that would be necessary for it. The Emergency Sustaining Fund that was begun under Father Kirk in 1943—scheduled to end in 1947 when it would have met its goal of

$680,400—did continue. But a report dated February 1, 1946, shows $100,718 in pledges of which only $54,918 were actually received. More fundraising was going to be needed. But Father Smith was not the man to provide it.

Francis P. Smith was born in Waterbury, Connecticut, on March 28, 1907. Following the tradition of Duquesne presidents Callahan and Kirk, he was a Duquesne alumnus, having graduated in 1930. He was ordained in 1933 and taught at St. Basil College, then at St. Mary's Seminary in Connecticut. He received his master's degree at Catholic University in 1939. He began work on his doctorate at Fordham, but his studies were discontinued when he received an assignment to teach philosophy at Duquesne University in 1940. He assumed the deanship of the College of Liberal Arts and Sciences in 1943 and was elevated to the vice-presidency to fill Father John Sullivan's vacancy in 1944. (Father Sullivan had left Duquesne to serve as an Army chaplain.) He was to serve as Duquesne's seventh president, until 1950.

At the June 3, 1945, commencement, Father Smith reiterated a standard article of belief at Duquesne when he expressed his philosophical support of a liberal arts program over a highly specialized technical program of studies that was becoming the trend at American institutions. He was, however, balanced in his approach, supporting the specialized professional schools but requiring a core of basic liberal arts courses.

Postwar Enrollment Boom

At the commencement ceremonies in the spring of 1946, the university conferred degrees on the 110 students who had been able to complete their studies from among the 200 who had entered as freshmen four years before. The situation was to change dramatically in the fall, when approximately 3000 veterans swelled enrollment to 4107. The next year the student body increased again, and by the fall of 1948 reached a postwar peak when 5280 students were enrolled. This made Duquesne's enrollment the eleventh largest among all Catholic colleges in the United States, outnumbering even Notre Dame. Over the next half decade, however, as the surge of veterans passed through the university, the size of the student body was to decline slowly by about 300 a year.

The Return of the Duke

Nothing so graphically illustrated the resurgence of campus life as the return of the *Duquesne Duke*. The final war issue had been printed on February 18, 1943. After a three-year hiatus, it resumed publication on May 9, 1946. During its absence, news in brief had continued on campus in the distribution of a typewritten mimeographed paper called the *Duquesne Durational*. The university rejoiced to have its old paper in publication again with several of its old staffers returning from military service to work on the paper once more. Of the 1943 staff, two had been killed in the war, the editor-in-chief was a correspondent covering war crimes in Manila, and the managing editor was still serving in the army as a courier for the State Department.

The *Duke* no longer cost a nickel but was distributed free of charge to the students, its cost covered by a student activities fee. It also appeared in a much reduced size. Before the war, it had been the size of a regular daily paper; now it was only 17 × 12 inches. Due to material shortages, it was only four pages, but the following year it grew to eight pages.

The Spring of 1946

In the spring of 1946, the *Duke* was full of the optimism of rebuilding. Many professors were already returning from war duty to pick up classes again. After three years of giving no award at all, the School of Business Administration awarded its McClelland Award for academic excellence to two seniors. The Red Masquers reorganized and scheduled their first production in the Campus Theater for the end of May. The Social Science Club made its debut. Although Lou "Doc" Skender had kept an intramural program alive during the war, Duquesne was to see intercollegiate competition again as Chick Davies returned to campus for his twentieth year of coaching basketball. Alpha Phi Delta announced that its May Frolic Dance was to feature the music of the Duquesne Swingsters playing together publicly for the first time in three years, with returning veterans forming a large part of the band. In announcing a nationwide tour of the Tamburitza Orchestra, the *Duke* referred to it for the first time as the "Tamburitzans," a name that was destined to endure. (The article also used the term "Tammie group" for the first time. This evolved into the familiar "Tammies.") The *Duke* also announced that the Commercial Education club, originally known as the Commedukes, had gone national as Pi Omega Pi; alumnus Father Charles Owen Rice gave the May Crowning address; the Alumni Federation pledged to raise $50,000 for the reinstatement of basketball and football; and Sigma Lambda Phi sorority was selected to host the semi-formal Graduation Ball. Although Gamma Phi and Kappa Sigma Phi fraternities had seen reactivated the previous school year, the fraternities were not yet strong enough to host dances, so the Harvest Ball which the frats had established in a downtown hotel ballroom in 1930 was now an informal affair held in the gym and sponsored by the College of Liberal Arts and Science.

The *Duke* also related more scholarly news, such as the high summer school registration for three sessions: pre, main, and post, offered for the second year. Also planned for summer school was a full year of study in German, Spanish, or French. Although graduate tuition remained unchanged, a fall increase of a dollar per credit would raise costs to $10 a credit.

The Fall of 1946

Picking up the pieces of university life that had seemed so easy that spring, proved somewhat more difficult to deal with when the flood of new students arrived in the fall of 1946. The start of school was complicated by other factors beyond the university's control. After the war, the nation, and Pittsburgh in particular, faced a wave of strikes that continued at near epidemic pro portions for several years. Although many of these work stoppages affected the university to a certain degree, it was the Duquesne Light Company strike that forced the university to close for three weeks. Although supervisory personnel maintained power to homes and hospitals, there was none for public buildings or the city's streetcar system. At the time, all of the colleges and universities in Pittsburgh were, to varying degrees, commuter colleges, and all closed during the strike. Classes finally resumed on October 14, a week before the strikes officially ended. It took weeks more before conditions returned to normal. The *Duke* did not appear until October 31. To compensate for the lost days, the annual retreat was postponed, and the Christmas vacation was abbreviated.

A sign of the times as Duquesne tried to right itself after the turmoil of the war years was an announcement in the school newspaper that anyone who had bought a Duquesne class ring during the war could have the red-orange sardonyx stone replaced with the traditional synthetic ruby. Materials shortages had made it unavailable during the war. (The Duquesne class ring after the war was priced at $32.40.)

Bursting at the Seams

When the school year did begin without further interruption, congestion from a student body that had grown more than fourfold over its wartime low nearly overwhelmed the campus. Every conceivable facility was employed. The Fitzsimons Building was used to capacity. More students than ever had to make the between-class dash from the downtown location to the Bluff, a difficult feat, resulting in much tardiness from exhausted students puffing up the hill. Conditions on the Bluff were impossibly crowded. The hallways were so congested that the administration ordered up and down staircases in Canevin Hall. This regulation was constantly violated by the ex-servicemen, so the *Duquesne Duke* claimed, who were doubtless impatient with a rule so reminiscent of military life. Cafeteria conditions were no better. The *Duquesne Durational* quipped that the veterans could hardly feel like civilians at lunch time since "there's a chow line a mile long." Once a student was served, there was often no place to sit. And there was no other place to go!

The opening of a student lounge in 1948 finally provided some relief. In a repeat of the 1939 problems, however, students were once again guilty of leaving newspapers on the floor, placing their feet on the furniture, card playing, and leaving candy wrappers. The administration closed the lounge for a few weeks after it opened. When it did reopen, the administration made a special, and valiant, attempt to end the card playing, principally because students were betting. On a single occasion, eight students were placed on probation for card playing. After that the ever resourceful young gamblers took to playing cards with their coats on, ready to run away at a moment's notice.

The enlarged student body also placed severe strains on the library. As veterans began flocking to the library for the summer sessions of 1946, the library reported overnight borrowing up 800 percent and seven-day circulation up 300 percent. The increased demand for essential resources led to stringent regulations by spring of 1947. With the ratio of books to students reaching a "dangerously" low level, more books were placed on reserve, much to the annoyance of the students.[24]

Parking was yet another area of frustration for the beleaguered Duquesne student. Always in short supply on the Bluff, street parking had long been taken by downtown office workers who parked there early, when spaces were still available. The sight of a city policeman issuing parking tickets was routine. One student declared that he wouldn't be able to continue his studies because he couldn't afford five dollars every week in parking tickets. Complaints from Duquesne fell on deaf ears at city hall, and many meetings between university officials and city planners came to naught. Finally, in October 1947, students took matters into their own hands. Led by the Veterans' Association, they set up a picket line protesting the parking of cars by downtown workers on the streets of the Bluff. Fearful of adverse publicity, the city's Bureau of Traffic Planning acted within the week. It posted two-hour parking limit signs on the streets adjacent to university properties. The *Duquesne Duke* rejoiced: "And so ends the parking worries of the students. The early morning fight for parking places is a thing of the past."

Veterans on Campus

Veterans had begun to enroll in the spring of 1946 and the character of the student body had changed again as a result. Men now outnumbered women six to one, a complete reversal of the wartime ratio, but they were older and often married. Approximately half of the great influx of students enrolling after the war did so under the Servicemen's Readjustment Act, or, as it was more popularly known, the GI Bill.

Veterans could receive full GI Bill payments if they carried a minimum of 12 credits. This amounted to a tuition allowance plus subsistence pay of $67.50 per month. But the veterans found life within this budget impossibly restraining in view of the high rate of inflation. By the beginning of November, some had jokingly organized as the "We Want to Make Some Money Club." Even the working vet was permitted to earn no more than $107.50 per month before his subsistence pay would be cut. The ceiling for combined earnings and subsistence pay was set at $175 for veterans with no dependents, $200 for veterans with dependents.

Duquesne's popularity as one of 31 preferred schools as reported by the Veteran's Administration lay partly in the fact that the larger, better-known schools soon placed a cap on admissions while Duquesne was willing to make room for any serious applicant. In January of 1946 Father Federici stated, "No qualified student has yet been turned away." Although not all of the veterans admitted to the university could be provided with dormitory space, 52 were housed on the third and fourth floors of the Administration Building, six men to a room.

The veterans' pursuit of an education was a hurried one. Having given years to the war, they were eager to make up the lost time. They won an exemption from ROTC and physical education requirements but received university credit for both of those courses. They had a limited period of time in which to secure their education before the benefits ended. Their determination to make the most of their opportunity, combined with the university's efforts to help them do so, sometimes made the traditional students feel like second-class citizens. When Mayor David L. Lawrence attempted (unsuccessfully) to secure lower-fare weekly trolley passes for veterans, the *Duke* bore this comment from one resentful student: "Students working their way through school deserve just as much consideration as the veterans. Everyone should get passes. Veterans have more money than we have, and if they can't afford the usual trolley rates, we certainly can't."

There was a lot of attention paid to the vets. GI wartime experiences were published in the *Durational* and the *Alumni Quarterly*. The *Durational* carried a column titled "Vets' News" to keep the ex-GI abreast of changes in Veterans' Administration rules. When the *Duquesne Duke* returned, it continued to carry notices and clarifications of requirement for veterans. In December of 1946 the university sanctioned the formation of an organization for veteran students known as the Duquesne University Veterans' Association. One of its acts was to establish a "cash your check here" program on campus to make it more convenient for out-of-town veterans to receive their subsidy payments.

Comments such as, "Vets get everything free," and, "The vets get too many privileges; even the school is being run for them," were registered with *Duke* reporters in the fall of 1946. In a sense, perhaps the school was being run for them. A thousand more came at the beginning of the second semester in February of 1947. By the fall semester veterans numbered 3122, making them 64 percent of the student body, and their number continued to rise. Many felt their presence had affected academic standards, though opinion was divided on which way—in a student opinion poll a majority thought that standards were rising, but a large minority felt that they were declining.

Bickering over the effect of the veterans continued for years. In an otherwise upbeat 1949 Christmas issue, the *Duquesne Magazine* editorialized about the appearance of what it called the "passing" student, "accentuated by a flush of veterans who were anxious to put in their four years and then snare a good job." An angry veteran countered that he and his fellows had actually raised standards on campus by their maturity and serious attitude toward studies. The veteran, he said, "has forsaken extra-curricular activities for his studies and has caused the death of the 'rah-rah' life on campus." The truth was that although slightly fewer As were given out in 1948 than in 1944, the overall distribution of grades remained largely stable.

The returning veterans were finding adjustment to civilian life in college not merely a financial strain but an emotional one as well. For example, when they first returned, those who had served as officers expected preferential treatment from ex-enlisted men, but the latter would have none of it. Also, many veterans declined the opportunity to join campus organizations that involved the mild but silly humiliation of initiations. Others opined that such organizations were clique-ridden and undemocratic. As a spoof, one group of young men began their own "fraternity," Alpha Bing Bing, and wore a distinguishing yellow sweater with a bottle-opener insignia. Having seen the horrors of war, they could not easily cast off the maturing effects of their experiences. They furthermore refused to submit to the indignities of freshman initiation by wearing dinks or parading through the streets in bizarre clothing. Like most postwar colleges and universities, Duquesne was largely a campus of freshmen now, with few upperclassmen to enforce the Freshman Rules. Despite all the publicity in the *Duquesne Duke* happily proclaiming the revival of campus organizations, its own survey revealed that 75 percent of the students belonged to no organization at all. With a wife, studies, part-time job, and a baby in the crib or on the way, most veterans did not have the time for such activities.

By the spring of 1948, so many students had children that the *Duquesne Duke* held its first Diaper Derby photo contest with 73 entries of children three years of age or younger. By the following year, although many of the veterans had already graduated and moved on, the contest still had 43 entries, several of them from two-child families and some whose mothers were university students.

A 1948 Disabled American Veterans' survey revealed that with average monthly expenses of $106 and subsistence pay of $65 ($90 with dependents), more than a third of the veterans had to work just to make ends meet. In March of that year, a subsistence increase to $75 was still far below expenses. It also was far below the $210 per month take-home pay earned by the average American worker in 1948. The *Duquesne Duke* carried articles on jobs held by vets, ranging from babysitting to bartending. Of course, many non-veteran students worked as well. Part-time jobs ranging in pay from 40 cents to $1.30 per hour were held by five-eighths of the student body.[25]

The GI bill had a life expectancy of four years from date of discharge or until July 25, 1951. Students whose benefits ran out before final examinations had to apply for special permission to complete their courses. This stipulation may have had a significant impact on enrollments. The number of veterans at Duquesne peaked at 3122 in the fall of 1947, constituting about 64 percent of the student body. Despite a drop in the number of veterans to 3000 in the fall of 1948, making them about half the enrollment, the total student body reached an all-time high of 5280. With the graduation of 966 in the spring of 1950, the largest commencement class in Duquesne history up to that time, the great surge of students had passed. In the four years following the end of World War II, the GI Bill made the dream of a college education a reality for many who otherwise would not have had such an opportunity. In this democratization of American higher education, Duquesne University was privileged to play a vital role.

The Administration Copes— And Congress Helps

When the flood of incoming veterans hit, the administration tried to simplify registration with a new procedure involving the distribution of course cards. Separate registration days for freshmen and sophomores, juniors and seniors were also introduced. Because of the volume of students, class schedules had to be picked up at the registrar's office rather than mailed as had previously been the case. A $15 activity fee was instituted to cover the use of the gym; participation in debates and intramurals; admittance to musical programs, dramatic productions, and athletic events; publication fees for the student newspaper and literary magazine; and use of the library, which had previously been covered by a wartime library fee.

Tuition income realized from the enlarged student body was not that great. In 1947–48 tuition covered only 68 percent of the expenses involved in running the university. Yet, the great rise in the student population necessitated additional facilities which would have to be hastily erected at a time when building costs were abnormally high, since construction materials and labor were both in short supply after the war. Moreover, the costs would be paid for during leaner years after the surge of veterans had passed.

Fortunately, Congress passed two important pieces of legislation: the Mead Bill for the distribution of surplus armed forces equipment to universities and colleges, and the Lanham Act, which covered the expense of moving and erecting surplus military barracks buildings. Under the Mead Bill, Duquesne received such things as cafeteria tables and chairs, which the *Duquesne Duke* said looked "suspiciously army-colored"—and a gigantic boiler from the Portsmouth Naval Yard. It was rolled across the gym floor and into a hole cut into the power plant wall to heat the growing campus.

Far more important was the Lanham Act, under which Duquesne received four barracks buildings. Two of the buildings, placed end to end as one long hall on the site where Trinity Hall was later erected, were used as classrooms. Another, overlooking Locust Street, was used for laboratories, and the third, located along Bluff Street, became an activities building and lounge. The university built garages under the student lounge and activities building. Used now by the priests at Trinity Hall, the garages survive as the sole reminder of the barracks. During the summer of 1947, the buildings were erected around the perimeter of the athletic field, which was still being used as an ROTC drill field. The Lanham Act required that the buildings be placed on level ground, and the scrimmage field was the only level ground of sufficient size to be found on the campus.

Notices were posted prohibiting smoking in the wooden buildings, but the university became more aware of the danger when a neon sign atop a downtown building caught fire and sparks blew toward the still uncompleted structures on the Bluff one night in late October. The Holy Ghost fathers rounded up a crew of students who helped stand guard over the buildings with fire extinguishers until Pittsburgh firemen succeeded in putting out the blaze below. The student newspaper issued weekly reminders of the no-smoking regulations, but they were regularly ignored until the *Duke* carried an article accompanied by photographs of students at Fordham University trying desperately to save their belongings from a barracks-building fire. This resulted in a crackdown on smoking in or near the wooden buildings and the installation of a fire alarm system. By this time, the buildings were looking clean and modern, and the University was considering facing them with brick and surrounding them with plantings to make them a permanent part of the campus.

Postwar ROTC

Though the United States had won World War II, the specter of war continued to loom. Consequently, the Reserve Officer Training Corps was restored to its prewar strength in the fall of 1946 and included Army Air Force ROTC, established at Duquesne with 138 cadets. In February of 1947 a professor of military science for the Army Air Force ROTC, Major George K. Sandman, organized a Duquesne Squadron of the Air Force Association with 37 members. Naval recruiters came to campus offering four-year enlistment packages and set up a naval recruiting office in the Fitzsimons Building. By the fall of 1947 the ROTC increased its staff by four to adequately train 300 elementary cadets and 160 advanced cadets.

A rifle team was organized, and in 1950 it succeeded in winning the prestigious Hearst National Perishing Rifle Regimental championship. The honorary ROTC society, Scabbard and Blade, inactive since 1942, was reactivated and joined by another, the Pershing Rifles. The Ninth Annual Military Ball, held January 15, 1948, was the only formal dance of the school year. Corsages were banned because of the high cost of flowers, but otherwise the evening was a splendid display of the importance and prestige that postwar Duquesne attached to ROTC. By the fall of 1948, Army ROTC had nearly doubled, with approximately 700 cadets. And ROTC administrators felt quite at home on the Bluff, as their offices were located in the same barracks building that contained the lounge.

Officers of the newly formed United States Air Force, no longer a branch of the army, appeared on campus to describe pilot training and nonrelated officer candidate opportunities in February 1948. Reflecting the division of the army and the air force as distinct military branches, the Eleventh Air Force ROTC group was eliminated as an operational unit at Duquesne and an Air ROTC command took its place, headquartered in Harrisburg. The Air ROTC now had its own society, a branch of Prop and Wing begun by 44 Duquesne cadets during their summer training at Langley Air Force Base, Virginia.

The National Guard began offering special opportunities with pay to World War II veterans who were willing to serve in the reserve. The National Guard also recruited from the ROTC.

Plans were announced in March of 1947 for Universal Military Training (UTM). All civilians between the ages of 17 and 20 were required to participate in this one-year training program. The proposal was an outgrowth of the compulsory military training for freshmen and sophomore men begun at Duquesne in October 1942, designed to replace physical education and required for graduation from every school in the university. Despite the military preparedness focus, the two-hour per week fitness course included boxing, wrestling, football, basketball, hand-to-hand fighting, military track, soccer, tumbling and calisthenics, and an obstacle course.

The Communist Threat

The reasons for military training were much changed in postwar America. The Soviet Union and international communism were perceived as grave threats to world peace. Even before World War II, communism had been given the cold shoulder on the Bluff. When a nationwide one-hour student "strike for peace" had been called for April 12, 1935, the *Duquesne Duke* had labeled it "red" and "communistic." On the appointed day, classes went on as usual at Duquesne, and the feature editor of the *Duke* decried the strike saying that the "Communistic movement's direct aim is the overthrow of American government." Perhaps as an answer to the editorial, vandals had painted the words, "REMEMBER THE WAR DEAD—NEVER AGAIN," signed with a huge hammer and sickle, on the board fence that lined the edge of the athletic field overlooking downtown. The university administration lost no time in having the sign painted over. Only days before the sign incident, the *Duke* had condemned American foreign policy in an editorial titled "United States Government Is Indifferent to Communistic Mexico's Reign of Terror" (May 25, 1935). But in an editorial in the spring of 1936 the *Duke* condemned the requirement of teacher loyalty oaths. Three years later, however, it reported without comment the new requirement that NYA students must take oaths of allegiance to the United States.

After the war, the entire international situation had changed dramatically with the beginning of the Cold War. At the local level, Pittsburgh, like many other cities, became a hotbed of

57. The very organized Rev. Raymond Kirk, C.S.Sp., succeeded Callahan as President of Duquesne University, 1940–1946. Kirk was an entirely homegrown product. A native of nearby Mt. Pleasant, Pennsylvania, he graduated from both Duquesne Prep School and the university. He took a doctorate of education at New York University, then spent a year of working in a parish of New York's Harlem. Then Kirk returned to teach in the prep school. He helped Duquesne's School of Education achieve its state certification and served as dean of the school. He had a gift for administration, and Duquesne was in for an onslaught of efficiency under his hand. Kirk faced a difficult task; he took over a university $450,000 in debt which also suffered from declining enrollments. His wartime administration helped Duquesne through a period when the university considered closing its doors for lack of students. The prep school, a part of Duquesne since its beginning, did close in 1941.

58. In 1942 officials seriously considered closing the university. Enrollment had fallen dramatically; seventy-one colleges across the country had already closed. But once again Duquesne's fortunes reversed. A 1942 army survey resulted in the selection of the university as a training site for the first group of 350 officers and cadets in the Army Air Corps. President Kirk's brother, the Pittsburgh City Treasurer, knew some serendiptiously placed people. Tuition, room and board for these cadets kept the university open. Cadets of the 328th College Training Detachment spent five months at Duquesne; one fifth left each month for flight training as new cadets took their place. Here cadets parade on Vickroy Street in 1943.

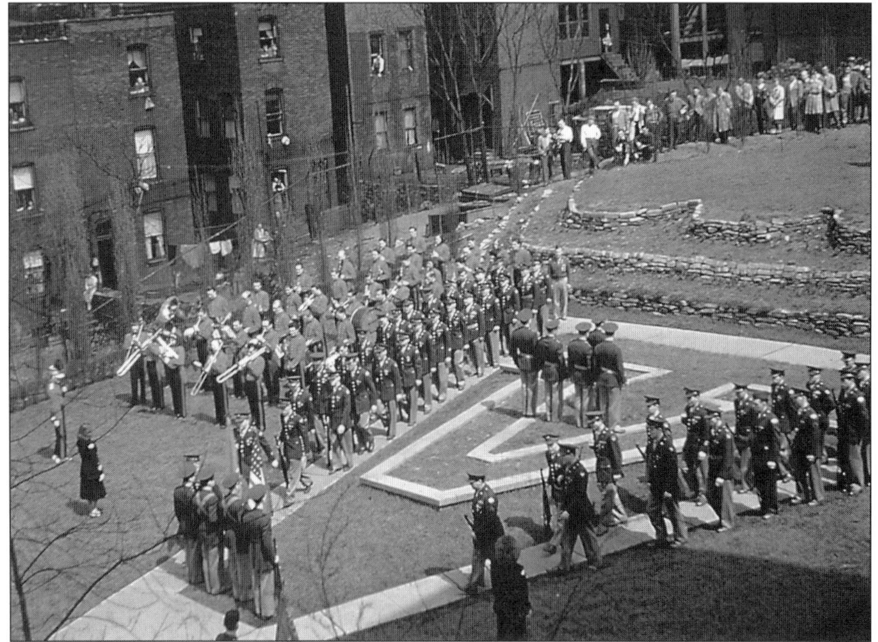

59. Even before the war ended, the University celebrated and offered thanks with the dedication of the Our Lady of Victory statue and garden, located between Canevin Hall and the library. Dr. Lester Pierce, founder of the Tamburitza Orchestra, first conceived of the statue and garden. The six foot statue of the Blessed Mother and Child was made in Chicago, by Daprato Studios. This photo shows the dedication on Labor Day, 1945. Two years later the garden was the scene of another service, in memory of those who did not return from the war. Each fall, the shrine was the center of Duquesne's Armistice Day ceremonies. In the past few decades, the university has added plaques in memory of alumni who servedin Korea, Vietnam, Grenada, Panama, and the Persian Gulf War.

60. Every campus building was over capacity, and service areas like the cafeteria and the library established increasingly stringent rules to spread their resources over the burgeoning student body. "Traditional" students began to resent their veteran colleagues, and there was bickering among the students. Additional facilities were a must, but despite enrollment income, money was still scarce. Tuition income in 1947–48 met only 68% of the university's operating expenses. Fortunately, after the war Congress allowed spare federal government equipment to be given to colleges and universities. In this 1947 photo, a boiler from the Ports-mouth Naval Yard is being fitted into a gymnasium window on Colbert Street for use in the adjacent power plant. Workers rolled it across the gym, cut a hole in the wall to the power plant, and connected the boiler to the campus heating system.

61. Reflecting the growth of the chemical industry during the war, the Chemistry Department was geared toward industrial research and development as well as teaching. In May 1949 the department dedicated its new laboratories in the North Barracks. So many veterans were interested in chemistry that additional laboratories were badly needed as the curriculum became less theoretical and more experimental. Now in new quarters with modern equipment, the chemistry department received its first research grants, totaling $5,500, from the Research Corporation of New York.

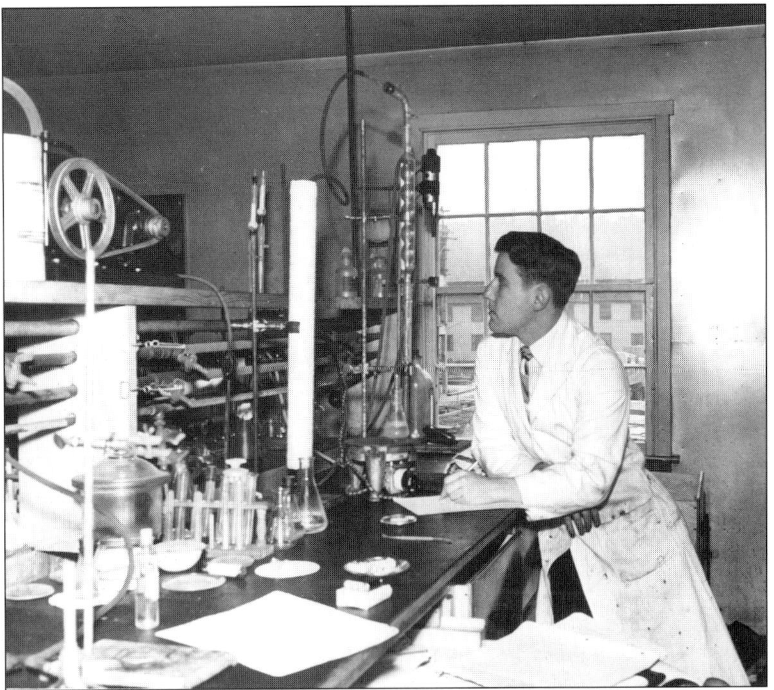

62. Under the Lanham Act, Duquesne received four barracks buildings. Two of the buildings, placed end to end on the site where Trinity Hall was later built, became classrooms. Another, overlooking Locust Street, became laboratories. Earlier, the university had purchased Quonset huts and placed them on the gym roof. These buildings, shown here in 1949, served Duquesne's needs long after the rush of veterans had passed.

63. Father Francis P. Smith, C.S.Sp., president 1946–1950.

The war years, the school's financial and accreditation problems all were a great strain on Father Kirk. He suffered a heart attack in 1940 from which he never really recovered. In 1946 his health forced him to resign as president of Duquesne. Having saved the university, Kird was succeeded by his vice-president, Father Francis Smith.

Like Callahan and Kirk, Smith was a Duquesne alumnus, graduating in 1930. He was ordained as a Holy Ghost father in 1933, taught at St. Basil College and St. Mary Seminary in Connecticut, and took his masters at Catholic University in 1939. He began his Ph.D. at Fordham, but left his studies for an assignment teaching philosophy at Duquesne in 1940. Dean of the College of Liberal Arts and Sciences in 1943, he became vice-president of the university in 1944. Under his administration the university experienced a surge of ex-G.I.s that filled the school to bursting. Fiscally responsible, Smith was a careful steward. Unfortunately, it was a time when the university needed a fundraiser and a visionary.

64. In the fall of 1946, approximately 3,000 veterans swelled enrollment to 4,107. By 1948, Duquesne reached a peak of 5,280 students. This postwar, overgrown student body meant long lines everywhere. These students are waiting to register for classes in September, 1947.

65. One of the four donated barracks, located on Bluff Street, became an activities building and lounge. The first floor served as the student lounge. Under the building, the university built garages. Used now by the priests at Trinity Hall, they are the sole reminder of the barracks.

66. Current Pittsburghers may find it ironic that parking was yet another area of frustration for the beleaguered Duquesne student. Always in short supply on the Bluff, street parking had long been taken by downtown office workers who parked early, when the spaces were still available. Duquesne's complaints fell on deaf ears, until, in the fall of 1947, students took matters into their own hands. Led by the Veterans' Association, they picketed in the street. Fearful of adverse publicity, the city's Bureau of Traffic Planning posted two-hour parking signs on the streets adjacent to university property within the week. The *Duquesne Duke* rejoiced: "And so ends the parking worries of the students. The early morning fight for parking places is a thing of the past."

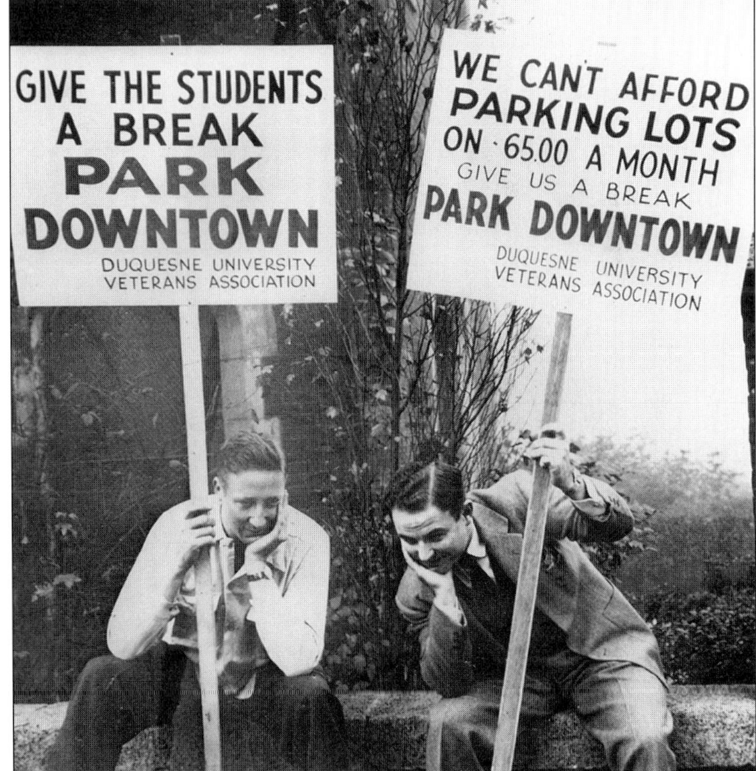

Pittsburgh *Post-Gazette*

Pittsburgh *Post-Gazette*

67. Compulsory ROTC training, begun in 1942, continued after the war as a UMT course — Universal Military Training. The course replaced physical education at Duquesne, and every school required it for graduation by 1947. Though the U.S. had won in WWII, the country still feared being caught unprepared for war. The Reserve Officer Training Corps was restored to its prewar strength in 1946, and a division of Army Air Force ROTC was established with 138 cadets. By 1948, Army ROTC had nearly 700 cadets. In this photo, students present themselves for a weekly drill.

68. Postwar shortages did not halt development of Duquesne's schools and departments. A model pharmacy, a gift of the George Kelly Drug Company, was built on first floor Canevin Hall in 1948. Since the professional practice of pharmacy required 2400 hours of actual dispensary work, most students held part time jobs to enable them to acquire this experience before graduation. A great deal of practice work took place in the George A. Kelly, Sr., Pharmacy.

69. The Department of Biological Science expanded considerably with the opening of Gregor Mendel Hall in 1949. The five story building located at 701 Forbes Avenue was thoroughly renovated. Cost of purchase and renovation: $107,000. This photo shows the renovation in progress.

70. Radio was popular on the Bluff almost from its beginnings, and, inevitably, Duquesne had the first collegiate radio station in Pittsburgh, which was named, appropriately, WDUQ. Establishing the new radio station meant installing two radio studios on the second floor of Old Main. Note the "Studio A" and "B" signs in the background of the photo. The self-named "Voice of Education in Pittsburgh" soon became the voice of Duquesne, and an outlet for everything from quiz shows to football games.

71. One popular show broadcast over the new WDUQ station was "Fiddle Faddle," a student-written variety show which developed into a half-hour comedy. Among the many stars who visited the campus was Rosemary Clooney, shown here on the air with "Fiddle-Faddlers" Al Bird and Al Hallaman.

72. Of all campus activities, sports at Duquesne rebounded from their hiatus during the war slowest. Football returned late and briefly, without its former glory. The strong coaching staff had been lured away to other schools when Duquesne disbanded its teams during the war. The team had no home field, which meant renting other area facilities for any home game. More importantly, they had no practice field; the administration, desperately trying to accommodate its huge postwar enrollment, had commandeered the scrimmage field as a site for army surplus barracks. In their first official year of play (1947), the team finished with two wins and eight defeats. In 1948, it had two wins and nine defeats. In this photo, the Dukes play in a near empty stadium. Other teams soon refused to play at Duquesne, where there were no fans and no box office receipts. In 1950, their coach of two years, Duquesne graduate Phil Ahwesh, was called to active duty in Korea. The university discontinued football in 1951.

73. Duquesne students made some show of support for their football team. Many banners and displays appeared in the week before the homecoming game against Villanova. WDUQ arranged to broadcast the festivities and the game. This photo shows the homecoming parade at the corner of Vickroy and Colbert Streets in the fall of 1950.

74. Members of the basketball team pose with coach "Chick" Davies at the end of his long career in 1948. He was a man who regularly shouted vulgarities at game officials, a man who had been known to take chewing tobacco from his mouth and throw it at a player during practice. And yet he won affection and respect that lasted long after people left his team — some of them to play professional ball. Throughout his 21-year career, Davies gave Duquesne one of the strongest basketball teams in the nation, one consistently known for its drive and persistence.

75. The Dukes in action against Villanova. During that first postwar season, the University of Tennessee refused to play a schedule game against Duquesne because one of the Dukes, Chuck Cooper (number 15 in the picture) was black. Coach Davies refused to pull Cooper from the team and Tennessee canceled at the last minute. The Dukes finished this first season with 20 victories out of 21 games, and Cooper and Joe Camic were selected for the Tri-state team. Cooper was All-American in 1950, and he became the first African American drafted to play professional basketball when he joined the Boston Celtics that fall.

76. After a 23-year hiatus, baseball officially returned in 1948. Tryouts attracted 150 students that spring. Like the university's other teams, the baseballers found themselves nomads. Practices were held at South Park, until the team was forced to move to the Aspinwall Hospital diamond. They won their first game at Forbes Field, then learned that, due to resodding, the field would be unavailable for the rest of the season. In announcing home games, the school newspaper often noted that no location had been set at the time of writing. Shown here is the 1950 team. Team pitcher and, later, Chairman of the Board of Directors, Carl Grefenstette, is in the last row, fourth from the left.

communist and anticommunist activity. In 1945 Father Kirk asked Reverend Charles Owen Rice, a diocesan priest who was a part-time professor in the Sociology Department, to start an Institute of Management-Labor Relations. The noncredit classes were enormous in their influence. It was estimated that perhaps half of all Pittsburgh-area union presidents and business agents attended them. And while they dealt mainly with themes having nothing to do with communism, Rice's biographer claims, that "these classes, together with undergraduate classes Rice was also instructing, would produce for him a whole generation of recruits to assist in his struggle against the communists."[26] Certainly the institute did promote anti-communist activities. In 1947 Rice authored a pamphlet, "How to Decontrol Your Union of Communists," with the help of Duquesne undergraduate students and the facilities of the institute. More than 30,000 copies of the ten-cent pamphlet offering "hard-headed advice on how to battle the Reds in one's own local" were sold.[27] The Institute of Labor-Management Relations lasted until 1950, when Rice was told that his services were no longer needed in the Sociology Department. Rice claims that U.S. Steel, which accused him of "poisoning young minds" in his undergraduate courses with union rhetoric, wanted his ouster from that department.[28]

The end of the Institute was by no means the end of the anticommunist activity on the Bluff. Communism was much on the minds of Duquesne students. When both elevators in the Fitzsimons Building simultaneously failed to operate in 1947, the *Duquesne Duke* article relating the incident was titled jokingly, "It's the Commies." More serious was another story by *Duquesne Duke* assistant editor, Paul J. Browne, titled, "I Was a Communist for Twenty-Four Hours." Browne related how he allowed a copy of the communist newspaper, *The Daily Worker*, to be seen by a sales clerk, policeman, bartender, etc., as he went about his business. The *Duke* staffer was amazed at how people's attitudes became suddenly hostile when they caught sight of the paper.

Despite the anticommunist frenzy that shook the country in those years, Duquesne managed to keep its operations stable, and there were no major disturbances.

Postwar School of Pharmacy

Even postwar shortages did not prevent the continued development of Duquesne's schools and departments. In 1945 the School of Pharmacy announced the publication of a quarterly magazine named *The Duquesne Pharmacist*. A thousand-dollar raffle with tickets priced at a dollar apiece defrayed publishing costs and purchased laboratory equipment as well. The school hoped the new publication would become as successful as its other one, *The Science Counselor*, then a decade old and still under the editorship of Dean Muldoon. That periodical was "supported by Duquesne . . . at considerable expense to the University. But due to its outstanding work in the field of science education, it has received the hearty support of the University Authorities."[29] *The Science Counselor* had a circulation of 3500 and was selected in 1951 for distribution in Germany. It ceased publication in 1967. *The Duquesne Pharmacist* lasted only till 1955.

Duquesne's Alpha Beta chapter of Rho Chi, the national pharmacy honorary fraternity founded at Duquesne in 1941, had the most stringent entrance requirements of all the honoraries on campus. Candidates had to have a B average and were not eligible for membership until the second semester of their junior year. In 1948 this elite organization had only 15 members and 30 alumni. The Pharmacy School also sponsored Lambda Kappa Sigma sorority and the Pharmaceutical Association.

This quest for excellence was the mark of the pharmacy school. It celebrated its silver jubilee in the spring of 1950 with a special pharmacy edition of the *Duquesne Duke* and a symposium at the William Penn Hotel with speakers concentrating on the growth of antibiotics. Dr. Hugh Muldoon, still dean of the school at that time, knew each of the pharmacy students—academically high achievers as a group—and taught many courses himself. Quality was maintained by limiting class size to 60. The first two years of study centered on theory. Junior-year courses were all supplemented by laboratory work, and the senior student concentrated on gaining actual pharmacy experience and preparing for the state comprehensive examinations. Since the professional practice of pharmacy required 2400 hours of actual dispensary work, the students held part-time jobs to enable them to acquire the necessary hours prior to graduation. Practice work was aided by a modern pharmaceutical store on the first floor of Canevin Hall. The George A. Kelly, Sr., Pharmacy, a gift of the George A. Kelly Drug Company, was officially dedicated in October of 1948.

Dean Muldoon, who kept bachelor quarters at the William Penn, dedicated his life to the building of the School of Pharmacy. He said that as a student he never saw the dean of the pharmacy school where he studied until commencement and vowed that would never be the case at Duquesne. He wanted to know "what each student is doing each day."[30] With apparent boundless energy, he appeared to come close to doing that. Plus he authored a 648-page text, *Organic Chemistry*, in 1948. Muldoon's national reputation was such that he was chosen as one of five American experts by the Headquarters of the Supreme Commander of the Allied Powers for a summer pharmaceutical mission to occupied Japan.

Postwar Science Studies

The Department of Biological Science underwent great expansion with the opening of Gregor Mendel Hall, dedicated on March 19, 1949. Dr. Tage Ellinger, head of the department, announced that 500 visitors had viewed the newly renovated facilities in a five-story building purchased by the university at 701 Forbes Avenue. Costing $107,000, it represented the department's second expansion in three years. In 1946, at a cost of $40,000, the university had acquired two quonset huts, which were erected on the roof of the gymnasium. Both were used as laboratories; one was given to biology, the other to chemistry.

Reflecting the growth of the chemical industry during the war, the Chemistry Department was geared toward industrial research and development as well as teaching. The four-year program was aimed at preparing students for highschool chemistry teaching, graduate work in chemistry, and medical school.

In May of 1949 the Chemistry Department dedicated its new laboratories in the North Barracks. So many veterans were interested in chemistry that additional laboratories were badly needed as the curriculum became less theoretical and more experimental. The Chemistry Department, now in new quarters—and expecting to outgrow them in three years—and supplied with modern laboratories, received its first research grants, totaling $5,500, from the Research Corporation of New York. The grants were given to promote the research of Drs. Hentzymant and Gawron. The department was getting other notice, too. In 1947 the chairman of the Chemistry Department, Dr. Tobias H. Dunkelberger, was selected to preview and review the Graduate Record Examination. Modest by later standards, these achievements represented a coming-of-age for the university and were the foundations for still greater achievements in the future.

Postwar School of Business Administration

As schools and departments throughout Duquesne registered their highest enrollments ever—the graduate school had 2296—the School of Business Administration had the majority of the veterans. Housed in what was unofficially called the "Fitzsimons College" were 1200 day students and 1700 evening students. In 1946 men outnumbered women 35 to one. In the spring of 1950, the U.S. Department of Labor announced that career opportunities were most plentiful for business administration graduates. On-campus recruiting by businesses for college graduate training programs became a springtime tradition. The School of Business Administration increased its liberal arts requirements and instituted required reading lists in the fall of 1946 to give its students a wider background and better prepare them to move into executive training programs.

Organizations in the School of Business Administration included the Society for the Advancement of Management (SAM), the Duchess Club (marking its silver anniversary in 1949), and the Evening Dukes and Duchesses, a newer club, established for the social, academic and professional betterment of its members and featuring evening lectures by faculty and leaders in industry. Beta Alpha Pi, the honorary business fraternity, was extremely active. Along with broadcasting a regular radio program, they also held banquets, hosted speakers, and held parties for the children at St. Paul's and St. Anthony's orphanages for which they collected toys and clothing. Once a year, at the Faculty Smoker, the fraternity hosted its "Quizdown," and the winner's name was inscribed on the "Little Brown Jug" prominently displayed in Dean Wright's office.

Other Postwar Changes

All departments seemed to share in the new enthusiasm on the Bluff. The Psychology Club held its first organizational meeting in the fall of 1948. The following year, the university approved its affiliation as a chapter of Psi Chi, the psychology honorary society. The year 1949 also saw the formation of the History Club.

The old activities building on Vickroy Street, its name changed to the "guidance building," became home to the dean of women, the university chaplain, and the dean of men and director of student welfare. The second floor held the testing departments of both the Psychology Testing Department which concentrated largely on research, and the University Testing Department. The latter was devoted mainly to guidance purposes, reflecting the country's new interest in IQs and aptitudes. The second floor also housed the university dispensary.

In February of 1948 journalism and advertising were separated from the English Department and reorganized as an independent department in the College of Liberal Arts and Sciences under Father Lauritis. This was to mark the beginning of dynamic developments in the publication of the *Duquesne Duke*, in newswriting and advertising courses, and in radio broadcasting.

WDUQ

Almost from its beginnings, radio was popular on the Bluff. In the 1930s the university made a substantial commitment to the medium in the form of a studio. In the 1940s that commitment was to result in the first collegiate radio station in the city.

When WPGH, a local radio station wishing to present a new college program for and by students of Pittsburgh's five colleges, issued a call for students to audition to do commentary, disc jockeying, musical renditions, or literary readings, Father Lauritis was interested. The Varsity Show began broadcasting on Saturday afternoons in the fall of 1948, and within the month, WEDO in McKeesport was presenting a Sunday afternoon show of college talent. CBS's celebrated "Columbia School of the Air," in which Duquesne students were frequent presenters, had been achieving popularity since the previous year. Father Lauritis wanted Duquesne to have an independent station of its very own, and put out a call for student tryouts for his proposed FM station in March of 1949. The new station was named, appropriately enough, WDUQ. By May his station was approved by the Federal Communications Commission on 89.3

megacycles. Two radio studios, each 19 × 22 feet, were installed on the second floor of the administration building. Tradition gave way to modernity when the steeple section of the 64-year-old cupola on the roof was removed to make way for the 16-foot broadcast tower. Owing to the station's small broadcast area, Father Lauritis formed the University Broadcast System of 14 FM stations to extend Duquesne's range. The network was first utilized to carry the Duquesne-Muhlenherg football game from Allentown on October 1, 1949.

The National Record Mart was enlisted to supply recordings for a Sunday afternoon opera series but mostly the university looked to its own resources to supply programming. Professor Zimmerman from business administration gave a 15-minute daily talk, the Tamburitzans performed regular Friday night broadcasts, and there was a daily broadcast from the School of Music. WDUQ also presented Catholic Theatre Guild productions and a children's program called the "Two to Twelve Club." By the beginning of October, the *Duquesne Duke* had begun to carry the weekly broadcast schedule. When a new Westinghouse transmitter was installed, it also necessitated the removal of the 16-foot broadcast tower on the administration building and its replacement with one 150 feet tall.

New shows continued to spring up: the Psychology Department's "Looking at the World;" a variety show, "Fiddle Faddle;" a disc-jockey hosted, "Campus Caravan;" "The Forensic League" featuring high school groups; the "Woman's Page;" the "World News;" the "World of Business;" the "Business Ticker;" and the Sociology Department's "Better Living." Religious programs included "Lady of Fatima," "Faith and Freedom," and "Lives of the Saints." Poetry readings were featured in the program called "Intermezzo." In addition to carrying Duquesne football games, the station also broadcast a daily "Sports Review."

The official birthday of WDUQ was December 15, 1949. A number of local announcers, including Rege Cordic, Paul Shannon, and Duquesne alumnus Ralph Fallert, were on hand for the occasion. President Smith cited Ted Kenney, a KDKA engineer, for his assistance in supervising the installation. At the dedication, WDUQ's power was increased from 10 to 2750 watts and its frequency was changed to 91.5 megacycles. The "Voice of Education in Pittsburgh," as the station called itself, could now reach all of Pittsburgh.

The progress that the station made in so short a time was heralded by the *Duquesne Magazine*: "The tottering baby of last August has shaken off its cellophane wrappings and taken on the cloak of respectability among the air-waves of Pittsburgh." The magazine also applauded the handful of students who stayed on the Bluff over the Christmas holidays to keep the station broadcasting daily—"a bit of the old *esprit de corps* that makes Duquesne what it is." The article also appealed to the students to get involved with the station by volunteering their services as scriptwriters, entertainers, or even by donating phonograph records to the station's music library.

WDUQ aired one of the nation's first telephone call-in shows, "Quick Quiz," on current events. In that time before telephone hookups, callers were not heard over the air; their answers were announced by the show host. By the fall of 1950, WDUQ was broadcasting the Carnegie Hall lecture series and the "Man on Campus" opinion poll. "Operation Learning," on the history of education in Pittsburgh, was a new effort for 1951.

WDUQ was never run entirely by students. B. Kendall Crane, a man with almost 20 years of experience in the field, came to Duquesne to teach evening courses in radio and helped with the installation of station apparatus. Crane became WDUQ's director and served in that capacity for 22 years. He encouraged live programming, especially dramatic productions complete with sound effects. Orchestras and bands performing in the city would be broadcast directly from the dance areas. Crane's favorite, "Fiddle Faddle," was a student-written variety show which developed into a half-hour comedy. Crane related how hectic the early broadcasts were:

> Many times when the program was going on the air, on Friday night, the last page was still being typed. But somehow or other, that page always got there. We shoved it under the door and the staff got it and went on.

The installation of a new public address system in the gym made it possible for WDUQ to enlist its music library in supplying music for university dances. An evening's music cost the sponsor $20. Duquesne's radio station did much to give added exposure to the university and for many it was not only the voice of education in Pittsburgh, but the voice of Duquesne.

Postwar Publications

The *Duquesne Duke*, with a circulation of 5500 by 1950, was recognized as one of the top collegiate papers in the country and was also one of the first college papers in the nation to install the Coxhead print process. The use of a composing machine and the offset or photolithographic, method of printing gave a clearer, cleaner product in which photographs could be reproduced more accurately. The *Duke's* photo contest reached new prominence with the new method, and a pictorial page became a weekly feature of the expanded paper. On March 5, 1950, the *Duquesne Duke* celebrated its silver jubilee with a 52-page special edition known as the "Big Duke." It had been cited as an honor paper by the Associated Collegiate Press for four consecutive semesters, 1948–1950. In a 1948 editorial, the paper applauded the university for its trust in the staff and the lack of censorship.

Sharing the administration building's third-floor location with the *Duke* was the *Duquesne Magazine*. It combined the literary works and reported news of all three sectors of the university: students, faculty, and alumni. The administration hoped that the magazine would pull alumni into a deeper involvement with the university and its current needs. The *Duquesne Magazine* first appeared in April of 1947, and within three years it received the National Scholastic Press Association superior All-American rating. This accolade notwithstanding, the university announced in the spring of 1951 that it was suspending publication of the *Duquesne Magazine* and returning to separate student and alumni periodicals. Presenting a balanced format for all three groups had proved too difficult for the student staff.

After the financial disaster of the 1929 *Monacle*, no yearbook was published until 1947, and it was likewise a disaster. In February of 1947, the Student Council even held a hop called the Sweetheart Ball to finance it. All 1500 copies went on sale May 1 at $5 apiece, and by fall the 800 remaining copies were reduced to $2 each. The working-commuting students of 1947 were no more interested in a yearbook than their working-commuting predecessors of 18 years earlier. Another yearbook would not be attempted until 1956.

Postwar Student Activities

Activities on the Bluff were coordinated by a new Student Council established in the fall of 1947. It proved to be more active than many students wanted. For example, it proposed fines for smoking in the barracks building or using the wrong stairs in Canevin Hall. Duquesne partially funded some of its activities through the sale of patron tickets to downtown businessmen. Such promotional efforts were so active, however, that some businessmen complained of their frequency.

One of the most dynamic organizations on campus was the National Federation of Catholic College Students (NFCCS). More commonly referred to as Catholic Action, the NFCCS had begun at Duquesne in 1941. During the war low enrollments forced it to affiliate with the Newman Club, but in 1946 it emerged as an independent and revitalized entity, although it still jointly sponsored activities such as the Sadie Hawkins Day Dance with the Newman Club. Among its activities was sponsorship of the intercollegiate May Day celebrations at Mount Mercy College, involving all of the colleges and universities in the city. Another was its hosting, in the spring of 1950, the national convention (over 800 persons) at the William Penn Hotel, with Archbishop Cushing of Boston as a special guest. The NFCCS was also in the religious forefront by sponsoring the first Cana Conferences in the city of Pittsburgh as preparation for students wishing to marry. In some ways the NFCCS was a transitional group, in that its concerns involved both those traditionally associated with college life and those that went beyond the confines of the university.

Community Involvement

The post-World War II student body was distinctly different and more practically tied to the larger community than previous generations at Duquesne. The Duquesne chapter of the Association of Childhood Education, formed in the fall of 1947, held a Christmas party for the first- and second-grade students at the nearby Forbes School in 1948.[31] Gamma Sigma music fraternity and Delta Mu Delta music sorority gave performances for orphanages, hospitals, and other institutions. Sigma Phi Delta sorority escorted children from St. Anthony's Village to the zoo. Beta Alpha Phi fraternity and Epsilon Eta Phi, the business administration sorority, held a Christmas party for 550 children at St. Paul's orphanage. Kappa Sigma Phi conducted a toy and clothing drive for St. Paul's orphanage. The Pan-Hellenic Council joined the Veterans' Entertainment Committee in supplying six or eight coeds to play cards, chat, and serve refreshments once a month at the Veterans' Hospital in Aspinwall. Requests for student entertainers for the veterans' hospitals led student thespian Don Brockett to write a show, which he performed with several friends. Together with other colleges and universities in the city, Duquesne participated in a choral group, a discussion group, and a journalism association. Community involvement also included public health aspects: syphilis and tuberculosis screenings and general physical examinations.

Marketing at Duquesne

One postwar phenomenon was the emergence of marketing on campus. Student representatives promoted Chesterfield cigarettes and Revlon cosmetics. The business manager of the *Duke* was the first to hold the position of Chesterfield representative on campus. He rewarded the best response to the paper's opinion poll with a free carton of cigarettes. Ads in the *Duquesne Duke* promoted study abroad and tours of Europe. Airline companies frequently advertised discounts for students returning home for the holidays with free airfare offered to any student who would serve as a representative in organizing group flights. Due to periodic rail strikes which wreaked havoc on the students' schedules, the airlines presented themselves as more reliable than the trains. Students could even take advantage of a company named Pittsburgh Stenographic Service. A student could dictate a research paper over the telephone and have it typed for 25 cents per page.

Bookstore Difficulties

An enlarged university forced the university bookstore, managed by Father William Hogan, to move into larger quarters in the basement of the administration building, where its opening was delayed by a shortage of lumber to build shelving. The bookstore had a difficult time securing all of the required textbooks and distributing them to the swollen student body. Despite much overtime spent in keeping bookstore shelves replenished, long lines formed each semester. Sometimes textbooks could not be secured until weeks after the beginning of the semester. While some students criticized the bookstore for incompetence, in reality it was postwar shortages and the inability of publishers to keep abreast of demand that were to blame. But by the fall of 1947, Father Hogan told the *Duke* staff, "We have been extremely fortunate this year in obtaining most of the necessary texts from the publishers. In only a few instances have we been unable to supply a particular text, and we hope to remedy that situation as soon as possible."

The bookstore's inventory expanded along with the student body. It stocked Duquesne T-shirts (including children's sizes), and a wide variety of gift selections. Even washing machines, television sets and electric mixers were on display, as the bookstore became a Westinghouse appliance franchise. In the fall of 1949 shoppers at the bookstore could boost their school spirit by buying a record album of Duquesne University songs, including the "Victory Song," the alma mater, the "Pep Song," the "Hike Song," and the "Dukes of Duquesne," all for $3.50.

The Postwar Tamburitzans

The Second World War brought hard times for the Tamburitzans, but it also provided some opportunities. Since their founding, the group had been composed entirely of men. The first woman to join the group was soprano soloist, Mary Verlich, in the 1939–1940 season. But as the men went off to war, it was the influx of young women, some not even affiliated with the university, that kept the group alive. The efforts of the Tamburitzan Scholarship Fund Committee and the dedication of the performers, who even as servicemen would join the troupe while on leave, maintained a nucleus for growth into a world-renowned institution after the war.

Although the group had begun as an orchestra, both singing and dancing entered the programs, and the original Eastern European emphasis had been expanded to include other cultural traditions, including American square dancing and even a Broadway revue. The 1946 program performed at the Nixon Theater for their Ninth Annual Concert included music and dances from Serbia, Slovenia, Bosnia, Dalmatia, and Croatia. Following intermission were selections from "New Yugoslavia" and Russia, popular American tunes, including Sigmund Romberg's "Desert Song," acrobatic dance, and a medley of service songs.

Folk Dancing

The postwar interest in traditional dancing encouraged Brunhilde E. Dorsch, eurhythmics professor in the School of Music, to begin the Folk Dancing Group. In its very first season, 1949–1950, the group gave performances at Duquesne and at Seton Hill College. Student interest was so great that Professor Dorsch gave folk and square dancing classes in the music school every Thursday. By the following October, the Folk Dancing group had lined up a busy schedule of performances, beginning with a Folk Festival in the campus theater. Their performances included Polish, Czechoslovakian, Jewish, Lithuanian, English, Scottish, German, Swedish, Greek, Brazilian, Mexican, and American dances.

Athletics Return: A Few Years of Football

Nothing so dramatically heralded Duquesne's postwar revival as the resuscitation of athletics. The announcement in the fall of 1946 that Charles R. "Chick" Davies would return to the Bluff to coach basketball was greeted with wild enthusiasm. The *Duquesne Duke* responded to complaints that the university wasn't reactivating football at the same time with the explanation that a football team would require long-range planning and a serious financial commitment. Football was played informally that fall under the coaching of Steve Sinko, who had assisted Buff Donelli as football coach at Duquesne. This was an experimental season of a freshman-squad football team playing local colleges and employing the new "T" formation. The excitement over the return of football caused the dean of men to announce the revival of the cheering squad as well. The all-male, four-member cheering squad appeared for the 1947 season, but they had their work cut out for them. They reported that the veterans wouldn't cheer, claiming that they felt self-conscious and that cheering seemed childish.

Duquesne's celebrity coach, Buff Donelli, had become an assistant coach at Columbia when Duquesne suspended football during the war. He was then offered the head coaching position at Boston College and invited Steve Sinko to join him as his assistant. Sinko resigned in January of 1947. Kass Kovalcheck, one of Buff Donelli's teammates when he played for Duquesne, was appointed head football coach after his release from the Navy. All-American Duquesne alumnus Johnny Rokisky served as his end coach for spring training. He was assisted by two other alumni, Johnny "Sandy" Yacina, who took over as end coach in August, and Joe Cibuls as line coach. Both Yacina and Cibulas had played on Duquesne's spectacular prewar teams and had their educations interrupted by military duty, Yacina at the close of football season during his senior year in 1941, and Cibulas in 1943 just before the beginning of his final semester. Both returned to Duquesne at the end of service to finish their degree programs in the School of Education. Al DeLuca, previously Sinko's assistant, was made freshman football coach and intramural director, Lou "Doc" Skender became assistant football and basketball coach, and W. John Davis, previously the graduate manager of athletics, was appointed athletic director. And a new position of moderator of athletics was designed and given to Father Salvator J. Federici. His role was to act as a liaison between the university administration and the athletic department and to guarantee that Duquesne's policy on athletics was upheld.

The first football season under Coach Kovalchek was holding at two wins and three losses by midseason, but the team was unable to score another victory and finished with a total of eight defeats. Nonetheless, Coach Kovalchek had high hopes for the following season. After spring practice in 1948, he announced, "Cooperation, spirit, and competition for first berths has been the keenest I've seen on the Bluff since 1927." But 1948 was no better; the "Kassmen" scored only two wins to nine losses, and Kass Kovalchek resigned at the end of the season.

Although the *Duquesne Duke* was doubtful of football's chances of success, even with alumni funding and support, Duquesne's president stood firmly behind the team. Father Smith declared, "I wish to reassure the student body that our plans for the return of the University football team to national prominence will be more effectually realized if all of us have more confidence and patience." After explaining in his open letter to the student body that part of the difficulty was the strength of the opposition for such a young team, he closed with, "Let all of us, then, in a spirit of faith and unity, look forward hopefully to the day when our program will come to complete achievement, this will take time."

Phil Ahwesh, another Duquesne graduate who had been a star under Donelli's coaching, had returned to Duquesne as freshman coach and stepped up into the head coaching position in the spring of 1949. One of Ashwesh's teammates, John Petchell, took over the freshman squad, which enjoyed a very successful season. The rebirth of school spirit was enormous when the varsity team won against Holy Cross. Students paraded through the city in a victory celebration that included visits to Pitt and Tech to sing Duquesne's praises. Pitt returned the favor by parading to the Bluff after one of its big wins. Many banners and displays appeared before the homecoming game against Villanova. As floats were prepared for the homecoming parade, WDUQ made arrangements to broadcast the festivities and game. Duquesne did not win its homecoming game, and as defeat followed defeat, school spirit evaporated. The scheduled student trip to accompany the team to Clemson was cancelled when only 25 students responded.

Lack of proper facilities was a persistent difficulty. Not only did the school not have a stadium, necessitating the rental of Forbes Field for home games, it no longer had a practice field. As the only level ground on campus, the scrimmage field became a victim of expansion as the site for the new barracks buildings. Football practice was moved across the river to Moore Field in the city's Brookline neighborhood. When other universities in the city happened to be playing, Duquesne could not draw enough supporters to cover the Forbes Field rental. Unable to offer visiting teams much of a crowd, Duquesne found it more and more difficult to schedule home games. Only two games in the 1949 season were played at home, and Duquesne's fortunes suffered. In view of the circumstances under which he competed, it was perhaps an accomplishment that coach Ahwesh's 1949 team scored two victories in eight games.

By the 1950 season Duquesne was able to schedule only two home games in a nine-game series. The only teams willing to meet them at Forbes Field were St. Bonaventure, coached by former Duquesne football coach Joe Bach, and Boston College, coached by Buff Donelli. Coach Ahwesh, a commanding officer in the National Guard, was called to active duty in the fall of 1950 during the Korean conflict. Phil Ahwesh and Father Francis R. Duffy, who agreed to serve as chaplain for Ahwesh's outfit, left on June 11, 1950. They were joined in Indiana by several members of the football squad who were called to active duty before the season got underway. He made the journey from Camp Atterbury, Indiana, for weekend games, but the university was unsure of how to proceed with Ahwesh under contract but unavailable for weekday practices. "Doc" Skender filled in as acting coach in what was to be Duquesne's last season. With a change in administration, intercollegiate football at Duquesne was discontinued in January of 1951.

Basketball Returns in Grand Fashion

Basketball's story was a far more glorious one. Returning for his twentieth contract year as head coach, in 1946–1947 Chick Davies led the Dukes to 19 straight victories before a loss to Georgetown. In the first season of postwar play, Duquesne received its third bid to the National Invitational Tournament in New York. It lost the first game of the tournament by one point to Utah, whom it had defeated in the regular season.

It was during the first postwar season that the University of Tennessee refused to play a scheduled game against Duquesne because the Dukes had a black player, Charles Cooper. The home game on December 23, 1947, was eagerly anticipated since Tennessee had two All-Americans and four other returning lettermen. Coach Davies refused to banish Cooper from the squad and Tennessee canceled at the last minute. The team finished its first season with 20 victories in 21 games. Cooper and Joe Camic were selected for the Tri-state team. Although he was only a freshman, Cooper was awarded a position as guard on the second team. He was selected as an All-American in 1950 and became the first African American drafted to play professional basketball when he joined the Boston Celtics that fall.

Chick Davies's attachment to Duquesne was deeper than basketball. Born in nearby Homestead, his own education was interrupted by service in World War I. After his discharge, he worked in the steel mills and did coaching on the side until recommended for the Duquesne position by a fellow Homesteader Hal Ballin, a previous coach. While coaching at Duquesne, Davies continued his own education by attending night school to secure his long-delayed high school diploma. Upon graduation, he immediately enrolled in Duquesne's College of Liberal Arts and Sciences, where he attended classes with his own players. Davies received a bachelor of arts degree in 1934 and a masters degree in 1938, resulting in his appointment to Duquesne's teaching faculty. It was a good bargain: Duquesne offered Chick the opportunity to secure an education, and he gave Duquesne one of the strongest basketball teams in the nation, consistently known for its drive and persistence.

For all his devotion to Duquesne, Chick Davies did not succeed in pleasing Father Smith. Although Smith characterized their relationship as a "clashing of temperaments," it was more than that. Smith disliked Davies' style, especially his habit of shouting vulgarities at the referees during games. Amazingly, Davies usually got away with these basketball court antics. During practice, Davies, who chewed tobacco, would throw his "chew" at any player who displeased him. Following the 1947–1948 season, his twenty-first, Chick Davies bade farewell to the team and to the university to become head coach at Homestead High School. Chick's last season at Duquesne resulted in 17 wins to six losses. One of the highlights for Chick that last year was the Varsity Alumni benefit game (sponsored by the Monogram Club) for which a number of Duquesne players of the past, some with professional careers in basketball, came back to play against their old coach's team.

Just as well liked as Davies was the athletic trainer, Brue Jackson, who had a successful second career as a night club entertainer. Players loved his jokes, impersonations, and songs, but they loved even more his expressions of concern for the athletes in his care, his encouraging words, and a practical demonstration of his concern—his massages. Brue was noted for his phenomenal ability to recall the names and faces of Duquesne's athletes and all the details of their college careers. He made the alumni feel as though they had truly come home.

Sports enthusiasts doubted Duquesne's chances at a winning basketball team after the Davies dynasty. The position of coach was given to one of his former players, Donald "Dudey" Moore, who had been coaching high school basketball since his graduation in 1931. With 13 returning lettermen in the 1949 season, he swept up 17 wins to five losses, stunning all the experts. The 1950 team chalked up 23 wins and was invited back to the National Invitational Tournament. Six hundred fans accompanied the team to New York to watch the Duke basketball team perform and were joined by 400 more for the second night.

Since the old gym on Locust Street was no longer large enough to accommodate the crowds, home games were played in the McKeesport Vocational High School gym or the Duquesne Gardens in Oakland. The Gardens, home court for the 1948 season, had a seating capacity of only a thousand, so athletic director Davis worked out a rotating system whereby students would be able to attend every third game. Despite a winning 17–6 season, there were still tickets left at game time, and attendance was eventually thrown open on a first come-first served basis. When Dudey Moore began fall practice with his initial team, he did not even have access to Duquesne's own gym for practice due to its use for university placement tests and other activities such as the Masquerade Ball. Worse still, part of the gym was used for storage. Daily practice had to be held at North Catholic High School.

Other Sports Also Make a Comeback

Spring sports also made a comeback. The tennis team opened its schedule on April 25, 1947, at McKinley Park. Handicapped by a lack of outdoor practice facilities, the team nevertheless won some impressive victories due to the heroic efforts of Joe Short, who was named an All-American in tennis. The team supplemented its limited seven-game schedule by joining the Pittsburgh Tennis Association to play regional teams, the first time a college had participated in the district circuit in nearly 50 years.

Father James Lavelle resurrected the golf team and led them to an opening match victory against California, Pennsylvania, at the Churchill Valley Golf Club. Although they had a mixed season, the 1948 season saw them undefeated.

Charles Muse, a semipro player who had managed minor-league baseball teams, enlisted the advice of all-time great Harold "Pie" Traynor in forming Duquesne's postwar baseball team in December of 1947. One hundred and fifty students showed up for tryouts, hoping for positions on this first Bluff baseball team since 1924. Practices were held at South Park; games were played at Forbes Field. The first year's schedule included sixteen games. Just as football and basketball suffered from a lack of home facilities, the baseball team also found themselves nomads. When they lost the use of South Park for practice, the team had to move to the Aspinwall Hospital diamond. Following their initial victory, it was announced that Forbes Field was to be resodded and would no longer be available for games. So uncertain were the circumstances under which they played, that in announcing the forthcoming games, the *Duquesne Duke* often had to report that the location for the home games was at the time of writing, not yet determined. Incredibly, the team managed to chalk up ten victories to five defeats in its first season.

In addition to his coaching duties, Muse, a 31-year-old veteran, was also a full-time student at Duquesne. He was a supportive and innovative coach. The 1949 drill season was preceded by the viewing of training films. Muse kicked off the 1950 season with a two-and-a-half-hour clinic in which the cheerleading squad acted out strategies on a miniature diamond marked off on the gym floor. Under his leadership and the pitching expertise of Carl Greffenstette, the 1949 team ended the season with 14 victories to four losses.

A notice for students interested in track appeared in November of 1947. Only 23 responded, and track never materialized that season. Despite another call in the fall, Duquesne was not able to field a team. Nor was the university able to take up hockey again, despite nostalgic articles in the *Duke* about the excitement of past play. A call for swimmers in the fall of 1950 also failed to produce enough enthusiasm to begin competitions. Once again, the lack of a facility for the sport was a discouraging consideration. Although the statement applied to far more than athletics, Father Vernon Gallagher summed up Duquesne's situation in 1947 this way: "Whatever limitations Duquesne suffers are due to lack of funds. Our only sin is the sin of poverty—if you can call that a sin."[32]

The resident student bowling league and softball league were quite popular. The bowling league teams traditionally played under the names of cigarette brands, but in 1947 the league switched to bird names—the Cardinals, Robins, Redbirds, Eagles, Orioles, Swallows, Sparrows, and Hawks—and went coed. They were back to all-male teams playing under the traditional cigarette-brand names the following autumn. The softball league sported names like the Clowns, the Hoopsters, the Freshman Hallers, the Raiders, the Red Sox, the Dreamers, and the Iron City Nine.

The Cost of Athletics' Return

Athletics had long ceased to be a moneymaker at Duquesne. In the three years before it was suspended for the duration of the war, athletics was earning about $91,000 a year, but it was costing the university about $135,000 a year. After the war, an activities fee had been instituted partly to make up for the shortfall. A sinking fund for athletics had also been established. For Smith, this was acceptable. "Sports," he wrote, "seem to be an established part of college life."[33] He never tired of saying, "We play big-time, or not at all."[34] It did not come without a price, and after the war, athletics was running oceans of red ink. By the last year of the Smith administration the deficit was three times the amount it had been just seven years earlier.

End of an Era

Apparently sports was the only area where Smith was willing to spend money. He refused to acquire land even when it was offered. During his term the Reliable Trunk and Bag Building at the corner of Boyd and Locust was up for sale. In 1948 a house on Locust Street where the university already held property was offered for $6,500. Both opportunities were refused.

This was not for lack of money, since Smith was most adroit at saving it. When he assumed the presidency, the university had a trifling $61,956 in savings and more than a third of a million dollars remaining on its debt. Thanks largely to tuition income, by the end of his administration, Smith had accumulated $2,029,463, an amount greater than the total university income in that year from all sources.

Smith was loath to spend money on the faculty, too, despite the fact that faculty pay raises was the reason given for a tuition increase in 1946. Two years later he wrote to the Holy Ghost provincial saying, "I am very wary of raising wages, considering how much more difficult it is to retract wages than not to increase them at all."[35] As dean of the college, Father Vernon Gallagher tried hard to change his mind. He later recalled that Middle States "wasn't all bad. As dean of the college I used it as a club to get Father Smith to improve faculty salaries (ever so little) so that I could recruit some Ph.D.s. We cracked the $3,000 (per annum!) level when I hired Dr. Olivia for the Psych Department in, I believe, 1948."[36] The faculty did eventually receive some pay increases, causing Father Smith to say that faculty salaries at Duquesne "compare with the median for all colleges, and more than favorably with Catholic colleges." He offered no statistics to back up his bold and entirely unfounded statement.

After the war, about 90 percent of American faculty members were covered by pension plans, but Duquesne's faculty was not among them.[37] At last, in the fall of 1949, under pressure from the Middle States Association, the university began a faculty insurance and pension plan. It was ironic that such benefits would come so late to the faculty. In 1941 Duquesne University was the first college in Pittsburgh to offer accident and medical insurance to students. (Students could collect up to $500 per accident for an annual fee of $5 for girls and $10 for boys.) The faculty plan included contributory life insurance coverage to $5,000 and annual pensions up to 25 percent of salary after age 65. Employees contributed two percent of annual earnings and the university paid the balance according to a schedule of age and salary factors. The cost of endowing the benefits package was enormous, consuming over half of the money Smith had saved. Funding it did not sit well with him, but he admitted, "We must inaugurate [the plan] if we are to maintain our standing with the accrediting agencies."[38]

The Smith administration was noteworthy for its penny-pinching policies. While it was true that the army barracks and quonset huts added much needed space, they, and even the "new" biology building, could scarcely be regarded as anything more than a temporary response to the long-term growth needs of Duquesne. And although Father Smith occasionally talked about fundraising, land acquisition, and the erection of new college buildings, nothing came of it. He was largely wedded to a make-do attitude that did not go unnoticed by the Holy Ghost Provincial, Father Francis H. McGlynn, who finally decided to "promote" Father Smith to the newly created position of Coordinator of Educational Activities of the Holy Ghost fathers. Although Smith was not pleased at the reassignment, he was not about to repeat Callahan's actions of 1936. The end of his tenure as president of Duquesne University was set as July 1, 1950, at which time he would be succeeded by Vice-President Father Vernon F. Gallagher C.S.Sp.

It would be unfair to say that the Smith administration had no accomplishments. The adjustment to the postwar conditions alone was a task of herculean proportions. In addition, the college radio station was founded, the student activities center was erected, and the university's indebtedness was lifted as well, with a fund provided for future expansion. Father Smith's support of athletics, costly though it might have been, brought a degree of public attention to Duquesne University that it otherwise would not have had. Finally, and most notably, he accommodated thousands of returning veterans as students, even amid severe postwar materials shortages. On the eve of his departure, the *Duquesne Duke* paid him deserved tribute: "He continually preached the gospel of 'love Duquesne, support the school, and contribute to its progress in every way.'"

6. A Master Plan

The 1950s was a decade of growth under one of Duquesne's most talented and charismatic presidents, one who devised a "master plan" for the university that endured long after he resigned in 1959.

Young Father Gallagher

Duquesne's eighth president was a native son, born in the Pittsburgh suburb of Sharpsburg, on September 26, 1914. Young Vernon F. Gallagher had been an altar boy at St. Mary's Parish where the Holy Ghost fathers had begun their ministry in 1876. After his ordination to the priesthood in 1939, he, along with Father Lauritis, attended the University of Pennsylvania, where he eventually earned a Ph.D. in English. Both men "contrasted the painful penury of D.U. with the awesome affluence of Penn."[1] It was at Penn that Gallagher vowed to remake the Duquesne campus if ever he got the chance. In 1950, after having served Duquesne as a professor, dean of the College of Arts and Sciences, and vice-president, he got that chance.

Father Gallagher returned from a tour of Europe to assume the presidency of Duquesne University at a time when key pieces were falling into place for an unprecedented expansion on the Bluff. Young, handsome, insightful, and intelligent, he had the necessary vision and leadership abilities to rally the community to support an ambitious building program for Duquesne University that became known as the "Master Plan." His original plan underwent many changes over the years, but the initial steps he took were to change the scope and direction of Duquesne's growth forever.

Others had prepared a good foundation for the able Vernon Gallagher to build upon. Father Kirk had established an alumni federation on which the university could rely for advice, support, and financial backing. Father Smith had cleared the university of the debt that had hobbled it since the Depression. He had even amassed a jubilee fund with which to launch a building program. All through the Korean War enrollment had declined—by the fall of 1953 the student body had fallen to 3685, a 29 percent drop in four years. But after the truce it began to climb slowly but steadily. The last year of the Gallagher administration it reached nearly 5000. This steady and predictable growth, about 6 percent a year, was invaluable in allowing realistic plans to be made for the future needs of the university. The postwar materials shortage was easing, and city revitalization in the form of the "Pittsburgh Renaissance" brought the support of Mayor David L. Lawrence and the Urban Redevelopment Authority in enabling Duquesne to secure the property and financial underwriting that would make building possible. Duquesne's Diamond Jubilee theme for the university's 75th anniversary was "Duquesne University Builds with Pittsburgh." The conditions and the temper of the times were right, and Duquesne University was blessed with a president who could effectively pull talent and resources together.

A Man of Varied Interests and Abilities

As a seminarian, Vernon Gallagher had shown exceptional musical talent. An accomplished tenor, he also played piano and organ, and even composed an operetta. But music was not his only creative expression. Father Gallagher also painted in oils and exhibited at the faculty shows which he originated in March of 1954. He loved gardening as well. In 1954 it was Father Gallagher who planned and designed the grotto of Our Lady of Lourdes at the west end of Bluff

Street. (The tufus rock arch grotto, the pool, and the gardens were built by Fathers Gallagher, McNamara, and Duchene with the assistance of the brothers of Kappa Sigma Phi. A greenhouse behind the library was built in the first year of his presidency for biological experiments. Students and professors soon began adding rare specimens to the collection, which included large fern trees, potted palms, and a 12-foot rubber tree used to decorate for special occasions on campus.)

Although he formally studied Latin and Greek, his interest in languages led him to learn French, German, and Slovak on his own. He was a talented professor and so enjoyed his interaction with the students that, even as university president, he occasionally substituted for English professors in teaching their classes. Father Gallagher's doctoral dissertation was on the poems by John Lydgate, written about 1421 and published as *The Life of Our Lady.* With apparent boundless energy, even while he was president of Duquesne, Father Gallagher completed his Ph.D. in English at the University of Pennsylvania in 1952.

Although "modest and humble in conversation," Father Gallagher was described as a "whirlwind" in the pulpit or on the speaker's platform. Always in demand as a speaker, he embodied an "unusual combination of artistic temperament and administrative ability."[2] Philosophically, Father Gallagher was a strong supporter of a wide range of knowledge and the liberal arts. When appointed dean of the College of Arts and Sciences, he expressed his views thus:

> The best positions are arrived at through keen competition, and the most successful applicants are those who attain to mastery not only of their chosen field of endeavor, but of a broad general culture as well. Even in an age of specialization, the liberal arts are with us still. We neglect them at our peril.[3]

A Youthful Administration

Vernon F. Gallagher, C.S.Sp., officially assumed the presidency on July 1, 1950, at the age of 36. The new vice-president, Father John Gerald Walsh, a native of Quebec, was only 34. So youth was the order of the day. Perhaps this was what made Father Gallagher's goal of "partnership" between staff, students, and community achievable. He began the tradition of the President's Faculty Reception and Tea to foster the partnership of president and faculty. And an indication of the openness of the Gallagher administration in building a partnership between the community and the university was the publication of his President's Annual Report, featuring enrollment, campus developments, research conducted at the university, student honors, ROTC events, athletics events, and a full statement of Duquesne's financial posture and development funds. This report was first issued in 1951.[4] He also revived the Priest Alumni Dinner suspended since the start of World War II. This annual event, begun by Father Hehir, was moved to the Monday closest to St. Martin's Day as a special tribute to Father Martin Hehir.

Father Gallagher announced in November 1950 that, as a Catholic university, Duquesne would begin all classes with the recitation of "The Lord's Prayer." During the Korean War, he initiated the practice of recitation of the rosary for world peace in the university chapel every half hour from 9 a.m. till 3:15 p.m. At his Armistice Day address, he explained his feelings on the current Korean conflict: "Education of mankind must supplant brute force. Only in this way can spirituality win over animosity."[5] But the education of which Gallagher spoke was rapidly losing ground to the brute force of which he warned; in that month alone, the university was to suffer the loss of 30 students to military duty.

The Korean War

The Korean War began in June 1950. When school began the following September, the *Duquesne Duke* outlined the new military draft regulations. A student called up for the service but already accepted into the university could take the physical and submit a certificate from the dean of his school to postpone induction until the end of the academic year. All ROTC cadets were exempt. So were veterans who had served active duty for 90 days before September 2, 1945, or who had served one year prior to June 24, 1948. However, the faculty and the athletic coaching staff were not exempt, and once again Duquesne felt the war-related impact of the departure of key men.

The *Duquesne Duke* of February 16, 1951, carried the obituary of First Lieutenant Robert Stylinger, class of 1949, the first Duquesne student to die in Korea. He was killed in action in January and was remembered at a Requiem High Mass by the brothers of Alpha Epsilon. Later came a report on the prison-camp death by starvation of Captain Philip J. O'Neill, a 1939 graduate of the School of Business who had made the army his career, had served in World War II, and had been a liaison officer when he was taken prisoner by the North Koreans.

With the draft situation a major concern on campus and the expression "upper one-fifth, deferred induction," commonly heard, Duquesne was selected in the spring of 1951 as one of a thousand sites at which special aptitude tests would be given to students seeking deferments. Many students purchased, for $1.35, *How to Prepare for Your Draft Test.* The number taking the three-hour written exam was so great that the Selective Service College Qualification Test was given three times between May 26 and June 30, 1951.

Pittsburgh's 375th Troop Carrier Wing was called to active duty at Donaldson Air Force Base, South Carolina, in October of 1950. Former Duquesne students there organized as the Red and Blue Club in honor of their alma mater. Duquesne's Air Force ROTC organization, Prop and Wing, became a chapter of the National Arnold Air Society, named for the late General "Hap" Arnold, in November 1951. Duquesne's chapter was named for William J. McKee, head cheerleader while at the university, who was killed in action in World War II.

By December of 1951 a drive to enlist students as part-time civil defense workers was in full swing. A demonstration on enemy aircraft identification was held on campus. Most importantly, the blood drive for the war front, so effective during World War II, was revived. The blood drives continued throughout the war with all the fanfare of a sporting event. Duquesne competed with other schools for the title of "bloodiest campus."

In March of 1952 Air Force ROTC numbered 400 students, and by October of 1953, Army and Air Force ROTC recorded their highest combined enrollment in three years: 355 for the Army and 365 for the Air Force. The end of involvement in Korea resulted in a budget cut and dropping of commissions for non-flight Air Force ROTC and a shift toward participation in the army branch. A notice appeared that same month for Korean veterans on the GI bill to get form sheets signed by instructors as a new, but much smaller wave of vets appeared on campus. By October of 1956, Duquesne had nearly a thousand veterans on the GI bill, more than a fifth of the student body. The Duquesne University Veterans' Organization was formed in May 1956 with 125 members; by 1958 that number had grown to 325. Their first major venture was to host a dance, "Winter Escapade," at the Buffalo Inn in South Park. They joined ROTC and Air Force ROTC in sponsoring a blood drive, the first at Duquesne in four years, for the veterans' hospitals. In its first year of operation, the Duquesne University Veterans' Association (DUVA) listed as its accomplishments a donation of $100 to Holy Ghost Seminary for Priestly Formation, 103 pints of blood collected in the drive, four socials, and a Lenten Mass.

The Cold War And the "Red Menace"

The Korean War was a three-year hot spot in the so-called Cold War that had begun after World

War II. This long struggle between the Soviet Union and the United States, and the countries allied with them, produced considerable fear and anxiety in the United States about communism that lasted long after the Korean War. Pittsburgh was a hotbed of communist activity and hence of anticommunist activity as well. As one writer put it, "Pittsburgh, with its industry and huge labor population, was a prime target for the American Communist movement."[6] Consequently, this was a city that took "the red menace" seriously. One of the leading area Communists was Matt Cvetic, whose son was a freshman music major at Duquesne. The younger Cvetic was ashamed of his father and of his name. Then suddenly, in February of 1950, Matt Cvetic testified before an astonished House Un-American Activities Committee that he was never a Communist, and that for the last nine years he had been working as an undercover agent for the FBI. The city was ecstatic. Mayor Lawrence proclaimed Matt Cvetic Day. The *Duquesne Duke* ran as a front-page story an article by Matthew J. Cvetic titled "I Thought My Dad Was a Communist." Cvetic wrote, "Today I answered roll in class with pride. No longer is the stamp of the red hammer a scythe over my name."

Cvetic's story became the basis of a Warner Brothers motion picture, *I Was a Communist for the FBI*. When it premiered at Pittsburgh's Stanley Theater in April of 1951 with Cvetic as guest of honor, searchlights lit up the sky, marching bands paraded, and two radio stations broadcast live from the lobby. Duquesne shared in the hoopla of the occasion when Cvetic, who was of Croatian descent, personally asked the Tamburitzans to perform at the theater prior to the movie.

Since the communist governments of Eastern Europe were closing Catholic schools and churches and imprisoning priests and religious in great numbers, the Roman Catholic Church was understandably even more anticommunist than it had been in the past. American Catholic colleges were equally vehement in their denunciations of communism. Owing to this, Catholic colleges were almost always above suspicion when a question of loyalty arose, as it often did in the postwar era. The FBI thus frequently hired agents from Catholic campuses, Duquesne among them. On occasion, the *Duquesne Duke* carried announcements such as, "FBI Seeks Young, Agile Non-Commies." By the 1960s so many had joined that the *Alumni News* reported, "Probably only two other universities in the U.S. exceed Duquesne in the number of alumni serving with the Federal Bureau of Investigation." The CIA was to join the FBI in becoming a regular recruiter on the Bluff.

The most organized and certainly most energetic of Duquesne's anticommunist efforts came from the History Department. In October 1951 Father John Schlicht began the Institute on Communism. Various guest speakers, including Matt Cvetic himself, spoke to "more than 90 labor leaders, and other professional men and women."[7] Not surprisingly, given the atmosphere of the day, the institute received wide coverage, including an article in the *New York Times*. In an editorial titled "Duquesne Shows the Way," the *Pittsburgh Press* heaped enthusiastic praise on the university because of the Institute. On Pittsburgh's WDTV television station, Schlicht told his audience, "In Communist writings Pittsburgh is singled out as one of the six fundamentally important centers to be attacked." And the city certainly counterattacked. Father Schlicht's Sunday afternoon program gained national attention that year when business and labor groups cooperated to hold "hearings" on communism. Each week two witnesses, one a former communist and the other a person who had lived under a communist regime, "testified" before a panel of three Allegheny County judges. Moreover, the Institute on Communism offered a one-credit course that was taught by a team of professors from the History, Economics and Political Science departments that prompted the report, "Nowhere in the country is such an extensive course being offered on this great threat to democracy."

Beginning in 1949, the university's Catholic students joined with other Catholic students in a May Day celebration intended to counteract communist celebrations occurring on the same day. Each year more than a thousand students marched in these candlelight processions, listened to sermons—Father Gallagher was among the most popular speakers—and sang hymns in "the biggest display of Christian fervor by students ever seen in this city.[8]

Father Gallagher repeatedly denounced communism and invited to campus those who did the same. In 1952 he wrote a guest editorial in *US Steel News* in 1952 that attracted considerable attention, and he received the Certificate of Merit from the Freedoms Foundation as a result of it. In the editorial he praised those "who bravely worshipped God" behind the Iron Curtain and concluded, "The unsung [heroes] who languish in the jails or swing from the gallows of the USSR keep burning a torch that no quantities of blood will extinguish."

The anticommunist efforts of Duquesne's leaders had results beyond any damage they may have inflicted on communism. For some time historians have recognized that at the height of the Cold War a major shift occurred in the definition of what was meant by loyalty to America and to its ideals. This was no longer defined exclusively as a belief in political democracy. With the advent of a virulent form of communism in Russia and Eastern Europe, capitalism came under heavy attack, and so, by 1950, a commitment to the free enterprise system coupled with strong anticommunism became the litmus test for American loyalty. As a Catholic institution in a city dominated by a Protestant elite, Duquesne was once suspected, however mildly, of being under foreign (i.e. Vatican) control. That perception was completely changed when Duquesne assumed its leadership role against the communist activities in the city. It didn't hurt that the Roman Catholic Church had stood shoulder to shoulder with the United States and Great Britain in its opposition to Soviet designs for communist world domination. The newspaper editorial on Father Schlicht's Institute on Communism titled "Duquesne Shows the Way" was characteristic of the city's new attitude toward Pittsburgh's Catholic university. Furthermore, as a result of its anticommunist role, Duquesne University became more integrated into the life of the community than it ever had been in the past. It is significant, perhaps even symbolic, that Father Gallagher's editorial in *US Steel News* should have preceded by just one year his being welcomed as the first Catholic priest to join the Duquesne Club, Pittsburgh's elite business club. Like a conjunction of the planets in the sky, the issue of anticommunism, Duquesne's greater community involvement, the university's need for corporate assistance in its plans for expansion, and the magnetic personality of Vernon Gallagher all came together at the right time for Duquesne's rise to a new prominence.

Gaining a High Profile

Father Gallagher was noted for having a very public face. His name appeared regularly as a speaker or participant in community events. In 1953 he was appointed, along with WDUQ station manager B. Kendall Crane, to the steering committee for Pittsburgh's new public television station, WQED. The June 18, 1953, issue of the *Pittsburgh Press* pictured him as one of the 100 young men selected from 1300 nominees as "outstanding leaders of the future—the young men most likely to write exciting new chapters in our city's progress." The selection was cosponsored by the Chamber of Commerce and *Time* magazine. Father Gallagher was one of three selected from this group to deliver principal speeches at the dinner in their honor.

Gallagher later stated that he never turned down an offer of a speaking engagement. He made use of every opportunity to gain publicity for Duquesne. Early in his administration, he actually sought out opportunities to speak, but by the middle and later 1950s, invitations were coming of their own accord.

By 1955 Father Gallagher had become so widely known that he was asked to deliver the prayer opening the 84th Congress. His prayer closed with, "Grant that, while the government is upon their shoulders, these educated agents of the free people may feel the power of Thy blessing and merit a full measure of that reward which is destined for all who undertake to be their brother's keeper. Amen." While in Washington, he was received by President Eisenhower, whom he presented with a book of essays written at Louvain University and translated into English at Duquesne. "I'll read it, too," Eisenhower reportedly told Gallagher.[9]

Father Gallagher and the Alumni

After announcing to the alumni at the first homecoming dinner of his administration that the job of running Duquesne University was too big for one man and that he needed their help, Father Gallagher mobilized the alumni into giving that help by having their offices at the William Penn Hotel redecorated and staffed with three employees. The alumni also returned to publishing their own paper, the *Duquesne University Alumni News*. This special focus on the alumni was long overdue. After the Kirk administration, they had been a neglected asset in assisting university growth despite the herculean efforts of a committed core through the Alumni Relief Fund and the fund for the shrine of Our Lady of Victory and their postwar involvement in the Athletic Sinking fund, the Judge Samuel A. Weiss Foundation, the Hugh C. Muldoon Pharmacy Alumni Foundation, and the Alumni Federation. In the fall of 1951, after a year's effort, current addresses could be found for only 7000 of the University's 20,000 alumni. Another year later, the Alumni Office had more than doubled this address list.

The President's Advisory Board

Early in 1952 Father Gallagher appointed Father George A. Harcar, C.S.Sp., dean of the School of Education, to the position of executive vice-president. Now Father Gallagher had more time for presenting Duquesne to the community while the soft-spoken, somewhat diffident Vice-President Walsh continued in charge of academic affairs and the new executive Vice-President Harcar took care of routine administration activities. In May of 1951 Father Gallagher had introduced Duquesne's first President's Advisory Board, a committee of 22 influential Pittsburghers composed of corporate presidents and vice-presidents, bankers, attorneys, real estate executives, a county commissioner, the mayor of Pittsburgh, a judge of the Court of Common Pleas, and the director of the Urban Redevelopment, all under the direction of Colonel Willard F. Rockwell, president of Rockwell Manufacturing Company. Colonel Rockwell was to remain as chairman of the President's Advisory Board until 1958, when he was succeeded by Edward J. Hanley, CEO of Allegheny Ludlum Steel Corp. In 1963 the board became the Duquesne University Foundation. William A. Seifert, Sr., a graduate of Duquesne's Law School and a senior partner of Reed, Smith, Shaw & McClay law firm, had considerable influence in the Pittsburgh business community, and it was he who made the President's Advisory Board possible.

Quite intentionally, only three members of the board were Duquesne graduates. Also intentional was the presence of men having religious affiliations other than Catholic, thus giving a more community-oriented and less sectarian focus to its fundraising appeals. However, it was acknowledged that more Protestant representation was needed on the board since "in the Pittsburgh area, corporate and foundation wealth is mainly in Protestant hands. The same is true of personal wealth."[10] The formation of this board was applauded by some as the "first truly effective lay leadership" at the university.[11] Certainly it was evidence of Duquesne's desire to reach out into the larger community. Likewise, the positive response of the business leadership was a confirmation of their faith in Duquesne University. Concurrent with its Diamond Jubilee, Duquesne launched a major fundraising effort that was to culminate in building a new Duquesne. But where?

Leaving the Bluff?

Although the Bluff had been Duquesne's home almost since its founding, the expense of acquiring the needed land raised the question of whether the university should remain at the same location or move. It was, perhaps, the consideration of this question that gave rise to a story so persistent that it can be considered a part of Duquesne's folklore. The story is that the Jesuits approached the Holy Ghost Fathers with an offer to purchase Duquesne from them, but when the offer was refused, they founded Wheeling Jesuit College in 1954. Gallagher avers that while the Jesuits were indeed looking to establish a college in the area, no such solicitation was ever made.[12]

Father Gallagher was of the opinion that Duquesne should move to some suburban location—he favored Bethel Park—where land could be purchased by the acre instead of the square foot. Only a few people favored moving, however. The Bluff, the majority pointed out, was at the edge of downtown and thus was served by virtually every public transportation system. It gave Duquesne an advantage over the Oakland area colleges since commuting students did not have to transfer. There was another obvious argument against moving. Duquesne already had made a substantial investment in land and buildings—and the investment was emotional as well as financial. Even first-semester freshmen knew that Old Main's bricks were made from clay literally scraped from the earth by the school's founders. The merits of these arguments carried the day, and Duquesne remained committed to the Bluff.

Finding a Base of Support

Duquesne hired a public relations firm, John Price Jones Company, Inc., of New York City, to assess the base of support and the prospects of a successful fundraising drive, and to present a strategem and timetable for the initial endeavor. The 111-page report, titled *A Survey, Analysis and Plan of Fund-Raising for Duquesne University*, was submitted in November 1951. In assessing the university, the Jones Report said, "Someone on the Bluff told us, 'Duquesne has always been a one-man university and always must be.' " The quote had a great measure of truth to it since the personality and abilities of its president have truly set the tone on the Bluff. However, Father Gallagher and his advisors were quick to see the value in further delegation of responsibility in view of the enormity of the building and fundraising tasks, so one of the Jones Report's first suggestions to result in action was the appointment of Father Harcar as assistant vice-president.

The survey also impressed upon the administration the necessity of educating the greater Pittsburgh community as to the nature of the university and its contributions to society at large. Among the misconceptions that Duquesne had to dispel was that as a Catholic institution, it was rigidly structured along doctrinal lines with little academic freedom. Nothing could have been further from the truth. For a religiously affiliated university, Duquesne exhibited a high degree of academic freedom. Professors were at liberty in the classroom to teach without interference from the Holy Ghost Fathers. Kirk's Sixteen Points were the sole exception to this venerable tradition. Duquesne had otherwise been remarkably fortunate in avoiding charges of classroom academic constraints even when other institutions had been attacked on just those grounds.

In 1955 Duquesne was challenged on the issue of academic freedom by a pamphlet written by a Dr. Elderkin, a professor emeritus from Princeton University. The pamphlet titled *The Roman Catholic Controversy on the Campus* accused Duquesne University of permitting a local pastor to "meddle: with a required, nonsectarian course on the Bible." In response, Father Gallagher pointed out that the premise of the entire pamphlet was in error as Duquesne offered no "nonsectarian" course on the Bible. There were Catholic courses offered, but as a Catholic institution, the content of those courses rightfully were in consonance with Church doctrine.

Duquesne was also a socially "open" institution, accepting students regardless of gender, race, or creed at a time when few other private schools did. Never having excluded anyone because of race—a practice commonly attributed to the Holy Ghost fathers' active ministry in the African missions—it could also lay claim to being the first Catholic college in the country to accept women. As college enrollments continued to rise toward the end of the decade, a Syracuse professor, Dr. Phillip Ward Burton, authored an article that was published in 1958 in the Sunday Magazine section of the *Pittsburgh Press* titled "Keep Women Out of College." His premise was that overcrowding could be minimized by dropping the number of women accepted by the nation's institutions of higher learning since a college education was not as crucial for success for women as for men. The article produced an outcry at Duquesne and was the subject for an editorial in the *Duquesne Duke*. At Duquesne, where the first woman had been graduated in 1911 and women had been routinely accepted by all the schools on an equal footing since 1926, the very suggestion of limiting coed admissions was unthinkable.

As to creed, the Jones report noted, "Fitness and moral character are the only tests applied to lay leadership, lay faculty, and the student body." A Jewish candidate for a faculty position at Duquesne later admitted that he was surprised that no one asked his religious affiliation. Upon his hiring he learned that a thousand students, about 20 percent of the student body, were not Catholic. Although by 1950 Duquesne had educated about 200 priests in the Diocese and another 150 throughout the country, it could also count among its graduates those who had gone on to become Protestant ministers and Jewish rabbis. This notwithstanding, the survey reported continuing and persistent misconceptions:

> Although this is a Catholic university—the only Catholic university in the Diocese or in the Tri-State area—it should be pointed out that it serves all without discrimination, although there is evidence that the public does not fully understand this. Underlying the instruction throughout the University is a clearly discernible ethical and moral philosophy which might be called basically Catholic, but which transcends sectarian lines. It is a way of life for all.

The survey also pointed out the need to make the community more aware of the services rendered by the university as a source of exceptionally well-trained manpower, a source of scientific knowledge, and a contributor to a better business environment, to the arts and culture of the city, and to an educational climate fostering preservation of the free enterprise system. The report recommended that the university convey to the city that in helping to make the Bluff "the future acropolis of Pittsburgh," it would be enabling a cultural as well as a material and aesthetic rebirth. And that, as a Catholic institution, Duquesne would serve as a strengthening force for moral values.

Father Gallagher Begins to Build

Father Gallagher had to plant the seeds of faith in Duquesne's future within the Pittsburgh community before beginning to build. He did this. Then he began the physical steps of Duquesne's expansion in the summer of 1951, using the funds designated by Father Smith for the jubilee celebration, gifts from alumni, and loans. The barracks classroom building was moved from the west side of the ROTC drill field to the middle to make room for the construction of a priests' residence. Gallagher later recalled, "When we built Trinity Hall, I was particularly sensitive about seeming to give the impression that I was taking care of the Holy Ghost Fathers before meeting the needs of faculty members and students."[13] Happily, these fears proved groundless. Gallagher writes: "As far as I could determine, though, people were generous in their attitude toward the first step in campus expansion. They did not know that I was commanded by the superior general to begin by housing the priests under one roof. Till then they were scattered all over the hilltop, a situation that was inimical to common prayers and community life."[14]

In a month-long procedure, the classroom building was carefully jacked up onto rails and moved 40 yards east while summer school classes were still being conducted without interruption inside. Construction of the priests' community house, Trinity Hall, was completed in time for an open house exhibit by each of the schools of the university in the new residence at the homecoming in November 1952. The three-story fireproof building featured a large commons room on the first floor and fifteen cubicles for altars in the basement where the priests could say daily Mass. Its chapel contained special stained glass windows designed by Father William Crowley, C.S.Sp., of the English Department, ten of which symbolized the fathers of the church and one, the influence of the Holy Spirit.

Immediately preceding the 1952 Homecoming, dedicated to the theme "The Duquesne of Tomorrow," was the groundbreaking ceremony for the new women's dormitory on the corner of Vickroy and Stevenson Streets. The university had long been delayed in beginning work on this desperately needed facility. Without governmental backing or the power of condemnation, and without the funds to buy out residents at inflated prices, the university had been forced to wait until the residents were willing to sell. And the process of acquiring land was painfully slow. During the first five years of the Gallagher administration, 1950–1955, only three acres were added through the purchase of some 38 homes and buildings. The cost amounted to more than a quarter of a million dollars per acre, and the properties that the university did acquire were scattered over the entire Bluff.

The Urban Redevelopment Authority

Soon after his appointment as president of Duquesne, Father Gallagher had approached the Urban Redevelopment Authority (URA) of Pittsburgh for eligibility as a private redeveloper of the Bluff. In June 1952, when the City Planning Commission certified the Bluff area as "blighted," Duquesne realized that it did not have the estimated two and a half million dollars needed to acquire the land necessary for campus expansion. Father Gallagher later admitted, "At this time it became evident that we had bitten off too much."[15] Although the university considered reducing the area to be acquired and allowing another private redeveloper to move in, Gallagher knew that he might never again have the opportunity to secure the remaining property and "we needed every square foot for the realization of our plans."[16] And at this time these plans embraced only the area between Bluff and Locust Streets. Only later were these plans extended to include all of the Bluff down to Forbes Avenue. At this point Father Gallagher approached the URA director, John P. Robin, "to admit defeat." The director encouraged him to proceed with the original plan and informed him of a provision for a federal loan to developers who could not immediately afford the purchase price. Duquesne University was to be the first in the nation to take advantage of this provision.

The Federal Housing and Home Finance Agency, unsure as to how to proceed, moved with extreme caution. Five years elapsed before Duquesne was notified (in 1957) that it was eligible for federal loans for land acquisition. Another five years were to pass before the first properties were acquired under the URA (in 1962). Duquesne itself was responsible for at least 19 months of this delay. When the university received word in April 1957 that it was eligible for federal loans it had just begun construction of Rockwell Hall. The administration was understandably cautious about undertaking yet another commitment until it had successfully completed this ambitious project. Father Gallagher later noted, "As anxious as I was to go along with Robin and Pease [Robin's successor], I did not want to go through the lengthly (and chancy?) process of seeking Vatican approval. Over the centuries social upheavals and anticlerical governments in Europe had taught the Church to be extremely wary of influences that could possibly deplete its resources. Much of Duquesne's holdings would have had to be pledged as collateral for a loan big enough to cover the URA's requirements, generous though they were. Then, even if I had obtained authorization to incur indebtedness of that magnitude, securing the loan would have been another hurdle. As one banker told me, " 'We are not interested in going into the education business if you default.' "[17]

The First Dormitory

By 1951, and without help from the URA, the university had purchased enough properties to build a women's dormitory. The new women's residence hall was planned to accommodate 250 students and was slated for opening in September of 1953. A ballot was prepared to select a name for the facility, either Redman Hall in honor of Kathryn Redman, Duquesne's first woman dean, or Blanchard Hall for Maria Gertrude Blanchard, Duquesne's head librarian for 17 years. Both were then deceased and both had served as dean of women. The name Redman Hall won, but in response to a letter sent by an alumnus, Elizabeth O'Connor, that the chapel in Fort Duquesne was named for the Assumption of the Virgin Mary, the name "Assumption Hall" was given to the building instead, and it was dedicated to the memory of Dr. Redman.

It was never intended that the women's dormitory remain as an isolated building blocks away from the existing campus buildings. Located directly across the street from Mercy Hospital, it was to demarcate the end of the proposed campus area. Thus, the erection of Assumption Hall was partly a strategic move designed to deter other would-be developers by staking Duquesne's "claim" on the Bluff. It was also tangible evidence that Duquesne was serious about its Master Plan. The completed plan was to encompass a campus of 28.5 acres at a projected cost of $13,300,000 for the land and buildings. "Duquesne does not dream of Georgian facades or Gothic spires," the Jones report said, "but it does hope tomorrow to have libraries, classrooms, and laboratories large enough to accommodate all students who seek an education on the Bluff." Although the dormitories were to be financed through self-amortizing loans, completion of the plan would require the raising of $8,300,000 in donations from alumni, friends, corporations, and foundations.

The Diamond Jubilee Campaign

Under the slogan "Duquesne University Builds with Pittsburgh," the Master Plan was praised and supported by the alumni and His Excellency, John F. Dearden, Bishop of Pittsburgh and chancellor of the university. Public enthusiasm for Duquesne's building plans was encouraged by the extensive building already taking place in the city's downtown, and especially the redevelopment at the Point with its park and the Gateway Center Project. Pittsburgh presented an image of a progressive city on the move, and

Duquesne was determined to be a part of that progress.

The first phase of the Duquesne University Development Fund, known as the Diamond Jubilee Campaign, swung into action under the direction of alumni John A. Robertshaw and M.C. Conick. The campaign was conducted in three phases: the first appeal was to "alumni, parents of students, and intimate friends of the University—in other words, to those who know Duquesne best and appreciate it most;" the second appeal to the Catholic population in the Diocese of Pittsburgh; and the third appeal to "individuals, corporations, and foundations in the community at large."[18] The drive officially began in mid-January, 1953, launched by a Special Development Issue of the *Duquesne Duke* with Judge Henry X. O'Brien, the university's very first *Duke* editor, returning to the honorary post. The paper, along with an artist's conception of the future campus, showing the individual buildings slated for construction over the next ten to 15 years, included an appeal from Father Gallagher to the students not to feel unimportant in the campaign amid all the publicity given to the other phases. The independent students' committee of the development drive set its own goal at $15,000. In less than a month more than a thousand alumni had pledged, and within two months the law school had far surpassed its quota in the student campaign, and the pharmacy and music schools exceeded their goals as well. The alumni held a "D-Day" of intensive calls and contacts for the Diamond Jubilee appeal in April, which proved to be so successful that the students followed suit by planning one of their own.

The university had no illusions concerning the socioeconomic status of its graduates or the possibilities for the drive's success. The 1950 President's Annual Report was a lesson in history:

> Some historic reference must be made here in order to explain the Alumni Association's present inability to provide substantial support for the University. Aside from sixty-two years of inactivity mentioned above, there is another major consideration: our student body is and has always been drawn from middle-class and laboring families. In providing easily accessible educational facilities in the center of Pittsburgh, we have made it possible for young men to work their way through college, graduate school and law school in great numbers. When this type of graduate becomes an alumnus, he finds that the task of establishing himself and his family socially and economically in the community leaves little in the way of surplus funds for the assistance of his school. This has been particularly true in recent years when much of his surplus income has been taxed away. Moreover, it takes more than one generation for a family to develop that economic security which will permit (both financially and psychologically) sizable alienation of its resources. It is to be hoped that, as the years go on, more generous aid can be anticipated from alumni quarters.

In the fall Colonel Willard Rockwell agreed to chair the business and industry phase of the campaign. Two hundred Duquesne alumni met in April 1954 to kick off the corporate drive.

The second phase of the campaign, following the appeal to alumni and friends of the university, was a plea to all the parishes in the Diocese of Pittsburgh. No such appeal to the larger Catholic community to support Duquesne had been launched since the Million Dollar Fund campaign of 1920 during the Hehir administration. October 4, 1953, was designated as "Duquesne Sunday" in all parishes of the diocese. Along with a letter from the bishop urging pastors to support the university's drive, the pastors were sent an outline to be followed in addressing the congregations. The homily was to stress contributions that the university had made: in the education of young Catholic men and women and members of religious orders, in aiding parochial schools through teacher-training for sisters, in assisting in formulating report cards and testing procedures, in supplying visual aids, in presenting educational programming for elementary and secondary schools over WDUQ, in scholarship aid, and in the services rendered by

Duquesne's Holy Ghost fathers in assisting with Masses in the parishes and teaching in the Diocesan Institute of Adult Education. Special Duquesne folders were distributed on Sunday, September 27, the day of the presentations, and pledge envelopes were placed in the pews for the October 4th drive. The university requested a pledge of at least one day's salary a year for three years. Pastors had a choice of authorizing a basket collection on October 4th or 11th or approving a committee for door-to-door solicitation during that period.

Some in the business community were surprised at Duquesne's solicitation. One senior and somewhat crotchety executive said to Father Gallagher, "Father Hehir ran a perfectly good school and he never asked me for any money," to which Gallagher replied, "Perhaps if he had, I wouldn't have to now."[19] But fortunately, this was not the attitude typical of the business community, and relative to earlier efforts, the campaign might be called a success. The 1951 annual report had disclosed a near-negligible $25,000 in annual alumni contributions and only $26,000 "in the form of research grants from government and industry." The results of the fundraising efforts were given in the 1953–1954 annual report:

Alumni and Friends	$ 579,541.41
Pittsburgh Catholic Diocese	286,931.87
Business and Industry	698,088.13
Foundations	15,000.00
Students	10,009.75
Clubs and Organizations	11,005.00
Total Contributions	1,601,576.15

The fundraising effort, begun in 1953, continued through the rest of Gallagher's administration. But by the end of the 1950s only about $3 million had been raised. Years later a presidential report looked back on these efforts: "Subsequent events showed we looked through rose-colored glasses in those days of 1953. The drive's goal of $8,300,000 proved far too extravagant for a University paradoxically making its debut as a community resource although it had functioned quietly as a community service for 75 years."

Assumption Hall Welcomes the Women

Modestly successful though the campaign was, Gallagher nonetheless decided to build. In February of 1954 the cornerstone of Assumption Hall was laid by Bishop Coleman F. Carroll, auxiliary bishop of Pittsburgh and a Duquesne alumnus. As the brickwork rose on Assumption Hall, the student newspaper reported that the coeds were becoming nostalgic about their "tenement campus" of small houses, fearing that dormitory life would be too formal. After moving into their new home, complete with recreation room and dining hall, however, they were pleased enough to celebrate with a Mothers' Tea in September 1954 in honor of the mothers of Duquesne's freshman students, and the next year, with their first formal dance. Assumption Hall even had its own two-page mimeographed newssheet.

The social life at Assumption was closely governed. Coeds were to be in their rooms by 11:00 p.m. Calling out the window was viewed as unseemly and was, in fact, a punishable offense. Shorts and slacks were forbidden outside the residence hall. "Loitering," as the *Code for Coeds* called it, was not permitted in or near the building after returning from a date. "Anyone kissing or embracing on the steps will be punished," the pamphlet threatened.

In the fall term of 1957 Assumption Hall was filled to capacity at 236 students. Thirty-seven women had to be turned away for lack of accommodations. And the demand for dormitory space increased as Duquesne slowly shifted from a locally oriented commuter school to one of regional renown.

A Better Student Lounge for the Men

With all that was being done for the women, the men on campus were feeling neglected, or so they claimed, despite their occupancy of St. Mary's Hall and ten university-owned houses on the Bluff. A 1957 report revealed that the University had housing for 173 men in St. Martin (21), St. Mary's (23), St. Joseph (15), St. Edward (9), St. Theresa (11), St. Thomas (15), St. Francis (13), Pius X (16), Holy Name (16), St. Catherine (19), and Liebermann Hall (15). Another 90 lived in the area in non-university housing. Thus only nine percent of the men were residents. The student government attempted to soothe their hurt feelings, whether real or feigned, by equipping the student lounge in the barracks building with two ping-pong tables, a pool table, an AM-FM radio, card tables, and games, and opening it to the men in the evenings. The coeds were invited to the opening celebrations replete with combo and refreshments. Unfortunately, the lounge had to close in the evening hours after the spring of 1958 due to lack of student supervisors. Similarly, a lack of supervisory personnel had forced the locking of the gym after intramural hours in 1954. The supervisions were needed primarily to keep non-student groups from using the facilities.

The Beginnings of Rockwell Hall

The administration's energies were now directed toward the most ambitious building project in Duquesne's history: the erection of what was to be named Rockwell Hall. The building would result in the campus facing Forbes Avenue, a principal artery in the city. In a physical sense, therefore, Duquesne would be ending its isolation on the Bluff; in a symbolic sense, the building was to be a public face to the world, reaffirming the community involvement that had already occurred.

Most of the properties on the block had already been purchased, and in an effort to persuade the holdouts to sell, some twenty buildings were razed in May of 1955 in preparation for what was then being called the Law and Business Administration Building. When at last the two remaining property owners did sell, it was to cost the university fully a third of the total expenditures for a block that had originally held 34 buildings. It was a painful but necessary process, one that, thanks to the powers of the URA to condemn properties, would never be repeated. With the "land war" finally over, in March of 1957, the Navarro Construction Company, which had built Trinity and Assumption halls, began work. Comprised of a ten-story classroom tower and an auditorium, the building was originally estimated to cost one and a half million dollars but actually cost about two and a half million. The architect, William York Cocken, who had designed the original Master Plan, sadly died only six days prior to the dedication of Rockwell Hall.

The need for a new building for the Schools of Law and Business Administration, both of which were still housed in the Fitzsimons building, was unquestioned. As the largest school at the university, Business Administration was in desperate need of classroom space. In 1957, some 1338 students were business majors out of a total enrollment of 4635. Yet the zoning classification of the Fitzsimons building as a commercial property, which permitted the rental of offices that produced income for the university, also made it illegal to expand classroom use to any more than half of the building. One of the university's renters at the Fitzsimons building was the Diocese of Pittsburgh. The rent charged by the university was so low that it did not even cover the annual taxes on that portion of the property. The diocese, however, later reimbursed the university.

The Library has Growing Pains

The library was proving less and less able to cope with more acquisitions and more students.

Students complained that the additional shelving meant a correspondingly smaller area for study tables. Having 60,000 volumes, the library was becoming little more than a repository. An editorial in the *Duke* in the fall of 1955 referred to the library as a place where students would take out books but could find no space for research. "Between looking for a parking space, a seat in the cafeteria, and a spot in the library, the harassed student hardly can think of going to class." The equally harassed and overworked librarians urged freshmen to use their library manuals and attempt to help themselves.

The male residents, who had long been scattered in numerous aging structures, were clearly in need of a dormitory, but Father Gallagher said in the spring of 1959, "I hope the boys won't mind if we hold off a bit on the men's dorm, but we have to think of first things first [meaning the library]."[20] Plans called for the building of a larger facility for upperclassmen and graduate students with the original library building designated as a freshman annex. The completed facility, originally slated at $1,500,000, was to accommodate 350,000 volumes as well as other research materials and to have a large reading area.

Other Building Projects

The Hall of Science, slated at $3 million in the original proposal, was to centralize the pure and applied sciences. Chemistry, physics, and biological science were to occupy the main part of the building, which was to have separate wings for pharmacy and nursing. The building was to give tangible expression to the interrelatedness of scientific knowledge.[21]

A permanent classroom building was becoming an absolute necessity. Projected at $1 million, it was to be shared by all schools and departments. Since the barracks buildings obtained from the army after World War II were in violation of a city code forbidding wooden buildings in the downtown area, the city had to reenact a special ordinance annually to permit their use. Intended only as temporary structures on campus, the classroom building had the additional disability of not being equipped with lavatories.

Estimated at $2 million, the student union had a lower priority than academic buildings, but it was finally being acknowledged as important. Duquesne students had always experienced a shortage of social and recreational facilities. By building a new student union, the university was recognizing the social aspects of college life as a valuable adjunct to education.

A field house was added to the slate by the university after the initial survey had been prepared. The Dukes had labored under the handicap of no home facilities ever since the war. The old gym held the intramural competitions but could not handle any expansion of the program. The athletic building to house basketball, track, tennis, and other sports would give Duquesne an adequate arena for intercollegiate competition once more.

Although not one of the considerations in the survey, as a Catholic institution, Duquesne dreamed of replacing its chapel with a larger one, seating a thousand. With so many pressing academic and recreational needs, plans for a new chapel were reluctantly shelved in 1957. A new School of Music and additional dormitories were more urgent needs.

Raising Money and Tuition

Students approaching graduation were requested to make a pledge of $40 to Duquesne University, payable over three years, as a parting gift. An official kickoff tea for the senior phase of the development drive was held at Assumption Hall. Alpha Epsilon fraternity made an initial pledge of $500. The class of 1957 pledged $16,000. John P. Roche, director and president of Heppenstall Company, agreed to lead the smaller business and industry drive for the Western Pennsylvania area.

In 1955, the Alumni Association had devised a novel plan: "International Card Parties."

Alumni and friends of the university from all over the world hosted card parties in their homes, charging their guests $1.50 per person to benefit the building program. But as the 1950s progressed, alumni giving decreased, and rising costs forced tuition increases three times during the Gallagher years. In the 1950–1951 school year, tuition was $12 a credit. By 1958 it had reached $20. In June of 1957, Duquesne ranked fourth in tuition charged in the city, below Chatham, Carnegie Institute of Technology, and the University of Pittsburgh, with only Mount Mercy ranking lower. But tuition income remained vitally important to the financial stability of the university. In 1953–1954, it accounted for 60 percent of total income, and under the demands of university expansion, along with Gallagher's efforts to increase salaries, it climbed to above 70 percent by 1958–1959.

In presenting the case for a tuition rise at a meeting of the Duquesne University Veterans' Association, Father Gallagher explained:

> In these days of personnel shortages, coupled with increasing enrollments, it is hopeless to think of acquiring and retaining good teachers without offering them adequate compensation. . . . Since our tuition rates also range far below the national average, and since the education of our students was further subsidized—not by state aid—but by the contributed services of 36 fathers and brothers who work night and day without a cent of salary, there seemed to be no alternative but to ask the young men and women of the university and their parents to bear a greater share of the burden.[22]

Despite the announced increase, by the spring of 1958, applications were up sharply from the previous year. The 3126 men students and the 1872 women students came from 30 states and fifteen foreign countries.

The value of teaching services from the Holy Ghost fathers—still referred to as the "consecrated endowment"—amounted to $200,000 per year. Salaries for other faculty accounted for 70.8 percent of the university's operation budget. As a result of both a general scarcity of teachers nationwide, and the parsimonious salaries Duquesne paid during the Smith years, the university had gradually fallen behind in the percentage of the faculty who had earned Ph.D.s.: 21 percent in 1953 (the year the university introduced formal contracts for all teaching faculty). Holy Ghost fathers at this time constituted a mere 12 percent of the faculty. Beginning in 1955, the Ford Foundation helped by making the first installment on a grant to provide an endowment for faculty salaries at Duquesne. By 1959 this grant amounted to $556,500, the largest ever received by the university up to that time.

In April of 1958, Dr. Thomas P. Melady, director of development, instituted yet another innovation to the building fund campaign. This involved the alumni "gifting" of life insurance policies by declaring Duquesne University as the beneficiary.

Fundraising efforts continued with asking the graduating seniors to contribute $50 each as a parting gift, with a class goal of $25,000. The final issue of the *Duquesne Duke* in the spring of 1958 showed that the seniors surpassed that goal with pledges amounting to $26,520. The alumni continued their annual "International Card Parties," and the Women's Guild hosted their annual "Pink Geranium Card Party" for the development fund.

A Fee for This and a Fee for That

Although the Holy Ghost fathers operated the school as efficiently as possible, students found that their tuition was accompanied by a host of other attendant fees, to say nothing of the fundraising campaigns. In addition to $16 a credit in 1955, a double room for a semester cost $65 for men in the small houses and $125 for women in Assumption Hall. The optional linen rental service added another $14 per semester. Board five days a week for a semester amounted to an additional $185. A $20 matriculation fee to reserve the student's place was applied toward the tuition but was not refundable if the student did not attend. Although the smaller fees were by no means unique to Duquesne, they were a source of annoyance to the students: a University fee of $12 for full-time students, $4 for part timers for auxiliary services; the library fee of $5 full time, $2 part time; registration fee of $1; ROTC fee of $1; and a condition-examination fee of $5 for any student wishing to be retested for removal of an E or X grade. Special schools and departments also had extra or attendant fees.

The cost of a college education pressured most students at Duquesne to work summers or part time during the school year. The *Duquesne Magazine* of November 1950 observed,

> Summer vacations are another mainstem of cafeteria conversation. The latest vacation trend seems to be away from resorts and into steel mills and business offices. Even the credit-tempting summer school takes second place to the lucrative offerings of industry. This summer, more spare time jobs are available, though certainly not plentiful.

When Reverend Englebert van Croonenberg was appointed director of student welfare, he was well aware of the number of students working their way through college. He posted off-campus job openings and supported the idea of a job placement bureau. In the spring of 1958, Duquesne established a University Placement Bureau to schedule an annual interviewing program with corporations for graduating seniors and former graduates. Various schools, most notably education and business administration, already had their own placement services, and on-campus recruiting was a common practice of corporations and the military, but the university hoped this central operation would help combat the effects of the recession for Duquesne students.

The Difficulties of Rockwell Hall

Duquesne's involvement in Pittsburgh's Bicentennial celebrations opened with the dedication of Rockwell Hall on November 16, 1958. It was decided to name the building in honor of Colonel Willard F. Rockwell, chairman of the President's Advisory Board and fundraiser extraordinaire. This truly devoted friend of Duquesne did not ask for the building to be named in his honor when he gave $226,000 to its building fund. With 54 classrooms, the new building was able to absorb all the activities from the Fitzsimons building, which was soon sold. When the classroom building was razed the following year, classes normally held in the barracks building were moved to Rockwell Hall. The School of Business Administration assumed 84,000 square feet on floors one to six, while the School of Law occupied 42,000 square feet on the seventh, eighth, and ninth floors. The John E. Laughlin Memorial Library was housed on the eighth floor, and the seventh held the Maurice and Laura Falk Moot Court. This model courtroom, complete with judge's bench, jury box, counsel tables, and spectator seating for 100, as well as a reception room, judge's retiring rooms, and a small lounge-library, was made possible through a $100,000 grant from The Maurice and Laura Falk Foundation. The air-conditioned building was equipped with four elevators. The ground floor, on which the main entrance was located, housed 28,000 square feet of administrative offices including the registrar, purchasing, cashier, and admissions, all of which were moved there from the administration building as well a some alumni offices, development, public information, and placement, which had previously been in the Fitzsimons building.

Also a part of Rockwell Hall was the thousand-seat Peter Mills Auditorium, named for the president of Moody Engineering Company. With a fully equipped cafeteria adjacent to the auditorium, it was designed to be converted as needed to a dining area. It also included a private diningroom named for another loyal Duquesne supporter, William A. Seifert, Sr. The auditorium displayed a mural behind the speaker's platform and specially designed stained glass windows. The Women's Guild Tea in honor of the mothers of the freshman students was moved from Assumption Hall to be the first social function held in the new auditorium.

Construction of the building was plagued from the start by difficulties in acquiring properties and by cold weather, a labor stoppage, and shortages of structural steel. Capping these events, just two weeks after its dedication, vandals smashed windows and pulled some of the aluminum letters denoting its name off the side of the building. When the building did open its doors to the students in February of 1959, additional problems appeared with excessive congestion at the elevators, cafeteria, and even at doorways, especially at the second floor facing Locust Street. This door, really the most used of all entrances, was too small to accommodate the throngs of students trying to use it during the change of classes . Moreover, the configuration of the lower floors was confusing, a feature compounded by the fact that the elevators did not reach the Forbes Avenue level. Adding to the confusion was the fact that the floor accounted as number one wasn't the first floor at all. Even an equestrian statue of the Marquis Duquesne, planned for the front of the building, arrived from the Netherlands broken into so many pieces that it could not be repaired. (The only remaining evidence of the planned statue is a concrete pad with protruding reinforcement rods located next to the Forbes Avenue entrance.)

These problems notwithstanding, the building enabled the university to host a wide variety of new activities, including the symphony band's Winter Pops Concert in December 1958, at which a new school song, "March on, Duquesne Dukes," was introduced.

The Law School Adds Day Classes

In 1958 the law school expanded by offering a day school division for the first time since its founding in 1911. The first year it had 117 evening students and 43 day students. Despite the excellent record of its graduates passing the state bar exams on the first sitting, the law school had been unable to receive accreditation from the American Bar Association because it automatically withheld approval of all schools having only evening classes. The association gave its provisional approval in 1960 and, after the customary two-year waiting period, its full approval in 1962.

The new building housed an extensive law library. The Honorable Henry X. O'Brien of the Court of Comon Pleas, a 1928 graduate of Duquesne's law school, took up the chairmanship of a campaign to raise $100,000 for the Laughlin Law Library, named for Duquesne's first dean of the law school.

The College of Liberal Arts and Sciences Develops a Strong Reputation

Cramped though they were as they awaited additional buildings, the schools and departments of Duquesne University continued to grow in progressive curriculum reform, academic offerings, and renown. The heart of the university, the College of Liberal Arts and Sciences, experienced dynamic growth in many disciplines. The Journalism and English departments continued to promote broadcasting and newswriting in conjunction with the university radio station, newspaper, and a new literary magazine. They also moved into television, and hosted community workshops on high school publications.

In the early 1950s the Philosophy Department experienced a rebirth with the arrival of scholars from the Netherlands and Belgium. The group included Dr. Bernard G. Boelen, an international lecturer from Louvain, Belgium, who had fled that country with his family because of threats he received as a response to his criticisms of communist philosophy; Father Henry S. Koren, C.S.Sp., from the Netherlands, head of the department of philosophy and a prolific author; and Father Englebert van Croonenberg, C.S.Sp., also Dutch, who became director of student welfare in addition to his teaching duties. Andrew G.

van Melsen came from the Netherlands in 1951 as a visiting professor. The Duquesne University Press published his *From Atomos to Atom* in 1952, the first in the philosophy series, and his *The Philosophy of Nature* in 1953. The fifth book in the philosophy series was *Truth and Freedom*, a copy of which Father Gallagher presented to President Eisenhower in 1955. Under Fr. Koren's leadership, the philosophy department achieved international recognition.

The science branch of the college continued to develop a reputation for research work though corporate grants. A leading department in the relatively new art of "grantsmanship" was the Chemistry Department. Though many of its research grants were from Pittsburgh-based companies, others were from outside the area. In the fall of 1952 the Chemistry Department began offering a program on the doctoral level. Noted professors in the department included Dr. H. Harry Szmant, who was appointed to serve for a year as "Professor Extraordinary" at the University of Oriente in Santiago, Cuba, and Dr. Oscar Gawron. The American Chemical Society held a "Symposium on Radioactivity" at Duquesne in December of 1958. Dr. Kurt Schreiber headed the department beginning in the fall of 1957, succeeding Father Moroney. He instituted a program of monthly conferences sponsored by the Chemistry Department.

Music School's Silver Jubilee

The music school celebrated its Silver Jubilee in the spring of 1951. The building that housed the school had ineffective lighting, broken tile floors, and unnecessary partitions until it was renovated that year, with modern soundproofing and lighting. A faculty of 23 taught 200 full-and part-time students. Musical ensembles from the school performed frequently for WDUQ, various campus functions, charity benefits, and hospitals and orphanages, as well as presenting an annual concert schedule. Talented students provided many original scores. One of the music school's 1956 graduates was Bobby Vinton, later to gain international fame as a popular singer.

A Duquesne Cap and Pin for the Nurses

The 1946 class of the nursing school was the first to receive a Duquesne cap and pin instead of those of Mercy Hospital, for in that year the school became independent of the Mercy program. Enrollment in the Nursing School continued to be high despite the eight additional credits it required.

In 1950 the *Bulletin* of the nursing school still used feminine pronouns in referring to the students, even though in that year it graduated its first male nurse, Albert Yamnitzky. In that same year, it graduated its first African-American student, too, Edith Payne. Duquesne did not consider race as a factor in its admission policy, but "because some of the hospitals in which the clinical work is taken do not take colored students," Payne took her classwork at Duquesne and, by special arrangement, completed her clinical work at the Lincoln School for Nurses in New York.

School of Education under Father Harcar

Father George A. Harcar, C.S.Sp., executive vice-president of the university from 1945 to 1951, also served as dean of the School of Education from 1944 until 1961. The graduate program in guidance and counseling and the programs in school administration for elementary principals, supervising principals, and administrative officers were approved for certification in 1952. Library science received certification in 1956. The school also initiated a nationally recognized summer conference on the study of Catholic school practices. In 1954 Harcar was the initial force behind the Institute on Catholic School Problems, "designed to acquaint priests with the special problems, practices, and procedures of Catholic education."[23] The School of Education had become increasingly involved in the science of learning, IQ and aptitude testing, and educational research, and in the 1950s undertook its own independent study of the reasons why teachers had difficulty reaching the "culturally deprived student."[24] This research was to have a great effect in the 1960s with the institution of various educational clinics on campus.

A Trade-Off—The Carnival for Football

Designed to fill the void in student life resulting from the discontinuation of football, the carnival, held for three days in early to mid-October, served as a rollicking entertainment fest, hosted by university organizations. When first held in 1951, the celebration was heralded by dorm displays. To form a midway, the university roped off Bluff Street from the administration building to Hooper Street. A variety show ran twice nightly at the Little Theater under the chapel, and a street dance was held on Vickroy. Prizes were awarded to the dormitory with the best display and to the organization with the most original booth on the midway. The festivities climaxed with he Carnival Ball at West View Amusement Park's Danceland. Plans for this first Duquesne Carnival included an array ranging from Hawaiian dancers to a shooting gallery, as well as the ever popular dunking booth and pie throws. Based on a Mardi Gras theme, the carnival commenced each evening at 8:00 p.m. and featured tent shows by fraternity and sorority thespians. The student body responded positively to the hoopla, which was fondly recollected by numerous photographs in the *Duquesne Duke*. In its very first season, carnival became an entrenched part of campus life.

Duquesne was not the first school in the area to have a carnival, but Duquesne's fall affair took on a special flavor as a welcome to new students—the Queen of the Carnival Ball was always to be a freshman—and a welcome back to upperclassmen. The second annual carnival, named for the Diamond Jubilee, was touted by Father James A. McNamara, dean of men and originator of the idea at Duquesne, as greatly improved:

> This year's Carnival was by far bigger and better than our first one. It was heartening to see the cooperation that was shown by the many students who pitched in.[25]

By the following year, fifteen different organizations, comprising approximately 500 students, worked on the carnival. That year the big highlight was the national broadcast of the Vaughan Monroe Orchestra from the campus theater.

The carnival of 1956 saw amusement park rides installed on campus operated by Beta Pi Sigma fraternity. The event was launched by fraternity members dressed as ancient Greeks running through the downtown streets enroute to the Bluff, bearing a torch and followed by a parade of floats. The carnivals also had yearly themes: "The Movies," "Television," "Around the World," and "Comic Books."

Freshmen of the Fifties

In an attempt to create a greater social bond among students, the administration revived the practice of freshman hazing on a limited scale in the fall of 1954. During freshman orientation the student government explained traditions, taught the school songs, and "encouraged" the newcomers to don their dinks and take part in hazing activities. For example, a sophomore "big sister" served as a guide for a freshman "little sister," who was expected to wake her big sister up with a song, make her bed, and show up at night to tuck her in and turn out the light. Safety pins were given out as demerits for little sisters who failed in their duties, and initiation week ended with a Kangaroo Court.

The student newspaper joined in the campaign by printing articles on the history of the university, the *alma mater*, the university seal, WDUQ, and campus organizations. Freshmen were encouraged to wear the beanies, not as a humiliation, but "to help the incoming student

77. Rev. Vernon F. Gallagher, C.S.Sp. (1950–1959). Duquesne's eighth president was born in the Pittsburgh suburb of Sharpsburg and was an altar boy in St. Mary's Parish, where the Holy Ghost fathers began their ministry. After ordination to priesthood in 1939, he attended the University of Pennsylvania, where he eventually earned a Ph.D. in English, finishing two years after he became president at Duquesne.

Gallagher had the vision and leadership to rally community support for an ambitious building plan. Under his dynamic hand the Master Plan developed, eventually resulting in the construction of three new buildings, the first major construction in nearly three decades.

An avid gardener, in the first year of his administration, he had a greenhouse built behind the library for biological experiments; students and professors added rare specimens to the collection over several years. Gallagher was young — just 36 — when he became president, and talented and energetic. He studied Latin, Greek, French, German, and Slovak. An accomplished tenor, he played piano and organ, and he painted in oils. In July 1958, he was elected provincial superior of the American Province of the Holy Ghost Order, in charge of priests in the U.S., Puerto Rico, and East Africa. Despite these new duties, he remained president of Duquesne until October 1959.

78. Despite his office, Father Gallagher was not averse to dirt. In 1954, along with designing and planning the Our Lady of Lourdes grotto, he helped Fathers McNamara and Duchene and the members of Kappa Sigma Phi build the tufus rock grotto with a pool and gardens, overlooking the Monongahela River Valley.

79. The completed Our Lady of Lourdes grotto. Designed by Gallagher, built by administration, faculty, and students, this shrine is a fine monument to Gallagher's goal of "partnership" between all branches of the university.

80. The President's Advisory Board, 1958, a committee of 22 influential Pittsburghers, among them corporate vice presidents, real estate executives, bankers, attorneys, the mayor, and the director of Urban Redevelopment. In a move bold for its time, President Gallagher appointed laymen to the Board, thus giving it a more community, less sectarian, orientation. Only three board members were Duquesne alumni. Some lauded formation of this board as the "first truly effective lay leadership" at the university. Their first order of business was organizing Duquesne's Diamond Jubilee, the first phase of the Duquesne Development Fund.

81. The first expansion project Fr. Gallagher undertook was the building of Trinity Hall. The first step was making room for the foundation. In a month-long procedure, one of the barracks classroom buildings was carefully jacked up onto rails and moved 40 yards east. Summer school classes of 1951 were conducted without interruption inside. The university continued to use the barracks until Rockwell Hall answered its space needs.

82. Until 1953 the Holy Ghost fathers lived in a number of locations on the Bluff under conditions not conducive to community life. Finally in 1952 Trinity Hall was built as a residential community house exclusively for their use.

83. This photo, taken on April 12, 1951, shows the state of the neighborhood at the eastern end of the Bluff. President Gallagher looked out over this landscape and saw it as Duquesne's new campus. Note Old Main, top center. Buildings that later became College Hall and the Music School are at upper right.

Pittsburgh *Post-Gazette*

84. After Trinity Hall and Assumption Hall (a women's dorm), Duquesne's administration turned its energies toward the most ambitious building project in its history: Rockwell Hall. Groundbreaking did not begin for another three years. Without government backing, or the power of condemnation, and with limited funds, the university waited until residents of smaller buildings on the Bluff were ready to sell. On the block intended for Rockwell Hall, which once held 34 buildings, two property owners refused to sell long after all the houses around them had been razed. This photo shows the two "holdouts" on the Rockwell site in 1956. When the owners finally agreed to sell 18 months later, these two houses cost over 30% of the total expenditures for the whole block.

85. Rockwell Hall, named for Colonel Willard Rockwell, chair of the new president's advisory board and an extraordinary fundraiser, was completed in 1959. It was the first campus building erected on Forbes Avenue, a principal artery of Pittsburgh. This 10-story, $ 2.5 million building was tangible proof that the university was growing, becoming more visible, and extending its lands and influence into the city.

86. Despite the large number of commuter students and the lack of group "houses" at Duquesne, fraternities and sororities were a strong social campus presence in the 1950s. In this photo, the fraternity members, dressed as ancient "Greeks," light torches on Vickroy Street to begin Carnival Week, October 1956. They ran through the downtown streets to the Bluff, bearing torches and followed by a parade of floats. Designed to fill a void in student life after football was discontinued, the Duquesne Fall Carnival was a rollicking entertainment-fest hosted by university organizations. The 1956 celebration saw amusement park rides installed on campus and operated by the Beta Pi Sigma fraternity.

87. To create a greater social bond between students, the Gallagher administration revived the practice of freshman hazing in 1954. During orientation, the student government explained school traditions, taught school songs, and "encouraged" newcomers to don their "dinks" (beanies) and take part in hazing activities. Here a freshman science student wears the "dink." This lab is in old Science Hall at the corner of Colbert and Vickroy Streets.

88. Freshman initiation week included requiring new students to avoid "Senior Walk," when changing classes (shown here in 1953).

89. The school paper, the *Duquesne Duke* and a popular KDKA radio show host sponsored a contest to select "Miss and Mr. Brickthrow of Duquesne University, 1959." This photo shows *(l. to r.)* students Arlene Niedzodski, "Miss Brickthrow," and Tom Mullaly, "Mr. Brickthrow." Mullaly threw his brick the farthest by hurling it over the side of the Bluff. Miss Brickthrow's qualifications (according to competition rules) were being "attractive and a female student of Duquesne." Shown with them (l. to r.) is the KDKA morning radio team, Karl Hardman, (radio name "Buffy Budekovitch"), host Rege Cordic, and Bob Trow ("Roquefort La Farge").

90. Tamburitzan alumni perform with Duquesne students, May 1956. The enthusiasm generated by the Tamburitzans after World War II endured through the 1950s. The Tammies even figured in Cold War Politics. After President Tito of Yugoslavia broke with Moscow's hard-line Communist philosophy, the U.S. State Department, looking for ways to build cultural connections with Yugoslavia, asked the group to visit that country. This 1950 trip was the first of several tours in Europe for the Tamburitzans, and it was such a success that a series of televised performances in Washington D.C. followed.

91. There was music of all kinds all over the Bluff in the 1950s. The Music School Opera Workshop closed its 1958–59 season with its biggest production ever, Gilbert and Sullivan's The Gondoliers, done in its entirety with 15 solos and a 28 piece orchestra. The proceeds were donated to the University Scholarship Fund.

92. Television fever was taking hold of the nation, and Duquesne was not immune. The Journalism Department began WDUQ–TV closed circuit television in 1956. The university's early use of this emerging technology is symbolic of the renewed vigor that attended the entire Gallagher Administration.

93. Rockwell Hall's new cafeteria held more students than the old one in Canevin Hall, but since enrollment continued to increase, tables were always full. Privately owned restaurants near campus helped relieve cafeteria congestion. One of the more popular was Albert's Grill at the corner of Hooper and Vickroy Streets.

94. Despite losing Coach Charles Muse to the Korean War draft in 1950, Duquesne fielded a strong baseball team for the next decade. Coached by Lou "Doc" Skender, the team was rated as one of the top eastern squads in 1952. In this photo, Dave Ricketts beats a hasty retreat to first base in a game with Indiana State Teachers College. Ricketts went on to play major league baseball with the St. Louis Cardinals and the Pittsburgh Pirates.

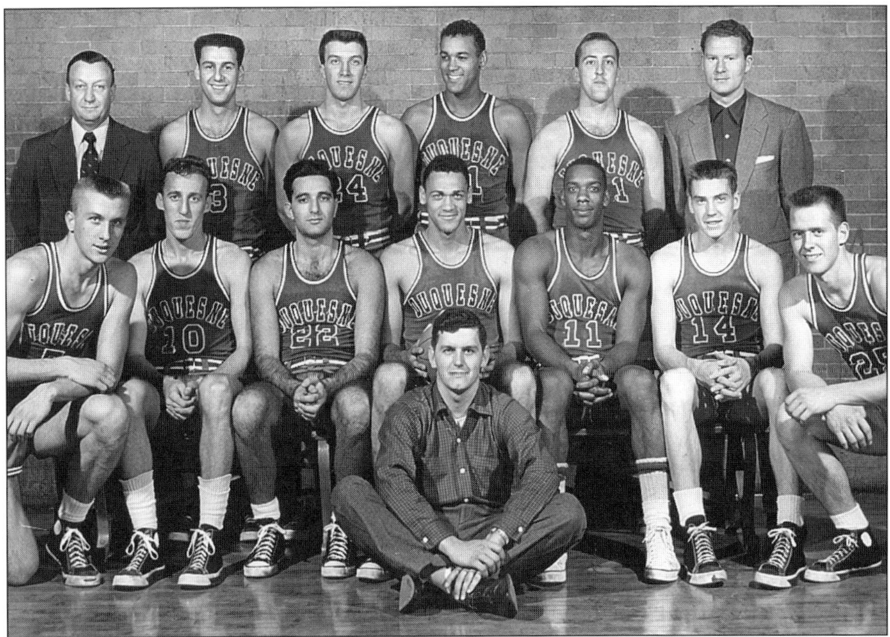

95. The 1955 National Invitational championship team. After a 19-4 regular season, the Dukes finally won it all at the National Invitational Tournament in New York, with wins over Louisville, Cincinnati, and Dayton. Basketball had replaced football at Duquesne as the sport everyone supported. In 1956, the university ended its fall homecoming in favor of a basketball festival to kick off the season. Three December days of activities included a float parade, a mass for the team, a dinner, pep rally, and motorcade to the Pitt Fieldhouse for the home game.

96. Coach Dudey Moore is held aloft by jubilant players following their 1955 National Invitational Tournament win. Five thousand people greeted the returning Dukes at the Pittsburgh airport, and the entire student body was invited to a testimonial dinner honoring the team. Moore's career at Duquesne tallied 144 victories to only 44 defeats.

become known."[26] Initiation week included the wearing of beanies and nametags at all times on campus and the avoidance of "Senior Walk," the sidewalk leading from the classroom building to Canevin Hall. Freshmen were also expected to know the *alma mater*, fight songs, names of the deans of the various schools, and the presidents of campus organizations, all of which they could be quizzed on by an upperclassman. A tug-of-war between freshmen and upperclassmen ended the week. Although some of the upperclassmen felt that the initiation was "stupid," the *Duke* reported that "no freshmen complained," and, in fact, most joined in enthusiastically.

Rege Cordic

Campus life sparkled with numerous sidelights, many of them formed in the fertile brain of Rege Cordic. The humorous morning-show host of radio station KDKA was extremely popular in Pittsburgh. Though having no official relationship with the university other than his support of WDUQ, Mr. Cordic delighted in taking part in campus parades and activities, often dressed in inappropriate costumes, along with Carman Monoxide, one of many comical sidekicks. Together with the *Duquesne Duke*, he sponsored a contest in October 1958 to select "Miss Brick Throw of Duquesne University, 1959," (hereinafter referred to as "Miss B.T.D.U.), [who] will not be required to throw bricks anymore than would, say, 'Miss Steamfitter of 1959' be required to fit steam. Her brick throwing ability will be taken for granted. She must, however, be an attractive female student of Duquesne University—end of qualification."

Dances—And the "Duke Box"

As late as 1953, dance corsages were still being banned at Duquesne because of the cost, but most campus dances were informal affairs where corsages would be out of place anyway. The Military Ball was an exception. The student government hosted a Welcome Back Dance at Syria Mosque known as the University Ball, but it was so poorly attended that it was discontinued. More popular were Carnival Ball and the Harvest Ball gym dance. Also, the Journalism Association always hosted a dance early in the year with an unusual theme, such as the 1950 Eight Ball. And then, of course, there were the traditional Christmas Ball, Easter Ball, and Graduation Ball every year, plus a variety of one-time benefit offerings for the building fund, such as the night-club theme dance sponsored jointly by the Holy Name Society and Our Lady's Sodality.

Informal dancing became a common recreation on campus. The old faculty dining room in Canevin was outfitted with a juke box dubbed the "Duke Box," and was opened nightly for dancing. The new dance room, called the Duke Box Room, became even more popular when pinball machines operated without coins were installed. But the "Duke Box" proved to be an annoyance for professors attempting to teach classes in Canevin during lunch time, and they successfully petitioned to have it unplugged at that hour.

Cards and Cigarettes

The prohibition against card-playing on campus continued throughout the Gallagher years. Because the Holy Ghost fathers were concerned about students betting large sums of money on the card games, students caught playing cards were immediately placed on probation. In a single incident in 1951, eight underclassmen were sentenced to probationary status. By 1959 the *Duke* was still reporting periodic unannounced "sweeps" of the lounge by university officials with more threatened. Some students took to playing with their coats on to speed their escape in the event of a surprise visit from the dean of men.

Cigarette smoking continued to be popular on campus, as evidenced by the large number of cigarette advertisements appearing in the

Duquesne Duke. In the late 1940s campus cigarette representatives began to appear among the student body, a practice that became so widespread that the "Cat's Meow" column of the *Duquesne Duke* in November of 1950 jokingly reported that there were "more cigarette company representatives on campus than smokers." As the decade progressed, information on the health hazards of cigarette smoking began appearing in the school paper, and an opinion poll was conducted on whether students would continue smoking in spite of the risks. Interviews from six students were printed. All six vowed to continue smoking. The response of Charles Biggs, Ed. '56, was typical. "I consider myself a moderate smoker and have not become alarmed by the controversial tie-in between cigarettes and lung cancer." Located just below this article was a large ad for L&M Cigarettes. Some switched to pipe-smoking, but in general the popularity of smoking on the Duquesne campus continued unabated.

Parking Woes

In the 1940s the students had successfully petitioned the city to have some Bluff area streets posted with limited time parking. But the imposition of a two-hour time limit was too short for a normal school day. The students petitioned for the removal of the two-hour parking limit on several Bluff area streets without success. Parking areas that the university made available were often only temporary. The students were able to park on the lot at the corner of Bluff and Stevenson Streets, for example, but when work began on Assumption Hall, that space was gone. Within weeks the students took to parking on the ROTC drill field, even uprooting fence posts and unstringing the locked cable to park their cars. Throughout the 1950s there were periodic complaints in the *Duke* about the students parking their cars at intersections, making it difficult for pedestrians to move about campus. Parking was a problem that was not soon to be solved.

A Great Decade for the Tamburitzans

The 1950s continued to be good times for entertainment, and the postwar enthusiasm generated by the Tamburitzans endured throughout the decade. The Tammies even figured in Cold War politics. After President Tito of Yugoslavia broke with Moscow's hard-line Communist philosophy, the State Department was looking for ways to build cultural bridges between that country—which still declared itself Communist—and the United States. Accordingly, government officials came to Duquesne and asked if the Tamburitzans would go to Yugoslavia. They were the first such American group to do so, and this 1950 tour was the first ever in Europe. It was such a success that upon their return a series of three televised performances in Washington, D.C., and a winter performance at Carnegie Hall followed. There they received honors as America's goodwill ambassadors. In addition, Duquesne University received plaudits for helping to create fissures in the Communist Bloc. The Tammies' return to Pittsburgh was a triumphant one. They held an Open House at the Fort Pitt Hotel, where they showed movies of their trip. Thereafter Open House became an annual event.

In the summer of 1952 the Tamburitzans embarked on a second tour, this time not under State Department auspices. They flew first to Yugoslavia again, where many had an opportunity to visit with relatives, and then to Paris, Lucerne, Marseilles, Venice, and Genoa. Successful as the trip was artistically, it created such financial stress that the group was forced to reorganize. Matt Gouze, the originator of the troupe and its longstanding head, left, and Walter Kolar, who had joined the Tammies in 1938 while a student at Duquesne Prep, took his place, assisted by former members Steve Kovacev, Charles R. Cubelic, and, in the roles of technical advisor and choreographer, Richard Crum. Father Vincent Deer, C.S.Sp., a missionary to Africa for many years, became the university liaison, spiritual director, and official photographer. The

Tamburitzans redefined their mission as one of cultural preservation and to this end made a commitment to accurate and authentic representation of the customs, dances, musical selections, and costuming of Eastern Europe. Mr. Crum made several research trips to Yugoslavia, recording music and dances on camera and audio tape, and collecting books, instruments, and costumes. They also phased out all non-European presentations, although other cultures were occasionally portrayed upon special request during overseas tours. The stipulation that Tamburitzan members must be of Eastern European descent, however, ended in 1954 when Byron "Butch" Powelson, of English-German descent, joined the troupe.

In 1953–1954, the troupe, appearing in costumes from Yugoslavia, performed under the vocal direction of Mr. Edward Sambol, who made both choral and solo singing more integral parts of the program. The chairs, music stands, and risers that marked their early instrumental presentations were discarded in favor of an open stage. Plans were made for a cultural center composed of a library, museum, and archives; and the 1955 Tamburitzans began their national tour in a new Greyhound bus.

In October of 1955 the *Duke* reported the formation of a "Tammie farm club" as junior Tamburitzan groups of children ages eight to sixteen sprang up in the Pittsburgh-area towns of McKeesport, Clairton, and Ambridge. The contribution made by the Duquesne University Tamburitzans to the revival of ethnic cultural interest in Pittsburgh resulted in Mayor David L. Lawrence's designation of March 3, 1957, as "Tamburitza Day." The interest in ethnic culture popularized by the Tammies fostered the production of a Pittsburgh Folk Festival in 1956 and again in 1957, replete with food booths, cultural displays, and costumed performances of ethnic songs, dances, and instrumental selections. It received wide coverage in all the area publications and became an annual event for several more years. Eighteen ethnic groups participated in the Fourth Annual Folk Festival, attended by 9000.

The Tamburitzans embarked on a new educational endeavor with the issuance of a bimonthly publication, *The Tamburitzan* in the spring of 1958. Circulating primarily to junior Tammie groups, the periodical contained news of the troupe's activities, the stories behind various songs and dances, and summaries of the histories of Slavic nations. Two nationally distributed albums, "Christmas in Croatia" and "A Balkan Concert," were recorded with RCA Victor in 1958 and were sold at the campus bookstore for $3.75 and $3.50, respectively. More money was raised when Director Kolar instituted Tamburitza classes for Tammie hopefuls. This was followed by a Tamburitzan Alumni Charm Clinic to benefit the building of Tamburitza Hall; instruction was given in voice, direction, wardrobe, makeup, and visual poise. The Duquesne University Tamburitzans were becoming so well known that choreographer and technical director Richard Crum was flown to New York to teach American Folk Dancing to a Russian troupe performing at the Metropolitan Opera House under the U.S.-Russian Cultural exchange. This extraordinary man, fluent in nine languages, taught the dancers in Russian. Though he eventually left Duquesne for Harvard graduate school in 1959, he continued to correspond regularly with the troupe.

Campus Dramatics

Duquesne's drama club, the Red Masquers, set on an ambitious performance schedule in 1950 under Mr. Frederic DeFeis. Offerings included Shakespeare's *Twelfth Night*; an Elliot Nugent-James Thurber comedy, *The Male Animal*; a Lenten play, *The Comedian*; and the Mary Chase comedy, *Harvey*. DeFeis also served as director for the spring musical, *The Vagabond King*.

In the fall of 1951, Richard Scanga, technical director for the previous year's Topper and Tails musical, headed the Masquers. They received their charter as a chapter of Alpha Psi Omega, a national dramatic fraternity, that year and ran a series of acting classes to encourage more students to join in the productions. They also took student Don Brockett's variety show from the previous spring on tour to local hospitals.

The big production for the Red Masquers in 1953 was George Bernard Shaw's *St. Joan*. In the fall of that year, the Red Masquers united with the new Duquesne University Vocal Workshop and 19 members of the Pittsburgh Symphony to perform the opera *Faust*—an artistic success if not a box office draw. The Opera Workshop had been added to the Vocal Conservatory department of the Music School in September of 1952 under Josephine McGrail. In its first year it performed the famed double bill of opera, Cavalleria *Rusticana* and *Pagliacci*, and the American opera, *Down in the Valley*.

With its mix of highbrow fare and presentations of more common appeal, the Masquers had something to please just about everyone. Contrary to reports in the *Duquesne Duck*, the special April Fool's Issue, the Red Masquers did not stage *The Ten Commandments, Minus One*, but did close their production year in 1957 with an awards dinner at which the Pittsburgh Drama Award, the Student Government Association Drama Award, and five "Sammy" awards, named for director Sam Meli, were presented. Notable among the student talents were John A. Griffin, Jim Sweenie, and Don Brockett.

More Music and Dancing

There was a lot of music at Duquesne in the 1950s, both for listening and for dancing. The Opera Workshop closed its 1958–1959 season with its biggest production ever, Gilbert and Sullivan's *The Gondoliers*, done in its entirety with 15 solos and a 28-piece orchestra. The proceeds were donated to the University Scholarship Fund. The Pan-Hellenic Council sororities staged annual variety shows beginning in 1951 under the title *Sorority Silhouettes*. Themes varied. The fourth show in 1954 was on coed life in 1929; the fifth was titled *Classical Delights*. In combination with the Intrafraternity Council, they also initiated Greek Sing as a semiformal affair at Carnegie Music Hall, with the awarding of prizes to the outstanding performing groups. Greek Night was moved to Peter Mills Auditorium in 1959 when the Intrafraternity Council held a talent show for members of all fraternities and sororities. Occasionally, shows were held by Greek organizations as benefits—and then there were their tent shows for the fall carnival!

And there was more. Gamma Sigma Music Fraternity formed its own dance orchestra in 1954, which first appeared at the fraternity-sponsored cafeteria dance in December, the Sno-Ball. The University Folk Dancers continued to be active, with performances in the campus theater and noon square-dancing classes in the music school. In 1955 they were replaced by the Duquesne University Square Dance Club, organized by eurythmics instructor Brunhilde Dorsch and Tammie choreographer Richard Crum.

And there was still more. Along with the Opera Workshop, the School of Music produced the Student Symphony, the Mixed Chorus, the Duquesne University Chamber Orchestra, the Trombone Quartet, and the Brass Choir, in addition to less formal jazz groups and combos. Mixed Chorus performed *Jeanne d'Arc* with the Pittsburgh Symphony in 1955. The Trombone Quartet made an appearance on the popular television show, *Ted Mack's Amateur Hour*, in 1958. Also that year a marching band was formed under the direction of Donald E. McCathren. The School of Music sold candy bars to buy band uniforms. That same year, the ROTC cadets formed their own marching band. And, of course, the Concert Choir, traditionally presented Christmas carols and sang at special masses.

Perhaps the most unusual musical offering at

Duquesne was founded by Robert Boudreau of the music school faculty in 1957. His American Wind Symphony, funded through a cultural grant from the Howard Heinz Foundation, performed on a barge fitted with an orchestra shell. The transportable stage tied up at Point Park for its summer Sunday and Thursday concerts before embarking on a performing tour of towns along the Ohio River, much in the tradition of nineteenth century showboats. While in Pittsburgh, the musicians, numbering about 60, were housed at Duquesne.

WDUQ: The "Voice of Duquesne" in the Fifties

One of the chief forums for Duquesne University's dramatic and musical productions was the university's own radio station, WDUQ-FM, still known as both the "Voice of Duquesne" and the "Voice of Education in Pittsburgh." Although the station only began broadcasting on a limited schedule in December 1949, within ten years it was a full-time, educational, noncommercial station, operating from two fully equipped studios, a control room, and a transmitter room in the administration building. It had also built an extensive musical recording library and newsroom equipped with a newswire service. Directorship still rested with B. Kendall Crane, who had assumed the duties in 1950. At 91.5 on the FM dial, the station broadcast programming from the Tape Network of the National Association of Educational Broadcasters, student-produced programs, shows from the large commercial networks, and play-by-play sports coverage. Its programming ran 85 hours per week. The Music School contributed the great bulk of WDUQ's original programming. Their commitment led to live concert performances nightly in the 1957–1958 school year.

WDUQ prided itself on its ability to run as a student station with auditions each fall for broadcasters and recruitments from the entire student body for nearly all of its personnel. The station's children's programming included the "Recorded Small Fry Show" and "The Playroom" for the preschool set. Daytime educational programming for elementary and secondary schools started in 1951 as the "School of the Air," followed by a series of taped programs in the fall of 1952 titled "In School Listening." WDUQ even hosted tours for elementary school students.

Public-interest programming in 1950 included such offerings as Congressman Buchanan's talk on combating inflation, the Carnegie Hall lectures series, the Carnegie Institute of Technology's Golden Jubilee, and a hallmark series on the history of education in Pittsburgh known as "Operation Learning." By January of 1952 WDUQ had 20,000 regular listeners. Continued input from the faculty was evident in such offerings as a three-month series on Shakespearean plays with commentary from the English Department and a novel educational experiment for inmates at Western Penitentiary with a series on social studies, history, English, and science.

Broadcasts of basketball games were an important staple in WDUQ's schedule. Along with the Duke's encounters, the station also carried Carnegie Tech's basketball games. Coverage was extended to high school football games in 1956.

In early 1954, radio station WJAS received a license to operate television station Channel 11. WDUQ and the Journalism Department set up their own TV workshop studio on campus. WJAS was already airing an extensive Sunday series through their radio station featuring shows from the Schools of Pharmacy and Music, and programs on literature, theater, the social sciences, a Red Masquer production, and a panel discussion as the "University of the Air."

With Father Gallagher and Mr. Crane on the steering committee for the new public educational station, WQED, the WDUQ staff was able to create an eleven-week series, *Senior Citizen*, for broadcast over WQED-TV. The Journalism

Department then set up its own closed-circuit system for use on campus.

Television fever was taking hold of the nation, and Duquesne was not immune. A television set appeared in the barracks building lounge in the fall of 1951 and in the cafeteria and student lounge in 1953. As the country fell in love with the medium, a survey of faculty on campus found them highly in favor of radio and television instruction.

Campus Journalism

The *Duquesne Duke* repeatedly received Class One Honor Ratings from the Associated Collegiate Press, with the additional laurel of being declared "Superior All-American," the top designation, every semester from the fall of 1948 through the spring of 1950 and again in the spring of 1952. The *Duke* was also given an excellent rating by the Catholic School Association. Excellence in writing the *Duke* was encouraged by Mr. Michael Peterson, who fined students a nickel for each mistake in his newswriting classes. WDUQ also had a fine box, known as the "Goof Box." Not surprisingly, student staff members occasionally deliberately tried to make their fellow students "goof" on the air by making faces or distracting them.

Duquesne Magazine, a student publication serving as a forum for students, faculty, and alumni, had received the National Scholastic Press Association's Superior All-American rating for 1949–1950 and first class honors for 1948–1949. It was thus a surprise when the university decided to suspend publication in the spring of 1951 on the grounds that representing so broad a spectrum of interests was proving too much for the student staff, and also because of "mechanical difficulties which arose, copy and material shortages, lack of personnel, and other reasons." It was succeeded by the *Overture*, published by the English Department. Whereas current news had been published continuously in the Duquesne *Duke*, the *Overture* published student literary works. The greatest effort of the *Overture* staff resulted in a spectacular edition for the Pittsburgh Bicentennial in 1958. Prominent Pittsburghers as well as students from the other major colleges and universities in the area were invited to submit works. Forty noted adult contributors joined the students in this outstanding volume. This bicentennial edition of *Overture* was under the direction of Ida Collura, whose sister Maria was also an English professor at Duquesne. Confusion between the two sisters, looking remarkably alike and teaching in the same department, promoted a *Duquesne Fluke* April Fool's issue to declare in a headline "One Collura Must Go."

The Alumni Organization began its own paper, the *Duquesne University Alumni News*, in the spring of 1951. The faculty kept itself informed through its own publication, *Faculty News*, first begun as a quarterly in 1952 and later superseded by *The Communicator*. And various schools and departments within the University continued to publish their own magazines, such as the Spanish *Estudios*, first released in January of 1952.

The graduate school offered a summer course in journalism education for faculty advisors to high school publications. This summer course spawned the Duquesne University Scholastic Press Association's annual all-day conference on high school yearbooks and publications. Duquesne also gave praise for outstanding high school publications at the Annual Newspaper Awards Day.

A 1954 Journalism Department survey of 125 alumni who had graduated since the department was founded in 1948 revealed that the vast majority of the respondents were employed in the journalism field. Four worked for local papers, eleven in the armed forces, one was doing Master's work at Columbia University, two were in the FBI, one was serving at the American Embassy in South Africa, one was working as a communications officer at Nicosia, Cyprus, and one was operating the university print shop on campus.

The Journalism Department, overseeing a host of special endeavors—ranging from WDUQ, to television production, to the *Duquesne Duke*, and to high school publications workshops—always maintained close ties with the media in the Pittsburgh area. In 1952 these associations made it possible for the department to set up internships in news, editorial, and advertising work for senior journalism students with the local weekly newspapers. That same year the department had also begun a speaker series for industrial editors.

In 1951, Duquesne's Journalism Association joined the American Society of Journalists, which cited Duquesne's Josie Carey, a pioneer in children's television programming, as "Pittsburgh Journalism Personality of the Year" in 1956.

Despite the previous financial disasters, a core of students began promoting the idea of a yearbook again in the spring of 1951 for the following year. A *Duke* editorial on how a yearbook would only be a waste of money and a lack of student momentum postponed any such undertaking for years, but a staff was finally recruited in the fall of 1955. To prevent the losses incurred by previous yearbooks, the books were sold on a pre-order basis with half the price as a deposit. A contest to name the yearbook resulted in *L'Esprit du Duc*. Six hundred were sold. After that the yearbook was truly a yearbook. In 1959, as a special feature, its staff announced the Hall of Fame to honor ten outstanding seniors. The yearbook also initiated the selection of the Duquesne Duke and Duchess, the male and female students at Duquesne who best exemplified the qualities of excellence (John Lelesch and Donna Dvorchak were the first). For a prepaid order, students could have their names imprinted in gold on the cover.

The Debate Team Grabs some Limelight

From its earliest days, Duquesne placed great emphasis on public speaking and debate, and in 1951 its team won the All-American awards and hosted the annual spring Novice Debate Tournament. Nevertheless, it was only occasionally that debate received mention in the *Duke*—until Professor Joseph Morice of the History Department took over the debate team in 1956. The Novice Debate Team that year went on to the regional eliminations, and the Varsity Debate Team hosted its third invitational tournament. The current events orientation of debate was reflected in student participation in other campus organizations, most notably in the Intercollegiate Conference on Government, the United Nations Club, the Young Republicans, and the Young Democrats. The university proclaimed that it would grant official recognition to the Young Republicans and Young Democrats only so long as both groups survived.

A Catholic Presence Remains Strong

A strong Catholic presence was accounted by many as the major strength of Duquesne. The National Federation of Catholic College Students was active in charity collections and fundraising, and in 1952 they branched out into catechesis by teaching in the new Confraternity of Christian Doctrine. Along with such practices as opening classes with the Lord's Prayer and rosary recitations in the chapel, Duquesne students also observed the ringing of bells at noon for the Angelus. The university agreed to house the archives of the Catholic Historical Society of Western Pennsylvania in the university library seminar room. Beginning in 1957 the university also celebrated Adoration Day, the national Pentecost observance.

Furthermore, Father Gallagher's involvement in the Holy Name Society led to the formation of a campus chapter of 41 Duquesne men in 1951. The resident coeds initiated Our Lady's Sodality, which they later opened to all women in Duquesne. In 1953 the Holy Name Society and Our Lady's Sodality members sang once a month at a Mass held at the county jail. The combined groups hosted a Christmas party at St. Paul's Orphanage for the first time in December of 1954, joining the NFCCS, fraternities, and sororities that worked for charitable causes. And the following year a new group, the College and University Relief Administration, sold holly and mistletoe to raise money for missions. Plus, Duquesne University participated in the newly formed Pittsburgh Intercollegiate Federation for Catholic Student Organizations.

A major celebration was held on campus in February 1952, commemorating the centenary of Venerable Lieberman, who revitalized the Spiritans in Paris after the French Revolution when he merged his Congregation of Mary with the Holy Ghost fathers. Students also actively celebrated the closing of Duquesne's Silver Jubilee with special pontifical Masses. They still participated in an annual retreat on Monday, Tuesday, and Wednesday of Holy Week, with classes canceled during the sessions and an opportunity provided for confession. May Crowning was still held at the university every spring at the Shrine of Our Lady of Victory, and May Day ceremonies were held in conjunction with area colleges and universities. The opening of Assumption Hall brought daily mass to its oratory for women students.

Catholic sentiments were expressed in a letter-writing campaign by students in 1952 to actress Ida Lupino, requesting that she decline offers to star in a movie on the life of Margaret Sanger, an early proponent of birth control. The actress responded in a letter published in the *Duquesne Duke*, thanking the students for their interest and sense of morality, and dispelling rumors that she would ever consent to playing such a role.

Duquesne had its own convent on campus next to Canevin Hall.[27] The Daughters of the Divine Redeemer, who were lodged there, cooked the meals at Trinity Hall and attended to its rooms and furnishings. Father Gallagher helped design and build them a garden shrine with a pool at the foot of St. Joseph in their cloistered garden.

Integration is Welcomed at Duquesne

Father Gallagher, was a staunch supporter of racial integration and did much to advance the cause at Duquesne. He spoke in the spring of 1952 at the Eastern Conference of Alpha Phi Alpha Negro Fraternity of the need for restraint in reacting to racial hostility:

> I realize that what is asked of the Negro today requires super human efforts. Self-preservation is a very basic instinct which exists—in all men—and it is natural to lash out against injustice.[28]

Alpha Phi Alpha became more prominent on campus when it produced the 1952 charity show, "Alpha Night of Stars." Its female counterpart, the Delta Sigma Theta sorority, was organized in 1946 but did not have the required ten members necessary for university recognition until 1953. African-American men enrolled in larger numbers than African-American women because of the opportunities in basketball and football. However, in 1953 Bobbie Jones, an African-American girl from Indianapolis, Indiana, was selected as the tenth Duquesne Darling by the *Duquesne Duke*, and the paper noted that her mother had also gone to Duquesne. Another African American, Audrey Nelson of the music school, was included in *Who's Who in American Colleges and Universities* in 1955.

In 1952 Duquesne began to offer financial aid "up to $100 per semester to Negro students." Most came to Duquesne because of its association with the Holy Ghost missionaries. They found a welcoming atmosphere on campus when they arrived. For example, the university celebrated Carver Day, honoring George

Washington Carver for his contributions to society, each January.

Duquesne's was not a common attitude in the 1950s, but it was one that sprang from the clear vision of the original Holy Ghost fathers, who knew that all people are valuable in God's sight, whatever their race.

Institute of African Affairs

The activities of the Holy Ghost fathers in the African missions were reflected on campus in a more dramatic way than the university policy of integration. The Institute of African Affairs was established on November 9, 1956, and received the apostolic blessing of Pope Pius XII, who applauded it as "a source of many benefits to all the people of Africa and to all those who strive to assist them materially, morally, and spiritually." Duquesne planned to offer both a bachelor's and a master's program in African Affairs Studies, the first comprehensive school on Africa in the United States. It was put under the direction of Father Francis M. Philben, C.S.Sp., who had spent six years in African mission work. A reception was held at the Provincial Headquarters in Washington, D.C., attended by church officials and government representatives from Belgium, Portugal, Great Britain, Morocco, Sudan, Liberia, Libya, and Ireland. A representative of the U.S. Foreign Aid Agency cited hopes that the institute would help fill a great need for personnel in the field of African-American diplomacy. Duquesne also joined a newly-formed African Studies Association that spring.

The first official activity of the new institute was to host a visit by Alione Diop of Senegal, French West Africa. Educated at the Sorbonne, Diop was a senator from 1946–1948, served on the French Colony Committee, and edited *Presence Africaine* in Paris. An official course in African studies was developed for the fall of 1957 as a graduate program. Applicants were carefully screened and required to attend an interview and pass an aptitude test in economics, history, political science, and sociology. All candidates were accepted on a probationary basis until they passed a January qualifying examination stressing the "meaning of a disciplinary study and its implied methodology." Courses were listed in the *Bulletin* under the various departments that offered them and were taught by faculty from those departments. With recognition by the U.S. Office of Education in 1959, the institute received substantial grants-in-aid, enabling it to operate with its own full-time and part-time faculty and offer extensive African-language programs.

The Alumni College

The Alumni College, originally begun in 1939, after a lapse of several years reappeared in February of 1953. After canvassing the alumni regarding their interests, faculty from four departments conducted a wide range of presentations dealing with mental health, economics, drugs, and literature. Each week brought 150 to 200 alumni and friends to the free lectures on topics like "T.V. and Your Child's Mind," "The Tobacco Controversy," "Our Lady and Music," and "Goodbye, Household Insects." In 1955 the Alumni College became the Community College. Following the presentations in the campus theater was a social with refreshments, all for a registration fee of $1 for a single night or $2 for the entire series. Lectures continued on "Hypnotism Holds No Fears" and "Why Can't Johnny Read?" The Seventh Annual Community College centered on a theme, "Healthy Thinking Is Happy Living," as presented from eight different viewpoints. The theme "Human Relations in a Geophysical Age" was explored at the October 1957 Community College. Turnout was great. In 1959 the new thousand-seat Mills Auditorium hosted an audience for lectures on the theme of "Leisure Living," focusing on the effects of additional leisure time on the economy, spirituality, learning, emotional tension, participation in government, poetry and literature, and music. In response to numerous requests, the Alumni Association published the eight lectures in a book, *Leisure Living*, available for $2.95.

The Community College was not the only forum for Duquesne professors to share their knowledge with the general populace. The University Speakers Bureau, operating since 1951, published a booklet, "Choose Your Speaker," in 1954 to assist groups in booking faculty speakers for social, civic, and religious groups. Duquesne professors contributed their services to teach in the Diocesan Institute of Adult Education as well.

Student Government Almost Dies

Student government at Duquesne was traditionally undervalued by the student body, which showed considerable apathy toward self-determination. In the Callahan administration, the Student Council had actually been disbanded in favor of the Dean's Council when not enough students chose to run for the vacancies. A strong student government following the Second World War, however, took over many of the functions of the fraternities in orienting new students and hosting dances. Student Council continued to host the Welcome Back dance, define the rules for social functions, plan homecoming activities, preside over freshman orientation, coordinate the carnival, and run the Community Chest drive. In March of 1951 Student Council members were issued armbands as aides in a new program of campus law enforcement. The Committee on Points and Keys was reestablished in 1953 to honor outstanding council members and those students who had "rendered unselfish service to the university and student body."[29] Nevertheless, elections had to be postponed due to a lack of candidates and, with only 11 of the 25 vacancies filled, not enough for a quorum, the Student Council died. Instead, the Welfare Committee handled fall activities through the Organization Presidents Association. The following fall a student government committee drafted a Student Bill of Rights and a new constitution, which was to be voted on by the student body—but less than a tenth of the students attended the meeting. The student body got involved with student government in at least one year during the 1950s, when it tried to impeach the Student Government Association (SGA) president. He was accused of (1) incompetence in not putting out a student directory and handbook, (2) failing to inform the students of SGA activities, and (3) imposing an unnecessary tax. Apparently sales of the student directory fell far short of the costs to produce it, and the SGA decided on a tax. Even here, though, apathy prevailed, and the impeachment movement was dropped. A revision meeting in the spring led to 15 proposals for the constitution committee, but only 19 percent of the students voted. Donna Dvorchak, who was later to be named Duquesne Duchess for 1959, reluctantly assumed the SGA presidency, and under her leadership, SGA finally had a strong and productive school year in 1958–1959. Along with producing an expanded yearbook and introducing the Duquesne blazer, SGA made the initial steps toward the formation of a Student Court to arbitrate campus disputes.

Resident Life in the Fifties—Lots of Regulations

In December of 1950 Father James F. "Black Mac" McNamara, C.S.Sp., took over the position of dean of men, freeing Father William J. Holt to handle his other responsibilities as chairman of the Student Welfare Committee and teaching Educational Psychology. Father McNamara published his list of rules for residents of the university-owned houses in February:

1. All residents must check in by 11 p.m. or one hour after university functions that continue past that hour.
2. Students must apply for late permission in special cases.

3. Hours are extended till 1:00 a.m. on Friday and Saturday.
4. Radios are to be off by midnight.
5. Card playing is forbidden during the day in the student lounge.
6. Occupants are responsible for damage to rooms and will be assessed as a group if no individual takes responsibility.

The Welfare Committee under Father Holt renewed enforcement of its ban on drinking at dances, much to the dismay of sponsoring groups, who feared a drop in ticket sales. The committee also organized a Council of Organization Presidents to govern work on the Carnival, the Community Chest drive, and a yearbook. Father McNamara began the 1952–1953 school year by reiterating the injunction against smoking in the wooden barracks buildings, a rule habitually disregarded by the students. Further regulations by the Student Welfare Organization in 1956 required that organizations respect the ban against social functions during Lent and submit a yearly report of activities, including a scrapbook. With new dance regulations in 1957, there were few functions on campus that did not have to submit to official regulations. Nevertheless, the mood was optimistic during the Gallagher years. When asked his impression of the atmosphere of Duquesne in 1955, Clarence C. Walton, the new dean of the school of Business Administration, told the Duke, "I like the willingness of our youngsters to work, and I like their friendliness."

Athletics: College Life without Football

Athletics continued to be a major part of campus life, but football, discontinued after the 1950 season, was sorely missed. Unlike his predecessor, President Gallagher was not willing to absorb the huge financial losses that football was likely to incur. Chuck Short, sports editor of the 1953 *Duke*, explained, "Duquesne quit the grid sport because the cleat marks were dragging too much red across the ledger sheets."

There were only two home games in the final season, with homecoming played at Pitt Stadium against Buff Donelli's Boston University team. That last homecoming was a nostalgic event, a reunion of Buff Donelli, Doc Skender, and Brue Jackson, all of whom had enrolled as Duquesne students in 1925. The team's performance was further hampered that year by the military call-up of Coach Phil Ahwesh, even though Doc Skender filled the gap as acting coach. The Dukes' October 27th win over St. Bonaventure resulted in an all-day celebration and the largest pep rally in Duquesne history. Students paid their traditional visits to the Pitt and Tech campuses. Carnegie Tech students stormed the Bluff the following week, jubilant over their homecoming victory over Case. Victories were rare, however, and Duquesne finished the season with only two wins to nine defeats.

When President Gallagher made the announcement in January 1951 that intercollegiate football was no longer to be played at Duquesne, he was acknowledging a changed situation in the sport. The big schools, especially the state universities, had "discovered" football and its potential for profit. Duquesne was by no means unique. "Hardest hit were the smallest schools of which over seventy dropped the sport in the first half of the 1950s."[30] Although students who had come to Duquesne on football scholarships could retain those scholarships even though they were no loner playing, Duquesne did what it could to help those who wanted to play to find positions at other schools.

Football was replaced by Carnival, which over the years took on many of the trappings of the football season, including dorm displays and a parade with floats. Homecoming for the alumni was centered around the building plan and a banquet, but without the traditional game. Phil Ahwesh was discharged from the army in

October of 1951 and returned to Duquesne, disappointed that there was no longer a team waiting for him, but gladdened that "many [Duquesne players] are now playing at various schools throughout the country."[31] Intramural touch-tackle football grew enormously, with twelve teams in play and the championship going to NFCCS the first year. Volleyball, badminton, and ping-pong were slated to begin in the expanded intramural program that November and softball in the spring.

In 1952, the homecoming theme was "Duquesne Builds with Pittsburgh." The next year homecoming became an alumni dinner affair held off campus. Homecoming in 1954 consisted of a special weekend at which the alumni dinner party was held at the new Gateway Plaza on a Saturday night, followed by the dedication of Assumption Hall on Sunday. The alumni also traditionally celebrated an Alumni Day in early June, which in 1955 was expanded to become a spring party. In 1956, Duquesne University ended its fall homecoming in favor of a basketball festival to kick off the season.

Ray Fleckenstein, sports editor for the 1954 *Duke*, proposed bringing football back on a limited basis to fill the void for the students and the alumni. His proposal included playing a Class B Schedule, hosting home games at major high school stadiums where residents might be drawn to attend, and awarding less inclusive, partial scholarships. Duquesne may have been able to afford the down-scaled involvement, but football remained dormant on the Bluff.

It was right that Duquesne should be celebrating its basketball team instead of holding a fall homecoming to mourn its late football team. In basketball the Dukes were certainly a force to be reckoned with, despite the absence of a home court. Although the season started off slowly, Coach Dudey Moore brought the Dukes to a 16–10 season in the winter of 1951 and captured a bid to play at the New York National Invitational Tournament. (Unfortunately, Duquesne lost to Wyoming in the first round.)

A preseason basketball reunion game brought 150 alumni players back in November 1951. They were defeated by Coach Dudey Moore's team, 50 to 31. The game occasioned the announcement of a new award for an outstanding senior basketball player in memory of Herb Brown, a Duquesne 1937 All-American who, as a navy pilot, was killed in action during the war. Duquesne was top-seeded in its fifth NIT bid, with four All-Americans, a 21–1 record (the best in the school's history), and Coach Dudey Moore was named United Press Coach of the Year. With an estimated million people watching the telecast in the Pittsburgh area, the Dukes beat Holy Cross, only to lose the NIT in the second game to St. Bonaventure. The disappointed Dukes then entered the NCAA tournament in Chicago, where they downed Princeton before suffering defeat at the hands of Illinois. Freshman Dick Ricketts, eligible to play under a recent ruling that fall, and sophomore Jim Tucker aided the team immeasurably, with Tucker named All-American that season.

Moore was pessimistic about his fifth season, but the Dukes won 18 games to 7 losses and went to the NIT again. After trouncing Western Kentucky and Tulsa, they lost to St. Johns, and, having won the consolation game against Manhattan, came in third. Duquesne students, welcoming back the basketball team, paid their traditional visits to neighboring campuses with disastrous results. The damage left in their wake caused one Pennsylvania College for Women (PCW, later Chatham) student to remark, "We cheered for you all season, and this is what we get."[32] The final action of that year's student council was to take up a collection for repairs at PCW and Tech.

In the fall of 1953 John "Red" Manning was appointed freshman coach and athletic director by Doc Skender. The gymnasium floor was refinished and the players outfitted with new warmup jackets and pants for what was hoped to be a great season. The old Iron Dukes: Becker, Urso, Melvin, Debnar, Kasperek, and Widowitz (Widdows), who first played basketball together in 1937, held their first reunion and wished the team well. The new UHF television station WENS, channel 53, scheduled broadcasts of four Duquesne games under the direction of Bob Prince, well known in radio sports broadcasting, where he was to become known as the "voice of the Pittsburgh Pirates." Rated in the preseason as best in the East, possibly in the nation, Duquesne won the Steel Bowl Trophy in December, the New York Holiday Tournament over the Christmas holidays, and, with a 23–2 record, was seeded first in the NIT Tournament. Dudey Moore was chosen coach of the Year by United Press again and was honored, along with Father Vernon Gallagher, by the Pittsburgh Junior Chamber of Commerce as among their selections for "Man of the Year." The Dukes did not quite live up to their promise. They defeated Niagara at the NIT only to lose to Holy Cross. President Gallagher nevertheless excused the student body from classes for a morning pep rally to welcome them back. The Dukes had set a new record number of victories—twenty-six—in a single season.

Because of the team's fine showing, an editorial in the November 1954 *Duke* reprimanded students for their lack of support at the beginning of the season. But Duquesne students had certainly developed interest as the season progressed, hitting a crescendo with "NIT Fever," and leading to a mass exodus to New York City for the tournament.

Coach Moore lamented his lack of big men (over 6'4"), but Duquesne at least was top-seeded once more in 1955. Considering Duquesne's luck at the NIT, top-seeding was referred to by the *Duke* as "the kiss of death." But the team was going strong: Dick Ricketts and Si Green, known on campus as the "Gold Dust Twins," were named All-Americans; Dudey Moore, with a career tally at Duquesne of 144 victories to only 44 defeats, signed a new three-year contract; and the Dapper Dan Club of Pittsburgh named him as "the man who did the most to publicize sports in the district during 1954."

The headline above a full-page picture of the Dukes in action at the hoop in the March 11th *Duquesne Duke* reads, "Is This the Year Dukes Reign?" After a 19–4 regular season, the Dukes finally took it all at the NIT with wins over Louisville, Cincinnati and Dayton. In a carefully planned strategy, Si Green and Dick Ricketts scored all 35 of the Dukes' points in the first half of the Dayton game, which ended with a score of 70 to 58. The students celebrated in a style benefiting champions, and an editorial in the *Duke* praised them for their lack of destruction in the New York hotels and for not running around to the other area campuses upon their return. Five thousand greeted the returning Dukes at the airport. The entire student body was invited to a testimonial dinner honoring the team.

To further celebrate the winning team, homecoming was moved to the beginning of basketball season in the fall of 1955. The Dukes won their opener against Carnegie Tech 61 to 25 and looked forward to a fine season. They took their fourth Steel Bowl Championship, but lost the Holiday Festival and finished the season with a 16–9 record.

The season almost came to a grinding halt in February when it was announced that the John Harris Gardens, home court for Duquesne, was to be razed. The Dukes were saved by a magnanimous gesture from the University of Pittsburgh, Duquesne's long-standing rival, to use the Pitt Fieldhouse for home games. The facility was not only convenient, it was a vast improvement over the Gardens. Duquesne was deeply touched by this prompt and generous offer. Doc Skender said, "It's one of the finest acts of sportsmanship I've ever known."

By the 1956–1957 season, Sihugo Green was gone and Duquesne's basketball greatness diminished. (Upon graduation that year, Sihugo Green was the first choice of the Rochester Royals; team co-captain Mickey Winograd went to the Philadelphia Warriors and was traded to the St. Louis Hawks).

The fall of 1957 saw bold changes in homecoming to revive a flagging school spirit, including the selection of a homecoming queen and slogan banners to replace the customary dorm decorations. The Dukes had finished the season with 10 wins to 12 losses, their first losing season in 24 years.

Dudey Moore accepted an offer to coach at LaSalle in Philadelphia. The move did not come as a complete surprise. New York University had approached Moore about coaching for them when his contract expired at the end of August. News also reached him that the freshman basketball team was to be disbanded. Rumors of an impending deemphasizing of basketball persisted, undoubtedly fueled by word of a proposed cutback in scholarships. The *Duke* accused the local newspapers of "bad press" in representing Duquesne's basketball team. The Duquesne team was even accused of unsportsmanlike "riding" of an African-American Cincinnati player as a racially motivated act. It was a peculiar charge indeed in view of the fact that Duquesne teams in previous year had fielded so many outstanding African Americans.

The coaching position fell to freshman coach John "Red" Manning, a native of Homestead, who had been coached by "Chick" Davies at Homestead High and by Dudey Moore at Duquesne, where he captained the 1951 squad. He took over the Duquesne Dukes with optimism despite the March *Duke* cartoon of Big-Time Basketball flying away. One of his teammates from his own playing days at the Bluff, Steve Garay from Sharon, Pennsylvania, came to coach freshmen basketball and cross country and to serve as intramural director.

Since the alumni had moved their homecoming celebration to the spring, the term "Basketball Festival" was adopted for the special three days of activities ushering in the new season in December. The event included a Tamburitzan performance at the new Peter Mills Auditorium, a special issue of the *Duquesne Duke*, a Mass for the team, a float parade, the Coronation Ball, a dinner, a pep rally, and a motorcade to the Pitt Fieldhouse for the St. Francis game. The team ended its first season under Red Manning with 13 wins to 11 losses, despite the fact that only 17 players had shown up for practice at the beginning of the season and the varsity team numbered only nine. The average crowd for a Duquesne basketball game ran between 700 and 800.

The race question came up yet again in the 1950s. Father Gallagher made a controversial decision that the team reject a bid to play in Louisiana's Sugar Bowl tournament over the Christmas holidays in the 1959–1960 season. Louisiana laws forbade blacks and whites to occupy the same stadium seats or to mix while participating in any sport. Assured that no segregation problems would arise, Doc Skender expressed interest in a bid, but the university decided against participation after it arrived. A sports editorial in the *Duke* was proud of the university's stand on a matter of principle, even though Duquesne had not a single black player on the varsity or freshman squads who might be affected. Others felt that the opportunity ought not be passed by precisely for the same reason.

The excitement that basketball generated did not easily transfer to other sports. The spring sports program existed in relative obscurity. Baseball had been resurrected by Charles Muse with the coaching assistance of Pirate great Pie Traynor, but Muse was called up for military duty in the fall of 1950 at the beginning of the Korean War. (Eventually, he worked as a scout for the Pittsburgh Pirates.) Lou "Doc" Skender filled in during his absence and coped with some very trying conditions. The limited gym practice facilities, combined with a cold, wet spring, resulted in an unprepared team, but they managed a 9–6 season.

In the 1952 season competition extended to include the University of Pittsburgh for the first time, with Duquesne the winner. With a 12–4 record, the baseball team was rated one of the top Eastern squads.

There was some renewed interest in the sport in 1955 when Ellen Conley became the first coed on the *Duke*'s sports staff interviewing the players. Then again, Dick Ricketts, basketball All-American, was the star pitcher, responsible for a 16-game winning streak that year.

In December of 1957 Duquesne was chosen as one of eight schools to participate in the new Western Pennsylvania Intercollegiate Athletic Conference. Although membership would not affect basketball, which was scheduled independently at a much higher level of competition, it did benefit the minor spring sports. In the conference, Duquesne played such teams as Waynesburg, West Virginia Wesleyan, St. Vincent, Geneva, and Pitt, either at Moore Field or in Munhall. When the *Duke* finished its reporting year, just before the big Pitt final, Duquesne's baseball record for 1958 stood at nine wins and four losses. Baseball star Fritz Binder received the B'nai B'rith trophy and went off to a scheduled tryout with the New York Yankees at the end of the season. The 1959 team scored its 100th victory under Doc Skender in a game against St. Francis, and finished with a good season.

Tennis continued to be coached by Paul G. Sullivan throughout the decade, although he was assisted by ex-Duquesne star Charlie Black in 1959 after his appointment as Western Pennsylvania's representative on the State Athletic Commission in February of 1955. The position of boxing commissioner had previously been held by Duquesne's John D. Holahan. Paul Sullivan offered his services free of charge. All-American Duquesne tennis player Joe Short assisted the 1952 team. They finished 4–2 for the season. The 1955 team had a losing season, despite the spectacular scoring of Charles Black. Si Green was also a member of that team.

New tennis courts were built behind Assumption Hall in the fall of 1955, easing the difficult situation of finding a home court at the area parks. The 1956 season boasted five returning lettermen and twins Dick and Ed Koselnik back from military service. But tennis suffered from a lack of players after that. A coed team was formed in 1958 that fared better than the varsity.

Golf had a very sporadic record, but the golfers truly operated at a disadvantage. For three years in a row they opened competition without a single practice session due to poor weather or a lack of practice facilities. The home course was Churchill Valley Country Club, yet the team was not allowed to practice there. They practiced at their own expense on public courses, never as a team, and were usually late for matches after attending classes all day, so they had no opportunity to warm up.

Duquesne had a difficult time keeping a cheerleading squad as well. Its all-male members were fiercely loyal, continuing their participation all through college, but graduations would find the squad down to a single man.

Pete Iole returned to campus as the Grand Duke in 1955. He had first appeared dressed in coat and tails in 1949 while attending night school. His public appearances ended following a motorcycle accident and he went on to the army reserve and work in South America for Gulf Oil until he finally amassed the necessary funds to finish his last year in the day school and pull his Grand Duke apparel out of mothballs. Pete graduated at last in the spring of 1956, and a new Grand Duke took his place at the games along with cheering squad captain Mossie Murphy's new recruits. For years, Mossie Murphy was synonymous with Duquesne cheering.

Spanish professor Reyes Carbonell, who had set three Spanish swimming records as collegiate champion of Spain and had a berth on the

Spanish Olympic team that was to have gone to Berlin just before the war, coached the swimming team in 1955. The "Aqua Men" scheduled their first four meets starting in December, but they never made it to competition. There were difficulties in securing the pool, and very few team members showed up for practice anyway.

Freshman basketball coach, Steve Garay, began the cross-country season in 1959 against Carnegie Tech—and lost. With only two experienced members, the team ended its first regular season 1–5.

Duquesne's rifle team, operating under ROTC auspices, but open to all for part of the competition, was a strong challenger during the 1950s. In 1950 and 1951, it placed first in the prestigious William Randolph Hearst ROTC National Tournament. The coeds formed their own 17 member team in 1952, although Michigan and Michigan State were the only other universities in the country with women's rifle teams. The girls' rifle team of 1953 had seven members, all freshmen, and Jean Degenhardt made the varsity team as its only coed. The team took third in the National Rifle Association Intercollegiate meet, and the ROTC squad placed seventh at the Hearst. They shot it out again at the Greater Pittsburgh Rifle League competition in 1955, taking three matches before being defeated, and placed third in the National Rifle Association competition. In the fall of 1956 the rifle team received recognition as an official varsity sport.

In the fall of 1957 the rifle team's opening shoot was in danger of cancellation due to an outbreak of the flu, but they ended the season with a spectacular 24 wins to 8 losses. Team captain, Bob Maguire, set a new scoring record. He became Duquesne's first All-American marksman as a member of the National Rifle Association team. After such a spectacular season, the team was disappointed by Coach Paul R. Elliot's departure for France, and although the Pershing Rifles placed second in the battalion drill at Gannon College in Erie in the spring of 1959, no mention was made of a varsity rifle team after Elliot's departure.

Following the conclusion of the basketball season, Duquesne held a special Sports Night. The first such event in 1952 witnessed Duquesne students pitted against blind wrestlers from the School for the Blind in Oakland, ping-pong and volleyball matches, and a basketball game between the varsity squad and the champion intramural team. The following year's event featured the city intramural championship games in basketball, wrestling, volleyball, badminton, and table tennis. Carnegie Tech took the intramural crown in volleyball and wrestling at the 1954 event, but the Chemets (Duquesne's Chemistry-premed team) beat Pitt for the city intramural basketball championship.

Touch-tackle intramural championships for the city were played just before the beginning of basketball season. An intramural softball program existed in relative obscurity since the games were played so late in the school year that they received little mention in the school paper. They suffered the same lack of attention that the varsity spring sport teams endured.

The WAA (Women's Athletic Association) at Duquesne organized five basketball teams for intramural competition in 1954. The following year, sorority teams challenged independents. The women continued their competitions with little publicity, but the Duquesne Duchesses of 1958, with a 12–1 intramural record, placed third in the thirty-four team Parks and Recreation Girls' Polio Benefit Tournament.

When Clare Marie Walsh became physical education director in the fall of 1955, she introduced basketball, volleyball, swimming at Oliver High, intercollegiate table tennis and a women's Ski Club, which made a trip to Seven Springs that winter, where the members spent most of their time sledding, if the pictures are to be believed. The students also went rock climbing at McConnell's Mill State Park in the early spring.

The final piece in Duquesne's athletic picture

was the Resident Bowling league, which continued strong, sponsoring both men's and women's competitions.

End of an Era

In July 1958 Father Gallagher was elected provincial superior of the American Province of the Holy Ghost Order. Although continuing as university president, he was now also in charge of priests in the United States, Puerto Rico, and East Africa. The order was to maintain its headquarters in Washington, D.C., although Father Gallagher intended to operate both offices from Pittsburgh. In November 1958, however, it was announced that the offices of the Holy Ghost Order in the United States were to be moved from Washington, D.C., to a 19-acre tract of land in Dorseyville, about 12 miles north of the campus. Father Gallagher took up residence at the farmhouse on the property, within commuting distance of Duquesne.

The strain of administering two institutions, the university and the provinciate, with all of the responsibilities that attended them was more than any single individual could manage, however. Father Gallagher had to make a choice. Citing "the overburdening demands of serving in the dual capacity as head of the Holy Ghost fathers and administering to the affairs of Duquesne," he announced at a press conference on June 19, 1959, his resignation as president of Duquesne University, effective October 1st. He later served as academic vice-president at St. Michael's College in Vermont.

Father Gallagher had already enlisted additional aid in administering his dual responsibilities by appointing Father Henry J. McAnulty, C.S.Sp., a former Air Force Chaplain, to the newly created post of administrative assistant to the president. McAnulty arrived on October 6, 1958. Few could have imagined what changes would eventually be wrought by his arrival, although McAnulty later said he knew immediately the purpose of his summons.

7. Redeveloping the Bluff

Duquesne had had several presidents whom the students respected and even admired, but none were so loved as "Daddy Hehir" had been—until "Father Mac," Henry Joseph McAnulty C.S.Sp., became Duquesne's ninth president in 1959.

"Father Mac"

"Father Mac," or more frequently, just "Mac," enjoyed talking with the students in chance encounters on the street or in the cafeterias. Almost as soon as he arrived, he began a presidential-student love affair that lasted throughout his tenure. There were perhaps a number of Holy Ghost fathers who knew Duquesne better than Henry McAnulty, but none who knew Pittsburgh and its people any better. Born in the Shadyside neighborhood of Pittsburgh on April 25, 1915, he was a sociable man who had many friends and much experience in dealing with people before he became Duquesne's president. He had majored in philosophy and English at Duquesne with no intention of becoming a Holy Ghost father. But following his graduation in 1936, he entered St. Mary's Holy Ghost Seminary, Norwalk, Connecticut, where he earned a bachelor of divinity degree. "It was an experiment," he later said of attending seminary, "but I just kind of stayed."[1] He was ordained in 1940. During World War II, Father McAnulty entered the Army Air Corps as a chaplain and served 15 years, reaching the rank of lieutenant colonel. Even after he left the air force, McAnulty stayed in the reserves and was later promoted to the rank of Brigadier General, the first Catholic so honored in that branch of the service.

Having resisted for several months Father Gallagher's entreaties to come to Duquesne as assistant to the president, Father McAnulty at last agreed in October 1958. The next year he became president, the last Duquesne president to be simply named to the position by the provincial—as had traditionally been the case—without a search committee. There was no formal installation ceremony.

McAnulty was new to academic life and later said, "When I came here I didn't know what a quality point was." But the chaplain-turned-president was a quick study:

> Even if I were a scholar, in America today the president is a fund-raiser and he is the one who has to create the climate in which the people can work. If he can do both of those, there are scholars hopefully among the deans and the administration and the academic vice president who can take care of that.[2]

Despite the presence of his predecessor as both provincial of the order and chairman of the board of directors of Duquesne University, from the beginning of his administration, Henry McAnulty intended to be his own man. But it wasn't always easy in the long shadow cast by Father Gallagher. McAnulty later recalled, "For the first year I would go anywhere—sometimes people would introduce me as Father Gallagher."[3] He told himself, "Okay, so you can't be Vernon Gallagher; you have to be Harry McAnulty."[4] And Harry McAnulty had a style that was all his own, one with a very high community profile. "I made myself visible," McAnulty recalled. "I attended everything from convocations to corn roasts, almost like I was running for office. . . . I had to sell myself. I had to convince them that even though I was Father McAnulty, that I was Henry—downtown they called me Henry—whom they could trust."[5] He made it his goal to help both Pittsburgh's elite and the community at large to recognize the contributions of Duquesne and its value to everyone in

Pittsburgh. On one occasion the father of Senator John Heinz, Mr. Jack Heinz, who was then patriarch of the family, was invited by McAnulty to visit the Bluff. He stood in front of Trinity Hall, looking at the campus, and said, "I didn't realize this was up here." So Father Mac's goal of manufacturing a high profile was a necessary one, especially if the Master Plan were ever to be realized.[6]

When McAnulty assumed the presidency, Gallagher's Master Plan was still largely on paper. It required more money than the alumni and the local Catholic population could possibly raise. Moreover, the Master Plan of 1951, with its bland set of look-alike buildings, no longer fit Duquesne's plans for the 1960s. Nor did it fit the requirements of the Urban Redevelopment Authority, which asked for three alternate versions of a new Master Plan, each having a detailed description of land usage.

Old Main

The New York architectural planning firm of Mayer, Whittlesey & Glass was hired to draw up the three versions, which were submitted to the university in October of 1960. All three versions envisioned razing the Administration Building and placing a student union on the site. Father Mac deliberately leaked the proposals to the news media, and as he had hoped, the alumni expressed their disapproval in a united voice. The beloved Old Main, instead of being demolished, would be renovated! As Father Mac said when addressing the Pittsburgh Rotary Club, "To most people, that building represents Duquesne. We can't tear it down."[7]

With help from the alumni, and at a cost of $700,000, the unsightly fire escapes were removed, the stairwells redone, and the wooden windows replaced with aluminum ones. With the installation of an elevator, the presidential offices could be moved from the first floor to the fifth. The exterior was sandblasted, removing the paint that had previously been applied to the stone courses only to run down over the brick. Unfortunately, the lofty chimneys that graced the building were much truncated, seriously detracting from the building's Victorian appearance. The completion of Old Main's renovation in 1966 ended its use as a classroom facility.

The Urban Redevelopment Authority

In their basic design, the three versions of the revised Master Plan were much the same. However, one version showed a field house and playing field directly on Forbes Avenue. Although this was entirely within the area designated for redevelopment, university officials had not seriously entertained the possibility that Duquesne might actually get the property. This was precisely what the Urban Redevelopment Authority did envision, and in September 1961 its board voted to make Duquesne the developer of most of the property between Locust Street and Forbes Avenue.[8] It was a happy and momentous turn of events. The addition of 11 more acres to what had previously been approved would increase the size of the campus from the originally projected 28 acres to about 39 acres.

The entire Bluff Street Project embraced 43 acres. Of this, only 26 acres were to be demolished, and of that about 21 were to be acquired for resale to Duquesne. The land was to be sold to the university not by the acre but by the square foot! It was Duquesne's equivalent of the Louisiana Purchase. Approximately 924,800 square feet were being made available at a cost to the university of $1.05 per square foot. The net effect of this transaction was that Duquesne was acquiring about $7.5 million worth of cleared land for less than a million dollars.

The new plan, complete with an actual model, was unveiled in June 1962. A 350-car parking lot added at the insistence of Pittsburgh City Planning, a field house, athletic field, ROTC building, and high-rise faculty housing were to occupy the newly added land along Forbes Avenue. The plan, grown now to a $24 million extravaganza, double the amount envisioned in 1951, included a complex of buildings for the liberal arts and sciences, a university center, an auditorium, and a music building. While very little of this plan would develop along the lines that the planning architects had imagined, one idea that was realized made a major contribution to campus development. Mayer, Whittlesey, & Glass wanted to restrict vehicular traffic to the perimeter of campus as much as possible. While leaving Locust and Colbert (McAnulty Drive) Streets open to traffic, their plan would transform Vickroy Street into a pedestrian mall to tie the campus together and give it a focus. The plan called it Academic Walk.

The new Master Plan retained the original plan's escalator from Forbes Avenue that would lift passengers directly into a student union on the Bluff. The plan also called for the building of a footbridge from Rockwell Hall across Locust Street to the upper campus. To the chagrin of generations of students and the aching bones of the faculty, this bridge would not become a reality until 1992.

The Library Addition

The library, according to President McAnulty's own report, had "reached the critical point."[9] Lack of space had not prevented the library from adding nearly 7500 books annually. When the new 32,000-square-foot, three-story addition opened in November 1961, the library, now more than doubled in size, practically exploded into the new space with its collection of 136,158 volumes.

The ultra-modern addition of light gray brick did not contrast well with red brick of the original 1939 building. Eventually an entirely new facility would be constructed. In the meantime, the library had capacity for a quarter million books, a statistic that head librarian Eleanor McCann and her staff seemed determined to test. They began acquiring new titles at a rate of 15,500 per year, nearly double the rate before the addition, and subscribed to nearly 2000 periodicals.

Strangely, much of the library's collection was ruled out of bounds for undergraduates, and the new addition's top floor was restricted to faculty and graduate students. The head librarian introduced other restrictive measures about which the *Duquesne Duke* complained from time to time. Sections of the ground floor, for instance, McCann ordered to be roped off as closed stacks when these had originally been intended as open stacks. Students who defied the rope—it could easily be ducked under—did so at the risk of being caught and scolded. Even the attempts of a faculty library committee to exert some control over the library proved ineffective without administrative backing, which it plainly did not have.

University Hall

Since space of every sort was needed, it came as so much manna from heaven when, in 1961, the Pittsburgh Testing Laboratory sold its building at the corner of Stevenson and Locust Streets to the university for the near-giveaway price of $76,806. The red brick building trimmed in stone was not an architectural masterpiece, but it did look somewhat like a college building. Although not what the Master Plan envisioned, the five-story building was a far cry from the many converted houses that the university was still using. Originally built in 1909 as the Old News Boys Home, the former orphanage-turned-laboratory had the merit of being immediately convertible into a number of university uses. Since it was at the Mercy Hospital end of the campus, only a block away from Assumption Hall, it had the further advantage of strengthening Duquesne's claim at the far end of the Bluff. Called University Hall, and renamed Des Places in 1981, most of the building was taken up by army and air force ROTC, which gladly gave up their post-World War II era barracks quarters on Bluff Street beside the administration building. The building also contained a women's gymnasium, the University Printing Shop, WDUQ, and a laboratory for the School of Nursing.

For years the university intended to raze the building as a part its new Master Plan, but lack of funds caused the administration to change its mind—permanently, as it turned out.

St. Martin's Hall

Father Mac did not forget the promise he made to the male students at the beginning of his presidency: to build a men's dormitory. The building, completed in August 1962, was erected on land that the university had purchased next to Assumption Hall on Bluff Street. The red brick was complemented by cast concrete window encasements that added a measure of visual interest. Named St. Martin's Hall after Father Martin Hehir, the dorm was a 15-story highrise housing 557 students. Funding for the $2.25 million building was obtained from the Federal Housing and Home Financing Agency. Duquesne had no difficulty securing the 3.5 percent loan, since the building would be self-amortizing if it had at least a 90 percent occupancy rate.

The *Bulletin* stated, "The new dormitory features three electronically controlled elevators, individual mail lockers, a commons room on each floor and a main recreation room. Rooms are arranged around a central service core containing laundry facilities, telephones, and a commons room. Each room features sofa-type pullout beds, built-in closets, book and trunk shelves, tack board, and adequate storage space. Single, double, and triple rooms are available." Unlike Assumption, however, St. Martin's Hall was built without cafeteria facilities. The university purchased the Industrial Rubber Products Building at the corner of Magee and Vickroy Streets and remodeled it into the residents' dining hall in 1962. Then, in 1971, Towers Dormitory was built, and in 1972 the dining hall, known as Union II, was razed.

Bluff-Area Residents React to Redevelopment

When public hearings on the Bluff Street Development Project were held before Pittsburgh City Council in July 1962, the smooth sailing suddenly turned rough. A small but determined number of angry residents refused to surrender their homes to the Urban Redevelopment Authority. At a council hearing, one charged Duquesne with a 12-year conspiracy, accusing the school of "planning that far back for the acquisition of properties for expansion."[10] Another said that Duquesne was "chasing" her out of the city, contributing to its population decline.[11] Most serious of all was the constitutional issue of separation of church and state. An attorney representing a Bluff Street couple claimed that resale of the condemned property to Duquesne would be illegal because it would be "committing public funds to the furtherance of a religious faith."[12] Underlying all of the questions of constitutionality or any of the other statements given at the hearings was still another reason that had long been suspected as the real motive behind the protests. That same attorney, according to *The Pittsburgh Press*, "indicated the opposition might disappear if the price is right."

Despite the angry rhetoric and some coverage of the hearing in the inside pages of the local newspapers, the City Council approved the Master Plan without delay. Although it was true that otherwise taxable real estate would disappear from the tax rolls, the neighborhood was undeniably in a state of decay, with no imminent signs of improvement. University officials were careful not to publicly call the area a slum for fear of further antagonizing the residents. But it was, in fact, a slum. In the end, the Urban Redevelopment Authority paid the homeowners—there were about 225 families living within the boundaries of the Bluff Street Project—considerably more than the true market value of their property. By way of illustration, one woman, who had purchased the house for $8,000 eight years earlier, received $24,000 for it.

The Bluff Street Project also involved the relocation of 47 businesses. They were not enthusiastic about starting over in new locations and joined the homeowners in complaining about the redevelopment project.

Threat from the Lunatic Fringe

The Bluff residents were not the only group opposed to Duquesne's redevelopment plans. The Bluff Street Project was also attacked by an extremist group calling itself Protestants & Other Americans United for the Separation of Church & State (POAU). It had taken notice of urban redevelopment projects in Pittsburgh and a number of other cities. In March of 1963 POAU called a protest meeting at the Soldiers and Sailors Memorial in hopes of drumming up enough public support to block the Duquesne University part of the Bluff Street Development Project. POAU charged that the use of urban renewal funds to aid Duquesne's expansion constituted a violation of the principle of separation of church and state.

Later, Father Joseph Lauritis, vice-president for university relations and director of development, answered for Duquesne. He said the University acquired the land "because they were the largest single developer that offered the city a reasonable plan for improving the land."[13] He also noted that, contrary to POAU's charge, "the Urban Renewal Project was open to anyone who wanted to undertake it, and the city felt that Duquesne could do a better job of redeveloping the area."[14] Finally, he pointed out that the POAU had filed suits against Fordham University and St. Louis University for land acquisitions under urban redevelopment, and in both cases the federal courts had ruled that such actions were not a violation of the Constitution. POAU had also questioned the constitutionality of selling such land to universities such as Duquesne below its true market value, but here, too, they were barking up the wrong legal tree. In the case of *64th St. Residences v. City of New York* (1958), the New York Supreme Court had upheld a contract whereby New York City conveyed land condemned via eminent domain by the Urban Redevelopment Authority to Fordham University, a sectarian (e.g., Catholic) institution, at approximately 44 percent of its cost.

In its ruling in favor of the City of New York, the court said: "Plaintiffs say that, because the city arranged to sell this land at a price much below what the city will pay for it, this necessarily amounts to a subsidy or gift. But what the city is buying is not the same as what Fordham is buying. . . . What Fordham is paying for is the re-use of the land. . . . The city benefits by the achievement of its valid municipal purpose of eliminating a slum." Those initiating the injunction proceedings against the city petitioned the Supreme Court of the United States to review the decision of the state court. The Court refused.

A POAU pamphlet was titled, "Urban Takeover: How Taxpayers' Money is Being Used to Give the Heartland of American Cities to the Roman Catholic Church." It pictured Father McAnulty and Robert B. Pease, director of the Urban Redevelopment Authority, looking at a scale model of Duquesne's Master Plan. In an earlier day the pamphlet might have had some real effect, but in the ecumenical atmosphere of the 1960s, it sank into obscurity. At the Methodist General Conference, Pease, who happened to be a delegate, denounced the "half-truths" in the pamphlet saying, "I deplore any anti-Roman Catholicism disguised as an effort to maintain the separation of church and state."[15] The Catholic bishop of Pittsburgh and chancellor of Duquesne University, Most Reverend John J. Wright, spoke at that conference and received a standing ovation. Such a thing had never before happened in Pittsburgh. Times had truly changed.

St. Ann's, West and East

At last, in December of 1962, the Urban Redevelopment Authority began to acquire land on the Bluff. The university was anxious to begin work on a second women's dormitory. The new Master Plan called for a long L-shaped four-story building that would match St. Martin's Hall in its general exterior appearance. The university already owned the western part of the site, and in 1963 it built St. Ann's West with a federal loan of $1,410,155. The following year St. Ann's East was completed, with a second federal loan, this time of $1,360,966. The buildings were five stories and seven stories, respectively, and had the capability of having more floors added in the future.

The erection of St. Ann's East caused the university's first run-in with its federal agency benefactor. The Federal Housing and Home Finance Agency (FHFA) flatly refused the university building plans, contending that with such a "large" dormitory, the student occupancy rate would fall below the amount necessary to generate income sufficient to meet the mortgage payments on the building. Father Mac, however, elected to proceed without the agency's endorsement, and the *Duquesne Bulletin* boasted of it, "A recreation room, snack machines, laundry facilities, and spacious lounge account for the students' description of this dormitory—'The Duquesne Hilton.'" The dorm, East and West, housed 500 students. Thus by the fall of 1964 when St. Ann's East opened, the university had housing for 1,324 students in three buildings. Not realizing that in a few years the need for more student housing would occur on a vastly increased scale, university officials believed that "Duquesne will never become predominantly residential."[16] About one out of five students were residents, a ratio that was expected to continue. Nearly nine out of ten were from Allegheny County. The addition of the dorms did little to cosmopolitanize the student body; in 1965 students were enrolled from 32 states and 28 foreign countries, but their numbers were small. States with the largest enrollments were New Jersey with 202, New York with 164, Ohio with 136, Connecticut with 58, and West Virginia with 40.

University Governance

The days when a president could run a university with a paternalistic, all-powerful hand were long past. No president, no matter how competent or well-intentioned, could make decisions affecting the fate of the university by himself. Father Gallagher had recognized this when he created the President's Advisory Board in 1954, composed almost entirely of laymen. But Father Mac believed that the board's lack of any real power affected the credibility of the university in the eyes of Pittsburgh's corporate elite and therefore impaired its fund-raising efforts. In addition, he said it felt "too close to the administration and had a tendency to approve whatever the Holy Ghost Fathers were doing."[17] Therefore, in October 1962 the board of directors of the University corporation empowered the president to organize his Advisory Board into a separate corporation. The new Duquesne University Foundation was founded to

- Review and interpret the university curriculum.
- Assist in planning for the university's long-range needs and goals.
- Supply advisory services to the university president.
- Plan and assist in getting support for the university from "all financial sources" in the community.
- Invest and manage funds, real estate and other assets acquired by the foundation and held in trust by it for the university.[18]

All 25 members of the old Advisory Board were invited to become members of the new foundation. E.J. Hanley, CEO of Allegheny Ludlum Steel Corporation, was named chairman.

Duquesne's charter had stated that, with the exception of the governor of Pennsylvania, all members of the board of directors had to be Holy Ghost Fathers, but in 1966, it was amended to allow laymen to sit on the board. With time, the number of laymen—and, beginning in 1970, laywomen—increased, and the board assumed primary governance over the administration of the university.[19] In 1971 the University Board of Directors and the Duquesne University Foundation were merged to form a single 46-member board of directors. Following the procedure they had used in 1963, the corporation asked its members to serve on the board of directors.

The Ecumenical Movement

There was no provision that the laymen on the Board of Directors had to be Catholic. Indeed, Father McAnulty desired that this not be the case. Duquesne University reached out to Protestants, Jews, and Orthodox Christians to a degree that had not been possible in the 1950s. The good relationship the University had with the Jewish community was especially noteworthy. Eight percent of the faculty was Jewish, a fact not lost on Pittsburgh's Jewish community, which did not fear to send their young to Duquesne. Moreover, the Jewish attorney Louis Little left the university a bequest of $25,000, some of which Father McAnulty (who served on the Board of National Conference of Christians and Jews) used to buy State of Israel Bonds. Also, the Rabbi Herman Hailperin Collection, valued at $20,000, was a gift from the Jewish Community to Duquesne. These 2,600 items on biblical interpretation, including six books printed before 1550 and some that were the only known copies in existence, reside today in the Duquesne University Library.

The change in outlook had come from the Vatican itself. In 1958 John XXIII had announced a general council and invited observers from other faiths. The spirit of ecumenism that he inspired quickly took hold on the Bluff. Indeed, Duquesne University was among the front-runners in ecumenical studies. Dr. Elwyn Smith of Pittsburgh Theological Seminary (a Presbyterian school) was appointed an adjunct professor in the Theology Department and taught a course in Protestant Christianity. The Duquesne University Press published its first issue of the *Journal of Ecumenical Studies: Catholic, Protestant, and Orthodox* in January 1964. It was edited jointly by Dr. Leonard J. Swidler of Duquesne's History Department and Dr. Elwyn Smith, with its purpose described as to "offer Christian theologians throughout the world a single forum for their opinions."[20] The *Journal* grew out of ecumenical dialogues begun the previous year through a grant from the Howard Heinz Endowment Fund. Within two years it was recognized as one of the world's leading publications in the field, and the members of its editorial board embarked upon a new endeavor, Ecumenical Week, March 1–5, 1965. In a one-faith-per-night format, public demonstrations of the Eucharistic liturgy followed by a public lecture were performed in Peter Mills Auditorium. The Presbyterian, Lutheran, Roman Catholic, Orthodox, and Methodist faiths were represented.

Though later generations would experience ecumenism as commonplace, in the 1960s such interfaith cooperation was still novel. Father Mac, long accustomed to such associations through his air force experience, unreservedly welcomed the new religious climate in America. It had allowed a Catholic to be elected president of the United States, but it had even more direct benefits for Duquesne. A decade earlier, Duquesne had championed the cause of anticommunism on behalf of the free world. In the 1960s, the new spirit of religious openness enabled the university to approach the larger society more positively than ever before.

The university's 1963–64 report celebrated the multireligious makeup[21] of its faculty, saying that "theology is taught in theology classes, not in chemistry laboratories," and noting that the faculty, regardless of religious affiliation, was "hired as authorities within their fields of competency."[22] The faculty was free to work in an atmosphere of unfettered inquiry, though, the report added, "They are not free to teach that Roman Catholicism is false. They are not free to teach that there is no God."

Faculty Size and Quality

It was remarkable that despite the efforts and resources being expended on improving the physical plant, the quality of the faculty at Duquesne, as measured in educational attainment, rose significantly. In 1953 only about 20 percent of the faculty held a Ph.D. or its equivalent, but by 1965 that number had doubled. The faculty size grew 75 percent in the ten years from 1955 to 1965.[23] But the student body grew at an even faster rate. To accommodate the burgeoning enrollment of the 1960s, some faculty were asked to teach extraordinarily large classes. Prior to 1961, truly large classes had been unknown on the Bluff, even though the practice of scheduling large classes had long been proliferating at other universities around the country. Beginning in September 1961, the theater beneath the chapel was used for introductory-level classes. More than 200 students crowded into the theater for such classes as Principles of Biology, Western Civilization, and Introduction to Political Science. Although they were assisted by graduate students, the teaching loads were still heavy enough to limit the amount of research the faculty could do. University support for scholarship was also pitifully small. The two $1,000 awards that did exist applied only to faculty publications in the fields of philosophy and theology.

In a university so tuition-dependent as Duquesne—it accounted for 67 percent of income in 1965–1966—the salaries were not high. The university reported the "minimum compensation of full-time faculty members" for the 1965–1966 academic year (not including overloads or summer pay) as follows: assistant professor, $5,833; associate professor, $6,416; professor, $7,500. In that year the Bureau of the Census reported median income for full-time salaried professional males as $8,500. When Father McAnulty was asked, "Can Duquesne pay enough to compete for outstanding professors?" he responded, "Yes, I think we can," but, significantly, he added, "Many professors can supplement their salaries in an urban area."[24] Despite the necessity for outside work, scholarly output in the 1960s was considerably higher than it had been a decade earlier.

The Faculty Senate

The faculty in the 1960s was manifesting a greater degree of interest in the governance of the university than it had before. Even this had historical roots, however. In the 1950s the American Association of University Professors (AAUP) had begun requesting data on faculty pay scales from colleges and universities. When Duquesne's AAUP Chapter asked Duquesne to take part in this survey, the administration declined to do so. The faculty then sent out questionnaires of their own to other faculty members and on the basis of this pressure persuaded the administration to join the survey. This constituted the earliest faculty action of its sort on the Bluff. But some faculty felt that it would be better to have an organization that was not subject to rules laid down by AAUP. Therefore, in 1962 the Faculty Senate began, with Dr. Foster Provost as its first president. Its first major achievement was to secure better retirement benefits for its membership. Today it continues "to debate, define, and help to resolve matters at issue among various parts of the faculty and between the faculty and the administration," as Father Mac requested of it back in 1966.[25]

A State-Related University in Pittsburgh

As Duquesne planned and built for the future, events were already in motion on another Pittsburgh campus that were destined to have an enormous long-term impact on the Bluff. At the

University of Pittsburgh, Chancellor Edward Litchfield had for years been spending considerably beyond the university's income. Borrowing and creative bookkeeping could no longer hide Pitt's massive $23 million debt, which came to light when Litchfield suffered a heart attack in 1965. The new acting chancellor appealed to the state for an emergency $5 million dollar appropriation. The Pennsylvania State Senate quickly approved it and Governor William W. Scranton signaled his intention to sign the bill when it passed the state House. The House held one day of hearings at Duquesne during which numerous officials paraded into Peter Mills Auditorium to testify on Pitt's behalf. Not wishing to capitalize on Pitt's financial distress, McAnulty did not oppose the state subsidy. He had, however, already gone on record regarding the plight of Pennsylvania's private colleges in an editorial saying, "Private higher education cannot survive the increasing financial competition from public institutions."[26] He did not ask for a state appropriation for Duquesne. Rather, he proposed that a state or even national scholarship program be implemented wherein money would be given directly to the student. The student could then use the money to attend either a public or private school. The legislature took little notice of Father McAnulty's editorial; a week after the hearing at Duquesne, it voted the entire $5 million that Pitt requested.

Within eight months the legislature was compelled to vote an additional $5.8 million "for regular maintenance," this, despite the fact that the original appropriation was supposed to carry the school to the end of the 1965–1966 fiscal year. Heads of private colleges in western Pennsylvania could not help but think that the state had financed one private university's construction program as well its faculty salary increases, while the remaining schools were laboring under responsibly tight budgets.

With the second appropriation, Pitt's trustees began to actively explore the idea of some form of state-relatedness. The state House Subcommittee on Education released a memorandum in December 1965, claiming "There is a great need to provide four years of low tuition college opportunities in various fields" and noting that "of the existing institutions . . . only the university of Pittsburgh is so constituted as to lend itself to such a conversion with the least amount of difficulty and expense." The memorandum also noted the Community College of Allegheny County that was "due to commence operations . . . next September," with its low tuition and the impact that it and a reduced tuition at Pitt would have on other area colleges. At last McAnulty's suggestion was given official notice: "Nor should we overlook the extraordinary value of the existing private colleges and universities. A continuing program of scholarship aid coupled with liberal loan programs must be expanded." Then in what must have given the private schools hope, the memo added in ringing tones, "It would be a tragedy of great magnitude if state action precipitated the decline and/or demise of these valuable schools of higher education."

Despite this high blown rhetoric, there was no consultation with any of the private schools in the area, all of which continued to be much concerned about the impact that a low tuition state university in Pittsburgh would have on their enrollments. Charles Simpson, chairman of the State Council of Higher Education, was thoroughly alarmed at the prospects of Pitt's tuition falling from $1,450 to $450 in a single year. He vowed to fight such a sudden drop, calling it "disastrous" for other Pittsburgh colleges. House majority leader K. Leroy Irvis, whose legislative district embraced the University of Pittsburgh, disagreed, saying that Carnegie Tech and Duquesne would not be adversely affected. Duquesne issued a press release disputing Irvis's ill-considered remark:

> The Very Reverend Henry J. McAnulty, President of Duquesne University, speaking for the administration and the members of the Duquesne University

Foundation, said that on the contrary, there is grave concern about Duquesne's future in private higher education in the face of any large and sudden reduction in tuition at Pitt.

> "Last year student tuition at Duquesne constituted 69% of our income dollar," Fr. McAnulty said. "Competition between figures of $1,300 and $450 a year can only cause students to look to the lower tuition figures. . . . This can only hurt Duquesne."

Days later Irvis wrote to McAnulty saying, "I want to take this opportunity to assure you that neither I nor anyone else working in the field of education here in Harrisburg is going to permit harm to come to Duquesne University through our efforts to aid the University of Pittsburgh." Irvis then promised to hold hearings at which the "representatives from private colleges and universities will be given an opportunity to explain their needs and problems."[27] The hearing was held, but nearly everyone, it seemed, favored state-related status. Politicians, businessmen, the clergy, and labor leaders vied with one another for newspaper coverage of their endorsements. Governor Scranton signed the bill on August 23, 1966, just in time for the beginning of the fall semester. Pitt's tuition did indeed fall from $1,450 to $450 per year.

Tuition Costs and Enrollment

Meanwhile, tuition at Duquesne and other private schools continued to spiral upward. The cost of a credit at Duquesne in 1950 was $12; by 1960 it had risen to $22, an increase of 83 percent. In the 1960s costs escalated even faster. Tuition went from $22 a credit in 1960 to $53 a credit in 1970, a rise of 140 percent, whereas the U.S. cost of living increased only 23 percent in the 1950s and 31 percent in the 1960s.

Despite the tuition increases, enrollment continued to rise. American colleges and universities were experiencing the effects of the baby boom generation reaching college age. Furthermore, larger percentages of high school graduating classes were pursuing higher education. High school students were barraged with statistics illustrating the relationship between a college degree and earnings potential. The number of students in American colleges and universities increased 111 percent in the 1960s, compared with a 35 percent increase the decade before.

Duquesne's student body increased by 50 percent in the 1960s compared with a 15 percent increase in the previous decade. When Pitt became state-related, Duquesne did experience a 10 percent drop in its freshman class, and sophomores and part-time students left as well, but the overall effect of Pitt's tuition reduction was not as bad as everyone had feared. The freshman class of 1968 numbered 7426.

As enrollments increased in the 1960s, the university continued to make a huge financial commitment for a projected student body of 10,000, a number that was expected to be reached by the year 1980. University officials planned to call a halt to the increasing size of the student body when it reached 10,000 because the physical plant would comfortably accommodate no more than that. They didn't have to, though, because that figure was never reached.

More New Schools in Pittsburgh

The education explosion of the 1960s brought a number of new schools to the city. In 1960 the Pittsburgh Business College transformed itself into Point Park Junior College. Four years later it became a four-year college granting both B.A. and B.S. degrees. By the mid-1960s the school had an enrollment of about 1700 students.

In 1962 the Pittsburgh School of Accountancy transformed itself into Robert Morris Junior College. In 1969 it became a four-year college, still with a business orientation, and its enrollment was about 3000. Both Point Park and Robert Morris had considerably less overhead than Duquesne and, as a consequence, charged less tuition.

The decade brought a third Catholic college into existence in the county. Duquesne and

Mt. Mercy College had operated extension courses at the Sisters of Divine Providence Motherhouse located about ten miles north of downtown Pittsburgh. In 1963 the Sisters began their own college. LaRoche College featured a liberal arts curriculum and by the 1970s had an average enrollment of about 700 students, many of them women in religious orders.

Since the early 1960s, the county commissioners had been seriously considering establishing a community college. McAnulty did not object to a two-year institution, but he could not ignore the fact that Point Park had been satisfied with its junior college status for only a short time. "The danger," he said, "lies in the fact that the community college may develop into a four-year academic college in questionable competition with other four-year colleges and universities."[28] The Community College of Allegheny County (CCAC) began operation in 1966, and at $300 a year, its tuition was the lowest in the city. Having multiple locations to serve a commuter student body, CCAC was a junior college offering both the liberal arts and technically oriented curriculum. Thus it attracted some students who otherwise may have considered Duquesne. Making the best of the situation, Father Mac decided to try to recruit qualified graduates from the CCAC—that is, to view it as a source of students rather than another competitor.

Educational Assistance

In varying degrees, nearly all of these schools duplicated programs offered on the Bluff—with lower tuition. Something had to be done to prevent a drop in the tuition-sensitive commuter enrollment. Toward this end, the Pennsylvania Association of Colleges and Universities (PACU), whose president was the president of Chatham College, and the commission of Independent Colleges and Universities (CICU), with Father McAnulty as president, lobbied in Harrisburg for the interests of private higher education. When in 1962, the presidents of Pittsburgh area colleges and universities began to meet informally, they discussed resource sharing. Soon this group, the Pittsburgh Council on Higher Education (PCHE), took on the added characteristic of offering "a common voice on matters that affect all of the member institutions."[29]

All three organizations were, in varying degrees, politically oriented, and with good reason. Father Mac later explained:

> It's easier for a legislator in Harrisburg to listen to a combined group than to a vested interest group. If I went as a president of a church-related school to a legislator, his job depends upon those other people too. But when PACU went to them, they listened.[30]

And the legislators did listen. The combined voices of these and other similar organizations caused a section to be added to the state's master plan that led to the creation of the Pennsylvania Higher Education Assistance Agency. It made grants to qualified students in both public and private institutions. Pennsylvania also set up the Institutional Assistance Grant (IAG). Unique in the nation, IAG gave funds to private colleges and universities based on the number of students who were eligible for state aid. Duquesne had the largest number of students receiving state aid and therefore received the largest amount from IAG.

In addition to state sources, Duquesne students were able to utilize a number of federal programs. Beginning in 1965, students at all colleges and universities were eligible for Education Opportunity Grants for financially disadvantaged families, Guaranteed Student Loans for middle-income families, and the Work-Study Program to enable students to work their way through college much as their parents had done under the Depression-era National Youth Administration. Under it, the students performed work for the institution where they were enrolled, with the federal government paying for 80 percent of the cost.

To a large degree, government financial aid kept Duquesne University competitive with the lower-tuition schools in the city. The available financial aid at Duquesne in the form of loans, grants, scholarships, and work-study amounted to $3,000,000 in 1967. By 1970, the total financial aid received exceeded $8,000,000 and was growing rapidly. At this writing, the amount of aid received annually exceeds $40 million, more than half of which is in the form of low-interest loans.

The College of Arts and Sciences

Almost since its founding, the School of Business Administration had been the largest in the university, but along with the national trend during the decades after World War II, the College of Liberal Arts and Sciences grew in enrollment. At last, in 1960, with 1382 registered, it became Duquesne's largest school, topping the business school by 194 students. And it was a trend that was to continue.

In 1961 the "Basic Studies" program for liberal arts freshmen included generous doses of history—12 credits of Western Civilization that replaced a four-credit requirement in American History—plus six credits of science (usually Principles of Biology), and 14 credits of a foreign language. The English requirement was revised, with four courses on facility in English, vocabulary, writing skills, and literature. The curriculum changes reflected a nationwide interest in increasing student knowledge in the sciences and humanities, often at the expense of the student's major field.

The Sciences and Grantsmanship

In the 1960s climate of industrial expansion and research, the number of science majors increased dramatically. To direct the growth of the science departments, a Science Advisory Committee was organized in 1961. Committee appointees came from major corporations and institutions, among them Carnegie Institute of Technology, Gulf Research, Heinz, Mellon Institute, and Allegheny Ludlum Steel, all interested in teaching and research in physical and natural sciences.

The science departments had been early beneficiaries of the increased availability of grant monies from Kennedy's New Frontier, responding to the perceived threat posed by Soviet scientific advances.[31] Then Lyndon Johnson's Great Society released a virtual avalanche of money for education that dwarfed New Frontier spending. Whereas the five largest grants in the fall of 1962 totaled $83,308, a single grant just two years later provided Dr. Oscar Gawron $250,000 to study certain operations of cell tissue. The grant was the largest in Duquesne's history up to that time.

A New Science Building

Despite the increased opportunities for research, facilities were strained past the breaking point. The faculty eagerly awaited a new science facility. The sad fact was that only one of the many structures used by the sciences was actually intended for laboratory use, the old Science Hall on the corner of Colbert and Vickroy Streets, built in 1916. The announcement in the spring of 1963 that the university planned to build a science center was an enormous psychological lift to the science faculty. The four-story building was to house pharmacy, biology, chemistry, and physics.

In the long list of buildings to rise on the Bluff during the McAnulty years, the science building was perhaps the most notable. Edwin Tucker, the president's trusted advisor, deserves the credit. McAnulty had neither the time nor the expertise to deal with planners, architects, and the maze of government bureaus to pilot his expansion and so in 1962, he appointed Tucker, assistant director of the Redevelopment Authority of Allegheny County and a lecturer in urban sociology at Duquesne, to the newly created post of director of university planning. In many respects, he was a man behind the scenes. Indeed, many faculty members did not even know he existed. But it was he who advocated a go-slow approach with the residents of the Bluff who had to be displaced for the expansion to become a reality. And it was he who talked Father Mac into hiring a noted architect for what would become a campus centerpiece—the science building. Tucker argued that even though money was critically short, Duquesne needed one or two buildings of significant architectural merit.

Architect Ludwig Mies van der Rohe, of world renown, came to Pittsburgh to view the campus and to select the site for the new building. He chose the land along Bluff Street overlooking the Monongahela Valley. Because Duquesne lacked space, Mies van der Rohe wanted to create the illusion of space. Therefore, the four-story black graphite-painted steel building was given extra wide hallways and stairwells. Too wide, some would aver, actually wasting space, but the building was 35,000 square feet larger than Rockwell Hall, making it the largest building on the Bluff at the time. The science-related operations of the university, which had been carried on in 14 scattered locations, including the old post-World War II quonset huts and army barracks, along with the ubiquitous Bluff-area houses, were at last to be united under one roof. Duquesne immediately doubled its freshman science enrollment and projected a freshman science class of 550 by 1980.

Construction proceeded rapidly, perhaps a little too rapidly. In a single day much of the steel beam construction was erected but not fully tightened and was left to stand for a weekend. When the city was struck by a high wind, a passing off-duty policeman saw the 200 tons of structural steel begin to wobble, then "all four stories came down like a lawn chair."[32] One-inch bolts securing the columns to the concrete base plates ripped through the heavy steel. The accident, along with a construction workers' strike in the summer of 1967, delayed the opening of the building for a full semester.

For Father Mac the science building represented a fundraising effort of herculean proportions. "We can't exist without the little people," he said, "but we have to have the big people too."[33] In January 1966, he hosted a kickoff dinner to a $7,000,000 capital campaign with the science hall as its centerpiece. "Whether or not we survive is no longer up to me," he told his audience. "We are going to need help to survive."[34] John J. Wright, bishop of Pittsburgh, pledged "a substantial amount" for Duquesne over the next five years. The special guest at the dinner was former Governor David L. Lawrence, who said that Pittsburgh owed a "staggering debt" to Duquesne for the education that it provided for many thousands of its young people.

Over 20 corporations, including U.S. Steel and Gulf Oil, gave sizable contributions. Grants were received from the National Science Foundation, and from the U.S. Department of Health Education and Welfare. Private foundations also gave large amounts. The Maurice & Laura Falk Foundation gave $200,000 and two lecture halls in the building were named in their honor. The Howard Heinz Endowment gave $100,000. The largest amount was given by the Richard King Mellon Charitable Trust. Its arrival was something of a surprise to Father Mac, who later described what happened:

> One day Joe Hughes, a representative of the Mellon Foundation, asked to see me. Understand that this was after five years of seeing them and promoting Duquesne. It was the day before Thanksgiving [1964] and he said "I thought I'd bring you a little Thanksgiving news. We've decided to give you two million dollars for the science hall."[35]

McAnulty asked if the building could be named Mellon Hall. It took six months for General Mellon to give his consent. At that time he gave the university a portrait of himself that still hangs in the lobby of the first floor.

After the building was opened, some unforseen circumstances occurred that added to the cost of the $8 million buildings. Traffic going through the Armstrong Tunnels that ran under the Bluff caused vibrations, which, although not felt on the surface, were easily detected by the sensitive scientific instruments used in Mellon Hall. The university had to install special vibration-absorbing devices under the laboratory tables.

In one gigantic step, Duquesne went from relatively poor science facilities to first class accommodations. State-of-the-art Mellon Hall was chosen "1969 Laboratory of the Year" by Industrial Research, Inc., of Indiana, and was featured on the cover of the May issue of *Industrial Research* magazine. Father McAnulty and a representative of the architect triumphantly made the journey to Chicago to receive the award.

The Psychology and Philosophy Departments

Duquesne was alone in the United States in presenting a holistic approach to psychology known as phenomenological psychology, as presented in the four- or five-year program leading to a Ph.D. Another pioneering effort was Duquesne's doctorate in pastoral psychology designed for priests, ministers, rabbis, nuns, brothers, and religious education workers. The pastoral psychology program required 20 hours of field work in state hospitals and clinics along with the classroom studies.

Duquesne's Philosophy Department was a source of pride for the entire university. It was chaired by Father Henry J. Koren, C.S.Sp., a native of the Netherlands, who was largely responsible for making Duquesne University a center for a modern philosophy known as phenomenological existentialism, based on the "openness of the human subject to all that is other than the subject."[36] The department also had professors specializing in the philosophies originated by Aristotle, St. Thomas Aquinas, and so forth; yet, there was virtually no factional strife among the 17 faculty members arising from their differing philosophies. Indeed, under Father Koren, the department was in full bloom with some 40 to 50 graduate students, a steady stream of noted visiting professors, and numerous publications of prestigious books. Since its program was unique and its faculty a distinguished one, the department had an international reputation.

In 1964 the pervasive and controversial Dr. John J. Pauson came to the department. The following year he was made acting chairman when Father Koren was asked to step down in view of the fact that he was also chairman of the Theology Department, and it was felt that the Middle States Association accreditation team, due to visit the campus the next year, would object to two departments being headed by the same person. Father Koren's health was not good—he had been taking up to eight aspirins a day—and he readily agreed to the change, suggesting that an outsider head the department. The academic vice-president, however, wanted Pauson. Since some philosophy faculty had begun to see Pauson as a divisive influence in the department, Father Koren recommended that he be made acting chairman rather than chairman so that he could be more easily removed should the need arise. This was agreed to.

Hardly had Pauson been seated when allegations of petty persecutions of some faculty and clerical students in the department were made. More serious were the complaints about Pauson's "deemphasis" on phenomenological existentialism. This new direction was being taken ostensibly to return the department to Thomism (the teachings of St. Thomas Aquinas), hence supposedly more compatible with traditional Catholic philosophy. Those who specialized in phenomenological existentialism were understandably upset—and so was the Psychology Department. It had developed a unique and successful program whereby its graduate students—it had about 60—were taking certain phenomenological courses offered in the Philosophy Department. This program would be in shambles if the Philosophy Department abandoned its contemporary orientation. The upshot of all this controversy was the dismissal of Pauson as chairman in January 1966, though he was retained as a faculty member, and Koren was again made temporary chairman.

At this point a new element entered the picture. The lay faculty, which until the 1960s had not shown much interest in the governance of the university, were beginning to demand more control. The day after Pauson was dismissed, the Duquesne University chapter of the American Association of University Professors (AAUP) met with McAnulty to discuss the propriety of the procedure leading up to this action. Two History Department professors threatened a faculty strike if Pauson were not reinstated. Although it was extremely unlikely that the Duquesne faculty would strike, the president nonetheless gave in and ordered that Pauson be reinstated as acting chairman on January 20, only two days after his ouster. Four days later, at a special AAUP meeting, the college dean acknowledged his "mistake" in improperly removing Pauson. Father McAnulty ended the meeting by asking that department disputes be settled by the department members themselves behind closed doors. He then read a statement, later released to the press, that welcomed faculty involvement in the determination of university policy. One faculty member wrote, "This public commitment of the university to some type of democratic structure, probably a senate and perhaps a policy permitting department members to elect their chairmen and the college to elect its deans, seemed to many the most encouraging forward step in the past fifteen years of administration-faculty relations."[37]

The receptive attitude of Father Mac toward sharing decision-making with the faculty—commonly known as "collegiality"—was seen by many as the result of his long absence from the order during his military career. The departure from authoritarian control was already far advanced on many college campuses, but McAnulty found on his return to the Bluff that collegiality did not enjoy universal acceptance among his confreres. Koren continued to press for the reinstated chairman's dismissal, which was heartily desired by many faculty members.

A departmental vote was taken on January 31, showing the department was evenly split. Pauson submitted his resignation. The meeting to elect a new chair was held on February 2, with the dean of the graduate school presiding. The philosophy faculty was still deadlocked, seven to seven, in their support of Pauson or Koren. Then a faculty member from the Pauson camp asked for a ten-minute recess. After the break, Dr. Pauson returned to the room with a graduate student from the Philippines who had been teaching some courses and announced that he had hired the student as a faculty member. Since a previous motion had been passed stating that all members of the department would be included in the election, the presiding dean approved this maneuver. Six faculty members then walked out in protest, charging that the election was "illegal and unethical." This left Pauson's supporters claiming that he was no longer acting chairman, but fully chairman, since the ten remaining faculty members still constituted a quorum.

In an effort to find a way out of the impasse, the philosophy faculty held a long meeting, this time presided over by the academic vice-president. A proposal to split the chairmanship in two, with Pauson directing the undergraduate program and Koren directing the graduate, was rejected by Pauson. The meeting broke up with no decision except to hold another meeting. Meanwhile, the faculty would be polled on the circumstances under which they could continue in the department. Nine members drew up a letter protesting any split in the department. Eight announced that they would resign if Pauson continued as chairman.

That night Father Koren fell extremely ill,

vomiting blood and collapsing in his bedroom. The aspirins he had been consuming in such quantity had eaten a quarter-inch hole in his stomach and perforated an artery. During his recovery in Mercy Hospital, he received flowers from Dr. Pauson followed by a letter from his attorney threatening legal action for Koren's supposed slander. The letter demanded an apology, which Koren refused to give. It was a moot point; Father Koren's illness left Pauson the victor, at least for the time being.

On February 19, the graduate students opposed to Pauson staged a demonstration. Three days later, a large number of faculty and students set up a picket line extending from the administration building across Colbert Street and down Vickroy Street. With the media in superabundance at both demonstrations, Duquesne was now advertising from the rooftops the very issues that Father Mac had hoped could be settled "behind closed doors." Few people could understand what all the excitement at Duquesne was about. One reason the dispute was so unclear, wags said, was "because nobody can get 'phenomenological existentialism' on a picket's placard."[38]

By the end of March, five phenomenological existentialist philosophers had handed in their resignations amid widely reported criticisms of McAnulty. They complained that throughout the crisis, the administration took a do-nothing stance, leaving them to Pauson's mercies. There was much truth to the *New York Times* analysis of the dispute: "The administration is scolded, in the name of democracy, for doing something or for doing nothing." The departure of the philosophy professors left the graduate program in psychology without a phenomenological orientation. The psychologists then also threatened to resign en masse and transfer in a body to another university. The efforts made to get the philosophy professors to change their minds were largely unsuccessful; only one reversed his decision.

The charges the departing professors made against McAnulty were unfair. He had indeed been active, but he wanted to act through the faculty itself. In January, following Pauson's reinstatement, he had announced the appointment of a committee "to study the 'policies, procedures and structures' at Duquesne . . . to solve present problems and to anticipate those of the future."[39] And on March 15, he appointed the President's Special Committee on Faculty Relations to help formulate a solution to the problems besetting the Philosophy Department. The five faculty members who resigned had refused to meet with the committee unless the university provided them with an attorney or protection from legal action. Since the university did not grant this demand, the committee received reports only from those faculty members loyal to Pauson.

In May, as the committee was collecting information, the dean of the graduate school confirmed the university's intention to continue an emphasis on phenomenological existentialism by announcing four new appointments to the Philosophy Department. All of the new faculty had backgrounds in existentialism.

On July 21 the President's Special Committee on Faculty Relations filed its report, recommending that a new chairman be found for the Philosophy Department. Father McAnulty declared the report classified partly because of the personal nature of much of its information, and partly because he was unsure that the report contained the entire story due to the refusal of the resignees to appear before the committee or to file a report. Two weeks later, Father McAnulty called a press conference to announce a search for a new chairman, a continuation of an emphasis on phenomenological existentialism, and though it was not stated, an official end to the controversy that had absorbed so much time and attention.

Father Koren resigned his chairmanship of the Theology Department and went to California to recover. Although he continued as editor/

director of the Duquesne University Press, he did so from a distance.

Reflecting on the affair years later, Father Mac said, "I really couldn't understand it."[40] Few could. The controversy might never have happened in an earlier day. By allowing the faculty to determine their own destiny, Father Mac had made the whole episode, painful though it was, a growing experience for the faculty and administration. It presaged the University Senate and a greater degree of democracy. For his conduct in the affair, the faculty nominated Father McAnulty for the American Association of University Professors' Alexander Meiklejohn Award, given to college administrators "in recognition of an outstanding contribution to academic freedom."

The Theology Department

The Theology Department broadened its curriculum, more than tripling the course offerings, in the fall of 1962. Although no major was offered, freshmen were required to take the course, "The Supernatural Life." With the broadening of selections, choices became less restrictive for upperclassmen, with sophomores given a choice among three courses, and juniors and seniors choosing from sixteen. The Theology staff, supplemented by two visiting foreign professors each year, beginning in the spring of 1963, attempted in the courses to dramatize the close relationship theology had with the primary area of study and with contemporary life. The first publication of Duquesne University Press's Theological Series, *Faith and the World*, also made its debut in 1962. An actual degree program leading to a bachelor of arts in theology, begun in the fall of 1964, increased to 37 the number of undergraduate fields at Duquesne in which a student could have a major.

Another new theology program, in Religion and Personality, was applicable to 19 areas for master's degree work. The Department began offering a master of arts in September of 1969 with the graduate-level courses offered on weekday evenings, Saturdays, and summers. Small as it was, the department was only able to offer the program in conjunction with the Philosophy Department. The degree mandated a minimum of 30 hours in philosophy and theology combined. Although scarred by developments in the Philosophy Department at the end of the decade, theology managed to survive and even prosper.

The Journalism Department

At the same time as the Philosophy Department's dispute, the Journalism Department had a dispute of its own. In 1965, it was changed to Communication Arts, with a curriculum deemphasizing the more practical technical aspects of journalism in favor of an increased number of liberal arts courses. The initial motivation for this change came from Associate Dean Samuel Hazo, whose own discipline was English and who felt that journalism majors were graduating with too little knowledge outside of the professional courses. The announcement of the change brought an immediate negative reaction from the students, Journalism alumni, and some faculty members. Even the Pittsburgh Chapter of the Association of Industrial Advertisers involved itself in what was rapidly becoming a community-wide brouhaha.

The alumni formed a Journalism Alumni Advisory Committee that wrote to Father McAnulty, advising that the existing curriculum was what was needed by students seeking careers in journalism, that it was "realistic."[41] The Advisory Committee then followed this up with a Declaration of Intent sent to nearly every important person in the university administration, including John J. Wright, the bishop of the diocese of Pittsburgh, whose position of chancellor of the university was strictly ceremonial. The declaration urged the university to restrict the curriculum changes to the graduate level.

Father Mac was astonished by all the controversy. "We are going to look into journalism again," he promised. "I didn't realize we had so many interested alumni. If Pittsburgh wants a particular kind of journalism, and we can afford it, we'll introduce it, even if it means setting up a separate School of Journalism."[42] The president then deferred the whole affair to the Journalism Department faculty and the college dean for resolution.

Samuel Hazo and Journalism Chair Cornelius McCarthy held a series of discussions with the journalism students and alumni and eventually announced a compromise. Beginning in the fall semester, those students already enrolled in the Journalism Department could, if they desired, continue under the old requirements, but new students would be subject to the new requirements of the new Communication Arts Department. Though that name would last for only a single year before returning to the old title, the changes were sweeping, and some were permanent. By the fall, the number of course offerings had been cut to 11, about a third of what it had been in 1965, and the number of credits needed to major in journalism had been cut by a fourth. The 92 journalism majors accepted the compromise only grudgingly, and two untenured faculty members eventually departed the Bluff. In 1974, however, when the department celebrated its silver anniversary, a record-high 215 majors were enrolled. In its printed 25th anniversary program, the department looked back on the 1960s, noting, "These years have seen the evolution from a newspaper-advertising-broadcasting sequence plan to the present broad communications program—incorporating both 'the other liberal disciplines as the raw material of the communicator' and on-the-job experience through internship in the field." This same publication boasted that a "gratifyingly high" 62 percent of its graduates were employed in the journalism field. The 1965 *Bulletin* had reported that more than 80 percent of its graduates were so employed. Journalism was to surface as an issue again in the 1980s.

School of Pharmacy

The School of Pharmacy, allied to the sciences but operating as a distinct unit, moved into the 1960s with a new dean, Dr. John S. Ruggiero. He had been groomed for the post as assistant dean under Dr. John G. Adams, who had been handpicked by Hugh C. Muldoon, founder of the school. Although Dean Adams served the school well, his heart lay in teaching. Once his five-year plan was launched and he was confident of Dr. Ruggiero's administrative abilities, he announced his resignation following graduation exercises in June of 1961 and returned to teaching and research at the University of Connecticut.

Dr. Ruggiero was barely 30 when he assumed the deanship and began working out details of the new plan. The five-year program, a national requirement for all accredited colleges of pharmacy, applied to all students enrolling after April 1960. The plan called for two years of pre-pharmacy in the College of Liberal Arts and Sciences, but acceptance standards had yet to be decided for admission to the final three years in the School of Pharmacy. Other areas of concern were the establishment of a pre-pharmacy student advisement program, creation of options for selection of majors in pharmacy, and the incorporation of student input in the School's decision-making policies. The staff numbered only six full-time professors, two part-time faculty members, and seven graduate assistants. Facilities were limited to eight rooms in Canevin Hall, an old house used for graduate research which was called the "Pharmacy Research Building," and a WWII quonset hut housing experimental animals. On the promise of a new science hall, still five years away, Ruggiero began increasing the faculty, more than doubling the full-time personnel. He also introduced new programs such as bionucleonics, toxicology, and electronics for scientists as specialties for both students of the school and in-service institutes for teachers, scientists, and others in the field. The small graduate program in pharmacy maintained a steady growth under his direction, with students branching into various Master's degree programs. Despite the lack of facilities, the school continued to reach beyond its circumstances in its quest for excellence. Rho Chi, the Honorary Pharmacy Fraternity, sponsored the Hugh C. Muldoon Memorial Lectures and the School held its own Pharmacy Seminars.

When the new Richard King Mellon Hall of Science finally became a reality in 1968, the fourth floor had been designed for the pharmacy school. The faculty and administration spent much time and effort on the planning and equipping of the facilities, including the Hugh C. Muldoon Model Pharmacy. Thanks to the new science building, the School of Pharmacy was able to conduct more research. On the basis of such research, it received permission to begin a Ph.D. in a pharmaceutical research program in 1969.

Dean Ruggiero, like Father McAnulty, was strongly supportive of decentralized authority. He placed much of the authority to organize departments in the hands of his department heads, and appointed an assistant dean to coordinate student advisement and direct alumni activities. In 1961 the School of Pharmacy began an annual continuing-education program for alumni. The school's reputation for a strong academic program, a highly qualified staff, and a superb new facility were essential in maintaining enrollments during this time of escalating tuition, especially in view of the lowered tuitions at the University of Pittsburgh.

The Duquesne School of Pharmacy was one of the first to recognize the importance of clinical experience. A liaison with Mercy Hospital gave its students an elective course in hospital dispensary work. Along with traditional retail dispensing, the course became a requirement in the 1960s. The master of science degree in hospital pharmacy thus obtained was converted into the doctor of pharmacy degree in 1967. After this successful program, Duquesne branched into other health-related fields in conjunction with Mercy and other area hospitals, devising a program leading to the bachelor of science in medical technology in 1968.

School of Business Administration

As noted earlier, the School of Business Administration at Duquesne had long had the largest enrollment, but it was surpassed by the College of Liberal Arts and Sciences in 1960. The following year, it was surpassed by the School of Education as well, but with 1188 students, it was still one of the largest in the university. It was continually offering new programs. Beginning in 1962 its Department of Educational Services taught management principles to small proprietors in the area under federal government auspices. In 1965 the school announced the beginning of a two-year program leading to a master of business administration.

In 1967 the Business Administration fact sheet listed the school's distinction as the only fully accredited school of business in the Western Pennsylvania-Western New York region. It was also one of the top five schools for its size in computer capacity. The school also claimed a high percentage of liberal arts courses in its curriculum, 50 percent, intended to offer its students a wide base of knowledge.

A change in the undergraduate curriculum in 1963 allowed students to choose one of three areas of concentration in place of the traditional business administration major: quantitative science (accounting, analytical methods, and finance), behavioral science (law, commerce, and managements), or economic science (economics). Students also had more freedom in course selection over a far broader range of offerings and could even select their own advisors.

School of Education

The School of Education received new leadership in the appointment of Rev. Philip C. Niehaus, C.S.Sp., to the deanship in 1961, after Father Harcar became vice-president of university relations. Under Niehaus's leadership, in 1964 the School of Education inaugurated a special education program for the instruction of the mentally retarded. Continued work in educating children in depressed areas revealed a greater incidence of mental retardation in disadvantaged school populations. Therefore, at the request of the City of Pittsburgh, Duquesne expanded its graduate-level program of educating the mentally retarded to the undergraduate level in 1965. A move within the city and county to establish special schools for the mentally retarded depended heavily upon qualified Duquesne School of Education graduates to staff them. In 1967 dual certification in special education with a major in either elementary or secondary education became available. The National Defense Scholarships and grants to students majoring in education brought an influx of highly qualified students to the school. Enrollment soared.

On the basis of several social-action education programs, the American Association of Colleges for Teacher Education (AACTE) cited Duquesne as "one of the top ten educational programs in the country." Underwritten by a grant from the Ford Foundation, the School of Education and the Pittsburgh Public Schools began an experimental team-teaching program for disadvantaged students in the city's depressed areas in 1963. Duquesne had supplied more than 85 percent of the interns used in team-teaching programs in the city since 1960. Through a collaboration with the Sociology Department of the College of Arts and Sciences, the School of Education designed a special curriculum to prepare teachers for work in culturally deprived areas that significantly reduced their turnover rate.

School of Music

The School of Music rapidly outgrew its accommodations in the early 1960s. Although classes were for the most part managed in the music building, faculty offices and practice rooms were scattered all over campus in the old houses that the university had acquired. Nevertheless, the School of Music was very successful. One of its accomplishments was to devise a master's degree in liturgical music for choirmasters and organists, done in cooperation with the Music Commission of the Diocese of Pittsburgh. This program emphasized the historical aspects of religious music, with courses in Gregorian chant, the history of the Roman rite, counterpoint, and choral conducting. Its faculty gave solo performances with the Pittsburgh Symphony, American Wind Symphony, Mendelssohn Choir, and other professional groups as well as creating original compositions.

The new School of Music was the first building completed under Phase I of the Master Plan. The old music building stood on the site of the proposed science center. The new one was renovated from the post office garage on Magee Street between Locust and Seitz. It opened for classes in the 1966 spring term. The architect, Edwin J. Gerard, designed a modern, three-story, buff limestone building, with aluminum windows and spandrels, affording 64,000 square feet of space. It was fitted with professional recording and listening equipment, Steinway pianos in all teaching and practice rooms, a Moeller organ, and five additional practice organs.

The new facility made it possible for the School of Music to accept more students. In 1964, there had been openings for only half of the applicants for the freshman class. After the opening of the new facility, the school increased enrollment to 295 undergraduates and 93 graduate students by 1968. Whereas the total university grew 4.4 percent in this period, the music school grew by 28 percent.

School of Nursing

After a long struggle, the School of Nursing had received accreditation of its general nursing program in 1954 and of its public health nursing program in 1956 from both the National League for Nursing and the State Board of Nurse Examiners. Much of the difficulty arose from Duquesne's inability to establish any control over the clinical aspects of nurses' training at Mercy Hospital, which felt caught between basic and graduate programs at Duquesne and the basic program at Mt. Mercy College. Duquesne even considered dropping its basic course and concentrating on graduate nursing programs at Mercy's request, but the difficulties were eventually resolved. In 1960 the basic nursing program, still four years in length, was shortened by one summer session so that seniors could graduate in the spring of their fourth year instead of the early August commencements at the end of their final clinical training. Enlargement of the teaching staff with a higher percentage of new faculty on the master's level, and arrangements with the C. Howard Marcy Tuberculosis Hospital, the University of Pittsburgh, and Mt. Mercy College, made it possible for the School of Nursing to consolidate work in the city and drop its out-of-town affiliations.

Financial assistance for nurses was made available through the army and navy nursing programs. There was also loan money available through the Nurse Training Act of 1964 for students enrolled in approved schools of nursing.

The School of Nursing had been directed since 1944 by Ruth D. Johnson, a fierce protector of her students' interests who had frequently clashed with Father Gallagher in seeking special provisions for them. The university was stunned by her sudden death in March 1962. Theta Pi Chapter of Alpha Tau Delta National Nursing fraternity established a scholarship fund in her honor.

Changes in the curriculum to create a better correlation between instruction and clinical practice in the formation of the courses Medical Surgical Nursing I, II, III, and IV and to focus on the family as a unit in the combined Maternal-Child Health Nursing course brought the National League for Nursing back to campus on October 1963. The board commended the new changes, praised the school for its faculty increases, and granted its approval in December. The School of Nursing's enrollment stood at 101 students in the Basic Nursing program and 185 in the general nursing program at the time. As recommended by the Nurse Training Act of 1964, the two programs were combined that year. Nurses could also be exempted from courses and receive the credits if they passed written and practicum examinations.

The poorly heated three-story brick house on Magee was stretched to capacity with 14 faculty members. In 1969, the School of Nursing moved briefly into a converted warehouse on Forbes Avenue but found a more permanent home the following year on the sixth floor of the newly completed College Hall.

Obstetrical training was offered at St. Joseph's Hospital in 1965 with pediatric experience at Mercy. St. Clair Memorial Hospital in Mt. Lebanon inaugurated a student nursing education program with the School of Nursing in 1966 at which time the school dropped its affiliation with St. Joseph's. The State Board of Nurse Examiners gave the School high commendations in 1966, the first year the nursing faculty was able to provide both classroom and clinical training. As with the rest of the University, the School of Nursing bowed to student pressure for representation on faculty committees in 1968. Student input made it possible for them to reverse the injunction against working during summer breaks at hospitals where they received their clinical experience, a practice the students felt absolutely necessary in funding their educations.

School of Law

In 1961 the law school celebrated its golden jubilee. The honored guest at dinner was Professor William H. Lacey, who taught the first law class ever held at the Duquesne Law School on September 25, 1922, at the George Building. At the Jubilee celebration, the school rejoiced in its 850 living graduates, among them 14 judges. In 1963 Duquesne's Law School issued its first law review journal. The school also offered one- and two-day institutes in Continuing Legal Education for local attorneys and jurists in association with the American Law Institute, the Pennsylvania Bar Association, and the Allegheny County Bar Association.

Duquesne's moot court at Rockwell Hall, a gift from the Falk Foundation in 1958, proved invaluable. Along with its use by the law school, it was used on occasion by the U.S. District Court, the Court of Common Pleas of Allegheny County, the Pennsylvania Commission on Human Relations, and the Pennsylvania Milk Control Commission. Rockwell Hall's proximity to the courthouse and City-County Building made it a viable alternative when official courtrooms were booked. The School of Law's John E. Laughlin Memorial Library was opened to students and all professionals in law on a 24-hour basis, seven days a week. When the new hours were offered in the 1962–1963 school year, it may have been the only law library in the country that never closed.

The Duquesne University Press

Many of the accomplishments of the 1960s were facilitated by the Duquesne University Press and the Philosophy Department. The press was the oldest university press in the city, publishing its first book, the diary of a World War I U.S. Army chaplain, in 1920, even though its official founding date was 1927. In its first 30 years, however, only eight titles were published and of those only one had any academic importance. Beginning in 1936, it published a quarterly, the *Duquesne Science Quarterly*, discussed in Chapter IV.

Until 1951 the press functioned on an informal basis and went largely unnoticed in the city of Pittsburgh, let alone the nation. But in that year Father Henry Koren became editor/director, and before the 1960s ended, the Duquesne University Press had gained an international reputation. To boost the Philosophy Department's reputation, Koren obtained permission to develop a visiting professor program. Deeming their lectures as too valuable to be limited to Duquesne students, President McAnulty authorized Koren to start a series of publications by the Duquesne University Press under the general name of *Duquesne Studies*. The first of these, the Philosophical Series, began in 1952. Under Koren's directorship, most of the press's publications concerned some aspect of a type of philosophy called phenomenological existentialism, and of these titles, most were from visiting professors. According to the Press's current director, Father Koren's "considerable genius lay in a combination of deep spiritual insight and devotion, a philosophical turn of mind, a literary fluency in most of the principal languages of Europe, and the ability to bring his ideas to reality through a gift of persuading people to aid him in his programs."[43]

In 1958 the Spiritan Series, devoted to the Congregation of the Holy Ghost, was begun. It contained historical works, documents, and writings of men who had prominent roles in the history of the order. In 1961, the Philological Series began. The English Department, which introduced a Ph.D. program in 1960, experienced increased attention when it began this series. The books were on English Renaissance literature. In 1978 the name was changed to *Language and Literature Series*, and its focus was narrowed to include only the works of Edmund Spenser, William Shakespeare, and John Milton. In 1963 the Psychological Series and the Theological Series were started. In 1965 the African Series was

97. During the Gallagher administration, Duquesne revitalized its alumni organization, and resolved never to neglect it again. Alumni activities were designed to keep alumni involved and supportive of their university. The 1959 Homecoming brought together a powerful group of supporters of the old school: *(l. to r.)* Bishop John Wright of the Pittsburgh Diocese; Willard Rockwell, whose fundraising efforts and generosity made possible Rockwell Hall; former Pittsburgh mayor, then Governor of Pennsylvania, David L. Lawrence; Father Gallagher, president of Duquesne 1950–1959; and Thomas J. Gallagher, the interim Mayor of Pittsburgh. Such individuals made Duquesne's building plans possible. When this photo was taken, Fr. Gallagher had turned his presidency over to Fr. Henry Joseph McAnulty just a few months earlier, and still served as chair of the University Advisory Board.

98. Rev. Henry J. McAnulty, C.S.Sp., President of Duquesne University, 1959–1980. He majored in Philosophy and English at Duquesne, graduating in 1936. He attended St. Mary's Holy Ghost Seminary of Connecticut, earning a bachelor of divinity, and he was ordained as a Holy Ghost Father in 1940. Beginning during World War II, he served as a chaplain in the Army Air Corps for 15 years. Later, as a member of the reserves, he earned the rank of Brigadier General, the first Catholic to do so in that branch of service.

When he became president, his predecessor was still provincial of the order and chairman of the board of directors of Duquesne — a hard act to follow, but McAnulty made the position his own. Having the longest tenure of any president save Hehir, "Father Mac" was beloved by Duquesne students, and he quickly created his own very visible place in the Pittsburgh community. "In America today," he said, "the president is a fundraiser and he is the one who has to create the climate in which people can work." He soon embarked on fulfilling the ambitious Master Plan envisioned by his predecessor but radically changed and enlarged it in the process.

99. Father McAnulty was a social man who had many friends and much experience in dealing with people before he became president of Duquesne, and he knew how to make the most of his talents. On a 1949 tour of Italy, Chaplain Henry J. McAnulty not only managed to get an audience with His Holiness, Pope Pius XII, he succeeded in standing directly beside the pontiff for this photo (middle right).

100. When McAnulty assumed the presidency, Gallagher's Master Plan existed largely on paper. Moreover, the master plan of 1951, with its bland set of lookalike buildings, no longer fit Duquesne's plans for the 1960s. In 1961 the consulting firm hired by the university submitted this model as a plan for Bluff redevelopment. The plan included a complex of buildings for science and liberal arts, a university center, auditorium, music building, a 350-car parking lot (added at theinsistence of Pittsburgh City Planning), a field house, athletic field, ROTC building, and high-rise faculty housing. Although actual development differed radically from this new model, some of its central features remained.

101. In the first of many groundbreakings during his administration, Father McAnulty sits atop a bulldozer, kicking off a major addition to the university library. The new 32,000-square-foot three-story addition opened in November 1961. The much needed addition to the library was viewed as a temporary measure, yet it served the university for 16 years. Fr. Edmund R. Supple, C.S.Sp., academic vice president, and Eleanor McCann, librarian, are standing.

102. The new addition was an ultra-modern structure of light gray brick that did not contrast well with the red brick of the original 1939 building, but the space it provided was crucial. The library, growing by 7,500 books annually, practically exploded into the extra space with its collection of 136,158 books. The new facility had room for a quarter of a million books, a statistic head librarian Eleanor McCann and her staff seemed determined to test. They began acquiring new titles at a rate of 15,500 per year and subscribed to nearly 2,000 periodicals. A jewel in these holdings was the Rabbi Herman Hailperin Collection, a gift from Pittsburgh's Jewish community. It held 2,600 books on biblical interpretation, including 6 printed before 1550 and some volumes that were the only known copies in existence. This collection still resides in the Duquesne Library today. Ironically, much of the library's holdings was ruled out of bounds for undergraduates, and the new addition's top floor was restricted to faculty and graduate students.

103. Father Mac, at the beginning of his presidency, had promised students a male dormitory, and by November 1961, St. Martin's Hall was under construction on land the university purchased on Bluff Street. The red brick, complemented by cast concrete window encasements, fit agreeably with the older university architecture. Named after Fr. Martin Hehir, the dorm was a 15 story high-rise that eventually housed 557 students. The new dorm had 3 elevators, individual mail lockers, a commons room on each floor, a main recreation room, laundry facilities, and telephones. Single, double, and triple rooms boasted sofa-type pull-out beds, built-in closets, and bookshelves. In this photo, Assumption Hall is to the right. To the left, an unbroken line of yet privately owned homes separated both dorms from the rest of the campus.

104. In 1962, the university began to acquire more land on the Bluff, space for a second women's dormitory. McAnulty's new master plan called for a long L-shaped building matching St. Martin's. St. Ann's West (built in 1963) and St. Ann's East, (1964) were both financed by federal loans, despite the fact that the Federal Housing and Finance Agency rejected the building plans as too "large." "Duquesne," they argued, "will never become a predominantly residential school." Father Mac initiated the projects anyway, and a few years later, a tremendous influx of students proved him right. Students described the dorms as "the Duquesne Hilton."

105. Literally thousands of nuns packed the campus on Saturdays, the vast majority pursuing degrees in education. The School of Education, under the leadership of Fr. Philip Neihaus, C.S.Sp., dean from 1962 to 1970, offered programs for teachers working in special education and in disadvantaged school populations. On the basis of several social-action education programs, the American Association of Colleges for Teacher Education (AACTE) cited Duquesne as "one of the top ten educational programs in the country." In this promotional photo, Father Neihaus looks on as a student explains a chemistry teaching aid.

106, 107. Because it stood on the site earmarked for the new science building, the School of Music moved on to more spacious quarters. In 1966 the old post office garage *(top)*, located on Magee Street, between Locust and Seitz, was renovated to house the School of Music building *(bottom)*. The architect, Edwin J. Gerard, designed a modern, three story building of buff limestone with aluminum window casings and spandrels. The 64,000 square feet of space was fitted with professional recording equipment, Steinway pianos in all teaching and practice rooms, a Moeller organ, and five practice organs. This new facility made it possible for the school to accept more students, and the music school grew by 28% in 4 years.

108. The School of Nursing also gained new space during McAnulty's building spree, albeit indirectly. The administrative offices of the School of Nursing occupied this house at the corner of Magee and Vickroy Streets from 1956 to 1967. The poorly heated three-story house was stretched to capacity with 14 faculty members. In 1970, the school found a home on the sixth floor of the newly completed College Hall. Students in this program took most of their general classes in other schools and performed practicum work at local hospitals. In 1966, however, the nursing faculty at Duquesne offered both classroom and clinical training on campus, and received high commendations from the State Board of Nurse Examiners.

109. For Father Mac, the science building represented his greatest fundraising challenge. In January 1966, he hosted a kick-off dinner to a $7,000,000 capital campaign with the science building as its focus. While the campaign garnered grants from U.S. Steel, Gulf Oil, the National Science Foundation, the Falk Foundation, and the Heinz Endowment, the Mellon Foundation made the largest donation, $2,000,000. McAnulty asked that the building be named after this benefactor. He received permission, and a portrait of General Richard King Mellon that still hangs in the first floor lobby of Mellon Hall.

Construction on the new science hall proceeded perhaps too rapidly. On a Friday, workers erected much of the steel beam construction, but neglected to tighten the bolts. Over the weekend the city was struck by high winds, and an off-duty policeman saw the 200 tons of structural steel begin to wobble, then "all four stories came down like a lawn chair." One-inch bolts securing the columns to the concrete base ripped through the heavy steel. The accident, along with a construction workers' strike in 1967, delayed the building's opening, and bumped its final cost to $8 million.

110. Of all the buildings that arose during McAnulty's tenure, the science building is perhaps most notable, thanks to Edward Tucker, lecturer in urban sociology and advisor to the president. He argued that Duquesne needed one or two buildings of significant architecture as a centerpiece for the campus. The world-renowned architect Ludwig Mies van der Rohe selected the site and designed the building. The Duquesne campus lacked space, and van der Rohe wanted to create the illusion of space. The four-story black graphite painted steel building has extra-wide halls and stairways. It was 35,000 square feet larger than Rockwell Hall, making it the largest building on campus at the time. Science classes and labs scattered throughout the campus in Quonset huts, army barracks, and ubiquitous Bluff houses were at last united under one roof. State-of-the-art Mellon Hall was chosen "1969 Laboratory of the Year" by Industrial Research of Indiana. After the building opened in 1968, scientists working there found a pervasive and surprising problem. Traffic going through the Armstrong Tunnels that ran under the Bluff caused vibrations which, though unfelt on the surface, were easily detected by sensitive equipment used in Mellon Hall. Special vibration-absorbing devices had to be installed under most of the building's laboratory tables.

111. Duquesne's Philosophy Department was a source of pride for the entire university. Father Henry Koren, C.S.Sp. was largely responsible for making Duquesne a center for phenomenological existentialism, a modern philosophy based on the "openness of the human subject to all that is other than the subject." Other professors specialized in more classical areas, Aristotle, St. Thomas Aquinas, etc. The department also formed an alliance with the psychology program, offering many courses integral to that curriculum's degrees. Under Koren, the department bloomed, with 40 or 50 graduate students and a steady stream of prestigious book publications. The department enjoyed an international reputation for scholarship. Koren also chaired the Theology Department and directed Duquesne University Press. Despite these successes, Koren was asked to step down as Philosophy Department head in 1965. Duquesne was about to undergo its accreditation review, and some thought the board might object to one person heading two departments.

112. As acting chair of Philosophy in 1965, Dr. John J. Pauson sparked a controversy that tested McAnulty's skills as an academic leader and brought the world-renowned department infamy rather than fame. Pauson strove to redirect the department's emphasis and created a bitter division among its faculty. When McAnulty dismissed Pauson as chair, professors from other disciplines began to take sides; some, from psychology, saw Pauson as endangering their own programs. Others objected to McAnulty's interference in department politics. The president reinstated Pauson and asked that the philosophy faculty settle their disputes among themselves. The conflict escalated, and by February 1966, faculty and students opposed to Pauson were demonstrating in front of the Administration Building, on the streets of Colbert and Vickroy.

113. The Tamburitzans widened the scope of their performances significantly during the 1960s, performing dances and songs from African and American cultures as well as Eastern European and Balkan music. They made national and international tours during university class breaks, including a broadcast of their own show over Voice of America radio and a performance at the 1964 New York World's Fair. This photo was taken during a 1962 performance in Italy.

114. In the 1960s, Duquesne's theater club, the Red Masquers, continued to do popular works rather than classics, maintaining director Sam Meli's practice of presenting current works with high student appeal. A fire in the campus theater in May 1962 did considerable damage and curtailed all productions for almost a year. The theater reopened with a new ceiling, floor, curtains, a light board, and a whole new season of plays. In 1967, Frank Thornton replaced Meli as producer-director, and he introduced an ambitious mix of classics and moderns. Here the Red Masquers perform *The Crucible* in December 1968. A considerable off-campus interest in the Masquers developed, and the Pittsburgh Drama League, after seeing another 1968 production, Van Itallie's Interview, invited them to repeat their performance in their community theater. Thereafter, performing at churches, high schools, and colleges all over southwestern Pennsylvania became standard practice during the Thornton years for the Red Masquers, and they earned a notable regional reputation.

115. Both the air force and the army had ROTC programs at Duquesne, and both boomed in the 1960s. Two years of ROTC was compulsory for all male students, except veterans and pharmacy students. The air force loved having one of "their" men as president of the college, and Fr. McAnulty was pleased to have them on campus. "Every time I made a speech," he noted, "I got another point towards becoming a general." On a more practical note, with enrollments ever growing, providing a phys-ed program for everyone was impossible, but because ROTC required weekly drill, a large portion of the student body automatically satisfied that requirement. The cadets drilled at noon in a variety of locations; in this photo they appear on one of Duquesne's short-lived "sport fields." The students disliked the mandatory service, and less than 25% took more than the required two years. Perhaps one of the most tangible effects of the Vietnam War on Duquesne life was the campus-wide decision to make ROTC training voluntary in 1969.

116. In 1964, the university broke ground for its next project, the student union. Again faculty member Edward Tucker urged engaging a noted architect, Paul Schweiker, Chair of the Architecture Dept. at Carnegie Mellon Institute of Technology. Few guessed that his "masterpiece" would be the most controversial building on the Bluff when it opened in 1967. In contrast to the mellow brick of the older buildings, or the crisp neatness of Mellon Hall (which faced it across the way), the student union was six stories of rough concrete softened only by natural oak, and it sported several other unusual features: The north and south walls were made entirely of glass, one interior wall was a full three stories high, much of the building was underground, and an enormous 28-foot ramp faced Mellon Hall. The students themselves took Schweiker to task for the "crude, dangerous" structure. Nevertheless, the building survived much as Schweiker had imagined it until the 1990s, when the administration completed significant remodeling.

117. Father McAnulty and Urban Redevelopment Director, Robert Pease, watch the demolition of the first Bluff building under the federal program on January 31, 1964. The entire Bluff Street project embraced 43 acres. On 26 of these, almost every existing house was razed. Duquesne acquired $7.5 million worth of cleared land for less than $1 million. For over eight years, Duquesne students and faculty dodged Bluff area demolitions and building construction on one street or another.

118. 1963 tennis team with coach Dr. Samuel Hazo, Duquesne English Professor (far right). This group made history when Liz Stockhausen (third from the right) became the first woman to play on Duquesne's varsity tennis team in 1961. Her brother and teammate, Paul, stands on her right.

119. When Father Mac ascended the presidency, students gained a president as enthusiastic about athletics as they were. Throughout the sixties, basketball reigned preeminent at Duquesne. Coach Red Manning built another winning team in two seasons, and in 1962 they returned to New York for their tenth appearance in the National Invitational Tournament's 25-year history. Pictured here is the 1961-62 team (l. to r.: Clyde Arnold, Bill Stromple, Willie Somerset, Coach Red Manning, Mike Rice, John Cegalis, Paul Benec). In 1964, the wandering Dukes finally found an official home court in the newly constructed Civic Arena, located within easy walking distance of campus.

120. Vickroy Street in the mid-sixties, before it was closed to traffic. While many details of McAnulty's model campus fell by the wayside, the Academic Walk did not. A focal point for student activities, Vickroy became a pedestrian mall in 1969.

121. In response to Fr. Gallagher's call for an active and informed alumni, many graduates formed groups that worked annually to support Duquesne, and their contributions continued throughout McAnulty's presidency. The Women's Guild of Duquesne University is one such group. With funds raised during activities like their annual Pink Geranium Card Party, they donated the campus crucifix in 1960.

begun. Some of these series consisted of only a few books, while others ran to more than twenty.

Most of the Duquesne University Press books were very well received, some titles appearing in half a dozen European languages and even in Japanese. Two books became classics in their fields as well as best sellers: William Luijpen's *Existential Phenomenology*, and Adrian van Kaam's psychobiography of Francis Libermann. Both books went through numerous reprints over a period of 30 years.

In addition to continuing the *Duquesne Science Counselor*, the press also published: *Duquesne Review: Journal of the Social Sciences*, beginning in 1956, *Annuale Mediaevale: Journal of Studies of the Middle Ages*, beginning in 1960, *Duquesne Hispanic Review: Journal of Spanish Language and Literature*, beginning in 1962, *Review of Existential Psychology and Psychiatry*, beginning in 1961, *The Journal of Ecumenical Studies-Catholic, Protestant and Orthodox*, beginning in 1964, *Envoy: A Monthly Newsletter of the Religion and Personality Program, Theological Seminary*, beginning in 1964 and *Humanitas: Journal of the Institute of Man*, beginning in 1965.

In 1965 the prestigious journal, *The American Scholar*, recognized Duquesne University Press as an outstanding example of what a university press ought to be. Two years later, Dr. Justus G. Lawlor, editor-in-chief of Herder and Herder, in an article in *America*, placed the Duquesne University Press first among all Catholic university presses, largely because of the philosophical and theological books that it had published. Such praises were well-deserved for when *The American Scholar* asked a group of leading academics to appraise the work of university presses in the United States, the only Catholic university press cited was that of Duquesne.

In 1967 the press published its hundredth book. At that time it was publishing some 12 titles a year, was financially self-sustaining, and even realized a small profit. From 1968 on, however, a crisis hit the publishing industry that included academic publishing. As costs soared, university presses began to run heavily into the red. The Harvard Press suffered a loss of half a million dollars in one year and those of a number of universities, including the Catholic University of America, closed their doors. The Duquesne University Press survived, but its output was much restricted.

The Institute of Man

April of 1963 saw the formation of a multidisciplinary study center known as the Institute of Man. The first of its kind in the nation, the institute united the fields of philosophy, psychology, psychiatry, sociology, anthropology, and theology in presenting a holistic view of humanity. Reverend Adrian van Kaam, C.S.Sp. of the Psychology Department originated the idea and founded the institute, with Father van Croonenberg as executive director. The inspiration was Father van Kaam's work as a theology student in Holland during the Second World War. In ministering to the needs of a church in hiding, he developed his theory of Christian character and personality formation as an "epiphanic theology," one that reveals the transcendent presence of God in everyday life. Following the war, as he was putting his theories into practice with everyday working people, he was requested by Monsignor Giovanni Batista Montini, later to become Pope Paul VI, to devote all his time to the development of his ideas. Father Vernon Gallagher, through Father Koren's suggestion, invited Father van Kaam and Father Engelbert van Croonenberg to Duquesne, where they joined the faculty, coinciding with Montini's hope that this epiphanic approach could be begun at a Catholic university as a model for Christian centers all over the world. While teaching in the psychology department, Father van Kaam promoted his ideas, eventually receiving permission to begin the Institute of Man as a subdivision of the Psychology Department. Three years later it became independent and was renamed The Institute of Formative Spirituality. Its first symposium, "Anxiety in Our Time," was held on April 19, 1964. Susan Muto was appointed assistant director of the institute and she was managing editor under van Kaam's editorship of *Humanitas: Journal of the Institute of Man*, begun in 1965, and of *Envoy: a Monthly Newsletter of the Religion and Personality Program, Theological Seminary,* and of the *Review of Existential Psychology and Psychiatry*. She also taught literature and formation theology. The four volume series *The Emergent Self*, 1968, was a combined effort of authorship that included Miss Muto, Father Van Kaam, and Father van Croonenberg.

During this period, students comprised of laity, clergy, and religious from the United States and abroad came to the institute, promoting its international reputation. Father van Kaam initiated a six-semester core program, praised by the Middle States Accreditation Association as a doctoral-style master's program.

Institute of African Affairs

Duquesne's Institute of African Affairs received increased impetus with the arrival of Reverend Alphons Loogman, C.S.Sp., in 1960. This 62-year-old missionary, one of the leading experts on Swahili, began teaching the language to six students at Duquesne in January. Immensely qualified for the task, Father Loogman had translated the New Testament of the Bible into Swahili and formed and edited a Swahili newspaper. He had also written numerous booklets on Africa dealing with topics ranging from grammar to native marriage customs. Under his leadership, the institute began teaching the West African language of Hausa in 1962, and Igbo, Bambara, and Yoruba in 1963. At the end of the decade, Duquesne was the only university in the Western Hemisphere that offered as a continuing part of its curriculum all four major languages of Africa simultaneously: Arabic, Hausa, Lingala, and Swahili.

By the time the African Institute celebrated its tenth anniversary on October 21, 1967, nine of the 100 National Defense Foreign Language fellowships were held by Duquesne students. Father Loogman finished a two-volume Swahili reference under a three-year HEW grant and grants provided the funding for extensive summer workshops. The institute sponsored publications in both the Duquesne University Press's African Series and the institute's own African Reprint Series. It also provided programs for Voice of America broadcasts in African languages, and its faculty and staff were greatly in demand as speakers on radio and television. At the end of its first decade, the Institute of African Affairs had 116 students enrolled, 22 of them pursuing a master's degree in the field. The institute supported such specialized offerings from the university's schools as the School of Business Administration's master of arts in the economics of African Affairs.

Concurrent with the growth of the program was the enlargement of the African Collection at the Duquesne University Library. Complementing the group of 1000 volumes in 100 African languages and 6000 volumes of African source material was the microfilm collection of all the archival and library holdings on Africa from the headquarters of Holy Ghost Fathers in Paris. Duquesne also received current materials from the embassies of African nations, government documents, catalogs of African collection holdings of other universities, and a vast assortment of periodicals, newspapers, and maps. At ceremonies to commemorate the 10th anniversary of the founding of the institute, Ahmadon Ahidjo, president of the Federal Republic of Cameroon, addressed the assembly, stating that although a university's traditional mission is to promote the search for truth and to develop pure knowledge of nature, man, and human societies, it is also necessary to "make the best use of the knowledge, techniques, and resources available to solve the distressing problems of hunger, ignorance, and disease."[44] President Ahidjo was awarded an honorary degree at the event, along with Joseph Palmer, the U.S. assistant secretary of state, and Archbishop Marcel Lefebvre, superior general of the Holy Ghost Order.

Dr. Thomas P. Melady, director of development and public relations at Duquesne under Father Gallagher, had prepared the groundwork for the institute in 1957. Author of six books on Africa, he was appointed U.S. ambassador to the African Republic of Burundi by President Nixon in 1969. The institute opened under the direction of Reverend Francis M. Philben, C.S.Sp., a former Holy Ghost missionary to Africa, as the fourth such institute in the country and the first to be sponsored by a Catholic university. Dr. Geza Grosschmid succeeded Father Philben in 1958. Although the institute operated as a division of the Graduate School, undergraduates and special students were granted permission to take the courses.

In 1964 Duquesne began an exchange program with the Afro-Asiatiches Institute in Vienna, Austria, which eventually brought one of Austria's most outstanding African linguists, Dr. Walter J. Pichl, to Duquesne.

Recognition of Duquesne's excellence in the field led to the University conducting the only Eastern summer program in African languages, linguistics, and area studies for the U.S. Office of Education beginning in 1966. This program, in joint sponsorship with the African language and study centers of Columbia, Howard, Indiana, Michigan State, Northwestern, Ohio, Syracuse, and Wisconsin Universities, was designed to prevent African studies from becoming too fragmented. The Institute provided accelerated language training for scholars from the University of West Virginia who were to teach in East African agricultural schools and initiated a program in Swahili and African Culture on the high school level at James C. Hawkins High School in Rankin, staffed by graduate students.

The White Genes Controversy

The director of the African Institute proved to be an embarrassment to the university when he appeared to endorse the theories of a wealthy Scot tish anthropologist, Dr. Robert Gayre. Lt. Col. Gayre believed that the wide variance in cultural levels in Africa resulted from Caucasian migration and the consequent introduction of white genes in coastal Africa prior to European colonization, thus explaining several more advanced civilizations. His theory held that the white race was intellectually superior to the Negro race because the rigors of the Ice Age had culled all the less resourceful and adaptable individuals from the gene pool. His theory concluded that the Negro race, saved from the test of survival by its tropical environment, had endured no such cleansing of its intellectually inferior population which continued to breed, lowering the general intelligence of the race. A proposed expedition hoped to find genetic characteristics in certain Africans that would prove white racial mixing in culturally advanced areas.

The African Institute at Duquesne went so far as to publish a booklet, "An Ethnological Survey: A Study of the Racial Drift of the African Littoral," presenting Gayre's theory, and the director was able to inveigle the university into announcing its support of the expedition on May 20, 1964. The director was quoted in *The Pittsburgh Press* as saying that the boat would carry guns and ammunition because "Some of the natives think that independence means you can shoot at whomever you want."

Over 50 fundraising appeals produced not one contribution. An unauthorized and brief-lived student newspaper called the *The Agitator* vehemently criticized the director of the African

Institute for supporting the venture, and to the credit of the faculty, at least one member wrote to congratulate the newspaper on its article. The director of the institute then sought, unsuccessfully, to have that untenured faculty member fired. Finally, since the "aims of the expedition were at variance with a basic philosophy at Duquesne which holds that all races are equal," the university leadership came to its senses and on July 24th revoked its support for the proposed expedition.

It was fortunate for the university that the whole affair ended as quietly as it did. Gayre's ideas soon lost favor with most scientists; and ironically at that very moment the African Institute was considering an expedition to try to prove Gayre's theory, Congress was passing the Civil Rights Act of 1964 designed to give equality to all Americans regardless of race.

Tamburitzans

The Tamburitzans widened their scope of involvement significantly during the 1960s. They continued the national tours during breaks, including a broadcast of their Maryland show over Voice of America. In July 1964 they performed at the New York World's Fair. In March 1965 they joined forces with the School of Music and the Red Masquers to stage Bedrich Smetana's comic opera, "The Bartered Bride," in its entirety. The Tamburitzan Cultural Center was established in early 1965 when the organization was able to purchase a building on the corner of the Boulevard of the Allies and Pride Street. The center housed the troupe's collection of Slavic costumes and crafts, as well as an extensive library of books, magazines, newspapers, and documents on Slavic languages, music, and literature.

The Tammies were called on by the U.S. State Department's Cultural Presentation Program in the 1967–1968 season. In 1950 they had performed their first European tour to Yugoslavia for the State Department to aid in establishing positive diplomatic relations with the new government. Now they were asked to embark upon an eight-week summer tour of Latin America with performances in Puerto Rico, the Dominican Republic, Curacao, Argentina, Uruguay, Peru, Ecuador, Panama, Nicaragua, Guatemala, and Mexico. The program prepared by "Los Tamburas" was composed half of Balkan and Eastern European Music and half of Americana from colonial times to the present. Along with the performances, they were also to participate in numerous lectures, dance demonstrations, and public activities.

The troupe, numbering 30, was recognized as the only collegiate performing group of its kind. Walter J. Kolar was still director, assisted by Steven W. Kovacev, and Richard Crum had returned from his leave to continue as choreographer and technical advisor. The troupe had a rough time on their 1967–68 Latin American tour because of the rigors of performing at high altitudes. In Quito, Ecuador, tanks of oxygen were placed backstage to assist the gasping performers, especially the horn blowers, who ran back to take a few gulps between selections. Following their strenuous Russian dance, three of the performers passed out. But the Tammies were a dramatic success, as evidenced by the 20,000 people who crowded into the town square to see them in Chimbote, Peru.

Still enjoying the plaudits they received, the Tamburitzans were invited by the State Department for another tour in the summer of 1969, this time to Moscow and nine other Soviet cities, plus Rumania and Poland. They were asked to do a performance of strictly American music, so, after much soul searching, they put together a program of cowboy songs, sea chantys, barbershop quartet, Negro spirituals, mountain songs, Dixieland jazz, and dances that included the Charleston, Cakewalk, Boogie-Woogie, hula, Eskimo Walrus Hunt, rock 'n' roll, and square dancing. They even included a Navajo performance. Slavic numbers were reserved for encores.

The Apollo moon shot took place while the Tammies were in Soviet Georgia. The Georgians toasted the Americans with champagne while the Tammies passed out Apollo buttons to their hosts. A novel sidelight to the trip was the filming of an hour-long show for Rumanian television while in Bucharest. They were enthusiastically received, often with standing ovations. That autumn, two musical groups, one from Poland and the other from the USSR, came to Pittsburgh as their guests.

Following the Tamburitzans' annual Communion Breakfast that September, a special room in the Cultural Center was dedicated to the memory of deceased members of the troupe in honor of director Kolar's wife, Jenny. The building was adorned by Rudolph Rohn's ceramic tile mosaic mural of Slavic dancers. During the 1969–70 season, they performed over a hundred concerts, produced two phonograph record albums, made an hour-long film, and produced a television documentary. They also restored complete affiliation with Duquesne University, from which they had become fiscally and organizationally separated in 1942.

WDUQ

WDUQ-FM, still under the direction of B. Kendall Crane, grew steadily, continuing to produce new programming, serving as a forum for Duquesne student opinions and a medium for Duquesne talent, informing the greater community of campus activities, and broadcasting the home basketball games. The Sociology Department's 13-program series, "Exploring the Child's World," was selected by the National Association of Educational Broadcasters for dissemination to 52 member stations. Thirteen other stations requested preview tapes. In January 1969, seventy-five alumni attended the first WDUQ Alumni Association reunion. The station was on the brink of another monumental step. In December, it applied for permission from the Federal Communications Commission to increase its power to 25 kilowatts and move its transmitter to Mt. Washington. At the same time, the station requested a change in frequency to 90.5 megahertz. Although the station officially had a radius of 35 miles, the signal actually carried far less in some directions because the broadcast antenna on the top of Old Main was said to be five feet below the surrounding hills. Therefore, Duquesne took advantage of an opportunity earlier in the year to acquire the former KQV-FM tower on Mt. Washington from Bell Telephone Company.

ROTC

Both the air force and the army had ROTC programs at Duquesne, and both were booming in the 1960s. Two years of ROTC was compulsory for all physically able male freshmen and sophomores except for veterans and students in the pharmacy school. The requirement was much disliked by the students, less than a fourth of whom went on to advanced ROTC. The record for actual commissions was even more dismal. In 1965 the entire program produced only 53.

In 1965 the university sent questionnaires to students who had been accepted into Duquesne but who did not register. Among the men who responded, unwillingness to take mandatory ROTC ranked fourth (behind financial reasons, academic preference, and "Did not care to attend an urban university") among the causes for choosing not to attend Duquesne. The university administration loved ROTC. With enrollments burgeoning, providing a physical education program for everyone was a practical impossibility, but because ROTC required a one hour weekly drill, that requirement was satisfied. Moreover, ROTC students were required to take two credits each semester with the military supplying the instructors and paying their salaries. Duquesne provided only the physical accommodations for the program and accorded the 15 ROTC instructors faculty status. The cadets drilled once a week at noon—it was called Common Hour—in a variety of locations: on Vickroy Street; on

Colwell Street across Fifth Avenue on the Lower Hill; and in what was called the Drill Building, a parking garage that was later to be remodeled into College Hall. In the mid-1960s about 1000 students were enrolled in ROTC. Air Force ROTC was the more popular. In the mid 1960s, 62 percent of the freshmen chose it.

The Air Force ROTC was pleased that the president of Duquesne was an air force man, and he was pleased to have them on campus. Father Mac continued in the Reserves even after he became president. "Every time I gave a speech, I got another point towards becoming a general," he recalls. "Then every summer I would go to Maxwell Air Force Base for two weeks."[45] In 1968 he was promoted to the rank of brigadier general.

Perhaps the most tangible effect of the Vietnam War on campus life was the decision to make ROTC voluntary in the fall of 1969. The decision was the result of action taken jointly by the faculty, students, and administration with the support of the Air Force and Army ROTC departments. As the Vietnam War wound down, fewer students elected to take it in their junior and senior years.

Veterans

The Vietnam War brought Duquesne students and graduates into active military service again. The *Alumni News* featured a separate listing for those graduates serving at the war front or in state-side support roles. The February 1967 issue featured a photograph of two alumni in Saigon, pilots of Air Force F-4C Phantoms who downed MIG-21s in an air battle over North Vietnam. That same issue showed Lt. Walter J. Marm, a recipient of the Congressional Medal of Honor, at a testimonial dinner where he received congratulations from an officer of the Knights of Columbus, Bishop McDowell, Father Gallagher, and Governor Shafer.

The Vietnam War produced another Duquesne class ring story. (The World War II ring story was related in Chapter 5.) The ring was found sixty miles from Saigon by a captain whose state-side station was Fort Eustis, Virginia, so he sent it there. The university bookstore, after being contacted by the post, searched its records and identified the owner as First Lieutenant Vincent C. Tamy, who confirmed that he had lost the ring when he slipped it into his pocket during a four- or five hour wait for a flight to Vung Tan. Alumnus and ring were speedily reunited.

Community Outreach

Always involved in serving the greater community, Duquesne sponsored an array of special programs and seminars, including a seminar on railroads, an Accounting Symposium, the Strub Series Lectures, and special convocations with visiting groups from Turkey, India, and Japan.

The School of Business Administration was especially busy in community outreach. In 1959, it had founded its Department of Continuing Education for area businesses. Renamed the Division of Educational Services in 1962, it reorganized and expanded its community-based program of in-plant training programs, seminars, and noncredit evening courses. In a pilot program that year, Duquesne worked with proprietors of stores in the Homewood-Brushton neighborhood of the city in cooperation with Action Housing, Inc. The program was so successful that Action Housing awarded Duquesne the contract to expand the program to Hazelwood in 1963, amid interest from the Small Business Administration in Washington, D.C. That interest led to a $150,000 grant from the federal government to cooperate with the Business and Job Development Corporation and the Small Business Administration in helping to carry out the Area Redevelopment Administration program in Pittsburgh.

One of Duquesne's more important roles in Lyndon Johnson's War on Poverty was in teaching business principles and new management techniques to small independent proprietors. By

1968 the School of Business Administration's Department of Educational Services, now replete with specialized short courses and certificates of completion for evening seminars and courses, made Duquesne "the only institution of higher learning in the Pittsburgh area consistently offering a broad range of study to the community at large without specific requirements."[46] The Continuing Education program was offering 42 different courses including six in real estate, which were being offered for the first time.

With the new impetus of federal, corporate, and foundation funding of educational programs, Duquesne became a well-frequented location for workshops, symposia, convocations, and forums. For example, in the summer and fall of 1966 alone, it hosted an Institute in Nuclear Science for high school science teachers, jointly sponsored by the National Science Foundation and the U.S. Atomic Energy Commission; an In-Service Institute in Physics for high school teachers of science and math, sponsored by the National Science Foundation; the Fifth Annual Workshop for High School Journalism Advisors, sponsored by the Newspaper Fund of the *The Wall Street Journal*; and the summer program in African Languages, Linguistics, and Area Studies, underwritten by the U.S. Office of Education. On March 30, 1968, the Foreign Policy Associations's Traveling Conference, cohosted by Duquesne's Political Science Department and the World Affairs Council of Pittsburgh, made the Duquesne Union the third stop on a twelve-city tour. Sessions dealt with foreign policy, alliances, the Communist world, emerging Asia and Africa, and world economy. The Diocese of Pittsburgh joined Duquesne in sponsoring the Convocation on Human Rights on November 3, 1968. Speakers and honorees included Mayor Richard Hatcher, the first black mayor of Gary, Indiana, Dr. Patrick Moynihan, one of the architects of the War on Poverty, and Caroline Jenkins Putnam, founder and president of Catholic Scholarships for Negroes, Inc. A grant from the Edgar J. Kaufmann Charitable Foundation helped underwrite expenses for the Duquesne University History Forum, first held as a single day of lectures in the fall of 1967. In 1969 it expanded into a three-day event including fifty presenters at the William Penn Hotel.

Duquesne had always been deeply rooted in the community, but increasingly throughout the 1960s, it assumed the leadership role of a major urban university.

The Alumni

Having discovered early in the Gallagher administration that the university had not kept up with its alumni, Duquesne resolved never to let it happen again. Alumni activities, programs, and publications were designed to keep alumni involved, informed, and supportive of Duquesne. In 1962, homecoming festivities for alumni included a tour of the newly completed glass-fronted library addition. On February 26, 1964, the Alumni Association invited its members to attend the Duquesne-St. Bonaventure basketball game at the Civic Arena and to gather socially in the assembly rooms afterwards. An unexpected 500 graduates attended! The Alumni Night basketball games continued to be very popular. The February 25, 1970, contest against Xavier brought the "gathering of the grads" to the Igloo Club, the Pittsburgh Penguin Hockey Club Room, following the game where the alumni were entertained by the Tammies. In 1964, the two-day homecoming celebration, dubbed "Positively Potpourri," featured a performance by the Brass Ensemble, a showing of the winning Carnival skit, and a special jazz concert by student Eric Kloss, a graduate of the Pennsylvania School for the Blind, who had been playing the saxophone since the age of ten. He had already performed on television and cut nine albums for Prestige Records by the time of his Duquesne debut. Then there was the football game featuring Duquesne's new club system team, now in its first season.

Of the 10,000 Duquesne graduates that lived or worked in Allegheny County, two-thirds became Alumni Association members. In 1962, the association sent out its first survey. The mailing of 16,000 questionnaires revealed a need for more intimate social alumni relationships, and so the association proposed an organization of 32 neighborhood clubs, averaging 250 members, referred to as "duchies," territories presided over by a duke or duchess. By December of 1964, there were 21 areas that had established clubs, including the Cleveland Club, which even published its own paper, the *Cleveland Duke.* The Washington, D.C., club was also very active.

The year 1966 witnessed a new high in alumni activity. The director of the Alumni Association reported that he was "convinced that our alumni club program is the best. It and the Duchy of the Year Program have been and are being studied and copied by several colleges and universities who are establishing or modifying alumni club programs." Yet, in the very next year, the Alumni Association enlarged its board of governors from 21 to 55 "to combat lack of interest and apathy on the part of members of the Alumni Association." Despite the social enthusiasm of the alumni Duchy Clubs, they were not rendering the type of assistance needed by the University to support its plans and functions. The goals of the newly enlarged board included assisting in attracting students of high academic standing and outstanding athletes to Duquesne, inviting back to campus alumni groups with common interests, organizing a committee to help secure scholarship and grant aid for students in bridging the cost gap between the public and private universities, organizing a homecoming weekend, reinstituting the community college lecture series, devising a procedure for awarding alumni recognition and medals, and organizing alumni tours.

Schools, departments, sororities and fraternities, special-interest clubs, and religious alumni organizations continued their activities for alumni. Father Gallagher had revived the Priests' Alumni Dinner in 1950 in honor of Father Martin Hehir. The dinners continued, with 100 priests in attendance at the November 10, 1961, dinner on the day the cornerstone was laid for St. Martin's Hall. The date was always chosen for its proximity to the Feast of St. Martin, Father Hehir's birthday. Corresponding to the Priests' Alumni with their fall dinner was the Sisters' Alumnae who held their annual reunion dinner in the spring.

Pharmacy continued to hold its annual alumni dinner, as did the School of Law. Speakers for the School of Law dinner included such notables as Byron R. White, first executive assistant to U.S. Attorney General Robert Kennedy (May, 1962), Senate Majority Whip, Mike Mansfield (April, 1961), and Senator Jacob Javits (May, 1964). The law school alumni also held an annual reunion. The eighth one included the dedication of the Laughlin Law Library, for which the alumni raised more than $50,000. The law alumni, like the pharmacy alumni, also funded a scholarship program.

Sigma Lambda Phi sorority alumnae held an annual luncheon, "Amid Autumn Leaves," to buy original paintings for the university buildings. Early purchases were displayed in Assumption Hall, St. Ann's, and the Greek Lounge of the Student Union. The Women's Guild of Duquesne University continued their Pink Geranium Card Party in support of university programs, one of many alumni groups that continued to function despite a lack of public recognition.

The biennial survey of Duquesne graduates of 1959, the third since the university began polling its alumni in 1955, had revealed that the graduates were desirous of more contact with the university, especially in helping them find a career. Duquesne opened a placement service in the fall of 1959, with a guidance library, staffing for periodic career conferences, and a system for inviting representatives of industrial firms and government bureaus to interview on campus. Services had also expanded to include career orientation programs conducted by representative groups of employers. By 1967, the Admissions Office began a college counseling and placement service of its own for children of alumni.

Student Life

In their design for the Master Plan, the architectural planning firm of Mayer, Whittlesey & Glass assessed the character of the Duquesne student body:

> One problem of education at Duquesne is especially difficult. Many students are commuting students who drive to and from the University *en masse*. The typical student arrives after breakfast, in time for his first class. He attends usually until lunch and then leaves campus at one or two. This typical student has traditionally, at Duquesne, been reluctant to engage in extracurricular activities, or to attend the evening lectures, or to become deeply involved in campus life.

But the number and variety of organizations at Duquesne belied this perception that the architectural planners had of the student body. Although 55 percent of the students were busy holding a job in 1966, the university reported no fewer than 81 student organizations and still more existed informally. Almost every graduating student listed participation in several organizations in the yearbook.

There was an attempt to imbue freshmen with a sense of belonging even before their first day of class. Welcome Week entailed mandatory, comprehensive, well-organized sessions for newcomers, designed to indoctrinate them into the spirit and traditions of the school and help them feel at home. Highlights included parental meetings with deans, student meetings with representatives of the schools, and a general academic orientation for students on study habits and how to make the most of their college experience in planning for a career. However, in the fall of 1963, the system to enforce the wearing of freshman dinks broke down entirely because of a lack of interest on the part of upperclass students. The practice of freshman initiation had ended. It was never resumed.

Duquesne University's fall carnival continued to be a popular tradition as it moved into its second decade. In 1963, the Alumni Association sponsored its first alumni night at the carnival with enthusiastic alumni returning to take part in the festivities that included six tent shows by "Greek Wags" and the thrills of the Midway. While the students went off to the Carnival Ball and the crowning of the Carnival Queen, the alumni took over the residents' dining hall for their own informal evening of singing, dancing, coffee, and donuts. Notable events in student life in the 1960s included the following:

- Duquesne participated in the General Electric "College Bowl" television competition in 1963, eventually losing to Bowdin College of Brunswick, Maine, in the first "sudden death" finish in the show's history.
- The Student Government Association, (SGA) established a student court system to arbitrate campus disputes.
- The Psychology Department opened a counseling center in 1960 for students and members of the university family, focusing on relationships and behaviors. It was operated by the graduate students.

Duquesne continued a plethora of professional, social, religious, creative, and special-interest campus organizations, some tied to, but not limited to, various departments. Students did not need to take journalism courses in order to write for the *Duquesne Duke* or work at WDUQ. They did not have to be speech students in order to participate in Red Masquer productions. They did not have to be music students in order to perform in the Symphonic Band. Anyone could contribute to the English Department's *Overture* literary magazine or join the Debate Club or dance within the Music Department's Folk Dance Club. The Collegiate Council for the

United Nations (CCUN), the Inter-Collegiate Conference on Government (ICG), the Young Democrats, and the Young Republicans were open to all. The only clubs with prerequisite conditions were the Assumption Hall Chorus, formed in 1959, for which one had to be a resident of Assumption Hall; the Cosmopolitan Club, which drew its membership from foreign students; and the National Federation of Catholic College Students (NFCCS), which retained its Catholic presence on the Duquesne campus, as did Kappa Sigma Phi Catholic fraternity. The Duquesne Chapter of the Knights of Columbus and Our Lady's Sodality of the Gallagher Administration had passed from the scene.

Professional groups were sometimes limited to honor students. The School of Business Administration sponsored the Society for the Advancement of Management (SAM), the Student Accounting Association (SAA), the Economics Club, established in 1959, Beta Alpha Phi honorary business fraternity (which still ran the annual Quizdown for the Little Brown Jug), Epsilon Eta Phi honorary sorority, and Delta Phi Sigma, the night school business fraternity. The School of Education also sponsored a large number of organizations. Along with the honorary fraternity, Kappa Phi Kappa, the honorary sorority, Kappa Delta Epsilon, and the honorary business education sorority, Pi Omega Pi, students could join the Association for Childhood Education International (ACEI) and the Student Pennsylvania State Education Association (SPSEA). The School of Pharmacy sponsored the American Pharmacy Association for all interested students and Lambda Kappa Sigma honorary sorority, Rho Chi honorary pharmaceutical society, and Phi Delta Chi honorary fraternity. Music students could belong to any of the ensembles or the Opera Workshop, along with Gamma Sigma fraternity or Mu Phi Epsilon sorority. The Journalism Association, open to all in the department for over a decade, was joined on the honorary level by Sigma Delta Chi fraternity and Theta Sigma Phi sorority. Nursing students could belong to Alpha Tau Delta honorary or the Duquesne University Four Year Nurses' Association (DUFYNA). Other professional clubs included the American Chemical Society and the Duquesne University Student Association of Commerce (DUSAC). Departmental honoraries included Alpha Psi Omega (Drama), Psi Chi (Psychology), Sigma Tau Delta (English), and a newcomer, Phi Gamma Mu (Social Science). The Pre-Med Club became Alpha Delta Epsilon. Army ROTC continued to sponsor Scabbard and Blade, Pershing Rifles, and beginning in the 1960–1961 school year, the Ranger Raiders, a green beret survival combat unit. Air Force ROTC continued the Arnold Air Society. In 1960 it also established a womens' marching corps known as Angel Flight.

The Greek-letter social fraternities and sororities continued to be an enduring part of college life on the Bluff. Nearly one out of ten students belonged to one of the ten fraternities or seven sororities (as compared to only 8 percent in the 1930s). Still others belonged to social groups such as the Sheiks, Playboys, or Rogues. Like the "Greeks" they claimed a table in Canevin Cafeteria as their rendezvous point. The Greeks displayed their letters at the tables, which for many commuter students became a second home.

Some fraternities and sororities were organized along ethnic or racial lines: Italian, Slavic, Jewish, black, etc. Some had a preponderance of students from areas in the county, South Hills, the East End, etc. They ranged in size from 61 to 21 members, but most had about 40 members. Whatever their size or composition, the Greeks made an important contribution to campus life. They designed and constructed floats, staged carnival shows, and raised funds for charity. They also conducted their own social affairs for members and alumni and participated in interfraternity events like the annual Greek Sing.

The Student Union

Duquesne had long needed a student union. The temporary lounge facilities that the students had been using for a quarter of a century no longer fit the image of a modern university. Moreover, a student union had been included as a part of the Master Plan, and the mortgage financing had already been promised by federal officials. The Federal Housing and Home Finance Agency had set aside $3 million for the building.

Again at the instigation of Edwin Tucker, the University retained a noted architect, albeit not as famous as Meis van der Rohe, to design the union. He was Paul Schweiker, chairman of the Architecture Department at Carnegie Institute of Technology. Groundbreaking for the Duquesne Union was held in October of 1964. Few could have guessed that Schweiker's "masterpiece" would be the most controversial building ever erected on the Bluff. In marked contrast to the crisp neatness of Mellon Hall, which faced it across the planned Academic Walk, the Student Union was executed in rough concrete softened by the use of natural oak.

The six-story building had a number of unusual features. Much of it was underground; its north and south walls were entirely glass; it had an interior wall three stories high that "would do justice to a cathedral;" and it had a system of ramps at either end, with a 28 foot cantilevered ramp defiantly facing Mellon Hall. It was expected that the enormous ramp would experience heavy noonday use when faculty and students entered the building for lunch, but as the ramp did not lead to the cafeteria, no such use ever developed, nor did it become a gathering place for students.

When the building opened in March of 1967, the reaction of the *Duquesne Duke* was, "Contrary to popular belief, no cars can be driven up the ramps . . . the ramps are actually glorified fire escapes." Some months later when Schweiker was the guest speaker at the Cultural Arts Committee's so-called ASK lecture series, the students unexpectedly turned his architecture talk into a question-and-answer session on the union. When they complained that the concrete was "crude," the architect retorted that it was deliberately "coarse" but not crude. When some students claimed that the glass walls were dangerous, the architect, plainly annoyed with the comments, replied that the windows took advantage of the excellent view which both sides of the building afforded, a fact that was undeniably true. He added that "students ought to be alert enough to keep from walking through the windows!"

Much later, in 1984, one person wasn't: the artist Henry Koerner was in the building, and while attempting to view the Civic Arena, crashed through a window. His injury required 30 stitches. The building survived as Schweiker had designed it until the early 1990s, at which time the administration began to paint or cover parts of the concrete. The otherwise gray interior was altered by the installation of a stained glass window at the west end of the ballroom. And in 1996 the main ramp was removed and replaced with steps.

Student Publications

Despite all the difficulties in getting the Duquesne yearbook off the ground in the 1950s, its place was assured by the 1960s. The 1959 *L'Esprit du Duc* received an All-American rating from the Associated College Press, and copies of the yearbooks from previous years were kept on hand at the bookstore for alumni who regretted not having secured one. The yearbook tended to be largely a photographic memory, with almost no text. Another publication, one that encouraged the more lyrically creative side of student talent, was the *Duquesne Magazine*, which reappeared in the 1960s. It featured mostly poetry.

The *Duquesne Duke* continued to print current campus news with no censorship from the administration. During the period of student unrest surrounding the Vietnam War, the *Duke* became very outspoken in its criticisms of the University administration and all regulation. English professor G. Foster Provost cited the university's tolerance of student criticism as freedom of the press, even when it was undeserved, and referred to this toleration as a sign of greatness at Duquesne. Alumni letters, though, urged the administration to clamp down on the *Duke*. Possibly the opportunity for the students to vent their feelings, justified or not, in the *Duquesne Duke* saved Duquesne from the massive demonstrations and riots that rocked other campuses. Although Duquesne students "avoided 'far-out' fringes of militancy," there had been demonstrations and mass meetings on campus by spring of 1966 over racial integration in Selma, Alabama, the function of the *Duquesne Duke*, the introduction of the new program in Communication Arts, and the dispute over Duquesne's emphasis on the teaching of existentialism in the Philosophy Department.

The university preferred to think that it was the caliber of students drawn to the Catholic atmosphere on campus and the emphasis on academic excellence at the university that were responsible for the lack of disruption. It didn't hurt that Duquesne was a pace-setter among church-related universities in relaxing regulations and granting students liberties. Although many interpreted policy changes in 1966 as "giving in," the administration felt that few students misused their new freedoms. There were no longer required hours for junior and senior resident women or for sophomore, junior, and senior men. Students on the men's and women's residence councils had the right to discipline students through counseling, campusing, or probation, and could even recommend suspension or expulsion to the deans. Amid the riots on countless campuses, Duquesne students were generally calm, and even their demonstrations were not destructive.

Athletics

When Father Mac ascended the presidency, the students gained a president as enthusiastic about athletics as they were. After Duquesne's defeat of the St. Francis basketball team on December 5, 1959, the students wanted school to be cancelled on Monday as a celebration. A crowd of several hundred proceeded to Trinity Hall and began to chant, "No school Monday! No school Monday!" Two Holy Ghost fathers came out to quiet the crowd. When they appeared, the students began a new chant, "We want the president." Father Mac, pleased that Duquesne was playing a fine game despite its inadequate facilities, agreed, to the horror of the faculty, who were suddenly a day behind in their lectures. He later recalled, "I guess I had my mind made up before I went out, but I thought about it. I thought, 'Well, I'm going to get it for this, but I don't care.'"[47]

McAnulty also gave a free day following the Pirates victory over the Yankees in the 1960 World Series. Duquesne was the only school in the city to declare a free day. Mayor Lawrence was pleased, but the faculty had had enough of this unorthodox practice. When the students appeared at Trinity Hall following the next athletic triumph, Father Mac did not appear. "They got the message," McAnulty later said. There were to be no more days off at Duquesne.

Throughout the 1960s basketball continued to reign preeminent among Duquesne University sports. But Red Manning's second season in 1960 proved a challenge to his strength of character. The team, slowly rebuilding after the departure of Dudey Moore, had a dismal eight wins to 15 losses. Fans were so disgusted after the mid-season loss to Carnegie Tech that "the Duquesne students hung their coach in effigy not once, but three times. All three dummies appeared within 50 feet of each other on the Hilltop campus last Saturday night."[48] But the mid-season slump of three consecutive losses was recovered by four consecutive victories to close the season. The team even speculated on the possibility of a NIT bid, though it wasn't to be.

Sophmore Willie Somerset proved a great asset to the 1962 team as it started its season with seven consecutive victories. Although rated ninth in the list of national basketball powers, the Dukes lost to Westminster late in the season. They finished with 20 wins to 5 losses and returned to New York for their tenth invitation in the NIT's twenty-five-year history. Despite their victories, the Dukes did not cover themselves with glory. The team was widely accused of unnecessary roughness and "dirty" play. The *Duke* sports editor defended them against "all the quotes, broadcasts, and articles," by explaining the nature of the competition: "On a few occasions the Dukes have been guilty of unnecessary roughness. The Dukes are certainly not blameless, few teams are. Because of Duquesne's big-time schedule, however, their faults are more readily noticed. We don't object to just criticism, only fanatical approaches." Victories over the U.S. Navy and Bradley brought Duquesne to the semi-finals in the 1962 NIT, but it lost to St. John's, 75–65.

Willie Somerset underwent leg surgery before the beginning of the 1963 season and was unable to play. The team still managed thirteen victories to nine defeats without its star scorer. The season was notable for the scheduling of five home games in the newly constructed Civic Arena, a showpiece of the city. Built as part of the Lower Hill Urban Renewal of which the Bluff Redevelopment was considered an extension project, the arena was within easy walking distance of campus and originally seated 12,000 for a basketball game. In the 1964–1965 season, the Civic Arena became Duquesne's official home court. It was also the site of the 1964 Steel Bowl Tournament for the first time in the bowl's ten-year history.

Duquesne made the NIT again in 1964 with Willie Somerset back on the team and averaging 25 points per game.

Somerset tied Si Green's average of 24.5 points per game. He smashed Greens's single-game scoring record with 46 points against St. Bonaventure and 47 against Xavier that season. The Dukes set a new high point per game record of 82.7, surpassing the 75.1 of 1960–1961.

Somerset's abilities were extolled in a *Pittsburgh Press, Roto Magazine* titled "The Duke's Wonderful Willie." At 5 feet 10 inches, he was the smallest man on the team, but his ability to jump was extraordinary. He could jump higher than players a full foot taller than he. The article noted that Somerset had over 100 scholarship offers but was attracted to Duquesne by its pharmacy school and through its unofficial recruiter, Mossie Murphy. The humorous Murphy went to Somerset's hometown of Farrell, Pennsylvania, where he made such a hit with the basketball star's mother that "she practically laughed Willie into Duquesne."

The university took pride in the team's accomplishments, especially its 16–6 record, in the *Duquesne Duke*, declaring, "The university is proud of the fine record of the varsity basketball team and recognizes the positive contributions it has brought to the university. The invitation to the National Invitational Tournament is a richly deserved award for continued excellent performance."

Claiming that "the university will continue to support all Intercollegiate activities which affirm and supplement the academic mission" of the school, Duquesne officials announced that faculty tutors would be sent with the team. The presence of the tutors may have made an important statement about Duquesne's academic mission, but was hardly necessary in preventing the student athletes from falling behind. Despite the fact that Duquesne had defeated Army in the regular season, Army took the first round against Duquesne in overtime. The team and its tutors went home earlier than expected.

There was no NIT bid for the 1965 team with its 14–10 record, saved from being a losing one by a four-game rally to conclude the season. In his last year at Duquesne, Willie Somerset was named All-American. The new Eastern Collegiate Athletic Conference chose to televise nationally the February 13th game against Providence as the "game of the week." The full 24-game schedule was carried locally by KDKA radio. In this seventh season for Red Manning, he made the "Century Club," marking his hundredth win.

The 1966 season continued Duquesne's moderately good fortunes on the court with a 14–9 record. The following year marked Duquesne's worst season ever, even exceeding the 8 wins to 15 losses in 1960 that resulted in Coach Manning being hanged in effigy. There were no hangings in 1967, but the 7–15 record left school spirit at a similar low.

Fortunes vary with the players and Duquesne was scoring high with a hundred points per game on four occasions in 1968. After an 18–6 season, Duquesne went on to the NIT, only to lose to Fordham in the first round. If the varsity team of 1968 looked good, the freshman team that year was remarkable. Coach Manning had five scholarship students: identical twins Gary and Barry Nelson, Jarrett Durham, Steve McHugh, and Tim Bradley. Frank Harrison and John Turek rounded out the team of only seven men, which left Duke fans wondering what would happen if more than two players fouled out. The Little Dukes were playing St. Francis and winning 59–57 when the "inevitable finally happened." With seven and a half minutes to play, "Gary Nelson drew his fifth foul and joined his brother Barry and Steve McHugh on the bench. And then there were four."[49] The Little Dukes managed to increase their lead despite St. Francis's one-man advantage.

> But things weren't too reassuring. With the Little Dukes in front, 71–66, Jarrett Durham was caught charging with 3:20 left. And then there were three. The St. Francis crowd howled and jeered, but not for long. The three Iron Dukes dropped into a zone defense around the basket. John Turek clogged up the middle of the lane while Harrison and Bradley each took a side.

They held out to win 79–76 and Red Manning could foresee a great season as these Little Dukes joined an already strong varsity team. Together they played basketball in 1969 the way Duquesne did at its best. They left for the NIT with a record of 19 wins to 4 losses.

Despite a slow start against St. Joseph's in the NIT, they managed to win 74–52. Victory was almost jeopardized when officials charged Gary Nelson with a foul committed by his identical twin and almost removed him from the game. Duquesne straightened out the confusion, kept Gary in, and copped the victory. But Duquesne lost a heartbreaker to North Carolina in the Eastern Regional competition of the NCAA, 79–78. They defeated St. John's in the consolation game, 75–72, prompting the *Duke* sports editor to look forward to a bright future:

> Duquesne's fine 21–5 season and gallant performance in the NCAA regionals also should make recruiting next year's freshman team a bit easier. The 1969 basketball on the Bluff could well have re-established Duquesne as one of the nation's basketball powers.

That year Bill Zopf was named All-American and Jarrett Durham, player of the Year by the Pittsburgh Chapter of U.S. Basketball Writers' Association. Red Manning was Coach of the Year.

In the following season, the team started strong, taking their third straight Steel Bowl Title. With a 17–7 finish, they were off to the NIT again, but once again failed to bring home the championship. They broke their single game total scoring record, though, in a game that ended 123–55 against St. Vincent.

The absence of scholarships, home fields, and student support continued to plague the spring sports. The baseball team, traditionally unsung heroes on the Duquesne campus, continued to score winning seasons. Doc Skender added a fall schedule of play to supplement the traditional spring season in 1961. After serving Duquesne athletics in capacities ranging from intramural director to director of athletics over several decades, Lou "Doc" Skender retired from his coaching career in 1967. The baseball team under his coaching had chalked up 227 wins to 96 losses. Doc was responsible for eighteen straight winning seasons and never a losing one. In his baseball coaching career, he brought four West Penn Conference Championships to Duquesne. Rich Spear picked up the coaching reins and continued the winning ways of his predecessor. Baseball's outstanding players at Duquesne during the 1960s included Herky Kress, Gary Wright, and Joe Gottron.

After a coaching career that dated from the 1920s, Paul Sullivan retired as tennis coach in 1961. He was replaced in the capacity by English professor Sam Hazo. Duquesne Athletic history was made when Liz Stockhausen became the first woman to play on Duquesne's varsity team in 1962. Her brother and fellow teammate, Paul Stockhausen, and Marty Katz played outstanding tennis for Duquesne. In 1967 Dr. Hazo passed on the tennis coaching position to Mike Kupersanin.

Golf continued to be played at local country clubs under the coaching reins of Dr. George Matlin, who brought the 1962 team to a 7–5 season, the best in Duquesne's golfing history. In 1964 he passed on the coaching position to Dr. Bruno Casile.

Cross-country, introduced in 1958 by Steve Garay, received greater emphasis when the coaching duties were passed to assistant basketball coach John Cinicola in the fall of 1960. Jim Jordan became coach of a new wrestling team, formed late in 1968. The team, claiming the ballroom of the new Duquesne Union as its home, posted a 1–9 record in its first season, dubbed "a year of experimentation."

Duquesne still hungered for football. Intramural teams of touch football had extended to city championship competition following Duquesne's decision to drop the varsity team in 1951. An intercollegiate touch football game was arranged with St. Vincent College in Latrobe in 1963, with buses transporting students to the game and subsequent party. The St. Vincent game became an annual event.

Eastern schools, especially those that had dropped football from their varsity sports programs, experienced the rising phenomenon of club football. The football club operated completely independent of the universities, supplying their own funds, equipment, players, fields, and coaching, although they had to acquire university permission to represent the school. Duquesne began club football in 1969 with Peter Kulyk and Sam Costanzo as co-chairmen of the Duquesne University Football Club. The team was known as the "Grid Iron Dukes." Joseph Nicoletti and Frank Lucido served as coaches with Pete Dimpirio, a well known local coach, advising. In its first season the team lost its opener to Niagara University, 20–0, and won only two of its six games. Football was back after 19 years, funded by dues paid by enthusiasts, players or supporters, and admission of $2 per game. Club football in the United States grew from 12 teams in 1965 to 71 in just four years.

Duquesne Establishes Sports Hall of Fame

Duquesne University established a Sports Hall of Fame in 1963, the fiftieth year of Duquesne basketball, to honor individuals who had made significant contributions to the school's athletic history. Area newswriters were invited to participate as members of the Selection Team. Honorees had to have been graduated from Duquesne for at least ten years. Sports eligible for recognition included boxing, football, hockey, and track, although they no longer held varsity status, as well as the current varsity sports of basketball, baseball, golf, tennis, and rifle. Paul Birch and "Chick" Davies were inducted for contributions to basketball at Duquesne during the first ceremonies, held at half-time during the West Point game at the Civic Arena. At that time, football inductees included "Buff" Donelli, Father Silas (Dan) Rooney, and Judge Samuel Weiss. Additional honorees were selected each year. In 1965 Mike Basrak and Dudey Moore were inducted during half-time ceremonies at the Civic Arena during the St. Bonaventure game. Boyd Brumbaugh and Herb Bonn were honored in 1966. In 1967 the honors went to 1898 baseball star, Ralph L. Hayes, the former bishop of Davenport, Iowa, and Raymond Kemp, a professor at Tennessee A&I who had been a football All-American in 1928. Observing his fiftieth anniversary of his vows in 1967, Brother M. Gerard "Jerry" Keating became the hall's first honorary member. The special classification was changed to "honorary and posthumous" the following year when the late Joseph J. Pesci was inducted. Other inductees for 1968 were George "Ganzy" Benedict for baseball and basketball and Dr. Aldo R. Mazzoni for football. Louis E. "Doc" Skender, "Synonomous with athletics at Duquesne University for forty-two years," was elected to the Sports Hall of Fame in 1969, along with the five original Iron Dukes of 1940. The sportswriters selection committee came up with another sterling list for 1970; Charles "Chuck" Cooper, who as Charlie Cooper became Duquesne's first black All-American, going on to a basketball career with the Boston Celtics, St. Louis Hawks, and Harlem Globe Trotters; Paul G. Sullivan, tennis coach for over thirty years; Kassian "Kass" Kovalchek, who coached Duquesne football in its prewar days; and honorary inductee, Cleveland Kim "Brue" Jackson, athletic trainer turned night-club entertainer.

The permanent-recognition plaques for the Sports Hall of Fame were kept in "Doc" Skender's office until the Duquesne Union was completed and later found a final home in Palumbo Center, Duquesne's fieldhouse.

Athletics at Duquesne had operated as an autonomous department under the management of an athletic director since Elmer Layden came to the Bluff in the 1920s. In 1967, however, Duquesne established an athletic committee including faculty members, administrators, students, alumni, and public relations personnel. Father McNamara, as vice-president of student services, had jurisdiction over athletics and used the committee as an advisory board in establishing policy. The committee was responsible for a review of budgets, approval of schedules, and recommending policy changes as needed, balancing athletics against other interests on campus.

Rousing interest and enthusiasm in Duquesne's athletics became the mission of ex-cheerleader Maurice "Mossie" Murphy. Mossie Murphy gained campus notoriety as captain of the cheerleading squad in the late 1950s, but graduation did not end his involvement. The *Duquesne Duke* saluted his efforts nearly a decade later in the following tribute:

> Mossie graduated from Duquesne in 1959 after a brilliant career in bufoonery from which the administration has not yet fully recovered. During his undergraduate years, Mossie emerged as the most avid cheerleader and greatest public relations man the Dukes have ever seen. He has never retired his megaphone, which really isn't needed, and surely the coming basketball season will be no exception to his spirited sessions of leading the student body in ear-splitting cheers.

Even the nationally distributed *Sports Illustrated* carried a story of Mossie Murphy's involvement as an unofficial basketball team recruiter. In the story, Coach Manning, Mossie Murphy, and a "gangling high school star" were lunching in the dining room of Pittsburgh's Pick-Roosevelt Hotel when Murphy spied Pennsylvania Governor, David L. Lawrence, at another table.

> Seizing his teen-age prospect, Mossie Murphy bounded over to the governor with outstretched hand and bellowed, "Hi, Governor! How's your son these days?" "Just fine," replied the governor, "and how are you?" Mossie warmly introduced his recruit to the governor, then strutted back to his table. The prospect was excited about meeting the

governor for the first time. Mossie should have been just as excited—he had never met the governor, either.

Legends such as Mossie Murphy kept athletics at Duquesne exciting even through the lean years and did much to battle the student apathy that, according to the *Duke*, plagued Duquesne athletics in all the pre-Murphy eras.

The Year 1968 Closes Out an Era

To the casual observer visiting the Bluff for the first time, 1968 must have seemed to be a very good year for Duquesne. The university had recovered from the trauma of the establishment of a state-related university in Pittsburgh. Indeed, with 7426 students, Duquesne's enrollment was higher than it had ever been. With a string of new buildings, about one per year, Father McAnulty could look back on his accomplishments with pride. After years of demolitions and piles of debris everywhere, the campus of the new Master Plan was beginning to emerge. It was in 1968 that traffic was banned from Vickroy Street, thus transforming it into the Academic Walk that Mayer, Whittlesley, and Glass had envisioned.

The faculty had better academic credentials than ever before, and they were steadily improving, with more grants and more publications. Two years earlier this had been recognized in a Middle States accreditation evaluation, which said that "faculty strength in many areas impressed the team." As a whole, the university's reputation and community profile were good and getting better. Duquesne looked as though the days of scarce resources were permanently in the past. The corporations and foundations were contributing to the university's building program more than ever before. The ambitions of Gallagher and McAnulty for a completed campus and a topnotch faculty seemed about to be realized. But a series of forces and events were developing, almost in a conspiratorial way, that would threaten the very existence of Duquesne University. These same forces would summon forth the very best qualities in the students, the faculty, the administration, and the larger community. The challenge was given, and it did not go unanswered.

8. One Hundred Years

After a decade in office, Father McAnulty's popularity continued to be high. He occasionally received criticism from the faculty, but he accepted it sanguinely. "I never remember thinking that any of their concerns were personal," he later said.[1] His high visibility in the community prompted a number of influential Democrats to approach him about running for mayor of Pittsburgh in 1973. His supposed candidacy caused a flurry of excitement in the local media, but being mayor was far from Father Mac's desires. He was focused on seeing Duquesne through a harrowing financial difficulty.

Part of the financial distress that Duquesne experienced can be traced to the erection of two additional buildings on the Bluff, neither one of which was funded prior to construction. Another problem was the low tuitions of competing schools. And the rising costs of operations coincided with the need to implement the Master Plan as promised to the Urban Redevelopment Authority. Duquesne's money problems in the 1970s were worse than they had been even in those dark days of the Depression.

Duquesne Towers

With a state-related university in the city and a county-supported community college draining off many of the cost-conscious commuting students, Duquesne's best prospect for survival lay in expanding dormitory facilities. This way an increased number of residents would replace the decreasing number of commuters.

"Both the experts in Washington and the experts in Harrisburg told us to build a large dormitory," Father McAnulty recalled. "So we built, and built, and built."[2] So convinced were the "experts" that additional resident students would automatically materialize that they convinced McAnulty to build a 17-story, 1238-bed dormitory. Yet the university was so heavily in debt from the construction of previously built dorms and academic buildings that it lacked the necessary credit rating for approval of any additional federal loans. Therefore, a $10.5 million private loan was arranged, payable over 15 years. The enormity of the risk he was taking weighed heavily on the president, but he hated the prospect of turning away applicants due to a lack of housing.

The architect for the new dormitory was V.M. Piland of Tulsa, Oklahoma. It was built by the Tandy Construction Company, also of Tulsa. Considering the spectacular view that the site commanded of the Monongahela Valley, it was strange indeed that only the resident assistants' rooms had windows directly facing it. Instead, the building was designed with six wings (shaped like two capital "E"s back to back) whereby only those rooms on the east and west ends of the building had an unobstructed view, and many of the east-facing rooms looked into the side of St. Martin's Hall. The windows of nearly all of the interior wings faced into the windows of other wings. Happily, the building was designed with many bathrooms and students did not have to walk far to use them. Men and women lived in separate wings. This arrangement was soon to be challenged by the students. Fraternities and sororities were permitted to request a block of adjoining rooms. Duquesne did not have Greek-letter houses, and having the freedom to reserve a wing did much to make up for the lack of them.

The cafeteria in the building was intended to serve all dormitory residents of the university, seating 2500 at a time. Normally it was quite adequate. The laundry facilities were a different story. The elevators reached the seventeenth floor of the dorm, but it had laundries—also separated according to gender—on the eighteenth. This meant that students had to carry their laundry up a flight of steps.

Strangely, the dorm was equipped with a swimming pool. The university had no pool, and a new athletic facility, the logical place for one, was not even on the agenda. But this dorm had a full, Olympic-sized (25 yards and six lanes wide) pool. Of course, it was made open to all Duquesne students.

Construction began in the summer of 1968, but the new dormitory was not ready in time for the 1969 fall semester as predicted. Therefore the university contracted with the nearby William Penn Hotel to rent three floors to house the students. When the building was completed, the university's finances were so precarious that a complicated lease/purchase arrangement was necessary to purchase the necessary furniture. Students first occupied the dormitory with the start of the spring term in January of 1971. The university asked the students to name the dorm. They came up with the name "Duquesne Towers," immediately shortened to "Towers."

No sooner was the building completed when problems began to develop. The windows leaked, and the galvanized pipe plumbing had to be replaced with copper.

Events were soon to show that the new dormitory was nearly twice the needed size. Since it paid for itself only if it had at least a 90 percent occupancy, Assumption Hall was closed entirely and its students, amid much grumbling, were moved to the new dorm. This was hardly a satisfactory arrangement, but the empty rooms of Towers had to be filled.

Fortunately, a number of downtown proprietary schools—business, art, and culinary—agreed to rent space from the university on a semester basis in Assumption Hall, and later in St. Martin Hall. Although the non-Duquesne dorm students ate in Towers Cafeteria, they did not become integrated into the fabric of student life. Over the years, an increasing number of Duquesne resident students rented more and more rooms, but not until the fall of 1992 were all of its dormitories once again entirely occupied by university students.

Cricklewood Hill Apartments

Filling the dormitories with Duquesne students was made more difficult by the availability of private housing in the neighborhood adjacent to the campus. Also, in 1967, a 20-story apartment house was constructed on Bluff land that the university had been unable to obtain from the Urban Redevelopment Authority.

This building, called Cricklewood Hill, had 316 apartments. It sat awkwardly surrounded on three sides by the Duquesne campus. Its appearance was intrusive, as the lower floors of the building, which contained a parking garage, were built up to the sidewalk, making the western part of Locust Street only 22 feet wide from curb to curb. Father Hehir's gymnasium was to be left forever in the shadow of the apartment building and Rockwell Hall remained an isolated peninsula of university property. Owing to Cricklewood Hill's unstable financial condition, the building was available for sale to the university on a number of occasions, but Duquesne's own shaky financial condition prevented it from purchasing the building and "completing" the campus.

Gradually, the building fell out of favor as its more affluent residents fled to Chatham Center or other locations. In 1992 the new owners of Cricklewood Hill changed its name to Cityline Tower Apartments, but they were no longer apartments in the conventional sense. The building had become a student dormitory. Duquesne students still rented units as private individuals—six floors were set aside for them—and the remainder of the building was rented by the downtown proprietory schools, which in turn rented it to their students.

College Hall

Visiting professors from Europe were astonished at the barracks offices of the world renowned Philosophy Department. Other departments in the College of Arts and Sciences produced similar reactions in professors who came to campus to interview for faculty positions. Moreover, as the student body grew, even the immensities of Rockwell Hall were beginning to be filled by an ever-growing schedule of classes. One by one, classrooms in the administration building were being converted to offices, further exacerbating the classroom shortage.

The university had asked the Urban Redevelopment Authority not to demolish the old Reick Garage. On occasion it had been used as a drill building by the ROTC, and more recently, for faculty parking, but its dreary interior was good for little else. The building was completely redone after a design by Edwin J. Gerard and Associates, the same firm that had remodeled the post office garage into the music school.

An otherwise bland exterior of Indiana limestone featured dark brown Italian mosaic glass tile surrounding every window. Shortly after the building opened, the tiles began to come loose and have gradually been raining down from the building ever since. Outside retaining walls and planter boxes were built from blocks torn out of Seitz Street, which, in the vicinity of College Hall, ceased to exist after the contractor built the southern extension to the building.

The six-story building was unique on the Bluff in that 175 faculty and departmental offices occupied the perimeter of the building, while 25 classrooms were placed in a windowless (and sometimes quite airless) interior. (In the 1990s the university undertook a multimillion-dollar air conditioning overhaul of the entire central system, which at last corrected these stifling conditions.) Offices and classrooms in such close proximity did not always make compatible neighbors.

Appropriately named College Hall, the building was to be home to every non-science department in the college. This included Classics, English, History, Journalism, Mathematics, Modern Languages and Literature, Philosophy, Political Science, Psychology, Sociology, Speech, Theology, the Graduate School, and the School of Nursing, the last of which occupied the entire sixth floor.

The building opened in the 1970 fall semester—just in time. The furniture from the History Department had just been moved out of its house on Vickroy Street when the entire staircase leading to the second floor gave way and came crashing to the staircase beneath it. Luckily, no one was on or under the stairs. In 1974 the appearance of College Hall was much enhanced with the addition of O'Carroll Plaza, popularly called Flag Plaza, between College Hall and Academic Walk. The plaza has three flagpoles for the American, Pennsylvania, and Duquesne University flags. A plaque at the base of the flagpoles commemorates John Patrick O'Carroll Sr., 1900–1974, professor of chemistry, dean of the College of Science, and superintendent of utilities and construction who "planned and supervised" the construction of Trinity, Assumption, and Rockwell Halls. In gratitude, the university had conferred on him an honorary degree of doctor of science.

Because College Hall was made from an existing shell, a savings of $1 million was realized. Still, the building cost about $3.5 million, and a great percentage of the cost was borne by the university. The Sarah Mellon Scaife Foundation gave $700,000 to the project, but this was not accompanied by enough other large donations. It was unfortunate that the last of the departmental homes to be built in the McAnulty administration should have contributed to Duquesne's financial crisis. The board of directors had authorized the construction of College Hall on the strength of a promise by the Duquesne University Foundation Trustees that they would raise $3.2 million, yet by December of 1969, a confidential report disclosed that the trustees had received only $800,000 in pledges and of that amount only $450,000 had been collected.

The Financial Dilemma of 1969–1973

In 1966 a reporter interviewing President McAnulty asked, "Are you keeping up with costs?" He responded, "Even though we're not in trouble now, we could be in about three years."[3] Few at the time realized how prophetic his words were. Throughout the 1960s the financial realities of a relatively sudden growth spurt had compelled Duquesne to redefine its age-old mission of providing low-cost education to the less affluent members of society. Instead, and by its own admission, it was providing "Catholic higher education to those who want it and can afford the necessary costs."[4] Having only a small endowment, Duquesne could not charge the same low tuition that the newly state-related status enabled Pitt to charge, nor could it equal the tuition of the county-supported community college system, or even that of the downtown business colleges. Duquesne had to offer its students something unique. As a Catholic institution, Duquesne sought to contribute "a substantial service to society by projecting a vision of God . . . and by sending its graduates into society as living witnesses to the rule of law . . . endowed with sound judgment, moral values and intellectual and professional skills."[5]

When he came to the presidency, Father Gallagher had inherited $2 million in the bank thanks to the parsimony of Father Smith, and he managed to achieve surpluses in every year but one. He left office in 1959 with a small surplus in the treasury, a remarkable achievement in view of the three major buildings he erected.

This was the situation when Father McAnulty assumed the presidency. His strongest efforts of fundraising could not keep abreast of his ambitious building program. Duquesne resorted to borrowing, and this is where its big money troubles began. In McAnulty's first ten years in office, university income more than tripled, growing by about a million dollars a year, but the growth was supported largely by bigger enrollments and substantial tuition increases. Contributions continued to account for only a small fraction of Duquesne's income, and neither they nor the tuition increases could stem the rate of growth of the university's debt. It was a rate that could not be sustained indefinitely.

Compounding the problem in 1969 were delays in legislative approval of state scholarship money. With the state taking as long as nine months to release the funds, Duquesne had lost many prospective freshmen because the school could not run the risk of admitting the students without assurance that their scholarships would be approved.

Duquesne's tuition for 1967–1968 had been $650 per semester, including the university fee. It slightly increased the next year. But in the year after that, it increased by $200. The 31 percent jump stunned both parents and students, yet the university, basing its budget on a projected enrollment that failed to materialize, knew it would still be operating at a deficit even with the increase.

On December 9, 1969, a confidential financial status report was given to the president. It did not make pleasant reading. The university had $50,000 on hand with no additional money due until the new semester began in January. Meanwhile, the treasurer's office was facing a December 19th payroll of $650,000, a $132,000 payment to the employees' retirement fund, and some $300,000 in regular monthly expenses. In addition, there were $315,000 in past-due invoices on College Hall that could be put off no longer. The entire amount came to $1,397,000. With less than $5 million in tuition payments expected the next semester, and all of the expenses of running a university continuing unabated, the university had no choice but to negotiate yet another loan.

Having postponed the money crisis as long as possible, Father McAnulty decided to make public the university's financial dilemma in a truly dramatic fashion. On Tuesday, April 21, 1970, he cancelled classes to address the students, faculty, and staff. With courageous candor, he explained just how desperate the university's financial circumstances were:

> Duquesne University faces a major financial crisis, something you all were made aware of—if you didn't know it before—at the end of last week in a letter jointly signed by me and Rita Ferko, the President of Student Congress . . . .
>
> How did Duquesne get into its present financial situation and just how bad is it? For most of its 91 years, Duquesne had been the low-tuition commuter college of the city of Pittsburgh. Several dramatic events have changed all that. Financially-plagued University of Pittsburgh had to go State-related and then drop its tuition to more than 50 percent below Duquesne's. Low-tuition community colleges sprang up all over the area. Perhaps even more significantly, and certainly more lasting, costs have spiraled for everything, from faculty salaries to the increased cost of simply maintaining and serving an expanded campus of new buildings and facilities. In an effort to balance our budget this year, we have already authorized a $200 a year increase in tuition to $1,800, and raised rates in the residence halls. Not enough. It is only 70 percent of the needed operating income.
>
> Up until last year, Duquesne University, with yearly help from friends, foundations and corporations, had been able to keep this ratio of tuition support in balance. Now that the difference has become $5,000,000 a year, our operating annual income for this year and for the foreseeable future has to come from other than our normal sources of private support.
>
> We are making every effort possible to raise money and solve our problems, but the time is growing short. Lending institutions which previously extended credit are concerned about our financial condition and expressing doubt that they can provide more assistance.
>
> The rumor is spreading of another tuition increase, which is one of the solutions being considered. We hope it won't be necessary, and Rita soon will be telling you about what she and a committee of students want to try as an alternative.[6]

The Student Council president, Rita Ferko, then addressed the assembly in the Student Union to outline the university's alternatives. The first alternative, to raise tuition again by an additional $400, would help alleviate the pressing deficit, but "it would restrict private education to only a select few who could afford it." The second alternative would be "to simply close our doors and say that education is just too costly," an injustice to the community that depended upon Duquesne. The third alternative, the one the students enthusiastically embraced, was for the students themselves to volunteer their help in support of the university, to work together to keep tuition down and the doors open. Under the chairmanship of student Pat Joyce, literally hundreds of students would work to seek the aid of corporations and alumni as representatives of the Duquesne Community. Their goal was to raise $1 million on their own.

Concluding with, "We all share the problem; we all must share the solution," Miss Ferko and Father Mac left for a press conference. Five hundred and fifty students immediately signed up to participate in the still-unnamed plan. By Sunday, May 10th, their ranks had swollen to more than 1,000, and by the time the program was ready for implementation in the fall, nearly 2,000, including new freshmen, were involved.

By no means certain of the students' chances for success, Father McAnulty, in anguish over how he was going to keep the university afloat, quietly approached Most Reverend Vincent M. Leonard, Bishop of Pittsburgh, about the possibility of diocesan governance and support. The diocese, however, was unable to assume responsibility for Duquesne owing to its own poor financial condition, so Father McAnulty looked toward his last option: lay leadership. He met with David Kurtzman, Secretary of Education for the Commonwealth of Pennsylvania, to consider making Duquesne a branch campus of Penn State under the state university network. This move would have totally changed the character of Duquesne and turned it into a secular school. It would have been a high price to pay. But, in any case, the state was not interested.

In view of these dead ends, the enthusiastic student response was heartening indeed. The task of redeeming Duquesne was formidable. The university had capital needs of $3 million and an operational need of an additional $2 million. The tuition increase still covered only 70 percent of the needed operating income, a fairly good ratio for schools with endowments and contributions to cover the shortfall, but impossible for Duquesne with only a small endowment other than the services of the priests themselves and with all other contributions channeled into the building program. Duquesne literally had no other resources on which to rely.

The Third Alternative

The students spent the summer of 1970 preparing a plan. The program, christened that summer the "Third Alternative," was to entail door-to-door canvassing, a phone-a-thon, a scholarship raffle, and a thank-you march from Altoona to Pittsburgh. While university officials spent the summer cutting the operating budget to the bone, the students adopted the slogan, "Duquesne needs a million dollars from someone, or a dollar from a million someones. BE ONE IN A MILLION." With the university submitting an operating budget paring the deficit of $2,750,000 to a surplus of $187,000, classes opened in August of 1970 with a mountain of faith and without any additional tuition increase beyond the $1800 previously announced.

Classes were cancelled for a second time on Thursday, September 10, 1970, as Father McAnulty delivered his "State of the University, Part II" address. Three thousand students jammed the Student Union ballroom to see Father Mac on stage with Third Alternative Chairman, Patrick Joyce; Allegheny County Commissioner, Leonard C. Staisey; and mayor of Pittsburgh and honorary co-chairman of the Third Alternative, Peter F. Flaherty.

Father Mac confirmed the fact that the financial crisis was still very real, and told the students that the contract on College Hall was unbreakable, and work on it had to continue. He explained that despite the belt-tightening budget, the cost of operating the university was $2 million more annually than it was receiving from tuition and all other sources. Also, the university had $5,109,000 in short-term debts falling due and no money to pay them. The failure of the state legislature to approve scholarship money resulted in fewer students and fewer residents at the William Penn Hotel, at which Duquesne had contracted to house a fixed number of students. An additional $2 million had to be taken from the operating budget for work on College Hall when the university's own fundraising efforts fell short of the projected goal.

Student chairman Patrick Joyce then presented the plan for the fall. Beginning September 14th, the students were to canvas the greater Pittsburgh area for contributions for eight weeks, "not going as beggars, but with a proud 92-year tradition behind us." Commissioners Staisey and Thomas Forester made a joint pledge of $1000 to start the campaign. Mayor Flaherty expressed the city's pride in Duquesne and "promised to knock on corporate and foundation doors in the city for the debt Pittsburgh owes Duquesne." He applauded the drive as the first of its kind in the country.[7]

And the corporate world did respond to the Third Alternative/Students to Save Duquesne. The Aluminum Company of America (ALCOA) donated its lighted Mt. Washington hillside sign to read "Help Duquesne U." There was also free on-the-air promotion time from local radio and television stations, and donations of billboards, buttons, and bumper stickers from an advertising company. The donated advertising was estimated to be worth as much as $20,000. A local alumni phone-a-thon raised $61,000 in pledges. Each evening students boarded buses to travel to various neighborhoods, where they spent three and a half hours a night going door-to-door soliciting donations. The raffle of a four-year scholarship to Duquesne netted $25,000 after deducting the $8,000 cost of the scholarship. The student drive even reached the front page of *The Wall Street Journal*:

> In this year of student protest, demonstrations, and anti-administration rhetoric and violence, it's unusual when college kids try to bail the college administration out of its financial troubles. But the idea is catching on at Duquesne, where the Third Alternative has swelled from a core of 12 organizers to more than 2000 volunteers hoping to raise funds to help pay off $5 million in short term debts coming due. Today the students begin solicitation in the city and suburbs with a goal of $1 million in contributions.

The community responded. One observer tells the story of an elderly woman on the Southside who, when asked if she would give a dollar to be "one in a Million," discovered that she had only 62 cents in her purse. She gave it all and insisted that the student volunteer return at the end of the month when she got her social security for the rest.[8] Yet, the student door-to-door effort raised only $300,000. The Richard King Mellon Foundation matched the amount as promised in a challenge grant, bringing the total to $600,000. Still the million-dollar mark had not been reached. Finally, touched by the efforts of the students who were willing to labor such long hours on the behalf of their university, and even to return during the summer recess to conduct a phone-a-thon, private sources and alumni contributions came in totaling $2 million.

Beginning on October 14, 1970, the original 12 organizers of the drive made a 96.4-mile march from Altoona to Point State Park in downtown Pittsburgh. This was the distance a million one-dollar bills would take if laid end to end. The marchers' number grew to a sizable crowd by the time they reached Pittsburgh's eastern suburbs. Professor Francis Thornton persuaded the manager of his apartment building in Monroeville to permit the marchers the use of the recreation room for the night. By the following day their ranks had grown to two thousand. Thornton and a number of other Duquesne professors joined the marchers for the last leg of the journey. The Vietnam era had generated many marches and demonstrations. He recalls some people, who apparently did not understand what the march was all about, shouting at the marchers "Get a job!" and "Take a bath!" They were a tiny minority, however, for the march received broad coverage in the media. Amid enormous publicity, the students made their way to Point State Park, where they held a rally and a thank-you celebration on October 17th. The program ended with a party in Duquesne's Student Union. The university later honored this student-sponsored effort by placing a bronze plaque, quite appropriately, in the lobby of College Hall. It reads:

> The Third Alternative Students to Save Duquesne. In 1970–71 when college and universities across the country faced similar financial crisis, Duquesne University stood uniquely alone.
>
> The students, united in support of their university, fought with initiative and determination to insure Duquesne's survival. This plaque is dedicated to their efforts and that same spirit that remains alive.

The Financial Crisis Ends

Although financial problems continued to affect Duquesne well into the 1970s, the year 1973 proved to be a turning point. After Kenneth Erfft was discharged (following the discovery that he had manipulated funds for personal gain) Father Mac appointed Father Frederick Clark, C.S.Sp, to head the University's financial affairs. Father Clark made some difficult decisions that alienated many, but he was determined to place Duquesne on a firm financial footing. He set up a system whereby literally every invoice was given to him for consideration. He spent only a given amount of money per day. Even deans had to queue up at the treasurer's office door as early as 7:30 in the morning and submit their invoices. When the money ran out, everyone still waiting in line was sent away with, of course, the chance to return the next day.

The Pennsylvania Higher Education Facilities Authority had been established in 1967 to enable colleges and universities to issue low-interest tax-free bonds to build new buildings. For reasons that remain unclear, Duquesne did not apply for a loan through it until the summer of 1972. After the federal government refused to lend Duquesne any more money, the university began borrowing from banks and insurance companies at marketplace rates. As the university's debt increased, it became a greater credit risk. Thus, the rate of interest it had to pay became ever higher. The $3 million that it borrowed to pay for College Hall was obtained at an extremely high 10 percent rate of interest.

When the state secretary of education, David Kurtzman, approved Duquesne's application to float a bond issue through it, the financial iceberg facing the university rapidly decreased in size. In January 1973 the university borrowed $3,385,000 through the Pennsylvania Higher Education Facilities Authority for a 5.03 percent rate of interest. It was more than enough to pay off the loan on College Hall and repay the money at half the old rate.

Tuition and Enrollment

Despite the financial crisis and the rising tuition, student enrollment continued to rise at Duquesne, to a record 8425 in 1971. Some were drawn by the publicity surrounding the Third Alternative: "While students saw many small schools closing up for lack of money, they saw the student body of Duquesne going out to help their school remain open. The honest and sincere attitude of students attracted many new students," said a member of the administration.[9]

Tuition went up again in the 1974–1975 school year, and enrollment decreased by 100 students, partially because of a significant decline in the School of Education's enrollments. The teacher shortage was over, and opportunities for education graduates were very limited.

By November of that year, the student government president announced that although the university would hold the line on tuition, the university fee and room-and-board charges would increase. An unforeseen drop in enrollment of 9 percent in January of 1975, the result of 400 mid-year graduations and a large number of dropouts and transfers, along with an increase in utility costs and the continuing inflation, had resulted in a shortfall of $600,000. With a decrease in contributions to the university as well, Duquesne found it necessary to suspend all funds for travel, faculty promotions, new equipment, and to lay off 38 employees of the Physical Plant Department. The board of directors stuck to its promise to hold the line on tuition for 1975–1976, but, as predicted, the university fee was raised by $45 and room and board increased by $100. The budget was based on a projected enrollment of 7500 following an enrollment the previous year of 8080. Each student would pay $76 per credit, or $2,530 for a full schedule of classes, with $1,400 for room and board.

But tuition was expected to climb again for the 1976–1977 school year by $300 if the state's $600,000 institutional assistance grant came through, and by an additional $30 above that if it didn't. The raise was to cover utility increases; a service fee payment on the newly acquired Geyer Garage, slated for renovation as the library; insurance; and a 6 percent faculty salary increase. The administration hoped to meet all of these additional expenses despite an anticipated drop in enrollment.

When the new budget was announced, the Student Government Association scheduled a rally, an opportunity for students to express their views on the tuition hike. Approximately 1200 of them boycotted classes to attend the rally. They were encouraged to write to the state legislators asking them to approve the full amount of the promised institutional assistance grant so that the tuition increase could be held to $300.

Even before this tuition hike took effect, enrollment dropped by another 609 students in the spring 1976 semester. The loss gave Duquesne an additional revenue loss of $443,764. Although faculty salaries made up $6,900,000 of a $22,800,000 budget, Duquesne's faculty salaries were still 14 percent below the national average. At the student government rally, the vice-president and treasurer of the university explained that even with the hike, Duquesne would be facing a $225,000 deficit, but some relief had been received in the form of a $100,000 donation from Alcoa Corporation. The academic vice-president proposed reviewing course enrollments and dropping obsolete courses, possibly with a resulting dismissal of some faculty. Since 60 percent of the faculty was tenured, though, this would not significantly reduce costs.

In 1977–1978, the budget was barely in the black despite an enrollment drop of 340, leaving a student body of 7117. Tuition stayed the same as in the previous year, although the university fee was raised to help finance the new library.

Steep tuition increases did nothing to help the enrollment figures, which continued to slide downhill. When Duquesne had celebrated its 50th anniversary in 1928, its enrollment of 3062 students had made it the seventh largest Catholic school in the country. When it observed its centennial in 1978, it had fallen to fourteenth place. In 1979 enrollment hit the lowest point in 17 years: 6605. The vast bulk of this decline occurred in the male enrollment.

Campus Unrest

When the Middle States evaluation team visited Duquesne in 1966, it reported, "Happily, there is little evidence of that dangerous tension between faculty and administration which at some institutions has badly torn the fabric of cooperative effort." The evaluators also noted the conspicuous absence of "serious student unrest."

The war in Vietnam and continuing racial tensions at home had combined to make many college campuses raucous and sometimes riotous places. Although the behavior of both students and faculty was a manifestation of the disturbances occurring within the larger society, it especially reflected what many contemporary observers called "the crisis of authority." College presidents and deans were convenient targets for those disaffected members of the campus community. No campus entirely escaped the unrest, and Duquesne had a share, but not nearly to the extent that many other campuses did. In May 1964 a renegade student newspaper appeared on the Bluff, aptly named *The Agitator*. Its editor stated its purpose was "to challenge, to confuse, to agitate," all in an effort to find "truth."[10] In January 1965 the *Commentator* began, claiming to be beyond the control of the administration as it searched for "opinion, ideas, and controversy."[11] October of 1968 brought yet another newspaper, *The University Vindicator*. Not really radical—it covered sports—this alternative to the *Duquesne Duke* promised to bring "fair, accurate, adequate, news coverage."[12] These student newspapers all charged five or ten cents a copy as they received no university funding, and all were short-lived.

To so boldly state that the university was a place where "no great questions cannot be asked," as the Holy Ghost fathers had done in "A Case for the Catholic University" in 1969, demanded that the administration respond judiciously in an atmosphere of student unrest and protest. Father McAnulty showed an openness to opinions that balanced the rights of the protestors and the duties of the university, and in no small measure accounted for Duquesne's lesser degree of disruption.

The Apostle of LSD

The willingness of the Duquesne students to test their administration's tolerance was publicly dramatized at the end of the 1966–1967 school year. On May 8, 1967, a former Harvard psychologist, Dr. Timothy Leary, spoke before a crowd of 1600 in the Student Union ballroom, having been invited by the Student Forum Committee. If Leary intended to shock his audience, he was an outstanding success. Sitting barefooted before an altar with a lighted candle and a flower in a vase, Leary spoke as four projectors splashed light on his face, his long hair, and his flowing white robes. Oriental music mixed with rock-and-roll sounds completed the desired effect.

Leary told his astonished audience that the powerful hallucinogenic drug LSD could help people find God and, indeed, would soon be approved as a sacrament by the Roman Catholic Church.[13] A firestorm of controversy followed his visit, centering around Father McAnulty. He was assailed on all sides, by the secular and religious press, by outraged parish priests, and by parents who had believed that Duquesne would insulate their children from dangerous or foolish thoughts. Many people were annoyed that Leary, whom they regarded as a charlatan, received $1000 for his speaking engagement. Ironically, some of the people who for so long had accused Catholic universities of being closed to unorthodox ideas were among Duquesne's severest critics in this matter. A number of Duquesne faculty members signed a letter in support of the president and in defense of freedom of thought. The controversy refused to go away. Finally, on May 18th, the university issued a press release saying that Leary's presence did not constitute Duquesne's endorsement of his beliefs. It also noted that the speaker's fee came from the Student Forum Committee's budget, not the university's general fund, a fact that did absolutely nothing to reduce public anger.

Father Mac answered every letter that was sent to him. His letters all said that "the University is committed to Catholic principles and does not endorse teachings to the contrary. We believe that truth, if it is to have real meaning, must be able to stand the test in the marketplace. Students are going to have to face these tests later in life and we hope in some way to prepare them." Years later, he commented, "I know priests who won't give to Duquesne and who are not favorably disposed towards Duquesne because Duquesne permits, even today, maybe questionable speakers, but in my opinion they don't know what a university is." On a less serious note, he also observed, "in those days they [the students] would invite the devil if he didn't charge too much."[14] He admitted, too, that he had wanted to attend the Leary presentation himself because "I was dying of curiosity, but I thought that would never be understood."[15]

Leary came relatively early in the age of unrest. In 1973 Jane Fonda, the Hollywood movie star whose support of North Vietnam earned her the undying hatred of millions, spoke on that very issue at Duquesne. She appeared with political activist, Tom Hayden. By that time, however, nearly all of the people who had earlier been shocked by Leary were inured to a seemingly endless parade of people dressed in bizarre clothing expounding equally bizarre philosophies. Fonda and Hayden spoke to a standing-room-only crowd of curious students, but virtually no protest followed. Of course, since Fonda spoke on October 2, 1973, she was addressing a dead issue; the war had ended the previous January. Her coming a few years earlier might have produced a different reaction.

In 1977 the Student United Nations of Duquesne extended an invitation to the murderous dictator of Uganda, Idi Amin. The story was carried by dozens of newspapers around the country. The State Department agreed to allow him in the country, but Father McAnulty refused permission for him to speak. The invitation was dropped with virtually no protest.

SDS

Duquesne was not without its radical elements. In the fall of 1968 the Students for a Democratic Society (SDS) virtually eclipsed the much less confrontational Students for Peace, associated with the Duquesne chaplain, who opposed the war in Vietnam. Radicalized by the riots that had occurred at the Democratic National Convention, these 43 SDS students, about a fourth of whom were also members of Students for Peace, were recognized by the university as a legitimate campus organization and, much to the annoyance of more conservative students and alumni, were given headquarters space in the Student Union.

Duquesne's SDS chapter picketed both George Wallace and Richard Nixon when they campaigned in Pittsburgh, protested the existence of ROTC, and tried to stop recruitment on the Bluff by the armed forces, the CIA, and by Dow Chemical Corporation. The group also demanded that the student handbook and the university curriculum be changed, and it wanted "an examination of the university power structure to determine its weak spots."[16] The administrative response to this ominous declaration was "typified by a restraint that would be [Duquesne's] hallmark in all subsequent events."[17] McAnulty's light hand could work to his advantage as well as his disadvantage.

In the charged atmosphere of 1968, the SDS did not have to wait long to find a cause against which it could focus its hostility. The university had appointed a Safety and Security Committee to oversee Duquesne's entire security operation which was then undergoing an enormous expansion. One of the many questions before it was to determine if the campus security officers should continue to carry liquid mace. On October 30, 1968, the SDS, the Students for Peace, and others sympathetic to their cause, staged a four-hour sit-in on the sixth floor of the Student Union outside of the office of Harry L. McCloskey, the dean of students. Led by a Philosophy Department professor, Stephen Levine, the SDS demanded that half of the committee consist of students who were elected by the students, and half of faculty who were elected by the faculty. They also wanted the administration to have one nonvoting observer.

McCloskey had neither the authority to grant such a demand nor the inclination to do so. He threatened to call the police. The group refused to leave, even when Father McAnulty came and talked with them. Finally, the Allegheny County Sheriff's Department was called. The sit-in turned into a media event as the administration and the demonstrators waited for the sheriff, who did not appear for two hours. While waiting, one press photographer speculated that perhaps the sheriff's people could not find an on-campus parking space. When the sheriff did arrive, he served a court order to the group. Facing arrest if they did not leave, the students left, but did gain an agreement from the administration to hold a student-faculty referendum on the issue of mace. Prior to the vote, a "forum" was held in the Student Union that attracted upwards of 300 students. The vast majority of Duquesne students were against the SDS, and many were openly contemptuous of SDS members as they attempted to pass out leaflets opposing mace. The vote in favor of using mace was a landslide—nearly 85 percent of students and faculty.

After the forum on mace, the university sought and was granted an injunction against Professor Levine's wife. She had joined her husband in the sit-in and the university wanted her to be banned from campus "until further notice" since she was neither a student nor a faculty member. When she had attended the forum on mace, she had been asked to leave by ushers from Alpha Phi Omega service fraternity acting on orders from the president of Student Congress.

On November 18th an announcement was made that a march would be held protesting Mrs. Levine's barring. Holding balloons and orange mums as peace symbols, about 40 marchers began at Rockwell Hall and made their way toward the Student Union. While en route they attracted a huge crowd of onlookers. A group of hecklers, mostly ROTC students, made chicken sounds and shouted, "Get a haircut!" and "Ranger Raider!" but the marchers ignored them and sang "Zip-a-dee-do-da." When the marchers reached the Student Union, Dr. Levine delivered an ultimatum threatening to resign unless the university apologized to his wife and rescinded the court injunction. Mrs. Levine then read her poem, "Is Auschwitz Coming to Duquesne?"

The *Duquesne Duke* reported that there were no incidents during the march, but Bill Trushel, a reporter for *WDUQ*, said that while he was recording Professor Levine's statement of resignation, "Mrs. Levine shoved her flowers into my microphone" and said, "Get out of here, you're my enemy. This is for poets only!" When the reporter refused to move, he claimed that "she then began smacking me on the head with the bundle of flowers she was holding."[18]

The march ended without a university apology. Father McAnulty received more letters from angry parents fearful of campus radicals, and the following month Professor Levine made good on his threat to resign.

Moratorium Day

Antiwar, antiestablishment opinion continued to be an inchoate force on the Bluff, as indeed it was on most other college campuses. The new Nixon Administration was winding down the war, but not fast enough to suit antiwar activists. In 1969 an umbrella organization, the Vietnam Moratorium Committee, called for a nationwide moratorium day on the war in Vietnam. At Duquesne the Students for Peace was the organizing force, and they were joined by the SDS, the Black Student Union, the chaplain's office, and the editorial board of the *Duquesne Duke*, which devoted an entire front page to promoting Moratorium Day.

October 15th was designated as a nationwide "day of education, informative dialogue between opposing sides on the war."[19] Duquesne's Student Congress decided to support the moratorium and to urge students to participate in antiwar-related dialogues and activities rather than attend classes. They requested that the Faculty Senate act in concert with them in supporting the moratorium. The senate wisely remained neutral. None of the deans would support calling off classes for the day.

Duquesne's chapter of the Young Americans for Freedom, a conservative organization, countered the moratorium with what they called the "Freedom Offensive." They threatened to bring charges against any students who interfered with their civil rights and against the administration if it allowed classes to be cancelled, thus denying them their contractual rights to an education. In addition, they promised to investigate the use of any student funds underwriting "leftist" organizations or activities and demanded that the administration crack down on such organizations that might cause destruction of property. The group began publication of a newsletter called *The University Other* in late 1969, claiming that the campus media's "coverage of events concerning conservatives has been biased, inaccurate, or nonexistent."

Duquesne University officials permitted the moratorium to take place on campus and allowed the faculty and campus ministry to participate as individuals. To do otherwise, they felt, would have been courting trouble. "The day started with an ecumenical service including music provided by seminary students, scriptural readings by the director of the campus ministry, and readings conducted by a member of the History faculty."[20] Following a "peace meal" of apples, bread, and cider, workshops were conducted on the draft, the ethics and economics of the war, violence, and other Vietnam-related issues. The Young Americans for Freedom, who so opposed the moratorium, were invited to debate the war with Vets for Peace, but they chose not to participate. The day's activities closed with a peace march to Point State Park. Classes were held as scheduled except for those that individual professors may have chosen to cancel. The day, which might have occasioned rioting, passed peaceably at Duquesne.

More Disorders

The quiet did not last for long. On the Sunday morning after Moratorium Day, a wooden "information booth" still under construction at the corner of Locust and Colbert Streets was burned. Campus activists claimed that it, and several others like it, were really guard stations aimed at the residents of neighborhoods adjacent to the campus.

Like nearly every other campus in the country, Duquesne began to experience bomb scares. During the day anonymous telephone calls caused the evacuation of classroom buildings. At night the calls were directed at the dormitories. The administration soon tired of reacting to the threats and decided to treat the calls on a "case by case basis." This inevitably meant not evacuating buildings every time a call was received. The university was uneasy about such a tactic and even sought legal advice concerning what its liability might be in the event of an explosion, but none ever occurred.

University Police

When Father McAnulty assumed the presidency, there was no daytime University security whatsoever beyond that afforded by the city police in their regular patrols. Campus police protection, such as it was, had been the responsibility of the Physical Plant Department. About the year 1950 a guard was hired to watch campus buildings in the evening hours. By the 1960s two unarmed security guards arrived on campus at 5:00 p.m. each evening. They departed at 1:00 a.m. leaving the city police with dogs as the sole protection through the rest of the night. This was something of a special favor that mayor Lawrence did for the university. At dawn even the dogs departed. During the day the chief activity of the city police seemed to be the writing of parking citations.

By the mid-1960s, there were several incidents reported of students being attacked and robbed, and by 1968 the campus was rife with outlandish rumors of impending violence. The dean of students, Harry McCloskey, writing in the *Duquesne Duke*, said, "One rumor has it that 35 commandos will surround St. Ann's, and at a given signal will seize the building. Another is that some Negroes from the Hill have set a date for the destruction of Duquesne University. These rumors are all false." The source of some of the rumors was to be the FBI. In 1967 and 1968, Duquesne alumni who had joined the FBI contacted university officials saying that the Bluff had been targeted by leftist individuals who were masquerading as students and were registering for classes. They also warned of potentially disruptive faculty. Such information apparently helped the administration make up its mind about forming a campus security force. Recalling the temperament of the times, Father Mac said, "the sixties had hysteria coming from every direction. Society was hysterical, not just the campus here."[21]

In the 1968–1969 school year, the Security Department was organized and made administratively separate from the Physical Plant Department. By the early 1970s, it had grown enormously, having 25 security officers and 19 building guards. It was larger at that time than it was ever to be again.

In an effort to improve relations between the students and the university police, and to provide still more campus security, in 1970 a student patrol was organized. Twenty male students wearing orange vests and armed with flashlights roamed the campus between 5:00 p.m. and 1:00 a.m., vilgilant for suspicious activities, which they reported to the university police via walkie-talkies. Since the students were in the work-study program, the federal government paid 80 percent of the cost. Each student received 20 hours of training. In the first three months after the student security force was established, incoming complaints fell 90 percent.

The student patrol was organized none too soon. In 1970 the university police voted for union representation by the International Brotherhood of Teamsters. Since the financially beleaguered university was unable to grant a satisfactory contract, the police went on strike in 1971. Fortunately, it was summer and the number of people on the Bluff was much reduced. Supervisory personnel, along with the student patrol, handled campus security. In any case, the Duquesne campus was in no great danger from outsiders; the striking police had set up picket lines at every entrance to the campus.

In 1969 the department had two unmarked and distinctly aged cars, one of which had been a taxi. But in 1973 the university leased four cars bearing Duquesne University Security department markings, and in 1975 the university began sending its officers to the Allegheny County Police Academy for 480 hours of training. Through special legislation, they were given the right to make arrests and to issue motor vehicle citations in the name of the state.

Student attitudes towards their police were as varied as the students themselves, but unlike many other campuses, Duquesne never experienced the sharp police-student confrontations so characteristic of this age of unrest.

African Americans on Campus

The Duquesne Security force had just been established when a fracas between a white security guard and a disorderly black student from another university prompted black leaders to demand that the security guard be fired. To improve relations with the African-American community, the university complied.

The African-American student population had risen dramatically during the Gallagher administration and continued to rise during the McAnulty years. In 1976 some 6.9 percent of the student body was classified as "minority," a figure that approached the percentage of blacks in the state. Father Mac's honesty with students served him well in his relations with African-American students. When the Black Student Union confronted him about a lack of minorities working on the renovation of College Hall in 1969, he went to the group's headquarters on the ground floor of Mendel Hall. McAnulty admitted to having some reservations about going alone at night to a basement room, lighted only by candles, to confront possibly hostile students of any race, and he explained that he had never even thought about the racial makeup of the construction crew, but he could not suspend work since that would cost the university $25,000 per day. He did offer to remedy the situation in future projects, however. In response to a student's charge that it sounded like the "same old B.S.," he said to come back in six months and see if it were just the "same old B.S." It wasn't, there were no more complaints on that score.

Despite its financial crisis, Duquesne opened the Counseling and Learning Department for Black Students in 1969, staffed with African-American counselors to help students adjust to college life on the Bluff. Many reported feeling stranded in an alien world of academia. Nearly two-thirds of second semester black freshmen were on academic probation. Their lack of ease and their self-consciousness resulted in a lack of classroom participation and thus a lower academic performance than they were actually capable of. The counseling program helped. Still, the attrition rate among black students was high, about 16 percent. More black students stayed when the center began offering assistance in finding part-time or summer employment, supplying referrals for off-campus living quarters and assistance agencies, and providing references for students who were not from the Pittsburgh area. The staff reported, "Although these services seem a bit mundane, our experience has shown us that it's these small services that many times spell the difference between adjusting to a new environment or being swallowed by it."[22]

Wishing a stronger tie with the academic affairs of the university, the department changed its name to the Counseling and Learning Research and Development Center some years later and moved from the student services area to the academic area.

The Status of Women

Like most other movements occurring in the larger society, the women's movement was manifested at Duquesne in a decidedly less radical form than at most other universities. Resulting from the complaints of women faculty members of unequal treatment, in 1971 an ad hoc committee was appointed to investigate the status of women at Duquesne. The committee's focus was on the 82 women who comprised 27 percent of the university's full-time faculty. Responses to questionnaires told of the slowness of promotions, the lack of important committee assignments, and generally a feeling by many women that "their contributions were belittled."[23] Nevertheless, the final question, "Are you aware of anything relating to the status of women at Duquesne, which you feel represents an inequity or is discriminatory in nature?" produced only 18 "yes" answers.

Salary inequities were found at every professional level—women faculty were being paid $759 a year less than their male counterparts; however, the committee did recognize "that certain factors such as publications, grants, longevity, etc. may legitimately explain some individual differences in salaries."[24]

In its 1966 report to the Middle States Accrediting Commission, Duquesne admitted that "no real effort has been made to place women in major or even minor administrative positions." This fact, so blithely reported by the university, did not escape the attention of the committee. Women were underrepresented in every area of policy-making, not only in the faculty, but also on the board of directors. They even received an insignificant number of the honorary degrees (4.2 percent).

Women students complained that they were "treated unfavorably in the allocation of funds for intramural athletics and of time for use of the university's athletic facilities."[25] Some also perceived a bias in the classroom that "usually found expression in comments indicating the particular professor's low opinion of the women students' academic ability and professional potential."[26]

In the words of the committee, "None of this sets Duquesne University apart from the rest of academia. Perhaps it merely corroborates the fact that Duquesne, like many institutions in our society, is subject to the historical perspective of women that has so long shaped the roles we assign to both men and women."[27]

Although many of the committee's 22 recommendations could not be implemented owing to a lack of money, one of its proposals—to establish a fund to redress salary inequities—may have been its most important initiative, and it was put into effect. In 1973 Mary Erhlich was appointed Duquesne's first Equal Employment Opportunities Officer, and the ad hoc committee became a permanent Committee on Affirmative Action.

Continuing Education

In the 1970s, the university reported a significant increase in the enrollment of women with interrupted educational careers, especially in the social services, where nursing and counseling were the most popular areas. In other words, these were older students. The School of Nursing, for example, had a student span of 18 to 54 years of age. In response, the University instituted a Credit Hour Bank where students could "sample" college courses by taking one or two classes a semester without the usual admissions requirements or fees (i.e., purely on a per-credit payment) and apply their banked credits held in escrow if they chose to enroll in a degree program at a later time.

Duquesne and the other Pittsburgh colleges and universities also offered enrichment and general-interest courses unrelated to degree programs for the general public. These courses drew a high percentage of senior citizens. The popularity of the college-centered Elder Hostel program encouraged schools to increase their informal education offerings and publicize them through senior citizen organizations. In the fall of 1979 Duquesne offered a 50 percent discount on tuition for any enrolling student 60 years of age or older. At the same time, it also reinstated the 50 percent discount for clergy and religious which had been discontinued during the financial crisis. The new discount, however, applied to any ordained or professed religious, whether Catholic, Protestant, or Jewish.

ROTC

ROTC almost became a casualty of the Vietnam War. When it was made voluntary in 1969, the number of students electing to take it plummeted. The number fell still further when the end of the military draft was announced in June 1973. By the fall of that year only 41 students were in the entire four-year program, and the army considered pulling out of Duquesne entirely. Enrollment everywhere was so low that the army placed Duquesne, Pitt, and Carnegie Mellon under one command. However, women were admitted into ROTC that year, and the program's enrollment slowly began to increase.

The army did reduce the program from sixteen to twelve credits. Equally important, the army-manual type of classes that depended on a captive audience were replaced by "soft" ones. Cadets could be seen rapelling from the outside walls of University Hall and playing intramural sports. Project Pride, a nationwide program, featured rock climbing, backpacking, and white-water rafting. Freshmen and sophomores no longer wore uniforms. The hated "common hour," the weekly drill, was abolished. By 1977 Duquesne's ROTC enrollment had increased to 173 male and female cadets. The cadet battalion commander of Duquesne's student corps that year was a woman. In the 1980s enrollment leveled off at about 100 students.

Air Force ROTC did not survive the enrollment drought, and it ended at Duquesne in June 1975. It was still available to Duquesne students, but they had to go to the University of Pittsburgh. Few were willing to make the journey.

Vietnam Veterans

After World War II and Korea, Duquesne had welcomed returning veterans. This tradition was to be revived even before the Vietnam War ended. When comedian Bob Hope made his annual Christmas tour to entertain the troops in Vietnam in 1969, he distributed forms to the soldiers asking if they were interested in attending college. The results of the questionnaires were sent to the colleges in the GIs' home states. Duquesne decided to admit all veterans of the Vietnam conflict regardless of their high school grades. The only requirement would be a high school diploma or its equivalent. Though other schools would do the same, Duquesne was perhaps the first.[28]

After it had been in effect for a year, in April 1971 the university announced the results of its calculated gamble: 73 percent of the veterans had achieved a 2.00 quality point average or better, and 92 percent had completed the fall term. The veterans' added maturity, self-discipline, and motivation had compensated for their lack of academic background.

Although Congress increased the GI living allowance from $130 to $175 per month in 1970, that amount, along with subsequent increases, was insufficient to maintain the veterans. Like the veterans of World War II, almost all of the Vietnam veterans had to find employment while in college. And like their predecessors, they formed their own organization, the Duquesne University Veterans' Association. In the early 1970s the group had a membership of 100. They were active in The Third Alternative, in counseling other Vietnam vets experiencing the psychological effects of that war, and in many other campus organizations. As a group, they were far more involved in campus life than their predecessors had been. They were also decidedly more conservative, a fact that was a cause of some concern. "At first, a lot of the students weren't sure about us," one Duquesne veteran said. "They thought we would be a bunch of flag-waving-rightwingers who would pull close-order drills in the cafeteria. But I guess that we're just regular guys." he added. Despite their participation in a war that did not enjoy wide support at home and even less support on college campuses, they were not a disaffected element on the Bluff.

Grade Inflation

The veterans who began to trickle onto the Bluff in the later 1960s returned to a campus that was very different from what it was just five years earlier. "Hundreds were in school just to hide from the draft, to get deferments," one professor recalled. "These students were very insolent and fed up. All the good students were very upset about this turn of events."[29]

The students' choices of subjects changed drastically. In the College of Liberal Arts and Sciences, students thronged to psychology, political science, sociology, and philosophy.

One of the by-products of the Vietnam Era was a phenomenon commonly referred to as "grade inflation." At virtually every campus in the nation an A or a B became far easier to obtain than had been the case in the early and mid-1960s. The students of that era had suffered through the results of soul-searching by American educators in the aftermath of the 1957 Russian launch of Sputnik I. Believing that the United States had fallen behind in the space race because of its educational system, leaders in the field saw to it that the curriculums everywhere were made more demanding, and teachers were encouraged to grade more strictly and assign more work. Courses that once required only a textbook soon required as many as six or seven additional paperbacks. Term papers became herculean class projects. At Duquesne, for example, nearly half the class taking the undergraduate biology course received either a D or an F and only 2.3 percent earned an A. In the basic U.S. history course only 1.2 percent received an A. "I always thought I was dumb," one alumnus recalls. "I didn't realize that others were getting similar grades because nobody wanted to talk about them."[30] He remembered the almost impossible task of balancing studying time with extracurricular activities and part-time employment (a necessity for a majority of Duquesne students).

As the Vietnam War heated up, professors faced the haunting prospect that giving a student an F or even a D might condemn him to possible death on the battlefield, since falling below a 2.0 grade point average made a college student liable for the draft. In addition, many college faculty members in the late 1960s and early 1970s claimed that students were less willing to study than their predecessors had been. Those who did not relax their requirements and grading standards faced near-empty classrooms. By the 1970s, the percentage of As given out was double that of the 1960s and the percentage of Ds had fallen to half of what it had been.[31]

Even inflated, Duquesne's grade distribution of the 1970s was still strict compared with that of many other schools. The practice of allowing students to decide their own grades, for a time quite widespread on some campuses, occurred only in several courses in the Psychology Department. However, the general grading scale never did return to the strictness of the pre-Vietnam War era.

Dormitory Visitation

In 1965 what "some claimed was just another example of 'giving in' to student demands for 'freedom'" occurred when the administration agreed to abolishing the curfew for most dorm residents. It was retained for freshmen and for sophomore women. In 1969 the curfew was lifted for sophomore women as well.

Having gained an easy victory regarding dorm "hours," attention shifted to a more sensitive issue. The students of 1971 wanted 24-hour visitation privileges—for visitors of either gender. Students threatened to move out of the dorms and into private apartments if they did not get their way on this issue. Because Duquesne was an in-town campus, close to city residences and foot traffic from the business district, the university had already experienced security problems in the dorms due to outsiders, but students responded to this concern with the suggestion that outsiders be screened upon entering campus, long before they entered the buildings. Additionally, the students said that they were taking responsibility for themselves and not relying on the university to supervise them. Some students proposed that several dorms be designated as coed housing with 24-hour visitation while other dorms house men or women under existing regulations. While deliberations dragged on, impatient women students in Towers dormitory decided to hold their own "Sixteenth-Floor Experiment" by inviting 21 male residents for a five-day simulation of the 24-hour visitation plan. Upon hearing about the experiment, Father Mac visited the 17th floor to meet with the students. As the 2 a.m. curfew drew near, the students had a change of mind. They decided to disband and allow the experiment to be conducted through official channels.

Father Mac was able to delay the issue for a full year. His point of view was that it was important to respond to student needs, but that it was not possible or even beneficial to "accede to all student demands." During the Easter and final-exams weekend of the spring of 1973, a regulated responsible visitation experiment took a tentative step and was expanded to weekends for the entire first semester in the fall. The program did not include freshmen. It was expanded to include limited coed housing, since the high number of women requesting university housing necessitated designating certain wings for women in the male Towers residence. Married students were also housed there and for the first time the University hired married resident directors. The president of Student Council announced in November of 1973 that "the students proved during the experiment that they can be responsible." By the spring of 1974, even the freshmen had visitation, although only on an experimental level that could be shut down if problems arose. After three years of discussion, the subject of visitation as an important issue finally sputtered to an end.

Student Disciplinary Process

The university proposed a disciplinary process outlined in the "Code of Student Rights, Responsibilities, and Conduct," completed in March of 1974. The dean of students was responsible for resolving cases of reported violations by students. Following an investigation, if the charges were warranted, official notification in writing of the charges would be sent to the student who had the option of defending himself before an administrative or a student judicial board. At the hearing, the student had an opportunity to make a statement and present witnesses. The judicial board, under advisement by a member of the dean of students staff, would determine guilt or innocence and recommend the appropriate sanctions if the student were found guilty. The proceedings were tape-recorded and the student notified of the board's decision in writing within five class days.

The Daily Nancy

The disciplinary process was quickly put to the test over the 1974 *Duquesne Duke* April Fools' Day issue, titled "The Daily Nancy," and accused of overstepping the bounds of decency in its stories with sexual overtones and references to individuals by religious background. Plus, it attributed several fallacious stories to students who had had no part in their writing.

Although the vast majority of the Duquesne community considered the issue harmless, if somewhat tasteless, some of the individuals whom it singled out for treatment, as well as a group of faculty and administrators, were much offended and wanted the responsible students to be disciplined. In a letter to President McAnulty they claimed, "Every member of the Duquesne University family and every alumnus has been soiled by this incredible manifestation of criminal (we refer to two cases of character assassination), sacrilegious, blasphemous, obscene, racist, and anti-Semitic journalism, inexcusable even in the light of past permissiveness and silence." They were also irritated by McAnulty's inaction which they addressed by saying, "Silence on your part makes a mockery of the Gospel, of the Church and her teachings, of all human standards and decency." They even went so far as to threaten that the president's continued silence would necessitate the involvement of the university board of directors and the Holy Ghost fathers.

The matter simply would not go away. The American Association of University Professors advised the students that they had abused the freedom of the press by attributing articles to those who had not authored them. The chairman of the Philosophy Department, while not condoning the publication, announced that occasional abuse of the freedom of the press was the price paid for extending that freedom and was, in the long run, less dangerous than censorship. Only one student was willing to press charges against the editor-in-chief and the executive editor of "The Daily Nancy." (Many were actually pleased to have been included as an indication of their position on campus.) At the hearing of the Student Judicial Board, the editors claimed that what they had written was no worse than what could be found in magazines sold at the bookstore and thus did not violate community standards of obscenity. They also claimed that the April Fools' Day issue had been an established tradition and was not taken seriously by students, faculty, or administration. They based their defense, without admitting that anything written was actually in bad taste, on the premise that poor judgment and a misguided sense of humor were not violations of the student handbook or the Code of Student Rights, Responsibility and Conduct. The Student Judicial Board agreed, ending the move to set up a censoring body.

Father McAnulty, though prepared to step in if the board had been too harsh, deliberately did not involve himself in this controversy. The pressure on him to intervene was considerable, since many in 1974 were uneasy with the new freedoms given to students. He, however, felt that the students should handle the responsibilities attached to those freedoms on their own and that an institution of higher learning should allow students the opportunity to make mistakes and learn from them. Moreover, he felt that once a procedure had been established to deal with campus problems, it would have been unfair to undermine it. In this age of unrest, the entire affair was a milestone in Duquesne's reaffirmation of student freedoms that on many other campuses were yet to be won.

Religious Stirrings

In some aspects of the general restlessness of the times, Duquesne's share may have been relatively small, but there was one area where it was decidedly in the forefront. Duquesne is credited with being the birthplace of the Catholic Charismatic movement.[32] It all began with two Duquesne University professors, William Storey and Ralph Kiefer, who were so interested in the Pentecostal / Charismatic movement within American Protestantism that they attended some prayer meetings in the home of an Episcopalian woman in January 1967. Kiefer and Storey waited for nearly a year before engaging the Ark and the Dove, a Roman Catholic retreat house near North Park about 14 miles north of Pittsburgh, for a weekend retreat in February 1968. The retreat involved about 30 Duquesne students who belonged to the Chi Rho Society, a university-recognized Scripture-study and prayer group. On the second day when a water pump broke, a number of the retreatants went to the chapel to pray for a miracle, for public health regulations would otherwise have required the retreat to be cancelled. Later, a student who was unaware that a plumber had arrived and repaired the pump, went to the kitchen and turned on the faucet. To her astonishment, water came out. She then ran to the chapel and announced the "miracle." Presently, "pandemonium broke loose and lasted far into the night. Spontaneous Scripture reading, spontaneous prayer, ecstatic utterances, speaking in tongues, tears, laughter, and prostrations overflowed from the chapel into other rooms."[33]

Not all of the Chi Rho members, however, were so moved. Some wanted nothing to do with such goings-on; others were concerned they had not received the Holy Spirit and Father Joseph A. Healy, C.S.Sp., the Duquesne chaplain, who was also in attendance, spent much of the night counseling these students. Believing that the devil had prevented these students from experiencing an indwelling of the Holy Spirit, the next morning, Professor Kiefer "took it upon himself to 'exorcise' some difficult cases,"[34] and, in fact, succeeded in converting several of them. "The retreat," Storey writes, "ended in a blur of happy confusion."

The following day Dr. Storey telephoned the Bishop of Pittsburgh, John J. Wright, to inform him of what had happened. The bishop "listened attentively but practically without comment." Later the bishop spoke to the nuns who operated the Ark and the Dove to get "their side of story," which doubtless was quite different from Storey's impressions. Although Storey was on intimate terms with the bishop, the latter "avoided ever mentioning the Ark and the Dove weekend," nor did he pursue the matter with any of the authorities at Duquesne. Thus, the first Catholic charismatic occurrence went virtually unnoticed by anyone outside the immediate circle of participants on that weekend in February. These events did not go unnoticed by like-minded people at the University of Notre Dame or at the University of Michigan at Ann Arbor, who were in close communication with the Duquesne charismatics. Six weeks later the Notre Dame group held their own charismatic encounter, and it did receive publicity.

Religious Strife

The Church hierarchy, unable to discern if charismatic occurrances were genuine manifestations of the Holy Spirit, was understandably reluctant to suppress these activities. It was quite a different matter, however, where issues of church discipline and practices were concerned. Father Healy, still the Duquesne chaplain, first aroused the ire of Auxiliary Bishop Anthony Bosco when, in 1971, he gave Holy Communion in the hand to those who indicated a desired to receive it in that manner. Since this contravened the method permitted by the National Council of Catholic Bishops, Bishop Leonard warned Father Healy against the practice. Healy stopped, but then resumed the practice in 1974. When an unidentified

122. In the 1970s, McAnulty focused on seeing the university through its financial difficulties, brought on by committing to two more buildings, Duquesne Towers and College Hall, and by low tuition rates at nearby state schools. Despite these problems, some argued that Duquesne's building plan had finally produced a true college campus and a firm identity for the school. This 1970 view of the Bluff shows an emerging campus with Duquesne Towers under construction (lower middle), College Hall nearly complete (middle) and the houses along Bluff Street all but gone.

123. The new Duquesne Towers (named by the students) had 17 stories and 1,238 beds, and it opened in the spring term of 1971. The building, planned by architect V. M. Piland of Tulsa, Oklahoma, was designed with six wings (shaped like two capital Es back to back). The building was nearly twice the size needed. To achieve the 90% occupancy crucial to their loan agreement, the administration closed Assumption Hall as a dorm and rented its space to other downtown businesses. Not until 1992 did the university have all its dorms entirely occupied.

124. One building that escaped razing was the old Reick Garage, shown here in 1969, just before its transformation into College Hall. It served for ROTC drills and faculty parking until its renovation by Gerard and Associates, the same firm that turned another brick garage into the new music school building in 1966.

Pittsburgh *Post-Gazette*

125. The newly completed College Hall opened in November 1970. As the student body grew, department and faculty offices were steadily squeezed out in favor of classroom space. At the same time, classrooms in Old Main were quickly being converted to administrative uses. College Hall was meant to relieve both shortages, to be home to every non-science department in the university. The six-story College Hall was unique on the Bluff in that 175 faculty and departmental offices occupied the perimeter of the building, while 25 classrooms made up a windowless (and sometimes quite airless) interior. An otherwise bland exterior of Indiana limestone featured dark brown Italian mosaic glass tile around every window. Shortly after the building opened, the tiles loosened, and they've been raining down, one by one, for over 20 years.

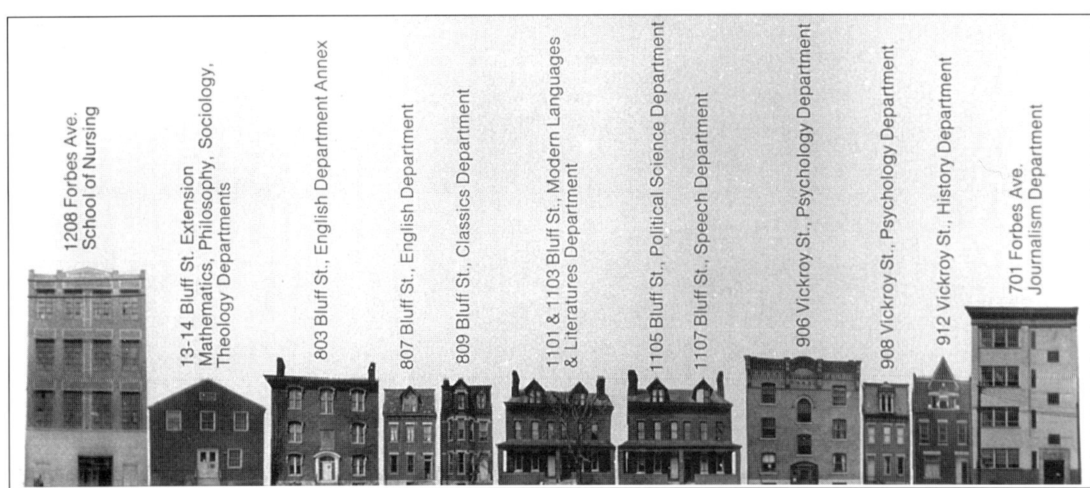

126. College Hall centralized offices that had been scattered all over campus in a variety of buildings, some in dubious repair. The new building opened none too soon; just after the History Department vacated their house on Vickroy Street, the second floor stairway collapsed. Here a brochure announcing the 1970 dedication of College Hall graphically illustrates the miscellaneous buildings that housed departmental offices before its completion.

127. In December of 1969, despite a 31% increase in tuition charges over two years, Duquesne had $50,000 on hand, and $1,397,000 in bills and loan payments due. The university, overextended in building and operation costs, was forced to take another loan. Having postponed the money crisis as long as possible, Father McAnulty chose to make public his dilemma dramatically. On April 21, 1970, he canceled classes to address the students, faculty and staff in a campus-wide meeting, where he candidly outlined Duquesne's financial plight. He noted that the University of Pittsburgh, through state support, had dropped its tuition to one half of Duquesne's; that costs for everything, from faculty salaries to building maintenance, had spiraled; and that the university had almost no endowment funds. In this photo, McAnulty (middle) introduces a new committee with a new, half-formed idea for fundraising; a month later, the Third Alternative Program, chaired by Patrick Joyce (lower left) was underway.

128. The leaders of the new fundraising program were (l. to r.) Leonard Staisey, the Third Alternative Honorary Chairman and Chairman of the Allegheny County Commissioners; Rita Ferko, President of the Student Council; Patrick Joyce, Third Alternative Chairman; and President McAnulty. Ferko motivated this fund drive by telling Duquesne students they had three possibilities for responding to the financial crisis: Raise tuition by $400, restricting education at Duquesne to "those who could afford it"; close the school; or volunteer their help in raising funds and cutting costs to keep tuition down and the school open. By fall of 1970, the committee had a plan, and nearly 2,000 students had committed to raising a million dollars in donations for Duquesne.

129. The student-initiated fundraiser, christened The Third Alternative, involved door-to-door canvassing, a phone-a-thon, a scholarship raffle, and a thank-you march from Altoona to Pittsburgh. The students attracted about $20,000 in free advertising — radio, television, billboards, bumper stickers — and they adopted a new slogan: "Duquesne needs a million dollars from someone, or a dollar from a million someones — BE ONE IN A MILLION!" Their neon message atop Mt. Washington, displayed free by the Aluminum Company of America (ALCOA), was more to the point.

130. Halfway through the eight-week fund drive, the original organizers of the Third Alternative Program made a 96.4 mile walk — the distance, they said, that a million one dollar bills would cover if laid end to end — from Altoona, PA, to Pittsburgh's Point State Park downtown. By the second day, the march had grown to 2,000 people. Some Pittsburghers, jaded with Vietnam era demonstrations and apparently ignorant of Duquesne's publicity blitz, shouted "Get a job!" and "Take a bath!" at the marching students and faculty. But these were a minority, and the marchers made their way amid enormous publicity to Point State Park. In this photo, taken in Market Square, they present a certificate of appreciation to the Pittsburgh Police and the local media. Notice President McAnulty in his usual place — the center of the celebration. The Third Alternative's strategies raised only $300,000, but their efforts attracted attention, respect, and $2 million in business and alumni donations.

131. Acting Duquesne President Edward L. Murray C.S.Sp., 1976–1977, accepted heavy responsibilities during Fr. McAnulty's one year leave of absence, taken when his physicians urged rest and leave from official duties. Years later, McAnulty said that the university's financial worries and increasing divisiveness among the administration contributed to his "burnout."

Murray, normally vice-president of academic affairs, addressed one controversy immediately by requesting the resignation of another vice-president, Darrell Rishel, who had alienated many students and the staffs of several campus services, including Residential Housing, the Black Learning and Counseling Center, and Career Planning and Placement. The Duquesne University Advisory Board ignored Murray's request and reelected Rishel to his position. It was unfortunate that the board was unwilling to support the Acting President's decision, and the administrative bickering continued. Nonetheless, the general operation of the university remained fairly smooth.

132. Here Father Joseph Healy, C.S.Sp., chaplain of Duquesne, offers Holy Mass in the University Chapel. Note that he wears a chasuble with the United Farm Workers insignia, whose strike he supported. Fr. Healy acted as advisor to Students for Peace, an activist group that opposed the war in Vietnam. Healy's support and practice of avant garde liturgical practices — giving Holy Communion in the hand to those who wished to receive it so, allowing women in the sanctuary of the university chapel to read the Epistle at mass — attracted the attention of diocesan officials. Under pressure from local Bishops Bosco and Leonard, who threatened to withdraw his authority to function as a priest, Fr. Healy resigned in 1974. It is ironic that these practices were shortly to be approved by the American Catholic Hierarchy.

133. Dean of the Law School, Ronald Davenport, who brought both improvement and controversy to the programs he oversaw, is shown here thanking an unidentified speaker in the Duquesne Room. Davenport's appointment at age 35 made him not only one of the youngest deans of law in the nation, but the only African-American dean of a major U.S. law school. A former president of the Pittsburgh Urban League, he increased the number of African-American law students at Duquesne from 2 to 40, and he significantly increased the number of women studying law.

But Davenport's growing program suffered from overcrowding and a high student-faculty ratio. Under his tenure, the law library, hobbled by a lack of space, could not increase its holdings. These problems were significant enough to threaten the school's accreditation. President McAnulty reappointed Davenport, overruling the Law School faculty's vote to dismiss him, but McAnulty's successor, Fr. Donald Nesti, was not so supportive, and Davenport resigned in 1981.

Despite the school's troubles, Duquesne Law graduates were very successful in passing the bar. In 1974, all 185 graduates passed on their first sitting. Duquesne was the only Law School in the state with a 100% success rate.

134. As part of the School of Music's "50 Grand Anniversary" celebration in 1977, Duquesne bestowed an honorary Doctorate of Music on composer Henry Mancini, a native of nearby Aliquippa, Pa. Mancini was the recipient of three Oscars, for best film score for *Breakfast at Tiffany's* and best song for "Moon River" and "The Days of Wine and Roses." He called the honorary doctorate "the biggest honor to come my way." Another musician so honored with an honorary doctorate was Duquesne alumnus Bobby Vinton, in the following year.

135. Bestowing an honorary Doctorate of Humane Letters on Her Serene Highness, Princess Grace of Monaco, was a highlight of the university's centennial celebrations in February, 1978. The degree acknowledged the princess's participation in a recital, "Birds, Beasts, and Flowers," hosted by the International Poetry Forum. The princess arrived in a Rolls Royce which drove up Academic Walk. She received her hood and degree in the Student Union Ballroom, in front of about 2,000 people. In this photo, standing beside Princess Grace is Forum Director, English professor Samuel Hazo.

136. Old Main, the first building of Duquesne University, has endured many trials and reworkings since the Holy Ghost Brothers began making the bricks for it in 1881. One of thegreatest trials was a fire, started by lightning, which destroyed most of the fifth floor. Other casualties included the campus theater, in which students had produced their plays since 1912. In this July 3, 1975 photo, Pittsburgh firefighters struggle to save the venerable building.

Pittsburgh *Post-Gazette*

137. Old Main, the morning after the 1975 fire. Sentimental attachment, not only at Duquesne but in Pittsburgh, to the 80-year-old building led the administration to rebuild the damaged structure rather than demolish it. Old Main had become the symbol of Duquesne University.

138. By the seventies, Duquesne had outgrown its library space once again; the 1939 building and its 1962 addition were over capacity for book storage and student accommodation. In 1976, the university moved to convert the old Geyer Garage, located directly across Locust Street from the original library, to a new facility. Once again, Duquesne engaged Edward Gerard Associates, an architectural firm that had already successfully renovated two buildings (the Music School and College Hall) for the campus. The new library, completed in 1978 (just in time for Duquesne's Centennial Celebration), had a capacity of 700,000 books and 6800 serial publications. Costing $5.2 million, this handsome and functional building was the last great building achievement of McAnulty's administration, and perhaps the best example of Gerard Associates renovating skills.

139. In the summer of 1972, the Duquesne University Tamburitzans, financed by a $90,000 grant from the Mellon Foundation, toured Czechoslovakia, France, Greece, and Bulgaria. They also spent a week studying Bulgarian folk instruments and dances. Here some troupe members join a street musician in an impromptu dance.

140. Brother Marie Gerard Keating, C.S.Sp., known on the Bluff as "Brother Jerry," was a familiar figure on campus for more than 50 years. Brother Jerry was ordained as a brother in the Holy Ghost Congregation in 1921, and came to Duquesne in 1924 as a chef. He became the dietician for the football team in an era when Duquesne was a college football power. Later, he left the kitchen for the gardens, becoming supervisor of landscaping for the 39-acre campus. A major accomplishment of Brother Jerry's is Duquesne's Victory Garden, dedicated in 1945, which honors those who have served in the armed forces. In his prime, Brother Jerry maintained more than 84 varieties of trees, shrubs and flowers in the six-acre garden. In 1974, Duquesne awarded Brother Jerry a Doctorate of Humanitarian Service. "Students exposed to Brother Jerry's philosophy," noted Father McAnulty, "have learned more from him than they ever could have in the classroom." Brother Jerry died in 1981.

141. The Rev. Edward A. Bushinski, C.S.Sp., teaching his famed marriage course. Over a 26-year career, Father Bushinski lectured more than 15,000 Duquesne students on the rudiments of successful marriage. *The Pittsburgh Press* referred to him as "Pittsburgh's version of St. Valentine." In 1978, Father Bushinski was recognized by the Faculty Senate with its Outstanding Teacher Award, and he was cited for excellence in teaching when receiving a Presidential Award for Excellence in 1981. He retired from teaching in 1988.

His brother, the Rev. Leonard A. Bushinski, C.S.Sp., was also a dedicated member of the Duquense community, teaching Scripture studies and later serving as the assistant archivist of the university. He died in 1991.

person who attended mass at the chapel reported that the priests distributed communion in a "disgraceful and irreverent manner,"[35] Bishop Leonard threatened to withdraw Healy's faculties (his ability to function as a priest) and those of another priest at Duquesne who was doing the same thing.

Healy also caused upset when he permitted women in the sanctuary of the university chapel and allowed them to read the Epistle at Mass. Though Father Healy was joined by two other Holy Ghost priests who held similar ideas, he nonetheless felt increasingly isolated from the other members of the order, most of whom did not approve of his actions. Father McAnulty took no position on the matter, as support for Father Healy could have brought ecclesiastical denunciation of Duquesne, something he was unwilling to risk.

Finally, in November 1974 the issue came to a head when "Bishop Bosco called Father Healy and reminded him of the penalties for breaking Church law."[36] Father Healy then resigned as chaplain and took a sabbatical. He did not return. The religious ferment on the Bluff, and in the Church as a whole, was a part of the general social upheaval of the times. It was ironic that these practices, once considered so radical, were shortly to be approved by the American Catholic hierarchy.

Controversy in the Administration Building

Through part of the 1970s Duquesne experienced a number of difficulties at the highest levels of university governance. The administration allowed vice-presidents and deans to act with a degree of independence that did not always contribute to the smooth functioning of the university.

The vice-president of Student Services, Darrell Rishel, seemed to live in a whirlpool of dissention. It was he who called the meeting of those ridiculed in the April Fools' issue of the *Duquesne Duke* in 1974 in search of an individual willing to press charges, and who subsequently brought suit on that student's behalf, prepared and presented the case, and proposed that the publications board censor student writing. Following the trial, two members of the Student Government Association had urged him to resign. However, the board of directors reelected him to the post the following day.

That same school year, Rishel received a report from the Housing Department that $200,000 had been lost to the university in uncollected fees. He then fired five resident directors and forced the housing director to resign. In April 1975 he notified the sports information director that his contract would not be renewed because of alleged incompetence, but a special committee appointed to review the sports director's performance recommended his retention. Claiming that the "student services administration was not receptive to the black philosophy," the Black Counseling and Learning Center requested that they be transferred from his jurisdiction to that of academic affairs.[37] In the spring of 1976, Rishel, claiming a "failure to develop and maintain an attitude and atmosphere of cooperation and communication with either superior or fellow student services staff members," fired the director and assistant director of Career Planning and Placement. After a due process hearing, they were reinstated in their positions and were transferred to the jurisdiction of the vice president for academic affairs.

It was in the midst of these goings on that Father McAnulty took a one-year leave of absence. The news release issued by the Duquesne News Bureau on October 15, 1976 said that McAnulty was "suffering from a central nervous disorder for which his physicians have urged rest and a leave from official duties." He had already been admitted to Mercy Hospital ten days before the news release. The exhausted president was suffering from what he later described in modern parlance as "burnout." Although the continuing financial crisis was undoubtedly the principal cause, the unceasing administrative bickering contributed to his condition. Even in the 1960s, McAnulty had not exercised a heavy-handed administrative control, but by the mid-1970s his governance had become lighter still.

Father Edward L. Murray C.S.Sp., vice president of academic affairs, having been named acting president during Father McAnulty's absence, requested Rishel to submit his resignation effective June 30, 1977, with the warning that if he refused to resign, his contract would be terminated. Father Murray rescinded his threat to fire Rishel prior to the meeting of the board of directors, but still demanded the resignation. The board ignored Murray's resignation request and reelected Rishel as Student Services vice-president. Even though it set up a committee to investigate Rishel, the whole unfortunate affair demonstrated just how far the board was willing to go in undermining the authority of the acting president.

Father McAnulty returned as president again in the fall of 1977. The vice-president of Student Services was eventually dismissed in May 1978. Father McAnulty said his reason for terminating the contract was that Rishel had made no attempt to get to know the students and was unpopular with both students and staff. The vice-president of University Relations was also dismissed following a mention in the report of the Middle States evaluation team of the need for more effective fundraising, which was the primary responsibility of that vice-president. The vice-president of Finance was leaving as well, because he intended to leave the priesthood.

At the end of June, Duquesne also lost its director of Admissions, who had accepted a position at another university and took four staff members with him. With a pressing need to recruit high school graduates for Duquesne, Father McAnulty had the director of counseling and career development assume the position of interim admissions director until another search committee could recommend a replacement. Duquesne entered its centennial celebration year—1978–1979—with a greatly changed administration.

Troubled Times in the Law School

When Louis Manderino resigned as dean of the law school in 1970, the faculty of that school voted that they had no objection to Ronald Davenport as his replacement. Nine years later a majority of that same faculty would sue the university to stop his reappointment.

Davenport's initial appointment at age 35 not only made him one of the youngest law deans in the nation, but also the only African-American dean of a major American law school. A former president of the Urban League of Pittsburgh, Davenport increased the number of African-American law students at Duquesne from two to 40. (The number of women law students also greatly increased.)

During the Manderino years, 1968–1970, the enrollment jumped from 472 students to over 600, yet the school continued to occupy only the top floors of Rockwell Hall. The faculty-student ratio was far too high, frequently resulting in overcrowded classes. The general lack of space made it impossible for the law library to increase its holdings or to serve its large number of students adequately. Although these conditions were noted by the Association of American Law Schools accreditation team during its 1973 visit, no improvements were made.

There were other problems having nothing to do with overcrowding. Dean Davenport had outside financial interests in a number of radio stations in Pittsburgh and other cities that frequently made him inaccessible to either students or faculty. Moreover, there were complaints that the dean ran the school in a highhanded, even dictatorial manner. Nevertheless, the faculty overwhelmingly voted for his reappointment in 1975, with the lone dissenter, who happened to be untenured, forced out by Dean Davenport in retaliation.

The dean had implemented a system whereby faculty pay raises were to be predicated on scholarship, which many called hypocritical, since the dean's own record of scholarly publication was practically nonexistent. By a vote of eight to six the faculty voted not to reappoint Davenport. But getting rid of Dean Davenport was not that easy. First, the dean questioned the legitimacy of the vote, saying that he and another part-time professor had not been permitted to vote whereas a librarian with "faculty status" had been. Aware that the librarian had voted against him, Davenport wrote her a letter saying that when her contract expired on June 30, 1979, her services would no longer be required. A number of faculty protested the firing, and the librarian promptly entered suit against Davenport and McAnulty. Having faculty status had indeed entitled the librarian to vote, and she had done so on previous occasions. Her position was not tenured, though, and she lost her suit against the university. Under the next dean she was rehired.

Despite the eight faculty "no" votes, President McAnulty reappointed Davenport to a third term. He gave a verbal slap on the wrist to the dean in a letter, saying that some students and faculty "have expressed certain concerns about your administration such as: absenteeism, unavailability, lack of input and consultation, and unity within the University. I know you will address yourself to these concerns."[38]

In February the eight law professors sued the university, claiming that their contracts gave them the right to appoint the dean. "McAnulty said the appointment of university deans 'traditionally' has been the responsibility of the administration of the university."[39] The university moved to have the case dismissed, but the court refused. The president of the Faculty Senate joined the fracas charging the administration with ignoring the "clearly expressed concerns of the faculty" and calling McAnulty's actions "a continuing failure of leadership."

With the law school attracting so much attention, in March of 1979 the American Bar Association (ABA) and the Association of American Law Schools (AALS) visited the campus for an inspection. Both associations decided not to challenge the dean's reappointment, though they warned of a follow-up evaluation at a later time. For most people, the issue was settled, but not in the minds of the eight faculty members who had entered suit. They had no intentions of withdrawing their case, which was still pending when the new university president, Donald Nesti, C.S.Sp., took office. Nesti was decidedly less enamored of Davenport than his predecessor had been, and in June 1981, the dean submitted his resignation.

The entire episode, played out as it was in the pages of the local newspapers—they even reported the firing of the librarian—was unfortunate publicity for the university. It was ironic that despite the tumultuous times and the cramped quarters, Duquesne's graduates still enjoyed a high rate of success in passing the bar. In 1974 all 185 of them passed it on the first sitting. Duquesne Law School was the only law school in the state with 100 percent success.[40]

Upheaval in the School of Nursing

The School of Nursing rewrote a portion of its curriculum under a phenomenological approach in 1973. The minutes of faculty meetings for 1974–1975 reflect the turmoil as the faculty learned the new philosophy and accommodated their teaching to cope with larger class sizes. The students also found the adjustment difficult and complained about inconsistencies in course requirements, a lack of definition in course outlines, and vagueness in the objectives in so-called "challengeable" courses in which students had to learn to identify a problem, develop a plan, follow through on the plan, and evaluate the results. The hospitals and clinics affiliated with Duquesne's School of Nursing were troubled with the new curriculum as well. This resulted in the formation of a School of Nursing Speakers' Committee to meet with nursing representatives of the agencies in explaining the purpose, objectives, and relevant approaches to nursing as taught at Duquesne. Other areas of controversy arose regarding the role of the proposed position of academic advisor and a move by the nursing administration toward promotion based on continued faculty education in pursuit of a doctoral degree for which no tuition reimbursement was given.

Faculty member Rosemarie Parse's "Systemic Inquiry" senior nursing course drew complaints from some students in 1975 for inconsistencies in grading, insufficient time in the clinical area, and a lack of teacher-student interaction on individual student projects. She, in turn, attacked Dean Regina Fusan for her handling of the complaints as an infringement on academic freedom. Divided loyalties within the school resulted in Regina Fusan's decision to resign as dean in August 1976. Her conservative and noninterventionist manner had not been appreciated by those who wanted a strong, decisive administrator who would fight for salary increases, faculty promotions, and the fullest consideration of their academic rights. She applied for a sabbatical leave and planned to return to the school as a student advisor, but upon her return was assigned as an advisor to the College of Arts and Sciences, ostensibly so that the conflicts within the School of Nursing could be resolved.

A search committee selected Rosemarie Parse, director of Duquesne's graduate nursing program, to replace Fusan as dean. Dean Parse completely revised the administrative hierarchy of the School of Nursing, identified several major new goals, began a program of faculty enhancement to encourage faculty to pursue further degree work, and began work on the development of a new undergraduate curriculum to address complaints about inconsistencies in the current courses. With a total enrollment of 699 students, the school also began an advisement and counseling service with each faculty member assigned a group of student advisees.

In 1978 the School of Nursing announced extensive curriculum changes for the freshman class along with a reduction in class size to increase student participation. New courses in nursing science and statistics were begun. The emphasis of the new curriculum was on nursing theory and existential thought, and took the form of a nursing model, not an integrated curriculum. The philosophy saw health as a process of becoming rather than a state of well-being. The students were to explore the value systems of their clients and decide upon a participatory program of health in a joint decision with the individual patient.

Students spent their freshman and sophomore years studying the philosophy and history of nursing and being introduced to nursing research. In the junior year, they were introduced to clinical work, with an emphasis on theory rather than application. In their senior year, they followed the treatment of patients in acute-care agencies, private homes, clinic settings, nursing homes, and schools to view the entire range of life stages within the context of the family.

The new curriculum was not warmly embraced. Students, parents, and individuals both inside and outside the university protested vehemently in letters and articles in the *Duquesne Duke*. Graduates of the 1973 curriculum, where the existential approach was first introduced, were receiving low scores on the state board nursing examinations, and hospitals accused the school of placing too much emphasis on theory and philosophy to the detriment of practical application and technical knowledge. The *Duquesne Duke* discovered that none of the hospitals that hired nurses produced by the new curriculum would recommend Duquesne to anyone interested in a nursing career. The school's reputation in the community plummeted.

Under mounting pressure, on June 8, 1979,

Father McAnulty finally relieved the dean, associate dean, and the assistant dean of their administrative duties while allowing them to teach in the graduate nursing program. But the National League for Nursing (NLN) placed the undergraduate nurse program on a first-warning basis, indicating that it did not meet their educational standards, and the Pennsylvania State Board of Nurse Examiners placed the school on provisional status. The curriculum had to be completely revised, although the philosophical framework was retained. Dr. Bruce Martin, dean of the School of Pharmacy, was made acting dean, the nursing school faculty and administration again devoted the requisite attention to the practical aspects of nursing. The school later received a letter of commendation from the Board of Examiners of the Commonwealth of Pennsylvania for progress made in meeting the program's deficiencies. But the NLN denied accreditation to the graduate nursing program, and it was eventually discontinued.[41]

Father Mac tried to reassure the nursing students to continue at Duquesne and to invite the new students by mailing out letters informing them of the administrative changes and asking for their input in the new program as Duquesne attempted to restore its "proud Nursing tradition."[42] In 1980 the NLN reaccredited Duquesne's School of Nursing, and the school began to achieve stability after the appointment that year of Dr. Carol Ann Smith, with credentials from Boston College, as the new dean.

Problems in the School of Education

Dissension arose in the School of Education when the president of the Faculty Senate was not permitted to attend the board of directors' executive session at which the reappointment of the deans of the Music School and the School of Education was to be voted upon. The Faculty Senate and the Student Government Association did have observer status at board of directors meetings, but were barred from executive sessions for voting on the reappointment of the music and education deans. The senate strongly objected to the closed session. Along with the dissension came disappointment when the school's accreditation was withdrawn by the National Council for Accreditation of Teacher Education (NCATE) in 1978. Membership in NCATE was voluntary and had no bearing on state accreditation. NCATE claimed that Duquesne failed to prepare elementary and secondary teachers satisfactorily at the bachelor's level and to adequately prepare elementary and secondary teachers, principals, supervisors, guidance counselors, and school psychologists. Only 25 of Pennsylvania's 83 institutions granting teaching degrees were approved by the NCATE that year.

The School of Pharmacy Survives a Financial Crisis

The 1975–1976 school year marked the fiftieth anniversary of the founding of the School of Pharmacy. The move from Canevin Hall to Mellon Hall in 1968 gave the school the space it needed to expand as new medical treatments such as radiology and pharmaceutical analysis emerged. The specialized pharmacy facilities in Mellon Hall included the model pharmacy, an animal operating room, an electronics laboratory, a bionucleonics laboratory, eight teaching laboratories, a manufacturing pharmacy laboratory containing basic pharmaceutical and manufacturing equipment, and separate tableting and aersol technology rooms. The school offered the only Ph.D. in pharmaceutical chemistry, specializing in pharmaceutical analysis, in the tri-state area, and it began the first baccalaureate program in radiological health in the region.

When Dean Adams resigned in 1961, he was succeeded by Dr. John S. Ruggiero, implementor of the five-year curriculum, who oversaw the move to Mellon Hall. He was succeeded in 1970 by Dr. Bruce D. Martin. As Dr. Martin assumed the deanship, the School of Pharmacy's future lay in doubt. The financial crisis affecting the entire university had so decreased enrollment of professional students in pharmacy that in December 1969, the university considered phasing out the School entirely. Enrollment was down to 223 undergraduates. The new facilities and expanded faculty resulted in a per-student cost of $4,500, whereas tuition income from each pharmacy student amounted to only $1,600. The faculty was able to convince the board of directors to delay the phasing out for several years. Along with delegating responsibilities to other faculty members, Dr. Martin selected Ralph R. Kreuer, a member of the school's first graduating class in 1928 and faculty member until 1943, as assistant to the dean. Dr. Kreuer proved a strong spokesman and recruiter, and devised a grant-sponsored tutoring program to help keep down attrition rates. Slowly, the enrollment grew and the school prospered.

The school devised the titles "clinical assistant" and "clinical associate" for part-time lecturers and instructors, recognizing the contributions of the professional staff of Mercy Hospital, who were unsalaried by the University. The financial crisis made it impossible to promote the medical technology program begun in 1969, but the program grew anyway, graduating its first students in the allied health area in 1972. A grant from Merck Company permitted Dr. Charles L. Winek to introduce new courses on drug abuse and begin student-produced programs on the topic in 1970–1971. Six undergraduate courses were offered during the summer of 1971, a program that was continued through subsequent summers and was actually showing a profit by 1973, supported by grants which allowed faculty to conduct research as well as teach during the summer.

By the end of the 1970–1971 school year, the faculty had grown to 14 full-time and 7 part-time members. The American Council on Pharmaceutical Education reaccredited the school in April 1972, after an extensive self-study by Duquesne and a site visit by two council members. The School became known as a leader in newer aspects of clinical practice in 1971–1972. The first Ph.D. was awarded in 1972.

Recruitment efforts raised the number of undergraduates to 315, and then the school cut its ties with the College of Liberal Arts and Sciences, and all its students, years one through five, became students in the School of Pharmacy. Now students were free of the worry of not being accepted into the School of Pharmacy after their first two years in the college, and the school once more had to consider placing a maximum number on class size. By 1974–1975, the year of the fiftieth anniversary, undergraduate enrollment stood at 508.

Federal money, directed toward the development of clinical pharmacy programs, aided the Duquesne program headquartered at Mercy Hospital. Competition for the limited number of positions in the clinical year at Mercy Hospital School of Medical Technology was based on scholastic performance during the three preparation years in the medical technology and radiological health programs. The programs were so strenuous and attracted such able students that the university earned a reputation for professional excellence in the cutting-edge areas of clinical pharmacy.

Independent funding was still vitally important to the school. By the 1973–1974 academic year, it was covering 20 percent of its $500,000 operational budget from sources outside the university and the rest from tuition and fees from the summer and regular semester sessions. The university still had to pay the extensive overhead on equipment, utilities, and debt service on Mellon Hall, but with 463 undergraduates and 69 graduate students, the school was once again on a firm financial footing. Nearly 70 percent of all undergraduates were receiving financial support through loans and grants from the school's scholarship committee, along with state, federal, and university loans and grants. Unfortunately, the Muldoon Chair, to be named for the school's beloved founder, was destined to remain a dream. By 1977 the alumni had pledged $50,000, an amount far short of the million dollar goal.

Participation in pharmacy organizations, which hit a low in the late 1960s, experienced an upswing, with new activities recorded by the Student American Pharmaceutical Association, Phi Delta Chi, Rho Chi, Kappa Psi, Lambda Kappa Sigma, the Graduate Student Association, and the Pharmacy Phorum which published three journals a year. After several years of preparation and piloting, the school implemented a college-controlled, mandatory student internship. A tribute to the school's preparation was the 100 percent pass rate of students taking the Pennsylvania State Board of Pharmacy examinations at the conclusion of the jubilee year.

A controversy occurred in 1978 following the disclosure that county morgue equipment had been installed and operated at Mellon Hall. The investigation resulted in a return of equipment and an end to research that had heretofore proved beneficial to both the county and the university. Dr. Charles Winek, a full professor of pharmacy at Duquesne, also served as chief toxicologist at the morgue, an alliance that had led to the installation of an atomic absorption spectophotometer in Mellon Hall because the morgue's power supply and ventilation system was inadequate for its operation. All this was done without the knowledge or consent of the Allegheny County commissioners. During the time it was in operation at Duquesne, it was used for official morgue work, as well. The county benefitted from discoveries made at the university, one being the breathalyzer later used by the county police. Unhappily for all, a reporter's zeal to expose what he imagined to be corruption in government required that the cooperation had to be officially ended, and the morgue had to undergo the extensive rewiring and renovation necessary to house the spectophotometer.

The African Affairs Institute Closes

In presenting the budget increases for the 1977–1978 school year, Acting President Murray promised to evaluate programs and eliminate those that had outlived their usefulness. The Institute of African Affairs, funded largely through federal grants since its inception in 1958, was continually starved for adequate resources. When the U.S. Office of Education funds were cut back in 1974, the institute reduced expenses by cutting the number of credits necessary for a graduate degree from 42 to 30. It survived, thanks to a Buhl Foundation grant of $50,000 over two years, and restructuring of the program enabled Duquesne to offer full master's degrees in two major African languages, Hausa and Swahili.

In 1976–1977, however, the institute received no federal funds at all. With only nine students, three of whom were undergraduates, and an operating budget of $80,000 annually, the university could not reasonably justify maintaining a program that employed six staff members. It was decided to phase out the institute gradually so that students could complete their graduate programs and faculty could be placed in other academic programs. The 1978–1979 academic year was the final one for the Institute of African Affairs. Most of the Institute's graduates moved into teaching in Africa or for American corporations that did business there. Father Joseph L. Varga, C.S.Sp. director, regretted its closing at a time when African nations were beginning to play stronger political and economic roles internationally.

Middle States Report: A Passing Grade

The 1977–1978 academic year brought the Middle States Association of Secondary Schools and Colleges back to Duquesne for its decennial accreditation review. The Middle States report noted the high level of involvement of faculty and staff in university planning as "an indication of the openness, candor, and desire for appropriate action to improve institutional performance which permeates Duquesne." The report also cited other strengths of the university:

> Other clear assets include the handsome new buildings on campus, including a spacious new library that will be opened next spring; the quality and leadership role of the Board; the sophisticated yet realistic organization and planning for fund raising that has been established on campus with frequently affirmed support by the Board; a general belief and commitment to the University that most everyone seems to share from Board to students, despite disagreements on how to resolve some problems; a student body that is loyal, concerned, and helpful (students through their own "Third Alternative" raised over a million dollars to save Duquesne in the doleful fiscal crisis of 1969–70 and the same dedication to help is still obvious); and a competent, responsive student services staff with an excellent program.

The report was not all one of praise. Problem areas cited included the declining enrollment, continuing financial difficulties, communications problems between faculty and administration and between various branches of administration, a lack of clarification of roles of administrative staff in the academic areas, an overly high percentage of tenured faculty, and the absence of a faculty development program. The team encouraged a capital funds campaign to lower the university debt of $25 million that was consuming nine percent of its budget. In summation, the team concluded:

> Duquesne has had a tough go of it in the past years, but an abiding sense of mission plus a willingness to make sacrifices have kept the University viable. . . . We found an institution fully aware of its problems and this is a healthy sign that it is prepared to make decisions concerning its programs and goal priorities for the next decade and then engage in a vigorous, systematic effort to find new resources that it will need to accomplish its goals.

Reaccreditation was approved.

Despite the controversies within several schools that had attracted much attention, most of the university had been continuing to operate smoothly, and this fact was duly noted by the inspectors. The university took seriously those trouble spots that were identified. Father McAnulty appointed a planning committee to help in developing a new academic Master Plan. Through the spring and summer of 1978, Helen M. Kleyle, associate vice president for academic affairs, chaired the 37-member committee to write a new mission statement and make recommendations for much-needed improvements in university administration.

One recommendation was to establish formal procedures for reviewing faculty members. Promotions had been handled in an informal manner, usually resulting automatically from seniority. The committee also recommended developing new programs to combat falling enrollments. A 12-year fundraising campaign was suggested, and it was advised that tuition increases be announced nearly a year in advance so as to allow the students to make adequate preparation. All of the committee's recommendations were accepted by the administration.

A New Library at Last

Even as the university was building an addition to the old library at the corner of Colbert and Locust Streets in 1962, plans were being made for still another addition in just three more years. But these three years had long since come and gone, and the Duquesne library was now sorely in need of space. The promised addition had not been built because the administration had been busy addressing construction needs even more critical than library expansion. By the 1970s, however, the library's space needs had become so great that the plot of ground set aside for the addition—the Student Union had been built next to it—was no longer sufficient to fulfill the requirement.

By 1974 the University had not yet decided upon the current location of the library when events were set into motion that came dangerously close to preventing Duquesne from ever being able to make the appropriate choice. In that year a local attorney announced plans to rehabilitate the old Geyer Garage directly across Locust Street from the original library and turn it into an apartment building. The property, still owned by the Urban Redevelopment Authority (URA) and zoned as commercial-residential, had been contracted to another developer, who had gone bankrupt. Supposedly, Duquesne had ended its land acquisitions, which for ten years had been conducted through the URA. Also, it had officially and amicably terminated its relationship with the URA in 1972, even though it still did not possess the land between Locust Street and Forbes Avenue in the vicinity of the Armstrong Tunnels where the garage was located. This did not mean that all hopes of gaining the property were abandoned, however. At the time, the site was being considered as a future home for the law school. University officials were aghast when the director "said the authority would not give the building to Duquesne University in order to maintain its policy of returning land to the tax rolls." Apparently, the days when the URA did all that it could to aid the expansion of Duquesne University were in the past. Duquesne's attorneys questioned whether the URA could transfer the property—it had a contract price of only $92,300—to another developer "without allowing the parcel to go up for public auction." Miraculously, the near-disaster passed. By 1976 the apartment developer had abandoned his plans for the property, leaving Duquesne as the sole interested party. Also, by that time the URA had reversed its position and was receptive to Duquesne's plans for the property.

With the last obstacles finally cleared, the University moved ahead at full gallop to convert the building into a library ready for the centennial just two years hence. Once again, the architects, Edwin Gerard Associates, were retained for the job. They were old hands at converting buildings for Duquesne, having done it twice before. Built originally as a printing plant in the late 1920s, and used most recently as a federal motor pool garage, the three-story building of reinforced concrete was still rock solid. The addition of two more floors effectively doubled the library space.

The space limitations in the old library had had a stifling effect on its operation. Even with the 1962 addition, the building had a stated capacity of 250,000 books. Yet it was attempting to house more than 300,000 books, making many of them inaccessible to patron use. And cramped as they were, the staff was unable to work effectively. When the new library opened in 1978, it had a capacity for 700,000 books and some 6800 different serial publications. With accommodations for 868 students, the seating capacity was triple that of the old library. There were faculty study carrells and a large special-collections area to house rare books and archival collections.

Costing $5.2 million, this handsome and functional building was the last great construction achievement of the McAnulty administration and perhaps the best example of Gerard Associates reuse of a preexisting building.

Centennial Celebrations

In the fall of 1978, Duquesne University put its troubles aside to celebrate its one-hundredth birthday. When the Pittsburgh Catholic College of the Holy Ghost had opened for classes on October 1, 1878, it had been doubtful whether it would survive the year. And now it had survived a century. The occasion was momentous, and to commemorate it in a truly fitting fashion, the University Relations Department researched the mechanics and arrangements of other institutional celebrations and activities that had been carried out across America for the nation's bicentennial in 1976. Almost a year before the anniversary date, a centennial chairman (Edgar B. Speer, chairman of the board of U.S. Steel Corporation) and honorary chairman (Arthur J. Rooney, chairman of the Pittsburgh Steelers) had been named. Mr. Rooney was a 1924 graduate of Duquesne's

School of Business and recipient of an honorary doctor of humanitarian service degree by Duquesne in 1975.

Long before the actual convocation, the university kicked off its centennial celebration on January 27, 1978, with a ten-foot-long birthday cake decorated with the centennial logo. The cake was the centerpiece of a university party for students, faculty, administration, and staff, the first official centennial event.

The second event occurred in February. Her Serene Highness, Princess Grace of Monaco, visited Duquesne to receive an honorary degree, having participated in the International Poetry Forum's recital, "Birds, Beasts, and Flowers," at the invitation of Dr. Samuel Hazo, Duquesne English Department professor and director of the forum. A movable stage was erected in the Student Union's ballroom at the opposite end of the room from the grand staircase to enhance the procession that preceded the presentation of an honorary doctor of humane letters, and the music school practiced diligently for its musical accompaniment, which included both national anthems. The princess arrived in a Rolls Royce which drove onto Academic Walk surrounded by a large welcoming crowd. She received her hood and degree before an enthusiastic audience of over 2,000. The magic and majesty of the event cast a glow of hope and optimism over campus, ushering in the university's second century.

On May 5, 1978, Duquesne University dedicated its Honors Day Program to the centennial graduating class. David Suskind delivered the commencement address to an audience of 1500. He spoke of the disenchantment of the preceding generation, who, burned out by depression and war, had become apathetic toward the world, creating a gulf between themselves and their children. He encouraged this new generation to change both their immediate society and the larger world. "You can go for broke on behalf of your deepest moral commitments." Another famous person in attendance was Luciano Pavarotti, who had served as a judge for the first Ezio Pinza Memorial Vocal Scholarship in 1975. He received an honorary degree of doctor of music.

In September came the dedication of the Duquesne Library Resource Center, followed by a reception and tour of the building, which had a special centennial historical display on exhibit. Later that month, Father Mac hosted a reception on the fourth and fifth floors of the administration building, from which vantage point the guests were able to enjoy a fireworks display launched from a barge floated down the Monongahela River. Part of the display was in the form of the official Duquesne centennial logo.

Founder's Day, October 1, 1978, opened with a Mass at nearby Epiphany Church, presided over by the auxillary bishop of Pittsburgh, John B. McDowell. The Founder's Day Mass was followed by a series of presidential lectures by Reverend Theodore Hesberg, C.S.C., president of the University of Notre Dame, Terry Sanford, president of Duke University, and Marver Hillel Bernstein, president of a Jewish university, Brandeis.

Five years earlier, the Pennsylvania Historical and Museum Commission had approved Duquesne University's application to have the Administration Building, "Old Main," designated as a historic landmark. The university requested that the designation be delayed until the centennial year. At that time the marker proclaiming the administration building as a historical landmark was presented to the university by the Pennsylvania Historical and Museum Commission on October 5, 1978. The inscription reads,

> Founded by the Holy Ghost Fathers from Germany in 1878, Incorporated 1882 as Pittsburgh Catholic College, named Duquesne University in 1911, the Catholic institution has served students of many faiths in liberal arts and professional studies.

Old Main had endured many trials and reworkings since the Holy Ghost Brothers began making the bricks for it in 1881. The building had served the university in various capacities over the years, weathering all movements to raze it and build something new in its place. It had even survived a lightning bolt in 1975 that caused a fire which destroyed the executive offices on the fifth floor along with several expensive paintings, including a sixteenth century Spanish painting valued at $216,000 and belonging to the Diocese of Pittsburgh. Smoke and water damage also affected the lower floors. But when it received its historical plaque in November of 1978, this venerable symbol of Duquesne bore no evidence of the tragedy that had befallen it just three years earlier.

The centennial celebration continued with addresses by faculty members from the History Department, an appearance by alumnus Bobby Vinton, who received an honorary degree of doctor of music and who also officially kicked off the "Great Centennial Phone-a-thon" to raise support from Duquesne alumni. Then, October 28, 1978, was declared Duquesne University Day in the city of Pittsburgh by Mayor Richard Caliguiri. The mayor and Father Mac served as parade marshals.

The calendar year and the centennial year closed on December 31, 1978, with a Tamburitzan benefit concert at Heinz Hall for the Performing Arts for the scholarship fund, followed by a New Year's Eve party at the Student Union ballroom. The party was titled, appropriately enough, "A Moment Between Two Centuries." In closing the centennial celebration, Art Rooney and Edgar Speer announced, "If there is one thing the centennial celebration has illustrated to us as chairmen, it is that the special educational opportunities offered by Duquesne University have been and will continue to be very important and precious to the people of Pittsburgh."

The Tamburitzans Thrive in the 1970s

The Duquesne University Tamburitzans were off to Paris for eighteen performances during the 1971 Christmas break. The All-American production was offered at the request of the State Department because their 1969 summer tour to the Iron Curtain countries had been so highly praised. Europeans particularly enjoyed Broadway, rock, jazz music and distinctly American dances ranging from square-dancing to the Boogie-Woogie. The Tammies had averaged a dozen curtain calls a night at their performances in 1971 and had been escorted around Paris to see the sights, ranging from the Louvre to the design studios of Christian Dior. In the summer of 1972, financed by a $90,000 grant from the Richard King Mellon Foundation, they toured Czechoslovakia, France, Greece, and Bulgaria. They also studied Bulgarian folk instruments and dances during a weeklong training session. The president of the Composers Union and director of the National Folklore Ensemble of Bulgaria, Philip Koutev, presented them with a gold medal for excellence. A Greek newspaper in Volos applauded them as "The best group of people America could or has ever sent here."[43] The Tamburitzans' final performance of the tour at the Burgos Festival was televised and broadcast through "Inter-vision" to an estimated 50 million in Bulgaria, Yugoslavia, Poland, the U.S.S.R., Czechoslovakia, Hungary, Romania, and East Germany.

By their fortieth anniversary, the Tamburitzans had nearly doubled the size of the ensemble to forty members. They also restructured their organization in the 1973–1974 season as the Duquesne University Tamburitzans Institute of Folk Arts (DUTIFA). Walter Kolar became director while Nicholas Jordanoff assumed the role of artistic director, the third artistic director in Tamburitzan history. With the new organization, the Tamburitzans were eligible to apply for and receive grants, including two major ones from the

U.S. Office of Education for the development of ethnic heritage curriculum study kits for use by elementary and secondary students. Hoping to acquire and develop a larger facility as a national folk arts center in the city of Pittsburgh, the Tammies launched a major fundraising drive. They also began offering symposia at Duquesne University of an academic nature. The first of these was on Romanian folk arts; the second, in 1976, on the folk arts of Yugoslavia. The performing ensemble traveled in a new private bus. The spring of 1976 also brought the awarding of DUTIFA's first master of folk arts degree and closed with a telethon through WIIC-TV to benefit the Tamburitzan Folk Arts Center.

Under Jordanoff, the performances took on a new look. Instrumental selections were arranged for larger groups of musicians; more attention was paid to vocal training, with choral singing presenting a wider variety of styles; dances were choreographed for larger groups in suites and often punctuated with small humorous sketches; and a wider range of folk and primitive instruments was employed. New, authentic costumes generally came from Eastern Europe, but the wardrobe department faithfully reproduced original costumes for the troupe while constantly designing new ones as the range of styles, periods, and ethnic variations increased.

In 1977–1978 DUTIFA entered into an agreement with Columbia Artists Management of New York to handle a percentage of the troupe's engagement bookings in the United States. With State Department and other government agency funding, the Tammies returned to Europe in 1978 for performances and training in Bulgaria. DUTIFA also sponsored a month-long folk arts festival in Blagoevgrad, Bulgaria.

The student Tamburitzans had a rigorous schedule imposed by the training and performance demands on the group, which made it especially difficult for them to devote large blocks of time to academic studies. Yet the Tamburitzan experience was so highly valued that belonging to the group became the dream of many aspiring musicians, singers, and dancers, who trained for years in junior Tamburitzan groups for the auditions. The Tamburitzan scholarship was one of the hardest-earned anywhere, yet the Tammies were exceptional students and always had a high percentage of members on the dean's list. Many did honors work in their academic areas, and many participated in a wide variety of activities, from the school newspaper to the concert choir. The Tamburitzans achieved such national prominence during this period that although most incoming freshmen had first heard about Duquesne through the basketball team, the Tamburitzans were an impressive second in spreading the university's reputation.

The Red Masquers Mix Classics and Moderns

In the 1960s, the Red Masquers continued to do popular works rather than classics, maintaining director Sam Meli's practice of presenting current works with high student appeal. A fire in the campus theater in May 1962 did considerable damage and curtailed all productions for almost a year. When the theater reopened with a new ceiling, floor, curtains, and lightboard, Meli put on Saroyan's *The Time of Your Life*. In December 1964 he directed what most campus theatergoers regarded as his best work, Tennessee Williams' *A Streetcar Named Desire*.

Frank Thornton replaced Meli as producer-director in 1967 and introduced an ambitious mix of classics and moderns beginning with T.S. Eliot's *Murder in the Cathedral* and Molière's *The Imaginary Invalid*. With his own play, *The Dawn of Fatty Pompeii*, Thornton started the practice, still followed, of offering original scripts by campus authors in minor productions. One of these was a translation by Fran Collechia, then chair of Modern Languages, of Carlos Solarzano's *Puppets*, which the Masquers also took on the road. A considerable off-campus interest in the Masquers developed. The Pittsburgh Drama League invited them to repeat their production of Van Itallie's *Interview* after seeing their Grotowski-style version on campus in 1968. Thereafter it became standard practice during the Thornton years for the Red Masquers to perform at churches, high schools, and colleges all over southwestern Pennsylvania, thus earning a regional reputation.

For a time during the early 1970s, the Red Masquers' reputation was further enhanced by skilled productions of English Restoration drama and eighteenth-century plays: *The Country Wife, The Contrast, The Rivals*, and *The Beaux' Stratagem*. The latter marked Jay Keenan's directorial debut with the Masquers and was performed in a festival at Bloomsburg University before playing on campus in 1975.

Before the fire that damaged Old Main and the campus theater in 1975, Thornton also directed Shakespeare's rarely performed *Troilus and Cressida* and Pinter's absurdist comedy, *The Birthday Party*. Thereafter, plays were staged in the Student Union ballroom. There was one notable exception when, at the suggestion of *Pittsburgh Press* drama critic and Duquesne alumnus, Ed Blank, Thornton negotiated the use of the Hazelett Theater on the city's North Side—later the home of the Pittsburgh Public Theater—and staged Jason Miller's *That Championship Season* there in 1976. In the late 1970s Jay Keenan assumed the role of producer for the Red Masquers.

Athletics: Basketball's Glory Fades a Bit

Basketball coach Red Manning looked at a team of promise for the 1970 season as an undefeated freshman squad joined an illustrious team. *Sports Illustrated* had ranked this team as one of the best in the country in the preseason and six players, the Nelson twins, Barry and Gary, Mickey Davis, Jarrett Durham, Bill Zopf, and Mike Barr, were to go professional. Expectations proved unrealistically high; the team scored 17 wins to 6 losses for the season. They even lost to Georgia Tech in the first round of the NIT. But, with only Zopf graduating and several promising sophomores joining the team, they settled down into a well-oiled machine in the 1971 season on a 15-game winning streak and an average of over ninety points per game. The opposition included top-rated teams like Notre Dame, De Paul, San Francisco, and Villanova, making their success even more impressive until they were downed by Boston College. They closed the season on a winning note, but lost in the NCAA tournament to an impressive University of Pennsylvania team.

Barry and Gary Nelson, Jarrett Durham, and Steve McHugh graduated that spring. Mickey Davis left Duquesne to play professionally. A transfer student was declared ineligible, and several others were injured or transferred during the year, leaving the team with very few players in the 1972 season. By midseason, the remaining seven, Barr, Billingy, Roebuck, Wojdowski, Harrington, Devine, and Montanez, earned the title "The Magnificent Seven" for their strong, tireless play. They were able to finish the season with a 20–5 record, although they received no post-season tournament bid. The team definitely deserved a bid; it was speculated that the tournament committee might have been worried about the possibility of injuries, penalties, or unforeseen circumstances reducing Duquesne to a team too small to play in competition.

Red Manning concluded his coaching career at Duquesne after sixteen years, following the 1973 season. The highlight of the year was a victory over Notre Dame, but losing the final game killed tournament hopes. The 1973 squad compiled a 16–8 record. As he moved to the position of athletic director, Coach Manning's career wins totaled 247 to 138 losses with a total of six post-season tournament teams.

Manning's assistant, John Cinicola, a Duquesne graduate, succeeded him. The first years for a new coach are always difficult—Coach Manning had been hanged in effigy after taking over from Dudey Moore. John's first-year squad won 14 out of 25 games; his second-year's team won only 12 out of 25. The fans were upset with this losing season, only the seventh in Duquesne's basketball history, but Cinicola was retained as coach on a one-year contract extension. A *Duquesne Duke* sports editorial stressed the stability of coaching in Duquesne's basketball history—there had been only four head coaches in fifty years. A Duquesne head basketball coach had never been fired, and when a new coach was hired, it was viewed at Duquesne as the beginning of a new era.

Eight schools, including Duquesne, founded the Eastern Collegiate Basketball League in 1977. Because of requirements that the league promote other sports as well, it was renamed the Eastern Athletic Association. The Eastern Eight—Duquesne, Pitt, West Virginia, Penn State, Massachusetts, Rutgers, Villanova, and George Washington—all played big-time basketball.

Duquesne had a superstar on the team for 1977, the first season of Eastern Athletic Association play. His name was Norman Nixon and his performance was so outstanding that he was honored at the pre-game ceremonies before the season's final game against Detroit. Detroit came to the game with a 22-game winning streak, but when Nixon, cited in the *Duquesne Duke* as "the greatest guard in Duquesne basketball history," took the court, the fans went wild. Nixon dazzled them, scoring 29 points to lead the Dukes to a 95–88 upset. Nixon's family had been brought from Macon, Georgia, to see his last regular season game for Duquesne, and he did not disappoint them. (Despite Nixon's efforts, the 1977 squad was a mediocre one.)

When Norm Nixon went on to professional basketball after graduation, the team worsened. Duquesne had never seen 17 defeats in a single season in its entire basketball history, and when this occurred under John Cinicola, his coaching contract became an item for discussion. He was offered another position within the university and assistant coach Mike Rice, another Duquesne graduate and former star, was given the position. John Cinicola was well liked at Duquesne and respected for his twenty years of coaching, so his firing was difficult for the fans to accept.

Coach Rice began strong. The team had a 9–4 record at midseason, but then sunk to a 4–9 record for the second half. Despite the poor showing at the end of the season, the fans were optimistic about the team's future prospects. Mossie Murphy still had an informal hand in recruiting with talented freshmen coming to Duquesne to play basketball, including Duquesne's first seven-footer. If the basketball glories of the past had faded during the lean years, the prospect of new laurels seemed brighter. Whatever the cost of the basketball program, it was supported by the administration because big-time basketball had helped to put Duquesne on the map.

During the financial crisis with its mountain of debt and high tuition increases, students seriously questioned Duquesne's supporting a basketball program. For the 1974–1975 school year the university spent approximately $430,500 on athletics, about 2 percent of its $23 million budget, but the return on basketball revenues was an insignificant $53,000 per year. As a consequence, $25 of the $205 university fee went to athletics. And university funding for all other intercollegiate programs was only $18,613. Yet 27 percent of students applying to Duquesne said they had first heard of the school through the basketball team. Also, the basketball team helped develop a school spirit, and, even when attendance was disappointing, it still provided wholesome entertainment. Attendance was up by 16,000 at the Civic Arena home games in 1979 after Duquesne joined the Eastern Eight. And it was obvious that the team was making a conscientious effort to hold down expenses without sacrificing quality.

In the fall of 1977 the Dukes Court, a support

organization for Duquesne athletics, was established. Dedicated to the financial, moral, and spiritual support of athletics, the group was university-sanctioned and operated under the athletic department. Father Hehir's gymnasium, now almost sixty years old, was refurbished with a new floor, lockers, and shower facilities so the basketball team could practice there, and the Dukes Court raised the necessary funds to construct and equip a weight room in the building. The group also purchased a video tape unit, supplied the baseball team with new uniforms, and sponsored social events for athletes, members, and alumni.

In 1975 Bob Prince was let go as the "voice of the Pittsburgh Pirates." His colorman, Nelson "Nellie" King (who had played for the Pirates) also got caught in the administrative crossfire. Both Prince and King were much beloved, and their firings caused an enormous public outcry. Nellie King came to Duquesne as sports information director and proved to be a valuable asset in promoting Duquesne's athletic program. He retired in 1993, and as of this writing, continues as an announcer for the Dukes' basketball games.

Football Returns Once More

After an 18-year hiatus, football returned to Duquesne in 1969. Known as club football, since it enjoyed no financial support from the school, it played its first season game during homecoming activities with a Sunday afternoon match against Niagara University. The first season ended with a 2–4 record, but the Grid Iron Dukes dramatically improved in their 1970 season with a 4–3–1 record. Club football at most universities was a shaky venture financially, backed only through alumni contributions, gate receipts, and student fees. The teams were so strapped that when the Grid Iron Dukes won an end-of-the-year forfeiture over St. Bonaventure, it was because the home team was unable to guarantee three quarters of the expenses incurred by the visiting Dukes as required by club rules. Such forfeitures were common. Home games were played at local stadiums.

The 1971 season was marred by tragedy when Clinton Eddy "Ed" Goodwin, a third-year pharmacy student, died following an early-season game injury in which his neck was broken. The parents still supported and encouraged the playing of club football at Duquesne despite their son's death. Ed Goodwin was remembered with a scholarship fund set up in his honor.

Dan McCann assumed the head coaching duties for Duquesne's club football team in 1970 and led the Dukes to a 7–1 record the following year. The 1973 team under his leadership was undefeated, winning the national club football title against Mattatuck Community College of Waterbury, Connecticut, 13–7, at Three Rivers Stadium.

The financial realities regarding club football hit hard in 1979 when Duquesne, with a 6–2 record, qualified for the playoffs against Westchester College of New York. Westchester was to be the home team and the national club football director could only offer $1,000 of the $2,500 necessary for Duquesne's team to make the trip. Coach McCann had to bow out of the playoffs rather than incur the debt.

The push to reestablish collegiate football at the Division III level of the NCAA had been growing for sometime, but the groundswell of interest following the financial difficulties, the high number of forfeited games, and the low prestige of club football by 1979 resulted in Duquesne's decision to reintroduce varsity football. Following NCAA approval, student fees were increased to guarantee the program an additional $18,000 to $20,000 per year. The Dukes hoped that scheduling small college NCAA teams in the area would cut travel expenses. In 1979, their first season of Division III, the Dukes won five out of nine of their games, several of them against club teams due to short notice in scheduling. They were able to schedule over half of their games against qualifying NCAA teams as required by the association for the 1980 season, including Carnegie-Mellon University, their old gridiron rival for the city championship back in the glory days of Bluff football.

Other Sports Struggle

The spring sports, baseball, tennis, and golf, labored under the dual hardships of lack of facilities and limited financial backing. They nonetheless benefited from having stable, competent, and dedicated coaching. Rich Spear coached baseball, still the unsung hero of Duquesne's sports picture. The team's home field and practice site was seven miles away, yet the team won consistently, winning the NCAA Division I batting title for the 1976 season.

Mike Kupersanin coached tennis. The team won 85 matches and lost only 44 in 1970. The university had three tennis courts on campus, but these were inadequate for competition play, so the team began playing competitively indoors at nearby tennis clubs for most of their home matches.

Golfers were coached by Dr. Bruno Casile. They still traveled to Churchill Country Club for the majority of their matches but also played at the North and South Park public courses. As the Eastern Eight expanded to promote sports other than basketball, Duquesne's golf team played teams in the new conference, coming in fourth at the fall of 1979 Eastern Eight tournament at Rutgers.

Although John Cinicola had revived cross-country in 1960, it faded out again early in the seventies. Fred deGroot and Dave McDonald reintroduced it late in the decade.

Wrestling, introduced to the campus late in 1968 on an experimental basis in the Student Union ballroom, was dropped as a varsity sport in 1974. The lack of permanent facilities and the cost of sustaining the program simply made wrestling unfeasible.

Soccer was becoming increasingly popular across the nation and Duquesne introduced a club team in 1971. It disbanded two years later, once again stifled by the lack of facilities.

Loyal alumni who had played on Father Louis Dietrich's ice hockey team in the 1930s had always wished for a resumption of ice hockey at Duquesne. Club hockey made an appearance on campus in 1971, and although its first contest against West Virginia ended pitifully with a 22–2 defeat, the club improved dramatically. Originally, the team suffered from a lack of funds, lack of experienced players, and from a practice ice rink that was closer to Butler than to Pittsburgh. James A. DePhillips took over as coach in the 1975–1976 season. Starting from the ground up, he recruited twelve freshmen and taught fundamentals. After joining the Western Pennsylvania Intercollegiate Hockey League in 1976, the Ice Dukes made the playoffs in the 1977 season and won the championship the following year.

Women's Sports Expand

The increased focus on opportunities for women in the 1970s led to a tremendous upsurge in athletic offerings for women. Duquesne had begun a women's basketball team, coached by Alice Walton, in 1929, not long after coeds won acceptance on the once all-male campus. But despite the annual Women's Athletic Association Play Days and periodic basketball, rifle, tennis, and other women's teams, women's athletics declined over the decades. The National Educational Amendment Act of 1972 in its Title IX requirement demanded the expansion of athletic offerings for women. Duquesne selected Eileen Surdoval as Women's Intramural Director in 1973. She secured the services of a coach for the women's student-directed basketball team and organized a volleyball team in 1974. Joan

Howarth began coaching the new women's varsity tennis team in 1978, the same year that a coed swimming team was formed. Duquesne's Athletic Department, in its commitment to continued expansion of opportunities for women, elevated Eileen Surdoval to the post of assistant to the director of athletics in 1977.

Because of the financial crunch affecting private colleges and universities in the 1970s and Duquesne's staggering debts from the building program, along with lost revenue from declining enrollments, the Master Plan under Father McAnulty was ended with the opening of the new library. Father Gallagher's dream of an adequate athletic facility remained a dream as Father McAnulty announced that Duquesne could not financially manage the building of a fieldhouse in the foreseeable future. With contributions below expectations for Mellon Hall, College Hall, and restoration of the administration building, a fundraising drive for a fieldhouse was out of the question. Duquesne was left with inadequate facilities to support the program. Father Hehir's gymnasium served for basketball practice and student use, but home games had to be played at the Civic Arena.

A few improvements did occur during the McAnulty years. In 1972, the Student Government agreed to a one-time $2-per-semester increase in the university fee to pay for a third of the cost of an athletic field. The construction project cost $100,000. Of this amount, $32,000 was paid by the University fee increase. The project included the seeding of the field, improvements to the driveway of University Hall, the creation of some parking spaces, and the lighting of Seitz Street between the field and St. Ann's Hall. Named for the dean of men, Harry McCloskey, the field was built for intramurals. Because McCloskey Field was not regulation size, the football team had to practice off campus, as did the baseball team, the hockey team, and the golf team. Tennis had the use of the three campus courts for practice, but it, too, had to go elsewhere for matches.

The athletic director, in his report to the university Planning Committee in 1978, stated that "the full athletic and recreational needs of the university and student body are not being met. Primarily this inadequacy results from a lack of facilities. For example, the university has less than 10,000 square feet of indoor athletic area where, by generally accepted standards, the area for a school of Duquesne's size should be more than 100,000 square feet." But the dreamed-for facility had to remain a dream.

Although Duquesne put much effort into preparing the Report of the University Planning Committee in 1978 to guide the university as it began its second century, the report failed to mention anything about athletics, despite the administration's support, especially of the basketball program, and despite the financial pressures to scale it down.

End of an Era: Father Mac Steps Down

In many ways the McAnulty administration was really three administrations. From 1959 to 1968, the mood and the direction of Duquesne was one of expansion and optimism. Enrollment figures were, with a single exception, ever upward. A generous federal government allowed, indeed encouraged, Duquesne to expand to cover nearly all of the Bluff. McAnulty became for Duquesne what Cheops was to ancient Egypt, a builder of extraordinary proportions. But unlike the grand edifices of Cheops that stand in mute testimony to past glory, Father Mac's buildings were not to be compared with the idle monuments to a pharaoh's greatness. They were long overdue functional buildings that announced to the world the new Duquesne, ready to meet the challenges of the future.

No one in those optimistic building-per-year times of the 1960s could have imagined the challenges of the 1970s. Spiraling college costs, campus unrest, and reduced federal help combined with the university's mounting debt, its crisis in leadership, and its declining enrollment to make 1969–1977 a difficult period.

Happily, the McAnulty years ended on the upside. In 1977 the president returned in good health. The university celebrated its hundredth anniversary with renewed faith in the future. The dedication of the new library gave tangible evidence of regained hope. It was the last great accomplishment of the McAnulty administration. The university's debt was high, but its income was higher still and its debt-service payments were manageable.

With the university on a steady course, Father Mac felt that it was time to step down from the position he had held for more than a fifth of a century. He had been president longer than any other man save Martin Hehir. McAnulty later said that he knew it was time to leave when he started to meet as freshmen the children of students who were enrolled at Duquesne when he had first become president.

Though he had contemplated retirement as early as 1978, he did not submit his resignation until May of 1979. He agreed to stay on until a successor could be found (which was not until July of 1980). The board promptly voted him chancellor of the university, a position that had traditionally been held by the bishop of the Pittsburgh Diocese.

In many ways Father McAnulty was a very ordinary man. He did not have a Ph.D. He never wrote a book. He had no previous experience in college administration. For fourteen years he had been an air force chaplain. A more unorthodox route to the presidency could scarcely be imagined. He did not want to be president of Duquesne University, but once the decision had been made, he threw himself into the task. But he did the job more like a Bing Crosby than a Winston Churchill or some other presidential type. He was low-key, sincere, and without guile—a gentle man.

At times he was almost too gentle, allowing schools and departments within the university the autonomy to alter curricula, manipulate elections, and carry on internecine bickering that all too often became public spectacles. This nonconfrontational personality trait that produced in him an aversion to firmly exercising power may have been a liability where the faculty was concerned, but it was an asset in dealing with the students. Describing him as "down-to-earth," a *Pittsburgh Press* article announcing his retirement said of him, "This undoubtedly helped spare the school from the destructive turbulence that swept other campuses in the 1960s and early 1970s." Anyone who could "spare a school from destructive turbulence" was no ordinary man after all. Father Mac was, in fact, quite an unusual man to preside over a university during those troubled decades—perhaps Heaven's hand-picked man. McAnulty had an assessment of his own:

> I have no regrets that I came into education by accident, but if I were starting over, I would not hesitate to get into education because, while there are very few overpaid people in education, I know a lot of wealthy people who don't get as much satisfaction out of life as a happy professor does or a happy clergy. I think they're the two best professions in the world. I was lucky enough to be involved in both.[44]

9. Strategies for a Second Century

The tenth president of Duquesne University was the first to be selected by means of a search committee rather than simply being named to the position by the Holy Ghost provincial. A subcommittee of the board of directors interviewed some 80 applicants before deciding on Father Donald Silvio Nesti, C.S.Sp., a 44-year-old former Duquesne professor. He assumed office on July 1, 1980.

A Pennsylvania native, Donald Nesti had attended Pennsylvania State University for one year before entering the Holy Ghost Seminary at Ferndale, Connecticut. He had received a B.A. degree in 1959 and a bachelor of divinity degree in 1964 from the Congregation's St. Mary Seminary in Norwalk, Connecticut. Ordained to the priesthood in 1963, Father Nesti received a S.T.L. degree in 1966 and an S.T.D. degree, the European equivalent of a doctorate in theology, both from Gregorian University in Rome. He earned a Master of Arts Degree in 1976 from the University of Pittsburgh and did postdoctoral work at St. Edmund's College, Cambridge University.

An accomplished musician on the French horn, and fluent in French, German, and Italian, the Reverend Donald Nesti was often described by his colleagues as a "Renaissance man." From 1970 to 1976 he was associate professor of theology at Duquesne. He wrote several book-length studies in his primary area of interest, the relationship between the Quaker and Roman Catholic faiths. From 1975 until his election as president, he was director of Immaculate Heart of Mary Seminary in Bethel Park, Pennsylvania.

The Inauguration

Father Nesti was formally inaugurated as president of Duquesne University on October 3, 1980. He was the first president to have an inauguration ceremony since Father Callahan's half a century before. The elaborate event included a buffet luncheon, a reception, a cocktail party, and an inaugural dinner. Over 3000 guests attended, including Lieutenant Governor William Scranton, and Mayor Richard Caliguiri. The affair cost the university approximately $60,000, and to many members of the campus community, the very grandness of the inauguration—some derisively called it a coronation—began the administration on the wrong foot. To Father Nesti, however, the ceremonies and festivities were quite appropriate.

In his inaugural address, Father Nesti called for creativity in improving Duquesne and promised that he would never allow the university to become a victim of apathy and discouragement. Moreover, he declared, "Excellence can only be achieved if our basic attitude is one of service rather than being self-serving."[1] The JAYCEEs selected him Man of the Year in the religion category, and 400 attended a tribute dinner held for him in his hometown of Clairton. The larger community appeared to be favorably impressed with Duquesne's new president.

The Honorable George Bush Makes a Visit

A highlight of the early Nesti administration was an appearance by Vice-President George Bush, already speculated to be Reagan's heir apparent and thus the object of much media interest. All of the local radio and television stations were on campus to record the visit for their evening news broadcasts on May 8, 1981. The Bluff was a frenzy of excitement as SWAT teams took up posts on top of university buildings. A helicopter surveyed the area from above, and officers scanned the crowd with binoculars. The press was restricted to a specially built media tower under the watchful eye of the Secret Service. The extraordinary security measures were prompted by the recent March 30th assassination attempt on President Reagan. The university police were leaving nothing to chance. The authorities even evacuated rooms in the dormitory that had windows affording a view of the speakers' platform on Academic Walk, much to the annoyance of the students and not without their verbal protest.

There were also about two dozen protestors who were kept at bay behind a wooden barricade, where they chanted, sang, and passed out leaflets against U.S. policy in El Salvador. At least one university official wanted Duquesne's director of public safety to remove the demonstrators altogether. Owing to the constitutional issue of free speech, however, the director refused.

After receiving an honorary doctor of laws degree, Mr. Bush spoke. Then, to the chagrin of university officials, he descended the steps of the platform and left the area. Father Nesti succeeded Bush to the rostrum and began to speak.

Changing the Guard

Father Nesti faced several important decisions early in his administration. First his academic vice-president, Father Edward Murray, announced his resignation in August of 1980. Then the deans of the Schools of Education and Pharmacy both declined reappointment. In none of these resignations was there expressed any animus toward the new president, though Nesti had announced that, along with balancing the budget, the creation of a new management team was a top priority.

The selection of an academic vice-president proved to be a difficult process. Father Nesti found none of the candidates presented by the faculty search committee to be acceptable. He convinced the board of directors to accept a procedure in which candidates were to be recommended by the board, "assisted" by a new Review Committee composed of representatives from the Council of Academic Deans, the Faculty Senate, and the Student Government. Instead of being allowed to select their own representatives, each group was to prepare a list of nominees from which the president would chose those whom he wanted. An indignant Faculty Senate refused to nominate any representatives to serve on the Review Committee. Nesti then appointed Dr. Stephen J. Miller to the position of academic vice-president, a candidate completely unknown to the search committee.

Other appointments were less troubled. Dennis C. Golden was named to the reestablished post of vice-president of student life, and James Allison was made vice-president of management and business. But changes in top personnel continued to mark the Nesti Administration. And the new academic vice-president's imperious behavior soon succeeded in alienating the faculty. After Dr. Miller spent $1.6 million on an unsuitable and useless computer system in 1983, Father Nesti "redefined" his role and replaced him with Dr. Carol Smith of the Nursing School as acting Academic VP, while retaining Miller as a special consultant. On the grounds that "no projects were identified for which Dr. Miller might be employed,"[2] he was finally dismissed.

The way in which the academic vice-president had been appointed was an indication of things to come at Duquesne under the Nesti administration. Nesti perceived the McAnulty administration as having been entirely too permissive of faculty privilege, a view shared by many who sat on the university's board of directors. He felt that the faculty had gained too much control over the governance of the university, and set out to do something about that.

The president's desire to gain greater control over the selection of department chairpersons is recorded in the Administrative Council minutes in December 1982: "It was thought appropriate to clarify that the process of choosing chairpersons is not a matter of election by the faculty of respective departments. Rather the faculty select one for nomination, who in turn is submitted to the President for his decision and final approval."

In a *Pittsburgh Press* profile at the end of his second year as president, Father Nesti was quoted as saying, in regard to the changes he anticipated making, "It's going to be intense and it's got to be quick."[3] The changes were to affect every employee, every student, every member of the university community, even down to the basketball team. His goals were stated as follows:

1. To achieve excellence in academic and non-academic programs.
2. To serve as models embodying the values held by the university.
3. To move the university into community service.
4. To bring students to an awareness of global issues, in keeping with the Holy Ghost fathers' commitment to missionary efforts throughout the world.
5. To reach out to the disadvantaged.[4]

Faculty Salaries—The Lowest of the Low

These goals were not to be achieved at the risk of increasing Duquesne's debt, for balancing the budget was a Nesti priority. In January 1982, he laid off 30 housekeeping and maintenance staff members and placed a freeze on the hiring of new personnel. Faculty salaries, rather than beginning to catch up with other schools, were frozen in 1981. In a survey of 15 Catholic-affiliated institutions in the Northeast, Duquesne ranked dead last.

In 1986, while the faculty at Carnegie Mellon University were receiving a six percent increase on a much greater base, Duquesne appropriated only two percent, and since that money was to be distributed on a merit system, some faculty could receive no increase at all. The Faculty Senate objected and called upon the university to "lend every effort to arrange a just and appropriate raise" for the faculty for the 1987–1988 academic year. Father Nesti, however, called for yet another two percent faculty salary increase. The Board of Directors approved a four percent performance-based salary increase. An outside report by the Cyert Committee completed on the university that spring cited low salaries as a potential problem area. And there were other problem areas. By 1988, graduate-student stipends and funds for scholarly research were far below what other institutions were paying.

So salaries were low, and merit-based pay increases were only two percent, whereas the cost of living was rising at a rate of 5.5 percent. Many faculty taught additional courses to earn enough income to live, leaving them even less time for scholarly research. The entire problem of salaries and raises played an important role in defining the deteriorating relationship between the administration and the faculty.

Tuition Rises Faster than Salaries

While faculty salaries were increasing at two or, at most, three percent a year, tuition and room and board increases were usually over six percent. Father Nesti had committed himself to a balanced budget, and that meant that most of the money had to come from student charges. In 1980 tuition was $117 per credit—about $3,510 per year—and room and board charges were $1,830 per year. By 1987 the full-time undergraduate student paid $198 per credit—about $5,940 per year—while room and board had skyrocketed to $3,048 per year.

Of course, federal education funding slashes were having a dramatic impact on enrollment in private schools. In 1983 Duquesne's freshman class dipped by 3.9 percent, not as much as had been feared, but the average family income of college-bound students in Pennsylvania was 14 percent below the national average while the cost of a four-year college education in the state was 17 to 19 percent higher.[5] Thus, the student pool from which Duquesne primarily drew had less to spend, while facing higher costs.

All together Duquesne provided $17.5 million in student aid in 1985 from state, federal, and private sources. Of the approximately 6500 students on campus, 5000 were receiving aid of some sort.[6]

Enrollment and Retention

For any college or university, the key to success lies in attracting qualified students and keeping them enrolled for their entire college careers. Concerns about enrollment and retention rates at Duquesne led to increased guidance and support services in the 1970s and to a student-satisfaction questionnaire in 1980. Students reported dissatisfaction with tuition and university expenses, parking facilities, class registration and scheduling procedures, and advising and grading practices. Academic quality, reputation, and size were the three highest-rated aspects leading to enrollment at Duquesne; cost was the greatest deterrent.

Duquesne initiated a new "Directions" orientation program in the 1981–1982 school year with a class kickoff, mock lectures to reflect actual classes, and directions to area churches and synagogues. The university also continued to sponsor the annual College Career Days on campus where high school students could meet with representatives of 100 different institutions. In order to make enrolling easier, Duquesne began accepting Mastercard and VISA.

The nadir in total enrollment during the Nesti years was reached in 1982, when the student body fell to 6299, down nearly 500 from what it was in 1980, down to its lowest point in 20 years. As considerable effort was expended in recruiting students, enrollment slowly grew by about a hundred students per year until peaking once again at 6738 in the fall of 1986. Beginning in 1984, the university sought the aid of alumni volunteers to make school visitations as part of the Admissions Action Marketing Plan, which also included student overnight visits to campus, high-school presentations, out-of-state recruiting efforts, and improved brochures. In 1986 the DART program, Duquesne Alumni Recruitment Team, was founded.

While still drawing 55 percent of its students from the Pittsburgh area, Duquesne found an increasing number of out-of-area and out-of-state students. Not only were the geographic origins of the student body changing, but its gender makeup was changing as well. For the first time in American history, the women students in higher education were in the majority. At Duquesne in the early 1980s, approximately 300 more women were enrolled than men, but by the end of Nesti's administration that figure had grown to more than 600.

Enrollments reflected shifting job opportunities, too, as the economy, especially in the Pittsburgh area, moved from the industrial sector to the service and information sector. In 1985, with the local market still described as bad, the College of Arts and Sciences still drew the largest number of students, 2237, followed by the School of Business with 1391. The School of Education had 810, Pharmacy 614, Nursing 405, and Music 309. The law school enrolled 636 students.

The admissions office considered the high school record as the prime factor in accepting applicants, followed by SAT scores (in 1981 the average was 455 for verbal and 485 for math skills), interviews, extracurricular activities, and alumni associations with Duquesne. In the mid 1980s, Duquesne was accepting 75 percent of its applicants, although only about half of those accepted actually enrolled.

Strategies for a Second-Century Campaign

Realizing the need for additional operating revenues and endowment funds, Duquesne announced a five-year $20 million fundraising drive in February of 1981. Called "Strategies for a

Second Century", the campaign was an enormous success. Then, in the summer of 1983, the news broke that businessman Noble J. Dick, who had never attended college but whose construction company had built Mellon Hall, had set up an educational fund in his name for Duquesne shortly before his death. The bequest was valued at $15 million, making it the largest gift from an individual donor ever granted to a Catholic college. The bequest formed a permanent part of Duquesne's endowment called the Noble J. Dick Educational Foundation, used largely to support faculty research.

The university's annual phonathon, some twenty years old in 1983, not only raised money, but also kept information on alumni up to date, gave the alumni a vehicle to express their opinions, and generally helped to publicize Duquesne. The university also made a parish appeal reminiscent of the Million Dollar Campaign of Father Hehir's time. Holy Ghost fathers or pastors who were Duquesne alumni made the presentations during mass on "Duquesne Sunday." In June of 1984 the university ran its first advertisement in the *Pittsburgh Catholic*, "To Remember Duquesne University in Your Will."

Thanks to all of these efforts, Father Nesti announced that Duquesne had surpassed its five-year Strategies for a Second Century Campaign with $20.1 million received or in pledges on February 1, 1985 (not including the Dick money), five months ahead of schedule. This marked the first time a Duquesne fundraising campaign had surpassed its goal. A luncheon was held at the Hilton Hotel for the workers, volunteers, corporations, and major individual contributors.

In the fall of 1986 the university was happily surprised by a $1 million dollar gift from Thomas J. Winschel, a 1954 graduate. Established as an endowment fund, this money represented the largest alumni contribution ever received by Duquesne.

Despite the success of the drive, less than $5 million could be earmarked for an endowment, however, since the vast majority of the $20 million raised was needed for construction, renovation, and operating costs. Thus, in the spring of 1987 Duquesne found itself formulating plans for another drive.[7]

Formula for Strategic Repositioning

The McAnulty administration had attempted to address the concerns of the Middle States inspection team that visited the campus in 1977 by completing a university self-study along with recommendations for the future. Every school was examined as to governance, finance, enrollment, academic standards, and student concerns. Even the campus ministry was studied. The result was a 200-page document released in September 1978 titled "Report of the University Planning Committee" and popularly known as the Bethel Document (because the committee met at the Holy Ghost provincial headquarters in Bethel Park, Pennsylvania).

The Nesti administration took little heed of this study and early in 1982 convened the University Planning Advisory Committee (UPAC) to conduct its own study, resulting in the Formula for Strategic Repositioning. The Nesti plan called for the redistribution of university resources based on program evaluations by the University Planning and Action Committee, with some programs strengthened and others phased out. The idea was for Duquesne to make a name for itself in the areas where it had a strong reputation and abandon those areas where it was duplicating offerings of other institutions or spreading itself too thin. The formula also called for an "integrative, systemic, and synergistic" core curriculum that "emphasized international and intercultural resources."

"Duquesne will not become a technical school. We will continue with our strength in the liberal arts and sciences," said Father Nesti. "I want to stress a liberal professional education."[8]

He had this ideal printed on all university stationery: "A liberal and professional education in the Catholic tradition." (At the same time a new letterhead was devised using the familiar Gothic Duquesne "D" and a form of lettering that is still the standard for the university).

The academic core curriculum that Father Nesti felt essential to the reestablishment of a strong undergraduate liberal arts framework was accomplished with much apparent input and consultation, periodic review sessions, and a faculty vote before implementation. But despite the outward appearance of collegiality, faculty members felt their role in academic decision-making was decreasing, especially in regard to Father Nesti's Five-Year Plan, begun in 1986.

The plan imposed new standards for tenure and promotion. Under Father McAnulty, who by his own admission left academics to the scholars while he built the campus, promotion and tenure and scholarly requirements had been the domain of the individual schools and departments. Each school had what amounted to a free hand to act as it saw fit. Now Father Nesti set the standards and made the decisions, and these included a demand for more scholarship. This reflected a national trend where the phrase "publish or perish" was commonly invoked. Some reform was past due, but inadequate salary increases and a low level of university support for scholarship continued to widen the rift between the faculty and the Nesti administration.

In July of 1980, the "Criteria for Promotion and Tenure at Duquesne," a product of the McAnulty administration, had been promulgated, but Father Nesti decided not to implement it. He established two other task forces instead to set new criteria for promotion and tenure, devise a method for faculty assessment, and develop an instrument for student assessment of faculty teaching. By 1984 a policy was in force through which ten elected senior faculty members, one each from the schools and two from the college, formed the Promotion and Tenure Committee. The tightening of requirements for promotion and tenure was amply illustrated in 1985 when the academic vice-president recommended only three candidates for promotion with tenure and denied recommendations to 14 others.

A move toward increased regulation of sabbatical leave occurred in 1982 following the Administrative Council's routine approval of a sabbatical request for a faculty member who had the support of the department chairman for his proposed project. Nesti then recommended that in the future "all projects related to sabbatical leave should be accompanied by a critique of the project from one external to the university."[9] The idea of asking outsiders to review sabbatical applications met with immediate faculty disapproval. It was widely interpreted as a lack of confidence in the competence of the Duquesne faculty. Father Nesti finally presented definitive guidelines for sabbatical leave in 1984 that did not include outside reviewers.

Earlier that same year, the Formula for Strategic Repositioning was followed up by yet another University Planning Advisory Committee: UPAC II. Derisively called Son of UPAC by the faculty, who had become weary of planning, UPAC II became lost in the morass of faculty-administration bickering.

The McCulloch and Schreiber Controversies

A controversy developed in March of 1984 when Nesti dismissed James A. McCulloch as Dean of the College of Arts and Sciences after 17 years of service. McCulloch had disagreed with the administration's decisions to combine departments and eliminate certain majors in the college. The Arts and Sciences faculty was outraged, not just because a dean whom they described as "a man of vision" had been dismissed, but also because the dismissal had come at an inappropriate time. It was too late in the year to conduct a proper search for a replacement. A member of the

English Department expressed the faculty's reaction: "Many of us are disenchanted and demoralized. The faculty must have a greater voice in decisions which affect us so much."[10]

The administration's desire to combine the positions of dean and graduate dean of the College of Liberal Arts and Sciences had long been resisted by the faculty. Finally, Carol Smith, vice-president for academic affairs, advanced a host of statistical information to justify this action. On April 12, 1984, she and her assistant vice-president, Benjamin Hodes, met with the faculty to discuss the proposal. Kurt Schreiber, the acting graduate dean, attended this meeting with the intention of demonstrating that the statistics were misleading: he contended the statistics of the graduate school of arts and sciences had been combined with those of other programs to "prove" declining enrollment. When Dr. Schreiber raised his hand, Smith refused to recognize him. Other faculty members demanded that he be permitted to speak. When this was denied, a large number of faculty walked out. Soon after, an angry Dr. Schreiber announced his resignation.

In a separate meeting, the Faculty Senate Council voted unanimously and the faculty in attendance voted 74–2 to call for the dismissal of Smith and Hodes for violating Schreiber's right to speak. Nothing came of this vote. Father Nesti did agree to the faculty demand that professors Jack Hausser and Bruce Martin be appointed acting dean and acting graduate dean, respectively. And in the midst of the McCulloch and Schreiber controversies, yet another, and far more public, controversy burst upon the scene.

The Duquesne Duke *1984 April Fool Issue*

On April 1, 1974, the *Duquesne Duke* had published its traditional April Fool's Day edition in a most untraditional manner. It had published what many believed to be an obscene paper. Father Mac had reacted in his usual sanguine manner and did virtually nothing about it. Although he endured some criticism for his nonreaction—to which he also did not react—the affair eventually lost its interest and died as a news story, just as McAnulty had expected.

Exactly one decade later, April 1, 1984, the *Duke* published another similarly obscene paper. But this time Father Nesti was at the helm, and he was not one to suppress a reaction. *The Weekly Douche*, as the paper called itself, pretended to be the student newspaper of a mythical school called Duke Wayne University having a president whom it identified as Rev. Donny Nesticles. Although most of the paper did not allude to sex, there was little on campus that escaped its satire. "Vulgar" and "tasteless" were the two most commonly used terms in the local media as they reported and discussed the story endlessly. The vice-president of university relations, Ken Service, stated, "We're very upset. It violates the principles and values we try to inculcate in our students," while student editor Linda Shirey admitted that it was "maybe a little too risqué." While the administration considered disciplinary action against the student editors, the Student Government Association wondered whether they should withdraw financial support of the *Duke* and if safeguards should be drawn up to prevent such a thing from ever happening again. Shirey protested that such sanctions would be too harsh for a paper intended only to amuse. She reminded the public that the *Douche* had printed a disclaimer on page one: "Hey, Fool! This April Fool's issue is not meant to offend or upset any individual or group. Our harmless (and slightly risqué) humor is our way of presenting the lighter side of life here at Duquesne University," and on page two, "The *Duke* staff reminds you that this is all in fun." But President Nesti told Shirey that the disclaimer had not prevented a large number of letters and phone calls calling the paper a disgrace and that he agreed with them.[11]

Shirey reportedly said, "The only thing we

can do is apologize." Some 30 members of SGA met to make their recommendations to Father Nesti, including that a letter of apology be printed on the front page of the next issue of the *Duquesne Duke*, charges filed with the judicial board for violating the organization's constitution, and all funding be suspended in September if the *Duke* staff hadn't met with local professionals of the Pittsburgh Chapter of Sigma Delta Chi Professional Journalism Society to establish practical guidelines. Senior editor John Wander stated, "So we erred, but we learned and are now going to correct our mistakes. Goodness, we're only human. What I'm really worried about is the future of the newspaper. Most of the offensive material was written by seniors but it's really the juniors and sophomores on the staff who are going to suffer. . . . All the fuss is over only five or six photos and copy; the rest of the issue is really mild."[12]

The Senate charged the editors with violating "an obligation to abide by accepted standards of responsible journalism and avoidance of libel, indecency, undocumented allegations, and attacks on personal integrity."[13] The SGA asked that the *Duke* be screened in the future by an editorial board before publishing. As the student editors worked on their apology page for the forthcoming *Duke*, the year's final issue, and while awaiting their judicial board hearing on April 16th, Father Nesti suddenly ordered a halt to publication, closing down the newspaper before the bureaucratic wheels had a chance to turn. Nearly everybody protested that action. It generated a second controversy even larger than the first. Nesti succeeded in casting himself in the role of censor and villain where only days before he had been the aggrieved party. A host of articles, letters to the editor, and editorials appeared in the local newspapers arguing for or against the university's right to censor or restrict publication. A *Pittsburgh Press* editorial said, "In a school noted for its work in law as well as for its work in theology and raising the human spirit, the right of free speech should not be denied."[14] A letter to the editor in the *Post-Gazette*, typical of those it printed, branded Father Nesti as a "Grand Inquisitor" who "would do better to exercise the duties of an educator."[15] Meanwhile, Shirey insisted that the university had no right to suspend publication since it gave no direct funding. Since the funding came from advertising, SGA, and student fees, she claimed "the university is not our publisher, the students are."[16]

The faculty-student judicial board decided that next year's *Duquesne Duke* must donate ten full-page ads to the student organizations that it offended, and that the student staff members must make a public apology to be printed in the faculty-administration publication, the *Duquesne Spirit*. The students editors were upset that the ten full pages of donated ads would mean a loss of $2,200 in advertising income, a fifth of the budget, meaning that paper would have to curtail its publishing schedule. Moreover, they doubted whether giving away ads could constitute restitution. An alumnus and former editor threatened not only to organize a protest at the administration building, but also to raise the money to print the year's final issue calling for Father Nesti's resignation for blowing this whole affair out of proportion.

Father Nesti wanted the guilty students to be expelled, but this option was not even seriously considered by the Judicial Board. Indeed, no punishment of any kind was meted out to individual students because the board could not prove who was responsible for specific articles. The *Duke* staff, in its own defense, called up a variation of an argument used by their predecessors ten years before: that the university bookstore sold reading material they considered even more offensive. A book entitled *101 Uses for a Dead Cat* was named. The staff also noted that the university Residence Council had shown an X-rated film on campus, *A Clockwork Orange*.

But the story was not yet ended. As letters to the editors in support of Father Nesti's decision began to appear in the area papers from the more conservative elements, the staff of the *Duquesne Duke* published 4000 copies of an underground paper they called *The Duquesne Duchess*. It cost $250 to print. Money was contributed by friends and alumni of Duquesne, the *Pittsburgh Post-Gazette, Pittsburgh Press*, and all three local television stations. It was printed with production help from the staff of the *Pitt News* at the University of Pittsburgh. Recapping the events of the spring, the paper named Father Nesti as the university's "Man of the Year." Linda Shirey explained, "We decided to use the criterion of *Time* magazine and name the person who has done the most to change the news, for better or for worse. He's the only logical candidate."[17]

The *Duquesne Duke* returned as usual in August of 1984 under the editorship of John Wdowiak, one of the editors on the previous year's staff. The new *Duke* had changed in size and design, with added entertainment sections and a police blotter. The staff committed itself to investigative reporting of campus matters and beefing up revenue from outside advertisers. The publication schedule called for 29 issues. Significantly, none was slated for April Fool's Day.

The *Duquesne Duke* made an amazing comeback. It suffered few financial reverses, for an appeals panel cut the number of required free pages in half and most of the offended organizations never claimed their free ads. The advertising department was aggressive enough to more than offset the loss. Although the *Duke* editor admitted that the staff felt a bit paranoid, as though "everybody was watching us, just waiting for us to make a mistake,"[18] in 1987 the *Duke* placed first with merit in the American Scholastic Press Association spring competition. It was cited for best sports coverage and received 945 points on a 1000-point scale, achieving perfect scores in page design, general plan, and editing.

The Guthrie Report

The timing of the 1984 April Fool issue along with the simultaneous McCulloch and Schreiber controversies could scarcely have been worse, involving as they did questions over the way that decisions were being made at Duquesne. It was over this very issue that Father Nesti, with approval from the board of directors, had gone outside the university for expert advice. Accordingly, in November 1983, R. Claire Guthrie of the Washington, D.C., law firm of Hogan and Hartson was retained to head what was called the Committee to Review University Administrative Operations. The idea was "to formulate recommendations for consideration by the entire university community regarding ways to strengthen academic management."[19] It produced what became popularly known as the Guthrie Report, which provided a remarkable outside look at the state of the university and the way in which it was governed. The conclusion: that Duquesne, they said, was "not at the brink of imminent disaster," but, owing to its narrow resource base, its "margin for error" was small.

A number of important situations had to be faced. The demographics of the Pittsburgh area pointed to a smaller pool of students, and, already, 800 dormitory beds were currently not being filled by Duquesne students despite the fact that 80 percent of all undergraduate applications were accepted. The enrollment figures were critical since nearly 90 percent of the university's revenues were derived from tuition and related sources. Furthermore, Guthrie and her colleagues found that what appeared to be a balanced budget in the ledger books actually contained a number of "hidden deficits." The freeze on salaries was one example. It had a "deleterious impact" on the university's long-term need to recruit and retain qualified faculty. Another hidden deficit was in the realm of deferred maintenance. University officials acknowledged that about $500,000 a year should be spent for repairs and general upkeep, yet only $100,000 was actually budgeted. There were other hidden deficits, too, in regard to money not being spent for scientific and instructional equipment, books, and so forth.

Noting Duquesne's commitment to collegiality (joint decision-making by the administration and faculty), the Committee pointed out that the multifaceted structure of the university was so arcane that "often it is not clear to those who must live within the regulations which of several procedures actually prevails in the consideration of a proposal or in the day-to-day management of the academic program." Duquesne, it seemed, was topheavy with committees and regulations.

The President, in particular, was hemmed in on every side by regulations. The committee also noted a "belief in some quarters that the central executive staff chooses to work in guarded secrecy," a conception that they believed to be unfounded. In fact, they asserted that it was difficult to determine what the university community expected of its president. They said that the language of university documents left the impression "that the president is not expected to act in executive fashion." The president was also "compelled to act on promotion and tenure recommendations without the advice of a faculty committee which represents interests beyond the departmental level." The committee recommended the creation of a university-wide promotion and tenure committee composed of teaching faculty and chaired by the academic vice-president, plus a new Advisory Council, supplanting the existing Administrative Council, to give the president the advice he needed.

A "vigorous program of scholarly research and publication" was urged for the faculty. Noting that some faculty members held outside employment, which invariably reduced the amount of time available for research, the report recommended that such employment be limited to one day a week.

Faculty reaction to the Guthrie Report was varied. Some, though not all, viewed the report as little more than an empowerment of Nesti and an attempt on his part to gain credibility and therefore acceptance of what had long been his aims. Nearly all were concerned with the report's demands for increased scholarship despite the noted faculty pay freezes, and felt that the urging of severe limitations on outside income-producing activities was unrealistic.

A Vote of No Confidence

The suggestions made in the Guthrie Report were translated into proposed amendments to the University Statutes in November 1984. A number of faculty members circulated a petition expressing concern about the proposed changes which they said would interfere with the University's "spirit of collegiality." In March 1985, they went a dramatic step further when they adopted a resolution of "no confidence" in the university directors and administration. They claimed in a 127–9 vote with 2 abstentions that "the board of directors has sustained in office an administration which has been incompetent to handle the affairs of the institution."[20] They were especially opposed to the abolishment of the Administrative Council in favor of a new Advisory Committee on which they would have more representation (eight faculty members, four students, and two administrators) but no power to place items on the agenda. The faculty further claimed that the administration had no clear plans for what areas would be encouraged and which would be phased out and was in disarray with two vice-president positions and three deanships unfilled. Patricia Watt, dean of students, resigned in August 1984. James Allison, dean of management and business, resigned in January 1985. Even physical plant co-director John Davis left in September, explaining that he had been there too long and was not objective enough to make the changes that were being asked of him.

Speaking on behalf of the administration, university spokesman Kenneth Service described the reaction as a "misunderstanding" since the new statutes did not deprive the faculty of authority in "legitimate decision-making areas."[21] Despite the faculty's lack of confidence in its president, the board of directors declared that it had no intention of dismissing Father Nesti. And Kenneth Service disputed the validity of the faculty vote saying that only 138 of the 313 faculty members participated in the vote. He also explained that while the administration viewed collegiality as an opportunity for the faculty to participate in the process and express its opinions, those views would not necessarily prevail.

The Student Government Association, in response to the faculty's "no confidence" vote, the first in Duquesne's 105-year history, voted 10 to 7, with two abstentions, against the administration. The students admitted that their vote was not a clear representation of the majority since students were leaving campus for spring break, but they felt the faculty discontent had adversely affected their classes. The Duquesne Corporation, the Holy Ghost Fathers' organization that owned Duquesne, met with the board of directors' statute-revision committee and urged that the board examine the revisions carefully and not pass them in haste.

This advice was not heeded. The board of directors approved the new statutes at its May 17, 1985, meeting. The Board also unanimously reappointed Father Nesti and all four of his vice-presidents for a one-year term. Two new vice-presidents and a new dean were brought in from outside the university community instead of being promoted from the ranks as had traditionally been the case at Duquesne, and the new Advisory Board was established in the fall. Its only function was to advise the president and administration regarding academic and policy issues, as opposed to the old Administrative Council, which implemented the policies of the board and made appropriate decisions and recommendations within their areas of responsibility. Things had changed. Many felt "collegiality" was becoming just a word at Duquesne.

Laval House

Several members of the board of directors had encouraged Father McAnulty to move out of Trinity Hall in favor of private, more luxurious quarters. They were influenced by other universities in the city which had impressive presidential houses, something that Father Mac believed utterly inappropriate for a Duquesne president. For him, it contradicted the Holy Ghost ideal of a community life. In vain did some board members argue that it would be easier for the president to entertain guests if only he had his own quarters. Father Mac responded that he could entertain in the Student Union or downtown.

When Father Nesti became president, these same entreaties were much better received. First the president had special private quarters arranged for himself on the first floor of Trinity Hall, where presumably he could entertain, but they proved unsatisfactory. When the Daughters of the Divine Redeemer grew too few in number to be able to staff Trinity Hall in 1984, their convent, the old Varsity Hall, fell empty. Father Nesti renamed the building Laval House, in honor of nineteenth century Holy Ghost missionary Father James Laval, and moved in.

Eventually Laval House was used for entertaining, but not in the way the board had envisioned. Late in his presidency, Father Nesti began to invite small groups of faculty members to Laval House for lunch. These lunches were not intended to be question-and-answer periods. They were strictly social affairs wherein the faculty could meet the president in an informal and pleasant setting and, it was hoped, develop a relationship of mutual trust.

A New Core Curriculum and the Five-Year Academic Plan

Father Nesti had dedicated himself to the academic revival of the liberal arts as the backbone of all academic studies. Duquesne established a program for a master's of liberal arts in 1982 that was Pittsburgh's only liberal studies program on a graduate level. By 1971 the rigid course requirements of Duquesne's core curriculum had been greatly relaxed. Indeed, much of the academic structure of degree programs all over the United States gave way to a vast array of elective courses as students were demanding freedom of choice in all areas of college life. In the new core, along with the emphasis on traditional subjects: writing and speaking, religion, philosophy, sciences, basic math, psychology, and the arts, there were, for example, requirements in computer use. As explained by Father Richard Conboy, executive assistant to the president, "We want to integrate the wisdom of the great civilizations with modern technology. Instead of just learning what Aristotle or Jesus Christ said, this must be applied to modern problems."[22] Under the direction of Constance Ramirez, the core committee began to develop Nesti's Formula for Strategic Repositioning into a workable plan in 1983. Implementation of the plan was underwritten in part by a $250,000 grant from the Pew Memorial Trust. Designed to cut across disciplinary barriers, the new core hoped to give students "knowledge of our essential human heritage and the capacity to analyze data, make logical decisions, and communicate ideas," according to Nesti.[23] Some changes were as follows:

- The Political Science Department began to phase out international relations, with no new majors offered due to a scarcity of interest.
- The graduate degree program was replaced by a similar program under a new Graduate Center for Political and Social Policy Studies in conjunction with the Sociology Department.
- The Art History Department and major were eliminated, with art history merged into the History Department.
- The master's program in history was placed on probation, cited for a lack of focus.
- The Classics Department was warned to increase the number of students majoring in the department.
- Anglican studies and some other special studies were terminated.
- The master's program in career studies was discontinued.
- The English Department's doctoral program, along with the social work and gerontology programs, were placed on probation.
- The Sociology Department included the development of a master's level program in gerontology in its five-year plan, as well as a juvenile criminal justice concentration on the graduate level.

While some schools and departments were cutting back, others were on the ascent. The Pharmacy School, itself in danger of being phased out in 1969, was now limiting class size. In 1986, Duquesne offered one of only a half dozen programs in the U.S. for a graduate degree in cosmetic science, dealing with the scientific and technological aspects of cosmetic products including formulation and quality testing. Also, Duquesne became the only school in the country to offer a joint master's of science / master's of business and administration degree in industrial pharmacy. This highly specialized program graduated its first class of two students in 1987.

When he came to Duquesne, Father Nesti had been interested in starting a doctoral program in theology, and this came into being in the fall of 1982. The program integrated related fields in a systemic study of Roman Catholic theology and moral theology. It was a unique program in the area and one of only a few in the nation. It was accompanied by a master's level pastoral ministry program for family and health-care ministers with a strong theological basis. A renewed interest in religion among college students was reported as a national phenomenon, although Duquesne had not suffered the great drop in attendance at mass that other Catholic institutions experienced beginning in the 1960s. The associate chaplain did report that participation and interest was on the rise at Duquesne, with 80 percent of the resident Catholic students attending Sunday mass, an increased number attending daily mass, and many students asking for special liturgical services. Theology courses drew more students even as enrollments fell in the early 1980s. So many students were interested in theology courses for their own personal development that the university even considered a new fee scale for noncredit students.

Forums for sharing scholarly research abounded at Duquesne. The History Department hosted its twentieth forum in 1986. Dr. Henry Samsonowicz, rector of Warsaw University, had participated in the 1981 forum and had received an honorary degree from the School of Business and Administration. The school had maintained a lecture and research exchange program with Warsaw University since 1973, but the firing of Samsonowicz from Warsaw University for his support of the Solidarity Union jeopardized Duquesne's program.

Beginning in 1974, Duquesne, the University of Pittsburgh, Carnegie Mellon, Carlow, and the Community College of Allegheny County, had jointly sponsored the Pittsburgh Symposium in World Literature. Held annually at Duquesne, each symposium focused on a specific author or topic. The 1983 symposium was devoted to the works of John Donne. An added highlight that year was a performance by Duquesne University's Madrigal Singers. Founded in 1981 by Dr. Robert L. Shankovich of the School of Music, the Madrigal Singers specialized in Medieval and Renaissance music. In 1982 they hosted the first of several madrigal dinners with a seven-course, candlelit, English feast accompanied by costumed pages, minstrels, jesters, magicians, and the singers themselves.

Throughout the 1980s the Symposium in World Literatures grew in size and stature. Eventually having grown to 15 colleges and universities, its name was changed to the Western Pennsylvania Symposium on World Literatures.

The university had also hosted the International Spencer Conference in the autumn of 1978. Funded by the National Endowment for the Humanities, it was seminal, resulting in the *Spencer Encyclopedia*, published in 1990.

Duquesne established the Simon Silverman Center for literature in the field of phenomenological studies in the university library in November 1980, and despite the lack of resources, other scholarly pursuits continued to be wide-ranging. For example, Professor Reginald Ney of the Physics Department went to the Marshall Islands to measure the level of radioactive isotopes in body-counting tests on inhabitants of the islands; and Dr. Marilyn Schaub of the Theology Department went to the Dead Sea Plain in Jordan to study the Early Bronze Age.

The activities of these departments was indicative of the academic interests of their respective faculties. Although the Nesti Administration pointed to a weakness in scholarship, the four Ph.D. departments in the College of Arts and Sciences were all involved in scholarship on an international scale. Except for the Chemistry Department, these departments failed to get much support from the university.

A New Building—Finally—For the Law School

As early as 1973 the university had begun to publicly discuss the construction of a separate building for the law school, as had been recommended by the American Bar Association after an inspection. By the end of the McAnulty administration, about $600,000 had been raised. It had been an uncoordinated effort. Only 18 days after McAnulty had contacted a major foundation, the dean of the law school had contacted the same one. The requests were for different size gifts for the same project and represented a great embarrassment to the university. In view of the error, it was strange indeed that the dean was given a free hand to conduct his own campaign until early 1979. According to a university report, "The results were, to say the least, not very impressive."[24] Father McAnulty continued to solicit funds in his role as chancellor during the Nesti administration. The largest single contribution came from Allegheny International Inc., made in honor of their long time CEO and Duquesne's first lay president of the board of directors, Edward J. Hanley.

Ground for the new building was broken in June 1981, and in September 1982 the Edward J. Hanley Hall was dedicated. Costing $4 million, it was the single most expensive construction in Nesti's Strategies for a Second Century fund-raising campaign. The building very nearly did not occur. President Nesti was reluctant to raise the indebtedness of the university and wanted 75 percent of the funding to be secured prior to any new construction. Several months after taking office, he seriously considered moving the law school back into its 1923–1932 home in Canevin Hall. The board of directors, however, voted to proceed with the project as originally planned.

Under Dean John J. Sciullo, the law school experienced a new vitality following its move into the new facility. The announcement of Sciullo's appointment as dean had received a standing ovation. The Duquesne Law School and that of the University of Pittsburgh held moot court competitions, funded by the Justinian Awards Benefit, an activity of the Allegheny County Association of Lawyers' Wives. The school initiated an honors program in which undergraduates with a minimum of a 3.5 QPA could forgo their last year as an undergraduate to enter the Law School. After a successful completion of their first year of law, they would then be awarded their undergraduate degree. In the summer of 1984 Duquesne's School of Law and the Pittsburgh Theological Seminary announced a new five-year program, split between the two schools, in which the student could acquire both a master of divinity and a juris doctor degree.

That same summer the law school founded its Paralegal Institute Program. Operating through the Center for Continuing Education, the Paralegal Institute awarded certificates on a part-time basis to students who already held bachelor's degrees. The on-campus program, taught by the law faculty, law librarians, and working paralegals, followed ABA guidelines.

The law school had always been active in another form of continuing education, the Duquesne University and Allegheny County Bar Association law symposiums for practicing attorneys. A concern for the larger society led to a special focus on the juvenile justice system in conjunction with the Sociology Department. In the spring of 1983 Duquesne helped sponsor a "Juvenile Justice Day," which provided an opportunity for people to hear all the judges in the juvenile court and attend workshops on alternatives to institutionalization, probation, and delinquency prevention. The following year, Philadelphia Common Pleas Court Judge Lisa A. Richette, author of *The Throwaway Children*, gave the keynote address to another day of workshops on the topic of juvenile justice. One of Duquesne Law School's distinguished alumni was recognized in 1985 as part of Black History Month. Percy Langster had been elected the first African-American district attorney in America in 1948, surprisingly in an almost all-white constituency in Lake County, Michigan.

The law school received reaccreditation from the ABA in 1988. An impressive 93 percent of the 1987 Duquesne law school graduates passed the state bar examination on their first try, more than 10 percent above the statewide average.

A Comeback for the School of Nursing

A dramatic comeback occurred in the School of Nursing under its new dean, Dr. Carol Smith. The school had suffered criticism and dropping enrollments as a result of its highly theoretical program and had been cited by the State Board of Nursing Examiners in September of 1979 as having too high a failure rate for students taking the state nursing board examinations. Appointed in 1980, Dr. Smith not only strengthened the basic undergraduate curriculum, but launched Duquesne's School of Nursing into prominence in the area of continuing education for registered nurses in the field. In 1982, responding to the American Nursing Association's recommendation that all beginning-level registered nurses have a bachelor of science degree, Duquesne initiated plans for such a degree program.

A gift from Seymour G. Heyison in memory of his wife led to the dedication of the new Margaret Heyison Nursing Resource Center in December of 1982 with facilities for practice laboratory experiences. Duquesne's nursing program was further enhanced by a European workshop study tour in 1983.

With Duquesne's School of Nursing's reputation reestablished in the area, Dr. Smith accepted the position of acting vice-president for academic affairs, and Dr. Joanne White took over. The School of Nursing expanded to the entire sixth floor of College Hall, with its own computer lab and learning research center. It also embarked upon a program for a master's degree.

The School of Business Administration Continues Strong

The American Assembly of Collegiate Schools of Business reaccredited Duquesne's Business School in 1981, putting it in select company, since less than a quarter of the nation's business schools were so accredited. Dr. Blair Kolasa, dean of the school and author of *The Social Responsibility of the Corporation*, was a strong advocate of ethical practices. A philosophy course on business ethics was strongly advised for undergraduates and was required on the graduate level. Kolasa, with strong ties to Warsaw University, was instrumental in the faculty-student exchange program with that institution. His decision to leave the deanship to complete research studies in 1984 initiated a nationwide search that resulted in the appointment of the acting dean, Dr. Glen Beeson. Changes in the school included a new student advisory group meeting monthly to discuss student concerns; offering the business bachelor's degree programs as evening courses; developing undergraduate courses in purchasing and entrepreneurship; increasing summer school offerings; adding a new master's program in management information systems to prepare students for business application programming, systems analysis, and data processing positions; offering a certificate program in international business in addition to the degree verifying completion of an international business curriculum, competency in a foreign language, and business and economic literacy; and securing program implementation grants from professional realty associations.

In recognition of the fact that women were entering business in ever increasing numbers, Delta Sigma Pi, the honorary business fraternity, became coed in 1982.

The School of Music Excels

Performing ensembles of the Music School figured prominently in the life of the Pittsburgh Community. The Wind Ensemble performed in the fall of 1980 for President Carter's visit to the city. The River City Brass Band, under the direction of Robert Bernat, gave their inaugural concert at Pittsburgh's Carnegie Music Hall in 1981. Duquesne also hosted the National Association of Pastoral Musicians convention in 1982, as well as conducting retreats and workshops for liturgical musicians in the area. The Jazz Performing Artist series became a campus hit as Duquesne, and WDUQ became almost synonymous with jazz in the area.

An area in which Duquesne's music school made a valuable contribution was in the musical training opportunities given to area youth. Dr. Robert Egan, who resigned as dean in 1981, had founded a program known as Bene-Duque in 1977 wherein students from kindergarten through eighth grade in the nearby disadvantaged Hill District attending St. Benedict the Moor School could learn flute, trumpet, recorder or clarinet for a dollar per week, with instrument rental at a dollar per month. Private piano lessons, given by student volunteers, cost $2.50 per week. Although the fees charged did not even cover repair costs for the instruments, the program stretched its grant money as far as possible to provide the service to over 180 students over eight years, some of them eventually enrolling as music majors at the college level.

In 1983 the school opened a Saturday noncredit program in music theory, musicianship, and jazz aimed at the advanced high school student and open to any Duquesne student. The program, known as DUET, Duquesne University Extention Training, expanded to include both jazz and sacred music, private lesson instruction on anything from harp to theater organ, and eurhythmics classes for children as young as three. Duquesne personnel directed both the Three Rivers Training Orchestra and the Children's Festival Choir. Duquesne University also helped sponsor the March of Champions, a show of precision drill teams preliminary to the International Championships in Montreal, Canada, in 1982.

Duquesne's School of Music had to be excellent to be competitive in the Pittsburgh area, which was noted for having such a high percentage of fine young musicians that schools from all over the country recruited there. Innovative programs involved audio recording techniques and an intern program with the Pittsburgh Symphony, Pittsburgh Opera, and Civic Light Opera. In 1987 the university outfitted the music laboratory with $60,000 worth of synthesizers, computers, and state-of-the-art recording equipment. The new laboratory, one of the most modern of any music school in the country according to Dean Kumer, not only included keyboard, an instrumental digital interface, recorders with editing devices, a graphic equalizer, and a 16-track mixer, but also included a piano and theory lab with 12 electronic pianos connected to a master board controlled by the professor.

The Institute of Formative Spirituality

The Ph.D. program in spiritual formation was inaugurated in 1980 as Dr. Susan Muto took over the directorship of the institute. Father van Kaam, founder and previous director, devoted his time to writing. That year also witnessed the beginning of a two-year master's program in formative leadership and ministry, a one-year master's program in ongoing formation, and a summer program. Courses included such topics as "Foundations for Living," "Spirituality and the Single Life," and even a course on art and meditation.

In 1988, a change in demographics, as older parishes and religious communities diminished in number, led to a drop in enrollment, and the institute began running a deficit. In 1994 the institute was phased out, though much of its work continued through the Epiphany Association. While at Duquesne, the Institute of Formative Spirituality awarded 25 Ph.D.s and 670 master's degrees. Father van Kaam and Dr. Susan Muto wrote 50 books and published over 300 articles alone or in collaboration. Dr. Carolyn Gratton of the Institute authored two other books on spiritual counseling and direction.

A Single Communications Department Emerges

University Hall was converted into a modern facility known as Des Places Communications Center in 1981, enabling the Graduate School of

Arts and Sciences to offer a new program leading to a master of arts degree in communications. The program was designed to prepare students to work as professional communicators in nonprofit institutions, business and industry, government and the public sector. Des Places, named for the founder of the Congregation of the Holy Ghost, was dedicated in a ceremony that included the awarding of the Ed King Memorial Award for Excellence in Pittsburgh Communications posthumously to an alumnus of the university, David Leherr, the late city editor of the *Post-Gazette*. (Ed King and his wife, Wendy, had hosted a call-in talk program called Party Line on radio station KDKA.)

The Bio-Communications program, a joint venture between Duquesne and Mercy Hospital, also moved into Des Places, under the name Medical Media Communication, later named Media Arts. Des Places also provided a home for the school newspaper and yearbook and WDUQ television studios.

Duquesne's Journalism Department encountered some competition from Point Park College with its announcement of the first master's program in that field in September 1981. Duquesne opened its master's program four months later, oriented more toward research than Point Park's program, with a heavy concentration on public relations and a liberal arts component involving political science and psychology. Although Point Park reported that public relations was gaining interest, their program was primarily geared toward newspapers and broadcasting. Duquesne, planning a sequence in radio, television, and print, promptly invested $45,000 in a typesetter and $109,000 in a font library. Duquesne had the advantage of a long established reputation for journalism, partly because the Duquesne University Scholastic Press Association (DUSPA) held its annual workshop for junior and senior high school newspaper and yearbook advisors and student staff members on campus each autumn.

In 1985, Father Nesti announced the merging of the departments of Journalism, Media Arts, and Speech Communications into a single Communications Department. This was done only for easier administration; none of the programs were slated for change.

The Institute for World Concerns

Among President Nesti's major goals for Duquesne was opening up the campus to the world through symposia, guest lecturers, faculty and student exchanges, and recruiting foreign students to campus. At his inauguration in the fall of 1980, he pledged his commitment to a "new-world-in-the-making." In reference to population projections for Third World countries, he promised, "Duquesne will serve and respond to the needs of these people by offering its finest intellectual resources to find answers to lighten the physical, social, intellectual, economic, and spiritual burdens that these people—as well as their counterparts in our country—face." The Institute for World Concerns was established the following year. George Gallup, Jr. spoke at its inauguration. Duquesne was already involved in a number of projects to increase knowledge and participation in world affairs, including the annual World Affairs Institute and the conference on world hunger cosponsored with Bread for the World Educational Fund. But the new institute, based on the commitment of the Holy Ghost fathers to the mission field, had its own mission statement and a permanent headquarters in Rockwell Hall. Invited speakers included Archbishop James Hickey, on the topic of American involvement in El Salvador; John G. Healey, executive director of Amnesty International, on "Human Rights in the 1980s"; Bishop Thomas Gambleton of Detroit, on the implications and validity of the U.S. bishops' pastoral letter on nuclear disarmament; and Anthony D.E. Quainton, U.S. Ambassador to Nicaragua, on the Sandinista government. Despite Father Nesti's deep personal devotion to the institute, after his resignation, Acting President Bonachea discontinued it in 1988 because Duquesne could not financially continue to support an organization of such scope.

Integrated Honors Program

Duquesne received a grant from the National Endowment for the Humanities to begin a scholars program in the fall of 1984. Students selected on the basis of grade point average, class rank, SAT scores, and recommendations from teachers and school officials followed a cross-disciplinary curriculum with a concentration on classic literary selections and intensive writing skills. A special section of the residence halls was set aside for these students to increase their dialogue with one another. In 1985 the program was extended to high school students who could enroll as juniors and seniors in an accelerated, honors-level, liberal arts program, banking their college-level credits until they enrolled at Duquesne or transferring them to another school after high school graduation. The opportunity to receive college-level credits before high school graduation was expected to draw exceptionally talented students to the Integrated Honors Program.

Duquesne and the Computer Age

Father Nesti likened the technological revolution brought about by the computer to the Renaissance and the Industrial Revolution. Accordingly, in 1980 the university purchased a computer system from Sperry Univac for faculty research, student instruction, and administrative applications, replacing the Control Data 3200 system. The College of Liberal Arts and Sciences piloted a computer literacy course in the summer of 1982. The president announced,

> We have no intention of abandoning our strong position in liberal arts and sciences, nor do we intend to require our students to become computer specialists. But we recognize the fact that our graduates must be able to understand the implications of new computer technology in their fields. We are attempting to interlock our traditional study areas with the high technology climate of the present and the future.[25]

The system was highly applauded when installed, but a year later it was pronounced "inadequate" by the dean of the business school. Not only was it common to wait an hour or more for a terminal to become available, but often the computer refused to accept the students' identification numbers, and even when it did, the system might "drop" an entire program. Purchase of the Sperrylink was perhaps the single most expensive error in Duquesne history.

In 1985–1986 the university began anew, with eight IBM personal computers in the College of Arts and Sciences pilot project writing center, and an additional million dollars for a 24-hour computer room in Towers dorm and 50 IBM personal computers in the business school. Fourteen IBM personal computers formed the nucleus for a computer lab on the third floor of College Hall in the fall of 1986 for word processing, computer science, and statistical applications. Graduate students at Duquesne were making significant contributions in the computer field, one having devised five programs in the WALTZ LISP linguistics system, and another having created an interactive program of rules of grammar and usage. Computers made their way into the Communications Department, the Music School, and the Foreign Language Department where new labs with video monitors, computer-aided instruction, and a complex casette system created a wide range of possibilities in tailoring instruction to meet the needs of each student in class.

Continuing Education

Adult career-related studies were centralized in the new Division of Continuing Education in the fall of 1982. Although the courses were taught by Duquesne faculty, Continuing Education handled all the management and records for business and industry, nontraditional learners, and health-care professionals. It also administered the offerings for clergy and religious, including summer institutes for priests at St. Paul's Monastery.

Functioning as a part of Duquesne's Continuing Education program, the Duquesne University Center for Management Development hosted its own seminars and workshops, targeted toward various sectors of managers and executives. An industrial relations professor, James Poindexter, established a center for labor and management cooperation in 1985 named ACCORD (Allegheny Center for Cooperative Resources Development).

When it founded its Small Business Development Center in 1981, Duquesne joined a statewide network of assistance agencies funded through the Small Business Administration. By spring of 1983, the center had won the praise of its area clients for its policy of contacting the client within 48 hours of the request for assistance; the quality of its counseling in identifying problems, suggesting methods of solving difficulties, and implementing efficient techniques; and for the helpfulness of the low-cost workshops and seminars. The center also moved out to various communities to present workshops, provide counseling, and conduct surveys in conjunction with the various chambers of commerce—in Wilkinsburg, Uniontown, the Beaver Valley, and Connellsville, for example. Duquesne's public relations classes in the School of Business and Administration produced marketing and publicity campaigns for companies who asked for such services. Such free services were seen as an opportunity for students to work in the real world of business.

Student Life Metamorphasizes Again

There was a resurgence of fraternities and sororities in the 1980s. One sociology professor observed, "It's all part of a larger trend back to an organized lifestyle, also exemplified by the renewed popularity of ROTC, proms, sports events, and even improved Scholastic Aptitude Test scores."[26] The civil rights upheaval, however, had had its effect on the Greek revival. "It used to be that one fraternity was Jewish, one was exclusively Italian, and you had to be a Catholic to get in, and that's no longer the case. They're looking for people who are interested in the fraternity and whatever its goals are, and it doesn't matter if you're white, black, Jewish, Christian or Arab," said James Fitzpatrick, assistant dean of students.[27] His claim was somewhat exaggerated, however, as Duquesne still had Alpha Kappa Alpha, a black sorority on campus, and few African Americans bothered to pledge the non-black fraternities and sororities.

Another transformation occurring was a more service-oriented, less "party" atmosphere. Instead of Hell Week there was Help Week, during which new pledges were put to work cleaning, gardening, painting, and repairing.

And there was all that charity work that Greek organizations had traditionally performed. Each organization had its own national philanthropies and local groups to support, plus all of them participated in the Interfraternity Council, which, for example, sponsored a Dance-a-thon every year to raise money for Muscular Dystrophy. With a total of $26,709 during the 1986 dance marathon, Duquesne qualified to send a representative to the Jerry Lewis Muscular Dystrophy Telethon in Las Vegas. Father Nesti encouraged generosity by good-naturedly allowing the group that donated the largest sum to shave his mustache. The honor went to Alpha Phi sorority for $8,000. Other unusual charitable collections included Alpha Phi Omega fraternity's annual Bath Tub Pull from the Bluff to Point State Park to raise money for the Western Pennsylvania Heart Association, and their calls from Santa Claus to children under eight years of age to benefit the Leukemia Society.

Duquesne had an official policy against hazing,

but one student had his jaw broken in an off-campus hazing, and one fraternity (Beta Pi Sigma) was placed on probation for spray painting "Betas FPC 85" on the Rt. 51 streetcar bridge in the Overbrook area of the South Hills.

The nine fraternities and six sororities on campus were not the only organizations to report dramatic growth in the 1980s. Membership boomed on the staffs of publications, in the professional societies, in the service organizations, in the honor societies, in the departmental clubs, and on the student governmental bodies. Intramural football, volleyball, basketball, and street hockey were popular, too. Charity work included the campus ministry's "Kick-in-a-can Soccathon" at McCloskey Field, where participants donated over a ton of canned goods in 1981 for the Pittsburgh Community Food Bank, and an Easter Party and a Christmas party for exceptional youth with Santa distributing toys donated by Goodfellows and the Pittsburgh Interline Club to almost 200 children in the Duquesne Student Union.

The traditional homecoming was reintroduced to Duquesne in 1984 under the name of Winter Festival. Beginning with a kickoff at the Rathskellar, the action moved to the Civic Arena for the Duke-Penn State game. A festival king and queen were announced at halftime, and the celebration moved back onto campus for the dance.

Another traditional festival was born in 1983 when the Duquesne German Club, along with DANK, the German American National Congress, hosted a Mardi Gras celebration known as the Rheinland Karneval to celebrate the tricentennial of German immigration to the United States. The Rheinland Karneval returned the following year with singing and dancing to the Peter Karsti Orchestra, door prizes for the best costume, comedians, clowns, musicians, jugglers, and the crowning of the Karneval Princess. This, too, became an annual event.

Alcohol on Campus

Difficulties with under-age drinking and the abuse of alcohol among those of legal drinking age plagued the university. Beginning in 1981, an alcohol awareness program helped. Focusing on students who had been guilty of disruptive behavior associated with drinking, it attempted to reeducate them on alcohol-use through lectures, quizzes on alcohol facts and myths, films, an alcohol use inventory, and group discussions. Of the 38 students in the first program, none had to repeat it.

The impetus for this program came from a television broadcast series, The Chemical People, produced for WQED public television as an outreach effort by Duquesne graduate, Mary Rawson. The public was so stunned by the extent of the alcohol and drug problem as presented by the broadcast that the number of task forces in Allegheny County grew from 40 to 120 in a year. The Chemical People Institute was headquartered at Duquesne. Several other efforts followed the broadcast designed to change the drinking habits of students. The dean of students, Patricia Watt, in association with the Panhellenic and Interfraternity Councils and the Union Program Board, held a Spring Alcohol Fair to share information through carnival booths set up on a variety of topics: drinking and driving, conscientious hosting of parties, alcohol and athletics, and physical responses to alcohol. The Resident Council hosted an Un-Bar Cabaret with a candlelit Bistro atmosphere, music, snacks, and exotic drinks including daiquiries, pina coladas, and margaritas, all with no alcohol.

The Nesti administration was more strict than previous ones had been on this issue. Fraternities complained loudly about its policies, which forbade them to host wet parties on campus. In an effort to circumvent the rules, some fraternities moved their parties to public banquet halls off of the Duquesne campus, but with predictable results; all reported smaller rush classes. A spokesman for Sigma Nu said, "I feel the alcohol policy has hurt all the fraternities because alcohol is what attracts people. They just don't come to hear about what the fraternities have to offer."

Alpha Phi Delta suffered the revoking of privileges after alcohol was reported present at their 1982 Valentine's Ball. They arranged for a tentative change in policy for the 1984 ball, allowing students over 21 to "bring your own bottle." Alpha Phi Delta catapulted into the news in 1985 when a pledge had to be hospitalized for overconsumption at a fraternity date party and again in 1988 when 13 students were arrested following "a full-scale, out-of-control drinking party where several fights had broken out." The party had been held at an off-campus site with buses transporting students from campus. Rumors circulated in the fall of 1986 that owners of local halls were refusing to rent to university organizations because of vandalism and noise. Even though facilities charged damage fees, owners were afraid to collect for fear of student retaliation. Students suspected that the Duquesne administration had sent out a memo warning the proprietors that the high percentage of minors in the university's student population might result in Liquor Control Board raids. In their dedication to circumventing rules, students were ingenious. The members of Tau Kappa Epsilon, for example, suspended for a series of violations, regrouped as a new fraternity, Delta Tau Chi, with a new constitution and free of its history with the administration. The Administrative Council approved two revisions for controlled use of alcohol in the fall of 1982: students who were over 21 were allowed to drink in their dorm rooms provided they kept the doors open, and parties in the resident lounges were allowed to feature kegs.

To many, the policy on alcohol was inconsistent. Social groups participating in the annual Carnival complained that their midway booths were not allowed to have alcohol, yet the Greeks, who were hosting tent shows, were permitted because the tents were considered separate "private" enclosures! Perhaps the most dramatic case to hit the news involved the Sheiks, one of Duquesne's few non-Greek social clubs. In 1985, during a hazing conducted off-campus, a student collapsed from overconsumption of whiskey and was rushed to Mercy Hospital, where his life was saved only by heroic medical intervention. The club was placed on official probation. The incident literally and figuratively sobered the campus for a short while, though the Sheiks continued proverbial bad boys, a term with which they were not uncomfortable, and managed to get themselves suspended at Carnival the following fall. Taking offense at a warning by the assistant dean of students to turn down their stereo, they proceeded to destroy their booth and sabotage other booths and tents. They were caught trying to unplug electrical cords during the evening performances. Perhaps they were just trying to keep up their reputation, which included having torn off the beaked headpiece and plucking the feathers out of the St. Joseph's basketball team's mascot's costume (replacement value $2,000) during a game in 1983.

Duquesne persisted in its educational efforts with the Alcohol Resource Center as part of the Dean of Students' office in 1983 and a new national student-operated program known as BACCHUS (Boost Alcohol Consciousness Concerning the Health of University Students) in 1986.

In 1983 the university decided to convert the Rathskeller, an on-campus establishment, into a full-service restaurant that served beer and wine. This did not help the alcohol awareness efforts! Though minors were barred after 9:00 p.m. and restricted to confined areas by ropes, this only prompted a rash of falsified ID cards as well as a sharp drop in business. After the restriction was lifted, the Liquor Control Board raided the Rathskellar in May of 1986, and apprehended 12 minors who were drinking at the time. The "Rat," as it was popularly called, stopped serving alcohol. Numerous attempts were made to reintroduce beer there, but without success.

Campus Safety

In 1981 the director of the Public Safety Department reported a rise in the campus crime rate. In the 1979–80 school year there were 474 reported incidents, compared with 330 in the previous year. The director attributed this to the dormitory visitation policy, since most of the crimes reported took place in the dorms, and most of these involved thefts.

The most bizarre theft, however, involved the library. A Pennsylvania man visited several university libraries in Pennsylvania and West Virginia and stole books that he feared could be used to make nuclear bombs. Before he was finally caught, the man had stolen about 1,800 books, some of them from Duquesne.

Many campus crimes involved vandalism, such as in a 1983 incident where rolls of pennies wrapped in electrical tape were thrown through the windows of Towers Dormitory. Also, the growing parking problem on campus was reflected in the large number of broken parking gates. For the most part, though, crime at Duquesne consisted of petty thefts and small acts of vandalism; very few violent acts were committed.

Fires and fire alarms presented a continuing headache for university officials in the 1980s. A rash of small fires at St. Ann's and St. Martin's dormitories led to a $1,000 reward offer for information, which in turn led to the conviction of the arsonist, a senior nursing student, and a 24-hour-a-day police patrol. When the university installed a new alarm system directly connected to a city fire station just a few blocks away, false alarms occurred at a staggering rate, sometimes as many as 50 in two weeks or eight a day. Each time an alarm went off, 16 to 20 men and five pieces of firefighting equipment arrived on the Bluff, and students were ordered to evacuate the building. At last it was discovered that faulty smoke detectors were causing the false alarms.

Racial and Ethnic Sensitivity Under President Nesti

Father Nesti committed himself to making Duquesne an international community by encouraging foreign students to attend the university, initiating overseas study programs, and making the atmosphere of Duquesne racially and ethnically sensitive. In 1982, Duquesne and the other universities in the city jointly sponsored a month of activities celebrating several ethnic groups with the Cultural Month of the Peoples and Nationalities of Yugoslavia. Beginning in 1984 the Duquesne University International Students Organization held an International Day on campus with arts and crafts exhibits, slide shows, a fashion show of native costumes, and performances of cultural dances. The event, open to the general public, was enhanced by contributions from the various embassies in Washington, D.C.

Duquesne was also sensitive to the Jewish community. In his annual Christmas message in the faculty newsletter, Father Nesti always extended his best wishes to those faculty members who would be celebrating Chanukah. When he realized that his annual faculty dinner was scheduled for Yom Kippur, he changed the date, insisting that Duquesne was a family of all faiths. Duquesne began holding Days of Remembrance of the Holocaust on campus in 1983. Duquesne recognized its fellow Catholics of the Orthodox faith as well with invitations to participate in the week-long program of prayer, reflection, and fellowship known as "Duquesne Alive."

Duquesne had made a commitment to increasing its African-American student population and supporting them academically and socially throughout their college careers with the institution of a special learning skills center in 1968. The center was cited in 1988 by the Pennsylvania State Department of Education for receiving its highest rating for the tenth consecutive year. Moreover, to encourage minority and disadvantaged students to plan for college careers despite the obstacles, a coalition of Duquesne, the

142. Rev Donald S. Nesti, C.S.Sp., President of Duquesne University, 1980–1987. This 10th president was the first to be selected by a search committee rather than simply being named to the position by a Holy Ghost Provincial. Out of 80 applicants, a board subcommittee chose Nesti, a 44-year-old professor who taught theology at Duquesne from 1970 to 1976. Ordained to the priesthood in 1963, Nesti's academic credentials were extensive; he had a B.A. (Holy Ghost Seminary), a bachelor of divinity (St. Mary's Seminary), an S.T.L. degree and an S.T.D. degree (the European equivalent of a doctorate in theology, from the Gregorian University in Rome), and a Master of Arts from the University of Pittsburgh. He also did postdoctoral work at St. Edmunds, Cambridge. He was fluent in French, German, and Italian, and he was an accomplished musician on the French horn. His colleagues often referred to him as a "Renaissance man."

143. Father Nesti's inauguration mass. Father Nesti is standing with arms upraised. He was the first Duquesne president to hold an inauguration in 50 years, an event that included a buffet luncheon, a reception, a cocktail party, and an inaugural dinner. Over 3,000 people attended, including Lieutenant Gov. William Scranton, and Pittsburgh Mayor Richard Caliguiri.

144. As early as 1973 the university had been publicly discussing construction of a separate building for the Law School. The school was cramped in its Rockwell Hall quarters, and Rockwell had no space for its expansion. McAnulty's administration had raised only $600,000 for the project. President Nesti, reluctant to increase the university's debts, did not support the project; he argued that the school should be moved to Canevin Hall, which had housed it originally. The board of directors voted to proceed with McAnulty's plans for building. Groundbreaking took place in June, 1981, and in September 1982 the Edward J. Hanley Hall opened. This photo shows the dedication of the new Law School building, September 17, 1982. Pictured (l. to r.) Father Nesti; U.S. Supreme Court Justice Byron White; Robert J. Buckley, CEO of Allegheny International; Mrs. Edward J. Hanley, for whose husband the building was named; and Father McAnulty.

145. Father Adrian van Kaam, C.S.Sp., founder and first director of the Institute of Formative Spirituality, teaches a class, part of a two-year master's program in formative leadership and ministry. An internationally known lecturer and writer, his psychobiography of Francis Liebermann, published by the Duquesne University Press, became a classic in the field of formative spirituality.

Pittsburgh Press

146. Nesti's governing strategies, which some described as "autocratic," threw much of the campus into turmoil. Sudden dismissals of and departures by popular administrators, a power struggle with the Tamburitzans, faculty senate objections to Nesti's handling of academic affairs, and student objections to campus rules created an atmosphere of discontent and mistrust that Nesti never overcame. This photo was taken when Nesti (left) and Academic Vice President Rolando E. Bonachea (right) met with students to discuss their grievances on April 7, 1987. To open the tense discussion, the chaplain asked all present to hold hands during the opening prayer. A *Pittsburgh Press* photographer caught this moment of the prayer, and the following day it appeared on the front page along with the story detailing all the day's unpleasant controversies. At the end of the year, the photo was reprinted as one of the *Press's* most memorable of 1987.

147. The Tamburitzans, ambassadors through ethnic song and dance since 1937, appeared throughout the U.S. and Europe during the early 1980s, and many of these performances were benefits. They now had eight Junior Tamburitzan schools in the Pittsburgh area. The growth and vitality of these community groups reflected the area's interest in keeping Pittsburgh's immigrant cultures respected and alive.

But the Duquesne-based Tamburitzans found themselves in an unprecedented battle with the Nesti administration. Their plans for their golden jubilee in 1987 included a 120-performance season and a 10-week tour of 26 countries in Europe and Asia, but most of these performances were canceled, and the jubilee year saw the Tamburitzans in decline. The Tamburitzan controversy was a major factor in the unraveling of the Nesti administration. By August of 1987, Nesti resigned as president; Dr. Bonachea served as interim president until the summer of 1988.

148. A highlight of Nesti's administration was an appearance by Vice President George Bush, who was presented with an honorary degree in 1981. Already Reagan's heir apparent, Bush attracted a great deal of media to the ceremony on the Bluff. Father Nesti is to the left of Mr. Bush and Elsie Hillman, Allegheny County Republican Chairman is on the right.

149. During fundraising activities for the Jerry Lewis Muscular Dystrophy Telethon in 1986, Father Nesti good-naturedly encouraged generosity by allowing the group that donated the largest sum to shave his moustache. This honor went to Alpha Phi sorority for $8,000.

150. Antonio Palumbo, a newer member of the Duquesne Board of Directors, made the recreation center possible with his pledge of $3 million. Duquesne named the new facility the Palumbo Center in his honor. Here Palumbo *(right)* presents Father Nesti with the first installment of his gift to the university.

151. After a few snags, groundbreaking for the new athletic-recreational facility took place in September 1986. It had been delayed by the Pittsburgh Planning Commission over parking issues; by the architects, who first submitted plans for a facility Duquesne could not afford; and by that ever-present problem, financing. Its supporters hoped that the new center would fill Pittsburgh's need for a mid-sized performance arena, something smaller than the 17,500 seats of the Civic Arena and larger than the 3,700 seats of the Syria Mosque. A 6,000-seat site available for concerts and other performances could help Duquesne financially and present the university in a positive light to the city and surrounding area, perhaps attracting potential students to the campus. The arena layout was flexible, with chairs on one side and bleachers on the other three and a moveable stage. With the first row of seats within five feet of the basketball court, there wasn't a bad game seat in the house!

And finally, Duquesne had what it had not had in more than 40 years: a home court advantage. The finished structure of the Palumbo Center received rave reviews architecturally, too. The gray block, trimmed in terra-cotta red and teal, subtle variations of the Duquesne colors, fit well with the red brick of campus. Since it sat near the foot of the Bluff, the red Spanish tile roof, with its pyramid-like slopes, created an interesting visual view from above.

152. Alumnus Maurice T. "Mossie" Murphy (class of '58), a prominent figure and political analyst in the Pittsburgh area, was one of Duquesne's most loyal and vocal proponents. For the last several decades, Murphy had been a permanent fixture at Dukes basketball games, often leaping from his midcourt seat to the floor to lead the crowd in cheers of "Shoo-shoo, rah-rah." Following Murphy's death in January 1997 at the age of 61, his seat in the Palumbo Center (seat 1, row G, section A-3) was retired in his honor. "That always has been and always will be Mossie's seat," said President John E. Murray, Jr.

153. Founded in 1964, the Duquesne University Sports Hall of Fame honors the university's athletic heroes. In 1985, the annual "Tip-Off Dinner" featured the induction of five well-known Duquesne athletes from several sports, pictured here with Father Nesti *(left)*: Dr. Fletcher Johnson (class of '54), who played basketball; Andrew J. Parlantieri ('51), football; Allan V. Bailey ('53), basketball; Arthur J. Roooney, ('24), football and baseball; and Joseph Maras ('38), football.

University of Pittsburgh, and Carnegie Mellon University selected 300 academically promising high school students to meet with their parents at Duquesne and commit themselves to scholastic excellence under the slogan "Kids Can Be Smart and Cool." And for all students who were experiencing academic difficulties, Duquesne initiated a Remedial Studies program with a concentration on English composition, Latin, psychology, and geology.

Beginning in 1982, an annual Black Week was held. And, in 1986, Father Nesti announced, "Because of the traditional missionary work of the Holy Ghost Fathers and the university's outreach to the community and its efforts at minority recruitment, it is most fitting that Duquesne University observe Martin Luther King Jr. Day out of respect for a man whose vision we share."[28]

In the spring of 1986, a black student filed charges of harrassment against three fraternity members for placing racist signs on his dorm room door and smearing jelly and ketchup on it. They denied the allegations, saying he had done the deed himself. Father Nesti chose to believe the black student despite his history of disruptive behavior. One of the members of Kappa Sigma Phi was permanently expelled from the dorms and put on behavioral probation. In addition, Father Nesti appointed the Task Force on Human Relations and Racial Discrimination, "not to apportion blame, but rather to help us all come to a better understanding of how we can function together as a community."[29]

The Red Masquers Try Some Different Things

The Red Masquers performed classical pieces such as Molière's *The Miser*; modern pieces such as *A Taste of Honey* and *Elephant Man*; the avant guarde piece, *A Coupla White Chicks Sitting Around Talking*; and even a musical, *You're a Good Man, Charlie Brown*. An unusual play for a Catholic institution was presented in 1983: *The Runner Stumbles*, about a 1911 murder trial of a Catholic priest who murdered a nun with whom he had been having an affair.

The Masquers experimented with new ideas in staging. The 1984 production of Shakespeare's *Twelfth Night* had the audience seated on both sides of a central rectangular stage. In 1985 *Dracula* was performed as a dinner theater. In cooperation with the Parish Council Educational Commission in the fall of 1983, *Mass Appeal* was presented in the Resurrection School gym.

Although an electrical fire made the campus theater under the university chapel unusable for staging productions, the Red Masquers continued to use the facility as a base of operations and for the storage of costumes and props. They were delighted, however, to be given the use of the former ROTC rifle range behind St. Ann's Hall in 1985. In a little more than a year, however, the Red Masquers were evicted from their new studio as the university prepared to raze the building in order to renovate McCloskey Field.

The Tamburitzans Increase their Fame

The eight Junior Tamburitzan schools of the Pittsburgh area—Ambridge, Duquesne, Monessen, Monroeville, North Hills, Rankin, South Hills, and Trafford—held their fourth annual holiday concert at Soldiers and Sailors Memorial Hall in November 1982. The growth and vitality of the community groups reflected a continued interest by the Tammies of Duquesne University to work within the Pittsburgh area. The staff served as consultants for WIIC-TV's series, *Pittsburgh's Wonderful People*, and Duquesne University Tamburitan Institute of Folk Arts (DUTIFA) sponsored the 1984 National Bulgarian Folk Festival in Pittsburgh. The exhibit mounted for this festival at the Tamburitzan cultural center traveled through the country under the auspices of the Bulgarian Committee for culture. As the scope of their operations broadened, the Tammies found the cost mounting greatly, as did the university, which started pressuring

DUTIFA to assume some of the cost of the Tamburitzan scholarships. In the fall of 1983, their economic situation was made worse when over a hundred instruments, mostly handmade and quite irreplaceable, were stolen. Despite the tightening financial picture, the Tamburitzans continued to do benefits, and their fame continued to grow. They performed regularly at Kennedy Center in Washington, D.C. In November 1984 they made their first appearance in Avery Fisher Hall at Lincoln Center. Sponsored by the Duquesne Club of New Jersey, the performance benefited the Tamburitzan Scholarship Fund. The following year, the Tammies were honored at a reception at the United Nations where a small ensemble performed in honor of their 50th anniversary on the eve of a major performance at New York's Carnegie Hall. As the Tammies prepared for their anniversary season, the ambassador from Yugoslavia presented them with 16 original costumes valued at $16,000. The Committee of Culture in Bulgaria donated 40 costumes valued at $20,000, and the Croatian Fraternal Union of America made a gift of $20,000 for the creation of 40 new costumes for the anniversary season. A generous grant from the National Foundation for Jewish Culture helped with the staging of the "Shtetl Scenes" in the performance program. Additional small grants totaling about $10,000 were pledged for more authentic and original costuming.

Forensics Joins the Debate Team

Duquesne won the state championship in debate in 1960, 1965, and 1967, and hosted its own tournament from 1955 to 1975, but in 1978 not a single student turned out for the debate team. It would have died completely except for the dedication of three students who paid their own way to participate in five tournaments and won back recognition and funding for the following year. By 1987 the group experienced its highest participation in 15 years and even considered reviving the tournament. The scope of the team's involvement widened to forensics, which included debate but also encompassed dramatic reading of poetry and prose, oratory, children's literature, radio announcing, salesmanship, and persuasive, informative, impromptu, and extemporaneous speaking.

WDUQ Undergoes Changes

WDUQ-FM underwent dramatic changes in the 1980s. The station had been gradually shifting from a student-run operation under the guidance of a few adult staffers to a professionally staffed station employing student interns, work-study students, and volunteers. The station also became a charter member of National Public Radio (NPR), incorporated in 1969. The station celebrated its 30th anniversary in the fall of 1980, with a reception and live broadcasts at the Duquesne Union ballroom. More than a hundred area media professionals attended the event, which focused on a nostalgic look at Pittsburgh radio's Golden Years. Rege Cordic, so instrumental in establishing and publicizing the station in its early years, hosted the event with Paul Long as co-host.

The nostalgic look back did not hinder WDUQ from redefining its image for the future. Although branching out to National Public Radio shows, *All Things Considered* and *Morning Edition*, WDUQ became primarily associated with classical music, jazz, and public affairs, for which it produced two local, magazine-format shows in 1982. WDUQ had also developed a reputation for ethnic radio shows in the native languages, including Hungarian, Indian, Irish, Italian, Scottish, and Yugoslavian. In 1985 John Gibbs became general manager and oversaw the extension of broadcasts to 24 hours a day. Station manager Judy Jankowski wrestled with what was to be WDUQ's special mission to the community. In response to the 1969 Carnegie Commission report that WDUQ put its money into alternative programming, she brought in a consultant from NPR to sort out the inconsistent programming of the station and decide where the focus should be. The biggest move was the elimination of all ethnic programming. This raised considerable controversy since the volunteer announcers were not notified in time to produce a farewell show. The station did make arrangements with a new area station, WYEP, to pick up the community programs that Duquesne was dropping.

WDUQ did not have a clear focus in the Pittsburgh area for a variety of reasons. Since it began as a university student-run station, the general public continued to perceive it as such, yet with 25,000 watts giving it a 70-mile broadcast radius, it had grown too large to be entrusted to student control. Students with little training were being given responsible positions in financial and broadcast management that counted for little on a resume in the professional world, which still considered them inexperienced. The station felt that students on work-study or as volunteers under professional training actually had better chances of entry-level radio positions after graduation. The station had no programming guidelines; programs came and went with changing course requirements in the department. Little had been done in terms of regulation as well. "We would go an hour or so without once giving the call letters," Jankowski reported.

With station meetings to establish the rules and reaffirm the commitment to news, public affairs, and jazz, WDUQ vaulted into professional status. Programming did acquire a distinct air and the use of professionals lent a continuity that made the station identifiable and familiar. Current-affairs shows broadcast by the station covered new ground. Auxiliary Bishop Bosco of the Pittsburgh Diocese spoke on the U.S. bishops' peace pastoral in 1984 as part of a series on nuclear disarmament, and the Third Global Town Meeting was broadcast by means of a national satellite hookup with the Soviet Union in 1985.

With its expansion and more professional standing, WDUQ had to take up fundraising as well. In 1981 the federal government gave $1 for every $2 raised by the station. When the Reagan Administration proposed cutbacks that would eliminate 50 percent of its public broadcasting funding by 1985, WDUQ embarked on a major fundraising campaign and raised $40,000 in 1982. Training simulators were bought so that students could practice off the air.

WDUQ's "ghost" station began operation in 1974. A community service station reading for the blind, the organization saved the cost of transmitting equipment and licensing by "piggybacking" its signal on a sideband of WDUQ. The broadcasts, transmitted on the same wavelength, could be unscrambled only by a coding device in receivers without dials given to designated blind subscribers. By 1985 the Golden Triangle Radio Information Center, Inc., broadcasting 65 different programs over 127 hours per week to approximately 2500 people, had built up its resources enough to expand the service to other certifiably handicapped. According to program director, Bill Pasco, "These people not only include the blind, but also people with dyslexia, severe palsy, or simply those in traction in hospital beds." Mercy Hospital and Central-Medical picked up the broadcasts on Pittsburgh's cable TV.

One more station made an appearance on campus. With WDUQ becoming a professional station, beginning September 26, 1983, Duquesne Towers cafeteria began its own campus television station, WDRC, broadcasting seven days a week during lunch and dinner. This effort of the Resident Council promised to be "a serious means of communication for all students," according to the communications vice-president and program director for the Council. As with several previous attempts to found a student station, it did not gain wide appeal. But it was resurrected again in 1988 under the same call letters. Originally planned as an FM station, WDSR

(Duquesne Student Radio) adapted to a carrier current system in which the radio signal was transmitted through the electrical wiring of campus buildings when no open FM frequencies were available. This attempt was also short-lived.

Criticism of the television station's facilities and instruction caused Duquesne to invite an outside committee to inspect and make recommendations for the new Des Places Communication Center. The upgrading of the facility was essential to prepare Duquesne for joining Warner Cable's educational channel 19 in 1983. University students produced their first program, *Duquesne Today*, premiering over the system on June 15 and featuring the Tamburitzans. A 1984 documentary "Computers and the College Student," part of the *Duquesne Today* series, won as the best collegiate TV documentary in the region in a competion by the Society of Professional Journalists / Sigma Delta Chi. With this success behind them, Duquesne was disappointed to hear in July 1984 that Warner Cable, claiming to have lost a half-million dollars a year in maintaining its five community cable access sites in Pittsburgh, planned to reduce the program. Duquesne had invested three years of planning and considerable expense to ready its Department of Media Arts for cable production and felt the move was being made prematurely by Warner, since most city schools had not yet been connected to the cable. But their protests went unheeded.

Athletics: Basketball Encounters Trying Times

Duquesne basketball encountered trying times on the Bluff in the 1980s. A series of coaches struggled with athletic ineligibility and scandals that filled the newspapers with the type of coverage that no school wants and cast shadows over the entire program. Coach Mike Rice took his fight to retain two of his star scholarship players all the way to President Nesti's desk. In August 1981 he was able to keep Bruce Atkins on the team after a successful summer school session, but lost 7'1" Ricky Tunstall, who failed to make the grade. This raised the question about the quality of Duquesne's recruiting and the university's responsibility in helping students in their studies. Accordingly, the Academic Support Services was restructured. Father Nesti described the role of the Academic Advisor of Intercollegiate Athletics as to "help our athletes before they get into hot water rather than to punish them when they do."[30] Professor Mike Kupersanin became the first to fill the new post.

After three winning seasons, with a 20–10 record in 1981, the Dukes were struggling with a 10–12 tally by mid-February 1982 when Father Nesti called a press conference to state his support of a "first-class basketball program."[31] He also announced that a blue ribbon athletic committee appointed the previous year had recommended that the school fund its athletic program more through donations, gate receipts, and media contracts and that the school appoint a full-time fundraiser for athletics. The committee also recommended increased financial allocations for intramural sports and intercollegiate women's sports, and a significant expansion of financing for men's basketball. Red Manning continued as Athletic Director with all the responsibilities of the university Athletic Committee—which was being disbanded—under his jurisdiction. Mike Rice, however, was discharged from his position as head basketball coach, even though the committee favored revamping the program without firing Rice. As Red Manning explained the change, "It is the university's feeling that long-range goals can be best accomplished by hiring a coach who fully understands and agrees with the president's concept of the role of intercollegiate athletics—in particular basketball—within the mission of the university."

Father Nesti's view of basketball puzzled some, including the newly appointed basketball coach, Jim Satalin. Although Nesti frequently attended the games, he was not particularly interested in whether the Dukes won or lost. He appreciated the team more for the spirit of cohesiveness it generated in the student body, who were, of course, more wildly supportive of a winning team. Although he was committed to "big-time" basketball, the academic potential of the players was of higher importance to him than their basketball skills. His displeasure with Mike Rice stemmed from that coach's recruiting of scholastically ineligible students solely on the basis of their athletic talent. Therefore, the charge laid upon Satalin was to recruit the best scholar-athletes he could find, not necessarily the best athletes. This put Satalin at a disadvantage, but Father Nesti proclaimed that a basketball program geared strictly toward competition exploited people, a practice he viewed as immoral.

Jim Satalin, after nine winning seasons at St. Bonaventure, had a losing season during his first year at Duquesne. He was nonetheless named *Pittsburgh Post-Gazette* Coach of the Year, Atlantic 10 Co-Coach of the Year, and *Duquesne Duke* Coach of the Year. He was praised for renewing camaraderie among the players and championing the university's commitment to academics. He was also applauded for landing Rick Suder and Emmett Sellers to play for the Dukes. One of the team members, Joey Myers, was selected as fourth best in the Atlantic 10 and part of the All-Atlantic 10 second team. Myers received the Sihugo Green Award for his outstanding play.

In December 1984, the Dukes lost another player, Tom Harvey, to academic ineligibility, but not because of his academic record. Satalin was accused of illegal recruitment by the NCAA because California Polytechnic State University, in what Satalin described as a vendetta, had complained that Harvey had been a student there, though never on the team, and had transferred for a semester to Victor Valley Junior College before coming to Duquesne. NCAA rules prohibited a four-year school from recruiting from a two-year school, but Harvey requested a restraining order in order to play at Duquesne and initiated an antitrust suit against the NCAA in federal court. Tom Harvey was lost to Duquesne.

Satalin also had to deal with the scandal of four of his players, including his star, Emmett Sellers, being accused of rape. With all four suspended from the team pending the outcome of the case, Satalin hoped for a speedy resolution and followed the story, day by day, in the newspapers. But the case was not resolved for over a year, while the team struggled through a 12–18 season. Even when the court acquitted them, the university suspended two for two years, making them ineligible to play, and suspended the other two, including Sellers, for a semester. Satalin had to look to January of 1986 before he could pump some depth into the team.

When the terms of suspension were over, Sellers proved to be spectacular and the Dukes had their first winning season since 1980–1981. In April 1986 Satalin's contract was renewed for three more years. Despite his 49–66 record at Duquesne, he was still considered one of the best floor coaches in the country. The requirement of a minimum of 12 credits per semester and 24 credits in an academic year for participation in varsity sports became policy in the fall of 1981. Student-athletes could also be dismissed for three failed courses in a semester.

The academic supervisor for intercollegiate athletics, Martin Snyder, designed a program that included tutoring service for all athletes, early preregistration for scheduling assistance, and mandatory study hall for all freshman basketball players. By midterm, grades in the pilot group averaged higher that those for the freshman class as a whole. One sign that athletic academic support at Duquesne was effective was the fact that none of Duquesne's five freshmen players were disqualified when the NCAA passed Proposition 48 in 1986. This required freshmen to complete a core curriculum of at least 11 courses, maintain a 2.0 average, and have a minimum SAT score of 700.

Good news and bad news attended Duquesne basketball over the next few years. On the good news side, a Duquesne player received a nomination for the Atlantic 10's pre-season second team in the fall of 1987. On the bad side, the Dukes were banned from the August 1986 NCAA postseason competition because Duquesne did not meet competitive standards in other sports—not enough women's or men's sports teams and not enough participants on the teams. For example, a swimming team had to have 11 swimmers participating in each of 10 meets. Neither the men's nor the women's swimming teams had that many competitors in any of their meets.

There was still more bad news. Another player was declared ineligible by the NCAA in February of 1988, this time because he had received $1,200 in summer pay from Duquesne supporter Mossie Murphy in what the association deemed an unacceptable pay scale for the hours and work involved. The player had to sit out seven games and pay back the money to regain his eligibility. To many it seemed that the NCAA watched Duquesne with uncommon closeness. The Dukes were also not able to sustain their winning ways. They finished the 1987–1988 regular season with a 10–20 record and lost in the second round at the Atlantic 10 tournament. Freshman Clayton Adams, named to the Atlantic 10's All Freshman team, broke Norm Nixon's freshman assist record with 163. Junior Co-captain Collin Dobbs ended the year with a total career point total of 1085 breaking the thousand-point goal.

Duquesne had other difficulties with the Atlantic 10 Conference, which the university joined in 1980. In the fall of 1983, Pittsburgh was excited about the fledgling Home Sports Entertainment network that was televising more local games from the Pirates, Penguins, Spirits, Dukes, and the Robert Morris and Carnegie Mellon basketball teams over cable. But the real money in television lay in contracts for coverage with the major networks and cable companies. The Atlantic 10 was unable to land any contract for its postseason tournament in the spring of 1984. The Atlantic 10 schools—Temple, Duquesne, George Washington, Massachusetts, Penn State, Rhode Island, Rutgers, St. Bonaventure, St. Joseph's of Pennsylvania, and West Virginia University—met that spring in Philadelphia to hammer out issues involving television coverage payment problems, marketing and promotion, schedules, sites and formats for championships and expansion, and the schools' reaction to the 45-second clock and three-point field goal rulings. When the Atlantic 10 still did not have a cable contract by the fall, Charlie Theokas, the new conference commissioner, made the rounds of the teams, meeting with the athletic departments and solidified the conference identification. In his opinion, the Atlantic 10 suffered from a lack of publicity and cohesiveness. The Big East, formed around the same time, had become a powerful entity because the teams in the conference were always mentioned as Big East teams in all their publicity, giving their conference high visibility and more power in negotiations with the media and merchandisers.

Duquesne suffered an unsettled athletic administration with Red Manning's resignation as athletic director in the summer of 1982. His duties were split among Eileen Livingston, the assistant athletic director; Jim Satalin, coach of the Dukes basketball team, and Dennis Golden, vice-president for student life. A realignment of duties in the fall of 1983 brought Eileen Livingston to the position of athletic director in charge of all intercollegiate teams other than basketball and all club and intramural programs. Nellie King became associate athletic director for community relations, and Jim Satalin was to handle the men's Division I program, the Dukes basketball team.

The financial strength of the program, especially competitive Division I basketball, rested on the Dukes Court booster club. Founded in

1977, the Dukes Court brought in $44,000 in 1981, $100,000 in 1982, and expected to raise $150,000 in 1983. The funds raised by the club were turned over to the university and used for salaries and expenses, primarily of the basketball team, Duquesne's only revenue generating sport, which generated only $72,000 in ticket sales for a season. Although the Dukes Court did not provide any funding for athletic scholarships, they did underwrite the expense of new equipment for the weight room.

The Women's Basketball Team Plays Well

The women's complement to the Duquesne Dukes, the Duquesne Duchesses, played excellent basketball. In 1983, the university lost coach Tom Welch, who had led the women to a 19–6 record, frustrated over the lack of facilities, his salary, and the tight budget for women's athletics. His successor, alumnus Paul Hindes, managed to lead the Duchesses to a 14–9 record and a Pennwood West Conference Championship in his first season. He resolved to increase funding for women's teams by pursuing a path of excellence: "I want to create some excitement at Duquesne. I want to develop a women's basketball program that this university has to notice."[32]

The women's conference, the Association of Intercollegiate Athletics for Women, was replaced by the National Collegiate Athletic Association in 1983, and the women transferred to the stiffer competiton of the NCAA the following season. To Bucknell's surprise, they played their best basketball of the season to defeat the host team at the Bucknell Tournament and advance to the finals. The Duchesses had a 1000-point scorer, too. Chrissi Stough scored her thousandth point in 1984, just two weeks after her twin sister did the same for Syracuse. And, as Paul Hindes expected, someone did notice how well the Duchesses were playing and gave them money. The organizational communications class held a Casino Night benefit and gave the proceeds, $692, to make repairs on the women's athletic facilities. Although not much considering what the university invested in the men's basketball program, it was the largest single donation to benefit women's sports at Duquesne. The Duchesses had a 16–13 record for their second season in Division I in 1985. Although they lost in the quarterfinals, they won their first Atlantic 10 playoff game against St. Bonaventure in 1987.

A step was made in recognizing the importance of the women's basketball program in the fall of 1986 when Nesti approved $161,000 in tuition-only scholarships for nonrevenue producing Division I sports. Sixty students received partial scholarships, although the only sports eligible were swimming, cross country, track, and women's basketball. Regardless of the quality of the program, with the exception of basketball, women's sports received no scholarships. Dennis Golden approached the Budget Committee to improve the program: "I asked for $40,000 last year to upgrade the women's programs, and I got $10,000."[33] By the fall of 1987 Duquesne was awarding 23 full athletic scholarships and 85 partials for all programs.

Other Sports Continue, and Rowing Begins

The lack of funding and support in the nonrevenue-producing sports—volleyball, cross-country skiing, tennis, golf, swimming—created an unstable situation regarding coaches. The NCAA regulations mandated a minimum number of sports programs, but they were initiated without enthusiasm and drew few participants. Bright spots were the winning Duchess tennis team and the rifle team.

In football, Pedro Bowman became the only player in Duquesne history to run more than 1000 yards in a single season in 1983. In hockey the Ice Dukes, having joined the Western Pennsylvania Ice Hockey League in 1976 and capturing the championship in 1979, continued their winning ways under the coaching of Mike Makin. The team swept the WPIHL championship again in 1982, 1984, and 1985. Hoping to become an NCAA Division III team, they played their first season as an independent in 1987–88 with a 12–9–3 season.

Gifts from the family and friends of the late Duquesne alumnus, Tom Grealish, funded a rowing team in 1986. Sixty-two potentials showed for the first call and the team got off the ground and into the water with 47 students, only three of which had had previous boating experience. Judging from the turnout, The Pittsburgh Rowing Association wondered why the area universities hadn't begun rowing earlier and hoped that Carnegie Mellon would be the next to enter competition. Duquesne University hosted the first collegiate crew regatta ever held in Pittsburgh in the spring of 1987, competing against West Virginia University and Mercyhurst College before a crowd of 100 spectators at the Point. The event was almost marked by disaster when the Gateway Clipper's *River Belle* cut off three crews under the Fort Duquesne Bridge. Fortunately no one was hurt and the shells were undamaged. On her return an hour later, the *River Belle* moved out of the way.

The Sports Hall of Fame

One of the traditions at Duquesne which kept the sports program in the eye of the student body and more particularly the alumni, was the Sports Hall of Fame. It inducted its first woman member, Elizabeth (Hochrein) Misher, highest scorer in the Duchess basketball team's history, in 1980. Bob Prince, former voice of the Pittsburgh Pirates, served as master of ceremonies for the Alumni Association tip-off night dinner in 1981 at which Joe Tucker, voice of Duquesne basketball for over 20 years, was given special recognition and Arthur "Jake" Strutt, football, 1930s; Elmer "Pickles" Kreiling, basketball, 1930s; and Thomas "Moe" Barr, basketball, 1960s, were inducted. The 1983 inductees included Irv Brynner, basketball, 1930s; Joseph Camic, basketball, 1940s; Robert Maguire, who established rifle as a varsity sport at Duquesne, 1950s; and Michael Barr, baseball and basketball, 1970s. A special inductee, William C. Kuenzig, established the Ryan Athletic Fund, the first and only endowment for Duquesne Athletics, funded by a gift of 1000 shares of Ryan Homes stock presented to Duquesne in 1972. The 1984 inductees included Sam Pratt, football, 1930s; Leo Elter, football, 1949–50; Ron Guziak, basketball, 1960s; and the "twin towers" of Duquesne basketball in the 1960s, Barry and Gary Nelson. Allan Bailey, Fletcher Johnson, Joseph Maras, Andrew Parlantieri, and Arthur Rooney were inducted in 1985.

The Palumbo Center

Construction on the long-awaited athletic-recreational facility envisioned in Duquesne's Master Plan was begun in 1986. The Pittsburgh-based architectural firm of Deeter, Ritchey, and Sipple Associates had won the design contract in October 1984, but the project had hit some major snags, the first of which involved parking. The Pittsburgh Planning Commission delayed approval while considering whether the area could support the additional parking requirements of a facility that size. The question also arose about how the university was to satisfy its own needs for parking space with the elimination of over 350 spaces on the building site itself. With the inclusion of a $4.6 million eight-story garage designed to hold 746 parking spaces, to be built concurrently with the new center, the city council gave approval on May 28, 1985. Then came another snag. Although the university had never projected more than $10 million for the recreation/convocation center, the architectural firm interviewed students, coaches, and administrators, analyzed all of their wishes, and arrived at a set of drawings for a facility costing $19 to $20 million (and charged Duquesne $600,000 for the plans.) The administration realized that the university could not afford such a complex and that the project would now be substantially delayed while a second set of plans, within the budgeted range, was prepared. The second set, estimating the construction costs at $10 million, cost the university an additional $300,000. Groundbreaking finally took place for the complex on September 3, 1986. Navarro Construction began work that same month.

The need for the new facility was undisputed. In February 1983 the university had reported that the cost just to open the doors at the Civic Arena was $7,500. This meant that the Dukes had to draw an average of 4500 fans per game just to break even, but the 13 home games of that season drew only 36,910 fans, an average of 2840 per game, woefully short of the needed amount. The administration reckoned that a substantial long-run savings could be realized if Duquesne owned and operated its own facility. Also, because it would be more suited to the size of the crowd, the facility would add excitement to the game.

Financing for the new recreation / convocation center was a distressing problem—until Antonio J. Palumbo, not an alumnus but a member of the university's board since 1985, pledged $3 million toward the new center, the largest grant ever received from a board member. Duquesne announced that the new complex would be named Palumbo Center in his honor.

As the Palumbo Center moved toward a completion date in the spring of 1988, David DiPetro, director of auxiliary services, began giving tours of the facility and booking engagements, primarily for concerts. The center filled a crying need in the city for midsized productions that would otherwise have been staged in a curtained-off section of the Civic Arena (seating capacity 17,500) or in the un-airconditioned Syria Mosque (seating capacity 3700). With approximate seating for 6000 depending upon staging, the Palumbo Center was in great demand. Without even knowing what the rock concert acoustics would be like in this athletic structure of hardwood floors, metal rafters, and plenty of concrete, DiCesare Engler booked eight summer concerts including names like Billy Ocean, Gloria Estefen and the Miami Sound Machine, America, and Joe Cocker. The complex had several features that made it attractive to concert promoters, particularly the convenient downtown location, the accessibility of the stage door for unloading heavy equipment, and the excitement generated by the stylish design of the structure itself. It was hoped that the draw of Palumbo Center as a concert site would not only help financially, but would present Duquesne in a positive way within the city and the surrounding area, making the university more visible and bringing potential students to campus.

Depeche Mode's sold-out electro-rock concert on June 11, 1988, the first event in the new center, was also the initial test of the acoustics for concert events. The *Pittsburgh Press*'s entertainment critic pronounced them similar to the Civic Arena "with the echoes common to spaces designed more for sports than music," but within the acceptable range for that type of performance.

The layout of the arena itself was very workable, with chairs on one side and bleacher seats on the other three, one side of which accommodated a movable stage during concert performances. Arranged in two levels, one red, the other blue, with the first row within five feet of the basketball court, there literally wasn't a bad seat in the house for sporting events. Jim Satalin looked forward to something Duquesne had lacked for several decades: a home court advantage. The athletic facilities included the main arena with a suspended running track, an auxiliary gym, men's and women's locker rooms and saunas, training and hydrotherapy rooms, a student lounge, a dance studio, a weight room, racquetball and squash courts, an activities deck, the athletic department offices, and improvements to McCloskey Field including bleachers, lighting, and an artificial surface.

The Palumbo Center received rave reviews from an artistic point of view as well. It succeeded in being both compatible with the red brick of campus, yet distinctive. The gray block building was trimmed in terra-cotta red and teal, subtle variations of the Duquesne colors. Since it sat near the foot of the Bluff, the red Spanish-tile pyramid-style roof was designed to create visual interest when viewed from above. Although it was essentially a square block, a sense of lightness was achieved through the use of translucent wall panels and a glass entrance supported by five teal support columns. The center's arduous path from dream to reality proved worthwhile. It was one of the most notable achievements of the Nesti administration.

Dennis Golden "Resigns"

In March 1987, both the Testing / Counseling Center and Health Services were removed from the purview of the popular Vice-President for Student Services, Dennis Golden, and placed under the jurisdiction of Dr. Rolando Bonachea, vice-president for academic affairs. Father Nesti announced that the decision had been the culmination of "intensive discussion and planning for over a year," yet none of the directors of the programs involved knew anything of the transfer until it occurred. And they were not happy with the transfer. Nor were the students, who appreciated Golden for his accessibility. Bonachea responded that all elements dealing with student well-being affected their academic performance, and thus should be under his jurisdiction. SGA called a meeting of student leaders to discuss their concerns about the transfer, the deeper issues of a lack of communication between administration and students, the lack of student input on student-related issues, social life, and the atmosphere of the Duquesne community generally. Golden himself, whose relationship with Nesti had been declining ever since he had refused to expel the students involved in the 1984 April Fool issue of the *Duquesne Duke*, "resigned" with no comment on March 28. Willard Fuller then declined the interim position due to what he said was a difficulty in working with the administration, and he resigned as well.

The Tamburitzans versus Dr. Bonachea

The Dennis Golden affair was soon overshadowed by a far larger controversy concerning the Tamburitzans. The Tammies' plans for their golden jubilee in 1987 included a 120-performance season, a reunion of former Tamburitzans, a gala dinner in April 1987 with a preview of the summer show, and a ten-week-long world tour of 26 countries in Europe and Asia during the summer. Then the first of many bombshells exploded. In February, Dr. Bonachea refused to allow the Tamburitzan bus to depart for the first scheduled performances, in North Carolina. He said that snowy conditions had rendered the Pennsylvania Turnpike unsafe. When Tammy officials told Bonachea that the State Police said the Turnpike was operating normally, it was to no avail. Then in March, university officials cancelled the Asian segment of the tour, citing insufficient funding. The student performers demonstrated in front of Father Nesti's home and demanded additional meetings with the administration. At this point Bonachea demanded that Walter Kolar, the director of DUTIFA, fire Nicholas Jordanoff, the Tamburitzan artistic director, Patricia (Pat) French, the public relations director, and Greg Shuga, the assistant tour manager and bus driver. Kolar asked for the reason for such an order. When none was forthcoming, he refused to carry it out. On March 26th Bonachea fired Kolar as well as all of the others. Only a year from retirement, Kolar had been with the Tamburitzans as a student, staff member, and director for 45 years. Jordanoff had been with the Tammies for

35 years. Pat French had been with the Tammies for 40 years.

The Tamburitzans and thousands of East-European ethnics who looked favorably on Duquesne were stunned. Thirty-two of the student performers returned to Nesti's home on the night of the firings and danced in protest. Once again they demanded a meeting with the administration. Fearful of what might happen next, Nesti spent the night of March 27 at the Hyatt Hotel off campus. "I figured I needed a good night's sleep," he said.[34] Extra campus police were assigned to guard the administration building. Nesti and Bonachea planned to hold separate meetings with the Tamburitzans, parents, alumni, and the Tamburitzan National Folk Art Corporation to explain their actions, but members of the troupe said that these separate meetings, tailored to individual groups, would effectively keep the parties involved from hearing a complete story.

Ken Service, vice-president for university relations, was another casualty of the Tamburitzan affair. He had sent a memo to Nesti on March 23 advising him to hold an immediate meeting with the Tamburitzans who believed "there is a planned effort to remove Walter Kolar and other members of the Tamburitzan staff," and that "Dr. Bonachea has dealt in an arbitrary and unduly harsh manner with certain students and staff members." Parents, too, he said, felt their children were being mistreated. The meeting never took place, and Service resigned his position at Duquesne eleven days later, a week after the firings.

A financial deficit was given as the reason for the shakeup. The administration said that the Tamburitzans were operating $100,000 in the red. The Tamburitzan leadership responded that much of the deficit was the result of plans for the world tour that the university had approved in the fall despite the fact that it would have to be subsidized—as all of their overseas trips were—while a nationwide tour would have produced a profit. They also pointed out that some of the deficit was the result of Dr. Bonachea cancelling two concerts that winter, ostensibly because of snow, the first of their concert obligations ever to be cancelled. French presented documents showing that Nesti and Bonachea had hampered fundraising efforts. One memo from Dr. Bonachea to Ken Service dated February 24th, read, "Effective today, you end the fundraising for the Tamburitzan World Tour."

Starting in January 1987, Dr. Bonachea had interviewed about 15 student members of the troupe with regard to reports, he said, of physical and verbal abuse and low morale. In so doing, he circumvented the channels of judicial board charges that normally were taken when a student had a complaint. One of the interviewed students said the vice-president "was digging for something." Another claimed he had "intimidated and twisted his way into the inner workings of the ensemble and pitted students against other students and staff. He created the so-called 'morale' problem so that he could make the staff look bad."[35] True, a handful of girls had complained that they had been shouted at during rehearsals and one said that she had had her arm twisted and bent backwards. But the other students replied that these "alleged" abuses were only attempts to encourage students to work harder and were no worse than what occurred on the football practice field or on the basketball court.

Dr. Bonachea felt that the Tamburitzan organization had become too autonomous. From 1942 to 1970, the Tamburitzans did operate semi-independently with salaries paid by the Tamburitzan Corporation. Even during these years, however, a university-appointed moderator sat on the board of the Tamburitzan Corporation. Bonachea had clashed with the Tammie staff within months of his arrival. He did not want them to communicate directly with the press and was angry at Jordanoff for expressing to a reporter his disappointment that Heinz Hall had cancelled the Tammies' traditional New Year's Eve booking in favor of a symphony. Then in the 1986–1987 school year, he informed Kolar that Sr. Dolores Montini of the campus ministry was to accompany the troupe on its world tour and have authority over the staff. This was much to the dislike of the Tammies. In addition, Dr. Bonachea ordered Kolar to shorten rehearsal time and monitor the number of breaks.

Although it was announced on March 27 that the Tammies would complete the remainder of their scheduled performances and continue with the abbreviated world tour, work on the production came to a grinding halt after the firings. The gala dinner meant to showcase the performance before they left on tour was postponed and then cancelled. The Tamburitzan files in the Duquesne University Archives contain many letters to President Nesti from groups angrily demanding the return of their money for the dinner. The executive director of the Mendelssohn Choir of Pittsburgh ended her letter saying, "It is a tragedy that the Tamburitzans' work, their 50th anniversary and world tour should be marred by this destructive action."[36]

Administration of the Tamburitzans was entrusted to the dean of the music school, Michael Kumer, but practice sessions for the tour show had stopped and outside choreographers designing the American numbers, which had been requested by the foreign governments, discontinued their efforts. Nothing further was done about processing the manifests, visas, and passports or confirming the bookings and travel arrangements. The Tammy students took a vote on whether to perform their current show on a world tour. They voted no. "How can you say yes to something that can change any moment?" one explained.[37] Kumer added, "It's one thing to have people planning a tour who have been doing it successfully for years. It's another thing to bring in a new team of individuals."[38] The students did not want to compromise the troupe's reputation by giving an amateurish show. In describing his feelings about the cancellation of the tour, which was to have concluded with a performance before Pope John Paul II in the Vatican, one member of the troupe expressed what was probably the opinion of many: "It's the destruction of a lifetime dream."[39]

When the chairman of the university's board of directors, A. William Capone, resigned in August of 1987, he recommended phasing out the Tamburitzan scholarships and reducing the Tammies to an extracurricular activity. He said that the work, 80 to 100 performances a year, was just too demanding for the students. French, however, claimed that such a move would change the whole concept of an amateur group with a professional show and an international reputation. "It would be the destruction of the preservation of our heritage. Duquesne has been unique in supporting this."[40]

The administration appointed Thomas A. Roncevic as acting managing director for 1987–1988. Under Roncevic's management, the Tammies had to cancel their first 14 shows of the 1987–1988 season that had been booked before the firings. They did not resume their performances until late August, and they had to shelve the New Year's Eve show. At the end of January, the university announced the appointment of Paul G. Stafura as managing director, and now the focus was on the ensemble with staff members no longer committed to teaching university courses. Thus the master's degree program ended. The Tamburitzan Corporation turned over its assets to Duquesne in exchange for a promise from the university to continue funding the Tamburitzan scholarships. Assets included a warehouse, the office building, the Tamburitzan summer camp property in Wisconsin, and other property in the Pittsburgh area. With Duquesne agreeing to continue the scholarships, the Tamburitzan National Folk Art Center also turned over two $50,000 state humanities grants that were to be used toward their scholarship endowment. Although the Tamburitzan Board was still charged with raising money for performance costs for the ensemble, the university would apply the grants to the Tamburitzan Scholarship Endowment, operated by Duquesne itself, and seek ways to increase its funding.

The Beginning of the End of the Nesti Administration

It should be understood that the Tamburitzan controversy played only a part, albeit a major part, in the unraveling of the Nesti administration. On March 29, two days after the Tamburitzan firings, and only one day after Dennis Golden's dismissal, the students wore red armbands to Greek Sing (which Golden had refused to cancel) to protest the administration's decision-making policies. The students demonstrated at Father Nesti's home with T-shirts, buttons, and banners asking, "Are Students Still #1 at Duquesne?" Coming together as they did, these controversies produced a groundswell of student discontent that engulfed the university and virtually paralyzed its administration.

President Nesti and Sister Dolores Montini, liaison for student concerns, met with student leaders and SGA members, hoping that the SGA could effectively communicate with the administration in solving student problems. Instead, claiming that the answers that Father Nesti had given in small groups were contradictory and that both Nesti and Bonachea had refused to speak to the Duquesne community at an open forum, the SGA affirmed a "lack of confidence" vote 19–1 on April 2, 1987, and called for Nesti's resignation. Actually, Father Nesti had not refused the open forum—he had just asked that certain conditions apply: that only students be permitted to attend, that questions be prewritten and submitted to SGA President Thomas McQuillan, and that the forum be held at the music school's Recital Hall. Saying that these demands were too restrictive, the students insisted on an open forum of students, faculty, and administration in a larger hall. On April 3rd, the day of the scheduled forum, for which a thousand people turned out, Father Nesti did not appear. The Vice-President for University Relations, Kenneth Service, resigned.

A letter from ten faculty members, including the president of the Faculty Senate, asking him to do the "large-minded thing" and resign met with a strong refusal. Then Father Nesti himself called an open forum a few days later at the Student Union ballroom. There he and other top administrators met with 1500 members of the university community for three hours. In a highly charged atmosphere, the students blamed Nesti for problems at the dorms and expressed their displeasure at his banning of alcohol at campus clubs and parties. Practically every interest group vented their particular complaints. Music students blamed Nesti for failing to allocate $150,000 for an organ. Other issues brought up were the Tamburitzan shakeup, the reorganizing of the Office of Student Life, and the recent firings and resignations. When Nesti said that Dennis Golden had resigned voluntarily and agreed to stay off campus by "mutual agreement," the disbelieving students booed him loudly. Nesti tried to gracefully close the forum by promising to make this the beginning of an ongoing dialogue. Obviously, it was too late. The president's popularity had reached the vanishing point.

The Faculty Senate urged both Nesti and Bonachea to resign "for the good of the university." A professor in the business school remarked, "They [Nesti and Bonachea] envision themselves as benevolent dictators, and I'm not sure the benevolence is there." The Senate joined the Faculty Council, SGA, and Concerned Friends of Duquesne University in calling for the resignations. On April 13 the board of directors met at an off-campus site and, unswayed by the climate of opinion, gave the administration another vote of confidence. At the same meeting, however, it also approved a special investigative panel to look into the administration of Duquesne. SGA president Tom McQuillan observed, "It's ambiguous to vote confidence and then ask for an investigation. Either you have confidence in him or you don't."[41] The Duquesne Corporation was also becoming increasingly alarmed by the situation and urged the board to take quick action because "a substantial lack of trust and confidence make it impossible for any official to govern."[42]

The investigative committee set up by the board became known as the Cyert Panel after its chairman, Richard Cyert, president of Carnegie Mellon University. Other members included Judge Lawrence Kaplan, of Allegheny County Common Pleas Court, Robert Wilburn, the President of the Carnegie, and Charles Parry, Chairman and CEO of Alcoa Corporation. During the time that the committee was investigating and compiling its report, additional events came into play. In May, Reverend Norman C. Bevan, provincial of the Holy Ghost Congregation in the United States Eastern Division, wrote a letter to the Duquesne Corporation demanding that the corporation take no action against any university official or administrator. He further ordered that the priests of the corporation rewrite the bylaws to enable it to turn over their power as owners of Duquesne to the seven-member provincial council and then resign. The members of the Duquesne Corporation had been discussing the possibility of their dismissing the chairman of the board of directors. Bevan did not want this to occur and therefore acted to prevent it from happening. The demand, calling upon their vow of obedience, threatened that if they did not comply, they would lose their good standing in the Order. Fathers Nader, Duchene, Dolan, Varga, and Fenner resigned immediately. Fathers Murray, Philbin, and Smith questioned whether the vow of obedience applied to an academic situation such as this and refused to resign. Ultimately, they too were forced to step down and all three did so prior to the final canonical warning. Thus ended the Duquesne Corporation as it had existed since the beginning of Pittsburgh Catholic College in 1878.

Student leaders convened the first SGA meeting to be held during a summer recess, with representatives coming from as far as New Jersey to meet at an off-campus apartment to consider actions of their own. They decided to cable Pope John Paul II at the Vatican to request his intervention. The Secretary of the Nuncio at the Vatican Embassy in Washington, D.C., responded, "We welcome the input, but it's very unlikely that the Holy See would get involved," because Duquesne, unlike Catholic University, was not a "pontifical university," chartered by the Vatican. SGA president Tom McQuillan felt the telegram was ill-considered and violated the SGA constitution. The SGA Senate then voted unanimously to impeach McQuillan for aligning himself too closely with the administration and to appoint Grant Bochicchio to succeed him.

In what some called an act of retaliation for speaking out against the changes in the Student Life Office at the April Open Forum, both Teresa Byrne, director of health services, and Keith Martin, director of Towers Dorm, were fired in June, despite excellent ratings of their performance on annual reviews. Regarding Byrne's dismissal, the assistant director of advisement and counseling stated that she could not maintain harmonious working relationships with staff and supervisors.

Father Nesti Resigns

The Cyert Committee Report was completed after 60 hours of hearings and shared with the board of directors on June 17, 1987. The report stated that Duquesne tried to do too much with the resources it had and was operating dangerously close to the edge, given its limited endowment. Alumnus Paul Sullivan responded in a *Post-Gazette* letter to the editor that Duquesne had always provided an education far beyond its means and that "I only hope that the

Post-Gazette and the Cyert Committee will never again proclaim an equation between millions in the till and excellence in the classroom."

The report praised Father Nesti's efforts at improving the quality of the university but cautioned that he "must concentrate on healing the wounds that have been opened in the community." It sharply criticized Nesti's management style and expressed reservations about his ability to retain enough support from the university community to administer effectively and "heal the wounds." The *Pittsburgh Post-Gazette* observed, in regard to the report's findings, "The best gloss on the controversy, however, seems to be that university president Donald Nesti pursued a commendable goal—a renewed commitment to excellence and accountability— in a clumsy and insensitive manner."[43] A month later, that same paper suggested that it would be better if Nesti resigned: "The *Post-Gazette* reluctantly has come to the conclusion, strongly implied in the committee report, that as well-intentioned and honorable a man as Father Nesti is, the university's troubles almost certainly will continue to mount until he steps down."[44] The board of directors, however, reappointed Nesti, even though he had offered his letter of resignation on July 15. Within a week of his reappointment, the last three priests of the Duquesne Corporation, Fathers Smith, Philben, and Murray, all with extensive background and experience in administration while serving at Duquesne, resigned their positions as ordered. Board Chairman A. William Capone charged that the Duquesne Corporation had never wanted Father Nesti as president and had been trying to do the president's job.

Having apparently won his battle to retain the presidency of Duquesne University, Father Nesti submitted a second letter of resignation on July 30, to become effective August 15. This time the board of directors accepted it with "profound regret."[45] The new provincial committee of the Holy Ghost Fathers had accepted the original letter of resignation, and since the Order had the authority to reassign him, their decision forced him to make good on his original decision to resign. According to a former board member and president of the Alumni Association, Ronald Bowes, "He obviously didn't get a vote of confidence from them. The Holy Ghost Fathers, the Congregation, thought it was in the best interests for him not to remain. That was probably the straw that broke the camel's back."[46]

Much speculation has been made concerning the relative importance of the president and the board in the governance of Duquesne University. A quote from the minutes of the board of directors is instructive: "During the last seven years, the Board has endorsed, almost without exception, all recommendations of Father Nesti and his staff." Claiming that his decision had nothing to do with Nesti's leaving, A. William Capone, one of Nesti's chief supporters, tendered his resignation as chairman of the Duquesne University Board of Directors on August 9th. His commitment to Duquesne University had brought him to the board in 1965. He had been honored as the third recipient of the Old Main Distinguished Alumnus award in 1985.[47]

An Acting President

Although the faculty and student leaders had called for the dismissal of Dr. Bonachea as well, the board appointed him acting president until a permanent replacement was named. The secretary of Concerned Friends of Duquesne University, a group consisting largely of alumni and parents of Tamburitzans, remarked, "That's like a clone being asked to assume the responsibilities of the president. There is no difference between Father Nesti and Dr. Bonachea."[48]

Dr. Bonachea stated, "I am saddened that the recent events have obligated the resignation of a very honest and decent man. Father Nesti loves Duquesne dearly, and gave everything to the university. Possessing a strength of character found in few others, he insisted on the correct decisions, even when they made him unpopular. Throughout his seven years as president, Donald Nesti put the university's students and future before all else. I'm certain that in the future, Duquesne's alumni and friends will recognize the good that his presidency brought to the university."

Saying that he was not autocratic, Dr. Bonachea elicited suggestions from the deans, professors, and students on the Five-Year Academic Plan and initiated an open door policy. He proclaimed a "Year of the Student," and made himself accessible to students by conducting weekly meetings with freshmen and occasionally took his lunches at the Student Union cafeteria and his dinners at Towers Dorm. He coached the fraternity-sorority All-Star softball team and held six campus pizza parties for students. Through a revitalized Student Life Division, he introduced the "Spring Fling." The new acting president met with 16 student groups and the faculty from all the schools.

These actions were seen by many as mere window dressing. The Faculty Senate criticized him for not including the faculty in his decision to merge the positions of vice-president for university relations and vice-president for management and business. He was challenged to admit to the injustices of the firings that had been done under the Nesti administration and to reinstate the dismissed staff. Bonachea refused that challenge. The tumult of previous years did subside, for a time, under his leadership. With a computerized system, he streamlined procedures for registration, transcript requests, and so forth, making life less stressful for students, at least in these areas, and under his administration the Office of Financial Aid monitored a record-breaking $21 million in grants and loans. The Advisement and Counseling Center was revised and improved and relocated in the chapel basement. The Office of International Education brought 50 new foreign students to campus. But a disaster lurked in the near future for the Bonachea administration.

The Middle States Evaluation

It was time for a routine accrediation inspection by the Middle States Association of Colleges and Schools. Aware of the difficulties that the university had been experiencing, Middle States offered to postpone the visit until a new president was seated. Perceiving this as a challenge to his own competence, Acting President Bonachea refused their generous offer. So the Middle States Task Force began the reaccreditation evaluation early in 1987, with a primary emphasis on assessing the university's goals as outlined in its mission statement. Happily, it found evidence of success in realizing those goals. Its initial findings reported a "high degree of satisfaction among alumni" and a high rate of employment among recent graduates. The university prepared its self-study that summer with the final draft ready for review by the end of August.

Then, the unthinkable happened. On February 26, 1988, the Commission wrote to Dr. Bonachea telling him of its decision "to defer reaffirmation of the accreditation" until a permanent president had been selected. The letter asked for a report not later than October 1, 1990, on some problem areas: financial planning, support for the graduate programs, faculty compensation, library resources, and perhaps most serious of all, "development of administrative effectiveness and governance based upon mutual respect and trust." For nearly a month, Dr. Bonachea sat on this letter and then on March 23, 1988, he issued a news release.

Although they understood that accreditation had not been withdrawn, merely delayed, the newspapers could not resist speculating what the ramifications would be if a school were to lose its accreditation: students would risk losing their federal financial aid and might be unable to transfer credits to other institutions. Attempting to control the damage to the university's reputation, Dr. Bonachea publicly announced, "The university is accredited unless the accreditation is taken away," but it was too late; confusion had set in and the public had the idea that Duquesne was in trouble. The timing could scarcely have been worse. High school seniors were making their decisions and sending their deposits to the colleges they had chosen. The real damage was not realized until Dr. Bonachea had departed the Bluff. In the fall of 1988, Duquesne's freshman class was down by 300 students and it would take four long years before that small class was to graduate.[49]

Dr. Bonachea Leaves for Salem

In the spring of 1988, Dr. Bonachea announced his decision to accept a position as president of Salem State College, in Massachusetts. Carl Grefenstette, of the presidential search committee, remarked, "We have received his news with regret because, clearly, Dr. Bonachea has done a remarkable job in his capacity as acting president and certainly he would have been a person the search committee would have taken a closer look at." Many members of the Duquesne community, however, interpreted Grefenstette's words as nothing more than a kind and harmless remark. Bonachea's close association with Nesti would forever hurt his image among a majority of students and faculty. In a parting interview, when asked why he had not distanced himself more from Father Nesti when advised to do so, Dr. Bonachea replied, "Because I, along with members of the board, knew the facts about the decisions he made. Father Nesti was right. In my opinion, he is a man of truth and principle who was determined to protect the welfare of each student."[50]

10. Renaissance on the Bluff

In a bold move—one not without its detractors—the Duquesne University board of directors selected a layman as Duquesne's eleventh president. For 110 years the university had been headed by Spiritans, priests of the Congregation of the Holy Ghost (with the exception of Rolando Bonachea in an acting capacity). But the Duquesne University Bylaws merely stated that a Holy Ghost priest should be given preference, and did not rule out other candidates. In fact, two lay finalists had been selected at the time Father Nesti was chosen. This time the Holy Ghost Provincial, Father Norman Bevan, actually encouraged the search committee not to limit themselves to a priest of the order. According to the *Pittsburgh Press*, alumnus Carl Greffenstette, who chaired the search committee, said that a letter from Bevan

> emphasized that the most qualified person for the job may not be a member of the order. Grefenstette noted the order's primary mission is not teaching, but working with the poor—a fact that reduces the potential number of Holy Ghost fathers with the qualifications to lead their only university in the United States.[1]

The committee had held a series of individual and small group interviews, conducted an open meeting with 200 members of the university community, and collected recommendations from all sources, drawing up a list of 132 candidates, before narrowing the field to four in April 1988. The finalists included one Holy Ghost priest, Rev. Eugene Hillman, director of the graduate program in liberal studies at Salve Regina College in Newport, Rhode Island. Some faculty circulated a petition backing Father Hillman, and it was signed by 105 faculty and staff, including 18 Holy Ghost fathers. The other candidates were Dr. Thomas P. Melady, a 1950 graduate of Duquesne and director of development under Father Gallagher, a former president of Sacred Heart University, and president of an economic research company in Connecticut; Dr. William A. Shields, president of the College of Great Falls, Montana; and—the winner—Dr. John E. Murray, Jr., Distinguished Professor of Law at the University of Pittsburgh.

Duquesne's First Lay President

John Murray's selection, on the first ballot, surprised many, including the man himself. He had never put himself forward as a candidate for the presidency of Duquesne. After his nomination, he had been interviewed once, and he was not even acquainted with Carl Greffenstette. When Chairman Thomas Murrin called to congratulate him on his election, an astounded Murray responded, "I haven't agreed to be president."[2] That he did soon agree was fortunate for Duquesne; John Murray turned out to be an excellent president. Pittsburgh's bishop, the Most Reverend Donald Wuerl, predicted he would, citing "his impressive credentials as a person, a Catholic, a respected educator and a legal scholar."[3] Moreover, the bishop applauded Duquesne's decision as a strong statement on the role of the laity in the Catholic Church.

Born in Philadelphia on December 20, 1932, John E. Murray, Jr. was the only son of a Philadelphia city policeman. Married with four children, Murray was recognized as a University Distinguished Service Professor of Law at the University of Pittsburgh, where, despite a full teaching schedule, he authored eight treatises and books used in law schools throughout the country. *Murray on Contracts* is still regarded as the premiere textbook on the subject. In addition, he served as a legal consultant for several Pittsburgh and Philadelphia firms and major corporations. This phenomenal productivity resulted from a self-proclaimed "workaholic" lifestyle that routinely began a 14-hour workday at 5:00 a.m. John Murray had attended La Salle University, Catholic University of America, and the University of Wisconsin, where he worked his way through law school playing jazz piano. He had begun his teaching career at the Duquesne University School of Law in 1959, and had served as acting dean of the law school during the 1966–1967 school year.

The Murray work-together style was a welcome relief to the Duquesne community. Soon after his appointment in May 1988, he declared "This is not going to be a secret society"; his administration would be an open one.[4] His orientation as a professor instead of an administrator helped break down barriers with faculty. The president of the Faculty Senate jubilantly exclaimed, "Instead of open warfare we're back to normal debate. It's a much, much more open process." A member of the History Department observed that Murray was "a polished, personable man," who "tends to think like a college teacher. He identifies himself as a professor. He talks about what it's like to be in front of a classroom—both the elation and the trepidation."[5] Indeed, he was soon teaching a night course on contracts in the law school, explaining, "I enjoy it immensely." His strong identification as an educator made him think of his teaching as a way "to make me feel like I'm earning my paycheck. I really don't believe I should be paid for being an administrator."[6]

But he was a good administrator. One of Murray's special gifts was for organization. He believed in selecting the right people for the right positions and in empowering them with decision-making capabilities. By the end of Murray's first year as president, the entire atmosphere of the university had changed to one of optimism. Freshmen enrollment had increased 16 percent, research grants were up by $700,000 to a total of $1.7 million, and the capital fund campaign had raised $38 million of its $50 million goal.

One of Murray's top priorities upon taking up the duties of president had been to gain reaccreditation by Middle States before the end of the year. Although accreditation had not been withdrawn during Bonachea's acting presidency, the decision to reaccredit had been postponed until the university had the opportunity to submit a plan regarding areas Middle States described as deficient—including that of administration. Although Middle States did not require this to be submitted until October 1, 1990, the necessary reports were prepared during the summer and Duquesne won its reaccreditation in August of 1988, less than two months after Murray assumed office.

In contrast to Father Nesti's strategic plans, Dr. Murray operated without a definitive five-year—or any-year—plan. Rather than locking the university into a prescribed course, he believed, "Opportunities arise, and we should be in a position to take advantage of them." With this flexible orientation, he considered all proposals on the basis of three criteria: first, whether the opportunity was compatible with and enhanced the university's mission; second, whether it enlarged opportunities for the students; and third, whether Duquesne was in a position intellectually and financially to undertake it.

By the end of Dr. Murray's second year, enrollment had grown to 7500, an increase of a thousand students since he took office, and the capital campaign had exceeded its goal. With characteristic optimism, the president announced that Duquesne was "now poised to become one of the great Catholic universities in the world."[7] And it was. In October 1990, a *U.S. News and World Report* poll ranked Duquesne as the ninth best Catholic university in the nation. Criteria for selection as one of the "best" included average SAT scores (1000), percentage of freshmen in the top quarter of their graduating class (57 percent), acceptance rates, percentage of faculty with doctorates (72 percent), and students to faculty ratios (17:1).

An eloquent speaker and a gifted professor, John Murray expressed a deep love of and commitment to the university. Upon his appointment, he cited the Catholic orientation of the university as a special strength: "At Duquesne it is the Spirit which gives life. That is why so many thousands have come to Duquesne for more than 110 years. That is why I have returned to Duquesne."[8] But he returned as a teacher—a teacher who was also a president—and perhaps this love of teaching is what made him such a good president. In his inaugural speech at the A.J. Palumbo Center on September 17, 1988, he admitted, "While this is certainly a great occasion, I confess it is only the second happiest day of my professional life." The happiest, he said, was the day he began a teaching career at Duquesne's School of Law in 1959.[9]

A Commitment to Moral Growth: "Virtuous" Not Just "Smart" People

Though a layman, Dr. Murray was a devoutly Catholic one, and in keeping with that, he made a commitment to an emphasis on moral values along with academic excellence: "The dominant concern of many American universities in 1988 is a concern for the moral growth of their students after almost a half century of neglect."[10] In an editorial on the failure of the nation's educational system in fostering a love of knowledge and the attitude of a perpetual student, Murray stressed the necessity of education based on absolute moral truths equal to scientific truths:

> We must convince our children, all of our students and ourselves that basic values of truth, honesty, loyalty, friendship, the preservation and enhancement of the family, self-discipline, a constant drive to improve intellectually and morally, and love for each other are the critical ingredients in the complete development of each member of society and, therefore, society itself. . . . As Jefferson said, we not only need smart people; we need virtuous people.[11]

Murray's commitment to moral values as an integral part of a college education was one from which he never wavered and was a topic on which he frequently spoke.

TQP Comes to Duquesne

A major part of Murray's organizing ability was directed at making the university run more smoothly. Largely at the behest of Thomas Murrin, dean of the business school, the concept of total quality performance (TQP)—"doing things right the first time"—was introduced. Murrin had developed the TQP program at Westinghouse Electric Corporation, where he had been vice-president with a strong background in manufacturing. In an unprecedented Saturday morning meeting, the entire faculty was called together to hear a presentation on the concept of TQP, and Duquesne began to reap the benefits of the practices that had revolutionized the business world.

President Murray Deals with Duquesne's Ancient Nemesis

Despite the tireless efforts of the Holy Ghost fathers through the consecrated endowment, a shortage of financial resources had been Duquesne's ancient nemesis, an enemy that must forever be kept at bay. In 1987 the Cyert Report had cited Duquesne's attempt to tackle more than it had the financial strength to accomplish as a major source of difficulty for the university. Its faculty and administration had frequently pushed ahead to initiate new programs on a financial shoestring and with meager compensation. Even after the financial crunch of the Nesti administration had been relieved by successful fundraising efforts of the Murray administration, Duquesne's Periodic Review to the Middle States Association admitted in response to one of their concerns, "We are aware that our endowment is still too small to enable us to meet our admittedly ambitions goals."[12] Much of the difficulty stemmed from the university's inability to tap the financial resources of the business community that in many ways profited from its services. The Holy Ghost fathers had pursued corporate fundraising tentatively. President Murray, as a corporate legal consultant, was quite comfortable in the business world, understood how it worked, and proved highly successful in generating gifts to Duquesne. Before his appointment, he had remarked, "I think there's a reservoir of good will to Duquesne that's capable of supporting the university very effectively. I'm convinced that the business community, the community in general, thinks Duquesne is a great community resource. No one wants to see it fail."[13] In his first two weeks as president, he raised two million dollars! It was only the beginning.

In his last year as president, Father Nesti had launched a major fundraising campaign with a target goal of $25 million, but the university suspended the drive due to the turmoil on campus. Under President Murray, the drive was resumed with a new target figure, $50 million, and a new name: "Spirit of the 90s." It was headed by alumnus Joe DeNardo, WTAE-TV meteorologist.

Large and small, gifts and pledges added up to $51 million by October 1990, fully 20 months before the campaign was supposed to end. Duquesne also made use of funding through the issuance of bonds under the auspices of the Pennsylvania Higher Educational Facilities Authority. As the university's financial posture improved, Duquesne's bonds were rated AAA. At the very time that the MBI insurance evaluators were visiting Duquesne to determine its bond rating, Dr. Murray received a letter confirming a multimillion-dollar gift from John Rangos.

The university kicked off a second major fundraising on April 12, 1995, when Dr. Murray announced a drive titled "Celebration of Excellence—Opportunity of a Lifetime." The campaign, slated to run through 1999, began with over $51 million in advance pledges toward the $100 million goal. In an unprecedented showing of loyalty and support, 98 percent of the Duquesne faculty and 93 percent of the staff pledged $1.36 million in the campus phase of the campaign before public fundraising officially started. In presenting the campus initiative, chaired by Father McAnulty, President Murray remarked on the phenomenal attainments and growth of the university: "We have achieved a unique and accelerating momentum. We have a window of opportunity that will certainly not be repeated during the careers of the faculty and staff who currently work at Duquesne, or, perhaps, at any time during the 21st century."[14]

The university also received more grants, among them: $1.5 million from the Richard King Mellon Foundation in September of 1990 for the Undergraduate Science Initiate Program; $1.5 million from Thomas J. Murrin, previous chairman of the university's board of directors, and his wife to establish Duquesne's first endowed chair—in Global Competitiveness—to be part of the School of Business Administration; $400,000 from Alcoa Foundation to begin a new computer lab in the Math Department, to develop an applied statistics program at the business school, and to purchase library materials for the law school; and $500,000 in grants from the Vira I. Heinz Endowment for programs in performance, composition, community outreach and music technology. In April 1994, John E. Connelly, who had already made a sizable contribution for the establishment of the School of Business Administration's Center for Entrepreneurship and Emerging Enterprise, announced a gift of $11 million, one of the largest donations by a single individual to a Catholic university. By the summer of 1995 President Murray had increased Duquesne's endowment to $42 million.

Scholarships and Financial Aid Increase

The additional revenue made it possible for Dr. Murray to announce in December 1988 that Duquesne would more than double the amount of financial aid to be awarded annually from $600,000 to $1.3 million, a figure that would eventually reach $17.5 million in 1995. As a response to Duquesne's historic mission to educate the poor and disadvantaged, a mission that had lapsed as tuition costs spiraled, one of the first student-aid funds to be increased was the Spiritan grants for minority students. Expanding in number from 10 awards to 25 and in value from $1,000 to $5,000 in 1989, Spiritan grants, awarded on the basis of academic merit and financial need, went to students from 11 states. The 1989 awardees were 71 percent African American, 15 percent Asian, and 11 percent Hispanic. "It is a matter of justice, rendering to each his due. Duquesne stands for this," said Dr. Murray, adding that the financial aid offered to disadvantaged students was "not yet enough."[15] By 1993 Spiritan Scholarships numbered 100.

Four new scholarship programs were created: ten full-scholarship Chancellor Awards, 100 Founders Awards of $5,000 each, 100 President's Scholarships of $3,000 each, and 50 Incentive Grants of $1,000 each. Further gifts and endowments brought even more in financial aid: Duquesne Light Company contributed $500,000 to the Henry J. McAnulty Scholarship Fund, in commemoration of the fifthieth anniversary of his ordination in October of 1990. President Murray and his wife created a scholarship fund for students whose circumstances caused them to fall just outside the qualification guidelines for other scholarships. It was established in memory of Dr. Murray's parents in September 1991. Marie W. Barry donated $100,000 to establish scholarship funds in the Schools of Pharmacy and Music in her name and that of her late husband Richard in October 1991.

Along with the scholarships and loans, students could also partially support their studies through 450 work-study positions on campus awarded on the basis of need. By the fall of 1994, however, the need had far outstripped the demand with 510 new work-study students cleared to compete for 225 openings. At that time, the entire program at Duquesne encompassed 1341 students who had been given work-study awards, but only 537 positions for which the students could interview. Work-study was federally funded at 75 percent, but, in order to provide more positions, Duquesne expanded its program until its share was almost 50 percent.

A Flat-Rate Tuition

Tuition for the 1990–1991 academic year, for a standard 15-credit load, was $8,850, an increase of 10.1 percent over the previous year. Room and board increased from $3,927 to $4,318, an increase of 10 percent for a double-occupancy room. Despite its price tag, Duquesne was rated by Barron's as one of the 300 best buys in college education in 1990.

In January of 1993, however, a faculty advisory committee discussed the possibility of a flat-rate tuition for students carrying 12 to 18 credits. Few schools were charging by the credit. The flat-rate tuition for full-time undergraduate students, with one fee consolidating the numerous additional fees paid by the students including activities, health, and orientation fees, became a reality in the fall of 1993. A tuition fee of $10,578 was charged for students enrolled in the College of Arts and Sciences, the School of Business and Administration, the School of Education, and the Nursing School. Students enrolled in the Schools of Pharmacy, Health Sciences, and Music paid a higher fee due to the special requirements of those programs. In a plan reminiscent of Duquesne's prepaid tuition of 1985, CollegeSure CDs, certificates of deposit that, when paid in full, could provide a child with the average cost of a college education, became available through credit unions, financial brokers, and various educational institutions, including Duquesne where the CDs were offered to alumni beginning in 1989.

Enrollment Rises and so do Ratings

By the fall of 1994, enrollment had reached 9000 students, the highest in the history of Duquesne University. In the years from 1988 to 1992 Duquesne's enrollment increased 29.5 percent while the growth rate for all private colleges and universities in Pennsylvania was only 6.1 percent. Why this dramatic rise in enrollments? Positive publicity about the university, active recruiting efforts, strong orientation programs to strengthen retention among freshmen, and even a novel program sponsored by the Residence Hall Association and SHARP to bring younger brothers and sisters to campus for a special Sibling Weekend all helped. The university also employed its mission ties to bring more international students to Duquesne. Recruiting trips to Canada, Latin America, and Asia resulted in an additional 97 new foreign students in 1989, bringing the total international enrollment to 292 from 72 foreign countries. Duquesne published its first issues of *World View* that year, a three-page newsletter put out by the Office of International Education. By the fall of 1991, Duquesne had 355 full-time and 78 part-time international students on campus, a total of 433, the highest international enrollment among all Pennsylvania Catholic colleges and universities.

In 1992 Duquesne reported that eight percent of its total enrollment consisted of minority students. The admissions office actively sought minority students as a participant in the South Eastern Regional Office—National Scholarship for Negro Students (SERO-NSFNS). As a member institution, Duquesne sent admissions officers to target cities with large minority populations. Minority enrollment in the fall of 1994 totaled 620 students including African Americans, Asians, Hispanics, and Native Americans.

The proportion of women to men in the student body had been increasing since the mid-1970s. In 1980 women comprised almost 52 percent of the student body. This figure continued to rise, and by 1994 women students comprised nearly 57 percent of the undergraduate enrollment.

Duquesne's increase in the size of its student body was not achieved by relaxing its admission standards. Incoming freshmen classes consistently demonstrated higher achievement levels in SAT scores. In the first six years of the Murray administration, the proportion of new students in the top fifth of their graduating classes had increased from 40 to 48 percent. The greatest percentage of growth occurred at the graduate level as a result of expanded program offerings. These changes were reflected in Duquesne's ratings in various college reports. *U.S. News and World Report* revised Duquesne's selectivity rating to "more selective" in comparing the years of 1990–1994. Their rating was based on several indicators: average SAT scores, freshmen who had been in the top tenth of their graduating class, and acceptance rate. Although Duquesne's acceptance rate was high, its increased reputation had resulted in fewer unqualified candidates applying.

Other significant advances cited by *U.S. News and World Report* included an increase in faculty members possessing doctorate credentials, from 71 percent in 1990 to 93 percent in 1994; student/teacher ratios that improved from 17 to 1 to 13 to 1; and a graduation rate that increased from 67 percent in 1990 to 72 percent in 1994. In 1996, that same periodical raised Duquesne's overall ranking to fall within the second tier of national universities. *Lovejoy's Guide to Four Year Colleges* cited Duquesne's increased variety of majors and strong accreditation, while *Peterson's* listed increased scholarship offerings as Duquesne's strength. The *Comparative Guide to American Colleges* in 1994 described Duquesne as having a "student body characterized by administrations equally concerned with professional/occupational goals and scholarly/intellectual interests."

Faculty Research and Teaching

Realizing that the greatest strength of any university lies in its faculty, President Murray made faculty salaries the highest priority in the university's financial plans. Within the first six years of his administration, salaries rose an average of 62 percent. The increased remuneration helped boost morale and draw talented educators to campus. From 1988 to 1993, Duquesne hired 162 faculty members, 40 to fill newly created program positions. Nearly all of these individuals possessed the highest degree in their fields.

Faculty evaluation and promotion procedures became better defined, including student evaluations of teaching and peer reviews, plus the establishment of a center for teaching excellence to assist faculty. As compensation and research incentives increased, so did the number of publications and presentations of scholarly papers by the faculty. Father Nesti's conflicts with the faculty over the respective values of teaching and research were still fresh in everyone's minds when Dr. Murray assumed office. Although convinced that research prevented a school from stagnating intellectually, the new president—always a teacher at heart—was also unwilling to sacrifice instruction for the sake of research. This basic commitment to education remains as one of Duquesne's greatest strengths.

This is not to say that research was neglected. Along with providing increased salary scales and larger blocks of available time for such pursuits, the Murray administration encouraged and rewarded outstanding achievement in research. Faculty development grants were available for this purpose, and for rewarding excellence in teaching, from the Noble J. Dick Educational Foundation, the Hunkele Foundation, and the Westinghouse Foundation, as well as from governmental and corporate sources. Moreover, to free the faculty to pursue research work, the administration reduced the number of years needed to be awarded a sabbatical leave from seven to six. Sponsored research at Duquesne experienced phenomenal growth, from $250,000 in the 1990 fiscal year to $1.7 million in the 1993 fiscal year, an unprecedented 580 percent. The vast bulk of the new funding went for research projects in the sciences.

The Academic Council approved the awarding of the title Distinguished University Professor to members of the faculty "who have brought special honor and recognition to their profession and to the university," in the 1989–1990 academic year. By unanimous vote of the Academic Council, the title was bestowed on Dr. Albert C. Labriola, Professor of English.

Student evaluations of faculty teaching effectiveness were consistently high through all the undergraduate and graduate schools and departments. Ratings for core curriculum courses were on a par with courses in major subjects.

Under the directorship of Dr. Dorothy Frayer, the Center for Teaching Excellence embarked on numerous ventures to improve even further the quality of instruction at Duquesne. Workshops to orient and prepare new faculty, adjunct faculty, and teaching assistants were followed by a series of luncheon seminars for new faculty covering such topics as teaching, academic support services, grants, developing a scholarly writing program, and documenting accomplishments for promotion and tenure. The center also conducted numerous workshops on such topics as improved teaching of the core curriculum, use of interactive media, student performance assessment, teaching for critical thinking, using computer networks, teaching learning-disabled students, and cooperative learning.

The Cooperative Learning Project was launched in the 1992–1993 school year, funded by an Institutional Incentive Grant from the Pennsylvania System of Higher Education and the Pew Charitable Trust. With educational research supporting the benefits of cooperative learning through peer instruction and student learning teams and its applicability to all disciplines, Duquesne launched a program of workshops to introduce the approach, faculty surveys to assess use of cooperative learning strategies, and study groups to explore applications in different fields.

Advisement

The Advisement and Counseling Center underwent many revisions, including, in 1994, a name change to Comprehensive Student Advisement. Each student was assigned a single faculty advisor, or mentor, to oversee his or her entire career at the university.

Beginning in the summer of 1994, the scourge of registration lines ended for Duquesne students with the on-line registration system. Instead of participating in a designated "pre" and "final" registration period, students could meet with an advisor, plan a schedule of classes, and have it immediately processed in one step, with the computer system compiling the roster for each class. A new student brochure, "I've Been Accepted . . . Now What?" was commended by the National Association of Academic Advisors as one of the six best in the nation.

The new supplemental learning program gave the departmental chairs the responsibility of setting up tutoring for students encountering difficulty. The five departments with the highest request rates for tutors—English, Math, Biology, Chemistry, and Physics—were given additional funding for supplemental instruction sessions.

The office of the Academic Supervisor for Intercollegiate Athletics (ASIA) had been started by sociology professor Michael Kupersanin in the early 1980s to oversee the academic needs of athletes. It continued to do this in the 1990s. Health Services was returned to the division of Student Life from Academic Affairs, reversing Father Nesti's unpopular move of 1987. The Career Services Center provided career advisements, credential service, a job hotline, government position listings, surveys of graduates, internships, job fairs and referrals, job search seminars, on-campus interviews, part time off-campus job listings, and a resource library.

A 1991–1992 survey, based on a 70 percent response, revealed that over 80 percent of Duquesne graduates found career employment, 14 percent went on for additional education, and 5 percent were still searching a year after graduation. In February 1995, Comprehensive Student Services initiated the SPACE (Seek Professional Advice on Careers and Education) program with a three-day fair in the Student Union ballroom.

Graduate Programs

The number of graduate students enrolled at Duquesne greatly increased following Murray's appointment, from 614 in the fall of 1989 to 808 in the fall of 1992. Graduation rates from post-baccalaureate programs for the corresponding spring terms rose by 49 percent, an indication of the efficiency of the programs. Financial aid available to graduate students increased, too, especially in biological sciences, chemistry, English, the newly established Social and Public Policy Center, and the master of arts in liberal studies.

New initiatives in graduate programs included degrees in Canon Law and Church Administration on a cooperative basis involving the graduate school, the law school, and the Catholic University of Leuven (Belgium). The document setting forth the parameters and basic requirements of a graduate canon law program was signed in Belgium by a delegation from Duquesne in June 1993. Students in the program studied for two semesters in Belgium and two semesters at Duquesne. It was only the third such program in North America.

The master of liberal studies (MLS) program

was reorganized and upgraded as a master of arts in liberal studies in 1994. Students also had the option of pursuing a combined Master of Arts in Liberal Studies (MALS) and Master of Business Administration (MBA).

A certificate program begun in 1992 in medical care ethics grew into a master of arts in health care ethics in 1993. The program received partial support from St. Francis Hospital.

The two-year program leading to a master of science in environmental science and management, inaugurated in 1992, provided instruction in environmental science, communication, conflict resolution, and national and international environmental public policy. Students were required to serve an internship in industry and regulatory agencies. Input from the state director of environmental resources and a corporate advisory board helped shape the program. With virtually no newspaper or television coverage, the university nonetheless received 200 inquiries concerning the new Environmental Science and Management program requiring a bachelor of science degree in biology, chemistry, physics, or engineering. Within its first two years, it managed to win a finalist position for the Three Rivers Environmental Awards.

A program developed jointly by sociology and political science professors led to the Graduate Center for Social and Public Policy in 1988, emphasizing the ethical dimension in the public policy process. The center, the first of its kind in this part of the country, focused on policy formulation and decision-making in response to local, regional, and national concerns.

Reflecting the role of chemistry in solving crimes by performing drug analyses, measuring blood alcohol levels, and informing the public about potentially dangerous chemicals, in 1989 the Department of Chemistry drew up a proposal for a master of science degree in forensic chemistry as a two-year program including an internship.

The fall of 1995 was set as the starting date for a new university-wide degree, a master of science in multimedia technology. The program emphasized practical applications in a variety of concentrations: education, communications, health care, and art. Along with instruction and technical experience in photography uses, graphical design, videography, sound, instructional design, and animation, the program also included an opportunity to continue work developing multimedia materials at Duquesne following completion of the degree.

A College of Arts and a School of Sciences

In 1938 the College of Liberal Arts and the College of Science had been merged into a single school called the College of Arts and Sciences. That arrangement would last for 56 years. In an effort to enhance the visibility of the science program at Duquesne, the Biology, Chemistry, and Physics Departments were separated from the college in August 1994. They were set up as the Bayer School of Natural and Environmental Sciences. Dr. Heinz W. Machatzke, who had come to Duquesne from the vice-presidency of Mobay Corporation as industrial science advisor and adjunct professor in 1989, was appointed dean. At the same time, the Environmental Science and Management graduate program was transferred to the new school. This program did not have its own faculty, but used faculty from other departments and schools, including law and business. By 1994 the environmental science program had enrolled some 110 students.

The setting up of a separate school occasioned some discussion among the faculty concerning the necessity for such a change. Most of the objection came from the liberal arts faculty, who saw the move as a dilution of the central role played by the college. A single dean, Dr. John J. McDonald, had assumed the administration of the College and Graduate School of Liberal Arts and Sciences on July 1, 1990, and the new position of associate dean was created in

January 1994. When McDonald resigned the deanship in 1994, it was filled on an interim basis by Dr. Constance Ramirez, who was then appointed dean of the newly named McAnulty College and Graduate School of Liberal Arts in the summer of 1995. Ramirez was the first woman dean of the college.

Departments in the College

During the Murray years, there were many developments in College departments:

• The Classics Department, host of a symposium titled "New Directions in Classical Archaelogy" in 1991, received a rich resource of 300 to 400 volumes on Greek and Latin from the late Reverend John P. Gallagher, C.S.Sp.

• The Communications Department instituted a pre-graduation review to help students meet graduation requirements. Also, in 1992 the department's Dr. Harper was elected president of the international Association for Communications Administration (ACA). In 1994 Des Places was renovated and Duquesne helped with financial support and assistance in planning the National Communication Ethics Conference in Michigan.

• The English Department's Distinguished University Professor, Dr. Albert Labriola, conducted his Milton seminars for high school teachers at Duquesne in the summers of 1990, 1992, 1993 and 1995, through National Endowment for the Humanities funding. Funded again for the summer of 1997, Dr. Labriola's was one of only 23 seminars nationwide to be so honored by the NEH. Another professor of English, Dr. Samuel Hazo, was formally installed as the state poet, the first poet laureate in the history of Pennsylvania, in 1993.

• In collaboration with the Department of Modern Languages and Literature, the English Department continued to host the annual Western Pennsylvania Symposium on World Literature each spring. And the department also brought the glories of literature to high school students through the English Festival at Duquesne in conjunction with the Western Pennsylvania Council of Teachers of English. In the spring of 1995, the third annual event, and the only such festival in the Commonwealth, 1200 high school students from 70 school districts in the Tri-State Area attended.

• The Department of Modern Languages and Literature initiated the study of Japanese in the 1990–1991 academic year. The department also coordinated study abroad programs in Italy, Germany, Spain, and France.

• The History Department continued to host its fall History Forum on subjects such as the family, urban history, the collapse of the Soviet bloc, and Catholicism in Pittsburgh. In the 1992–1993 academic year, the department received two grants: one from Allegheny County to inventory and evaluate the artifacts at Soldiers and Sailors Memorial in Oakland, and another from the Annenberg Foundation to conduct a month-long seminar entitled, "Discovering America: The Peopling of Pennsylvania."

• The graduate history program was greatly aided when the provost appointed a trained professional, Paul Demilio, to oversee the university archives in 1993.

• In 1995 the history department broadened its art history program by beginning a studio arts program as a history concentration. The arrangement of essentially fine arts classes being offered through the Department of History was not unusual, but Duquesne's art studio program was designed not to prepare students for a career in studio arts, but to complement the art history major with an understanding of artistic processes and to satisfy an interest in art production from the general student body. Because of this mission, admission to the program was by "self selection" rather than portfolio assessment. The interdisciplinary program was to operate on two tracks: the traditional fine arts track, and the more commercial track of illustration and computer imaging.

• In order to increase awareness of Duquesne's programs in mathematics and computer science, the department hosted the high school math supremacy competitions sponsored by the Mathematics Council of Western Pennsylvania beginning in 1989. The department completely renovated its fourth-floor College Hall quarters with the latest in computer designs, dedicated September 1992 as the Alcoa Mathematics and Computer Science Center.

• The Department of Philosophy hosted the 28th annual meeting of the Society for Phenomenology and Existential Philosophy in 1989, commemorating the birth centenary of Martin Heidegger.

• After the Psychology Center building was razed, the department moved to College Hall, and later to Rockwell Hall. The department continued to offer phenomenologically oriented therapy and community outreach services.

• Before the collapse of the Soviet Union, the Political Science Department served as the contact agency for U.S. institutions, corporations, and research institutes interested in joint projects with the Soviet Union.

• Duquesne's dean of the College and Graduate School of Liberal Arts and Sciences officiated at the graduation ceremony for master's degree candidates of the Spiritan International School of Theology in Enugu, Nigeria, in May 1993. This outreach to Africa, stemming from the Holy Ghost Fathers' mission work and Duquesne's international mission, was probably instrumental in Duquesne's hosting of the African Church as Peacemaker Colloquium in October 1994. Although the representative from Rwanda was unable to attend, African bishops from Mozambique, Sudan, Benin, Burundi, Angola, Liberia, Nigeria, Eritrea, South Africa, and Zimbabwe shared their stories of tragedies and discussed strategies for conflict resolution among the peoples of Africa. The university offered a special gift to each bishop—a full-tuition scholarship, to be bestowed on one of their citizens, for graduate studies at Duquesne toward a master of arts degree in conflict resolution and peace.

• The director of the pastoral ministry program, Reverend Patrick Malloy, announced new master's degrees in campus ministry, social ministry, and parish ministry for the fall of 1995.

• The bishop of the Diocese of Pittsburgh, The Most Reverend Donald Wuerl, became a University Distinguished Service Professor in the fall of 1990.

The Sciences

The Biology Department offered a new major in microbiology in the fall of 1989 and in following years received significant grants from the National Institutes of Health. Since there was only a five percent acceptance rate on initial projects funded by NIH grants, Duquesne was honored to be a grant recipient. The Biology Department also received special recognition as an accomplished and qualified program when the National Science Foundation funded its Summer Undergraduate Research Program in 1994.

The Chemistry Department's chapter of the American Chemical Society Student Affiliates was recognized as an outstanding one in 1989, 1990, and 1993. Research at Duquesne included the Air Force Office of Scientific Research project on oxidation of fuels, robotics education and research through use of a Hewlett Packard Company Optimized Robot for Chemical Analysis (ORCA), microwave chemistry, and the use of the Inductively Coupled Plasma-Mass Spectrometer.

The Kresge Foundation and R.K. Mellon Foundation provided funds for x-ray diffraction apparatus for the Physics Department for the study of crystal structures. The Physics Department worked on replacing old equipment with state-of-the-art apparatus and implementing curriculum suggestions from an outside collegiate investigative report.

The new Bayer School of Natural and Environmental Sciences containing biological sciences, chemistry and biochemistry, physics, and the Center for Environmental Science and Management, formed in 1994, offered a wide array of degree programs, as well as certificates in environmental science and environmental studies.

When the Human Resources Building (the old Science Hall erected by Father Hehir in 1916) at the corner of Colbert and Vickroy Streets (McAnulty Drive and Academic Walk) and the Psychological Counseling Center next to it (purchased in 1928 for use as the library) were declared unsafe and beyond repair, the way was clear for an entirely new building. They were demolished in January 1994. That same year work began on a new science hall. Costs were estimated at $7.8 million for the red brick structure. Opened in time for the 1996 spring semester, the three-story building essentially completed the "old" campus. It was even designed to complement Old Main and Canevin hall. In the spring of 1995 Bayer Corporation endowed the new school with $2 million to be matched by the university. In return, Duquesne University named the building the Bayer Learning Center. Since 1989, when Dr. Murray had announced the university's new science initiative that "would respond to the national need for critical research and bridge academics and industry for the improvement of science education," the sciences had experienced phenomenal growth. From 1989 to 1995, undergraduate enrollment had increased 200 percent, graduate enrollment had increased 250 percent, faculty had increased 75 percent, and $8 million in new grants for the sciences had come to the university. The amount of research conducted on campus led the university to expand even further.

Advances in the Business School

The School of Business Administration had begun a 56-credit program leading to a master of science in information systems, accredited by the American Assembly of Collegiate Schools of Business, in 1988. A restructuring of its programs in 1995 enabled students to compress work for the bachelor of business administration and the master of business administration into five years. The School also initiated several cross-discipline dual masters' programs.

In a move reminiscent of classes in the university's old downtown location in the Fitzsimons Building, Duquesne's School of Business's Continuing Education had moved downtown again in 1984 to offer certificate programs in accounting and financial analysis at the U.S. Steel Building and Mellon Bank Building. In 1989 the business school began offering a master's of business administration at USX's Mon Valley Steel Works as part of Duquesne's service to the community.

A $1.5 million gift from Thomas and Marie Murrin in 1990 gave the university its first endowed chair, a School of Business Administration position in global competitiveness. Following the sudden death of Glen Beeson, Thomas Murrin was the unanimous choice of the search committee as dean of the Business School in December of 1990.

In 1993, Murrin announced the development of the university's Executive Faculty, an elite group of more than 50 leading business, government, and labor executives who would teach classes in the School of Business under the course professor. This body grew from the School of Business Administration's Advisory Boards of local business executives in accounting, human resources management, law administration, management, management information systems, international business, marketing, and real estate.

Globalization and TQM

Duquesne's business school was well aware of the development of the global marketplace, as evidenced by the following:

- A cooperative agreement with the Euro-Schulen-Organisation (ESO), a consortium of 23 private West German universities, in 1990 made it possible for ESO German graduates to enroll in Duquesne's MBA program, for Duquesne to participate in faculty exchanges, and for Duquesne graduates and undergraduates of the business school to study at ESO institutions in Germany.

• An exchange agreement signed in the fall of 1991 sent 20 Duquesne business students to the Universidad de Alicante in Spain while English teachers from Spain came to Pittsburgh to gain fluency.

• Nineteen faculty members of the School and four businessmen spent two weeks in Japan in 1993 to study Japanese business and culture in another international venture. In the spring of 1994 seventeen students from the Estonian-American Business College in Tallin, Estonia, visited the campus for a four-week English and business-related program.

• A student-exchange program was finalized with the Institut Commercial de Nancy in Nancy, France, with two French students attending Duquesne in January of 1994.

• An alliance also permitted Duquesne business students to study at Budapest University of Economic Sciences in Hungary.

• An agreement signed in the spring of 1995 with Bayer AG Miles, Inc., a wholly owned subsidiary of Bayer, allowed three or four students in Business and Science to participate in internship studies in Germany for up to three months. Forty Pakistani students were accepted for work towards an MBA in the fall of 1995 following the signing of an agreement with the National College of Business Administration and Economics in Lahore, Pakistan, the previous October.

Antonio J. Palumbo made another generous gift of $1.5 million in the fall of 1991 for renovations to Rockwell Hall. Digital VAX computers were donated by Ketchum Communications and Digital Equipment Corporation. As a result, Duquesne was able to fully implement President Murray's total quality management (TQM) vision. A mini-course on the concept was offered to faculty and an accredited graduate school in TQM was established. Duquesne was partnered with Westinghouse Corporation through the Quality Forum in the 1993 business education program.

A revised undergraduate core curriculum in the school in the fall of 1993 brought four new courses: Global Business Perspectives, Operations Management/TQM, Communication Ethics, and Comprehensive Case Study. In keeping with a global economic view, students also had to meet a new foreign language requirement. A revised curriculum for the graduate program was implemented in the fall of 1994 on four major themes: globalization, ethics, technology management, and, of course, TQM.

Service to Community Businesses

Duquesne's business school was on the cutting edge of business techniques and philosophies. And the community benefited. A $420,000 grant from the owner of the Gateway Clipper Fleet in 1993 led to the creation of the John E. Connelly Center for Entrepreneurship and Emerging Enterprise to offer education and training services for new and existing area businesses. In its first year, it announced plans to establish a supplier-training center through a national consortium and to help business owners and executives partici-pate in an eight-day instructional program in Tokyo. The Connelly Center also agreed to serve as the temporary, and possibly permanent, home for a corporation of industrialists from the Tri-State area who hoped to make the region into a High Performance Manufacturing Zone by organizing meetings with labor union members, school board members, bankers and regulators in their attempts to draw new, competitive industries.

In conjunction with the School of Education and industry professionals, the School of Business Administration organized Duquesne's Leadership Institute in 1993. In 1995 the institute made plans to host 16 CEOs and COOs (Chief Operation Officers) from Egypt for four weeks for instruction in crisis management, GATT, privatization, human resource development, organizational change, international finance, government reorganization, and creating a stock exchange.

The business school continued to serve as a valuable community resource through its Small Business Development Center, which prepared and presented programs in several communities and held an annual Home-based Business Conference beginning in 1988. Through BIAS, Business Intelligence Access System, made operational in the fall of 1994, business owners could access information from all over the world. The Center for Leadership in Ethics sponsored both roundtable discussions and distinguished speakers.

African-American Business Goals

In an attempt to increase the pool of qualified African Americans in the business world, Duquesne's School of Business Administration provided financial assistance, student support services, transfer services, career planning and placement, an academic advisor, a peer mentor, and two scholarships for any African-American student with a 3.2 or better GPA. The university also began the Black Accounting Scholars program to identify qualified high school candidates, provide financial assistance through scholarships and internships, and assist academically with mentoring, a learning skills center, and workshops.

Revisions in the Law School

In 1989, applicants to the law school had increased 25 percent over the previous year with only one in 12 being accepted. At the other end of the program, 93 percent of graduates passed the Pennsylvania Bar Exams on the first attempt and 92 percent were able to find positions within six months of graduation. So the law school was doing well, but it decided it could do better, and it revised the curriculum to include more flexibility. Seventeen new courses were added as the school developed a specialization in trial tactics. A $50,000 grant from McCardle Foundation enabled it to design a courtroom with jury room and judge's chambers. Although appellate cases without a jury had been heard on the Bluff, the law school hoped to encourage the use of its facility for criminal jury trials from the Allegheny County courts so that students would have more opportunity to observe cases being argued.

Dean John J. Sciullo worked out an exchange program with the China University of Political Science and Law in 1991. Under this agreement, two Chinese professors visited Duquesne in the spring of 1993 to make presentations to law students and local firms. In return, Duquesne organized a week-long workshop for American attorneys in Beijing in April of 1994. In 1993, Dr. Sciullo returned to teaching as the deanship passed to Nicholas P. Cafardi, university vice-president and general counsel. The American Bar Association granted approval for the law school to open a summer school at the China University of Political Science and Law in Beijing for June of 1995 to be taught by faculty from both schools. According to Dean Cafardi, "This reflects the university's vision of the legal future which is that legal practice will increasingly become more international, especially in commercial law." Actual faculty exchanges with the Judicial School of the Republic of Costa Rica were slated to begin in the fall of 1994 following the signing of an agreement with that school the previous summer. And in 1995 the law school signed an agreement with Moscow State University to exchange faculty and library resources. The school's Continuing Legal Education conference for American lawyers was scheduled for Ireland in June of 1995 through a collaboration with the law school of University College in Dublin.

In 1993 the Sarah Mellon Scaife Foundation established an endowed chair in law and economics with an annual grant of $150,000. This gift served as the impetus for the establishment of the Duquesne Institute of Law and Economics. Then the Pennsylvania Supreme Court decreed new legislation requiring registered lawyers in the state to participate in ethics and professional conduct courses, and Duquesne responded with its first Continuing Legal Education Ethics program in March 1993.

Duquesne's law school received a HUD grant to provide legal services to the Pittsburgh communities of East Liberty and the Hill District. Training of eight law students and community legal professionals for the services began in February 1995.

The premier moot court competition in the region, the Gorley Cup, was won by the Duquesne School of Law team six out of eight times. The school also participated successfully in the Corporate Law Competition at Widener University.

The School of Education Grows

Reaccreditation of the School of Education by the Pennsylvania Department of Education was secured in November 1990. Duquesne's Counselor Education program received national accreditation from the Council for the Accreditation of Counseling and Related Education Programs in the 1992–1993 academic year, after being cited as the outstanding program in the Commonwealth for 1989 by the Pennsylvania Counselors Association. Rapid growth in enrollments brought the total in the School of Education to 400 undergraduates and 756 graduate students in the spring of 1990. By the time it celebrated its 65th anniversary on April 21, 1995, the school could boast of more than 12,000 graduates.

A "Teacher of the Year"

The director of student teaching and associate dean of undergraduate education, Dr. Kenneth Burrett, was selected "Teacher-Educator of the Year" by the Pennsylvania Association of Colleges and Teacher Educators. Designer of a number of innovative programs in the school, he was particularly proud of the Professional Employment Program that placed math and science teachers in summer business and industry jobs where they gained experience in the practical applications of their fields, and in a program enabling college graduates to gain methodology and student-teaching work in a one-year program leading to certification.

International Initiatives

- A grant allowed the school to send a group of educators to Hungary in cooperation with four other area universities, in the summer of 1990 and again in 1991.
- In a unique pilot program, seven students from Duquesne participated in student-teaching in West Sussex, England, in the fall of 1990, where three of the seven were offered positions in English schools. A group of undergraduates returned to that institution in May 1991 to examine differences in American and English methods of teaching reading and mathematics.
- Student-teaching placements at the Holy Ghost colleges of Blackrock and Rockwell, Ireland were initiated.
- Duquesne's School of Education faculty joined the U.S.-Soviet Global Thinking Project as Advisory Committee members in the Pittsburgh Schenley High School and Leningrad School 239 link in 1991.

IDPEL

Duquesne's Interdisciplinary Doctoral Program for Educational Leaders (IDPEL), a very flexible program for school superintendents, principals, supervisors, teachers, psychologists, and professors, was the only program in the country to meet the American Association of School Administrator's Professional Standards for the Superintendency when they were published in 1994.

Since the learning team consisted of professionals with heavy time demands, the program supplemented the number of actual meetings with sharing of ideas through electronic mail (e-mail). Several universities were already creating programs based on the Duquesne model when it was only halfway through its first cohort of 36. Although 70 individuals had expressed interest in the program while it still had a year and a half to go, the School of Education decided to begin a new cohort every three years so as to allow sufficient time for staffing of dissertation committees and ensure the quality of the program.

New Equipment and Facilities

In February 1992 President Murray dedicated the School of Education's new computer facility, one of 22 fully equipped student computer labs on campus. The School of Education also opened a new multimedia lab in Canevin in October 1994. And when an anonymous benefactor endowed the university with $600,000 for various multimedia facilities throughout campus, the School of Education won the privilege of having the first. Truly innovative in arrangement, the center had eight banks of tables, tethered at one end by the computer connections, that could be swiveled around to form classroom, learning pod, or computer bank arrangements. Instructors could use a ceiling-mounted projection unit to display data from individual computer screens, footage from video, cable TV, and satellite downlink, or even his or her own notes written on a six-by-eight-foot screen.

Project Genesis and Kidlink

The school had provided computer literacy coursework in the city's Wilkinsburg schools and had conducted a middle school-high school summer computer camp in 1991 and 1992. Now it made plans for the implementation of a computer network, Project Genesis, using the equipment donated by Digital Equipment Corporation and Ketchum Communications, Inc. for humanitarian purposes: serving as a free communication link for area educators. Students of ages 10 to 14 could participate through Duquesne as the service provider in Kidlink, where children all over the world could enter into thematic discussions and academic projects. Duquesne's assistance enabled teams of mathematics teachers in nine area school districts to gain access to the Internet and receive assistance in computing technology.

Helping the Mentally and Physically Challenged

The School of Education worked with the Autism Society of Pittsburgh and the Allegheny Intermediate Unit-Exceptional Children's program to sponsor a summer Autism Symposium on campus in 1989. A gift of the Danny Cope Collection on Autism and the NFL Charities Research Collection on Autism made Duquesne's School of Education the repository of the most comprehensive collection of books and writings on the subject in the country. Moreover, Duquesne's student chapter of the Council for Exceptional Children received national recognition for its work with mentally retarded adults from the Catholic organization, The National Apostolate with People with Mental Retardation.

Supporting Family and Community Values

In connection with the Pennsylvania State Middle School Association, the School of Education's Center for Character Education, Civic Responsibility and Teaching created an action plan for school districts and communities for education in family and community values. The school did extensive work throughout the 1994–1995 school year with program design and implementation for middle school students.

The School of Music also Grows

The School of Music experienced great growth, with the graduate program averaging 115 students per semester and the overall enrollment reaching 350 in the 1990–1991 academic year. The School also reported an increasing caliber of incoming students. That year's freshman class entered with the second highest average SAT scores in the university and with 40 percent of the students from the top ten percent of their high school graduating classes.

Distinguished musicians made appearances on campus, including Morton Gould, American composer; Lorin Maazel, musical director of the Pittsburgh Symphony; Witold Lutoslawski, Poland's renowned composer/conductor; and operatic soprano Martina Arroyo. A Steinway concert grand piano, a gift to the music school, was unveiled and dedicated on February 11, 1990, with a performance that included members of the school's faculty and the university president himself, Dr. Murray, at the keyboard.

The university also served as home for the Pittsburgh Opera Center, which expanded its summer training program into a nine-month curriculum with master classes presented by opera greats. A gift of $100,000 from the Christian A. Johnson Endeavor Foundation helped start the Duquesne University Opera Center. In 1995, that organization awarded Duquesne one of the largest foundation grants for an arts program, $1 million over four years, for the Legends of Opera series.

Duquesne joined the technological revolution in the field of music with a revolutionary new program, Emphasis on Music Recording Technology, featuring state-of-the-art digital sound processing equipment and computer hardware and software, gifts of the Women's Guild of Duquesne University and a number of contributing electronic and computer firms. A 1991 grant from the Vira I. Heinz Foundation funded renovations to the Recital Hall. An additional grant from the foundation in May 1992 was designated for performance and composition program development, community outreach, and music technology. In its efforts to establish itself as a contemporary music leader, the School of Music founded the new Contemporary Music Ensemble, expanded the summer composers' conference, and planned a new international music festival.

The School of Music also began several outreach programs at the City Music Center for non-degree students of all ages, including conservatory-type classes for pre-college students. Classes in Suzuki string instruction, jazz, and music technology, were targeted for groups ranging from pre-schoolers to high school students. For adult learners, there were lessons in jazz and sacred music certification for church organists. Duquesne also allied with the Ozanam Cultural Center in the city's Hill District to provide piano and string instrument instruction to inner-city youths.

The Vera I. Heinz Foundation gave a three-year endowment grant to the City Music Center of $33,000 for financial aid to the center's disadvantaged students in the spring of 1995. That year the school moved into its third decade as hosts of the Mid-East Music Festival. Duquesne had a long-established reputation in music therapy, supplying 90 percent of the music therapists working in Allegheny County.

In response to a nationwide shortage of church musicians and choir directors, Duquesne offered a 50 percent tuition reduction to any student working at least 20 hours a week as a music minister at a church or synagogue, without regard to religious affiliation.

The School of Nursing

In 1990 the School of Nursing received reaccreditation for its undergraduate program and initial accreditation for its graduate program from the Board of Nurse Examiners. This time the examiners found no concerns to report to the board. Indeed, the school achieved its highest passing rate for graduates on the State Board of Nurse Examiners licensure examinations in 1991 at 95 percent.

Emphases in Nursing

Ethics became a major focus in the school in 1991, and the school held its first Nursing Education Institute in 1992. Experienced nurses participated in a Gerontology Nursing Institute on campus in the 1993–1994 school year.

With the Palumbo School of Business Administration and the Rangos School of Health Sciences, the School of Nursing made plans to participate in an interdisciplinary collaborative education project for continuous quality improvement in health care.

The school's doctoral program began operation in the fall of 1994 with an emphasis on preparation of nurses as researchers, on updating the organized body of nursing knowledge about nursing, health and health care delivery, and on care of the chronically ill, disabled, or dying.

International Ventures

• Associate Dean Joanne White, Dr. and Mrs. Murray, and an American delegation of health care professionals visited Nicaragua in 1992 to assess conditions in the country and formulate a voluntary humanitarian aid plan through the Nicaraguan American Nursing Collaboration project.

• The school conducted its first course in Managua on emergency and trauma care in October 1994, followed by a course in intensive care nursing in January 1995, and three more seminars in the spring and summer of 1995.

• Duquesne's commitment to international improvements in health care led the School of Nursing to open an International Nursing Office to coordinate the School's work in Nicaragua with activities of Project Hope and the World Health Organization.

• The dean of the Nursing School, Dr. Mary deChesnay, signed a sister school agreement with Polytechnical University in Nicaragua during one of the trips to assist the school in building a research component for implementation of the first master of nursing degree in that country.

Wellness Programs

In 1994 the School of Nursing initiated a nurse-managed, free wellness clinic for St. Justin Plaza, a high-rise, independent-living facility for the elderly on Mt. Washington. Also, using funds from a HUD grant, the schools of Nursing, Pharmacy, and Health Sciences prepared a wellness program for the K. Leroy Irvis Towers in the Hill District, based on the School of Nursing's Gerontology Clinic at St. Justin's.

Mylan School of Pharmacy

In September 1995 the university announced that the School of Pharmacy would be known as the Mylan School of Pharmacy in honor of the Pittsburgh pharmaceutical company that had so generously supported the university. At this point, the school had been enjoying its most successful decade to date. By 1989, Duquesne pharmacy graduates could look forward to some of the highest starting salaries as compared to almost any other field of study, and averaging more than the national average for other pharmacy school graduates. Enrollments reflected the program's success. By 1992 the fall freshman class of 217 students represented the largest in the pharmacy school's 67-year history. In fact, Duquesne was the sixth largest of the nation's 75 schools of pharmacy.

Experience in practical applications had always been a strength of the pharmacy school with its early dispensing and retail internship through the George Kelly Model Pharmacy in Canevin Hall. In the 1990s it continued strong in the area, helped along by a five-year grant from Thrift Drug to develop a practice simulation laboratory including a community pharmacy model, an institutional pharmacy model, a sterile products area, and a drug information center.

The brothers of Duquesne's Beta Gamma Chapter of Phi Delta Chi pharmaceutical fraternity won the Emory Thurston Presidents' Cup as the top pharmacy school chapter in 1992—the eighth time they had done so. Delta Epsilon chapter of Kappa Psi pharmaceutical fraternity celebrated its 25th anniversary that year and the Tau chapter of Lambda Kappa Sigma International pharmaceutical fraternity its 60th.

The School of Pharmacy implemented a drug education and assistance program in 1988, and the school faculty voted to make participation in the school's educational symposium about the disease of chemical dependency a requirement for graduation. Furthermore, Phi Delta Chi produced a video presentation to educate high school students on the subject. It was received so enthusiastically that the group produced a second, "Tackling Steroids," in 1993. Copies of these videos were added to the Prevention Materials database of the National Clearinghouse for Alcohol and Drug Information.

In its own international move, the School of Pharmacy signed an agreement with Kobe-Gakuin University of Kobe, Japan, in May of 1991 to effect faculty exchanges and shared publications.

The Rangos School of Health Sciences

Duquesne entered the field of allied health services with a bachelor's degree program in perfusion technology through the Pharmacy School and Mercy Hospital in 1990. Perceiving a need for more professionals in the health sciences, it opened its first new school in half a century, the School of Health Sciences, that year. Jerry Martin, former dean of the School of Health Related Professions at the University of Pittsburgh, was the dean. Allegheny General Hospital offered a scholarship endowment fund of $100,000 annually for health science students. The home selected for the new school was Father Hehir's old gymnasium on the corner of Locust Street and McAnulty Drive. John G. Rangos, Sr., a member of the university board of directors, and president and CEO of Chambers Development Company, donated $2 million to the new school, about half the necessary capital to convert and equip the building. Construction proceeded at breakneck speed and on October 18, 1991, the John G. Rangos Sr. School of Health Sciences was dedicated.

The new school offered degree programs in athletic training, health records administration, perfusion technology, physician assistant, and physical and occupational therapy. The university wasted no time in putting together the various components and seeking accreditation. Because of the diversity of departments, accreditation had to come from a different entity for each one.

The Physician's Assistant program received outstanding reviews from the AMA and was thus eligible for a federal training grant. It provided the only entry-level master's degree program in its field in the United States.

The new school experienced skyrocketing enrollments (from 296 in 1991 to 759 in 1994), quickly filling all available spaces and creating additional demand for further expansion. It received more than ten applications for every available seat, making it the most competitive school in the university. Within two years, the school had outgrown its new quarters and the university set to work planning a fourth floor to the building.

The fourth floor became the home of the Sports Medicine Institute, jointly funded and operated by Duquesne and Allegheny General Hospital. Physicians from Allegheny General provided instruction in the new anatomy lab and multimedia instruction center, also occupying the fourth-floor addition.

In the fall of 1993 the school implemented a new six-year program for a bachelor of science degree in athletic training and a master's degree in physical therapy. By far the most selective program in the university, enrollment was limited to just two or three students per academic year.

In one of the first health-care-focused projects funded by the National Institute of Standards and Technology, Duquesne received $2 million for a joint project of the Department of Health Information Sciences and a commercial enterprise on Patient-Oriented Management System (POMS), integrating business and clinical computer applications in improving patient care processes and cutting health care costs.

Duquesne also operated a university-wide Pre-Health Professions program for students preparing for admissions to schools in medicine, osteopathy, veterinary practice, dentistry, optometry, podiatry, and chiropractics.

Continuing Education Continues . . . and Innovates

In pursuing its mission to enable older persons to reenter the university as painlessly as possible, the Division of Continuing Education instituted a Return to Learn program in 1994. These on-site, free lunch-time sessions were designed to build confidence in and provide information to students who were older than 25, which College Board statistics revealed to be 45 percent of the 10.6 million attending U.S. colleges. At Duquesne those aged 25 and over represented 15.9 percent of enrollments (896 students). The Division of Continuing Education even raised funds for endowed scholarships for its older students.

Opening in September 1992, the Saturday College enabled a Continuing Education student to receive a degree in just four years by attending only on Saturdays. Offered in response to community requests, the Saturday College program expected 30 to 40 students when it opened, but registered 135. The average student in the program was 38 years old and most probably already in the professional world, wishing to advance a career. Only 20 percent were first-time college students. The bachelor of science and professional studies degree included various years of emphasis on organizational leadership and professional communication. The Saturday College won a 1994 Distinguished Program Award for its innovative nature.

Vincentian Academy—Duquesne University

Many graduates of Duquesne Prep had longed for the day when Duquesne would operate a high school again, as it had for most of the life of the university. Since the closing of the prep school in 1941, several unsuccessful attempts had been made to reopen it. Finally, in the summer of 1994, Dr. Murray and Sister Charlene Reekel, VSC, superior general of the Vincentian Sisters of Charity, jointly announced the creation of the first university-affiliated international baccalaureate (IB) program in the world at Vincentian Academy-Duquesne University. The sisters had operated Vincentian High School since 1927, and the students already enrolled there would complete their studies under the existing curriculum. But beginning with the freshman class in the fall of 1995, students at the school would be enrolled in an international baccalaureate program, one recognized as a mark of excellence throughout the world. So rigorous is the IB course, offered at less than 500 institutions worldwide, that graduates are qualified to enter any college or university as second-year students.

As in Duquesne's early days, when the Holy Ghost fathers tried desperately to make education as affordable as possible, tuition was held to the minimum possible—in this case, $7,000 annually, a figure far less than other IB academies, and even less than the cost per public school pupil in the Commonwealth. And this was despite the extended calendar of 210 instructional days. Derek Whordley, dean of the School of Education, undertook the presidency of the new academy program. Although open to students of all

154. Dr. John E. Murray Jr., President of Duquesne University, 1988–present. Duquesne's board of directors broke with 110 years of tradition when they chose a layman as the university's 11th president. Murray differed from earlier presidents in other ways; he was not a native Pittsburgher, nor a Duquesne alumnus. He was born in Philadelphia in 1932, the only son of a policeman. Murray attended LaSalle University, Catholic University of America, and the University of Wisconsin, where he worked his way through law school playing jazz piano. He began his teaching career in Duquesne's Law School in 1959, and he served as acting dean during 1966–67. He moved on to the University of Pittsburgh, where he was University Distinguished Service Professor of Law. Despite a full teaching load, he wrote eight treatises and books used in law schools throughout the country. *Murray on Contracts* is still regarded as the premiere textbook on the subject. He served as a legal consultant to several Pittsburgh and Philadelphia businesses. A self-labeled workaholic, he started teaching a night class on contracts soon after accepting the presidency at Duquesne. His outstanding scholarship and his orientation as a professor instead of an administrator did a great deal to bridge old rifts on the Bluff. Murray also had a gift for organization. He believed in selecting the right people for the right jobs, then empowering them with decision-making capabilities. He was also very successful in attracting generous donations to Duquesne; in his first two weeks as president, he raised two million dollars.

155. Dr. Murray meeting with Pope John Paul II, 1993. Though he was the university's first lay president, Dr. Murray was a devoutly Catholic one, and he made a commitment to emphasizing moral values and "campus ministry in the Catholic tradition." In one speech, Murray stated that "the dominant concern of many American universities . . . is a concern for the moral growth of their students after almost half a century of neglect."

156. Many on the Bluff saw the chapel as the heart of the university. In celebration of its hundredth anniversary, the Duquesne Chapel underwent renovation and received a new sound system. In 1996, a new cupola with chimes topped the roof.

157. The rededication of the chapel took place on its 100th anniversary in 1994. Duquesne's mission to educate in "the Catholic tradition" did not preclude other traditions of worship. In addition to an ecumenical prayer room in the Towers Living-Learning Center, a room near the chapel was renovated to create a private praying place for Muslim students. The chapel hosted activities such as Bible study groups every night. Duquesne established a telephone number at which students looking for guidance could contact a priest 24 hours a day, and a renewed interest in the sacramental presence accompanied the rededication ceremonies.

158. President John E. Murray was a phenomenal fundraiser, and he made a sizeable endowment his goal. His campaign, "Spirit of the '90s," increased Duquesne's endowment to $42 million by 1995. In April 1994, John E. Connelly, who had already made a sizeable contribution toward establishing the School of Business Administration's Center for Entrepreneurship and Emerging Enterprise, announced a gift of $11 million — onc of the largest donations by a single individual to a Catholic university. In this photo, Murray accepts the first installment of this gift from John Connelly at the annual alumni luncheon.

159. The Duquesne University Chamber Singers and Choir, under the direction of Dr. Brady Allred, joined with actor James Earl Jones in "Exultate," a program of poetry and music, at Pittsburgh's Trinity Cathedral in November 1992. The event was sponsored by the International Poetry Forum, directed by Duquesne English professor Samuel Hazo. Here, University Provost Dr. Michael P. Weber shares an informal moment with Jones.

160. Two older structures, the Human Resources Building (originally the Science Hall built in 1916 at the corner of Colbert and Vickroy) and the Psychological Counseling Center (purchased in 1928 to expand the library), were declared unsafe and beyond repair in 1993. In 1994 they were demolished, and work began on a new science hall. The $7.8 million red brick structure was designed to complement Old Main and Canevin Hall. The Bayer Learning Center, named in recognition of a $2 million donation from the Bayer Corporation, opened for classes in January 1996.

Douglas C. Booth

161. In order to increase awareness of Duquesne's mathematics and computer science programs, the department hosted the high school math supremacy competitions sponsored by the Mathematics Council of Western Pennsylvania beginning in 1989. The department also renovated its fourth floor College Hall quarters with the latest in computer designs, and in September 1992, the facility became the Alcoa Mathematics and Computer Science Center. Despite its steady metamorphosis of colleges and facilities, classroom instruction remained fundamental at Duquesne. This photo shows Donato DeFelice, math professor, in action.

162. An eight-story garage built during the Nesti Administration represented the university's first serious effort to address the long-standing parking problem on the Bluff. Although it's 746 spaces were deemed adequate at the time, demand soon exceeded the supply. President Murray, recalling his own experiences at other urban universities, set at the parking problem with a will. From 1992 to 1996 some 1,800 additional spaces were provided in three separate additions. Duquesne's garage, shown here from the Locust Street side, had become the largest single facility in the city.

163. In 1994, as part of its beautification projects, the university installed arched gateways at campus entrances. Shown here is the McAnulty Drive entrance at Forbes Avenue.

164. With many projects and speakers, Murray stressed the importance of service to the global community. One notable visitor was Nicaraguan President Violeta Chamorro. On her first visit in 1992, she spoke on Nicaragua's need for help in the areas of education and health care. With her help, Duquesne "adopted" and supported a high school in her country. Through the World Health Organization and Allegheny General Hospital, the university brought 20 Nicaraguan nurses to campus for additional training. In the spring of 1993, she returned to speak at graduation ceremonies for the School of Education, and Duquesne awarded her with an honorary doctorate in humanities.

165. Murray made sure that the new optimism at Duquesne was reflected in the campus image. Between 1987 and 1995, he spent $36 million in renovation and new construction. In 1992, he fulfilled a decades-old promise to save commuters the climb from the bottom of Shinghiss Street up to the intersection of Academic Walk and McAnulty Drive — perhaps better known as Heart Attack Hill. A covered "skywalk" extending across Locust Street to the sixth floor of Rockwell Hall finally became a reality, and new elevators in the building kept traffic moving.

166. Duquesne welcomed the addition of the Arthur J. Rooney athletic field — Rooney played football during his college days at Duquesne. Located on the site of the Mellon Hall faculty parking lot, the field was designed to meet NCAA regulations for football, baseball, soccer, lacrosse, and softball. Fitting the field into the Bluff's limited flat area required an ingenious and careful scheme. Terraced seating banked the Academic Walk side and hillside seating filled the other three. Portable bleacher seating was erected for the football season. The entire field was recessed six feet, painstakingly dug so as not to disturb the Armstrong tunnels that ran beneath it.

167. Perceiving a need for more professionals in the health sciences, Duquesne opened its first new school in half a century, the John G. Rangos, Sr. School of Health Sciences. The home selected for the new school was Father Hehir's old gymnasium on the corner of Locust Street and McAnulty Drive, which was quickly converted and equipped for its opening in 1991. The new school offered degree programs in athletic training, health records administration, perfusion technology, physician assistant, and physical and occupational therapy. Within two years, the school had outgrown its new quarters, and the university set to work planning a fourth floor to the building.

The new floor (pictured) became the home of the Sports Medicine Institute, with its own entrance on top of the Bluff near the skywalk from Rockwell Hall. The Institute is jointly funded and operated by Duquesne and Allegheny General Hospital.

Douglas C. Booth

168. Duquesne's growth in enrollment, programs, and buildings, as well as its enhanced public image and academic reputation, owe much, of course, to the leadership team that continues to guide the university through the 1990s: Rev. Charles J. Fenner, C.S.Sp., Secretary of the University; Dr. Michael P. Weber, Provost and Vice President for Academic Affairs; Dr. John E. Murray, Jr., President; Rev. Sean Hogan, C.S.Sp., Executive Vice President for Student Life; and Isadore R. Lenglet, Executive Vice President for Management and Business.

Douglas C. Booth

169. In late spring 1996, Duquesne began construction of a new living-learning center, located at the end of Academic Walk between St. Ann's and Towers. The exterior of the new dormitory was designed to closely resemble the new Bayer Learning Center building, using brick and limestone with a Gothic style roof. Unlike existing dormitories, the new building plan features an apartment style of living, with each unit containing two bedrooms, living room, an efficiency kitchen and bath. Each unit will accommodate four students.

creeds, the school would reflect the faith of its founding institutions as "a Catholic school in the great Vincentian and Spiritan traditions," according to Dr. Murray, who often reminded his listeners of society's need, not only for superiorly educated youth, but also for moral leaders. Within three months, the school had received more than 280 inquiries from parents.

"DUQ3" and other Technological Marvels

In 1992 Duquesne began implementation of Duq3, part of the Internet system, that enabled students to communicate via electronic mail from the computer labs on campus and through telephone modems for off-campus access. The service was offered free of charge to students and faculty members, who could also receive instruction on the network through the Center for Communications and Information Technology (CCIT). DuquesneNet electronic mail and internet connection allowed graduates to stay current in their fields through access to information at the university and use of university access to world information, faculty advice and counseling, and professional education. DuquesneNet was installed in the A.J. Palumbo School of Business Administration in 1995 and scheduled to be available to other disciplines within two years.

Also in 1992, the library began placing its card catalog on the Integrated On-Line System. Students and faculty were able to use the on-line catalog system from stations within the library, dorms, and offices. They were also able to access information in the FIRST SEARCH database from within the library.

The library also received a new name as it became the Gumberg Library early in 1995. Stanley R. Gumberg, a 1950 graduate of Duquesne and chairman of the board of J.J. Gumberg real estate and development company, and his wife Marcia were on campus for the dedication, proclaiming the library "one of the most computer-advanced academic libraries in the region."

The New Palumbo Center

The A.J. Palumbo Center, completed in the spring of 1988, and McCloskey Field, which was renovated as part of the same project, received a workout from the students that exceeded expectations. There were, for example, ten separate aerobics classes that fall, and the use of the weight room was so great that the university allocated $10,000 for new equipment and repair of existing equipment in early 1989. The Palumbo Center proved to be such a popular venue that the city and county officials filed a formal appeal challenging its tax-exempt status as a university building. The university compromised, offering to pay a property tax based on the number of concerts held at the center. Duquesne became the first institution of higher education to reach an agreement with the county. Palumbo received such heavy use, especially with concert equipment, that the floor in the main arena had to be replaced after eight years.

The Parking Problem . . . Again

A parking garage was built concurrent with the Palumbo Center, but the demand for parking soon outstripped its capacity. In 1991, 70 students camped outside the physical plant building to purchase parking permits when the doors opened in the morning. Freshmen waited in vain, as no permits were issued to them.

A new garage on Locust Street, opened in the fall of 1992, failed to satisfy parking needs for long, especially since the university lost 320 spaces when the Mellon Hall surface lot became the Arthur J. Rooney Sr. Athletic Field, and expected to lose more along Bluff Street when a proposed Science Center was built. An additional facility at the corner of Magee and Locust Streets was completed in September 1993, but almost predictably, once again demand increased to meet the available supply and by 1994 a small waiting list had formed. By the fall of 1995, yet another two floors had to be added to the existing garage.

Reworking the Campus

A new look was given to the central campus with the reworking of Academic Walk. The street had been vacated by the city and turned over to the university in 1967 but little had been done to improve its appearance. Work to create a park-like setting began in 1991, and the street was dedicated in a ceremony in November of that year. Laval House stood as the only original residential building of the old neighborhood amid a stonework paving, a Clock Plaza east of Canevin Hall (donated by Dean Murrin), Victorian lampposts, and a fountain in front of Canevin Hall. As a crowning touch for campus beautification, arched gateways were built at campus entrances. Dr. Murray truly was building what he referred to as "a renaissance university in a renaissance city," a goal toward which he donated his personal bonuses in 1990 and 1991. Between 1987 and 1995, Duquesne spent $36 million in interior and exterior renovations and new construction.

There were changes of a more utilitarian nature as well. For anyone who attended Duquesne as a commuter and climbed the hill to the Bluff—it was popularly called Heart Attack Hill—each day, the 1958 plan to install an escalator would have been welcome indeed. But, alas, as with many other parts of the Master Plan, the escalator was never to become a reality. Finally, though, in 1992, President Murray made good on a decades-old promise to build a footbridge from Rockwell Hall to the upper campus. The difference in elevation from the bottom of Shingiss Street to the intersection of Academic Walk and McAnulty Drive is 107 feet, a distance about equal to the climb from the foot of the Statue of Liberty to the crown. A covered "Skywalk" across Locust Street was erected, leading into the sixth floor of Rockwell Hall. At the same time, another set of elevators was installed in Rockwell Hall that supplemented the existing elevators by going to the Forbes Avenue concourse level. This was a great improvement. Academic Walk was then extended across McAnulty Drive to the crucifix behind the administration building where it joined the new skywalk.

The university also replaced a footbridge across the Boulevard of the Allies on the Bluff side of campus. The bridge had been erected by the Pennsylvania Department of Transportation in 1954, but had been weakened by a collision with a truck in 1991 and pulled down by a backhoe in 1993. Students walking from the South Side had been trying to cross the boulevard at rush hour, jumping the Jersey barrier in the center. In the interest of safety, Duquesne secured permission to replace the old bridge with one in the Victorian style of the campus gates, decorated with Duquesne's gothic "D."

In celebration of its hundredth anniversary, the Duquesne chapel was renovated and given a new sound system. In 1996 a new cupola with chimes was added to the roof to symbolize the chapel's importance as the heart of the university.

Changes in the Student Union

The Itza Pizza Restaurant, closed during reconstruction of the Student Union's first floor, reopened as The Off Ramp in the fall of 1992, transformed from a pizza parlor to an upscale cafe offering a deli bar, non-alcoholic beer and wine, and featuring entertainment through the College Coffee House Circuit. Much to the delight of the students, the cafe honored resident meal tickets for those who wanted a change from cafeteria meal service. And other alternatives were provided after that. A joint effort between the university and the ARA Food Services led to the construction of a Burger King and a Pizza Hut in Rockwell Hall in 1993. Dunkin' Donuts and Freshens Yogurt joined the "Rockwell Expressway" in 1994.

The new food plan was, in a way, symbolic

of the flexibility of the new administration. Prior to the Murray administration, resident students were required to purchase a full meal plan, their tickets valid only at Towers Cafeteria. The new plan allowed them to eat in Towers, in the Student Union, or in any of the fast-food restaurants on campus.

Many cosmetic changes were made to the Student Union throughout Murray's presidency, none so radical as the 1996 facelift. The great ramp was removed and replaced by stairs and a fountain. At the same time, the ground level floor on the Locust Street side of the building was extended to accommodate an enlarged campus bookstore.

The Arthur J. Rooney Athletic Field

Football was being played at South Stadium at a cost of about $35,000 a year when the university began breaking ground for the Arthur J. Rooney Athletic Field in May 1993. Duquesne's plan to initiate soccer as a Division I level sport spurred the decision to build an on-campus field. President Murray decided to name it for Steeler founder Art Rooney, who had played football during his college days at Duquesne, and proposed the idea to his son Dan, also a Duquesne alumnus. Located on the site of the Mellon Hall faculty parking lot, the field was designed to meet NCAA regulations for football, baseball, soccer, lacrosse, and softball. It required much ingenuity to fit the field into Duquesne's limited flat land on the Bluff, though. Terraced seating was installed on the Academic Walk side and hillside seating filled the other sides. Portable bleacher seating was erected on the Bluff Street side beyond the sidewalk, extending over a strip of parking spaces, for the football season. The entire field was recessed six feet, requiring care as it was dug so as not to disturb the Armstrong Tunnels that ran beneath it. The price tag for the field was $2.5 million.

Although nothing was stated publicly, university officials hoped that the new field would attract more male applications so as to even out the male-female ratio in the student body, and would allow Duquesne to move into Division I play as required by the NCAA.

A regrettable spin-off of the new Rooney Field was that the annual carnival was moved from the site to McCloskey Field. There it was held with uniform, commercially designed midway booths in place of the more imaginative student efforts of the past.

Arrangements were made with the Pittsburgh Steelers to cover much of the field with a climate-controlled "bubble", 70 feet high, so that they could practice there in the later months of the football season. In 1995 the Beard family contributed half the necessary funds to build a press box on the Bluff Street side of the field, necessary to comply with NCAA and Metro Atlantic Athletic Conference rules. This "gothic" structure, planned in keeping with campus gates and decorations, has a games operations personnel room, rooms for visiting and home-team coaches and visiting-team radio crew, facilities for the home-team film unit, a VIP box, and concession stands in the archways underneath.

International and Minority Students

Duquesne's commitment to a racially and ethnically mixed student body has never slackened, nor has it been confined to recruiting students from this country. In the 1990s the number of international students increased, many from Third World countries. The Duquesne University International Students Organization celebrated this diversity with an annual showcase of culture and talent, including dances and musical performances in the Student Union ballroom. The fifth annual International Students Week in the spring of 1995 featured a Mass, an exhibit at Les Idees Gallery in the Union, vendors selling items from around the world, ethnic foods for lunch, an evening program of food-tasting, fashion show, cultural performances, and dancing, and a night of Caribbean music at the Off-Ramp.

Among the many student and faculty exchange programs at Duquesne were the American Ireland Fund, which developed a graduate fellowship in honor of its co-founder, Pittsburgh Steeler president and Duquesne alumnus Daniel M. Rooney, and the German-American organization, DANK, which continued to host its annual Rheinland Karneval.

The Black Student Union received funding from the university to support its Black History Month each February. Unfortunately, the campus was, like most others in the nation, vulnerable to racial unrest, and in the fall of 1989, the Black Student Union's carnival booth was vandalized. The administration was, however, generally successful in promoting racial harmony on campus as the 1990s progressed.

Greek Social Societies

Although the traditional fraternities and sororities continued to increase in popularity on campus, some 34 male and female students formed another alternative group in 1988, Alpha Upsilon, with no written rules, no fees, no mandatory attendance at meetings or at social functions. Since their unofficial status denied them the right to advertise, they relied on word of mouth to recruit and inform students of meetings and functions. The group was so casual about its lack of organization that the only pledging activity scheduled was an optional city-wide scavenger hunt.

A move on campus in the 1980s to eliminate hazing as part of fraternity and sorority pledging had gained general acceptance by 1989, when Zeta Beta Tau fraternity ceased hazing on a national level. The move to ban hazing was strengthened by state laws, including one passed by the Pennsylvania legislature in 1991. Duquesne established a policy officially banning hazing activities that same year. Also in 1991, Delta Sigma Theta went on record for the elimination of hazing. Instead, emphasis was placed on the positive side of Greek life. In March 1994 the social fraternities and sororities united in sponsoring Greek Week. Among the activities scheduled was a fundraiser for United Cerebral Palsy. Fraternities and sororities also continued to sponsor couples for the annual Dance Marathon for Muscular Dystrophy Research in the fall. Thus, service activities became more and more prominent among the "Greeks."

Alcohol Banned on Campus

The controversial policy allowing groups in enclosed areas to have alcoholic beverages during the carnival, while those sponsoring open booths were banned from consuming alcohol, ended in 1989 with a unilateral policy forbidding alcohol at Carnival. State and federal policies, including the Drug-Free Schools and Communities Act Amendments of 1989 requiring Duquesne to certify the implementation of a program to prevent illegal use of drugs and alcohol on campus, dictated the new rules. The university was relieved to find no evidence of infractions of the new ruling or any sign of a decrease in attendance at the 1990 carnival. The year before, fraternity members had worn black armbands to the Carnival tent shows in protest. By 1994, however, when the carnival was combined with homecoming, and alumni flocked to campus to recapture the carnival spirit, strict enforcement of the alcohol ban was accepted.

The Interfraternity Council executive board was responsible for enforcing the university's prohibitions against underage drinking on campus. In 1994, when a freshman was served alcohol at a Sigma Tau Gamma function and became involved in an altercation on campus, the council sanctions against the fraternity included mandatory attendance of the fraternity's executive board at a regional leadership meeting in Cleveland, mandatory participation of all the brothers in the University's Duck Days alcohol-awareness program, and 20 hours of on-campus service from each of the brothers. Fraternity members were warned that anything less than

100 percent compliance would result in their being banned from the Interfraternity Council and suspended from campus activities. Harsh as the ruling was, such strong measures curbed the growing difficulties with campus drinking that had so marked the 1980s.

Government efforts to stem underage drinking led to state liquor control officials pressuring schools to issue false ID cards to undercover agents. The program, begun in the fall of 1992, allowed officers access to fraternity and university parties with student ID cards and permitted them to testify at university judicial board hearings. Duquesne, along with the other area colleges, refused to cooperate, labeling the operation as "deceitful."[16]

In a less intrusive effort, faculty members could secure $500 grants by attending three training sessions on alcohol awareness information and incorporating the information into already existing classes. Seven Duquesne professors took advantage of the opportunity by implementing the additional alcohol-awareness instruction in 1993.

The Pendulum Swings Back in Residence Halls—and Security Tightens

In contrast to the 1970s when students pressed for openness in housing, including coed floors and open-visitation policies, the 1980s and 1990s witnessed cries for more structure and regulation in the dorms. In 1989, complaints from the women about a lack of privacy led to a reorganization of Towers with side B designated as all-female and side A all-male on certain floors. There were other types of segregation as well. The seventeenth floor became designated as an intensive study area, and some wings were declared smoke-free and chemical (i.e. alcohol)-free. Some "interest wings" were permitted, coed and otherwise, such as the one for the Tammies, which even had Tamburitzan murals painted on their hallway walls, and also for sororities and fraternities. The university found that these wings, housing students who had a common bond, were marked by a decrease in violence, rude behavior, and even profanity.

The university also tightened visitation policies and beefed up security. Door buzzers were installed at St. Ann's so desk aids could control entry into the building. A panic bar on the stairway lobby door of St. Martin's prevented unauthorized entry, and nonremovable screens were placed on windows (above the height ruled accessible by fire codes) to prevent students from "hoisting beer through their windows" according to the Campus Director of Public Safety. Following a rash of thefts and vandalism in the fall of 1989, further temporary regulations prohibited non-university guests from signing into the dorms after 2 a.m., although those of the same sex were allowed to stay, with a prepared guest pass. Students who had visiting friends who were not Duquesne students protested in vain. After Towers residents had to be evacuated six times in December of 1991 because of arson or criminal mischief, the university employed its campus police to patrol the dorm and insisted that all visitors be signed out of the building by midnight until the problem was resolved.

The dorms became more comfortable and attractive as well as safer. The Student Life Office tried to be responsive to student suggestions, such as the installation of televisions in the laundries and the construction of a convenience store including a pizza parlor in the Towers cafeteria in 1989. Moreover, dorms were continually upgraded with new carpeting, lighting, ceilings, and so on as necessary. Even the Towers cafeteria was renovated, at a cost of $100,000, with new carpet, neon signs, vertical blinds, plants, and new laminate tabletops and countertops in the 1989–1990 school year. Housing renovations in the spring of 1994 began the conversion of three separate rooms into suites of two double-occupancy bedrooms and a common study lounge. Dorm life became so appealing that Duquesne experienced a shortage of available space in the fall of 1994. Study lounges at St. Ann's were converted into three-and four-person suites to temporarily accommodate the overflow. As the number of students enrolled at the university continued to increase, the percentage of commuters hit its lowest figure in five years. Duquesne's policy guaranteed on-campus housing for undergraduates who requested it, but by the fall of 1995 graduate students were forced to find their own off-campus housing. By 1996 the university was preparing to build yet another dormitory.

Campus Crime in the 1990s—Not That Bad at Duquesne!

In 1991 Duquesne University ranked as one of the safer campuses in Pennsylvania. This did not mean that the campus was totally free of crime, but most crimes involved theft rather than personal attacks. In 1992 the university recorded 54 thefts, 13 acts of vandalism, six incidents of public drunkenness, and four alcohol regulations violations on campus for the entire 12 months.

Some student theft had to be viewed as semi-pranks, as when three Duquesne University students were accused of stealing a city parking meter. Father Hogan, vice-president of student life, posted bail. He said he had posted bail in the past and had never been let down by the students involved, and that he would continue to advance bail money for minor cases. (In this case, charges were dropped.)

In 1989 the Public Safety Department reestablished the Student Patrol, focusing attention on preventing thefts from the College Hall and Rockwell Hall writing and computer labs. Students wishing to use the facilities during off-hours could receive escort services from the university police. But violent crimes were never a major problem at Duquesne. Other than theft, drinking posed the main difficulty. Students residing in the uptown residential neighborhoods near the campus occasionally clashed with residents, usually provoked by noisy student parties.

And student parties were a major source of contention. In April 1992, for example, some 248 people were arrested at parties held at off-campus houses rented by Duquesne students. The charges of underage drinking and disorderly conduct led to the university's decision to suspend eleven of the students for a semester, but eight had their suspensions lifted by an appellate board. Increasingly, students took recourse to the appeal process that was open to them both inside and outside the university. Three students suspended as a result of a 1992 off-campus party filed a civil complaint with the Allegheny County Court of Common Pleas and won permission to complete the spring semester until a full hearing could be conducted. Controlling student behavior continued to be a challenge to the administration as indeed it was at virtually every campus. Nevertheless, crime was, and continues to be, less serious at Duquesne than at most other universities.

A Very Active Student Government

Along with their defined tasks of serving as a forum for student input, the Student Government Association (SGA) made some bold ventures in the 1980s: consulting with administration on policy, dispensing activity funds to campus organizations, planning student programming and social events, coordinating campus-wide celebrations, and operating the Student Senate and the Student Judicial Review Board. In 1988 Duquesne hosted the first International Students Conference with representatives from Canada, Sweden, Switzerland, and Great Britain. Student approaches to problems on campuses around the western world were discussed and documented in *The Duquesne Report: A Student Agenda for the Future*. The student delegates concluded that membership in a student union would be voluntary or involuntary on the basis of the national situation rather than on international decisions, that governmental interference in student unions should be opposed, that governments should examine their educational systems to prove that they do not discriminate against any members of society, and that non-governmental money was having a negative effect on undergraduate education, with reduced funding in the humanities and social sciences in favor of technological and scientific support.

U.S. News and World Report listed Duquesne University as one of the country's best college values in its 1992 education issue, and SGA conducted its own survey to confirm or contradict this judgment. The three-out-of-five rating on the majority of questions in the five areas surveyed (academic advisement, student rights, plus/minus grading, teaching effectiveness, and Duquesne University perceptions) seemed to indicate some "discontent" but no serious problems from the 285 who filled out the survey.[17]

The Persian Gulf War

On January 17, 1991, the headlines in the *Duquesne Duke* proclaimed, "U.S. BEGINS WAR." The *Duke* printed a message from President Bush to college newspapers, and in the same issue three editorials gave diverse viewpoints on the war, one of which scolded Duquesne students for being more interested in "the visitation problems for Towers residents" than in the war. This was not true; every available television on campus attracted a crowd of viewers who watched the nonstop reporting of the conflict. Few Duquesne students participated in the antiwar demonstration held in Oakland.

A small number of students had already been called for military service just before the end of the fall semester in 1990. The university determined to help those students who were in the military reserves as well as the small number of faculty and staff who were also reservists. Students called to duty during the semester were to be awarded either credit for the coursework or a refund depending upon how far work had advanced, and the university decided to award staff and faculty the difference between their regular salary and government compensation for the time they were in the military. The war, however, was extremely brief and few lives on the Duquesne campus were disrupted because of it. After the troops were recalled, Duquesne honored those students, faculty, and alumni who served by dedicating a plaque on the shrine of Our Lady of Victory.

Visitors to the Bluff

As part of the celebration of a millennium of Christianity in the Ukraine and the return of property to the religious communities in the former Soviet Union that had been confiscated under the Communist regime, Achille Cardinal Silvestrini, prefect of the Church's Supreme Tribunal at the Vatican, spoke at Duquesne in the fall of 1988 on the progress in world recognition of religious freedom through the efforts of Pope John Paul II. Cardinal Silvestrini was also president of Villa Nazareth, a cultural and educational center in Rome that housed students at nearby universities and had maintained an exchange program with Duquesne since the McAnulty administration.

A short-lived but highly publicized controversy attended a visit from President Bush in May 1992. The Republican Party had rented the Student Union for his talk at a $1,000-dollar-a-plate fundraising luncheon in support of his reelection bid. Other than the invited guests, no one was permitted in or even near the building. The luncheon was attended by 340, while the Pittsburgh and university police kept 60 protesters at a safe distance. When the university's general counsel was contacted by the Allegheny County solicitor regarding the legality of a tax-exempt institution renting out its facilities, the situation was explained to him and the matter seemed to be closed. But then "the great god of publicity overtook him."[18] Glorying in the limelight, the solicitor told the local news media that he was contemplating a challenge to the building's tax exemption. The solicitor, a Democrat, also denied any political objective, a disclaimer believed by absolutely no one.

Local radio and television stations carried the story, and a blistering editorial by the *Pittsburgh Press* accused Duquesne of "dipping into politics."[19] The editorial took no note of the fact that the president's talk was an outline of his plan for revitalizing cities and thus was not strictly political.

President Murray, however, had no intention of taking the attack lying down. In response to statements that Duquesne was endorsing a political candidate, jeopardizing its tax-exempt status, and denying students access to their own building, he responded in a letter to the editor that George Bush, as holder of an honorary degree from Duquesne, had as much right to rent the facility as any other alumnus. He also noted that Duquesne paid taxes on noncollegiate entertainments and a 26 percent parking tax. Adding that a university official had been in contact with the county solicitor in the matter, Dr. Murray pointed out that students were not denied access to their union building because of the president's visit, but, in fact, there were few if any students on campus at the time since graduation had been held the week before. And this was the reason Duquesne had agreed to use of the facility when no hotels were available. Dr. Murray's reasoned and comprehensive letter put an effective end to the controversy.

That same year (1992) Duquesne had another famous visitor, Nicaraguan president Violeta Chamorro. Both her niece and granddaughter were Duquesne students. She spoke on Nicaragua's need for help with educational and health-care systems and received Duquesne's offer to "adopt" and then support a high school in her country. Duquesne also arranged through the World Health Organization and Allegheny General Hospital to bring 20 Nicaraguan nurses to Duquesne for training. Several Duquesne administrators, along with Richard White, president of the university's board of directors, who had met Chamorro while doing research in Nicaragua for his doctorate on international relations, accompanied her to New York, where she attended a special United Nations session on children and was honored at a dinner. At the dinner, various Duquesne personnel agreed to coordinate national relief efforts in medical and surgical supplies and in educational materials. President Chamorro returned to Duquesne the following spring to speak at graduation ceremonies for the School of Education and to receive an honorary doctorate of humanities.

On April 12, 1996, the Law School hosted a "reunion of Robert F. Kennedy's closest advisors in the Justice Department." The panel included a host of major figures from his time as Attorney General, including Archibald Cox and Nicholas Katzenbach. Mrs. Ethel Kennedy accepted a posthumous honorary degree on behalf of her late husband.

ROTC is Discontinued

U.S. Army budget cutbacks necessitated the discontinuation of ROTC at Carnegie Mellon University in 1990 with interested students at that university required to take the courses at the University of Pittsburgh. When the ROTC program at California University of Pennsylvania was in danger of closing in 1992, the school became an extension center of Duquesne. California still had its own program, but Duquesne acted as a so-called "host" school. In addition, Duquesne instructors taught ROTC at Washington and Jefferson College in Washington, Pennsylvania. Duquesne was also the downtown hub school for ROTC training as students from Point Park and Robert Morris Colleges took their course work on the Bluff.

The ROTC headquarters at Duquesne was not easy to find, however: it moved from Canevin Hall to the old gym in 1989, where it remained for a mere year and a half until the renovation began for the new School of Health Sciences. It then relocated on the tenth floor of Rockwell. By

1994 about 80 students were enrolled in ROTC.

Then, in 1996, as a cost-cutting move, the federal government ended a number of ROTC programs, including Duquesne's. The announcement ended 61 years of ROTC on the Bluff.

The Red Masquers Finally Find a Home

From the old ROTC rifle range building, to the physical plant building, to the gymnasium of Des Places Communication Center, the Red Masquers moved again and again until finally they found a home at renovated Rockwell Hall. Here they set up headquarters and stored costumes and sets and props. The old Peter Mills Auditorium was eliminated in favor of smaller rooms, one of them a state-of-the-art theater for the dramatic troupe, having 220 surrounding seats, a computerized lighting system, and a $10,000 amplified stereophonic sound speaker system. (The new facility was also convertible into four large-group lecture-hall classrooms through the use of movable partitions.) The Masquers made their debut performance at the new theater, the opening of their 76th season, with the February 1992 production of Oliver Goldsmith's *She Stoops to Conquer*. Under the direction of Jay Keenan, the group celebrated its 80th season in 1994–1995 with a controversial dark comedy of Philadelphia ghetto life, *Gemini*; a program of plays written, directed, and acted by students entitled *Premiere Performances XVIII*; Shakespeare's *Two Gentlemen of Verona*, set in a 1920s art deco motif; and their first improvizational comedy troupe on campus.

The Tamburitzans

In April 1993 the Tamburitzans felt the reverberations of the ethnic fighting in the former Yugoslavia between Croats and Serbs. Giving a performance before a largely Croatian audience in a suburb of Youngstown, Ohio, they eliminated all Serbian dances from their performance. This brought complaints from some members of the troupe and from a leader of the Serbian community in Pittsburgh. President Murray defended the action, saying that to do otherwise would be like "playing a Japanese song on an American radio network during World War II."[20] A *Post-Gazette* editorial denounced the decision, saying the Tammies were "overly responsive to the politics of the day."[21] It noted that the Croatians themselves did not demand that Serbian numbers be dropped; rather the gesture was made by the director of the Tamburitzans. Emotions ran high enough that on May 9 a bomb threat against the Tamburitzans forced the cancellation of a performance in Charleroi, Pennsylvania. Afterwards, the group did not eliminate any dances from its performances, regardless of the ethnic makeup of the group for which it was performing.

Under managing director Paul Stafura, the Tammies kept good relations with the Duquesne administration, though Duquesne began reducing their scholarships. A $100,000 grant from the State of Pennsylvania in 1994 helped, but only about 20 percent of Tamburitzan alumni supported the ensemble that year. Still, considering the students' safety on the road of vital importance, the university had at least bought the Tammies a new bus costing over $260,000 early in the Murray administration. Despite financial difficulties, the Tammies continued to entertain successfully.

Radio and Television on the Bluff

The decision to convert WDUQ-FM, 90.5, radio station from an amateur, student-operated station to a professional one was controversial when made in the late 1970s, but the station's success was undisputable. By 1994 it was acclaimed as the most listened-to public radio station in metropolitan Pittsburgh, with audience figures of over 111,000. Through grants from the Corporation for Public Broadcasting, the station installed a digital audio production studio to produce nationally distributed programs on campus instead of having to use outside facilities. New director Scott Hanley assumed the post in 1995 just as federal budget cuts severely reduced funding for public broadcasting. WDUQ's pledge drive netted an additional 40 percent to meet the shortfall in its most successful drive ever.

Nevertheless, funding difficulties along with equipment problems caused several delays. After these were resolved, Duquesne Student Radio, WDSR, 97.7 FM, located on the ground floor of Assumption Hall, finally began broadcasting in 1988. In a parody of the motto printed on the university's stationery, "Liberal and professional education in the Catholic tradition," the station adopted the motto, "Quality rock-n-roll in the liberal arts tradition." Unlike other student radio attempts on campus, WDSR survived, despite financial, managerial, and morale problems, compounded by a burglary over the semester break in the 1989–1990 school year. The rock-and-roll emphasis was revised to include rap, heavy metal, classic rock, and jazz. The station also hosted a talk show that covered such controversial subjects as date rape, alcoholism, homosexuality, and affirmative action.

In the 1994 football season, the station made a major step forward in offering live sports coverage for the first time with new equipment that enabled transmission using cellular phones. Towers, St. Martin's, and St. Ann's dorms had cable access to the station.

The university completed wiring the campus for a closed, circuit television station, DUQU, channel 36, in the fall of 1990. The station broadcast from the studios installed in Des Places Communication Center with program development and technology supplied by the university Center for Instructional Resources. Duquesne had built its studio to broadcast over one of the Warner Cable community-access educational channels until Warner, claiming extensive losses, began cutting the number of such stations in 1984. The new station broadcast campus events and activity announcements, conferences, educational programs, movies, and a campus news show. By 1993 the campus cable channel was airing original programming produced and hosted by Duquesne students, including "My Friend Anita," a comedy on the lighter side of campus life on The Bluff, and "Visual Radio," a music video program on alternative artists.

The Duke *and the President*

University presidents typically have troubles with the student newspaper at least once during their administrations, and President Murray was not to escape the tradition. It all started on a Monday morning, February 13, 1989, when the *Duquesne Duke* staff reported to their office in the student union only to find that the locks had been changed. The Student Government Association (SGA) Student Senate had called a locksmith after voting to suspend the paper's publication—they said because of "illegalities in Rebecca Drumm's election to the post of editor-in-chief and the existence of an unauthorized, off-campus bank account." The *Duke* staff, however, and, in particular, editor-in-chief Rebecca Drumm, claimed that the lockout resulted from the SGA opposition to an advertisement for a contraceptive-counseling service. SGA President Harold J. "Happy" Meltzer had said that if the ad appeared again, the SGA would "have no choice but to examine the operation of our student newspaper, which has been entrusted in good faith to you and the current editorial board," since the ad "can in no way be seen as consistent with the mission statement of the university and the values and traditions upon which Duquesne University was founded and operates."

The staff received aid from *The Penn* of Indiana University of Pennsylvania and the *Observer-Reporter* of Washington, Pennsylvania, in publishing *The Free Press* on February 16, 1989. Although the staff circulated a petition asking for students and faculty support in reinstating the *Duke*, it was time for examinations and most students were too busy to be aware of anything else.

SGA voted unanimously to reopen the *Duquesne Duke* on February 16, but suspended Ms. Drumm from acting as editor-in-chief until she was cleared of charges. Eventually she was cleared of the most serious charges, involving the misuse or theft of university property and tampering with the election process. She was, however, found guilty of two lesser violations of the student conduct code, and was barred from further participation in university extracurricular activities and placed on probation until graduation. Editor Drumm appealed the Judicial Board decision, but to no avail. A preliminary audit uncovered extravagant expenditures from the *Duke* account for gifts and banquets, with only a tenth of the money spent from the account from March 1987 to February 1989 having been used for proper business expenses. The decision was made that the *Duquesne Duke* would be audited annually at the same time as the university audit.

The *Duquesne Duke* soon resumed publication under the supervision of a publications board composed of faculty, students, and an off-campus media representative. Dr. Murray was criticized for his failure to step in, and for allowing the SGA too much authority. He responded that his administration had no intention of stepping in forcefully when the situation did not merit such a reaction:

> I believe in using my influence with student organizations and discussing critical issues with them without imposing solutions from on high. This is also a part of the educational process. It is important to arrive at workable solutions to problems with students in a free and open discussion. That is what we do at Duquesne.[22]

The *Duquesne Duke*'s traditional April Fools' Day issue made a reappearance in 1992, as the *Duquesne Puke*, subtitled *The Bluff School for the Terminally Apathetic*. Proving that even students learn from experience, the *Puke* contained harmless stories such as President Murray turning down an offer from heaven for "a position . . . at the right hand of God" to remain at Duquesne. The paper continued to flourish, and the Society of Newspaper Design awarded the one of 13 national prizes for graphic design excellence in 1993 and 1994.

The Debate Team Distinguishes Itself

After a glorious history under Joseph Morice, Duquesne's debate team had died out following his retirement, but it was revived again in the 1994–1995 school year by Bob Frank as part of a forensics program that included public speaking, poetry, and prose. The new team immediately distinguished itself in competition, being one of 30 U.S. schools selected to host the British debate team in a competition between the two nations.

Campus Ministry "In the Catholic Tradition"

Duquesne's mission to educate in "the Catholic tradition" meant encouraging more than Catholic devotion. In addition to the ecumenical prayer room in the Towers Living-Learning Center (renovated in the summer of 1994), a storage room above the chapel was renovated for the 50 Muslim students on campus who asked for a private room in which to pray. Activities were scheduled every night, such as Bible studies and the RCIA program for those interested in studying about the Catholic Church. The chaplain invited others to use the room as well, insisting that it was large enough for several activities. Students were provided a telephone number for contacting a priest for guidance 24 hours a day, and renewed interest in the sacramental presence accompanied the rededication of the university chapel in 1995.

Believing that true faith is reflected in Christian service, Campus Ministry organized two annual service trips. Over Thanksgiving Break, students traveled to Appalachia, and during Spring Break, they went to Immokulee, Florida, to lend a hand to those in need. The December 1992 National Student Campaign Against Hunger and Homelessness Workshop in Washington, D.C., inspired the Urban Plunge in 1994. Students spent 48 hours immersed in the needs of the poor in the inner city, sleeping in shelters and helping individuals at agencies and parishes during the day. Campus Ministries also organized students to take part in the annual CROP Walk to end world hunger.

Athletics Boom: Men's Basketball Improves

If basketball coach Jim Satalin and the Dukes thought the new Palumbo Center would give them the edge they needed to become a winning team, they were sadly disappointed, as was the rest of Duquesne. By February of 1989, as the Dukes stood 10–14 with only a 5–10 standing in the Atlantic-10 Conference, President Murray expressed disappointment in the progress of the program and indicated that he had informed Satalin "there are times when it may be necessary to make a change."[23] The official dismissal came shortly thereafter. Athletic Director Eileen Livingston was dismissed as well.

The *Pittsburgh Press* had reported several irregularities in the program under Satalin. Several former players and a former assistant coach said he had regularly violated recruiting rules by having the players tryout, had withheld players' meal money on at least three occasions following on-the-road losses, had encouraged unproductive players to leave the program and give up their scholarships, and had not been active as a recruiter. Of the 31 players recruited on scholarship by Satalin, only seven graduated. Following his firing, Satalin criticized the university administration for not supporting him against the charges leveled in the *Pittsburgh Press* articles, which he claimed were false.

Brian Colleary, previously athletic director at Marist University in New York, was selected for the same post at Duquesne, and he assisted in the decision to award John M. Carroll, assistant coach at Seton Hall, a five-year contract as basketball coach. Carroll, who was credited with the recruiting expertise that brought Seton Hall to the runner-up position in the NCAA championship game, was elated: "This is probably the most exciting day of my life, except for the day I got married. I knew all along from day one, when the opening came up, that this was the job I wanted."[24] Given the late start Duquesne had in recruiting, rebuilding the team was a challenge, especially in view of Duquesne's rule requiring a 2.0 grade average every semester for an athlete to remain eligible, the strictest ruling in the Atlantic-10 Conference. Three hundred Duquesne fans, at a school that had become more and more apathetic during Satalin's coaching reign, turned out just to see the first practice at midnight in mid-October. Those fans witnessed the slow return of Duquesne's fortunes on the court. And slow it was. The first year the Dukes finished with a 6–21 regular season, and 5–13 in conference play. They managed to take the first game only to be defeated again by Temple for the third straight year in the Atlantic-10 Tournament. But they had their best record in five years when they finished the 1990–91 season 13–15.

The Dukes tied that record the following year, their last in the Atlantic-10 Conference, before joining the Midwestern Collegiate Conference in the fall of 1992. Duquesne's participation in the Midwestern Conference lasted a single year before the university returned to the Atlantic-10. They finished the 1993 season by tying the previous year's 13–15 record, winning the first round in the Midwestern Conference championships for a fifth-place finish. Junior center Derrick Alston was named to the All-Conference second team and freshman guard Kenya Hunter to the All-Newcomers team.

The decision to leave the Midwestern Conference followed Dayton's departure, making the conference one team short of the six teams with five continuous years of membership necessary to participate in the NCAA tournament. After returning to the Atlantic-10, the 1993–94 team made it to the second round of the NIT championship. One of Carroll's first recruits, Derrick Alston, became the second highest scorer in Duquesne's history, with 1903 points. In the spring of 1994 he posted two Atlantic-10 highs: a 21.3 points per game average and a field goal average of 56.1 percent, and received the First Team All-Atlantic-10 Conference honors. When Alston graduated in 1994, he was selected in the second round of the National Basketball Association amateur draft by the Philadelphia 76ers.

The 1994–95 Duke basketball season received wide coverage, with eight games scheduled to be televised on ESPN, ESPN2, Prime Network, and KBL, and the entire schedule broadcast over WJAS Radio. The team, however, despite some promising newcomers, suffered from a lack of strong veterans. Athletic Director Brian Colleary announced the firing of John Carroll, stating that Duquesne could not be content to let its only athletic moneymaker struggle for the .500 mark. The team finished the 1995 season with 10 wins to 18 losses.

New basketball coach Scott Edgar, a native of nearby Penn Hills, came from the head coaching position at Murray State in Murray, Kentucky. He impressed the Duquesne community with his friendliness and cordiality in contrast to Carroll's toughness. Duquesne hoped that just such a winning personality would help the university draft the best talent the area had to offer, as well as some prime candidates from the rest of the country.

The strict academic requirements were a cause of continuing concern in the Athletic Department. In 1988 athletic director Eileen Livingston and basketball coach Jim Satalin had proposed new eligibility standards in which a player with a stipulated full schedule of classes could play with a minimum of a 1.6 average in the first year, a 1.8 after the second, and a 2.0 after the third and any other eligible years. The vice-president for student life, Reverend Sean Hogan, had said that the proposal would not even be considered, so the mandated 2.0 had been maintained. Coach Satalin had also opposed Proposition 42, prohibiting high school athletes who scored below 700 on the SAT from receiving athletic scholarships, but Livingston had differed with him there.

In 1989 Duquesne offered all student athletes, who had attended on scholarship within the last 10 years and who were not playing professionally, an opportunity to complete their degrees free of charge. This offer came from the university's Center for Academics and Sport. Support for student athletes at Duquesne was strong enough for the university to rank first in the Atlantic-10 Conference and surpass all national averages in the graduation rates of athletes and other students in Division I colleges.

The survey released by the *Chronicle of Higher Education* compared the number of entering freshmen in the fall of 1984 with the number of graduates in 1989, and did the same for the number of recruited athletes in that same period. Duquesne graduated 69.7 percent of its entering freshmen as compared to a national average of 40.7. Among freshman athletes, 95.2 percent graduated as opposed to a national average of 56 percent, and among freshman basketball recruits, the percentage of graduates was 66.7 as compared to the national 42.1 percent. A survey released by the NCAA in 1992 revealed that Duquesne finished second only to Rutgers among the Atlantic-10 schools in athlete and non-athlete graduation rates, at 70 percent. On overall athlete graduation rates, 91 percent of Duquesne's baseball players graduated, while 86 percent of the men's basketball players graduated. Duquesne committed itself through the athletic support programs to graduating scholar athletes. The 125 institutions of the National Consortium for Academics and Sports initiated a national Student-Athlete Day to honor athletes who had attained spectacular levels of academic excellence and leadership.

Basketball's Lady Dukes

The Duchesses, renamed the Lady Dukes in 1990, had some great talent, especially on the 1991–92 basketball team that was seeded eighth in the Atlantic-10 tournament. Although the Lady Dukes were eliminated in the semifinal rounds, they managed to beat topseeded West Virginia in the quarterfinals. Darcie Vincent, despite foot and knee surgery, became the Duquesne Duchesses's all-time leading scorer by breaking Kathy Redilla's 1989 record of 1312. The Lady Duke's head coach, Renee DeVarney, stepped down following the 1992–93 season after four years and a record of 28–85. The players had great respect for her recruiting abilities and knowledge of the game, but looked forward to resuming Atlantic-10 play under new coaching.

The new coach, Dan Durkin, began turning things around for the Lady Dukes. His first season record was an overall 9–18, but the Atlantic-10 conference tally of 6–11 was the best in women's basketball since Duquesne had joined the conference. His second season brought the Lady Dukes a 10–16 record, due to a great extent to the enthusiasm generated by All-American guard, Korie Hlede. A freshman at Duquesne playing her first season of American basketball after leaving her native Croatia, Korie put on a sensational performance, capturing the attention of the media and the NCAA as she broke Duquesne's women's freshman scoring record.

Division I Football

The NCAA attempted to balance sports participation by prohibiting Division I schools in basketball from fielding Division II or III teams in football. The ruling gave Duquesne's football team an uncertain status since Duquesne had neither the facilities nor the capital to play Division I football. The NCAA felt justified in insisting that a wide spectrum of sports be offered, but pinning eligibility for conference championship play in basketball on the number of participants who showed up for swimming or cross-country competitions or the division of play of the football team made little sense. However, Duquesne made plans to construct an athletic field on campus and hire a full-time football coach so that the Iron Dukes could play at least half their schedule against Division I-AA teams. In 1992 Dan McCann announced his retirement in favor of a full-time coach after a 91–73–3 overall record at Duquesne. Duquesne promoted assistant coach Greg Gattuso to the head coaching position. Gattuso was presented an immediate challenge when Duquesne entered Division I-AA nonscholarship football in the 1993 season. The first game in the new Rooney Athletic Field was played against Mercyhurst on October 23, 1993. It was the first time that varsity football had been played on the Bluff since 1929. The Iron Dukes finished their season with a 4–6 record, and the 1994–95 team posted its first 6-win season since 1989. The university received nationwide exposure when on October 31, 1994, the first Duquesne football game was televised on the ESPN network. In 1995, the Iron Dukes won both their conference with a 9–1 record and the ECAC Championship.

Baseball: End of an Era

The baseball team felt the end of an era as well in 1993 when Rich Spear, coach for 24 years, retired in the midst of the season. Spear felt he had just burned out with two full-time jobs: director of intramurals and baseball coach. The previous week, the Diamond Dukes had been beaten by Notre Dame in a four-game series after nearly taking two of the four. Spear's reaction: "We played with all the effort possible. It's very difficult to be so close to an outstanding team, almost pulling off an upset, and losing."[25] After a 344–265 career coaching record, Spear turned to his duties as intramural director and left his assistants to finish the season. Coach Mike Wilson labored to bring the team back to the win column. Duquesne baseball finished its 1995 season with a 17–35 record.

The Ice Dukes

The Ice Dukes proved to be winners under the coaching of Jim Koch. They closed the 1988 season with a 12–9–3 record, and surprised the experts—after starting the 1989 season with four straight losses—by finishing with a record of 16–7–2. After a 12–8–1 season in 1990, they won a four-team tournament on March 10 and 11, and a second tournament, the Keystone Classic, in early April. Then luck and experience gave out, leading to a disappointing season in 1991 and the departure of Jim Koch. Matt Heufelder, a 1990 Duquesne grad and past star for the Ice Dukes, took on the head coaching position in October 1991 with his assistants, Ray Conway and Chris Vaccaro, working with him as a close team. In his first year as coach, Heufelder led the Dukes to some remarkable tournament play that saw them emerge as a surprise finalist despite a depleted team due to illness and injury. They lost to Kent State in the championship, but finished the 1992–93 season 15–7–1, totaling 31 game points, the most in three seasons. They then went to their first American Collegiate Hockey Association (ACHA) Division II National Championship, where they were able to come up with two ties to offset their loss. The Ice Dukes seemed very successful at finding fresh talent. Huefelder closed the 1995 season 10–13–2 with a team comprised mostly of freshmen and sophomores.

Women Athletes Ask for Equal Treatment—and Win Some Honors

In the spring of 1992, women athletes at Duquesne asked for equal treatment with the men. Assistant Director of Athletics Paul Hightower responded, that he "couldn't see how female athletes are discriminated (against) here," but the women had no difficulty finding instances. The women's locker room, although furnished with carpeting and a couch, was small and meager compared to the men's locker room, equipped with TV, VCR, and cable. When the Lady Dukes played Temple in a regular season game, they were embarrassed to be relegated to the auxiliary gym while a high-school game got preference in the main gym. A track and cross-country team member said that males not only received more attention from the coach during the season, but at one meet, when new T-shirts were passed out, only the male athletes got them. Assistant Athletic Director Dan McCarthy revealed that double the number of athletes participated in men's sports as compared to women's sports: 167 men to 82 women.

Yet women at Duquesne boasted some remarkable athletes. Duchess volleyball player Stacy Gilligan was named Atlantic-10 Rookie of the Year in 1991 after twice making Rookie of the Week. With her assistance, the team improved from the previous year's 6–24 record to a 1991 record of 12–13, qualifying for the Atlantic-10 tournament for the first time. Under the coaching of Ray Bobak, in 1993 the team placed third in the Atlantic-10 Conference. Volleyball received its first-ever full-time head coach, Kerry Miller, in 1995.

Lori Bishop set a new school record in cross-country in 1988. Her time of 19.20 on the 3.1-mile course against St. Francis was a great improvement over the old record of 20.21 on a 2.8-mile course. She and two other Duquesne runners lost what appeared to be a sure victory against Westminster in 1990 when they missed a sharp turn and got lost. According to Bishop, "We were so far off the right course that we passed an Amish man on the path and asked him if he had seen the rest of the runners."[26] But Duquesne did not lose its way to the winner's circle in cross-country. Early in 1991 the men and women swept the Walsh Catholic Schools Invitational, and swept the freshman honors in the Atlantic-10 for three consecutives meets. The track team was spectacular that spring as well, breaking five school records in a meet against IUP and another seven the following week at Carnegie Mellon. Under seven-year coach Tony Brano, the 1994 cross country team finished fourth out of 24 teams in the National Catholic Championships.

The women swam well, too. In 1991 the 23 Duquesne swimmers recorded all-time personal bests in 67 of 69 races as the women finished third and the men fourth at the President's Athletic Conference Championships. The following year, the Lady Aqua Dukes won the President's Athletic Conference Championship while the men placed second. The men and women's teams set 47 records, 32 by the women's team. Their triumph in achieving their first team championship earned Coach of the Year honors for the women's swim team head coach, Wayne Becker. Duquesne did consistently well in these events. In the 1994–95 school year, the men's track team had a 3–0 meet record and the women, 2–1. The Lady Aqua Dukes surpassed the men swimmers with an 8–4 record to their 6–5.

A Wide Variety of Sports

The women had a contingent on the crew team as well. Indeed, two-thirds of the 50 member team were women in 1989. The team, set up through the Grealish Memorial Fund, was only three years old when it won four medals in five events at the second annual Head of the Ohio Regatta. The team headed to Philadelphia to compete against schools with strong rowing traditions for their first Head of the Schuylkill Race in October of 1988. Coach Jeff Howe was pleased by their performance as the men finished 18th out of 30 entrants, and the women in 15th out of 25. Later, the team held a 24-hour row-a-thon fundraiser in the lobby of Towers dorm, with Coach Lowe rowing the first half-hour. Finances improved that fall when the Three Rivers Rowing Association built a boathouse to house the equipment of local universities and Duquesne no longer had to rent space in a private facility. In 1992 the men's eight-oar team placed first and set a course record in the Head of the Ohio race. Duquesne came home with three third-place medals in other events. The arrival of a Vespoli-8 fiberglass boat to replace the heavier wooden one was celebrated by the team in 1993. They planned another fundraiser to outfit the boat with new oars and a new cox box. The parents of crew team member Christen Thompsen set up a memorial fund to benefit the team after her death in the fall of 1993. The four-person, 10-oar scull that the fund provided was gratefully received by the team in the fall of 1994.

Duquesne had dropped wrestling in 1972 due to the difficulties of holding it in the Student Union ballroom, but a new NCAA change in revenue distribution if Duquesne added at least one more Division I sport brought wrestling back to campus. A 12-member squad under the direction of former North Allegheny High School coach Gus De Augustino was granted exclusive use of the Des Places Communication Center gym in 1991, sending the Red Masquers searching for a new home. The Dukes hoped to be part of the elite Eastern Wrestling League, one of the top Division I conferences in the country by 1992. By 1994 Duquesne had won the Eastern Qualifiers for the NCAA nationals. For such a young sport on campus, wrestling proved to be incredibly strong. The 1995 team finished its season 9–7–1.

Golf and tennis continued to be played at Duquesne. Nellie King's jovial attitude softened the golf team's tough times in 1992 as they finished last in their only year of MCC tournament play. But Rich Regalla proved a shining star and four-time medalist for the team that year.

Jim McKenna coached the tennis team

through some successful years, including the 11–7 season in the spring of 1988. The tennis team coached by Tony Martin hosted the Duquesne Invitational at South Park at the conclusion of the fall season in 1992 following a 5–2 season. By 1995 the men were playing an impressive 20–13 season. The Lady Dukes tennis team finished sixth in the MCC Tournament in 1992, the first time in 12 years that they finished higher than last place. Making superb strides, the Lady Dukes finished their 1994–95 year 13–9.

In the spring of 1994, Duquesne announced the addition of a men's and a women's soccer team to begin competition in the fall. Plans were to inaugurate the sport as an intramural and elevate it to varsity competition in the Atlantic-10 conference the following year. The idea of fielding a soccer team was part of the impetus in the building of Rooney Field. The women's coach was Shelly Heisey, a Mt. Lebanon High School All-American in the sport; men's coach Dave Kasper had been All-American at the collegiate level at the University of Maryland. In their first season, the men finished with an amazing 5–0–2 record and the women had an even better season at 6–4–1. Both the men and women played as soccer club teams in this initial year.

Among other new sports to appear on campus was lacrosse, also played as a club sport. The team organized during the first semester of the 1990–91 school year and played its opening game against Carnegie Mellon that spring. Although they lost 6–3, CMU's coach congratulated them on the quality of their play, surprised at how well they did for a first-year team. The previous school year, 1989–90, witnessed the inaugural run for the ski team under Andrew Sepelyak, operating also as a club team, raising their own operating funds and grateful for gifts from Corleone's Pizza and the Dukes Court for helping with funding. As a member of the Allegheny Collegiate Ski Conference, founded in 1980 with three schools—and by this time up to 17—the Duquesne Ski Club participated in its first alpine event competition at Tussey Mountain in 1990, where the men's team came in last but the women's finished "a miraculous sixth" out of 13 teams. The rifle team finished second in the sectionals and was ranked 18th out of 57 teams in the NCAA in 1995.

Intramural Program

A rundown on the intramural program in 1992 found it flourishing at Duquesne, with four football leagues, one soccer league, a successful tennis tournament, and a street hockey league. The intramural football leagues were comprised of a women's league, a freshman league, an independent league, and a fraternity league. Believing that the purpose of intramurals was to increase socialization and bonding, intramural director Rich Spear expanded the program into the noncompetitive areas of aerobics, karate, women's weight training, and even a walking club. The newly established walking club boasted only 12 members, mostly university employees, but expected 40 or 50 joining as the group became more established and well-known. In his attempt to involve as many individuals as possible, Spear found that the confined community on the Bluff made it possible to develop more enthusiasm and heighten the rivalries in the team sports. New offerings in 1994 included racquetball competitions.

Athletics Encouraged by Murray Administration

The university made several attempts to promote athletics and encourage enthusiasm on campus. In the spring of 1990 plans were laid for the Dukes Court Student Athletic Booster Club for the following autumn. For a student membership fee of $10, the club supplied a window sticker, a subscription to the Dukes Court newsletter (its name was later changed to *On Guard* and still later to *Reserved Seat*) an invitation to all Dukes Court events, a special meeting with the coach and players, and a reception at a Dukes home basketball game. The University's Sports Information department kicked off the 1991–92 basketball season with a preview of the team consisting of refreshments along with a chance to socialize with the coaches and other fans, a summary of the upcoming season by both the men's and women's coaches, a question-and-answer period, a women's scrimmage, a slam-dunk contest, and a men's scrimmage. Season tickets for Lady Dukes' basketball games were made available for the first time. Before the home game against the University of Massachusetts that season, the Athletic Department and SGA sponsored a "Turf Gate I" party on McCloskey Field. Following the group relay race, face painting, disc jockey dancing, free food and drink, the fans followed the Duke's mascot (a student dressed as a duke) in "One Hundred Steps to Insanity" to the Palumbo Center for the game.

The 1992 school spirit program included pompoms, placards, signs, Duquesne logos, a "red carpet" introduction of the players, the Big Band, and game instructions sheets explaining when to clap, stand, and count down. The Duke Shop at Palumbo Center's Gate A opened that year, selling athletic gear and apparel during home games. Cable network KBL covered nine of the season's home games. Athletics at Duquesne gained popularity for both the player and the spectator.

In 1987 Dan Snurr had organized Duquesne's Big Band, a 25-member jazz band dressed in formal black tuxedos, to support the basketball team by pumping up the crowd before the game, during time out, at intermission, and after the game. Much as Duquesne appreciated this free student effort, Dr. Derek Whordley, dean of the School of Education, began a survey in 1994 on student interest in rebuilding "The Pride of Duquesne," an official Duquesne 100-member marching band. Duquesne had had a marching band until it was disbanded when varsity football ended on the Bluff in 1951. When cleanup efforts following the 1975 fire in Old Main uncovered the band's recordings from the 1930s and 1940s, interest in the band was revived. From the initial 1994 interest group of twelve students, the Pride of Duquesne had grown to a 70-member troupe, 40 musicians and 30 auxiliaries, when they took the field under the direction of Sam Hazo, Jr., for their first show in 50 years that fall.

President Murray Bids Farewell to "President McAnulty"

When the 1992 April Fools Day Issue of the *Duquesne Duke* had as its cover story President Murray turning down a position "at the right hand of God" because of his "strong commitment to this wonderful university," the students touched on a concern close to Duquesne's heart. In January of that year, President Murray withdrew his name from consideration for the presidency of Catholic University of America. In March, he turned down an endowed chair at the University of Pittsburgh's Law School. The faculty, staff, and student body feared that the dream of revival on the Bluff might well fail if Duquesne's president were to leave. But he didn't. The *Pittsburgh Press* referred to his early administration and the changes it had brought as "the Miracle on the Bluff." It was. And it continued.

By the fall of 1994 more than 60 new programs had been started and two new schools founded. Everywhere physical improvements to the campus continued to be made. With a national reputation that continued to rise, the Duquesne of 1994 was not the Duquesne of 1988. More students than ever before were seeking admission.

In his fundraising efforts more than a quarter of a century earlier, Father McAnulty could only point to plots of ground strewn with the rubble of demolished houses and tell prospective donors what buildings were planned if only the resources would be forthcoming. In the 1990s

President Murray could point with pride to those finished buildings. Much had been accomplished. But John Murray was not a man to forget that he stood on the shoulders of his predecessors.

Father McAnulty had remained at Duquesne in the capacity of University Chancellor, a position that had normally been reserved for the bishop of the Pittsburgh Diocese. Still immensely popular, Father Mac was honored by a university-wide celebration of the fiftieth anniversary of his priesthood in 1990. The university renamed Colbert Street in his honor. President Murray regularly stopped into his office to chat and ask his opinion.

On June 10, 1995, Father McAnulty celebrated a wedding Mass in the university chapel and he returned to the priests' residence in Trinity Hall in an upbeat mood. Sitting down to relax in the community room, he then suffered a massive heart attack. He was 80 years old. In the funeral Mass at St. Paul's Cathedral, thousands of his old friends—and he had thousands—turned out to bid him a last good-bye. Speaking for the Duquesne community, Dr. Murray said of Father Mac, as he had often done before alumni gatherings, "He was the president of Duquesne University. He will always be the president of Duquesne University."

Notes

Notes to Chapter 1

1. The order was founded by Father Claude Poullart des Places. Gradually, two distinct but related organizations emerged, the Seminary of the Holy Ghost and the Congregation of the Holy Ghost. From the date of its founding and up to the French Revolution, the seminary educated some 1,600 priests, achieving considerable status as a center of higher learning.

2. The order was restored in 1804, but growth was slow until Father Francis Liberman and his confreres, the Holy Heart of Mary, entered the congregation in 1848. His successor, Father Schwindenhammer, continued the congregation's missionary work and also established seminaries and colleges, including Blackrock College (1860) in Dublin, Rockwell College (1864) in Tipperary, Braga College in Portugal, and a French seminary. Henry J. Koren, C.S.Sp., *The Spiritans: A History of the Congregation of the Holy Ghost* (Pittsburgh: Duquesne University Press, 1958), pp. xix, 15–35, 125.

3. Father Strub's own biography is worthy of mention. He was born in Strasbourg in 1833. He entered the Congregation of the Holy Ghost and was ordained in Dakar, Africa, in 1858. James L. Snyder, "Duquesne University, 1878–1953," *Catholic Educational Review*, December 1952, p. 649.

4. It should be noted that the Holy Ghost Fathers were not the only order to suffer the effects of the *Kulturkampf*; the Jesuits were also banished from Germany.

5. There were 17,110 foreign-born Irish and 15,957 foreign-born Germans—21 percent of the city population of 156,389—in 1880. U.S. Department of the Interior, *Compendium of the Tenth Census, 1880* (Washington, D.C.: Government Printing Office, 1928), pp. 380, 390.

6. Andrew A. Lambing, *A History of the Catholic Church in the Diocese of Pittsburgh and Allegheny*, (New York: Benziger Brothers, 1880), pp. 477–78.

7. Bishop O'Connor had attempted to establish a college (actually a high school) in 1844, but it closed four years later. Another was started in 1848, but it closed after only three years. Still another, the Pittsburgh Catholic Institute, likewise failed after only three years. Such a failure rate for Catholic colleges nationally was not unusual, however.

8. *The Hierarchy of the Catholic Church in the United States*, (New York: The Office of Catholic Publication, 1886), p. 339.

9. Ibid.

10. *The Catholic*, August 29, 1878, p. 6.

11. Cassock and broad-brimmed clerical hat.

12. *Blackrock College Annual—Centenary, 1860–1960*, Aug. 1961, pp. 71–72.

13. "Fifty Years of Service: An Historical Sketch of Duquesne University," *Duquesne Monthly* 35, no. 9 (June 1928), p. 313. This 38-page article has no byline, but the title page states, "Published Monthly During the School Year by the Students of Duquesne University." The editor-in-chief was Thomas F. Henninger; the assistant editors were Michael A. McNally, Thomas P. Mulvaney, John M. Lambert, Ralph L. Hayes, John F. Murphy, John P. Desmond, George M. Haber, Charles O. Rice, and George E. Kelly.

14. Both the Classical and Commercial course cost $6.00 per month. The Preparatory was $5.00, Piano $3.00, Violin $2.00, other instruments $1.00, Drawing $2.00, and Vocal Music was no charge.

15. A brochure proclaimed the philosophy that the college was "a school where the religious and moral training of the pupil is combined through instruction in every branch of a liberal education." The Classical curriculum required curses in English, Latin, Greek, German, French, history, geography, mathematics, physics, chemistry, astronomy, and the natural sciences. The commercial curriculum consisted of English, grammar and composition, bookkeeping, correspondence in English, practical arithmetic, geography, and history. The Preparatory curriculum included English, grammar, spelling, reading, arithmetic, geography, and penmanship.

16. Various numbers have been given for the first class ranging from as low as 30 to as high as 45 students, but 40 is the number most commonly cited. An article in *The Catholic*, July 19, 1879,

states that "the number of pupils on the books of the institution last October was thirty. At the close of the scholastic year it had reached ninety-one."

17. James L. Snyder, "Duquesne University, 1878–1953," *Catholic Educational Review*, December 1952, p. 650.

18. The School was incorporated as a private organization having a legal address. It was also under the control of seven directors who had the power to transact the business of the school. Clees states that "Keeping the legal address in Pittsburgh was significant for it later separated the principal office or place of business of the school from the religious headquarters of the congregation, a factor which later proved to be important in the continuing growth of the University." William James Clees, "Duquesne University: Its Years of Struggle, Sacrifice, and Service," D.Ed. Diss., University of Pittsburgh, 1970, p. 20.

19. The Bluff was known by various names. An 1830 map of Pittsburgh shows it as Ayres Hill with present-day Bluff Street labeled as Bank Street. The Bluff was also known as Goat Hill and Pigeon Hill, but by the time the college moved there, the name Boyd's Hill was in common usage.

20. James D. Van Trump and Arthur P. Ziegler, Jr. *Landmark Architecture of Allegheny County Pennsylvania*, (Pittsburgh: Pittsburgh History & Landmarks foundation, 1967), p. 69.

21. The brickyard was located on the western half of the hill with its works, office, kilns, and stables. Later it was sold, probably because of the school's need for money. Although some histories state that the brickyard continued until 1920, a 1910 plat map shows no evidence of it. There was, however, a brickworks east and south of what would later be College Hall, but it would have been too far away from Old Main to have been a nuisance.

22. The layer of stone lying just below Bluff Street was so hard that the basement (actually the sub-basement) was not extended to Colbert Street and remains only a partial basement under the western half of the building. Francis A. Danner C.S.Sp., "Sidelights on the Early History of Duquesne University," (unpublished manuscript, Duquesne University Archives, 1938), p. 1 in the first numbering system. (This manuscript has four sections and three numbering sequences.)

23. *The Pittsburgh Commercial Gazette* of April 23, 1884 estimated the crowd at 10,000. Whatever the size of the crowd, it was supposedly the largest throng of people ever to gather at a religious event in the history of the city. Pope Leo XIII sent a blessing.

24. In 1881 several priests, including Father Power, had contracted smallpox and been nursed by the Sisters of Mercy, whom Strub said "merited our heartfelt gratitude and special thanks. By their generosity and tact they prevented notoriety and, consequently, great loss for us. No one suspected the danger that threatened us and our enrollment suffered no decline."

25. Father Willms was transferred to Millvale, a suburb of Pittsburgh.

26. Father Murphy was born in County Kerry in 1854 and educated at Blackrock College. After his ordination in Paris in 1878, he was prefect of studies and vice president of Rockwell College until he left Ireland for America.

27. It should be noted that Blackrock and Rockwell Colleges were not degree-granting institutions. Although both were called colleges, they educated boys only up to 18 years of age.

28. Father McCabe prepared the play. Father Willms had also prepared a play, this one in German, that had been well received: *The Egyptian Joseph*.

29. Clees.

30. In 1951, in preparation for a possible nuclear war, civil defense authorities took a survey of alternative water supplies. The university reported the well as its potential water source should the need arise. Evidence of the capped well remains today as a circle in the concrete behind Old Main.

31. "Fifty Years of Service," p. 313.

32. Shingiss Street, which now ends at Locust Street, at this time extended as an unpaved street intersecting with Bluff Street.

33. Francis A. Danner, C.S.Sp., "Sidelights on the Early History of Duquesne University," (unpublished manuscript, Duquesne University Archives, 1938), p. 5 in the first numbering system.

34. *Duquesne Monthly*, December 1914, p. 149.

35. The first team fielded was captained and coached by an underclassman, Dan Barr, later to become a prominent businessman in the city. Both Henry McDermott and Edward Galway were part of the first team and later entered the priesthood and returned to the college to teach and to coach.

36. Michael Kupersanin, "Intercollegiate Athletics

at Duquesne University in Historical Perspective." unpub. Ph.D. Diss., University of Pittsburgh, 1980, p. 31.

37. Paul G. Sullivan, "Forty Years of Hill Athletics," *Football Program*, 1928, Duquesne University Archives, p. 6.

38. Ibid.

39. Ibid., May 1901, pp. 15–16. The game was played on the college playing field. The *Bulletin* contended that the short left field helped the Pirates and congratulated the Holy Ghost team for getting nine hits, including a home run.

40. Actually, of the six sections in the sanctuary, each containing two windows, one on either side, all but the last two sections were built in 1894. The difference in the exterior brick between the two parts can still be seen.

41. It is 70 feet long, 42 feet wide, and 42 feet high from the pavement to the central elevation.

42. The organ was built by the Didinger Company of Philadelphia. It has since been rebuilt and remodeled.

43. "Fifty Years of Service," p. 326. Father Murphy returned to America as Provincial in 1906 and established the Apostolic College of the Holy Ghost near Philadelphia. He returned to Ireland in 1910 as Provincial, and in 1916 he was made Bishop of Port Louis, Mauritus.

Notes to Chapter 2

1. He was born near Kildysart, County Clare, in 1884 and graduated from Blackrock College in 1877, having received a traditional classical education. Father Hehir taught at Blackrock for three years, went to Paris to receive his theological training, and was ordained there in 1883.

2. Reports of the Immigration Commission (Washington, D.C.: 1911) vol. 33, pp. 717–731. These figures are rounded off to the nearest whole percentage point. The report states that statistics were compiled only for college students, and do not include the grammar or prep schools. They apply to "second-generation immigrant children," meaning American-born children of foreign-born parents. The term Bohemian probably applies only to Czechs. The report identified some 113 students as "third-generation immigrant."

Historians have ventured a number of explanations for the high percentage of Irish and German students. The most obvious is that the Irish and Germans had more time to assimilate American culture and climb the socioeconomic ladder as opposed to the more recent arrivals from Eastern and Southern Europe. Others have noted that both Irish and German Catholics tended to avoid non-Catholic schools since they came from societies where such institutions were often viewed as instruments for the proselytization of Catholic youth away from their faith. Still other historians have averred that Southern and Eastern Europeans made a greater effort to preserve ethnic identity.

3. Snyder, "Duquesne University, 1878–1953, p. 655. A number of popularly written histories of Duquesne allude to the legend that Father Hehir had two groups of student files: one labeled "those who can pay" and the other "those who cannot pay."

4. "Fifty Years of Service", p. 329.

5. Peter Robers, "Immigrant Wage-Earners." *Wage Earning Pittsburgh* (New York: Survey Associates, Russell Sage Foundation, 1911), p. 33.

6. Weiss, "Duquesne University: A Case Study," p. 183.

7. Letter from Bishop Canevin to College and University Council, October 1, 1910. "Historical Documents of the American Province of the Holy Ghost Fathers," v. 15.

8. Francis X. Hanley, "Evolution from College to University: Administration of Martin A. Hehir, C.S.Sp., 1899–1931." Unpublished D.Ed. dissertation, University of Pittsburgh, 1961, p. 265.

9. Letter from Henry S. Drinker, Council member, to Rev. Patick J. Ryan, Archbishop of Philadelphia, October 11, 1910. "Historical Documents of the American Province of the Holy Ghost Fathers." v. 15.

10. Clees, "Duquesne University: Its Years of Struggle," p. 43.

11. Letter from James A. Flaherty to Father Hehir, October 20, 1910, quoted in Clees, p. 43.

12. Court of Common Pleas #2 No. 169, July 1911.

13. Because of an accident of history, it has frequently and erroneously been said that Duquesne University traced its beginnings to Western University of Pennsylvania. In 1838 a splinter faction left that institution and founded Duquesne College. It went out of existence in 1849, nearly four decades prior to the founding of Pittsburgh Catholic College. It has no connection to the present Duquesne University.

14. Weiss, p. 184.

15. Hanley, p. 42.

16. Grand Duke 1926, p. 46.

17. The members of the first graduating class were John R. Clark, Francis B. Cohan, Thomas Daugherty, Paul J. Friday, Henry J. Gelm, Bernard J. McKenna, Oscar G. Meyer, Edward M. Murphy, Frederick W. Ries, Jr., Henry J. Schmitt, Henry J. Thomas, and Francis Wolf.

18. The law school's original location was in the George Building, 430 4th Ave. It moved to the Vandergrift Building in 1914, the Maloney Building in 1921, Canevin Hall in 1924, Fitzsimons Building in 1932, Rockwell Hall in 1958, and the Hanley School of Law in 1982.

19. Until 1975 governors were limited constitutionally to one four-year term in office.

20. In a report the university filed in 1919, the amount shown is only $11,875.

21. Originally day classes were conducted on the main campus. After the University puchased the Vandegrift Building in downtown, both day and evening classes were held there. Downtown was to remain as the location for business courses until Rockwell Hall opened in 1959.

22. *Duquesne Monthly*, vol. 22, pp. 32–33.

23. The drama school went through a series of name changes: School of Oratory, School of Drama and Speech Arts, School of Theatre Arts and Dramatic Literature, and School of Drama. The number of graduates, mostly women in later years, when Duquesne became coed, was never very large, averaging about three students per year.

24. "Fifty Years of Service," p. 335.

25. The Pre-Medical Department used Science Hall, a two-story chemistry laboratory at the corner of Vickroy Street (now Academic Walk) and Colbert Street (McAnulty Drive). This red brick structure had vaguely Gothic windows and was a familiar landmark to generations of students. Used as offices following the completion of Mellon Hall, it was razed in 1994. The Bayer Learning Center was erected on the site. Science Hall was built on an unoccupied part of a lot that extended to Ivanhoe Street, on the corner of which stood a three-story house that the university first began renting in 1913. The house and property were owned by Julia Scanlon. In 1915 she sold them to Duquesne for the sum of one dollar. Named St. Martin's Hall, the house was first used as housing for lay faculty (probably unmarried men). In the 1920s it was a student residence, then later student offices, and still later was used as offices for the History Department. Finally, it was razed as part of the redevelopment of the Bluff.

26. *Duquesne Duke*, March 8, 1934.

27. *Pittsburgh College Bulletin*, November 1907, p. 55.

28. William Brashler, *Josh Gibson: A Life in the Negro Leagues*, (New York: Harper and Row, p. 7), 1978.

29. *Duquesne Monthly* June 1917, pp. 333–34.

30. In 1908, the North Braddock High School Team refused to play the Duquesne Prep School. *Pittsburgh College Bulletin*, November 1908, p. 58.

31. In 1910, the year in which Pittsburgh Catholic College applied for a university charter, only 2.9 percent of persons ages 18 to 24 were enrolled in a degree-granting institution. By the fiftieth anniversary of the University in 1928, that number had more than doubled to 7.1 percent of the population. *Historical Statistics of the United States*, (Washington D.C.: Government Printing Office, 1975), p. 383.

Notes to Chapter 3

1. This figure includes the prep school. *Official Catholic Directory* (Milwaukee, WI: M.H. Wiltzius Co., 1921), vol. 36, p. 519.

2. Hanley, p. 62.

3. Professional fundraisers, F. A. Converse of Buffalo and W. J. Clifford of Chicago, accepted the management of the campaign. The executive committee consisted of William Magee, mayor of Pittsburgh; Judge Ambrose B. Reid; Mrs. Enoch Rauh, head of the Allegheny County Health Department; Bertrand W. Lewis, cashier and later vice president of Mellon Bank; and Paul J. Friday, who was in the first graduating class of the Duquesne Law School.

4. *Father Hehir Scrapbook*, Duquesne University Archives.

5. Letter dated August 15, 1920. *Duquesne Monthly*, vol. 29, p. 23.

6. *Duquesne Monthly* 28, pp. 3–5.

7. Clees, p. 61.

8. *Father Hehir Scrapbook*, undated newspaper clipping.

9. *Pittsburgh Catholic*, Oct. 28, 1920.

10. *Pittsburgh Catholic*, November 11, 1920.

11. In 1921 the average earnings in the United States was $1,233. Paul H. Douglas, *Real Wages in the United States: 1890–1926* (New York: Augustus M. Kelly Publishers, 1966) p. 392.

12. *Pittsburgh Catholic*, November 18, 1920, p. 8.

13. Ibid, November 18, 1920, p. 1.

14. Hanley, p. 68.

15. No archival records of the Million Dollar Fund campaign could be found. This figure was given in a report done for President Gallagher titled "A Survey Analysis and Plan of Fund-Raising for Duquesne University," by John Price Jones Company, Inc. New York, NY 1951, p. 47. It lists only the $300,000 figure and does not say if that includes the $169,495 given by the Holy Ghost Fathers.

16. Danner, "Holy Ghost College, Duquesne University." Unpublished, undated manuscript, Duquesne University Archives, p. 23.

17. The wall, made of 10,000 cubic yards of concrete, does not actually hold back the earth. It is a 36-inch thick covering meant to stabilize the hill. The wall slopes at a 1/4 inch to 1 inch ratio and is topped by yet another smaller vertical wall built behind a drainage culvert. "The New Liberty Bridge Approach," *William Penn Points* vol. 10, no. 6 (March 15, 1928), p. 16.

18. *Duquesne Duke*, March 20, 1930.

19. Although this part of Shingess was not officially vacated by the city until 1949, the county commissioners agreed to the university's takeover of county property adjacent to the retaining wall in 1930.

20. The discus-thrower, chosen for its appropriateness to a gymnasium, is, coincidentally, equally appropriate to the Rangos School of Health Sciences which occupies the building since its conversion in 1992.

21. *Duquesne Monthly* 37, February 1930, p. 127.

22. Clees, p. 60. Breil also wrote the music for *Intolerance* and *Cabiria*.

23. *The Pittsburgh Chronicle Telegraph*, October 7, 1920.

24. He is not to be confused with Bishop Richard Phelan, Bishop of Pittsburgh, who was present at the laying of the cornerstone for the Administration Building in April 1884.

25. Hanley, p. 73.

26. Snyder, p. 658.

27. *University Ad Hoc Committee on the Status of Women at Duquesne University*, 1972, p. 7.

28. In a telephone conversation, the archivist at DePaul University stated that there is "some evidence" to suggest that women were enrolled prior to 1914, but that no actual records exist to support this assertion.

29. In the Summer of 1909, Marquette University established a special eight-week program for women (no men were permitted in the class), but it is doubtful if they received college credit.

30. Snyder, p. 658.

31. This data was taken from a handdrawn list, ca. 1935. Duquesne University Archives.

32. *Duquesne Monthly*, vol. 35, p. 307. She and her husband, the Mexican Consul in Pittsburgh, both taught Spanish.

33. Mary E. Rice, "The Co-ed's Progress," *Duquesne Monthly* LXIII, no. 6 (February 1936), p. 28.

34. *Duquesne University Bulletin*, 1925, pp. 30–31.

35. Clees, pp. 81–82.

36. Clees, p. 82.

37. "Fifty Years of Service," p. 345.

38. *Duquesne Duke*, May 7, 1954.

39. "Fifty Years of Service," p. 343.

40. "Fifty Years of Service," p. 344.

41. "Fifty Years of Service," p. 344.

42. *Grand Duke* 1926, pp. 147–148.

43. Interview with Father Henry J. McAnulty, February 25, 1993.

44. Sullivan, "Forty Years of Hill Athletics," p. 10.

45. Kupersanin, pp. 58–59.

46. Elmer Layden (with Ed Snyder), *It Was a Different Game*, (Englewood Cliffs, NJ: Prentice-Hall, 1969), p. 53.

47. Ibid., p. 56.

48. Ibid., pp. 56–63.

49. Ibid., p. 65.

50. Ibid., p. 66.

51. Ibid., p. 74.

52. From an interview with Mr. Clair Brown February 27, 1979, cited by Kupersanin, p. 64.

53. Layden, *It was a Different Game*, p. 75.

54. *Pittsburgh Catholic*, January 23, 1930, p. 8.

55. *Duquesne Monthly*, February 1924, pp. 156–157.

56. Sullivan, p. 8. Before William Campbell,

who coached for only a single season, the basketball coaches were, Father Eugene McGuigan, 1915–1920, and 1922–1923, and Ben Lubic, 1921. Alexander Hogarby was first coach, 1913–14, 1914–15. McGuigan coached 1915–16–1919–20, 1921–22–1922–23. Ben Lubic coached 1920–21.

57. "Fifty Years of Service," p. 311.

58. Weiss, p. 184.

59. Francis M. Crowley and Edward P. Dunne, *Directory of Catholic Colleges and Schools, 1928* (Washington, D.C.: National Catholic Welfare Conference, 1928), p. 121. Villanova is also 36 years older than Duquesne. Moreover, it had the advantage of starting out on a 197 acre campus, in the long run an important factor in the school's expansion, since, at this writing, Villanova's enrollment exceeds that of Duquesne.

60. The small office was on the second floor of Old Main, directly above the Bluff Street entrance. Interview with Msgr. Francis Glenn, March 15, 1993.

61. Testimonial speeches, quoted in Hanley, p. 94.

62. Clees, pp. 90–91.

63. Hanley, p. 96.

Notes to Chapter 4

1. Einstein postulated a closed universe in which parallel lines eventually converged, whereas Euclid envisioned parallel lines continuing indefinitely.

2. *Duquesne Monthly*, January 1932, (39:4), p. 125.

3. Father Callahan also graduated from the prep school. His postgraduate work was at the Holy Ghost Apostolic College at Cornwells Heights and at the Gregorian University in Rome. He returned to Duquesne after ordination to teach languages for a year before his assignment to Ferndale Holy Ghost Seminary in Norwalk, Connecticut, as an instructor in philosophy and theology. He then served as pastor of a church in Chippewa Falls, Wisconsin, for seven years.

4. Interview with Msgr. Francis Glenn, March 16, 1993.

5. The university's financial report for that year shows $399,348.07 in "ordinary" income, and an additional $51,000.00 in "building fund" income. In 1928 there was a carryover cash balance from previous years of $39,588.43. Much of this was apparently used as down payments on the various property purchases.

6. The Fitzsimons Building, now razed, was at 331 Fourth Avenue between Wood and Smithfield streets. A 1934 financial statement reported, "The carrying charge on this building is less than the rent previously paid by the University for much less space." Historical Documents, vol. 70, p. 274.

7. The rent that the Fitzsimons Building generated, $22,875 per year, covered not only the mortgage, $11,575 per year, but the other costs attendant to the building's operation: utilities, taxes, and maintenance. A financial statement shows a small positive cash flow for the building of $25.54 for a one-year period, 1933–1934. Historical Documents, vol. 71, pp. 232, 251.

8. The university may not have had a full-time superintendent of buildings and grounds, however, after World War II. The September 26, 1940, issue of the *Duquesne Duke* identified Father Salvator Federici as "Superintendent of Buildings and Grounds and instructor in History."

9. Koren, *Serpent and the Dove*, p. 317.

10. Adam Di Vincenzo, "Graduation—Then What? Problems Faced by Departing Seniors Create Interest," *Duquesne Duke*, May 31, 1934.

11. John Augustine, "After Graduation, What?" *Duquesne Monthly*, October 1937, p. 16.

12. Ibid., p. 40.

13. Snyder, p. 660.

14. Larry Cooney, "The National Youth Administration," *Duquesne Monthly*, December, 1938, vol. 46, no. 4, p. 25; and *The Duquesne University Bulletin*, 1937–1938, p. 33. The tuition fee was $8 per credit hour.

15. *Duquesne Duke*, October 4, 1934.

16. *Duquesne Duke*, October 3, 1935.

17. *Duquesne Duke*, April 2, 1936.

18. The *Duquesne Duke* of October 20, 1938 gives an interesting history of St. Mary's along with all the myths that surrounded it.

19. *Duquesne Duke*, September 29, 1932.

20. *Duquesne Duke*, October 3, 1929.

21. The total membership for all fraternities was 157, and for sororities, 88.

22. McGown later became western regional director of the NYA and his work as NYA director at the University was taken over by John D. Holahan, athletic manager, who marshalled university resources and labor for the Spring Folk Pageant.

23. Walter W. Kolar, *Duquesne University Tamburitzans: The First Fifty Years Remembered* (Pittsburgh: Tamburitza Press, 1986), p. 10.

24. Early in 1936, just a few months before Dr. Lloyd's death, his son, Rollo, a young screen actor in Hollywood, filled in as a guest speaker at his classes. Earlier, his daughter had filled in as director on occasion when he was hospitalized.

25. The renovation, costing $1,500, included two electric chandeliers, 20 wall bracket lights, floodlights for three altars, and a new gold and silver tabernacle door.

26. A story of men from Mars invading New Jersey done so realistically that many people took it for a true newscast.

27. Charlie McCarthy was the name of the dummy used by the ventriloquist, Edgar Bergen, who had an immensely popular radio program.

28. This was a common practice at the time in American higher education, the theory being that high schools varied greatly in their preparation of students for college, thus rendering class standing a less than valid indicator of potential success or failure in college.

29. Snyder, p. 601.

30. Historical Documents, vol. 71, p. 171.

31. One of the great difficulties at the time was that diploma schools of nursing in Pennsylvania and across the nation did not at that time require a four-year high school diploma for admittance. The university, however, did. Potential degree students who did not possess high school diplomas petitioned the university for a waiver of this requirement, but it was denied. Eventually the Commonwealth of Pennsylvania, in setting the high school diploma as a requirement for admission to a school of nursing in 1935, made provision for those who had previously graduated from nursing schools to obtain their diplomas. A State Board of Nurse Examiners served as an accrediting body for schools of nursing operated by hospitals and universities and set the standards regarding licensing, faculty, curriculum, students, laboratory space and equipment.

32. The affiliated agencies were the Public Health Nursing Association of Pittsburgh, the Tuberculosis League of Pittsburgh, St. Francis Hospital, Pittsburgh Hospital for psychiatric nursing, and Gallinger Municipal Hospital in Washington, D.C. for communicable diseases.

33. Mary Tobin resigned due to poor health in 1944; the university, in gratitude for her contributions and accomplishments, awarded her the title of dean emeritus. Eileen R. Gimper, *The School of Nursing of Duquesne University, 1937–1979*, Ph.D. dissertation, Univ. of Pittsburgh, 1983.

34. Ralph Munn, director to Dr. J.J. Callahan, October 8, 1934, Historical Documents, vol. 66, p. 293.

35. The minutes of the board of directors for November 30, 1938, records the bid for the library as $58,000, but the final cost for the library was $67,000. See Financial Report and Property Acquisitions, 1927–1943, p. 6. The university treasurer was authorized to borrow an additional $20,000 for its construction. See Minutes, April 17, 1939.

36. Elmer Layden, *It was a Different Game*, pp. 90–91.

37. *New York Times*, October 18, 1936, p. 4L.

38. *Duquesne Duke*, January 7, 1937.

39. Layden, p. 91. According to the *Duquesne Duke*, Jan. 21, 1937, p. 3.

40. Kupersanin, p. 84, citing his interview with Dr. Kenneth Duffy, Duquesne, 1936, director of WDUQ, November 19, 1978.

41. *Duquesne Duke*, May 5, 1930, p. 3.

42. Kupersanin, p. 92, citing the Middle States Evaluation Report, 1940, D.U. Archives.

43. Koren, *Serpent and the Dove*, p. 316.

44. Hanley, p. 105.

Notes to Chapter 5

1. At the same time, the Board approved the provincial's appointment of two other Holy Ghost fathers, Rev. John J. Sullivan as Vice President and Rev. Edward Rectenwald as treasurer. Board of Directors, Minutes, February 9, 1940.

2. Snyder, p. 662.

3. See Raymond E. Callahan, *Education and the Cult of Efficiency* (Chicago: University of Chicago Press, 1962).

4. *The Bulletin Index: Pittsburgh's Weekly Newsmagazine*, February 6, 1941, p. 8.

5. Policies and Regulations Concerning appointments to the Faculties of Duquesne University, Duquesne University Press, 1940, pp. 6–7.

6. Historic Documents, vol. 71, p. 295. This was a statement in a letter by Dr. Wilson Farrand, chairman of Middle States to Dean Muldoon dated March 1, 1935.

7. Koren, *The Serpent and the Dove*, p. 318.

8. The course, which was full-time for two weeks, began with glider training. "Beginning their day with reveille at 6:30, the men have a full schedule until taps at 10 p.m. Every morning, including Saturday, they have four classes. At 12:30 they leave for Bettis Airport where they receive their flight training. Two evening classes complete their day." Bettis Field is now the site of a Westinghouse Electric Corp. plant in the Borough of West Mifflin.

9. *Duquesne Duke*, May 15, 1941, p. 1.

10. *Duquesne Duke*, March 7, 1940.

11. *Duquesne Duke*, January 8, 1942.

12. *Duquesne Duke*, January 15, 1942.

13. *Duquesne Duke*, February 12, 1942.

14. Layden, p. 64.

15. *The Duquesne Alumni Federation Quarterly*, September 1943 (3:3), p. 7.

16. *Historical Statistics of the United States: Part I*, 1975, p. 383. In 1940 there were 1.39 million students in college. By 1944 that number had declined to 1.10 million. The national decline of 20 percent in these years was mild when compared to Duquesne's 51.6 percent decline.

17. Interview of Father Henry J. McAnulty by Perry K. Blatz, August 21, 1990, p. 119.

18. President's Annual Report, 1944–1945.

19. Ibid.

20. President's Annual Report, 1944–1945.

21. Blatz, p. 119.

22. *Duquesne Durational*, May 4, 1944.

23. *Duquesne Durational*, February 15, 1946.

24. *Duquesne Duke*, March 20, 1947.

25. Forty students were employed by the University in the cafeteria, bookstore, library, and offices. Students worked as sales and stock personnel in department stores, in warehouses, mills, post offices, and gas stations. Some explored career-related work at pharmacies, newspapers, youth programs, playgrounds, clinics, and settlement houses, as well as by playing in local bands or by giving music lessons. *Duquesne Duke*, January 15, 1948.

26. Patrick J. McGeever, *Rev. Charles Owen Rice: Apostle of Contradiction* (Pittsburgh: Duquesne University Press, 1989), p. 105.

27. McGeever, p. 102.

28. Author's interview with Charles Rice, September 7, 1993. See also McGeever, pp. 138–39.

29. *Duquesne Duke*, April 17, 1947.

30. *Duquesne Duke*, April 19, 1950.

31. Forbes School was located at the corner of Forbes Avenue and Stevenson Street. The site is now occupied by a Mercy Hospital parking garage.

32. *Duquesne Duke*, April 17, 1947.

33. Smith to Collins, October 7, 1948. Holy Ghost Archives, RG 38 H–98.

34. *Duquesne Duke*, May 5, 1950.

35. Smith to Collins, October 7, 1948.

36. Vernon Gallagher, in letter to the author. January 3, 1994.

37. Smith to Collins, October 7, 1948.

38. Academic Report from January 1946, to June, 1949. In Duquesne University Archives.

Notes to Chapter 6

1. Vernon Gallagher to the author, January 3, 1994.

2. *Duquesne Duke*, September 1959, Welcome Back Issue.

3. *Duquesne Magazine*, May 1950, vol. IV, p. 7.

4. *A Survey, Analysis and Plan of Fund-Raising for Duquesne University*, November 1951, p. 17, Duquesne University Archives.

5. *Duquesne Duke*, November 17, 1950.

6. Jeffrey Zaslow, "When the Red Scare Hit Pittsburgh." *Pittsburgher Magazine*, March 1980, p. 62.

7. *Duquesne Duke*, December 7, 1951.

8. *Duquesne Duke*, April 27, 1951.

9. The book *Truth and Freedom* was written at Eisenhower's request when he was president of Columbia University. It was translated by Father Henry J. Koren, C.S.Sp. See Gallagher Scrapbooks, Duquesne University Archives.

10. Dr. Melady to Fr. Gallagher, February 15, 1958. Duquesne University Archives.

11. Jones, pp. 41–42.

12. Interview with the author, December 10, 1993.

13. Vernon F. Gallagher to the author, January 3, 1994.

14. Ibid.

15. Letter from Fr. Gallagher to Very Rev. Fr. L.J. McGinley, S.J., president of Fordham University, January 5, 1957, Duquesne University Archives.

16. Ibid.

17. Vernon Gallagher to the author, January 3, 1994.

18. *Duquesne University Alumni News*, December 1952, (2:5).

19. Interview with Father J. Gerald Walsh, September 17, 1993.

20. "Duquesne Builds with Pittsburgh," *Pittsburgh Press*, Roto, May 17, 1959.

21. *Courage and Imagination*, Duquesne University Development Fund, 1952, MMs, p. 9.

22. *Duquesne Duke*, March 21, 1958.

23. *Ripe for Jubilee*, p. 6.

24. Ibid.

25. *Duquesne Duke*, October 3, 1952.

26. *Duquesne Duke*, September 15, 1955.

27. The building had previously been called Varsity hall and later was named St. John's Hall as a men's dormitory. The original St. John's Hall on the early campus was the hospital of Dr. Walters, a building that later was renamed St. Mary's. The convent building had most recently been used as the Tamburitzan dormitory. At this writing it is known as Laval House.

28. *Duquesne Duke*, May 23, 1952.

29. *Duquesne Duke*, March 13, 1953.

30. Rob. Ruck, *Sandlot Seasons: Sport in Black Pittsburgh* (*Champaign, IL*: University of Illinois Press, 1987) p. 198.

31. *Duquesne Duke*, October 5, 1951.

32. *Duquesne Duke*, March 20, 1953.

Notes to Chapter 7

1. Interview by Perry K. Blatz, July 31, 1990, p. 4. In Duquesne University Archives.

2. Blatz, pp. 74–75.

3. Blatz, p. 79.

4. Ibid.

5. Ibid., p. 101.

6. Blatz, p. 96.

7. *The Pittsburgh Press*, January 25, 1962.

8. A single surviving land use map dated November 16, 1960, and revised June 2, 1961, shows the university occupying the land between Locust and Gibbon Streets. (Gibbon was parallel to Locust and about midway between it and Forbes Avenue). In separate discussions with the author, both Fr. Joseph Duchene and Fr. William Crowley aver that the Urban Redevelopment Authority wanted Duquesne to take still more land between Forbes and Fifth Avenues. The city objected to that much land being taken off of the tax rolls, and in any event the university felt that it would be overextended and was quite satisfied with Forbes as its "natural" northern boundary.

9. Annual Report, 1959–1960, p. 4.

10. *The Pittsburgh Press*, July 3, 1962, p. 15.

11. Ibid.

12. Ibid.

13. *The Pittsburgh Press*, March 28, 1963.

14. Ibid.

15. *The Pittsburgh Press*, May 7, 1964.

16. *Duquesne University: People, Programs, Policies*, Spring 1966, pp. vi–18.

17. *The Pittsburgh Press*, February 19, 1963.

18. *Pittsburgh Post-Gazette*, February 19, 1963.

19. At its meeting on November 17, 1966, the board approved as new members E.I. Goldberg, representing the Alumni Association; W.J. Blenko, J.L. Propst, and E.J. Hanley, representing the Duquesne University Foundation; and P.C. Cross as a lay educator (he was the director of Mellon Institute) not connected to the university. In 1970 Hanley was elected the first lay chairman of the board of directors of Duquesne University. At the same meeting the following *ex officio* titles were admitted to membership: the president of the Duquesne University Women's Advisory Board; the president of the Duquesne University Women's Guild; the mayor of the city of Pittsburgh; and the chairman of the Allegheny County Commissioners. Also admitted were S.A. Weiss and D.L. Frawley.

20. *Report of the President, 1963–1964*, p. 12.

21. The 1966 report to Middle States gave this religious breakdown of the faculty:

	Number	Percent
Catholics	200	68
Protestants	54	18
Jews	24	8
Other	4	1
None Listed	11	5

22. *Report of the President, 1963–1964*, p. 17.

23. In 1955 there were 181 full-time and 78 part-time faculty. By 1965 the faculty had grown to 317 full-time and 74 part-time faculty. Of these 319 were men and 72 were women. Some 34 were religious.

24. *The Pittsburgh Press*, June 19, 1966.

25. Duquesne University, News Release, August 4, 1966.

26. *Duquesne Alumni News*, December 1964, 1.

27. K. Leroy Irvis to Henry J. McAnulty, March 7, 1966.

28. *This Week at Duquesne*, May 4, 1964.

29. Pittsburgh Council on Higher Education, Statement and Purpose and Background, 1966.

30. Blatz, p. 111.

31. The grants included $32,000 to the Chemistry Department from the National Science Foundation for a two-year study of chemistry and biochemistry of sulfur amino acids; $7,866 to Dr. Bernard T. Gillis of the Chemistry Department from the U.S. Public Health Service for a study of alkylated carboxylic and amino acid hydroxides; $16,977 to Dr. Oscar Gawron of the Chemistry Department from the Division of General Medical Sciences, U.S. Public Health Service, for work on enzymes in the Krebs cycle; $16,445 to the Chemistry Department from the Research Grants Branch, National Cancer Institute; and $10,000 to the school of Pharmacy from the Division of Biology and Medicine, U.S. Atomic Energy Commission.

32. *The Pittsburgh Press*, May 29, 1966.

33. Blatz, p. 98.

34. *The Pittsburgh Press*, January 26, 1966.

35. Interview with R.K. Mellon Foundations, March 2, 1994.

36. This definition was supplied by Father Koren to the author, June 11, 1995.

37. Michael Strasser, "Report to the President's Special Committee on Faculty Relations," RG Philosophy Department Dispute, 1965–1966 in Duquesne University Archives.

38. *National Catholic Reporter*, March 23, 1966.

39. *The Pittsburgh Press*, January 26, 1966.

40. Blatz, p. 147.

41. Letter from Daniel A. Torisky to Henry J. McAnulty, January 25, 1966.

42. *The Pittsburgh Press*, June 19, 1966.

43. John Dowds to the author, March 10, 1994.

44. *Duquesne University Alumni News* 18, no. 2 (December 1967), p. 2.

45. Interview with the author, January 14, 1994.

46. *Duquesne University Alumni News* 18, no. 4 (May 1968), p. 1.

47. Blatz, p. 103.

48. *Duquesne Duke*, January 21, 1960.

49. *Duquesne Duke*, March 15, 1968.

Notes to Chapter 8

1. Blatz, p. 145.

2. Blatz, p. 113.

3. *The Pittsburgh Press*, June 19, 1966.

4. "A case for the Catholic University," by the Holy Ghost Fathers, Duquesne University, 1969, p. 2.

5. Ibid., p. 14.

6. *Duquesne University Alumni News* 20, no. 4 (May 1970), p. 1.

7. Fitzpatrick, pp. 113–114.

8. Fitzpatrick.

9. *Duquesne Duke*, August 24, 1972.

10. *The Agitator*, May 11, 1964.

11. *Commentator*, January 6, 1965.

12. *The University Vindicator*, October 3, 1968.

13. *Pittsburgh Catholic*, May 11, 1967.

14. Blatz, p. 136.

15. Ibid., p. 137.

16. Minutes of Students for a Democratic Society, September 26, 1968.

17. William Nicholsen and Stephen Strasser, "It Was Hardly A Columbia," June 23, 1994, p. 1.

18. *Duquesne Duke*, December 6, 1968. The WDUQ reporter's story was corroborated by the December 5, 1968 issue of *The University Vindicator.*

19. *Duquesne Duke*, October 24, 1969.

20. Fitzpatrick, p. 98.

21. Blatz, p. 114.

22. "Progress Report, 1970–1971," Counseling and Learning Department for Black Students, compiled by George D. Harris and Joanne A. Walker, Duquesne University Archives, p. 8.

23. Report on the Status of Women at Duquesne University, 1972, p. 28.

24. Ibid., p. 83.

25. Ibid., p. 85.

26. Ibid., p. 84.

27. Ibid., p. 72.

28. *The Pittsburgh Press*, April 4, 1971.

29. *The Daily News*, McKeesport, Pennsylvania, September 11, 1981.

30. Interview with James P. Homer, April 25, 1994. Homer graduated in 1966 from the School of Business.

31. Report to Middle States Association, Aug., 1966, p. B–2., Self-Study Report to the commission

on Higher Education Middle States Association, November 1977, p. 98.

32. See *America*, July 20, 1968, p. 43. It says that the Catholic Pentecostal movement "was born at Duquesne University." See also *Newsweek*, June 16, 1975, p. 48, which says, "[The Catholic charismatic movement] was founded at Duquesne University."

33. Storey manuscript, 1994, p. 5.

34. Ibid., p. 6.

35. *Duquesne Duke*, November 14, 1974.

36. *The Pittsburgh Press*, November 17, 1974.

37. *Duquesne Duke*, September 2, 1975.

38. Henry J. McAnulty, C.S.Sp., to Ronald R. Davenport, January 2, 1979.

39. *Pittsburgh Post-Gazette*, February 10, 1979.

40. Much of the information in this section resulted from interviews by the author with Henry J. McAnulty, C.S.Sp., May 11, 1994; Robert S. Barker, May 12, 1994; and Margaret K. Krasik, May 12, 1994.

41. Gimper, pp. 91–102.

42. Henry J. McAnulty and K.S. Rensel, in letter to students in the School of Nursing, June 8, 1979, Duquesne University Archives.

43. *The First Fifty Years Remembered*, p. 68.

44. Blatz, p. 207.

Notes to Chapter 9

1. *Duquesne Duke*, October 17, 1980.

2. Academic Council Minutes, May 10, 1983.

3. *Pittsburgh Press Roto Magazine*, June 27, 1982, cover story.

4. Ibid.

5. *McKeesport News*, July 3 and 12, 1985.

6. *Pittsburgh Post-Gazette*, September 23, 1985.

7. *Pittsburgh Post-Gazette*, July 29, 1987.

8. *Duquesne Duke*, February 3, 1983.

9. Administrative Council, April 13, 1982.

10. *Pittsburgh Press*, March 15, 1984.

11. *Pittsburgh Post-Gazette*, April 7, 1984.

12. *Greensburg Tribune-Review*, April 8, 1984.

13. *Pittsburgh Post-Gazette*, April 10, 1984.

14. *Pittsburgh Press* editorial, "Spring on the Bluff," April 12, 1984.

15. *Pittsburgh Post-Gazette*, April 14, 1984.

16. *Valley Independent*, Monessen, PA, April 12, 1984.

17. *McKeesport Daily News*, April 28, 1984.

18. *Pittsburgh Post-Gazette*, April 8, 1985.

19. Nesti Papers. Guthrie Committee. Charge to the Committee to Review University Administrative Operations, November 30, 1983.

20. *Pittsburgh Post-Gazette*, March 26, 1985.

21. *Pittsburgh Post-Gazette*, March 26, 1985.

22. *Duquesne Duke*, March 24, 1983.

23. *Pittsburgh Post-Gazette*, October 31, 1985.

24. RG University Project/Alternatives, n.d., pp. 2–3.

25. *Allegheny Journal*, August 1, 1983.

26. Pete Bishop, "Greek Revival," *Pittsburgh Press*, February 5, 1984.

27. *Pittsburgh Press*, February 5, 1984.

28. *Duquesne Duke*, April 17, 1986.

29. *From the Desk of the President*, March 17, 1986.

30. *Catholic Accent*, Greensburg, PA, October 9, 1980.

31. *Duquesne University Record* 9, (December 1980): 2.

32. *Duquesne Duke*, April 14, 1983.

33. *Duquesne Duke*, October 23, 1986.

34. *Pittsburgh Press*, April 5, 1987.

35. *Pittsburgh Press*, April 26, 1987, letter to the editor.

36. *Pittsburgh Press*, April 5, 1987.

37. *Pittsburgh Press*, undated article from the personal papers of Bruce C. Martin.

38. Ibid.

39. *Pittsburgh Press*, undated article from the Martin papers.

40. *Pittsburgh Post-Gazette*, August 27, 1987.

41. *Pittsburgh Press*, April 14, 1987.

42. Ibid. Statement by Father David L. Smith, chairman of the Duquesne Corp. It should be remembered that the Duquesne Corporation, composed entirely of Holy Ghost fathers and chaired by the provincial, is the actual owner of Duquesne University. On the organization chart, it is supreme, located above the board of directors.

43. *Pittsburgh Post-Gazette*, June 20, 1987.

44. *Pittsburgh Post-Gazette*, July 20, 1987.

45. *Duquesne Duke*, September 4, 1987.

46. *Pittsburgh Press*, July 31, 1987.

47. This is an excerpt from a paper written by Board member A.P. Levinson. It was read to the entire board on April 20, 1987 which then voted

unanimously to present it to the Cyert Committee. See Minutes, Special Meeting of the Board of Directors of Duquesne University, April 20, 1987.

48. *Pittsburgh Press*, July 31, 1987.

49. *Pittsburgh Press*, March 24, 1988.

50. *Duquesne Spirit*, June 15, 1988, p. 8.

Notes to Chapter 10

1. *Pittsburgh Press*, Bill Zlatos, April 5, 1988.

2. Interview with Dr. John E. Murray, Jr., December 20, 1994.

3. *Pittsburgh Post-Gazette*, May 6, 1988.

4. *Pittsburgh Press*, May 12, 1988.

5. *Pittsburgh Post-Gazette*, December 5, 1988, Quotes from Victoria Hartung and Jean Hunter.

6. *Pittsburgh Press*, October 22, 1989.

7. *Pitttsburgh Post-Gazette*, October 16, 1990.

8. *Duquesne University Spirit*, June 15, 1988.

9. *Pittsburgh Press*, September 18, 1988.

10. *Pittsburgh Press*, September 18, 1988.

11. *Pittsburgh Press*, July 1, 1991.

12. *Duquesne University to Concerns Identified by the Middle States Periodic Review Site Committee*, p. 4.

13. *Pittsburgh Post-Gazette*, April 5, 1988.

14. *The Duquesne University Times* 4, no. 30 (April 1995).

15. *Pittsburgh Business Times-Journal*, April 10–15, 1989, p. 23.

16. *Duquesne Duke*, October 1, 1992.

17. *Duquesne Duke*, September 17, 1992.

18. *Pittsburgh Press*, May 17, 1992.

19. *Pittsburgh Press*, May 14, 1992.

20. *Pittsburgh Post-Gazette*, May 5, 1993.

21. *Pittsburgh Post-Gazette*, May 7, 1993.

22. *Pittsburgh Press*, February 24, 1989.

23. *Pittsburgh Press*, February 21, 1989.

24. *Pittsburgh Press*, April 18, 1989.

25. *Duquesne Duke*, April 22, 1993.

26. *Duquesne Duke*, September 20, 1990.

Index